DAVID IN THE FOURTH GOSPEL

ARBEITEN ZUR GESCHICHTE DES ANTIKEN JUDENTUMS UND DES URCHRISTENTUMS

herausgegeben von

Martin Hengel (Tübingen), Peter Schäfer (Berlin),
Pieter W. van der Horst (Utrecht), Martin Goodman (Oxford),
Daniël R. Schwartz (Jerusalem), Cilliers Breytenbach (Berlin)

XLVII

DAVID IN THE FOURTH GOSPEL

The Johannine Reception of the Psalms

BY

MARGARET DALY-DENTON

BRILL
LEIDEN · BOSTON · KÖLN
2000

This book is printed on acid-free paper.

Die Deutsche Bibliothek - CIP-Einheitsaufnahme

Daly-Denton, Margaret:
David in the fourth gospel : the Johannine reception of the psalms / by Margaret Daly-Denton. – Leiden ; Boston ; Köln : Brill, 1999
(Arbeiten zur Geschichte des antiken Judentums und des Urchristentums ; 47)
ISBN 90-04-11448-3

Library of Congress Cataloging-in-Publication Data

Library of Congress Cataloging-in-Publication Data is also available

ISSN 0169-734X
ISBN 90 04 11448 3

© Copyright 2000 by Koninklijke Brill nv, Leiden, The Netherlands

All rights reserved. No part of this publication may be reproduced, translated, stored in a retrieval system, or transmitted in any form or by any means, electronic, mechanical, photocopying, recording or otherwise, without prior written permission from the publisher.

Authorization to photocopy items for internal or personal use is granted by Brill provided that the appropriate fees are paid directly to The Copyright Clearance Center, 222 Rosewood Drive, Suite 910 Danvers MA 01923, USA. Fees are subject to change.

PRINTED IN THE NETHERLANDS

For Michael

TABLE OF CONTENTS

Foreword xi
Abbreviations xiii

General Introduction.. 1
  A David, the "Good Shepherd" 1
  B David in the Fourth Gospel 5
  C Literary Considerations 9
  D Terminology and Methodology for this Study 13

1 Johannine Usage of the Psalms in the Context of Early
    Christian Usage: A Preliminary Look.................................... 21
  A Introduction 21
  B The Psalms in the Synoptic Gospels 21
      1 Synoptic Quotations of the Psalms 21
      2 Synoptic Allusions to the Psalms 23
  C The Psalms in the Fourth Gospel 27
      1 Johannine Quotations of the Psalms 27
      2 Johannine Allusions to the Psalms 30
  D Statistical Analysis: Comparing John with the Synoptics .. 31
      1 Ratio of Psalm to Scripture Quotations in Mark 31
      2 Ratio of Psalm to Scripture Quotations in Matthew 32
      3 Ratio of Psalm to Scripture Quotations in Luke............ 33
      4 Ratio of Psalm to Scripture Quotations in John 33
      5 Overview of Statistical Analysis 34
  E The Psalms Quoted in the Fourth Gospel: A Profile
      of their usage in the NT 38
      1 Ps (21)22 39
      2 Ps (33)34 40
      3 Ps (40)41 41
      4 Ps (68)69 42
      5 Ps (77)78 43
      6 Ps (81)82 44
      7 Ps (117)118 45
  F Psalms Used in the NT and Not Quoted in the Fourth
      Gospel 46
      1 Ps (30)31 47
      2 Ps 8 48
      3 Ps 2 49

    4 Ps (90)91 52
    5 Ps (109)110 52
  G Conclusion 56

2 Davidic "Authorship" of the Psalms 59
  A Introduction 59
  B David's Musicianship 61
  C David's "Authorship" of a Corpus of Psalmody 65
  D The Liturgical David: Founder of the Temple
      and its Cult 72
  E The "Autobiographical" David: The Historical
      SuperscriptTradition 79
  F David the Prophet 91
  G The "Sapientialized" David 94
  H David as Compared and Contrasted with Moses 98
  I David as Psalmist in the Johannine View 102
  J Conclusion 110

3 The Psalms Quoted in the Book of Signs 115
  A Introduction 115
  B Psalm (68:10)69:9 in John 2:17 118
  C Psalm (77)78:24 in John 6:31 131
  D Psalm (77)78:16.20 in John 7:38 144
      Excursus: The Johannine Reception of Ps (77)78 161
  E Psalm (81)82:6 in John 10:34 164
  F Psalm (117)118:26 in John 12:13 176
  G Overview of the Five Citations in the Book of Signs 188

4 The Psalms Quoted in the Book of Glory 189
  A Introduction 189
  B Psalm (40:10)41:9 in John 13:18 191
  C Psalm (68:5)69:4 in John 15:25 201
  D Psalm (21:19)22:18 in John 19:24 208
  E Psalm (68:22)69:21 in John 19:28 219
  F Psalm (33:21)34:20 in John 19:36 229
  G Overview of the Five Citations in the Book of Glory 241

5 Other Psalms Present in the Fourth Gospel through
    Allusion and Echo 243
  A Introduction 243
  B Substantial Allusion: Ps (88)89 245
  C More Transitory Allusion 251

    1 Ps (39)40 252
    2 Pss (41-42)42-43 253
    3 Ps (22)23 and Ps (94)95 258
    4 Allusion to David's Psalms and the Shaping of
       Johannine Christology 265
  D Echo: Ps (109)110 and Ps 8 270
  E Johannine Resonances of Ps 1-2: An Intertextual
     Relationship? 278
  F Overview of Fourth Gospel Allusions to the Psalter 286

6 Shades of David in the Fourth Gospel Presentation
   of Jesus 289
  A Introduction 289
  B The Synoptic Presentation of Jesus in Terms
     Reminiscent of David 289
  C Echoes of David's Story in the Johannine
     Passion Narrative 292
  D Reminiscences of David Elsewhere in the Fourth Gospel.. 302
    1 David Anointed by Samuel 303
    2 David as Shepherd 308
  E The Johannine Jesus as the Expected "David" 309
  F Overview of Davidic Features in the Johannnine
     Portrayal of Jesus 314

General Conclusion 317

Bibliography 325

Indices 348

FOREWORD

This work is a revised version of a doctoral thesis presented at the School of Hebrew Biblical and Theological Studies, Trinity College, Dublin in 1996. The thesis remains substantially as submitted in 1996. I decided to confine the revisions to editing, attempting to make the work more audience-friendly and "fine tuning" the argument. The list of works consulted and quoted remains as it was in 1996. To have engaged seriously with works which have come out since the thesis was submitted would have prolonged the revision to an impractical extent.

I wish to thank Prof. Seán Freyne, my supervisor for the thesis, for so liberally sharing his time and knowledge with me. In the early, somewhat tentative stages of my work, his faith in its potential and his enthusiasm for what he clearly regarded as a joint project gave me the confidence I needed. I emerged from each consultation with him laden not only with gifts of the mind, but with books from his personal library on indefinite loan — a measure of his generosity. Above all, I have been personally enriched through his exceptional capacity for calling his disciples friends.

I am grateful to the School of Hebrew, Biblical and Theological Studies at Trinity College for granting me a share in the Elrington Scholarship. I also express my thanks to Prof. Werner Jeanrond of Lund University who was Head of Department for a short period during my time as a graduate student. I appreciate too the efficiency and helpfulness of the staff of the Berkeley Library, Trinity College.

For visiting reader's privileges and invaluable assistance, I wish to thank the staff of the Library at the Catholic Theological Union and the Jesuit Krauss McCormick Library, both in Chicago. I am also grateful to Bríd O'Brien and Mary Cunningham of the Library at the Milltown Institute, Dublin and Patrick Jones, Director of the Irish Institute of Pastoral Liturgy.

Dr Lomán MacAodha, one of those rare friends on whom one can "inflict" one's thesis in conversation, sustained me with his understanding of the scope of the work and with concrete practical help. At a difficult stage, when the waters had risen to my neck, my friend Seán Dooney, a specialist on governmental structures, sensed my near despair and invited me to talk through the argument of the thesis with him. This helped me to impose a structure which would eventually control the chaos.

Among the many others who helped in various ways, I wish to thank my mother, relatives and friends who offered encouragement and made allowances for my prolonged neglect of them, especially as the work neared completion. I am grateful to Dr John Page and to all my colleagues of the International Commission on English in the Liturgy for their interest in my studies and for the opportunities they have afforded me to discuss my ideas. My special thanks are due to Prof. Kathleen Hughes, Professor of Liturgy at the Catholic Theological Union, Chicago. Dr Maarten J. Menken of Utrecht graciously allowed me pre-publication access to some of his material. It was through the kindness of Dr Gerard Norton and thanks to his assistance with the deciphering, that I was able to consult the DSS microfiches. I also acknowledge the support and interest of Dr George Brooke, Dr Gervase Corcoran, Brendan Devitt and Hugh MacCaffery. I am grateful to Dr Kieran O'Mahony and Joan Deane for the assistance of their computer expertise and to Dataproducts Imaging Supplies Division (Europe, Africa & the Middle East) for their sponsorship of the printing.

I wish to thank Prof Martin Hengel of Tübingen for his help and advice concerning publication of the thesis and Mr Theo Joppe and Ms Willy de Gijzel of Brill for their patience, helpfulness and expertise.

Finally I wish to thank Michael, a supportive friend during the early stages who became my fiancé during the course of the work, and who waited patiently until the thesis was within sight of completion to become my husband. Without his regular demands for progress reports, his willingness to take second place, temporarily, to "David" and his unfailing support, this thesis would not yet have seen the light of day.

ABBREVIATIONS

ABD	Anchor Bible Dictionary
ANE	Ancient Near-Eastern
ANRW	Aufstieg Und Niedergang Der Römischen Welt
BCE	Before Common Era
BDB	Brown, Driver, Briggs Hebrew-English Lexicon
BeO	Bibbia e Oriente
Bijdr	Bijdragen, tijdschrift voor filosofie en theologie
BIOSCS	Bulletin of the International Organization for Septuagint and Cognate Studies
BSac	Bibliotheca Sacra
BTB	Biblical Theology Bulletin
BZ	Biblische Zeitschrift
CE	Common era
CRINT	Compendium Rerum Iudicarum ad Novum Testamentum
DACL	Dictionnaire d'archéologie chrétienne et de liturgie
DeltBibMel	Deltion Biblikon Meleton (Athens)
DJD	Discoveries in the Judean Desert of Jordan
DRev	Downside Review
DSS	The Dead Sea Scrolls
ET	English translation
ETL	Ephemerides Theologicae Lovaniensis
EvangQuart	Evangelical Quarterly
GCS	Griechische Christliche Schriftsteller
HBT	Horizons in Biblical Theology
HJPAJC	History of the Jewish People in the Age of Jesus Christ
HTS	Hervormde Teologiese Studies
IBS	Irish Biblical Studies
Int	Interpretation
JBQ	The Jewish Bible Quarterly
JETS	Journal of the Evangelical Theological Society
JNES	Journal of Near Eastern Studies
JSNT	Journal for the Study of the New Testament
JSP	Journal for the Study of the Pseudepigrapha
LAB	Liber Antiquitatum Biblicarum
LCL	Loeb Classical Library
LS	Louvain Studies
LSJ	Liddell-Scott-Jones, Greek-English Lexicon
LTP	Laval théologique et philosophique,
LumVie	Lumière et Vie
LumVit	Lumen Vitae
LXX	Septuagint
MT	Masoretic Text

NAB	New American Bible
NCB	New Century Bible
NEB	New English Bible
NedTT	Nederlands Theologisch Tijdschrift (The Hague)
Neot	Neotestamentica
NGTT	Nederuits Gereformeerde Teologiese Tydskrif
NJB	New Jerusalem Bible
NJBC	The New Jerome Biblical Commentary
NovT	Novum Testamentum
NRT	La nouvelle revue théologique
NT	New Testament
NTS	New Testament Studies
OL	Old Latin
OT	Old Testament
OTP	Charlesworth (ed.), The Old Testament Pseudepigrapha
PG	J. Migne, Patrologia Graeca
PIBA	Proceedings of the Irish Biblical Association
RevistB	Revista Biblica
RevQ	Revue de Qumran
SBL	Society of Biblical Literature
Scr	Scripture
SEÅ	Svensk exegetisk årsbok
RevAT	Revue Africaine de Théologie
RSV	Revised Standard Version
RTL	Revue Théologique de Louvain
SE	Studia Evangelica
SJT	Scottish Journal of Theology
ST	Studia Theologica
TDNT	Theological Dictionary of the New Testament
Tg. Ps.-J.	Targum Pseudo-Jonathan
TJT	Toronto Journal of Theology
TSol	Testament of Solomon
TyV	Teología y Vida
VT	Vetus Testamentum

David, the 'Good Shepherd' (Photo Zodiaque).

GENERAL INTRODUCTION

A. *David, the "Good Shepherd"*

The illustration at the beginning of this study shows a carved capital in the south nave of the Romanesque basilica at Vézelay, half way between Paris and Lyons. It depicts a lion with its paw on a lamb's head being forcibly restrained by the young David who, at the peril of his own life, has jumped on to the lion's back and put his two hands into its mouth. David, the shepherd who risks his life for the sheep, is portrayed in Vézelay not just as a figure from OT history, or even as an ancestor of Jesus, but as a prefiguration of the Good Shepherd who lays down his life for the sheep. The inspiration for the particular connection between David and Jesus which the Romanesque sculptor has brought to expression in this capital comes directly from the Fourth Gospel (cf. John 10:11.15). In fact, this sculpture captures, more elegantly than any verbal explanation could, the intuition which this study seeks to verify and interpret: that David has an important role in the Fourth Gospel.

The Vézelay capital illustrates the transformation that occurs when an already evocative scene from the Jewish Scriptures is reproduced in a Christian liturgical context. In fact this "quotation" in stone might well be described as a visual instance of intertextuality and thus a paradigm for our understanding of the early Christian reception of "The Psalms of David." The literary theory of intertextuality acknowledges that texts do not exist in isolation. When a quotation from an earlier work is introduced into a later work, it brings in its train manifold resonances of other texts already associated with it. Intertextuality is thus "less a name for a work's relation to particular prior texts than a designation of its participation in the discursive space of a culture."[1] Furthermore, the quoted text is itself transformed by its incorporation into a new context. The reception of the quotation as part of the later work will therefore depend on factors

---

[1] Jonathan Culler, *The Pursuit of Signs: Semiotics, Literature, Deconstruction* (London & Henley: Routledge & Kegan Paul, 1981) 103. "Any text is an intertext; other texts are present in it, at varying levels, in more or less recognizable forms: the texts of the previous and surrounding culture. Any text is a new tissue of past citations." Cf. Roland Barthes, "The Theory of the Text" in Robert Young (ed.),*Untying the Text: A Post-Structuralist Reader* (Boston, London & Henley: Routledge & Kegan Paul, 1981) 32-45, at 39.

far more complex than the reader's mere awareness of the original source. Intertextuality thus involves an exploration of the unconscious presuppositions, the *déjà lu*, which readers bring to a literary work.²

This visual citation of 1 Sam 17:34-5 depicts the account David gives of his shepherding exploits by way of assurance to Saul of his readiness and ability to fight Goliath in defence of the nation—

> Your servant used to keep sheep for his father; and when there came a lion, or a bear, and took a lamb from the flock, I went after him and smote him and delivered it out of his mouth...³

Already in its original context this speech points beyond its immediate referent. This is a figurative presentation of David's credentials for another kind of shepherding, kingship.⁴ It was from devoted shepherding such as that described in 1 Sam 17:34-5 that God took David, "to be shepherd of Jacob his (*sc.* God's) people, of Israel his inheritance" (Ps (77)78:70-72). There would be many an occasion when David's kingship would be exercised at the risk of his life. In Israel's collective memory, the image of David the shepherd-king, fighting "in the name of the Lord of hosts" against seemingly impossible odds (1 Sam 17:45) was enhanced with more and more detail as psalms traditionally attributed to him were retrospectively linked with various incidents in his career. The record of "all the hardships he endured" (Ps (131)132:1) was thus enshrined in the Psalter. There the voice of David could be heard praying, when surrounded by foes: "deliver me, lest like a lion they rend me," and singing "praise to the name of the Lord, the Most High" who had never failed to

---

² The term *déjà lu* refers to what Barthes elsewhere calls *les citations sans guillemets*. "The intertext is a general field of anonymous formulae whose origin can scarcely ever be located; of unconscious or automatic quotations, given without quotation marks..." Barthes, "Theory of the Text," 39.

³ Unless otherwise noted, all English translations from Scripture are from the RSV. The archaic pronouns (thee, thou, thy, thine) and verbal forms (art, hast *etc.*) have, however, been changed to conform with current English usage.

⁴ It is a *topos* of ancient Near Eastern monarchic ideology that the king is expected to prove himself fit to rule during a period of battle with the wild beasts in a hostile wilderness or desert setting. Philo drew on this tradition in his life of Moses: "... the chase of wild animals is a drilling ground for the general in fighting the enemy, and the care and supervision of tame animals is a schooling for the king in dealing with his subjects, and therefore kings are called 'shepherds of their people,' not as a term of reproach, but as the highest honour. ...the only perfect king...is one who is skilled in the knowledge of shepherding" (*Mos.* I, XI, 61, trans. F. H. Colson, *Philo*, LCL (Cambridge MA/London: Harvard University Press/Heinemann, 1959). This idea is also believed to underlie the reference to Jesus being "with the wild beasts" for forty days in Mark 1:13. For the lion as *l'adversaire par excellence des rois*, see E. Beaucamp, *Le Psautier*. Sources Bibliques. 2 vols. (Paris: Gabalda,1976, 1979) I, 113.

rescue him.⁵ In the ongoing development of this tradition represented by the extra-canonical psalms, the young shepherd, already a psalmist, prays to be delivered "from the paw of the lion" (cf. 1 Sam 17:37)—

> ...Shall I descend to Sheol by the mouth of the lion?
> Or shall the lion maim me?
> Is it not sufficient for them to ambush my father's flocks:
> and to tear a sheep from his sheepfold?
> They are even wishing to slay me...⁶

The young shepherd's struggle with the wild beasts would provide Judaism with a rationalization for the "adoption" of the image of Orpheus charming the trees, birds and wild animals with his music as a depiction of David.⁷ Early Christian iconography would gradually assimilate the Orpheus figure to that of the Johannine "Good Shepherd" and transform the "wild beasts" into the sheep of his flock.⁸ Since Orpheus was principally a cultic founder and composer of hymns, this could not have occurred if David the shepherd had not been remembered as psalmist. As Jean Magne puts it, "Orphée a été "davidisé" avant de devenir le "bon pasteur."⁹

The change wrought upon the 1 Sam 17:34-36 scene by its introduction into Vézelay demonstrates the transformative effect of quotation. If the young David tackling the lion carries a considerable "freight" of associations into his new context, he also acquires there a whole new *persona*, that of prophetic prefiguration of Jesus. David's

---

⁵ See Ps 7, "A Shiggaion of David which he sang to the Lord concerning Cush the Benjaminite," vv. 2 and 17.

⁶ From Ps 152 (5ApocSyrPs 4). See J. H. Charlesworth and J. A. Sanders, "More Psalms of David: A New Translation and Introduction" in J. H. Charlesworth (ed.), *The Old Testament Pseudepigrapha*, Vol. II (New York: Doubleday, 1985.) 616.

⁷ Until the discovery of the Qumran version of Ps 151, the earliest evidence for an Orphic David was a Jerusalem mosaic, dated *ca.* second century CE. This is reproduced in J. A. Sanders, *The Dead Sea Psalms Scroll* (Ithaca, New York: Cornell University Press, 1967) 99. Sanders first proposed an Orphic David in 11QPsᵃ Ps 151. See *The Dead Sea Psalms Scroll*, 98-101. Cf. J. Magne, "Orphisme, pythagorisme, essenisme dans le texte hebreu du Psaume 151?" (*RevQum* 8 [1975] 508-47) and "'Seigneur de l'Univers' ou David-Orphée?" (*RevQum* 9 [1977] 189-96). For a dissenting voice, cf. J. Strugnell, "Notes on the Text and Transmission of the Apocryphal Psalms 151, 154 (= Syr II) and 155 (=Syr III)" in *HTR* 59 (1966) 257-281, at 280.

⁸ The "Orphic" fresco in the Roman Catacomb of Callistus (second Century CE), departs from the classical model, adapting it towards a portrayal of the Good Shepherd. Instead of wild animals there are two sheep. See Henri Leclercq, "Orphée" in F. Cabrol and H. Leclercq (eds), *Dictionnaire d'Archéologie Chrétienne et de Liturgie* (Paris: Libraire Letouzey et Ané, 1936) Vol. 12, 2735 - 55, at 2738.

⁹ Jean Magne, "Orphisme," 535.

new setting, a Christian liturgical space, resounds with the psalms which he is believed to have composed in prophetic anticipation of Jesus. Within this environment, it is taken for granted that lines from these psalms such as "Zeal for your house will consume me," or "He who ate my bread has lifted his heel against me" find their full meaning on the lips of Jesus.[10]

The Vézelay capital is thus the visual equivalent of the typological reading of the story of David found in liturgical texts and biblical commentaries of the patristic and medieval periods. For those schooled in this tradition, prophetic intimations of Jesus were to be found in even the most apparently insignificant details of David's story. Bernard of Clairvaux, for example, represents the full flowering of this interpretive tradition. In the concluding sentence of his *De Diversis* Sermon 100, alluding to John 10:11 and 1 Sam 17:40, he compares the five smooth stones which David puts into his wallet with what the "true David" carries in his: *Habet etiam pastor bonus panem in pera, hoc est verbum Dei in memoria*.[11] In this allegorization of the five stones, Bernard shows himself heir to a tradition reaching back into pre-Christian Judaism.[12] For the medievals, David's role as psalmist was an integral feature of his prefiguration of Jesus. They received the "Davidic" reading of the psalms, as inherited from Judaism, further overlaid with a rich development of Christian and Christological *relecture*.[13] This had a particular attraction for these authors, gifted, as they were, with an extraordinary familiarity with the

---

[10] Ps (68:10)69:9, quoted in John 2:17, and Ps (40:10)41:9, quoted in John 13:18.

[11] Bernard of Clairvaux (1090-1153) may even have seen the David capital when he visited Vézelay to preach the Second Crusade there in 1146. The *verbum Dei in memoria* is explained elsewhere, in Bernard's Sermon, *De David et Golia, et quinque lapidibus* (Sermo IV pP) as five different kinds of scriptural "word"—*verbum comminationis, promissionis, dilectionis, imitationis et orationis*—which David carries in the *pera* of his memory. Cf. also *Sent.* II, 68. References are to the abbreviated titles in the 8 volume critical edition of Bernard's writings, *Sancti Bernardi Opera*, ed. Jean Leclercq, C. H. Talbot and H. M. Rochais, (Rome: Editiones Cistercienses, 1957-77).

[12] For early Jewish interpretations of David's five stones see J. Magne, "Le Verset des trois pierres dans la tradition du Psaume 151," *RevQum* 8 (1975) 565-591. In these allegorizations the number of stones varies: from three, to five, to seven. Thus in two early Arab recensions of Ps 151, the subject of Magne's article, David uses three stones which represent Abraham, Isaac and Jacob. In traditions which keep to the biblical five stones, Moses and Aaron are also mentioned. To these five, other traditions add another two stones representing God and David, e.g., *LAB* 61:5. See L. Ginzberg, *The Legends of the Jews* (Philadelphia: Jewish Publication Society of America, 1941) IV, 87.

[13] In a Christian interpretation of the psalms, the God spoken about or spoken to is the one whom Jesus called his Father. In a Christological reading, the psalms are seen as fulfilled in Jesus who is the speaker, the one spoken about, or the one addressed. See Balthasar Fischer, "Christological Interpretation of the Psalms Seen in the Mirror of the Liturgy." *Questions Liturgiques* 71 (1990), 227-35.

Psalter acquired during the daily hours of psalm singing to which they were committed as monastics or clerics. Again, Bernard may be cited as an illustration. For him the individual who speaks in David's psalms is really Jesus. Therefore spontaneous recollections of snatches of psalmody recalled from the liturgy are *verba Verbi*, words of the Word who is the true singer of the Songs of Zion.[14] The Vézelay sculptor and Bernard stand more than a millennium downstream from the NT source of this interpretive tradition. Having caught a glimpse in their work of the river in full spate, we now proceed to find and explore one of its headwaters—the Fourth Gospel.

B. *David in the Fourth Gospel*

The Psalter is the most frequently cited book of the Hebrew Scriptures in the NT. Not only is it is quoted over one hundred times (according to the 27th edition of the Nestlé-Aland text), but there are very few NT writings that show no trace of its presence in the form of either allusions or echoes.[15] The Jewish attribution of the Psalter to David is crucial for an understanding of the role of psalm quotations, allusions and echoes in the NT. Unlike modern critical scholarship, early Christian exegesis followed its contemporary Judaism in attributing the psalms to David, just as the Pentateuch was attributed to Moses,[16] Lamentations to Jeremiah,[17] and the Wisdom literature to Solomon.[18]

---

[14] See Bernard's *Super Cantica* Sermons, SC 32.4. For Davidic authorship of the psalms, see *SC* 32.8 (referring to Ps 26:8), *SC* 32.9 (referring to Ps 131:4-5) and *SC* 34,2 (referring to Ps 7:5). For a Christological reading of Pss 9:35, 68:2-3 and 24:18, see *IV HM*, 11. Psalm references are to the LXX - Vg. numbering.

[15] Possibly only Philemon and 2-3 John lack allusions to the Psalter. However, the presence or absence of citation is not necessarily an indicator of the importance of an OT passage for NT writers. 2 Sam 7, a foundational text for NT Christology, is cited only once in the NT, at Heb 1:5. On this point, see D. Moody Smith, "The Use of the Old Testament in the New" in James M. Efird (ed.), *The Use of the Old Testament in the New*, 3-65 (Durham, NC: Duke University Press, 1972) 4.

[16] The report in Deut 31:24 that Moses wrote "this Torah" on a scroll was taken to refer to the entire Pentateuch (Ezra 3:2; 7:6; Neh 1:7-9; 8:1.14; 9:14; 10:30; 13:2). See R. E. Friedman, "Torah (Pentateuch)" in D. N. Freedman (Editor-in-Chief), *The Anchor Bible Dictionary*. 6 Vols. (New York & London: Doubleday, 1992) VI, 605-22, at 618.

[17] According to 2 Chr 35:25, Jeremiah uttered a lament for Josiah which was preserved in a collection of laments. This may be based on an erroneous identification of "the Lord's anointed" in Lam 4:20 (written in the wake of the 587 events) with Josiah (ruled 640-609).

[18] Solomon's great reputation for wisdom is based on such passages as: the dying David's injunction to his son, "Act according to your wisdom"(1 Kgs 2:6), Solomon's prayer for wisdom (1 Kgs 3:9, pseudepigraphically expanded in Wis 9), the visit of the queen (1 Kgs 10:6-7), the concluding remark on his acts and his wisdom, said to be preserved in "the book of the acts of Solomon"(1 Kgs 11:41).

By the late Second Temple period, this attribution was by no means limited to what we nowadays would call "Laments of the Individual." It extended to the entire Psalter. There was a sense, then, in which even historical recitals or celebrations of Torah in the Psalter would be received as connected with David. The exact nature of the connection is something quite foreign to our modern Western concept of authorship. We will explore this is Ch. 2, but at this stage, we simply note that David flourished as psalmist in a culture where pseudepigraphy was an accepted part of literary activity.

The authority with which Davidic "authorship" had invested the psalms would be maximised by the NT authors. The notion, derived from the attribution to David, that the psalms were, in some sense, prophetic would enhance the effectiveness of psalm allusions and quotations as components of NT preaching, worship and apologetic. For the early Christians, Jesus was the "new David" in whose name King David had prophetically written his hymns. And so, for them, the psalms were about Jesus (Luke 24:44). In modern scholarship, once this attribution became historically discredited, its significance tended to be overlooked. With the more recent application of literary theory to the biblical text however, we have come to see that Davidic authorship of the psalms is part of the *déjà lu* which shaped the NT *relecture* of the Psalms.

David's "voice" was particularly audible in those psalms where the author laments, prays and utters praise in the first person singular. Early Christianity shared with contemporary Judaism the conviction that these psalms were actual utterances of David. The interpretive tradition (reflected in the biblical superscripts) whereby particular psalms were linked with incidents in the life of David was to set a precedent for the Evangelists in their presentation of Jesus as a "Davidic" figure. The identification of the "I" in these psalms as the David of the narrative traditions allowed the Evangelists to see David as prophetic of Jesus, not only in "his" psalms, but also in the events which were believed to have occasioned them. Furthermore, the "Davidlike" features in the Evangelists' portrayal of Jesus demonstrated that the Davidic hope, as expressed in the Latter Prophets (e.g., Ezek 34:23; 37:24; Hos 3:5; Jer 30:9), was fulfilled in him. The presentation of Jesus in terms reminiscent of the "historical" David and suggestive of the expected David, which is a feature of all the gospels, is, therefore, intimately connected with reference to the psalms.

This study focuses on the Fourth Gospel as an exemplification of the early Christian reception of the psalms. We will show that this Gospel contains more quotations of the psalms than any of the synoptics, and that it is particularly rich in allusions to the psalms and in echoes of their phraseology. We will find that it is occasionally quite independent in its psalm usage, that some of the psalm passages that it quotes occur nowhere else in the NT, while other psalm passages that are very much in evidence in the rest of the NT do not appear in John, at least not on the surface of the text. This is a highly cultic gospel in which the narrative is entwined around the Jewish cycle of feasts and many of the discourses of Jesus are presented as having been uttered in a context of worship, that is, in the milieu of psalmody.[19] Its portrayal of Jesus is that of the glorified Son, as encountered in the worship of the Christian assembly. Thus it is a work that has been shaped by the liturgical experience of a community which treasured the Jewish Scriptures, and in particular the psalms, as texts that bear witness to Jesus (John 5:30).

The "Davidlikeness" of Jesus is, perhaps, a neglected strand in the multi-hued texture of the Fourth Gospel. The Johannine presentation of Jesus as a Moses figure, "the Prophet like Moses," has been the object of several detailed studies.[20] The idea of Jesus as a David-like figure has tended to be regarded as a synoptic phenomenon. It has been noted, for example, that the Johannine Jesus is nowhere called "Son of David."[21] It is also frequently remarked that in the Fourth Gospel explanations of Jesus in terms suggestive of Davidic messianism, residues of earlier gospel tradition, are put on the lips of characters who have not yet reached full faith.[22] It is claimed that these opinions function in the narrative as challenges to the reader

---

[19] This has been demonstrated effectively by Aileen Guilding. Even though the details of her proposals concerning the lectionary background to the Fourth Gospel have not met with wide acceptance, she is surely correct in her primary insight that "the starting point for its (sc. the Fourth Gospel's) interpretation is to be found in first century Jewish temple worship and synagogue preaching." See *The Fourth Gospel and Jewish Worship* (Oxford: Clarendon Press, 1960) 2. As David E. Aune has shown, Jesus is depicted in the Fourth Gospel as he was experienced in the context of worship. See *The Cultic Setting of Realized Eschatology in Early Christianity* (Leiden: E. J. Brill, 1972).

[20] The title of this study is an intentional echo of one of these studies, T. F. Glasson's *Moses in the Fourth Gospel* (London: S.C.M., 1963). See also Wayne Meeks, *The Prophet King: Moses Traditions and the Johannine Christology* (Leiden: Brill 1967); J. Louis Martyn, *History and Theology in the Fourth Gospel* (Nashville: Abingdon, 1968) especially pp. 104-11; M. E. Boismard, *Moïse ou Jésus; Essai de Christologie Johannique* (Leuven: Leuven University Press, 1988).

[21] John Ashton mentions the absence of the title "Son of David" from the Fourth Gospel as one of "two negative facts" to be taken into consideration before assuming that "King of Israel" is a messianic title in John. See *Understanding the Fourth Gospel* (Oxford: Clarendon, 1991) 262.

[22] E. g., M. de Jonge, *Jesus: Stranger from Heaven and Son of God*, (Missoula: Scholars, 1977) 50.

to go beyond an inadequate category for understanding him. It is noteworthy, however, that the Fourth Gospel also relegates the category of "Prophet" to this status (John 4:19, 6:14, 7:40, 8:52, 9:17). That does not make it any less worthy of attention, as the literature shows.

Reception studies are concerned with the received ideas of a reading community, the influence these ideas have had, the way they have stimulated the development of alternative views and how they themselves have undergone metamorphosis. Without in any way denying the "Prophet-like-Moses" traits of the Johannine portrait, this reception study will demonstrate that Jesus is also shown as a new/ideal David figure in the Fourth Gospel, and that Davidic motifs form an important and perhaps underestimated current in Johannine thought.[23] It will argue that a strong inter-textual link between the Fourth Gospel and the biblical traditions about David—as remembered and as expected—adds a particular resonance to the Johannine reading of the psalms.

C. *Literary Considerations*

This is a study of the way in which a later text (the Fourth Gospel) uses an earlier text (the Psalter) and how, like the David scene on the Vézelay capital, the earlier text is transformed by its incorporation into the later. As T. S. Eliot explained, anticipating later theorization about intertextuality, existing works are modified by their introduction into a new work. The past is altered by the present as much as the present is directed by the past. In his essay, "Tradition and the Individual Talent" (1919), he suggests that true individuality lies not in the aspects of a poet's work in which it least resembles the work of others, but in those parts "in which the dead poets, his ancestors, assert their immortality most vigorously."[24] In a similar way, the individuality of the creative mind responsible for the Fourth Gospel is powerfully sensed when the voice of David, the poet par excellence of Israel, is heard in the text. This voice is not just a source or even an influence, but is, to use Eliot's metaphor, a "new compound" formed from two elements, the Psalter and the story of Jesus, combined under the catalytic effect of an early Christian re-

---

[23] Gunter Reim believes that the title "Son of David" has in fact "cast its shadow" on the Fourth Gospel references to Jesus as "King" which reflect Johannine acceptance, but at the same time, re-interpretation of the title. See *Studien zum Alttestamentlichen Hintergrund des Johannes Evangeliums* (Cambridge: University Press, 1974) 248.

[24] T. S. Eliot, *Selected Essays*, (London: Faber & Faber, 1932) 14.

flection which encompassed worship, preaching, Scripture study and writing. The existing "work" of David, the Psalter, once re-read in a new work, the Fourth Gospel, is thus irrevocably altered. It is this transformation that has enabled the Johannine community to find in the Psalter both testimony to Jesus' divine status and a vehicle for its own worship "in spirit and truth."

The guises in which the Psalter appears in the Fourth Gospel, as in the NT generally, range from actual quotations where the author gives notice that an earlier source is being used, through allusions where the author refers recognizably to a work known to the ideal audience, to echoes which, to quote John Hollander's explanation, "constitute a kind of underground cipher message...or perhaps a private melody or undersong hummed during composition" and heard only by a particularly attentive reader.[25] The capacity to invoke other meanings is essential to the concept of echo. As allusion, literally word-play, is of its nature an adaptation or accommodation of an earlier work, its revisionary power is easily recognized. But quotations too, even if lexically they appear to be faithful representations of the cited text, are equally distortions, radical reinterpretations of the original voice, that generate new signification.

These three modes of reference to an existing text—quotation, allusion and echo—function on a "sliding scale" of diminishing intentionality on the part of the author and decreasing visibility on the surface of the text, requiring a correspondingly increasing competence on the part of the reader. Authors quote intentionally, their allusions may plausibly be presumed to be intentional, but they can echo an earlier work quite inadvertently. Quotations, because they are "sign-posted" in the text by a formula of quotation, are of their nature obvious. Allusions, although more fragmentary and periphrastic, must still be recognizable if they are to perform their function. Echoes, however, are covert, faint, blurred, subliminal, often as small as a single word or as elusive as a particular cadence or turn of phrase. Verbal echoes may consist of as little as one word. Thematic echoes may not even have any actual words in common with the source text. Structural echoes may occur when a more extended OT passage can be perceived as functioning like a framework or as generating the sequence of thought in a NT passage. Readers are directed by the author to perceive quotations as such. They are presumed by the author to be able to recognize allusions to material that inhabits the shared "portable library" or, as the the-

---

[25] John Hollander, *The figure of Echo: A Model of Allusion in Milton and After.* (Berkeley: University of California Press, 1981) ix.

ory of linguistics would have it, the "presupposition pool" of author and reader.[26] They need a well trained ear to hear echoes.

Obviously, it is important to establish criteria for each category. This is fairly straightforward with regard to quotations. References to Scripture introduced by an introductory formula such as "This was to fulfil the Scripture..." (John 19:24) or "Is it not written in your Law ...?" (John 10:34) are clearly quotations. The Evangelist alerts the reader to their presence in the work. There are exceptions, however, the cry of the dying Jesus, "My God, my God, why have you forsaken me?" (Mark 15:34; Matt 27:46), for example. Obviously this is a quotation from Ps (21)22. Another quotation from Ps (117)118:26 in John 12:13—"Blessed is he who comes in the name of the Lord."—is introduced in direct speech without an introductory formula. Clearly, though, its narrative setting functions *in lieu* of such a formula and its textual fidelity to its source is beyond question. Matthew's second quotation of this psalm passage (Matt 23:39) illustrates well the transformative power of quotation. The referent for the Lucan parallel (Luke 13:35) is clearly the entry of Jesus into Jerusalem (Luke 19:38) with the possibility of an eschatological reference, perhaps to the destruction of the Temple, at a more figurative level. In Matt 23:39, the eschatological reference is inescapable, as the entry into Jerusalem has already taken place. In fact, its position at the opening of Matthew's eschatological discourse (Chs 23-24) requires such a reading if it is to make sense.[27] The new context which Matthew creates for the quotation thus imposes the eschatological interpretation which is inherent, though latent, in Luke's version.[28]

Generally speaking, allusions manifest substantial repetition of words from the precursor work, although there can often be a strong case for thematic allusion even where there is minimal verbal contact. This means that the dividing line between allusion or echo can be somewhat blurred. The distinction seems to lie in the realm of authorial intent. If the "point" of a passage would be lost, were the reader to miss the reference to Scripture, then this is likely to be a

---

[26] Hollander, *Figure of Echo*, 64. The term "presupposition pool," is explained with reference to the biblical text in P. Cotterell and M. Turner, *Linguistics and Biblical Interpretation* (London: SPCK, 1989) 89 -95.

[27] As Hans-Joachim Kraus explains, "Only when the Messiah (as Son of Man) comes from heaven will he really be the "coming one"...Only then—and this is the meaning of this saying—will Ps 118:26 be fulfilled." See, *Theology of the Psalms: A Continental Commentary*, trans., Keith Crim (Minneapolis: Fortress, 1992) 193.

[28] A similar Christian "eschatological" interpretation of Ps (117)118:26 occurs in *Didache* 9—"May the Lord come and may this world pass away! Amen! Hosanna to the house of David!" The *Didache* is dated 100-150, with the possibility of some passages being earlier.

case of allusion. For example, the Fourth Evangelist clearly intends the readers to see a connection between Jesus' words to Nathaniel—"...you will see heaven opened and the angels of God ascending and descending upon the Son of Man" (John 1:51)—and Jacob's dream (Gen 28:12). Without recognition of the Genesis allusion, they would be at a disadvantage and quite unable to experience the meaning effect of the passage.

In contrast, a NT passage in which there is an echo of Scripture can be read quite satisfactorily "at face value." For example, the Johannine Jesus' warning about the branches that do not abide in him withering, being thrown into the fire and burned (John 15:6) is quite intelligible as part of an extended viticultural metaphor. An attentive reader may, however, catch here an echo 2 Sam 23:6 where David is presented as saying—

> "But the godless are like thorns that are thrown away
> ...and they are utterly consumed with fire."

A deeper, more enriching level of meaning opens up for such a reader, in this case, as we will see, a reading which draws one of several Johannine lines of comparison between Jesus and David. For such a reading to be plausible, it is not essential to show that the author intended to echo Scripture; it could simply be be part of the *déjà lu* which the author has brought to bear, even unconsciously, on the writing.

Since an echo may be fleeting, often no more than a single word, we need certain controls lest we slip into "parallelomania." So the echoed text must be reasonably distinctive. The claim that the author is echoing Scripture in a particular passage must be in line with what we know of the conventions for Scripture interpretation during the NT period. It must also cohere with the author's general line of argument.[29] In practice, we tend to discern echoes by hunches and intuitions which we then seek to verify by using criteria such as these. Yet, while such controls have their place, we must acknowledge, in the end, that the nature of echo is such that it resists schematization.

For modern readers it will frequently be what John Hollander calls "the genially open philological cf." in the margin or the footnotes which suggests the presence of an echo.[30] Our task, as students of the NT, is to discover the intended audience as readers, who did

---

[29] Useful criteria for the testing of echoes are presented by Richard B. Hays in *Echoes of Scripture in the Letters of Paul* (Yale: Yale University Press, 1989) 28-32.
[30] *The Figure of Echo*, 88.

not have the benefit of *marginalia*, to try and hear the resonances which scriptural references would have created for them. This involves trying to stand alongside them, within what Hollander calls "the caves of ambience and the chambers of meaning," that is, sharing, as far as possible, the presuppositions, the *déjà lu* which they brought to their reception of the Gospel. In this way we may begin to learn what they made of it.

In his descriptions of the elusiveness of echo, Hollander's frequent recourse to imagery from the world of music is most enlightening and appropriate for this study of intertextual reference to a text which has always been transmitted in song—

> Echoes can be so faint and fragmentary that they seem to enter a poem as tonal quality, or shading of voice, even as harmonic partials, accompanying a fundamental pitch, enter and shape its world of timbre rather than being heard in their own right....The reader of texts, in order to overhear echoes must have some kind of access to an earlier voice, and to its cave of resonant signification, analogous to that of the author of the later text. When such access is lost in a community of reading, what may have been an allusion may fade in prominence; and yet a scholarly recovery of the context would restore the allusion, by revealing an intent as well as by showing means.[31]

If Fourth Gospel borrowings from the Psalter, are to make their full referential impact on us, we need access to the "cave" or ambience of signification in which author and ideal readers heard the voice of David. We need to attune our ear to the overtones that this voice carried for them and to hear, as they did, echoes of the biblical traditions about David resonating in "sympathetic vibrations" with the psalms.[32]

D. *Terminology and Methodology for this Study*

This study adopts a predominantly, although not exclusively, synchronic approach to the Fourth Gospel reception of the psalms. It views the Johannine reception of the psalms as what Hans Robert Jauss has called "a synchronic cross-section of a moment in the process of reception."[33] A synchronic method is congenial to an ex-

---

[31] Hollander, *The Figure of Echo*, 64
[32] The production of sympathetic vibrations is an acoustical phenomenon whereby vibrations can occur in an object as a result of similar vibrations in a neighbouring body.
[33] See "Literary History as a Challenge to Literary Theory," a translation of Chs 5-12 of *Literaturgeschichte als Provokation der Literaturwissenschaft* (Konstanz:1967), in Ralph Cohen (ed.), *New Directions in Literary History* (London: Routledge & Kegan Paul, 1974), 32-33.

ploration of the way in which the Gospel's intertextual reference to the psalms functioned among its original readers. Marinus de Jonge describes the original audience of the Gospel as "people who did *not* take its prehistory into account."[34] Certainly, they would not have been engaged in a textual comparison of the "definitive version" of the Gospel with earlier recensions. However, the form in which the Gospel has come down to us confronts us with the obvious care the Evangelist has taken to preserve an earlier narrative source, even to the point of creating the occasional *aporia* in his text. As Robert T. Fortna has pointed out, Johannine Christians would have brought a memory of that source to their reception of the Gospel. Thus, the modern redaction-critical method may have some similarities to the way the original readers would have perceived and understood the Gospel. Like that of the redaction critic, their reading involved "comparing the old with the new."[35]

In the course of this study, we will discover that certain psalms which had a decisive role in the shaping of the kerygma are apparently absent from the Fourth Gospel. This study proposes that, in a similar way to what Fortna has described, the original readers would have brought to their reception of the Gospel text a memory of these psalms being quoted with reference to Jesus. This memory would have sensitized and alerted them to even the most fragmentary echoes of these psalms in the Gospel text. An awareness of this memory can amplify these echoes for us, rendering them audible, and enabling us to "track" their generative role in the formation of Johannine Christology. It is in this sense that diachronic considerations will have an important, even if ancillary, place in this study. To read the Fourth Gospel purely synchronically would be to hear polyphonic music as homophony, to notice only the chordal progressions without enjoying the contrapuntal interplay which accounts for so much of "The Pleasure of the Text."[36]

In keeping with its synchronic bias, this study envisages a single implied author who functions as the narrator and is responsible for the text as we have received it. The name John, masculine personal pronouns, and the terms "the author" and "the Evangelist," are used in

---

[34] M. de Jonge, *Jesus: Stranger from Heaven and Son of God* (Missoula: Scholars Press, 1977) 198.

[35] Robert T. Fortna, *The Fourth Gospel and its Predecessor: From Narrative Source to Present Gospel* (Philadelphia: Fortress, 1988) 8-9. For another critique of a purely synchronic approach to the Fourth Gospel, see Mark W. G. Stibbe, *John's Gospel*, (London & New York: Routledge, 1994) 74-75.

[36] Title of a book by Roland Barthes, *Le plaisir du texte* (Paris: Editions du Seuil, 1973).

this study as designations for this writer.³⁷ This does not, of course, constitute a denial of the ample evidence in the text for several editorial and redactional hands. It is rather an aspect of the particular approach which this study adopts.

Textual matters concerning the prehistory of the Johannine form of the psalm quotations, other recensions of the Greek Psalter agreeing more closely with the Hebrew, alternative renderings which may have persisted in later Greek translations, would be outside the scope of this study. Detailed work, diachronic in approach, attempting to recover the *Vorlagen* for the Johannine Scripture citations has been published in recent years, notably by M. J. J. Menken and B. Schuchard.³⁸ This study draws amply upon their research. In many instances, their findings contribute important exegetical insights which support and strengthen its argument. In keeping with its intertextual methodology, it takes up those insights and interprets them from a somewhat different perspective. The generic term "Septuagint" is used in full awareness that in the NT period the term was fairly elastic and the Greek text itself was not fixed.³⁹ It is widely recognized, however, that, even when variants are taken into account, the Evangelists agree much more with the Greek Scriptures than with the Aramaic or Hebrew versions.⁴⁰ In this study, the term "LXX" refers to our present best possibility of access to the Greek text which Johannine Christians knew.⁴¹

As this study concerns the psalms, both as received in Judaism and as employed in the NT, it will be necessary to use both the Hebrew and the Septuagintal numbering. Where the discussion centres around Jewish interpretive traditions, the Hebrew numbering is used. Where it focuses on the Greek Psalter and NT intertextual ref-

---

³⁷ The fact that some of these designations are masculine is not intended as an exclusion of the possibility that authorial activity of women may have contributed to the Gospel. For that possibility, see Sandra M. Schneiders, *The Revelatory Text: Interpreting the New Testament as Sacred Scripture* (San Francisco: Harper, 1991) 185.

³⁸ Maarten J. J. Menken, *Old Testament Quotations in the Fourth Gospel: Studies in Textual Form* (Kampen: Kok Pharos, 1996); Bruce G. Schuchard, *Scripture Within Scripture: The Interrelationship of Form and Function in the Explicit Old Testament Citations in the Gospel of John*. SBL Dissertation Series 133 (Atlanta: Scholars Press, 1992).

³⁹ "In short, we can detect at least six uses for the term "LXX" in antiquity: the earliest Greek translation of the Pentateuch, the earliest Greek translation of the entire Old Testament, Origen's koine, Origen's completed fifth column, any authoritative Greek text, and the entire Greek tradition." See Leonard Greenspoon, "The Use and Abuse of the Term 'LXX' and Related Terminology in Recent Scholarship," *BIOSCS* 20 (1987) 21-29, at 28.

⁴⁰ See Bruce C. Chilton, *A Galilean Rabbi and his Bible: Jesus' Use of the Interpreted Scripture of his Time*, (Delaware: Glazier, 1984) 89.

⁴¹ Alfred Rahlfs (ed.), *Septuaginta: Id est Vetus Testamentum graece iuxta LXX interpretes* (2 vols.). Stuttgart: Deutsche Bibelgesellschaft, 1979.

erence to the psalms, the Septuagintal numbering is usually preferred. The text will always indicate which numbering is being used. When, to avoid confusion, both Septuagintal and Hebrew numbering are required, for example, when a psalm is first introduced into the discussion, the Septuagintal and Hebrew numbering will appear as follows: Ps (40:10) 41:9.

In order to make this book accessible to those who do not know New Testament Greek, some translations of the Greek are provided. Obviously, it would not be possible to translate every instance of Greek in the book, especially where the argument depends on Greek vocabulary and verbal forms. We have provided a translation at the beginning of each section and wherever a new psalm quotation or allusion is introduced. We have also provided a translation of the Septuagint where it is necessary for the reader to understand that it differs from the Hebrew text. Elsewhere, Scripture references will enable readers to follow the discussion by referring to their own ET of the Bible.

Any consideration of the textual form of quotations needs to be balanced by a consciousness that a text such as the Fourth Gospel comes from a culture which "exhibits a strong bias towards orality, with even literates expressing little confidence in writing."[42] Even though the ancients produced significant literary works, they remained convinced that the spoken word was the real means of communication. The written text was always intended for reading aloud. *A fortiori*, this must be said of a text like the Psalter whose function was largely liturgical. In the ancient world, the acts of both writing and reading were, in fact, inconceivable without vocalization.[43] Reading aloud was necessary for the comprehension of a text written in lines with a consistent number of letters, using numerous abbreviations, and having neither punctuation nor separation into words. Paul Achtemeier alerts us to the implications of this for the study of intertextual reference in an ancient text.

> The shape of written texts in late Western antiquity, with their absence of all visible indications of organization of thought, also must be taken into account in our consideration of references in one text to another. In such written texts, the location of a given passage would be extraordinarily difficult: aside from the need to roll and re-roll, there would be no visible indication of where various parts of the

---

[42] See P. J. J. Botha, "Living Voice and Lifeless Letters: Reserve towards Writing in the Graeco-Roman World," *HTS* 49 (1993) 742-759 at 742.

[43] See, for example, Luke 1:63 where the expression ἔγραψεν λέγων indicates that it is in the act of writing that Zechariah shows that he has regained his speech. Note also that Philip hears the Ethiopian reading (Acts 8:30).

composition began or ended. Nor would there be a way, once the passage was located, of referring to it by paragraph or page so that others could find it. A reference meant the words itself. All of that simply means, I would urge, that authors did not "check references" in the way that modern scholars do (or ought to do!). In light of the pervasive orality of the environment, and the physical nature of written documents, references were therefore much more likely to be quoted from memory than to be copied from a source.[44]

The reliance on memory in the ancient world and the relatively limited amount of literary material available meant that first century readers and hearers would be alert to biblical allusion and echo to an extent which we today find difficult to imagine.[45] The way in which the pervasive orality/aurality of the culture, ensured an effective "filtering" of the Scriptures through interpretive tradition, is equally difficult for us to comprehend fully.[46]

The question of orality also has implications for the use of Jewish sources which postdate the NT period. Given the importance attached to memorization in the preservation and transmission of the Scriptures in Judaism, a record of oral interpretive traditions is sure to contain genuine reminiscences of earlier periods. From the point of view of dating, however, the *Targumim* to the Writings are probably to be classed, with Onkelos and Jonathan to the Prophets, as unknown in Palestine, in their written form, before 1,000 CE.[47] Does this indicate that we should dismiss the Psalms Targum and, even more certainly, the *Midrash Tehillim* as too late to be of any direct importance for a NT study?

In his article on the dating of Targumic literature, Anthony D. York draws attention to the two NT passages which allow us to claim, on the basis of textual evidence, that the Targum to the Psalms existed in the NT period: Matt 27:46—Ηλι ηλι λεμα σαβαχθανι; —"Eli, Eli, lama sabachthani?"—(possibly an Aramaic form of Ps [21]22:1, although this has since been disputed[48]) and the quotation in Eph 4:8—

---

[44] Paul J. Achtemeier, "Omne Verbum Sonat: The New Testament and the Oral Environment of Late Western Antiquity," *JBL* 109 (1990) 3-27, at 26-27.

[45] Cf. Chilton, *A Galilean Rabbi*, 68-69.

[46] Donald Juel cites a modern example of "the interpretive power of tradition." People today are "convinced by a special form of argument" that certain biblical texts are "messianic"...simply because they are part of Handel's *Messiah*. See *Messianic Exegesis: Christological Interpretation of the Old Testament in Early Christianity*, (Philadelphia: Fortress, 1988)16.

[47] See Anthony D. York, "The Dating of Targumic Literature," *JSJ* 5 (1974) 49-62.

[48] Joseph Fitzmyer, writing on 4Q243, holds that the name "El" found in this fragment "puts an end to the debate whether the words of Jesus on the cross in the Matthean form...were really Aramaic or half Hebrew and half Aramaic, as has been at times maintained." See "The Aramaic Language and the Study of the New Testament," *JBL* 99 (1980) 5-21, at 14-15.

Ἀναβὰς εἰς ὕψος ᾐχμαλώτευσεν αἰχμαλωσίαν,
ἔδωκεν δόματα τοῖς ἀνθρώποις.

When he ascended on high he led a host of captives;
he gave gifts to human beings.

—which is generally believed to reflect the Targum to Ps (67)68:19.[49] Of course, there is no evidence to show that this particular Targum existed in written form.[50] The most we can say is that these passages *may* reflect what was eventually to become the written Targum.[51] However, even if textual evidence allowing us to bring forward the dating of the written Psalms Targum were to be found, we still could not claim that any single manuscript contained all that ever existed of the Targum, much less that there was one official, uniform text. As York warns—"Given the assumption that the New Testament and the Targumim were contemporaneous, one still has to establish that the text of the Targum we have today corresponds to the text of New Testament times, and this is no easy task."[52]

Some would contend that the use of later Jewish midrashic material in NT study is inappropriate because of the lack of evidence that the developments they contain were known in the first century.[53] On the other hand, there are those who would include the later Jewish material among the possible sources for traditions reflected in the Fourth Gospel. John Ashton, for one, would count among the "'Jewish' sources" for the Fourth Gospel the Old Testament Apocrypha and Pseudepigrapha, the *Targumim*, the *Odes of Solomon*, the Samaritan Writings, the Dead Sea Scrolls...as well as the rabbinical material and various works of Jewish mysticism." In his opinion, "Together, these constitute a vein not likely to be exhausted for many years."[54] Lindars too notes the Fourth Evangelist's familiarity with ideas not found in the primitive gospel strands and known to us only from rabbinic sources.[55]

---

[49] York, "The Dating," 56.

[50] For oral transmission of the Targum in NT times, see Birger Gerhardssohn, *Memory and Manuscript: Oral and Written Transmission in Rabbinic Judaism and Early Christianity* (Copenhagen: G. W. K. Gleerup / Lund: Ejnar Munskgaard, 1961) 29 and Ch. 5, "The Importance of Public Worship for the Preservation of the Text."

[51] York, "The Dating," 61.

[52] York, "The Dating," 62.

[53] For Raymond Brown, e.g., "appeal to later Jewish midrashim is methodologically weak." See *The Death of the Messiah: From Gethsemane to the Grave* (London: Chapman, 1994) 1447.

[54] Ashton, *Understanding*, 26.

[55] E.g., the point of controversy found in 5:17, the rabbinic argument in 6:45, and the idea of the hidden Messiah in 7:27. See Barnabas Lindars, *The Gospel of John* (London: Oliphants, 1972) 37.

An important feature of the Jewish sources to which we will refer in this study is their haggadic character. As R. Bloch has pointed out,

> ...the *aggadah*, essentially homiletic in nature, represents an intrinsically religious meditation on immutable sacred texts; it is much less subject to fluctuation, to adaptation to ever-changing circumstances, than is the *halakah*, whose nature is essentially practical. Thus the *aggadah* has a much more stable nature, one more apt to conserve extremely ancient traditions.[56]

The conservative nature of Jewish exegesis is thus particularly evident in much of the Jewish material we will be using in this study. This is especially so in view of the liturgical nature of the Psalter and the homiletic character of its interpretive expansions. The axiom of David Daube is surely apt: "The Haggadah is a piece of liturgy, and it is more difficult to expurgate liturgy than almost any other kind of literature."[57]

The charge of anachronism would certainly be justified if one were to insist that a direct genetic relationship exists between a given NT passage and an interpretation found, for example, in the *Midrash Tehillim*.[58] However, the methodology of intertextuality allows one to make other than genetic connections between texts. Surely too the exegetical insights of Jewish authors of the first millennium steeped in the Hebrew Scriptures have, at the very least, as much chance of reflecting an ongoing Jewish style of exegesis that had its roots in antiquity, as those of modern academics.

In assessing the value of these sources for a NT study, perhaps the most one can expect is to be able to recognize a late interpretation, though even with this modest hope there is a problem. For example, it would, at first, appear unlikely that a reading of Ps (40:10)41:9,

---

[56] See R. Bloch, "Methodological Note for the Study of Rabbinic Literature," in W. S. Green (ed.), *Approaches to Ancient Judaism: Theory and Practice*, Brown Judaic Studies I (Missoula: Scholars Press, 1978) 51-75, at 54.

[57] David Daube, *The New Testament and Rabbinic Judaism* (London: Athlone Press, 1956) 9.

[58] The dating of the *Midrash Tehillim* was discussed by William Braude in the 1957 introduction to his English translation, *The Midrash on Psalms* (New Haven: Yale University Press, 1959) xxv-xxxii. Braude held that it was compiled in the 9th century CE, that it continued to be elaborated as late as the 13th century, but that it may contain material from a collection of homilies on the psalms known to have been in existence in the 3rd century CE. He noted that it reports the *dicta* of two first century rabbis, Hillel and Shammai. This last point would nowadays be treated with a little more caution. In literature of this kind, attribution of a saying to a venerable rabbi of the past is notoriously unreliable as it may simply reflect a desire to invest an opinion with an aura of authority. "The tacking on of a revered rabbi's name to a saying hardly guarantees its authenticity." See J. P. Meier, *A Marginal Jew: Rethinking the Historical Jesus*. Vol. I, "The Roots of the Problem and the Person," Anchor Bible Reference Library (New York: Doubleday 1991) 272.

preserved in the *Midrash Tehillim*, which refers to those who ate David's bread as his disciples in the House of Study goes back to the NT period. True, it was in much later Judaism that David came to be revered as a "rabbi."[59] However, one would have to acknowledge that such a development did not take place overnight. As we will see, David's reputation as a sage is already well established by the first century CE, and the quotation of this very verse in John 13:18 may well be an early testimony to it.

This brings us to the possible contribution that NT studies, which take account of the *Midrashim* and *Targumim* might make to Jewish studies. In the case of this study, the Fourth Gospel may be found to preserve Jewish readings of the biblical text known until now only from rabbinical sources. Something similar happened when, for example Ps-Philo or the DSS were found to contain interpretations of Scripture which had previously been regarded as the products of rabbinical Judaism.[60] Again, a note of caution is in order. In positing an influence of the Jewish interpretive tradition at some stage of the development of a NT text we should always bear in mind the possibility "that rabbinic documents may reflect (rather than underlie) Christian teaching."[61]

In so far as the Psalms Targum and the *Midrash Tehillim* retain elements of earlier interpretations found in older sources, they do afford, at the very least, valuable illustrative parallels. Striking convergences between these Jewish sources and the Fourth Gospel may even suggest that interpretations of the psalms, later incorporated in the Targum and Midrash, may go back as far as the first century CE and may even have influenced John's composition. We will use the Jewish sources with caution, in full awareness of the problem of depending on material which found written form long after NT times. We will therefore attach more credibility to material that is supported by the witness of other NT writings and such independent sources as Philo, Josephus and the Apostolic Fathers.

---

[59] In *y. Ber.* 1:1, e.g., we find "Rabbi David ben Jesse" who, in the speeches which scripture puts in his mouth, talks Torah and does Torah deeds. See Jacob Neusner, *Messiah in Context: Israel's History and Destiny in Formative Judaism* (Philadelphia: Fortress, 1984) 88-90.

[60] On this point see A. T. Hanson, *The Prophetic Gospel: A Study of John and the Old Testament* (Edinburgh: T. & T. Clark, 1991) 20.

[61] Chilton, *A Galilean Rabbi*, 44.

CHAPTER ONE

JOHANNINE USAGE OF THE PSALMS IN THE CONTEXT OF EARLY CHRISTIAN USAGE: A PRELIMINARY LOOK

A. *Introduction*

At the outset, several questions arise. Does the Fourth Gospel quote or allude to the psalms more frequently than the synoptics do? What proportion of Fourth Gospel OT reference do psalm quotations actually represent? Does John draw on the same psalms as the synoptics? Or conversely, are there psalms which have a high profile in the synoptics and/or in other NT writings and yet do not appear to be functioning in the Fourth Gospel?

Our approach to Johannine psalm usage is firstly to situate it in the context of wider NT psalm reference in order to show its distinctiveness. It is especially important to achieve a profile of the synoptic pattern of usage of the psalms so that the particular features of the Johannine usage can emerge more clearly. In this chapter we confine ourselves, as a first step, to quotations and and then to clear verbal allusions. The other less overt forms of intertextual reference discussed in the General Introduction are, of their nature, not easily quantifiable. As they do not lend themselves to the form of analysis used in this chapter, they will be dealt with in Chs 3—5. We begin with an overview of synoptic psalm usage. As we are simply identifying psalm quotations and allusions at this initial stage, English translations of the psalms will generally suffice.

B. *The Psalms in the Synoptic Gospels*

1. *Synoptic Quotations of the Psalms*

In all three synoptics, Jesus is represented as quoting a psalm and as attributing it to David when he poses the question about Ps [109]110:1—

> The Lord says to my Lord: "Sit at my right hand,
> till I make your enemies your footstool."[1]

---

[1] Mark 12:36; Matt 22;44; Luke 20:42. Mark's and Matthew's variant form of this psalm verse—"till I put your enemies under your feet"—is discussed on p. 54 below.

In all three synoptics, Jesus concludes the vineyard parable with the passage from Ps [117]118:22-23—

> The stone which the builders rejected
> has become the head of the corner.[2]

Although the verbal form of the quotation varies, all three synoptics report the song of the crowd at Jesus' solemn entry into Jerusalem as Ps (117)118:26—

> Blessed is he who comes in the name of the Lord.[3]

Both Matthew and Luke introduce this quotation a second time in a pericope from "Q," where Jesus declares, "You will not see me again until you say, 'Blessed is he who comes in the name of the Lord.'"[4]

In the "Q" account of the temptation of Jesus, there is also the devil's quotation of Ps (90)91:11-12—

> He will give his angels charge of you...
> On their hands they will bear you up,
>   lest you strike your foot against a stone.[5]

There are only two other explicit quotations of the psalms in the synoptic accounts of the ministry of Jesus, both Matthean. Matthew 13:15 quotes Ps (77)78:2 to show that Jesus' policy of speaking in parables fulfils scriptural prophecy

> I will open my mouth in parables
> I will utter what has been hidden
>   from the foundation of the world.

Matthew 21:16 also portrays Jesus as claiming that Ps 8:3—

> Out of the mouths of babes and sucklings
> you have brought praise.

—...is fulfilled in the children crying out in the temple, "Hosanna to the Son of David."

Finally, in both Mark and Matthew, the dying Jesus prays using the opening line of Ps (21)22—

---

[2] Mark 12:10; Matt 21:42; Luke 20:17.
[3] Mark 11:9; Matt 21:9; Luke 19:38. Matthew interpolates "to the Son of David." Luke has, "Blessed is the king who comes...."
[4] Matt 23:39; Luke 13:35. We noted in the General Introduction how Matthew's quotation exemplifies the principle that even lexically faithful quotations generate new signification. On "Q," see J. S. Kloppenborg, *Q Parallels: Synopsis, Critical Notes and Concordance* (Sonoma CA: Polebridge, 1988) 158.
[5] Matt 4:6; Luke 4:10-11

My God, my God, why have you forsaken me?⁶

It is possible that the Evangelists' intention was to depict Jesus as praying the whole psalm. In NT times, psalms were identified by their *incipit*. ⁷

2. *Synoptic Allusions to the Psalms*

So far, we have confined ourselves to explicit citation of the psalms in the synoptics. We move now into the area of allusion. Here we find Ps (109)110:1 again. In all three Jewish trial narratives, Jesus declares that his judges will see him sitting at the right hand of God.⁸ Mark's gospel concludes with the statement that Jesus "was taken up into heaven and sat down at the right hand of God" (Mark 16:19).

The synoptic accounts of the baptism and transfiguration of Jesus all include an allusion to Ps 2:7—

> The Lord said to me, You are my Son...

The allusion is particularly clear in Mark 1:11 and Luke 3:22 as the second person singular of the psalm is retained. Matthew's baptismal *bath qol* (Matt 3:17) and all three accounts of the transfiguration (Mark 9:7, Matt 17:5, Luke 9:35) use third person singular.

There is a noticeable intensification of allusion to the psalms in the synoptic Passion Narratives. Referring to his betrayer as "one who is eating with me," (...ὁ ἐσθίων μετ' ἐμοῦ), the Markan Jesus alludes to Ps (40:10)41:9—

> Even my bosom friend in whom I trusted,
> who ate of my bread, has lifted his heel against me.

(cf. Mark 14:18). Matthew is much more inclined than Mark to weave elements from his OT sources into the texture of the narrative. This is characteristic of his midrashic style of OT reference.⁹

---

⁶ Mark 15:34; Matt 27:46.

⁷ For Jewish examples of this practice, see the quotations from the *Midrash Tehillim* on p. 99 and 195 below.

⁸ Mark 14:62; Matt 26:64; Luke 22:69.

⁹ This is exemplified with particular reference to the psalms, by Matthew's account of the visit to the child Jesus by the μάγοι (Matt 2:11). Elements from scripture passages which Matthew sees as fulfilled in this incident provide the material for his narrative. Ps (71)72:9-11.15, e.g., is drawn upon to tell of the homage paid to Jesus (καὶ πεσόντες προσεκύνησαν αὐτῷ), the giving of gifts and the mention of gold among these gifts. Isa 60:6 has clearly also "contributed" the frankincense. By evoking the contexts from which these elements are drawn, these details point to the meaning of the story, that this child is the Son of David (the "Solomon" to whom the psalm's superscript refers) to whose light all the nations, as represented by the wise men, are already beginning to come. See Kraus, *Theology of the Psalms*, 195. The Passion Narrative provides further examples of

So, for example, in Matthew it is the action of the traitor putting his hand in the dish with Jesus that recalls Ps (40:10)41:9. Thus the reference to the disloyal table companion in the psalm takes the form of a thematic allusion—"He who has dipped his hand in the dish with me will betray me" (Matt 26:23). Like Matthew's, Luke's allusion to Ps 41:9 (Luke 22:21) is thematic rather than verbal: πλὴν ἰδοὺ ἡ χεὶρ τοῦ παραδιδόντος με μετ᾽ ἐμοῦ ἐπὶ τῆς τραπέζης (But behold the hand of him who betrays me is with me on the table).

We suggested above that the placing of the *incipit* of Ps (21)22 on the lips of the dying Jesus may have been intended to portray Jesus as praying the whole psalm. This would be supported by the fact that the three synoptic crucifixion scenes include further strong allusions to Ps (21)22. In Mark 15:24 the soldiers divide out Jesus' garments among them, casting lots for them (...καὶ διαμερίζονται τὰ ἱμάτια αὐτοῦ, βάλλοντες κλῆρον ἐπ᾽ αὐτὰ τίς τί ἄρῃ.). This is a clear allusion to Ps (21)22:18—

> They divide my garments among them
>   and for my raiment they cast lots.

Later, in 15:29, Mark describes the crowd as "wagging their heads" (κινοῦντες τὰς κεφαλὰς αὐτῶν) in derision of Jesus. This recalls Ps (21)22:7—

> All who see me mock at me
>   they make mouths at me, they wag their heads.

Matthew uses the same three elements from the psalm: the dividing of the garments, the wagging of heads, and the *incipit*. He also makes the scoffers echo v. 8 of the psalm:...πέποιθεν ἐπὶ τὸν θεόν, ῥυσάσθω νῦν εἰ θέλει αὐτόν ("He trusts in God: let God deliver him now if he desires him."), a further allusion to Ps (21:9)22:8—

> He committed his cause to the Lord; let him deliver him,
>   let him rescue him, for he delights in him.[10]

---

what K. Stendhal has called Matthew's "targumizing procedure" with regard to OT reference, notably the thirty pieces of silver (Matt 26:15 alluding to Zech 11:12) and the story which this detail generates (Matt 27:3-10). See *The School of St. Matthew and its Use of the Old Testament* (Lund: Gleerup, 1968) 127.

[10] The possibility of allusion to Wisd 2:18 should also be noted, especially in light of the continuation: "... for he said, "I am the Son of God." The theme of the innocent sufferer persecuted for his piety (See especially Wisd 2-5) is sometimes suggested as a background to Matthew's Passion Narrative, e.g., by A. E. Harvey in *Jesus and the Constraints of History* (Philadelphia/London: Westminster/Duckworth, 1982) 148. Martin Hengel, *The Atonement: The Origin of the Doctrine in the New Testament*, (Philadelphia: Fortress / London: SCM, 1981) 41, attributes the fact that "features of the suffering of the righteous man appear" in Matthew's Passion Narrative to the "rabbinic training" of Matthew who "makes

Luke's use of Ps (21)22 in the passion narrative is less extensive than Mark's: no "wagging of heads" and no quotation of the *incipit*. Instead, in Luke 23:46 the dying Jesus prays, adding a filial note to a line from Ps (30:6)31:5—Πάτερ, εἰς χεῖράς σου παρατίθεμαι τὸ πνεῦμά μου. ("Father, into your hands I commend my spirit.")

Finally, Mark 15:36 where Jesus is offered vinegar to drink (δραμὼν δέ τις [καὶ] γεμίσας σπόγγον ὄξους περιθεὶς καλάμῳ ἐπότιζεν αὐτόν...) alludes to Ps (68:22)69:21—

> They gave me poison for food,
> and for my thirst they gave me vinegar to drink.

In Matthew, the soldiers offer Jesus "wine to drink mixed with gall" on his arrival at Golgotha (Matt 27:34). The mention of "gall" here (the LXX equivalent of "poison") and of vinegar later (Matt 27:38) possibly indicates an understanding of the parallelism in Ps (68:22) 69:21 as a description of two separate actions.[11]

Luke's infancy narratives exemplify a particular kind of allusion to the psalms which is not readily quantifiable. They set out to show OT characters as foreshadowings of the protagonists in Luke's story and thus to demonstrate that the Hebrew Scriptures are prophetic of Jesus.[12] Although, strictly speaking, there is no allusion to the psalms in the infancy narratives meeting the criteria established for this discussion, there is a high degree of intertextual reference to the psalms. In particular, the diction of the Psalter is used *passim* in the Canticles of Mary (Luke 1:46-55) and Zechariah (Luke 1:67-79). As the following examples from the Canticle of Mary show, these consciously imitate the psalm genre.[13]

---

the Messiah Jesus into an exemplary saddiq." However, Hengel insists that such features are always "in a messianic key." We touch here on the issue of the exegetical warrant for regarding the speaker of the psalms used in the Passion Narratives as David and, by extension, the Messiah, a question which will surface frequently in this study. Suffice it to say at this stage that, while the Wis 2-5 background need not be excluded, the primary reference is most probably to the psalm in view of its association, through David, with the Messiah.

[11] In Mark, Jesus is offered "wine mingled with myrrh" (Mark 15:23), and vinegar (Mark 15:36). See Brown, *Death of the Messiah*, 942.

[12] An allusion to Mal 4:5, e.g., in Luke 1:17 indicates that John is to be another Elijah, "turning the hearts of children to their fathers..." The declaration of the angel that nothing is impossible with God (Luke 1:37) links Mary with Sarah (Gen 18:14). Luke's description of Jesus increasing in favour with God and humankind recalls the boy Samuel (1 Sam 2:26), just as Mary's Magnificat recalls Hannah's prayer (1 Sam 1:11) and song of praise (1 Sam 2:1-10). Like Judith, Mary receives a blessing (Jdt 13:18) and responds with a canticle of praise (Jdt 16:1-7).

[13] Brown believes that these canticles come from a pre-Lucan Jewish-Christian source. He thinks that they have their closest parallel in the Jewish hymns and psalms attested in the literature from 200 BCE to 100 CE such as 1 Maccabees, Judith, 2 Baruch, 4 Ezra, the Qumran Hodayoth and the Qumran War Scroll.

Luke 1:49-54	Psalms
For he who is mighty has done great things for me,	
and holy is his name.	(110)111:9 Holy and terrible is his name!
And his mercy is on those who fear him from generation to generation.	(102)103:17. But the steadfast love of the Lord is from everlasting to everlasting upon those who fear him
He has shown strength with his arm, he has scattered the proud in the imagination of their hearts	(88:11)89:10. You scattered your enemies with your mighty arm
and exalted those of low degree	(17:28)18:27. For you deliver a humble people but the haughty eyes you bring down.
	(112)113:7. He raises the poor from the dust, and lifts the needy from the ash heap.
he has filled the hungry with good things...	(106)107:9. For he satisfies the one who is thirsty and the hungry he fills with good things.
he has helped his servant Israel, in remembrance of his mercy...	(97)98:3. He has remembered his steadfast love and faithfulness to the house of Israel

In this survey of the extent of psalm usage in the synoptics, we have found that five psalms are quarried for explicit citations—

Ps (109)110 and Ps (117)118 common to all three synoptics
Ps 8 and Ps (77)78 unique to Matthew
Ps (90)91 used in Matthew and Luke (from Q)

Ps (109)110 appears again in the form of allusion in the synoptic Jewish trial narratives and in Mark at the conclusion of the Gospel. In all three Passion Narratives there are allusions to the disloyal table of companion of Ps (40)41 and to the vinegar drink of Ps (68)69. Several allusions form an extended structural echo of a whole section of Ps (21)22. Reference to the Psalter intensifies in the synoptics as the narrative moves from the pre-passion sequence— the solemn entry into Jerusalem, the hostile confrontations which follow, the trial of Jesus—into the Passion Narrative proper.

See his *The Birth of the Messiah: A Commentary on the Infancy Narratives in the Gospels of Matthew and Luke*, (London: Chapman, 1993) 349-50.

C. *The Psalms in the Fourth Gospel*

1. *Johannine Quotations of the Psalms*

What appear to be formal quotations in the Fourth Gospel are not always so. Sometimes the "Scripture" introduced by a formula of quotation is not found *verbatim* anywhere in the OT. Before proceeding with our analysis, we pause to ask what this apparent imprecision says about the author's understanding of ἡ γραφή ("the Scripture"). Perhaps it is a matter of the total witness of the Jewish Scriptures which, because they come from God, are also the Father's witness to Jesus.[14] Thus, for example, without referring to any particular passage of Scripture, The Johannine Jesus can contend that Moses wrote of him (John 5:46). Similarly, the Evangelist can claim that Isaiah saw Jesus' glory (John 12:41). With even less precision, John can say of the disciples, "for as yet they did not know the Scripture, that he must rise from the dead" (John 20:9). This is similar to the general reference in 1 Cor 15:4 to Jesus' death and resurrection being "according to the Scriptures" (κατὰ τὰς γραφάς). We are not to demand of this witness the level of precision to which modern critical tools have accustomed us. In this context, it is important to keep in mind the orality issue and the *haggadic* nature of Scripture citation in the Jewish world contemporary with the NT (both mentioned in our General Introduction). Only then can we come to some sense of how a "citation" which might have been intentionally, and even tendentiously, adapted by the author, or which might be a collage of various biblical passages, could carry full scriptural authority for its hearers.

In the Fourth Gospel, there are seven readily identifiable psalm quotations with a formula of citation or, in the case of John 12:13, a narrative setting which functions in lieu of such a formula. We present them in the verbal form in which they appear in the Fourth Gospel—

> John 2:17 quotes Ps (68:10)69:9—
> Ὁ ζῆλος τοῦ οἴκου σου καταφάγεταί με.
> "Zeal for your house will devour me."

> John 6:31 quotes Ps (77)78:24—
> Ἄρτον ἐκ τοῦ οὐρανοῦ ἔδωκεν αὐτοῖς φαγεῖν.
> "He gave them bread from heaven to eat."

---

[14] See Raymond Brown, *The Gospel According to John I-XII* and *The Gospel According to John XIII-XXI*, Anchor Bible Vols. 29 & 29A, (New York & London: Doubleday, 1966/70) 228, 929, 987. From now on, Brown's commentary will be referred to as *John I-XII* and *John XIII-XXI*.

John 10:34 quotes Ps (81)82:6—
Ἐγὼ εἶπα, Θεοί ἐστε.
"I said, 'You are gods.'"

John 12:13 quotes Ps (117)118:26—
Ὡσαννά· εὐλογημένος ὁ ἐρχόμενος ἐν ὀνόματι κυρίου.
"Hosanna! Blessed is he who comes in the name of the Lord."

John 13:18 quotes Ps (40:10)41:9—
Ὁ τρώγων μου τὸν ἄρτον ἐπῆρεν ἐπ' ἐμὲ τὴν πτέρναν αὐτοῦ.
"He who ate my bread has lifted his heel against me."

John 15:25 quotes Ps (68:5)69:4—
Ἐμίσησάν με δωρεάν.
"They hated me without a cause."[15]

John 19:24 quotes Ps (21:19)22:18—
Διεμερίσαντο τὰ ἱμάτιά μου ἑαυτοῖς
καὶ ἐπὶ τὸν ἱματισμόν μου ἔβαλον κλῆρον.
"They parted my garments among them,
and for my clothing they cast lots."

There are three occasions in the Fourth Gospel where the source of a text apparently presented as a citation of Scripture is not immediately evident:

John 7:38—
ποταμοὶ ἐκ τῆς κοιλίας αὐτοῦ ῥεύσουσιν ὕδατος ζῶντος.
"Out of his belly (RSV: heart) shall flow rivers of living water."

John 19:28—
Διψῶ.
"I thirst."

John 19:36—
Ὀστοῦν οὐ συντριβήσεται αὐτοῦ.
"Not a bone of him shall be broken."

The introductory formula in the first of these, John 7:38, καθὼς εἶπεν ἡ γραφή (as the Scripture has said), indicates that the Evangelist regarded what follows as a Scripture quotation. We will therefore treat it as such. For reasons which will become clear as this study progresses, it will be taken as a composite citation of Ps (77)78, vv. 16 and 20. The second "Scripture" is that apparently quoted in

---

[15] Strictly speaking this is the Fourth Evangelist's approximation of the psalmist's reference to his enemies as οἱ μισοῦντές με δωρεάν, but since the author presents it as a quotation, introducing it with a formula, we will include it among the quotations.

John 19:28, but not readily identifiable. Again, there appears to be a formula of citation: ἵνα τελειωθῇ ἡ γραφη (that the Scripture might be fulfilled). The giving of vinegar in response to Jesus' cry would suggest that Διψῶ introduces the Johannine equivalent of the "vinegar to drink" motif from Ps (68:22)69:21 found in all three synoptics. The "Scripture" in John 19:28 will therefore be treated as such, although as our study unfolds, we will find that this is just one of several possible layers of reference. Our third not-readily-identifiable "Scripture"—Ὀστοῦν οὐ συντριβήσεται αὐτοῦ—could be from either the prescriptions concerning the Paschal Lamb in Exod 12:46 or Ps (33:21)34:20. It may even have been intended as a composite citation of both. It is frequently pointed out that in the Fourth Gospel "images which are apparently inconsistent tend to be used" and that consequently John "can never be analysed in such a way as to pin upon any text a single interpretation."[16] We will therefore consider the implications, should there be a psalm quotation in John 19:36, without excluding the likelihood of a simultaneous allusion to the unbroken bones of the Paschal Lamb.

Of the ten explicit psalm quotations in the Fourth Gospel, only four are paralleled in the synoptics—

> "Blessed is he who comes in the name of the Lord."
> "He who ate my bread has lifted his heel against me."
> "They parted my garments among them ..."
> "I thirst."

The first of these is the only psalm passage that is actually quoted in all four gospels. The synoptic parallels to the second, third and fourth are not quotations but allusions. In fact, some of them might even be better categorized as echoes, for example, Luke 22:21— "The hand of him who betrays me is with me on the table." While the synoptic references to the Psalter tend to be concentrated mainly in the passion narrative, John's are spread more throughout the whole work.[17] The Johannine tendency to bring forward elements of the passion tradition into the account of the ministry, might partially account for one of the three psalm quotations occurring outside

---

[16] J. N. Suggit, "John 2:1-11: The Sign of Greater Things to Come" (*Neot* 21 (1987)141-158 at 153 & 146.

[17] With the exception of Matt 13:35 ("I will open my mouth in parables," quoting Ps [77]78:2), the synoptics do not introduce quotations from the Psalter until the passion sequence begins. The Lucan Jesus' statement "You will not see me until you say, 'Blessed is he who comes in the name of the Lord'" (LXX Ps 117:26 at Luke 13:35) pertains to the passion sequence as it anticipates the crowd's acclamation in Luke 19:38. As we have seen, the Matthean parallel (Matt 23:39) occurs after the triumphal entry of Jesus into Jerusalem.

the passion sequence, Ps (68)69:9 in John 2:17. However, as will be argued in Chs 3-4 below, there is more involved here than simple transposition. The selection of particular psalm verses, the verbal form in which they are quoted and their location in the text show that they have an integral role in the unfolding of the argument of the Gospel as a whole. The Fourth Gospel also gives evidence of considerable independence in its reference to the Jewish Scriptures. It contains nine Scripture quotations that do not occur at all in the other gospels or, with the exception of Isa 53:1, anywhere else in the NT.[18] Of these nine quotations that are unique to John, six are from the psalms.

2. *Johannine Allusions to the Psalms*

Surprisingly, perhaps, verbal allusion to the OT is quite rare in the Fourth Gospel. It is interesting to find that the Greek New Testament of the United Bible Societies, which uses bold type for references to Scripture, identifies only two Johannine passages which would meet our criteria for allusions: the reference to the angels ascending and descending on the Son of Man (2:51, alluding to Gen 28:12) and the speculation of the crowd that the Christ is to be of the seed of David and is to come from Bethlehem (7:42, alluding to 2 Sam 7:12 and Ps (88)89:3-4).[19] Johannine scriptural allusion tends to be thematic rather than verbal and of such subtlety that it veers towards echo. It is this that prompted the comment of Charles Goodwin, "It is remarkable how rarely John quotes the Scriptures. In John 1-20 there are only about half as many Scripture quotations as in the shorter Gospel of Mark..."[20] In fact, the apparent infrequency of Scripture reference in the Fourth Gospel is quite deceptive.[21] As Goodwin too acknowledges, the Fourth Evangelist has an immense repertoire of biblical words, expressions and turns of phrase by means of which he can evoke the great currents of OT thought, even without precise reference to their biblical expression. The highly allusive quality of his writing is an indication of the

---

[18] Ps (68:10)69:9, Ps (77)78:24, the composite citation from Ps (77)78:16 & 20, Isa 54:13, Ps (81)82:6, Isa 53:1, Ps 68:5, Ps (33:21)34:20 (and/or Exod 12:46) and Zech 12:10. Isa 53:1 is quoted in Rom 10:16.

[19] *The Greek New Testament*, ed. B. Aland a.o., 4th rev. ed., (Stuttgart: Deutsche Bibelgesellschaft, 1993).

[20] "How Did John Treat His Sources?" *JBL* 73 (1954) 61-75, at 62. 65.

[21] See Brown, *John I-XII*, lix-lx. See also, making the same point, Barrett, noting that John has 27 direct quotations from Scripture compared with Matthew's 124, Mark's 70 and Luke's 109. C.K. Barrett comments that John uses scripture "in a novel manner, collecting its sense rather than quoting." See "The Old Testament in the Fourth Gospel," *JTS* 48 (1947), 155-69, at 155-56.

depth and fecundity of what A. T. Hanson calls "the scriptural springs of his thought,"[22]

When, however, the Fourth Evangelist decides to refer overtly to "the Scriptures" he shows a distinct preference for formal citation over verbal allusion. Thus, for example, the Johannine equivalent of the synoptic allusions to the dividing of the garments motif is a formal citation of Ps (21:19)22:18 in John 19:24. John is concerned to be seen to be quoting Scripture. It appears that he wants his readers to "search the Scriptures" for themselves and to find eternal life in these writings which bear witness to Jesus (John 5:39).

D. *Statistical Analysis: Comparing John With the Synoptics*

The most we can state with any precision is the proportion of Scripture quotations represented by psalm quotations in the four gospels.[23] But even this modest task is fraught with risks of distortion, as frequently there is little functional distinction between quotations and allusions, especially in cases where the volume of the precursor text reappearing in a gospel allusion is substantial.[24] We should also remember that the presence or absence of explicit quotations is not always a reliable indicator of the importance of a particular text. 2 Sam 7, for example, a foundational text for Christology is explicitly cited only once in the NT, at Heb 1:5. It is one of several passages which, according to Juel, are rarely or, in some cases, never cited in the NT, "either because their presence could be taken for granted or because their major function was to provide links with other, more readily applicable portions of the Scriptures."[25]

1. *Ratio of Psalm Quotations to Scripture Quotations in Mark*
Three of fourteen formal Scripture quotations in Mark are from the psalms.

---

[22] Hanson, *The Living Utterances of God: The New Testament Exegesis of the Old.* (London: Darton, Longman & Todd, 1983) 122.

[23] For our present purposes, quotations are citations which the author presents as quotations, either by prefacing them with an introductory formula, or by giving them a narrative setting which functions *in lieu* of a quotation formula. This applies even if the citation is not an exact reproduction of any version of the biblical text known to us.

[24] E.g., the allusions to Mic 7:6 in Matt 10:35-36 and to Hos 10:8 in Luke 23:30 in which the volume is substantial but there is no formula of quotation. Note also how the reference to Isa 6:9-10 ("see and not perceive ...") borders between quotation and allusion in Mark 4:12, is definitely amplified into a quotation in Matt 13:14-15, and becomes a comparatively "light" allusion in Luke 8:10.

[25] Juel, *Messianic Exegesis*, 59.

Mark 12:10 quotes Ps (117)118: 22-23
("The very stone which the builders rejected...)

Mark 12:36 quotes Ps (109)110:1
("The Lord said to my Lord, Sit at my right hand ...)

Mark 15:34 quotes Ps (21)22:1
("My God, my God, why have you forsaken me?")[26]

2. *Ratio of Psalm Quotations to Scripture Quotations in Matthew*

In Matthew, we find the following categories of explicit citations of Scripture. The fourteen quotations found in Mark appear as fifteen quotations in Matthew.[27] As in Mark, three of these are from the psalms. There are ten "special Matthew" quotations—where the narrator employs an introductory formula which stresses the fulfilment of prophecy. One of these is from the psalms—

Matt 13:35 quotes Ps (77)78:2
("I will open my mouth in parables ...")[28]

There are four quotations in the "Q" temptation narrative (Matt 4:1-11), one of which is from the psalms—

Matt 4:6 quotes Ps (90)91:11-12
("He will give his angels charge of you..."[29]

A further eight quotations occur on the lips of Jesus in the course of teaching and debate. They are usually introduced by formulae such as "You have heard that it was said to the men of old..." or "Have

---

[26] The other formal quotations in Mark are as follows:
Mark 1:2-3 quotes Mal 3:1 ("my messenger") and Isa 40:3 ("voice in the wilderness").
Mark 4:12 quotes Isa 6:9-10 ("see but not perceive...").
Mark 7:6-7 quotes Isa 29:13 ("This people honours me with their lips...").
Mark 11:17 quotes Isa 56:7 ("...house of prayer...") and Jer 7:11 ("...den of robbers...").
Mark 14:27 quotes Zech 13:7 ("I will strike the shepherd...").

[27] Matthew "corrects" Mark's conflation of two different passages in Mark 1:2-3.

[28] The other nine "special Matthew" quotations are as follows:
Matt 1:23 quotes Isa 7:14 ("Emmanuel").
Matt 2:6 quotes Mic 5:2 ("And you, O Bethlehem...")
Matt 2:15 quotes Hos 11:1 ("Out of Egypt ...")
Matt 2:18 quotes Jer 31:15 ("A voice is heard in Ramah......").
Matt 4.15 quotes Isa 9:1-2 ("Land of Zebulon......").
Matt 8:17 quotes Isa 53:4 ("He took our infirmities......").
Matt 12:18 quotes Isa 42:1-4 ("Behold my servant......").
Matt 21:5 quotes Zech 9:7 ("Tell the daughter of Zion....").
Matt 27:9 quotes Zech 11:2 and Jer 32:6-9 ("the thirty pieces of silver").

[29] The other three quotations in this narrative are all from Deuteronomy.

you not read ...?" None of these is from the psalms.[30] Two other "fulfilment" quotations occur in direct speech of Jesus in a context of controversy, the first unique to Matthew, the second in a "Q" passage. Both of these are from the psalms.

> Matt 21:16 quotes Ps 8:3
> ("Out of the mouths of babes and sucklings...")
>
> Matt 23:39 quotes Ps (117)118:26
> ("Blessed is he who comes in the name of the Lord.")

Out of a total of thirty eight explicit Scripture quotations in the Gospel of Matthew, therefore, seven are from the psalms.

3. Ratio of Psalm Quotations to Scripture Quotations in Luke

Luke's gospel is, of course, the first part of a two "volume" work, so an analysis confined to the first "volume" runs the risk of distortion. In fact, reference to the psalms is particularly frequent in the Acts of the Apostles. In the gospel of Luke, however, the following quotations of Scripture occur. Luke has nine quotations in common with Mark and Matthew, one of them significantly extended (Luke 3:4-6). As shown above, these include three quotations from the psalms. As in Matthew, the four quotations in the "Q" temptation narrative (Luke 4:1-13), include one from the psalms. Three other explicit quotations of Scripture are unique to Luke. These include one from the psalms—

> Luke 23:46 quotes Ps (30)31:5
> "Father, into your hands I commit my spirit."[31]

Out of a total of sixteen explicit Scripture quotations in the Gospel of Luke, therefore, five are from the psalms.

4. Ratio of Psalm Quotations to Scripture Quotations in John

Of John's thirteen readily identifiable Scripture quotations, seven are from the psalms (see page 27-28 above).[32] Three other "Scrip-

---

[30] This is not the statement of the obvious that it might, at first, appear to be. The Fourth Evangelist apparently regards the psalms as part of the Law (John 10:34). The eight quotations are found as follows: Matt 5:21. 27. 31. 33. 38. 43—all from Pentateuchal sources; Matt 9:13; 12:7—both quoting Hos 11:1.

[31] The other two quotations unique to Luke are as follows:

> Luke 2:23 quotes Exod 13:2.12 ("Every male that opens the womb...")
> Luke 4:18-19 quotes Isa 61:1-2 ("The Spirit of the Lord is upon me...")

[32] The other six quotations are as follows:

> John 1:23 quotes Isa 40:3 ("Make straight the way of the Lord.").
> John 6:45 quotes Isa 54:13 ("They will all be taught by God.").

tures" explicitly cited by the Fourth Evangelist, but not fully reflecting any known Scripture passages, also appear to be non literal quotations from the psalms (see p. 28 above). We would estimate, therefore, that the Psalter is the source for ten of the sixteen quotations found in the Fourth Gospel.

5. *Overview of Statistical Analysis*
Our findings in this section may be summarized as follows:

Mark	21%	of Scripture quotations are from the psalms.
Matt	18%	of Scripture quotations are from the psalms.
Luke	31%	of Scripture quotations are from the psalms.
John	76%	of Scripture quotations are from the psalms.

The limitations of this statistical analysis must, however, be stressed. These percentage figures refer only to explicit citations while, as we have already begun to see, the psalms are strongly present in the gospels in other more subtle ways. The table which follows takes account of one of these ways—verbal allusion. However, its limitations too must be kept in mind. It is the contention of this study that the psalms function in the Fourth Gospel not just through citation and verbal allusion, but through more covert modes of intertextual relationship such as thematic allusion and echo. Since these utterly defy statistical analysis, a table such as this can offer only a partial view. Even at this preliminary stage of our investigation, however, it would appear that the psalms do have a considerably stronger presence in the Fourth Gospel than they do in the synoptics.

The overview of intertextual reference to the psalms in all four gospels presented in this table shows where John corresponds with the synoptic tradition and where he differs. It shows that several psalms provided material for more than one quotation or allusion. Evidently the gospel writers' interest was not confined to isolated phrases which seemed pertinent to Jesus, but would appear to have extended, at least in some cases, to the psalm as a whole. The first four columns show where the psalm verses either quoted or verbally alluded to appear in the gospels. The references to quotations are in bold face. Those to verbal allusions are in plain type. The fifth col-

---

John 12:15 quotes Zech 9:9 ("Fear not, daughter Zion...").
John 12:38 quotes Isa 53:1 ("Lord, who has believed our report...?").
John 12:40 quotes Isa 6:10 ("He has blinded their eyes...").
John 19:37 quotes Zech 12:10 ("They shall look on him whom they have pierced.").

Of these only two are paralleled in all the synoptics: Isa 40:3 and Isa 6:10. The Zech 9:9 quotation is also found in Matt.

umn headed "Other" extends the lines of comparison beyond the four gospels to other NT appearances (through quotation and allusion) of the psalm verses used by the gospel writers. In fact, there are only three texts involved here: Acts, Hebrews and 1 Pet. Given the Lucan connection, it is not surprising that there are convergences between the synoptics and Acts, for example, Stephen's dying prayer modelled on Jesus' quotation from Ps (30)31. The author of Hebrews shares with the synoptics an interest in Ps 2 and Ps (109)110:1 as testimonies to Jesus' divine sonship and heavenly exaltation. In view of 1 Peter's extensive use of the psalms,[33] the appearance of what seems to have been an important "plank" of early Christian preaching is not surprising.

The table on pages 36-37 shows that John has four psalm verses in common with the synoptics: the acclamation from Ps (117)118, the dividing of the garments from Ps (21)22, the betrayal by one who partakes of table fellowship from Ps (40)41 and the giving of the vinegary drink from Ps (68)69. As mentioned above, the first of these, εὐλογημένος ὁ ἐρχόμενος ἐν ὀνόματι κυρίου ("Blessed is he who comes in the name of the Lord."), is the only psalm passage quoted by all four Evangelists. As all actually quote the line, the references in the table appear in bold face. However, in the cases of the other three, the chart shows bold face for John and plain type for the synoptics. The Johannine explicit citations are paralleled by allusions in the synoptics. In the case of Ps (21:19)22:18 the synoptic allusion is paralleled by both an allusion and a formal quotation in John. The other five Johannine psalm quotations are completely independent, not only of the synoptics, but of all other NT writings, as indicated by the absence of any parallel in the "Other" column.

Finally, the table also shows that John and the synoptics differ in the amount of material they draw from certain psalms. On the one hand, John makes more extensive use of Ps (68)69 than the synoptics.[34] On the other hand, in the case of two psalms, Ps (21)22 and Ps (117)118, John quotes from only one verse while the synoptics use

---

[33] Both in formal quotation (e.g., an extended quotation from Ps (33)34:12-16 in 1 Pet 3:10-12), and in allusion and echo (e.g., 1 Pet 1:17, where a single sentence takes up phraseology from no less than three psalms—"invoke as Father" from Pss (88)89:27, "according to his deeds" from Ps (61:13)62:12, "with fear" from Ps 2:11.

[34] The chart shows three quotations from Ps (68)69. On purely textual grounds, John 15:25 could be a quotation of either LXX Ps 34:19 or LXX Ps 68:5, but since John already quotes twice from Ps (68)69, it is possible that he has the same psalm in mind here too.

Quotations and Allusion to the Psalms in the Four Gospels

[Quotations in bold type; Allusions in plain type]

Ps 2

v. 7—... Υἱός μου εἶ σύ... ("You are my Son")

Matt	Mark	Luke	John	Other
3:17	1:11	3:22		Acts 13:33
17:5	9:7	9:35		Heb 1:5, 5:5

Ps 8

v. 3—... ἐκ στόματος νηπίων... ("Out of the mouths of babes...")

Matt	Mark	Luke	John	Other
21:16				

Ps (21)22

v. (2)1—Ὁ θεὸς ὁ θεός μου... ("My God, my God...")

Matt	Mark	Luke	John	Other
27:46	**15:34**			

v. (8)7—... ἐκίνησαν κεφαλήν... (they shook the head ...)

| 27:39 | 15:29 | | | |

v. (9)8—... σωσάτω αὐτόν, ὅτι θέλει αὐτόν ("Let him save him....")

| 27:43 | | 23:35 | | |

v. (19)18—... διεμερίσαντο τὰ ἱμάτιά μου... (They parted my garments...)

| 27:35 | 15:24 | 23:24 | 19:23, 19:24 | |

Ps (30)31

v. (6)5—εἰς χεῖράς σου παραθήσομαι τ. πνεῦμά μου. ("Into your hands...")

Matt	Mark	Luke	John	Other
			23:46	Acts 7:59

Ps (33)34

v. (21)20—ἓν ἐξ αὐτῶν οὐ συντριβήσεται. ("Not a bone of him will be broken.")

Matt	Mark	Luke	John	Other
			19:36	

Ps (40)41

v. (10)9—... ὁ ἐσθίων ἄρτους μου...("The one eating my bread...")

Matt	Mark	Luke	John	Other
26:23	14:18	22:21	**13:18**	

Ps (68)69

v. (5)4—...οἱ μισοῦντές με δωρεάν... ("...those hating me without cause...")

Matt	Mark	Luke	John	Other
			15:25	

v. (10)9—ὁ ζῆλος τοῦ οἴκου σου κατέφαγέν με... (Zeal for your house...)

			2:17	

v. (22)21—εἰς τὴν δίψαν μου ἐπότισάν με ὄξος. (In my thirst...vinegar)

27:34.38	15:23.36	23:36	**19:28**	

Ps (77)78

v. 2—ἀνοίξω ἐν παραβολαῖς τὸ στόμα μου ("I will open my mouth in parables.")

Matt	Mark	Luke	John	Other
13:35				

v. 24—... ἄρτον οὐρανοῦ ἔδωκεν αὐτοῖς... (He gave them bread of heaven)

			6:31	

vv. 16.20—ὡς ποταμοὺς ὕδατα (... waters like rivers...)

			7:38	

Ps (81)82

v. 6—... ἐγὼ εἶπα Θεοί ἐστε... ("I said, 'You are gods...'")

Matt	Mark	Luke	John	Other
			10:34	

Ps (109)110

v. 1—Εἶπεν ὁ κύριος τῷ κυρίῳ μου...("The Lord said to my Lord...")

Matt	Mark	Luke	John	Other
22:44 26:64	**12:36** 14:62 16:19	**20:42** 22:69		**Acts 2:34** **Heb 1:13, etc.**

Ps (117)118

v. 22—... λίθον, ὃν ἀπεδοκίμασαν οἱ οἰκοδομοῦντες... (The stone...rejected)

Matt	Mark	Luke	John	Other
21:42	**12:10**	**20:17**		Acts 4:11 1 Pet 2:7

v. 26—...εὐλογημένος ὁ ἐρχόμενος...(Blessed is he who comes ...)

21:9 **23:39**	**11:9**	**13:35** **19:38**	**12:13**	

two, three or even four. When we come to consider thematic allusions, structural allusions and echoes of these psalms in the Fourth Gospel, we will find that the Johannine use of Pss (21)22 and (68)69 is possibly more extensive than might at first appear. This is where statistical analysis reaches the limit of its usefulness. However, even at this early stage we should note that the Matthean reference to Ps (21)22, as shown in the chart, is a valuable witness to early Christian reflection on the psalms. It seems from the synoptics, and especially from Matthew that the whole "narrative" of Ps (21)22 exercised a generative influence on the passion story. In Chs 3 – 4 below, we will be positing a similar tendency for Fourth Gospel psalm usage.

E. *The Psalms Quoted in the Fourth Gospel:
a Profile of Their Usage in the NT*

So far, we have established that the gospel writers quarry a total of eleven psalms for quotations and verbal allusions. The Fourth Evangelist uses seven of these psalms, one of them, Ps (68)69, possibly on three occasions, another, Ps (77)78, possibly twice. It is to these seven psalms that we now turn our attention. At this stage, we are looking at the psalms as individual poems, without contextualizing them in the over-all structure of the Psalter.

We have already found that there are synoptic parallels to four of the psalm verses quoted by John, but that the other five are used nowhere else in the NT. We have also found that in two cases, Ps (21)22 and Ps (117)118, additional verses to the one quoted by John are used by the synoptics. We now widen the circle of our investigation to see if any such additional verses are used by other NT authors apart from the Evangelists. Firstly, we note briefly the particular character of each of "John's psalms." We then profile its usage in the wider NT context. We then tentatively situate the Johannine reference in relation to the usage of the psalm in other early Christian circles. This section will help to create a more accurate picture of the reception of these seven psalms in early Christianity which will prove valuable as a background when we come in Chs 3 – 4 to treat the Johannine reference in more detail. Since in this section we will have frequent occasion to refer to the Greek text, we will use the Septuagintal psalm and verse numbering in the body of our text.[35]

---

[35] The following works have been consulted for this section: Sigmund Mowinckel, *The Psalms in Israel's Worship*, trans. D. R. Ap-Thomas, 2 Vols., (Oxford: Blackwell, 1967); Artur Weiser, *The Psalms: A Commentary*, (London: SCM, 1962); W. O. E. Oesterley, *The Psalms: Translated with Text-Critical and Exegetical Notes* (London: SPCK, 1962); Mitchell Dahood, *Psalms I, II & III*,

1. *Ps (21)22*
This is a psalm of an individual sufferer which falls into two parts; a lament sequence (vv. 1-22) and a proclamation praising God's deliverance (vv.23-32). The distress involved in the psalm is probably illness. According to the concluding verses (vv. 28-32), referring to the salvation of the nations, possibly a liturgical addition, the deliverance of the worshipper is to have world-wide consequences. Jacquet believes that this psalm "porte en filigrane une authentique signification messianique." He explains this with reference to the psalm's vision of all the nations turning towards Israel's God. The ordeal of the worshipper becomes in its liturgical recitation a lesson for Israel. Because the sufferings of the just one provoke an intervention on the part of God, they hasten the coming of the reign of God in the world.[36]

Lament sequences in the psalms have provided what has been described by William L. Holladay as "a primary tool in the early church for the theological interpretation of the passion narrative."[37] Several features may have contributed to the particular appeal of this psalm as a testimony to Jesus:[38] the absence of any mention of the psalmist's sin, the unusual freedom from anger and vindictiveness against enemies, the striking intimacy of the psalmist with

---

Anchor Bible Vols. 16, 17 & 17A (New York: Doubleday, 1968 & 1970); Leopold Sabourin, *The Psalms: Their Origin and Meaning* (New York: Alba House, 1974); Louis Jacquet, *Les psaumes et le coeur de l'homme: etude textuelle, litteraire et doctrinale*, 3 Vols., (Gembloux: Duculot, 1975, 1977 & 1979); Beaucamp, *Le Psautier;* Kraus, *Theology of the Psalms;* Carroll Stuhlmueller, *Psalms I* and *Psalms II*, Old Testament Message Vols. 21 & 22 (Wilmington, Delaware: Glazier, 1983). In what follows, we will refer to these works by the surnames of their authors. In noting the character of each psalm discussed in this and subsequent sections, we are guided by Sabourin's system of classification which follows the approach initiated by Gunkel and further developed by Mowinckel. We are conscious, however, of a certain reserve in contemporary psalm study towards the perceived atomism of the *Gattungsforschung* approach in favour of an appreciation of the structure of the Psalter as a whole. As this study unfolds, it will become evident that this more holistic approach has much to contribute to our appreciation of the Johannine reception.

[36] Jacquet, I, 519-20.
[37] Holladay, *The Psalms Through Three Thousand Years: Prayerbook of a Cloud of Witnesses*, (Minneapolis: Fortress, 1993) 119. See also Meier, *A Marginal Jew*, Vol. 1, 170.
[38] In this study the term "testimony" is used in the general sense of an OT passage which an NT author regards as bearing prophetic witness to the validity of early Christian claims about Jesus. It is not used in the specialized sense associated with the work of Rendel J. Harris on systematized collections of OT prooftexts found in patristic authors which Harris believed dated back to a stage behind the NT writings. See *Testimonies against the Jews and the Mohammedans: With Some Proof of the Existence of a Lost Apostolic Work, a Testimony Book* (Cambridge, University Press, 1916-20).

God.[39] As we have seen, the lament sequence in Ps 21 has furnished material for the narrative enactment and formal quotation in John 19:23-24 and is used extensively in the synoptic passion narratives. There is evidence that, at least in some circles, the praise sequence was read as a testimony to the resurrection. Heb 2:11-12, for example, puts v. 23—διηγήσομαι τὸ ὄνομά σου τοῖς ἀδελφοῖς μου...—on the lips of the risen Jesus and makes the point that he is not ashamed to call those who belong to him his brothers. Perhaps the Fourth Gospel gives us a hint that its author too read the whole psalm in this way when, after the resurrection, the Johannine Jesus refers to those to whom he has manifested his Father's name (John 17:6) as his "brothers" (John 20:17).

2. *Ps (33)34*

This is a hymn in which a person who has prayed in distress and received God's help praises God and offers sapiential insights on the experience for the encouragement of others. An acrostic piece, this "Thanksgiving of an Individual" is an example of learned psalmography, composed in the wisdom tradition, possibly for cultic use as evidence of piety. It stresses the principle of retribution—reward for the good, punishment for the wicked—common in sapiential literature.[40]

Ps 33 is not used in the synoptics. As we have seen, the quotation in John 19:36 is most probably a composite reference to v. 21 of the psalm and to Exod 12:46. The rules for life from the wisdom tradition found in vv. 12-23 are quoted as part of an exhortation in 1 Pet 3:10-12. In a similarly sapiential vein, Heb 12:14 also alludes fleetingly to v. 15 of this sequence—... ζήτησον εἰρήνην καὶ δίωξον αὐτήν. 2 Tm 3:11 echoes Ps 33:20—

πολλαὶ αἱ θλίψεις τῶν δικαίων,
καὶ ἐκ πασῶν αὐτῶν ῥύσεται αὐτούς.

Corresponding to the psalmist's πολλαὶ θλίψεις is a list of all the author has undergone for the gospel. Then, echoing v. 20b, he adds: καὶ ἐκ πάντων με ἐρρύσατο ὁ κύριος. Again in 1 Pet, alluding to v. 9 of

---

[39] Concerning the psalmist's intimacy with God, Stuhlmueller, 146, remarks, commenting on v. 1, "We never feel abandoned by strangers, only by those close to us." In a similar vein André Feuillet writes of the psalmist, "... son angoisse est avant tout celle d'un ami de Dieu qui ne peut pas supporter de le sentir si lointain. "See "Souffrance et confiance en Dieu: Commentaire du Psaume XXII," *NRT* (1948) 137-149, at 143.

[40] Oesterley, 214, notes that every verse of the didactic section of the psalm (vv. 11-18) "has its parallel, sometimes verbal, in one or other of the Wisdom books."

the psalm—γεύσασθε καὶ ἴδετε ὅτι χρηστὸς ὁ κύριος...—and perhaps indulging in word play on the homophones, Χριστὸς and χρηστὸς,[41] the author reminds his addressees that they have tasted the kindness of the Lord—ἐγεύσασθε ὅτι χρηστὸς ὁ κύριος (1 Pet 2:3). The κύριος of the psalm is, of course, God. In 1 Pet the κύριος is Jesus. In fact, the author's whole exhortation to spiritual worship in 1 Pet 2:1-10 has been described as a midrash on Ps (33)34. In this midrash what the psalm says of God and the joy of worship in the Temple, is applied to Jesus and the spiritual worship offered by believers in and through him.[42] The Johannine quotation from this psalm stands well within the tradition which sees the psalms as "a resource for the Evangelists in supplying details for the crucifixion story."[43] Nevertheless, John's choice of v. 21 as a testimony to Jesus is quite unparalleled in the NT writings.

3. Ps (40)41

This is a poem by an individual who is either undergoing illness or has just recovered.[44] The author rehearses his sufferings, focusing particularly on the aspect of other people's evident satisfaction at his plight. It is in the course of this that the reference to the disloyalty of an intimate friend (v. 10) occurs.[45] The tradition associating this verse with Judas, reflected in all four gospels, would appear to have

---

[41] Χρηστὸς (meaning "kind" or "useful") was a familiar proper name in the Greco-Roman world, often given to slaves. Suetonius apparently confuses this name with Christos when he tells of the Emperor Claudius' expulsion of Jews from Rome because of riots instigated by Chrestos (Claudius 25). The impact of the scribal confusion known as itacism is evident in the transmission history of 1 Pet 2:3. The fragmentary 3rd-4th century papyrus, **P**[72] has Χριστὸς. The itacism works in the other direction in the transmission history of the only three NT passages where the word "Christian" appears—Acts 11:26; 26:28 and 1 Pet 4:16. In all three, the variant Χρῆστιανοι ("Chrestians") is found in the uncorrected Codex Sinaiaticus. See Michael J. Wilkins, "Christian" in David N. Freedman (Ed.), *The Anchor Bible Dictionary* (New York/London: Doubleday, 1992) I, 925-26. On itacism, see Bruce M. Metzger, *The Text of the New Testament: Its Transmission, Corruption and Restoration*, 3rd Edition (New York & Oxford: Oxford University Press, 1992) 189-91.

[42] Jacquet I, 715.

[43] Holladay, *The Psalms Through Three Thousand Years*, 119.

[44] Depending on the reading one adopts, this psalm is either a thanksgiving for recovery from sickness (Weiser, Sabourin, Jacquet) or a supplication during illness (Dahood, Sabourin). Its present form may even represent a liturgical adaptation of an original lament psalm (Stuhlmueller). The fact that it ends on a doxological note is not conclusive. The final verse may not have originally belonged to the psalm as it is the doxology marking the "seam" between Books 1 and 2 of the Psalter.

[45] In a culture where violation of the law of hospitality was a heinous crime, v. 10 describes the attitude of a particularly odious enemy. For meal sharing as an earnest of fidelity to an oath, see Gen 26:30; 31:54.

arisen because of the aptness to the passion story of the one verse describing the chilling contrast between table sharing and betrayal, and not because of any particular relevance of the psalm as a whole. There is no significant reference to any other part of this psalm in the NT.[46] At this preliminary stage, we can at least see that, although the Fourth Evangelist's choice of v. 10 is not distinctive, he does heighten the sense of scriptural fulfilment by introducing it as a formal quotation.

4. *Ps (68)69*

This is a lament of an individual who passes from a complex mixture of prayer in distress and confession of sin to imprecation against his enemies and finally to praise for God's anticipated intervention on his behalf. It may have been composed by a sick person. Certainly the speaker in the psalm is someone severely hounded by persecutors. One of the "afflicted" (v. 33, עָנָו), he becomes a witness to God's gracious presence and effective provision of justice, to be manifested in the hoped for transformation of his destiny.

The extensive use of this psalm in the NT indicates that it was "of particular importance for the kerygma of the early church.[47] In fact, Lindars has shown that almost every line of vv. 22-29, the psalmist's prayer for revenge against the enemy, is quoted or alluded to somewhere in the NT.[48] As we have already seen, all four gospels allude to v. 22—καὶ εἰς τὴν δίψαν μου ἐπότισάν με ὄξος. The Fourth Gospel goes further, prefacing what appears to be a "narrative citation"—Διψῶ—with the authorial note, ἵνα τελειωθῇ ἡ γραφή.[49] The quotation of v. 10 (... ὅτι ὁ ζῆλος τοῦ οἴκου σου κατέφαγέν με) in John 2:17 is unique among the gospels and unparalleled in the NT. However a quotation of the continuation of this verse (... καὶ οἱ ὀνειδισμοὶ τῶν ὀνειδιζόντων σε ἐπέπεσαν ἐπ' ἐμέ.) in Rom 15:3 shows that the interpretation of Ps 68 as prophetic of Jesus was not confined to the gospel writers. There is thus good reason for suspecting that the Johannine quotation, Ἐμίσησάν με δωρεάν (John 15:25), which does

---

[46] Luke's borrowing of the phrase found at v. 14, Εὐλογητὸς κύριος ὁ θεὸς Ισραηλ..., for the opening of his *Benedictus* (Luke 1:68) is simply a case of using the phraseology of the Psalter to write in the psalm genre. He could equally have found the phrase in Pss 71:18 or 105:48, both conclusions to books of the Psalter.

[47] Kraus, 177.

[48] See Barnabas Lindars, *New Testament Apologetic: the Doctrinal Significance of the Old Testament Quotations* (London: SCM, 1961) 105.

[49] As noted above, Mark (15:23.36) and Matthew (27:34.48) record two drinks offered to Jesus. The full parallel pair in Ps 68:22—καὶ ἔδωκαν εἰς τὸ βρῶμά μου χολὴν καὶ εἰς τὴν δίψαν μου ἐπότισάν με ὄξος may have suggested this, especially in view of Matthew's detail that the first drink contained χολή.

not correspond fully to any biblical text, was intended by the author as a reference to Ps 68:4—οἱ μισοῦντές με δωρεάν.[50]

Within the logic of the early Christian *relecture* of the psalm, Judas becomes the target of the imprecatory section. Thus Luke adapts v. 26 of the psalm (...γενηθήτω ἡ ἔπαυλις αὐτῶν ἠρημωμένη, καὶ ἐν τοῖς σκηνώμασιν αὐτῶν μὴ ἔστω ὁ κατοικῶν...) to make it applicable to Judas, changing the pronouns to the singular (Acts 1:20). There are several indications in the NT that the imprecatory section of the psalm was also used to demonstrate that the opposition and hostility experienced by the early Christians were foretold in Scripture. Paul's extended quotation of vv. 23-24 in Rom 11:9, for example, forms part of his attempt to make sense of the "unbelief" of Israel. V. 24 of the psalm (... σκοτισθήτωσαν οἱ ὀφθαλμοὶ αὐτῶν τοῦ μὴ βλέπειν) included in Paul's citation, may have performed quite a similar role in the Johannine characterisation of the inability of "the Jews" to believe in Jesus as blindness. (John 9:39-41. cf. 12:40, quoting Isa 6:10). Against this background, it is understandable that Christian groups suffering persecution would have found in the imprecations of Ps 68 a promise of their ultimate vindication by God. Thus in Rev 16:1, the command to the seven angels to pour out the seven bowls of the wrath of God shows distinct traces of Ps 68: 25— ἔκχεον ἐπ' αὐτοὺς τὴν ὀργήν σου, καὶ ὁ θυμὸς τῆς ὀργῆς σου καταλάβοι αὐτούς. Similarly, the influence of v. 29 of the psalm, ἐξαλειφθήτωσαν ἐκ βίβλου ζώντων, on several passages in Revelation suggests that Ps 68 encouraged hard-pressed believers with a promise of their enemies' ultimate destruction. The psalm seems also to have contributed to the idea expressed by Paul in Phil 4:3 that his collaborators are all enrolled in "The Book of Life."[51]

5. *Ps (77)78*
This is a synopsis of Israel's history in the form of a hymn. It presents the historical traditions of Israel, not as preserved in written

---

[50] Ps 34:19, which also contains the phrase οἱ μισοῦντές με δωρεάν, is another possible source for the "quotation" in John 15:25.

[51] The idea is found in Ex 32:32 where Moses begs to be blotted out of God's book if the people are not forgiven, in the Isa 4:3 reference to those who have been "recorded (written) for life," and in Dan 12:1 where those whose names are found written in the book are to be delivered at the time of trouble (Cf. 1 En 47:3). However, the expression βιβλίον τῆς ζωῆς in Phil 4:3 and in Rev 3:5, 13:8, 17:8, 20:12.15, 21:27 has its closest OT counterpart in Ps 68:29—ἐξαλειφθήτωσαν ἐκ βίβλου ζώντων. While obviously individual words alone are not adequate indicators of psalm usage, in this instance the presence of the verb ἐξαλείφω in Rev 3:5 (... καὶ οὐ μὴ ἐξαλείψω τὸ ὄνομα αὐτοῦ ἐκ τῆς βίβλου τῆς ζωῆς...) does strengthen the case for the influence of Ps 68.

archives, but rather as communicated and inculcated in solemn cultic proclamation. In this recital of selected events in Israel's past, interpretation is the overriding concern. According to Ps 77, the history of Israel culminates in the choice of Jerusalem as God's sanctuary and the anointing of David as king. The Davidic *terminus ad quem* of the historical schema and the author's tendency to censure the Northern tribes (the ancestors of the Samaritans, referred to in the psalm as "Ephraim") no doubt reflect theological polemic and the related controversy about the place of worship.

The only explicit citation of Ps 77 in the NT, apart from that in John 6:31 (and possibly another in John 7:38), is in Matt 13:35.[52] Here Jesus' practice of teaching in parables is presented as the fulfilment of the prophecy: ἀνοίξω ἐν παραβολαῖς τὸ στόμα μου, φθέγξομαι προβλήματα ἀπ' ἀρχῆς, that is, Ps (77)78:2. Matthew's version of the psalm verse appears to be an intentional adaptation. As Stendahl has demonstrated, "The quotation is entirely dependent on the form it has in Matthew to fulfil its purpose."[53]

6. *Ps (81)82*

This psalm consists of an oracle from Temple prophecy combined with a short concluding prayer. The oracle itself, is presented in the context of a lawsuit (ריב) in which God arraigns and sentences subordinate "gods." "Those who are mighty on earth, whose representatives tower into the heavenly world, are brought to judgement."[54] The psalm insists, in keeping with the self revelation of God in the Mosaic covenant (Exod 34:6-7), "that true divinity, whether in the person of God or among God's representatives, is ultimately decided by concern for the weak and destitute."[55] Borrowing from the religious myths of neighbouring cultures the idea of a divine council, the psalm reflects a stage of Israel's journey towards monotheism. However, a distinctively Israelite feature of the psalm is the close connection it makes between God's judgement and God's sovereignty. This stress on just judgement shows how minimally the psalm is in fact tied to the polytheistic root of the concept which it has adopted.

---

[52] Stuhlmueller (*Psalms* II, 30) sees several futher allusions to Ps (77)78 : to v. 3 in 1 John 1:1-4, to v. 18 in 1 Cor 10:8, to v. 37 in Acts 8:21, to v. 44 in Rev 16:4. These would probably be better described as echoes and even then would still be somewhat questionable.

[53] *The School of Matthew*, 116-117.

[54] Kraus, 198. According to Mowinckel (I, 150-151), "iniquity in the history of mankind, of nations and states, is what forces Yahweh to interfere...Under the rule of such powers Israel has become poor and needy and oppressed."

[55] Stuhlmueller, II, 41.

The Fourth Gospel is certainly unique in its quotation from Ps 81. The only other occasion when it might be claimed that an NT writer shows any awareness of this psalm is Matt 18:20 which could be a case of contact with a halakhic reading of the second line of the psalm, "In the midst of the gods he (God) holds judgement."[56]

7. *Ps (117)118*

This psalm obviously presupposes an accompanying ritual. It may, in an earlier form, have been a victory song of a king entering the gates of the city at the head of his army. Its present form would suggest that it was sung during a liturgical procession beginning in the city of Jerusalem and ending in the Temple. It appears to have been composed for performance by a soloist, alternating choirs, priests, and the assembly, although it is impossible to assign precise verses with any degree of certainty. There are indications in the text that it had strong associations with the feast of Tabernacles.[57] It also concluded the "Egyptian Hallel" recited at Passover,[58] Tabernacles and Pentecost. Within the psalm itself, elements of individual thanksgiving (vv. 2-19) are incorporated into a community thanksgiving. The community is referred to by the sacral title, "Israel," the designation for the people when gathered for worship.

The special attention accorded this psalm in the NT must owe something to its great significance in Judaism. We have seen that the acclamation from Ps 117:26, Εὐλογημένος ὁ ἐρχόμενος ἐν ὀνόματι κυρίου, is the only psalm passage quoted in all four gospels, and that both Matthew and Luke quote this verse twice. Verse 22 of Ps 117, —λίθον, ὃν ἀπεδοκίμασαν οἱ οἰκοδομοῦντες, οὗτος ἐγενήθη εἰς κεφαλὴν γωνίας—quoted by all three synoptics at the conclusion of the parable of the vineyard, appears to have had quite a wide appeal to NT authors. Luke introduces it into Peter's speech in Acts 4:11. For the author of 1 Pet, who quotes it fully (1 Pet 2:7), the risen Jesus is the living corner stone of a temple into which believers are being built.[59]

---

[56] According to an interpretation of Ps (81)82:1b preserved in *m. Abot* 3:6, God judges among the judges. Since judges had to be a minimum of three, this verse was believed to show that the Shekinah rested even among only three men sitting together occupied with Torah. It is plausible that an earlier form of this exegetical argument may have contributed to Matt 18:20.

[57] These are principally the reference to tents in v. 15, the acclamation "Hosanna" in v. 25, the description of God as a light shining on the people in v. 27, and the mention in the Hebrew of v. 27 of the festal bundle of branches (*lulab*) carried in procession. Cf. *m. Sukka* 4, 5.

[58] Mark 14:26, Matt 26:30.

[59] The Isa 8:14 reference to "a stone to make people stumble," which the author of 1 Pet identifies with the rejected stone of Ps 117:22 explains the "commentary" following the quotation of the psalm verse in Luke 20:17. In the light of the

Three other phrases from Ps 117 occur in the NT writings. Foremost among these is v. 16—... δεξιὰ κυρίου ὕψωσέν με, δεξιὰ κυρίου ἐποίησεν δύναμιν—which itself echoes Moses' song of victory (Exod 15:2), the prototypical "psalm" in which the entire history of Israel converges. In Acts 2:33 Luke has Peter claim, alluding to Ps 117:16, that the risen Jesus is τῇ δεξιᾷ οὖν τοῦ θεοῦ ὑψωθείς. Another similar allusion to this verse is found in Acts 5:31—τοῦτον ὁ θεὸς ἀρχηγὸν καὶ σωτῆρα ὕψωσεν τῇ δεξιᾷ αὐτοῦ.[60] The role that these texts indicate for Ps 117:16 in early Christian worship and preaching could suggest a contribution of reflection on the psalm to the special Johannine use of the verb ὑψόω. Ps 117:6—... κύριος ἐμοὶ βοηθός, οὐ φοβηθήσομαι τί ποιήσει μοι ἄνθρωπος—is recalled to the readers of Hebrews as something that they can themselves say with confidence (Heb 13:6). Paul's description in 2 Cor 6:9 of those who share in the apostolic ministry as παιδευόμενοι καὶ μὴ θανατούμενοι carries definite echoes of Ps 117:18—παιδεύων ἐπαίδευσέν με ὁ κύριος καὶ τῷ θανάτῳ οὐ παρέδωκέν με. Finally, an allusion to v. 24 in the χαίρωμεν καὶ ἀγαλλιῶμεν of Rev 19:7 may hint at the extent to which Ps 117 had become part of early Christian worship.

F. *Psalms Widely Used in the NT and Not Quoted in the Fourth Gospel*

In order to appreciate the distinctiveness of the Johannine reception of the psalms it is important to take account of certain psalms which seem to have been highly influential in the development of the kerygma, as shared by both the synoptics and Paul, but which, at first sight, do not seem to have contributed to the Johannine synthesis. With reference to general NT usage of the psalms, Kraus speaks of certain psalms as "'star witnesses' in the proclamation that the

---

connection between these two texts, it is likely that Ps 117:22 has influenced two passages in Paul: Rom 9:32-33 and 1 Cor 3:11.

[60] Whether these Lucan texts are regarded as allusions to Ps 117:16 or to Ps 109:1 depends on whether the dative of δεξιά is understood in terms of location or instrumentality. Both readings are grammatically possible. See M. Zerwick, *Analysis Philologica Novi Testamenti Graeci* (Rome, Scripta Pontificii Instituti Biblici, Editio Quarta, 1984) 258. Reading τῇ δεξιᾷ in Acts 2:33 *localiter* (to use Zerwick's terminology) makes a good introduction to the quotation of Ps 109:1 in 2:34. However, Luke's use of the verb ὑψόω from Ps 117:16 suggests that reading τῇ δεξιᾷ *instrumentaliter* and thereby regarding it as an allusion to Ps 117:16 might be the better option. There is also in favour of this reading the fact that Ps 109:1 uses the word δεξιός meaning "right as opposed to left" whereas Ps 117 uses δεξιά (sc. χείρ) meaning "right hand," the word used by Luke. See W. Bauer, *A Greek-English Lexicon of the New Testament* (Second Edition), translated by W. F. Arndt and F. W. Gingrich (Chicago: Chicago University Press, 1979). Cf. the note to Acts 2:33 in H. Wansbrough (General Editor), *The New Jerusalem Bible* (London / New York: Darton, Longman & Todd / Doubleday, 1985) 1803.

promises of God had been fulfilled." These are (in the LXX numbering) Pss 2, 21, 68, 109 and 117.[61] As we have seen, two of these, Pss 2 and 109, are neither explicitly quoted nor clearly alluded to in the Fourth Gospel. There are also two other psalms quoted in the synoptics but not in John: Ps 30 used by Luke and Ps 8, used by Matthew, While these, particularly Ps 30, may not be quite "star witnesses" we will consider them briefly for the sake of completeness, before proceeding to the more puzzling problem of the surprising absence of Fourth Gospel reference to such important psalms as Pss 2 and 109.

1. *Psalm (30)31*

This anthological lament of an individual sufferer draws on several other psalms and on the Book of Jeremiah. It was probably occasioned by serious illness, although the exact nature of the psalmist's suffering is unclear. It moves in a progression from expressions of confidence and supplication to thanksgiving and didactic praise.

The prayer inspired by v.6 (Εἰς χεῖράς σου παραθήσομαι τὸ πνεῦμά μου...) which Jesus says before he dies (Luke 23:46) and which is echoed by Stephen in Acts 7:59, is a particular Lucan touch. Jacquet notes that Jesus cites the psalm "avec cependant un accent filial."[62] Luke's usage of Ps 30 appears to stem from his interest in prayer rather than from any particular Christological motivation or widespread usage of the psalm as a passion testimony.[63] There is, perhaps, a hint of "passion" usage in Matt 26:3-4, although the influence of Ps 2 may be stronger.[64] There is nothing to suggest that Ps 30 has any role in the Fourth Gospel.

---

[61] According to the Hebrew numbering used by Kraus, Pss 2, 22, 69, 110 and 118. See *Theology of the Psalms*, 180.
[62] Jacquet I, 671.
[63] In Jewish piety "Into your hands I commend my spirit" [Ps (30:6) 31:5] is a prayer before going to sleep.*b. Ber.* 5a states that at bedtime even a scholar should recite one verse of supplication such as "Into your hands I place my spirit; you have redeemed me, O Lord God of truth." (Quoted by Brown in *Death of the Messiah*, 1069). The impetus for Luke's use of Ps 30 could come from this tradition, if it goes back to the NT period. However, Kraus (197) would favour a "Christological motivation" behind the use of this psalm verse. "As Messiah, Jesus is the bearer of the divine πνεῦμα (Luke 4:18). He surrenders to his God the spirit with which he had been anointed (Luke 4:18, 21)."
[64] The gathering of the Jerusalem leadership to take counsel (Matt 26:3-4) may echo Ps 30:14—ἐν τῷ ἐπισυναχθῆναι αὐτοὺς ἅμα ἐπ' ἐμὲ τοῦ λαβεῖν τὴν ψυχήν μου ἐβουλεύσαντο. When compared with Mark's straightforward statement that the chief priests and scribes were seeking to arrest Jesus by stealth and kill him (Mark 14:1), the Matthean version with its psalm allusions not only highlights Matthew's redactional contribution but also exemplifies his characteristically midrashic style of OT reference.

2. *Psalm 8*

This hymn in praise of God as creator is so rich in royal terms and imagery, that it is thought to have been composed originally in honour of a reigning Davidic king viewed as maintaining the stability of the universe through his rule in God's name. It speaks in regal terms of God's commission to humankind to rule over creation.[65]

It is in the context of Jesus' royal entry into Jerusalem that Matthew quotes from v. 3 of the psalm—ἐκ στόματος νηπίων καὶ θηλαζόντων κατηρτίσω αἶνον (cf. Matt 21:16). The author of Hebrews identifies the psalm's υἱὸς ἀνθρώπου, briefly made less than the angels and subsequently crowned with glory and honour, as Jesus (Heb 2:9). Also in a royal vein, Paul uses the psalm to delineate his notion of the cosmic rule of the exalted Christ. He presents Jesus in 1 Cor 15:20-28 as the one under whose feet God has put everything in subjection. Paul's allusion to Ps 8 here is nuanced by his clarification of the word πάντα. In the new context in which Paul sets it, πάντα no longer refers to all created things but to all the enemies of humanity, the last of which is death. What is actually happening in this introduction of the "enemies" is a conflation of Ps 8:7 with Ps 109:1. The significance of this and its implications for the Fourth Gospel will be explored below in the discussion of Ps 109. In a similar mode, Paul makes a fleeting reference to Ps 8:7 in Phil 3:21 where he speaks of the power of Jesus to subject everything to himself (... ὑποτάξαι αὐτῷ τὰ πάντα). There is also an allusion to Ps 8:7 in Eph 1:22—... καὶ πάντα ὑπέταξεν ὑπὸ τοὺς πόδας αὐτοῦ καὶ αὐτὸν ἔδωκεν κεφαλὴν ὑπὲρ πάντα τῇ ἐκκλησίᾳ... Here too there is the same tendency to link Ps 8 with Ps 109:1 (cf. Eph 1:20).

In the milieu where so many of these early Christian writings circulated, a context where formative Judaism in all its diversity, Hellenistic syncretism and incipient gnosticism intermingled, Ps 8 proved a useful text. It enabled NT authors to fit Jesus into a world view which took for granted the existence of various divine beings, angels and spirits conceived of as personal powers.[66] John 1:51 indi-

---

[65] Note the royal title, "our Lord" (see 1 Kgs 1:11.43.47), "majestic" (v.1.9), "crown...with glory and honour" (v.5), "dominion" and "under his feet" (v.6 Cf. Ps 109:1). In Ps 8 there is evidence of strong interaction with the Genesis creation stories which also employ royal imagery to depict the role of humankind in the world. God has raised them from dust to kingship (Gen 2:7. cf. Ps 112:7) and has appointed them to rule the earth (Gen 1:28). See Walter Brueggemann, "From Dust to Kingship," *ZAW* 84 (1972) 1-18.

[66] The "Colossian error " (Col 2:8.18), for example, seems to have involved belief in and worship of angelic powers that mediated between God and the world and influenced the cosmic order. See E. Lohse, *A Commentary on the Epistles to the Colossians and to Philemon*, Hermeneia Series (Philadelphia: Fortress, 1971) 96-98.

cates that the Johannine circle shares at least the belief in angels. While there is no clear evidence of direct influence of Ps 8 on the Fourth Gospel, it is noticeable that its role in several NT writings touches on some of the concerns of the Fourth Evangelist, in particular Jesus' divine status and his cosmological role as pre-existent Son. The claim that God has given Jesus power over all flesh (John 17:2) might even, perhaps, reflect a Johannine *relecture* of Ps 8:7.

3. *Psalm 2*

This psalm has its roots in the royal rites of the Davidic dynasty. While the exact nature of the psalm's original *Sitz im Leben* remains obscure, it is generally accepted that Ps 2 is a liturgical chant for a royal anniversary or a royal birth. It dramatises the oracle of Nathan (2 Sam 7: 5-16) recalling the exploits of the dynasty's founder as a guarantee of the future stability and permanence of his line. The psalm clearly envisages Jerusalem as the residence of a reigning Judean monarch. When it could no longer be sung in honour of an incumbent king, it continued to foster Israel's conviction that God would honour the covenant with David.[67] The hope for a dynastic revival of David's line was never completely abandoned and was to surface from time to time in popular uprisings. With the passage of time, however, it was increasingly focused on a non-political fulfilment of the promises to David. The eventual linking of Ps 2 with the sapiential Ps 1 to form a prologue to the Psalter is indicative of this development.

As we have seen, the principal gospel allusions to this psalm occur in the synoptic accounts of the baptism (Mark 1:11, Matt 3:17 and Luke 3:22) and the transfiguration of Jesus (Mark 9:7, Matt 17:5 and Luke 9:35),[68] where the *bath qol* contains a clear verbal allusion to the divine oracle addressed to the anointed king in Ps 2:7, Υἱός μου εἶ σύ. 2 Pet 1:17 also makes an oblique reference to it. In Acts 13:33 Luke has Paul quote a fuller version of Ps 2:7—Υἱός μου εἶ σύ, ἐγὼ σήμερον γεγέννηκά σε.[69]

---

[67] PsSol 17:23-27 (first century BCE) speaks of the expected "Son of David" in the language of Ps 2.

[68] The additional designation of Jesus as ὁ ἐκλελεγμένος along with the use of the third person in Luke 9:35 means that here the resonances of Isa 42:1 may be stronger than those of Ps 2:7. As Kraus has shown, however, this nuance of God's choice is already implicit in Ps 2:7. It is to be explained by 2 Sam 7:14 ("I will be his father and he shall be my son.") and Ps (88)89:26-27 ("He will say to me, 'You are my father...' and I will make him my firstborn son."). There is also a possible allusion to Gen 22:2.17 in the designation of Jesus as ὁ ἀγαπητός in all three synoptic accounts of the baptism and in the Markan and Matthean transfiguration scenes. See Kraus,*Theology of the Psalms*, 181.

[69] The fuller form of the declaration used in Acts 13:33 appears also in the Western text of Luke's account of the baptism (Luke 3:22). C. H. Dodd, *According*

Luke is responsible for a formula quotation of another part of Ps 2 in Acts 4:25-6. A prayer of the persecuted community of believers includes the first two verses of the psalm—

Ἵνα τί ἐφρύαξαν ἔθνη
καὶ λαοὶ ἐμελέτησαν κενά;
παρέστησαν οἱ βασιλεῖς τῆς γῆς,
καὶ οἱ ἄρχοντες συνήχθησαν ἐπὶ τὸ αὐτὸ
κατὰ τοῦ κυρίου καὶ κατὰ τοῦ χριστοῦ αὐτοῦ.

The assembling of the kings and rulers against the Lord and his Anointed is believed to have taken place in the plotting which led to Jesus' death. While Herod's involvement in Jesus' condemnation may not be merely based on Ps 2, there is nevertheless the strong likelihood that the story of Herod and Pilate becoming friends (Luke 23:6-12) is the outcome of imaginative reflection on the connivance of the kings and rulers in the psalm.[70] Matt 26:3-4—Τότε συνήχθησαν οἱ ἀρχιερεῖς καὶ οἱ πρεσβύτεροι τοῦ λαοῦ...καὶ συνεβουλεύσαντο ἵνα τὸν Ἰησοῦν δόλῳ κρατήσωσιν καὶ ἀποκτείνωσιν.—would be a similar example. We have already seen here a "hint" of Ps 30 in the "taking counsel together," but Ps 2 would seem to have furnished συνήχθησαν. Neither is this early Christian application of the "gathering together" motif from Ps 2 confined to the gospels. In one of at least five allusions to Ps 2 in Revelation, v. 2 provides the phraseology for the author to describe the ordeal to be endured by his readers: Καὶ εἶδον τὸ θηρίον καὶ τοὺς βασιλεῖς τῆς γῆς καὶ τὰ στρατεύματα αὐτῶν συνηγμένα ποιῆσαι τὸν πόλεμον μετὰ τοῦ καθημένου ἐπὶ τοῦ ἵππου καὶ μετὰ τοῦ στρατεύματος αὐτοῦ (Rev 19:19).[71] Its function is not to remind the reader of Ps 2 *per se*. So complete is the appropriation of Ps 2 by this group, that the psalm's phraseology reminds them of Jesus' passion and of his ultimate triumph in which they hope to share.

---

to the Scriptures: The Substructure of New Testament Theology (London: Nisbet, 1952 / Fontana, 1965) 32, thinks it conceivable that Luke gave the full form in both places and that the prevailing textual tradition assimilated Luke 3:22 to Mark 1:11. If this is so, the case for the baptismal *bath qol* as an evocation of Ps 2:7 is greatly strengthened.

[70] This idea has been taken up by, for example, Etienne Trocmé in *The Passion as liturgy: A Study of the Origin of the Passion Narrative in the Four Gospels* (London: SCM, 1983) 70. He regards Luke 23:6-12 as "a kind of *midrash pesher.*" Brown, *Death of the Messiah*, 1453, agrees that, for the purposes of early Christian appropriation of Ps 2, Herod is a 'king' and Pilate is a 'ruler' and that together the two exemplify the Gentiles and the Israelites gathering against Jesus the anointed servant of God. See also "Psalm 2 in Luke/Acts: an Intertextual Study" by W. J. C. Weren in *Intertextuality in Biblical Writings: Essays in Honour of Bas von Iersel* (Kampen: J. H. Kok, 1989) 189-203.

[71] Cf. Rev 2:26-27, 11:15, 12:5, 19:15.19.

The importance of Ps 2 in the synoptics is in marked contrast with its apparent absence from the Fourth Gospel.⁷² The lack of a Johannine parallel for the synoptic use of Ὑιός μου εἶ σύ can be easily explained by the decision of the Evangelist not to include the two stories which provide a setting for the pronouncement of the oracle. In fact, none of the four different ways in which early Christianity understood the ἐγὼ σήμερον γεγέννηκά σε of the Ps 2:7 oracle would be consonant with Johannine Christology. Kraus has schematised the four "possible" readings of the σήμερον as the baptism of Jesus, the transfiguration, the resurrection and the ascension. The Fourth Gospel does not recount a baptism of Jesus; John the Baptist is primarily a witness (John 1:7). A transfiguration narrative would be redundant in the Fourth Gospel; Jesus' glory is always visible to the eyes of faith (John 2:11) and, besides, in 12:28 the "transfiguration" and "agony" of the synoptics are conflated in line with the Johannine perspective. The suggestion implicit in the synoptic application of the psalm oracle to Jesus, that he became Son of God at some point in time, for example, at his resurrection or ascension,⁷³ would have jarred with the Fourth Evangelist's views on Jesus' preexistence (See John 1:1, 17:5) and with his concept of the whole passion as the "lifting up" of Jesus. However, given the prominence of the theme of Jesus' divine sonship in the Fourth Gospel, it would be surprising if a psalm which functioned as a basic testimony to Jesus' status as Son of God in early Christianity, has played no role in the Fourth Gospel. On the analogy of the synoptic Passion Narratives, there is a strong likelihood that v. 2 may have contributed to the Johannine account of the plotting which led to Jesus' death. Moreover, an interpretation of the Ps 2:7 oracle which comes close to the Johannine perspective is found in Hebrews where it is quoted twice (Heb 1:5, 5:5). On the second occasion the oracle is adduced to show that Jesus did not glorify himself. Coming in a work which has many affinities with the Fourth Gospel,⁷⁴ this reading of the psalm hints at another possible route by which Ps 2 might have entered Johannine thought. At this stage these must remain mere suggestions for further exploration.

---

⁷² Some editors regard Nathaniel's confession , Ῥαββί, σὺ εἶ ὁ υἱὸς τοῦ θεοῦ, σὺ βασιλεὺς εἶ τοῦ Ἰσραήλ (John 1:49) as an allusion to Ps 2:7.

⁷³ The quotation of the oracle in Acts 13:33 is open to such an interpretation. Cf. Rom 1:4.

⁷⁴ The affinities between these two works are particularly noticeable with regard to their use of the psalms. In both texts, vocatives in psalms are understood as addresses to the exalted Jesus as God. Cf. Ps 44:7 and Ps 101:26-28 in Heb 1:8-12 and Ps 34:23 in John 20:28.

4. *Ps (90)91*

The original setting for this psalm is clearly pilgrimage to the Temple. Within the sanctuary, under the shelter of God's presence, a pilgrim expresses confidence in God (v. 2). A priestly exhortation assures him that God's protection goes with him on his dangerous homeward journey and throughout his life (vv. 3-13). The psalm concludes with an oracle spoken in God's name (vv. 14-16). In Second Temple Judaism, Ps (90)91 was particularly associated with driving away evil spirits. The Qumran Psalm Scroll, 11QPsAp[a], for example, contains a recension of Ps 91 apparently for exorcising demons.[75]

Ps (90)91 is used—or rather, misused—by the devil in the "Q" narrative of the temptation of Jesus (Matt 4:1-11; Luke 4:1-13). The devil's suggestion that this verse applies to Jesus as "Son of God" may reflect a messianic reading of the psalm, perhaps along the lines of an interpretation preserved in the Psalms Targum.[76] However, the evidence for such an interpretation is late and could represent a re-messianising of the psalms under the impact of Christian claims. More likely, there is a certain ironic intent in the account of an attempt by Satan to misuse a psalm well known for its apotropaic qualities. In Luke 10:19, Jesus cites v. 13 of the psalm at the victorious return of the seventy disciples—ἰδοὺ δέδωκα ὑμῖν τὴν ἐξουσίαν τοῦ πατεῖν ἐπάνω ὄφεων καὶ σκορπίων. The psalm's promise of the sight of God's salvation (v. 16) may also have contributed to Luke's portrayal of Simeon (Luke 2:30). There is nothing to suggest that Ps 90 has any role in the Fourth Gospel.

5. *Psalm (109)110*

This is an oracle which originated in the rituals of the Davidic dynasty. As Jacquet explains:

---

[75] J. A. Sanders, *The Psalms Scroll of Qumran Cave 11*, DJD IV (Oxford: Clarendon, 1965) 93. Cf. Émile Puech, "11QPsAp[a]: Un Rituel d'Exorcismes. Essai de Reconstruction." *RevQum* 14 (1990) 377-408.

[76] In the Targum, the second person singular address in vv. 3-8, inculcating trust in God, is spoken by David to his son Solomon. In Jewish exegetical tradition (See Wisd 7:17-22; Jos. *Ant.* 8.2.5, 45-49), Solomon is credited with exorcistic powers. In v. 9 Solomon addresses God: *Quoniam tu ipse Domine fiducia mea*...and God replies with the promise of angelic protection quoted in Matt 4:6 and Luke 4:10-11. The theme of David's mastery over the wild beasts may also have suggested the application of this psalm to Jesus (See v. 13). If an interpretation along these lines underlies Matthew's and Luke's use of Ps (90)91, the point of the quotation would be that Jesus should demonstrate his Messiahship by claiming the angelic protection promised to David's son. All quotations of the Psalms Targum in this study are taken from *Biblia Sacra Polyglotta* of Brianus Vvaltonus [Brian Walton] (London: Thomas Roycroft, 1657) Vol. III.

> Premièrement le psaume doit son origine à une circonstance extraordinaire, qui a surexcité à l'extrême, en Israel, le sentiment national et éveillé la foi en un triomphe définitif du Peuple de Dieu sur tous ses ennemis, et au cours de laquelle s'est révélée l'action d'un homme exceptionelle à la fois Roi (1-3) et Prêtre (4-7)...Historique en son origine, mais résolument tourné vers l'avenir...et par le fait même, déjà messianique *in nuce* (cf. 2 S 7:8-16), le Psaume prit dans la suite devant les échecs nationaux et dynastiques, surtout à partir de l'Exil, une coloration de plus en plus "eschatologique."[77]

For Jacquet, the most likely candidate for the original referent of the earliest form of the psalm is David who blends prophetic, royal and priestly prerogatives. R. Tournay has suggested, however, that it may date from the 4th or even 3rd century BCE and that it is written in a deliberately archaic style in order to appear "Davidic."[78] The psalm's enigmatic character allowed it to attract a rich and varied corpus of expository traditions in formative Judaism, several of which will be referred to in the course of this study.

It appears that in Jewish exegesis of the NT period, Ps 109 was believed to refer to the mysterious origin of the Messiah. This is the presupposition behind the question raised by Jesus concerning v. 1 of the psalm—

> Εἶπεν ὁ κύριος τῷ κυρίῳ μου Κάθου ἐκ δεξιῶν μου,
> ἕως ἂν θῶ τοὺς ἐχθρούς σου ὑποπόδιον τῶν ποδῶν σου.

—in Mark 12:35-37, Matt 22:41-46 and Luke 20:41-44. What is at issue here for the communities behind this story is the problem of "reconciling descent from David with the dignity of Κύριος."[79] This verse was widely used in early Christianity as a testimony to the heavenly exaltation of Jesus. It is fully quoted with reference to his ascension in Acts 2:34. In the synoptic trial narratives, Jesus uses a phrase inspired by the psalm, ἐκ δεξιῶν καθήμενο(ς) τῆς δυνάμεως, in combination with an allusion to Dan 7:13 to refer to his role as eschatological judge (Mark 14:62, Matt 26:64, Luke 22:69).[80] Mark concludes his gospel by telling that Jesus was taken up into heaven καὶ ἐκάθισεν ἐκ δεξιῶν τοῦ θεου (Mark 16:19). The status of Jesus as

---

[77] Jacquet, III, 203.
[78] R. Tournay, "Recherches sur la chronologie des Psaumes, " *RB* 65 (1958) 321-357 and "Le Psaume CX" *RB* 67 (1960) 5-41.
[79] Kraus, *Theology of the Psalms*, 186.
[80] The circumlocution in Mark and Matthew (ἐκ δεξιῶν...τῆς δυνάμεως) reflects Jewish reverence for the divine Name. In contrast, Luke's more "Gentile" rendering (ἐκ δεξιῶν τῆς δυνάμεως τοῦ θεοῦ) corresponds to the direct mention of God by Stephen in Acts 7:56 (ἐκ δεξιῶν τοῦ θεοῦ). The absence of the reverential circumlocution in Acts 7:56 is a masterful touch on the part of Luke which adds dramatically to the offence of Stephen's speech.

the exalted one seated at the right hand of the Father is mentioned in terms drawn from Ps 109 in several Pauline and Deutero-Pauline writings: Rom 8:34, 1 Cor 15:25, Eph 1:20, Col 3:1. For the author of Hebrews, Ps 109:1 is a key text to which he returns frequently (Heb 1:3.13, 8:1, 10:12-13, 12:2). The other passage from Ps 109 which appeals to him is v. 4b—Σὺ εἶ ἱερεὺς εἰς τὸν αἰῶνα κατὰ τὴν τάξιν Μελχισεδεκ. It appears in Heb 5:6.10, 6:20 and 7:3.17.21 where it is used to develop the idea of an eternal priesthood of Jesus.

In 1 Cor 15:25 it is evident that Paul's application of Ps 109 to Jesus has extended beyond the phrase Κάθου ἐκ δεξιῶν μου to its continuation: ἕως ἂν θῶ τοὺς ἐχθρούς σου ὑποπόδιον τῶν ποδῶν σου. He construes the "until" as the period of Jesus' reign until the τέλος, during which all his enemies, and ultimately death, are to be subjected to him.[81] However, as noted above in the discussion of Ps 8, in alluding to Ps 109:1 Paul does not actually refer to God as putting Jesus' enemies under his feet as a footstool. His synonymous wording...ἄχρι οὗ θῇ πάντας τοὺς ἐχθροὺς ὑπὸ τοὺς πόδας αὐτοῦ...owes more to Psalm 8:7—πάντα ὑπέταξας ὑποκάτω τῶν ποδῶν αὐτοῦ.[82] In fact, Paul proceeds to quote this very verse of Ps 8 within a few lines (1 Cor 15:27). This is just one instance of the widespread tendency in the NT to conflate Ps 109:1 and Ps 8:7 which we have already noted. It is evident in the Markan and Matthean form of the question about the Son of David—... ἕως ἂν θῶ τοὺς ἐχθρούς σου <u>ὑποκάτω τῶν ποδῶν σου</u> (Mark 12:36, Matt 22:44). In Eph 1:20, following close on the reference to God making Jesus sit ἐν δεξιᾷ αὐτοῦ ἐν τοῖς ἐπουρανίοις, comes the above mentioned allusion to Ps 8:7—... καὶ πάντα ὑπέταξεν ὑπὸ τοὺς πόδας αὐτοῦ (Eph 1:22). Similarly, the author of Hebrews obviously connects these two psalms. The Ps 109:1 oracle (quoted in Heb 1:13) was addressed to no angel but to the one of whom Ps 8 testified, πάντα ὑπέταξας ὑποκάτω τῶν ποδῶν αὐτοῦ (Heb 2:8).[83]

As with Psalm 2, in the case of Ps 109 the Fourth Gospel confronts us with another instance of distinctive usage of the OT. This

---

[81] Cf. the form of the paraphrase of Ps 109:1 in Heb 10:12-13—...ἐκάθισεν ἐν δεξιᾷ τοῦ θεοῦ, <u>τὸ λοιπὸν ἐκδεχόμενος</u> ἕως τεθῶσιν οἱ ἐχθροὶ αὐτοῦ ὑποπόδιον τῶν ποδῶν αὐτοῦ. Luke gives expression to a similar tendency to 'theologize' on the 'until' in Acts 3:20-21 where the exalted Jesus appears as a "Messiah designate," waiting until the time of complete fulfilment.

[82] The NJB gives a false impression of verbal allusion to Ps 109:1 in its mistranslation of this verse—"For he is to be king until he has made his enemies his footstool..."

[83] Neither David M. Hay, *Glory at the Right Hand: Psalm 110 in Early Christianity* (Nashville: Abingdon, 1973) nor Juel, *Messianic Exegesis*, Ch. 6, "Christ at the Right Hand," trace this variant of Ps (109)110:1 to the influence of Ps 8.

is the psalm most frequently quoted in the NT and perhaps most formative of the kerygma.[84] Yet it is apparently not used by the Fourth Evangelist.[85] Obviously, the suggestion of elevation from a higher to a lower status inherent in v. 1 would not have appealed to an author who thought of the earthly life of Jesus as the descent from heaven of the pre-existent Word and his return to where he was before. There is also in the early Christian *relecture* of Ps 109, as outlined above, a hint of a certain type of subordination to God which would not have resonated with the Johannine perspective in which a Jesus who makes himself equal to God is no blasphemer (John 5:18; 10:33).[86] In addition, the interpretation of the "until" in terms of a second coming of Jesus would not fit with the realised eschatology which predominates in the Fourth Gospel.

It is inconceivable, however, that the Fourth Evangelist would not have encountered traditions about Jesus couched in terms drawn from Pss 2 and 109, particularly from the Υἱός μου εἶ σύ and the Κάθου ἐκ δεξιῶν μου. It can only be concluded that he had cogent reasons for avoiding expressions which did not fit into his theological schema. Thus the silence of these psalm passages in the Fourth Gospel is, in its own way, as eloquent as the quotation of other passages. The silences reveal an author who is selective in his use of the material available to him, incorporating into his text only the Scripture passages that are conducive to the theological thrust of his gospel.

There is also, nevertheless, the possibility that material emanating from early Christian reflection on Pss 2 and 109 (perhaps from the latter as conflated with Ps 8) has, in fact, been incorporated into the Fourth Gospel but has been so utterly transformed that it is not immediately obvious. Thus Chapter 5 below will propose that these psalms do actually function in the Fourth Gospel, but in the form of covert allusion which, to use Hollander's expression, may have "faded in prominence with the passage of time."[87] An awareness of

---

[84] The "sit at my right" motif appears in Matt 22:44; 26:64; Mark 12:36; 14:62; 16:19; Luke 20:42-43; 22:69; Acts 2:34-35; Rom 8:34; Eph 1:20; Col 3:1; Heb 1:3.13; 8:1; 10:12-13; 12:2.

[85] In what is perhaps the most detailed study of the early Christian reception of Ps (109)110 to appear in recent years, Hay, *Glory at the Right Hand*, there is no reference to any Fourth Gospel passage which incorporates an allusion to Ps (109)110. The most Hay allows is that there are several points of contact between early Christian interpretation of Ps (109)110 and Johannine thought.

[86] The Fourth Gospel does maintain, however, a fine balance between Jesus' subordination to God and his equality with God, thus avoiding ditheism. See John 5:19-23. 30; 17:3

[87] See Hollander, *Figure of Echo*, 64.

the various ways in which these psalms function in the NT generally, such as has emerged in this section, is an important step towards the recovery of these intertextual echoes in the Fourth Gospel.

G. *Conclusion*

From our analysis so far, it has emerged that David, *qua* psalmist, is important in the Fourth Gospel in that quotations from "his" psalms represent about 75% of explicit Scripture citation—as compared with an average of about 25% in the synoptics. The Fourth Gospel contains ten psalm quotations drawn from seven psalms. In the three cases where there is a synoptic parallel to its usage of a psalm verse, the Fourth Gospel exhibits a preference for formal citation over verbal allusion. It quotes five psalm verses used nowhere else in the NT. One of the psalms which it quotes, Ps (81)82 is used by no other NT author. The distinctiveness of the Johannine usage of the psalms is also evident in the fact that the two psalms most widely used in the NT, Pss 2 and (109)110 are never explicitly cited in John. It remains, of course, to be seen whether perhaps these two psalms might have influenced the Johannine text in a manner less overt than actual citation.

Of the seven psalms quoted in the Fourth Gospel, four, Ps (21)22, Ps(40)41, Ps (68)69 and Ps (117)118 are treated as prophecies fulfilled in the events leading up to the death of Jesus, as in the synoptics. John's use of Ps (68)69 is more extensive and, because of his particular chronology, more spread throughout the gospel as a whole. Nevertheless his three quotations from Ps (68)69 stem from this mode of psalm usage as does his unique use of Ps (33)34 which is quite unlike any of the other references to this psalm in the NT. The quotations from Pss (77)78 and Ps (81)82, on the other hand, are somewhat different in that they do not emanate from the passion testimony tradition. This, coupled with the fact that they both come from psalms which do not have a Davidic superscript, raises several of the issues which this study will seek to address.

In our statistical analysis we have also attempted to reckon and compare the extent of less formal intertextual reference to the Psalter in the gospels, but any such attempt must be approached with a *caveat*. The play of allusion and echo, which accounts for much of the influence of the Old Testament on the New, simply defies numerical analysis. This is particularly true of the Fourth Gospel. As we have seen, it exhibits a surprising sparseness of calculable verbal allusions. However, it is well known that it manifests an extremely skilful form of OT reference in an abundance of thematic allusions and echoes, far beyond what is found in the synoptics. Given the fact that less formal inter-textual reference to the Jewish Scriptures in John is particularly subtle and given what we have already established of the Evangelist's penchant for the psalms, it is to be expected that the Psalter would be one of the threads intricately worked into the finely woven fabric, the *textum subtile* of the Fourth Gospel. This study will show that, even if at times this thread creates only the merest of flecks, its distinctive hue pervades the work from start to finish.

It will be the task of Chs 3 - 5 to examine more closely the guise in which the psalm citations and allusions appear in the Fourth Gospel and to assess the extent of their integration into the flow of the Johannine argument. This will involve entering imaginatively into the presupposition of Davidic "authorship" with which the earliest Christians approached the Psalter. The next chapter explores this attribution and its implications for the Johannine reception of the psalms.

CHAPTER TWO

DAVIDIC "AUTHORSHIP" OF THE PSALMS

A. *Introduction*

The semiotics of literature has shown that a reader's approach to a text can never be autonomous. It is always conditioned by cultural conventions and presuppositions. Culler has described the reader as "the repository of the codes which account for the meaning of the text."[1] The Johannine milieu, as a site where various codes from Jewish tradition and Greek philosophy converged in a unique manner, accounts for the particular reading of the psalms which we find in the Fourth Gospel.[2] If we are to discover the basis upon which references to the psalms in the Fourth Gospel were received, we need to make explicit the implicit presuppositions that such a community would have brought to their reading of them, insofar as this is possible.

In dealing with presuppositions, we are confronted by what Roland Barthes termed "un mirage de citations," a complex web of all the intertextual codes and discursive conventions which go to make up a culture.[3] While we cannot identify each individual code and trace it back to its source, it is possible to reconstruct certain salient features of what Jauss calls the "horizon of expectations" on the basis of which a work was created and received. We can do this by considering the work against the background of other works which the author could expect his contemporary readers to know either explicitly or implicitly.[4] When we try to envisage the "horizon of expectations" which the Psalter would have opened up for the

---

[1] *Pursuit of Signs*, 38.
[2] On the contribution to the Fourth Gospel of various intellectual strands from its contemporary Roman Hellenism "characterized in many respects by a kind of religious universalism or syncretism," see George MacRrae, "The Fourth Gospel and Religionsgeschichte," *CBQ* 32 (1970) 13-24.
[3] Barthes explains codes as follows: "Alongside each utterance one might say that offstage voices can be heard: they are the codes. In their interweaving, these voices (whose origin is 'lost' in the vast perspective of the *already written*) de-originate the utterance; the convergence of the voices (of the codes) becomes *writing*, a stereographic space where the...codes...intersect." See *S/Z: A Structuralist Reading of Balzac's 'sarrasine,'* trans. Richard Miller (Oxford: Blackwell, 1990) 21.
[4] Jauss, "Literary History," 23.

early Christians, we immediately encounter their presupposition that David was its "author." In this chapter, we consider what Walter Brueggemann has called David's "literary future."[5] We explore certain salient features of the figure of David the psalmist as developed in the memory and imagination of Second Temple Judaism and as inherited by early Christianity.

As mentioned in the General Introduction, the rabbinical writings, the Targumim (especially the Targum to the Psalms) and the *Midrash Tehillim* cannot be used *en bloc* as evidence for 1st century CE perceptions of David as psalmist. They do, however, show the destination of trajectories which began with the inner-biblical and extra-biblical exegesis that we will explore in this chapter. Since these trajectories leave traces of their passing in the NT writings, there are many instances in which the NT confirms that later Jewish writings have preserved much earlier interpretive traditions. Our portrayal of David as psalmist will, therefore, owe much to the image which formative Judaism constructed out of the biblical and post-biblical traditions.

In this chapter we will have occasion to refer frequently to the narratives in 1-2 Sam and 1 Kgs 1-2. In our century, these have been analysed from perspectives as diverse as redaction and source criticism, comparative sociology, archeology and literary studies.[6] It appears that there is no consensus regarding the dating and consequent interpretation of these writings. As this is a reception study, we adopt, in this chapter, what might be called a "final form" reading.

---

[5] Walter Brueggemann, *David's Truth in Israel's Imagination and Memory* (Philadelphia: Fortress, 1985) 13.

[6] The two "landmark" studies of the David materials are: Leonhard Rost, *Die Überlieferung von der Thronnachfolge Davids*, (1926) translated by Michael D. Rutter and David M. Gunn as *The Succession to the Throne of David*, (Sheffield: Almond, 1982) and Martin Noth, *Überlieferungsgeschichtliche Studien I* (2nd ed. 1957) translated by Jane Doull and revised by John Barton, Michael D. Rutter, D. R. Ap-Thomas and David J. A. Clines as *The Deuteronomistic History*. Sheffield: JSOT Press, 1981. Rost posited a 10th cent. BCE "Succession History" (2 Sam 11-1 Kgs 2). While his theory that this narrative basically intends to ask, "Who is to sit on the throne after David?" (1 Kgs 1:20) is currently questioned, and while there is at present no consensus on the exact beginning or ending of the "Succession History," Rost's identification of this textual unit remains widely accepted. Noth proposed that a post exilic author is responsible for Deuteronomy and the Former prophets. While subsequent scholars have preferred to think in terms of one or several post-exilic redactors, Noth's basic intuition concerning the similar language and ideology of these works is still accepted.

B. *David's Musicianship*

An early intimation of David's role as psalmist is found in the biblical account of the Rise of David.[7] This strand of the David materials is an unambiguous celebration of his reign characterized by the repeated "refrain" that God was with him.[8] In this tradition, David's musicianship is an accomplishment, like eloquence or competence in war, which fits him for kingship. 1 Sam 16:14-23 tells of David's arrival at Saul's court as a skilled musician. The description of him "playing with his hand"(v. 23) to drive away the evil spirit, even though a reference to purely instrumental performance at this early stage of the tradition, was to become the taproot of the later conception of David as psalmist. Or perhaps, if we envisage a post exilic author, we might see that David's role as psalmist is being "read back" into the narrative tradition. According to the Rise of David narrative, the lament that David is said to have composed for Saul and Jonathan (2 Sam 1:17-27) is to be taught and is apparently preserved in a certain "Book of Jashar" (v. 18). Here we have an important reference to David's poetic and musical output being transmitted as part of a collection fixed in writing.

Josephus' retelling of biblical history is one of several works which exemplify the reception of this image of David in the first century CE. In describing the young David's therapeutic music making for Saul, he uses terms that are noticeably psalmic compared with the biblical terms which refer to a non-vocal and non-liturgical instrumental performance. For example, according to Josephus, Saul's physicians search for someone to sing powerfully and play upon the harp (ἐξᾴδειν δυνάμενος καὶ ψάλλειν ἐπὶ κινύρα). The verb ψάλλειν most likely carries here its original meaning, "to pluck" or, by extension, "to play (a stringed instrument)," but here a non-biblical reference to David's singing is expressed in the combination of the two verbs ψάλλω and ᾄδω which is a familiar idiom of the Psalter.[9] The LXX, in contrast, has Saul's servants seeking simply an accomplished instrumentalist: ἄνδρα εἰδότα ψάλλειν ἐν κινύρα (1 Sam 16:16). Again, according to Josephus, David is to play and sing hymns over Saul (ψάλλειν τε καὶ τους ὕμνους

---

[7] The Rise of David (1 Sam 16 - 2 Sam 5:5), also known as "The Apology of David" is best understood by comparison to the ANE tradition of court apology or royal justification. See P. Kyle McCarter Jr, "The Historical David," *Interpretation* 40 (1986) 117-129 at 118.

[8] The claim that "God was with David" (1 Sam 16:18; 18:14; 2 Sam 5:10, etc.) is the *leitmotif* of the entire composition, providing what McCarter has called a "theological undergirding" for the transfer of the kingship from Saul's line to David's. See P. Kyle McCarter Jr, "The Apology of David," *JBL* 99 (1980) 484 - 504, at 494 & 499.

[9] E.g., LXX Pss 26:6, 32:3, 56:8

ἐπιλέγειν),[10] while, in the LXX, Saul is looking merely for a skilled player of a stringed instrument, ἄνδρα ὀρθῶς ψάλλοντα. Josephus' Saul has no other physician than David who restores him to himself by singing hymns and playing on his harp (λέγων τε τοὺς ὕμνους καὶ ψάλλων ἐν τῇ κινύρᾳ) In his expansion of 1 Sam 19:9 (*Ant.* VI, 214), Josephus has Saul, spear in hand, ordering David to sing a psalm and some hymns (τῷ ψαλμῷ καὶ τοῖς ὕμνοις ἐξᾴδειν). The LXX states simply: καὶ Δαυὶδ ἔψαλλε ταῖς χερσὶν αὐτοῦ. Obviously Josephus is reading into the narratives of David's youth the figure of David the psalmist that he has encountered in his Jewish religious studies.

A similar David emerges from the extra-canonical Ps 151.[11] He is a maker of musical instruments with which he gives glory to God. In fact, this composition even suggests that the practice of psalmody in David's youth was the reason for God's choice of him. We quote the first two strophes—

> I was the smallest among my brothers,
>   and the youngest among the sons of my father;
> and he made me shpherd of his flocks,
>   and the ruler over his kids.
>
> My hands made a flute,
>   and my fingers a lyre:
> and I shall render glory to the Lord,
>   I thought within myself...[12]

Sanders sees this psalm as a poetic midrash on 1 Sam 16:7, "The Lord looks upon the heart," supplying what the Lord saw in David's heart: the desire to "give glory to the Lord" in song.[13]

A further example of the later reception of biblical traditions about David's musicianship is found in the *Liber Antiquitatum Biblicarum (LAB)* of Pseudo-Philo.[14] LAB contains a "Davidic" composition

---

[10] The psalmic character of Josephus' terms does not come through in the Loeb translation: the physicians search 'for one with power to charm away spirits and play upon the harp,' and David is to 'strike the strings and chant his songs' over Saul (*Ant.* I, 166). See R. Marcus and H. St-J. Thackeray, *Josephus*, LCL (Cambridge, MA & London: Harvard University Press, 1988) V, 249-50.

[11] This composition is extant in Greek (LXX Ps 151), in Syriac (5ApocSyrPs1) and in Hebrew (11QPs^a 151 A & B, Col. XXVIII, 2-14). It is the most well attested of what appears to have been quite a proliferation of extra-canonical psalms of David in circulation in the NT period.

[12] Charlesworth and Sanders, "More Psalms of David," *OTP* 2, 612.

[13] *DJD* IV, 58.

[14] The earliest extant manuscripts of *LAB* of Ps-Philo date from the 11th cent. CE and are in Latin. They are thought to translate a Greek version of the original Hebrew which was composed in Palestine during the first century CE, prior to the destruction of the Temple. See D. J. Harrington, "The Biblical Text of Pseudo-Philo's 'Liber Antiquitatum Biblicarum,'" *CBQ* 33 (1971) 1-17 and "Pseudo-Philo:

presented as: *psalmus quem psallebat in Saulem ut recederat ab eo spiritus iniquus (LAB* 60:2-3. Cf. 1 Sam 16:14-23). David addresses the evil spirit:

> ...do you not remember that you were created from a resounding echo in the chaos?
> But let the new womb from which I was born rebuke you,
> from which after a time one born from my loins will rule over you.[15]

We can see here how the tradition of David as psalmist has been assimilated to that of David as exorcist. Josephus' assumption that David's exorcistic music making is a vocal performance and the inclusion in the Qumran list of David's compositions (11QPs^a XXVII) of four "songs to be sung over the stricken" suggest widespread interest in imaginative expansions of 1 Sam 16:14-23. There is, therefore, a strong possibility that Ps-Philo knew several apocryphal apotropaic psalms of David and may be incorporating at least elements of them into this psalm.[16] As John Strugnell cautions, "In this type of literature the final redactor selects from earlier material as much as he composes."[17]

Perhaps the clearest statement of David's musicianship and poetic gifts dating from NT times is found in Josephus' *Ant.* VII, 305 where he describes a David who is not only proficient in Greek poetic metre, but is adept in instrument making and a master of performance technique.

> (David), being now free from wars and dangers, and enjoying profound peace from this time on, composed songs and hymns to God (ᾠδὰς εἰς τὸν θεὸν καὶ ὕμνους) in varied metres—some he made in trimeters, and others in pentameters. He also made musical instruments and instructed the Levites how to use them in praising God on the so-called Sabbath day.

A New Translation and Introduction," *OTP* 2, 297-377, at 299. Cf. D. Flusser "Psalms, Hymns and Prayers" in M. Stone (ed.), *Jewish Writings of the Second Temple Period: Apocrypha, Pseudepigrapha, Qumran Sectarian Writings, Philo, Josephus,* CRINT 2, 2 (Assen/Philadelphia: Van Gorcum/Fortress, 1984) 551-77, at 574. For the Latin text, see Daniel Harrington (ed.), *Pseudo-Philon, Les Antiquités Bibliques, Tome I* (Paris: Les Editions du Cerf, 1976). The author re-tells biblical history from Adam to David in a narrative which interweaves the biblical account with legendary expansions. "Pseudo Philo reflects the milieu of the Palestinian synagogues at the turn of the common era." See Harrington, "Pseudo-Philo," 300.

[15] Trans. Charlesworth and Sanders, *OTP* 2, 373. The reference to David's offspring is most probably to Solomon as exorcist.

[16] This exorcism addressed to the evil spirit is quite unlike the canonical psalms. It alludes to the type of speculation about the original silence before creation and the creation of spirits that is encountered in 1st - 2nd century CE apocalyptic literature, e.g., 2 Bar 3:7; 2 En 29:1; Jub 2:2.

[17] "More Psalms of David." *CBQ* 27 (1965) 207-216, at 208.

The motivation behind this statement is Josephus' determination "to elicit from the cultivated world respect for the much calumniated Jewish people"[18] His Hellenized David refutes the charge that the Jews have not produced marvellous, outstandingly wise people such as inventors of the arts.[19] It shows the extent to which, by Josephus' time, Davidic authorship of the Psalter had become a matter of course.

Philo is responsible for the most extensive corpus of writing from Hellenistic Judaism outside the Land of Israel. Since so much of his work exemplifies a biblical *relecture* which is coloured by Greek culture, it has significant contacts with the Fourth Gospel.[20] His exegetical work is mainly on the Pentateuch. This, no doubt, reflects Alexandrian synagogue reading practice and the special interest which the Pentateuch held for Jews living in Egypt. [21] For Philo, the rest of Scripture, Prophets, Psalms and Proverbs especially, is a kind of commentary on the Pentateuch, almost "secondary Scripture."[22] Mention of David in his writings, therefore, occurs only incidentally. However, several remarks made in passing throughout his works reveal a view of David very much in line with what we can establish from other sources of the period.

For Philo, David, being a king, is naturally the ὑμνήσας of God (*Conf.* 149), a gift for poetry being a *sine qua non* for kingship in the royal ideology of his cultural milieu.[23] In *Plant.* II, IX, 39 David, as psalmist, is described as θεσπέσιος, a term which is properly used of the voice as "divinely sounding" or "divinely sweet."[24] In *Conf.* 11.39

---

[18] Emil Schürer, *The History of the Jewish People in the Age of Jesus Christ* (Edinburgh: T & T. Clark, 1973-87) I, 48. In further references this work appears as *HJPAJC*.

[19] Louis H. Feldman, "Josephus' Portrait of David, "*HUCA* 60 (1989) 129-74.

[20] The most obvious aspect of Philo's work which invites comparison with the Fourth Gospel is his speculation on the Λόγος. See R. Bultmann, "The History of Religions Background of the Prologue to the Gospel of John" (1923) in John Ashton (ed.), *The Interpretation of John* (Philadelphia: Fortress & London: SPCK, 1986) 18-35, at 27. Other points of contact with the Fourth Gospel are Philo's portrayal of Moses, see Meeks, *The Prophet King*, 100-31, and his allegorization of the manna, see Peder Borgen, *Bread from Heaven: An Exegetical Study of the Concept of Manna in the Gospel of John and the Writings of Philo* (Leiden: Brill, 1965).

[21] Borgen, "Philo of Alexandria" *ABD* V, 333-42, at 336.

[22] See David M. Hay, "Philo's View of Himself as an Exegete: Inspired, but not Authoritative," in David T. Runia, David M. Hay and David Winston (ed.), *Heirs of the Septuagint: Festschrift for Earle Hilgert* (Atlanta: Scholars, 1991) 40-52, at 45.

[23] According to Dio Chrysostom's Second Discourse on Kingship, for example, Calliope, the muse of oratory and epic poetry is the attendant of kings. And Alexander is reported as saying that a king should be able to accompany his hymns and chants in honour of the brave on the cithara. Dio Chrysostom 1:63-65 (Second Discourse 24); 66-67 (Second Discourse 28).

[24] H. G. Liddell and R. Scott, *Greek-English Lexicon*, revised by H. S. Jones (Oxford: Clarendon Press, 1961) 795. In further references, this work appears as *LSJ*.

David, though not actually mentioned by name, is clearly the disciple of Moses (τῶν Μωυσέως γνωρίμος) who wrote Ps 30 (31), Τῷ Δαυιδ συνέσεως in the LXX. Philo's emphasis on David's discipleship of Moses is part of his preoccupation with Moses.[25] In one reference to it, however, Philo uses a telling technical term which has nuances of inspired musical activity, calling him ὁ τοῦ Μωυσέως δὴ θιασώτης (*Plant.* II, IX, 39). The term Θιασώτης refers to a member of a mystic guild or confraternity (θίασος).[26]

As we explore the various "salient features" of the "horizon of expectations" on the basis of which the Psalter was received as Davidic in NT Christianity, we will be referring again to the sources drawn upon in this section.

C. *David's "Authorship" of a Corpus of Psalmody*

It is impossible to pinpoint a precise date by which the Psalter was fixed in its present form.[27] If Dahood's reading is correct,

ס[פרים חומשים

in 1Q 30, a poorly preserved fragment of a collection of liturgical texts, may be the earliest reference we have to the most obvious structural feature of the Psalter, the division into five books.[28]

4QMiqsat Ma'ashe Ha-Torah ("Some Precepts of the Torah") also contains a reference to a corpus of writings associated with David. The text is in poor condition, but it is possible to discern what appears to be a designation for the tripartite biblical canon.

בספר מושׁה [ו]בספר[י] הנ[ב]יאים ובדוי[ד במעשׂי] דור ודור[29]

In the translation and reconstruction by F. García Martínez, the immediate context of this reads:

---

[25] For Philo, Moses is not only prior to the great Greek philosophers, but is "the very father of philosophy from whom all Greek thinkers take their best ideas." See John Dillon, *The Middle Platonists: A Study of Platonism 80 B.C. to A.D. 220* (London: Duckworth, 1977) 143.

[26] The term Θιασώτης is found in particular with reference to devotees of Dionysus in their revels. See *LSJ*, 801.

[27] For the current *status quaestionis*, see David M. Howard, Jr, "Editorial Activity in the Psalter: A State-of-the-Field Survey," in J. Clinton McCann (ed.), *The Shape and Shaping of the Psalter* (Sheffield: Sheffield Academic Press, 1993) 72-82.

[28] Dahood, *Psalms 1-50*, xxxi. According to the editors of this fragment, "si la lecture ספרים est exacte, il s'agit du Psautier." See D. Barthélemy and J. T. Milik, *Discoveries in the Judean Desert: Vol. 1, Qumran Cave I.* (Oxford: Clarendon, 1955) 132-33.

[29] From section C, lines 10-11 of 4QMMT in the reconstruction by E. Qimron and J. Strugnell in *Discoveries in the Judean Desert X: Qumran Cave 4* (Oxford: Clarendon Press, 1994) 58.

...to you we have wr[itten] that you must understand the book of Moses [and the words of the pro]phets and of David [and the annals of eac]h generation.³⁰

In the translation and reconstruction by Elisha Qimron and John Strugnell the same passage reads:

...we have written to you so that you may study (carefully) the book of Moses and the books of the Prophets and (the writings of) David [and the events of] ages past.³¹

What is of particular interest here is the interpretation of דויד. Qimron and Strugnell see a reference not merely to the Psalms of David, but to the Hagiographa. They regard this as "a significant piece of evidence for the history of the tripartite division of the canon."³² Otto Betz believes that דויד means the Psalter and that the partly reconstructed words במעשי דור ודור refer to the Books of Chronicles. He also draws attention to the similarity between Luke's ...ἐν τῷ νόμῳ Μωϋσέως καὶ τοῖς προφήταις καὶ ψαλμοῖς (Luke 24:44) and this "very early description of the canon."³³

As mentioned briefly above, in recent psalm study there has been a shift away from the atomistic classification of individual psalms according to *Gattung* (hymn, lament, royal, didactic etc.).³⁴ The greater appreciation of the Psalter as a coherent literary whole is, in fact, a recovery of the way in which it was received in NT times. Among the various explanations of the rationale behind the biblical order of the psalms which have been offered, that of G. H. Wilson appears to have received the most support. Wilson has shown that the ordering of the Psalter "is the result of a purposeful, editorial activity which sought to impart a meaningful arrangement which encompassed the

---

³⁰ F. García Martínez, *The Dead Sea Scrolls Translated: The Qumran Texts in English*. 84. Translated by W. G. E. Watson (Leiden: Brill & Grand Rapids: Eerdmans, 1994) 79, lines 95-96.
³¹ Qimron and Strugnell, *DJD X*, 59, Section C, lines 10-11.
³² Qimron and Strugnell, *DJD X*, 59.
³³ O. Betz, "The Qumran Halakah Text Miqsat Ma'ase Ha-Torah (4QMMT) and Sadducean, Essene, and Early Pharisaic Tradition" in D. Beattie & M. McNamara (ed.), *The Aramaic Bible: Targums in Their Historical Context*. (Sheffield: Sheffield Academic Press, 1984) 176 - 202. Cf. also the similar conclusions of L. H. Schiffman in "The New Halakhic Letter (4QMMT) and the Origins of the Dead Sea Sect," *Biblical Archaeologist* 53 (1990) 64-73, at 66.
³⁴ "In genre analysis, it is widely recognized that the assumptions of scholarship are enormously speculative concerning the proposed history of ideal genre, and tend toward reductionism. The problem of genre analysis is compounded by the fact that in much of scholarship, the notion of genre has been reified so that the specific psalm must submit to the proposed genre." W. Brueggemann, "Response to James L. Mays, 'The Question of Context'," in Mc Cann (ed.), *The Shape and Shaping*, 29-41, at 30. For a study of the composition and theology of a section of the

whole."³⁵ In his view, the psalms that mark the "seams" between books of the Psalter and the theological leitmotifs within each book reveal a progression in thought regarding kingship and the Davidic covenant:

> Book 1: from Ps 2 where the sovereignty of YHWH is extended to the king, to Ps 41 where David expresses his assurance in the face of his enemies.
>
> Book 2: from Ps 42 to Ps 72 where David prays for his son; the covenant passes to his descendants.
>
> Book 3: from Ps 73 to Ps 89 which recalls the Davidic covenant, now failed, and expresses the hope of its future extension to David's descendants.
>
> Book 4: from Ps 90 (A Prayer of Moses) to Ps 106 with its strong Mosaic motifs. The answer to the "failed" covenant is, YHWH is king, Israel's refuge long before the monarchy existed. Ps 106 ends with the plea: "Gather us from among the nations."
>
> Book 5: from Ps 107 (which refers to the "gathering" as accomplished) to Ps 145, the climax of the Psalter. David implements the final verse of Ps 145 by "speaking the praise of the Lord" (cf. Ps 145:21) in the concluding *Hallel*, Pss 146-150.³⁶

From this mere sketch of Wilson's theory, the significance of the attribution to David emerges as conspicuous. Also significant is the placing of Pss 1 and 2 as a prologue to the collection. This has important implications for a Davidic reading of the Psalter.

> The profane nations and rulers in Ps. 2 are identified with those who walk the way of sinners and the wicked in Ps. 1. Opposite these, one finds the divine king depicted in the language of Nathan's oracle as one who, by contrastive implication, walks in the way of the righteous. Consequently, David is represented in Ps. 2 both as author of the Psalms and also as one who qualifies under the injunction of Ps. 1 to interpret the Torah as a guide to righteousness...By his association with Ps. 2, David, who is, in canonical terms, the chief architect of the Psalter, is fully in accord with the ideals of Ps. 1. The entire Psalter, therefore, is made to stand theologically in association with David as a source of guidance for the way of the righteous. In this fashion, the Psalter has gained, among its other functions, the use as a source for wisdom reflection and a model of prayers based on such a pious interpretation of the Torah.³⁷

Psalter demonstrating the more holistic approach, cf. Erich Zenger, "New Approaches to the Study of the Psalms," *PIBA* 17 (1994) 37-54.

³⁵ Gerald Henry Wilson, *The Editing of the Hebrew Psalter*, SBL Dissertation Series 76 (Chico, CA: Scholars, 1985) 199.

³⁶ Wilson, *The Editing*, 110-228.

³⁷ Gerald T. Sheppard, *Wisdom as a Hermeneutical Construct: A Study of the Sapientializing of the Old Testament* (Berlin: de Gruyter, 1980) 142.

Even if the five books had reached their present form by the first century CE, Book 5 may have been still "open ended."[38] As mentioned above, a proliferation of extra-canonical "Psalms of David" appears to have been in circulation in the NT period, Ps 151 being the most well attested example.[39] The presence of Ps 151 in the LXX means that it must predate the second century BCE.[40] In the LXX it has the following superscript:

Οὗτος ὁ ψαλμὸς ἰδιόγραφος εἰς Δαυιδ καὶ ἔξωθεν τοῦ ἀριθμοῦ· ὅτε ἐμονομάχησεν τῷ Γολιαδ.

This superscript is also found in the Syriac, but not in the Qumran version. Instead, in 11QPs[a] Ps 151 is entitled "A Hallelujah of David the Son of Jesse" and the lines referring to David's combat with Goliath appear under a further heading: "At the beginning of David's power after the prophet of God anointed him." The absence in the 11QPs[a] version of anything corresponding to the words ἰδιόγραφος and ἔξωθεν τοῦ ἀριθμοῦ is striking. Apparently at Qumran there was no need to justify the inclusion of this composition among the psalms of David.

The Dead Sea Psalms Scroll 11QPs[a] where Ps 151 is found has been paleographically dated to the first half of the first century CE,[41] It contains a mixture of forty canonical and seven extra-canonical psalms, all presented as of equal standing, that is, without any textual indications of differentiation.[42] The scroll raises questions about

---

[38] This is the conclusion of J. A. Sanders on the basis of the greater frequency of variations towards the end of the Psalter in Qumran Mss. See "The Qumran Psalms Scroll (11Q Ps[a]) Reviewed," in M. Black and W. A. Smalley (ed.), *On Language, Culture and Religion: In Honor of Eugene A. Nida* (The Hague: Mouton, 1974) 79-99, at 98. Wilson, *The Editing*, 121, speaks of "a certain looseness in pss arrangement which continued until ca. A. D. 50 and apparently died out soon thereafter."

[39] According to a letter from the Nestorian Patriarch Timothy I (780-823) to Sergius, Metropolitan of Elam, first published in *Oriens Christianus*, I (1901) 299-313, more than 200 psalms of David were found ca 686-7 in scrolls discovered in caves near Jericho. This letter is quoted and discussed by John Strugnell in his "Notes on the Text and Transmission," 258. Cf. also Menahem Mansoor, *The Thanksgiving Hymns*, (Leiden: Brill, 1961) 2. Among the Cairo Geniza discoveries is a fragment of a medieval manuscript containing further extra-biblical "Songs of David." According to David Flusser, "Psalms, Hymns and Prayers," 568 - 69, their language and style point to a composition date prior to 70 CE.

[40] Charlesworth & Sanders, "More Psalms of David," 612. In fact, the LXX recension may be the closest to the original Hebrew composition. See M. Haran, "The Two Text Forms of Ps 151," *JJS* 39 (1988) 171-82.

[41] Charlesworth and Sanders, "More Psalms of David," 609. Cf. Sanders, *DJD IV*, 9. For this dating, cf. also Y. Yadin, "Another Fragment of the Psalms Scroll from Qumran Cave 11 (11QPs[a])," *Textus* 5 (1966) 1-10, at 1.

[42] The fact that the canonical psalms, all from the last two books of the Psalter, appear in a non-MT sequence suggested to Sanders that 11QPs[a] reflected a stage in the canonization process when this part of the Psalter was still "fluid." See *The Dead*

which there is much disagreement: whether the extra-canonical psalms were regarded as "biblical,"[43] what their intended function was.[44] Whether the supernumerary psalms in 11QPs^a originated in Qumran or were simply copied there we cannot be sure. But we can be certain that those involved in what we would call their composition would not have regarded themselves as original authors, but rather as heirs and interpreters of a tradition. In the opinion of Sanders, the lack of any distinguishing marks or variations in layout shows that in Qumran the validity of such a concept of authorship was accepted without question. There was no more doubt about David's "authorship" of these compositions than there was about his "authorship" of the canonical psalms. All were regarded as examples of his phenomenal literary output in various psalmic genres, a total of 4,050 compositions as listed in a prose note inserted towards the end of the scroll.

Sea Psalms Scroll, 13. Wilson, *The Editing*, 89, accepting Sander's theory, noted the importance of distinguishing between the fixation and the triumph of a particular form of the Psalter. 11QPs^a could thus represent a particular local tradition. Others have explained the scroll's content and order as driven by liturgical requirements. See M. H. Goshen-Gottstein, "The Psalm Scroll (11QPs^a): a Problem of Canon and Text," *Textus* 5 (1966) 22-33 and Shemaryahu Talmon, "Pisqah Be'emṣa' Pasuq and 11QPs^a," *Textus* 5 (1966) 11-21. P. W. Skehan, "A Liturgical Complex in 11QPs^a," *CBQ* 35 (1973) 195-205, agrees with this "liturgical" hypothesis, but adds that 11QPs^a could also have been a "library collection" honouring David as the psalmist par excellence. In a later variant of the "liturgical" hypothesis, Talmon suggests that 11QPs^a is "an ancient compilation of liturgical poems which served the members of the Qumran community as a kind of breviary." See *The World of Qumran From Within* (Jerusalem: Magnes & Leiden: Brill, 1989) 245-6. In his more recent writing, Sanders insists that 11QPs^a and several other as yet unpublished fragments which include MT and non-MT psalms side by side call for "a review of the extent of the Psalter as referred to in other ancient literature." See *Canon and Community: A Guide to Canonical Criticism* (Philadelphia: Fortress, 1984) 13.

[43] Talmon deduces from the content of 11QPs^a the variegated nature of the craft practised in the Qumran scriptorium where "scribes were busy...with copying sanctified literature while creativity of a biblical or quasi-biblical stance continued." He includes also the *Hodayoth* and possibly the Temple Scroll as evidence of such creativity. See "The Textual Study of the Bible—A New Outlook," in F. M. Cross and S. Talmon (ed), *Qumran and the History of the Biblical Text* (Cambridge MA & London: Harvard University Press, 1975) 321-400, at 337.

[44] See S. E. Farrell, "Le rouleau 11QPs^a et le psautier biblique," *LTP* 46 (1990) 353-68, at 365-66, for a convenient summary of the three main hypotheses: 1. 11QPs^a reflects a stage when the canonization process was not complete and the content of Book Five of the Psalter was still fluid (Sanders & Wilson). 2. 11QPs^a owes its order and content to liturgical requirements (Talmon & Goshen-Gottstein). 3. 11QPs^a is a library collection, "a reflection on the liturgy rather than a composition for a directly liturgical purpose" (Skehan). For a summary of the first hypothesis see Wilson, "The Qumran Psalms Scroll Reconsidered: Analysis of the Debate," *CBQ* 47 (1985) 234-42. With reference to the second, "liturgical" hypothesis, see Talmon, "Pisqah Be'emṣa' Pasuq," 11-21. For the "library collection" hypothesis, see Skehan, "Jubilees and the Qumran Psalter," *CBQ* 37 (1975) 343-47, at 343.

And David, the son of Jesse, was wise, and a light like the light of the sun, and literate, and discerning and perfect in all his ways before God and men. And the Lord gave him a discerning spirit. And he wrote 3,600 psalms; and songs to sing before the altar over the whole-burnt perpetual offering every day, for all the days of the year, 364; and for the offering of the Sabbaths, 52 songs; and for the offering of the New Moons and for all the Solemn Assemblies and for the Day of Atonement, 30 songs. And all the songs that he composed were 446, and songs for making music over the stricken, 4. And the total was 4,050. All these he composed through prophecy which was given him from before the Most High.[45]

This prose insert is preceded at the top of col. xxvii by 2 Sam 23:7. It seems likely, therefore, that the preceding column, which is damaged at the bottom, would have contained the biblical passage known as "The Last Words of David" (2 Sam 23:1-7), in the title of which David is referred to as נעים זמרות ישראל[46] and where he declares,

> The Spirit of God speaks by me,
> his word is upon my tongue (2 Sam 23:2).

2 Sam 23:1-7 has apparently been included in 11QPs^a as "a 'Davidic' psalm among psalms...clearly just as 'Davidic' as the psalm that precedes it in II Sam 22, which is also Psalm 18!"[47]

The enumeration of David's compositions in 11QPs^a suggests to some that David is being presented as even more prolific than Solomon who, according to the Hebrew of 1 Kgs 5:12, wrote 3,000 proverbs and 1,005 songs. Others see it as part of a glorification of David, not to be taken literally as a claim that these thousands of songs actually exist.[48] It could thus, as Sanders has suggested, be

---

[45] Col. xxvii, 2-11, known as 11QPs^aDavComp. See Sanders. *The Dead Sea Psalms Scroll*, 137.

[46] Among the varied translations for this designation of David are: "The sweet psalmist of Israel" or "the favourite of the songs of Israel" (RSV), "the singer of Israel's psalms" (NEB), "favourite of the Mighty One of Israel" (NAB), "the singer of the songs of Israel" (NJB).

[47] Sanders, *The Dead Sea Psalms Scroll*, 10. In fact, the description of David in 11QPs^aDavComp as "perfect" (תמים) relates back to 2 Sam 22—v. 24, "I was perfect (תמים) before him," and v. 26, "With the perfect (תמים) you show yourself perfect."

[48] So writes Menahem Haran drawing a comparison with the record of Solomon's prolific output in 1 Kgs 5:12-13 which does not refer to known texts. Haran denies that the psalms in 11QPs^a were attributed to King David. One of his arguments is that the scroll contains Ps 134 which is not attributed to David in either the MT or the LXX. Its *incipit* is damaged, but there would not, he claims, have been room for a superscript. Haran, however, fails to explain why the 11QPs^a versions of Pss 104 and 123 have Davidic superscripts, contrary to the MT. 11QMelch shows that the lack of a Davidic superscript does not inhibit Qumran scribes from attributing psalms to David. See "11QPs^a and the Canonical Book of

compared to the claim of the Fourth Evangelist that if all the works of Jesus were to be written down, the world itself could not contain the books that would be written.[49] It may even be the case that the idealization involved in attributing 4,050 compositions to David stretches into the future. Ben Zion Wacholder argues that the enumeration of David's poems in 11QPsªDavComp refers to a great eschatological Psalter containing 3,600 psalms, that is, 150 (the number of the canonical psalms) X 24 (the value of דויד).[50] It points to the descendant of Jesse of Isa 11:2 on whom the Spirit of the Lord will rest, rather than back to the memory of the historical David.[51] This futuristic reading of 11QPsªDavComp may be confirmed by the Targum of the Former Prophets where "the last words of David" become "the words of the prophecy of David that he prophesied for the end of the world, for the days of the consolation that are to come." The Targumic reading of the דיד האחרנים of 2 Sam 23:1 as a future figure may preserve interpretations of the "oracle of David the son of Jesse" (2 Sam 23:2) current at the time of the Qumran scribe's activity.[52]

With regard to the canonical psalms in 11QPsª, it is perhaps significant that the compilers show a preference for psalms in the first person singular, even to the point of changing occasional plural pro-

---

Psalms," in Marc Brettler and Michael Fishbane (ed.), *Minhah le Nahum: Biblical and Other Studies Presented to Nahum M. Sarna in Honour of His 70th Birthday* (Sheffield: Sheffield Academic Press, 1993) 193-201, at 200-01.

[49] John 20:3; 21:25. Sanders, *The Dead Sea Psalms Scroll*, 158.

[50] דוד normally has a value of 14, but written דויד, as in the Qumran scrolls and 1-2 Chr, it has a value of 24. See Ben Zion Wacholder, "David's Eschatological Psalter: 11Q Psalmsª," *HUCA* 59 (1988) 23-72, at 35. Skehan has noticed that, in fact, several of the numbers used in 11QPsª DavComp are multiples of 150—the total of 4050 compositions, the 3600 psalms and, by implication, the remaining 450 other poems. See his "Qumran and Old Testament Criticism" in M. Delcor (éd.) *Qumrân: sa pieté, sa théologie et son milieu*, (Paris: Duculot & Gembloux: Leuven University Press, 1968) 163-82, at 168.

[51] Ben Zion Wacholder regards Is 11:1 as "perhaps the most crucial text" for understanding the whole conception of Davidic authorship of the psalms. In Isa, it announces a literary unit (Chs 11-12) in which a new era is associated with the presence of a descendant of Jesse. The phrase, "in that day" (Is 11:10.11; 12:1.4) refers to a second exodus when this Davidic figure will lead the people in a new "Song at the Sea" (Is 12:2 quotes Ex 15:2). This song will include the words—

Give thanks to the Lord, call upon his name;
make known his deed. among the nations (Is 12:3).

—i.e., the *incipit* of Ps 105 which, according to 1 Chr 16:7, David appointed to be sung "on that day" by Asaph and his brethren. See "David's Eschatological Psalter," 26-27.

[52] 2 Sam 23: 1. 3. See *Targum Jonathan of the Former Prophets*, trans. D. J. Harrington & A. J. Saldarini, The Aramaic Bible, Vol. 10 (Wilmington DE: Glazier & Edinburgh: Clark, 1987) 203.

nouns in the MT to the singular.[53] As we will see, the first person plural by no means excludes David as "speaker" in the psalms, since David speaks in the name of the nation. However, it could be that some of the non-MT "singulars" in 11QPs[a] represent either a tendency to adapt the canonical text in order to strengthen the impression of Davidic authorship or, perhaps scribal error arising from the presupposition that the individual who speaks in the psalms is David.[54]

D. *The Liturgical David: Founder of the Temple and its Cult.*

Another strand of the early David materials recounts his story from the anointing at Hebron to his eventual subjection of all the surrounding Philistine tribes (2 Sam 5:6-8:18). Followers of Rost's "Succession Narrative" theory would see the portrayal of David in this narrative as designed to bolster Solomon's legitimacy. Others would see this as a David-focused document, concerned to legitimize Jerusalem and the centralization of the cult in the Temple.[55] The glorification of David peaks at Nathan's oracle (2 Sam 7), a foundational text, initially for Israelite kingship ideology, subsequently for messianism and ultimately for Christology. It is in this passage that we first hear of David's desire to build the Temple. As an ideal ANE king, he must found, organize and officiate in the cult.[56] It is this narrative that preserves the memory of David leading the rituals in celebration of the transfer of the ark to Jerusalem, an image of David which not only establishes him as Temple founder, but, in its later reception, enhances his reputation as psalmist.[57]

---

[53] E.g., Ps 122:2 (My feet are standing...). This is paralleled by the singular "throne" in v. 5 against the MT plural, "thrones." In Ps 141:7, "my bones" replaces the MT "our bones."

[54] E.g., the 11QPs[a] variant of Ps 119:152, "Long have I known from knowledge of you that you have founded me for ever." (Cf. the MT, "Long have I known from your testimonies that you have founded them for ever."). This variant may, as Sanders suggests, indicate that the verse, and indeed the whole *Koph* section of Ps 119, was understood in Qumran as a prayer of David referring to God's promise through Nathan (2 Sam 7). Sanders, *The Dead Sea Psalms Scroll*, 18.

[55] For a useful summary of the divergent views, see J.W. Flanagan, "Samuel, Book of" in ABD V, 957-65.

[56] See Othmar Keel, *The Symbolism of the Biblical World* (London: SPCK. 1978) 278-79, especially Ch. 3, "The King as Temple Builder and Priest." Biblical tradition represents all the kings from David (2 Sam 6:15) and Solomon (1 Kgs 8) to Hezekiah (2 Kgs 19:15-19) as leading the liturgy.

[57] The account in 2 Sam 6 may derive from another strand of tradition identified as "The Ark Narrative." This strand is thought to include 1 Sam 4:1b - 7:1, possibly 1 Sam 2 and possibly also 1 Sam 6. Cf. McCarter, "Apology of David," 489.

The memory of David's dance before the Ark (Cf. 2 Sam 6:14) has clearly influenced a passage where Philo speaks of the soul—

> ...disporting itself in virtues, leaping and skipping by reason of abundance of great joy, having set before it, as enjoyment outweighing thousands of those that men deem sweetest, the worship and service of the Only Wise (τὴν τοῦ μόνου θεραπείαν σοφοῦ). One after taking a sheer draught of this bright joy, a member indeed of Moses' fellowship, not found among the indifferent, spake aloud in hymns of praise, and addressing his own mind cried, "Delight in the Lord" (Ps 36:4), moved by the utterance to an ecstasy of the love that is heavenly and Divine...while his whole mind is snatched up in holy frenzy by a Divine possession, and he finds his gladness in God alone.[58]

Between the David who danced before the ark and the David identified by Philo in this passage as the "author" of the psalms,[59] there is a long process of metamorphosis. An important "milestone" in this development is the work of the Chronicler. He devotes a chronologically disproportionate amount of text to David in his history (1 Chr 10-29).[60] Selectively "editing" the earlier materials of Samuel and Kings, he builds on the strands in the David traditions which remember him as poet/musician and as man of faith, inferring from them David's composition of Temple psalmody. He creates a cultic David, sponsor and promoter of the Temple liturgy. His work, complete by about 400 BCE, presupposes an established corpus of psalmody associated with David.[61] Out of concern to legitimate the liturgical function of levitical singers in the Second Temple,[62] the

---

[58] *Plant.* II, IX, 39. "Holy frenzy" renders the Gk: οἶστρος, an insane passion, madness, *lit.* a sting ; a term used of the Bacchic Maenads (Euripides, *Bacchae* 665). See LSJ, 1210. "Gladness" renders ἐνευφραινόμενος. See ἐνευφραίνομαι (=εὐφραίνομαι) LSJ, 737.

[59] There are in this passage several thematic echoes of some of David's "hymns," notably Ps 83(84):10—"One day in your courts is better than thousands." The verb εὐφραίνω, used in the above passage by Philo, occurs over 50 times in the LXX Psalter.

[60] 1 Chr opens with a summary mention of all who came before David in 9 chapters of genealogies, as if history were leading towards the moment of his appearance. It has been estimated that the Chronicler's narrative of David's 33 year reign accounts for a third of the space allocated to the 450 year story of Israel from the reign of Saul to the edict of Cyrus. Cf. William Riley, *King and Cultus in Chronicles: Worship and the Reinterpretation of History*, JSOT Supplement Series 160 (Sheffield: JSOT Press, 1993) 54.

[61] "Then on that day David first appointed that thanksgiving be sung to the Lord by Asaph and his brethren" (1 Chr 16:7). Excerpts of Pss 105, 96 & 106 follow in the text. Cf. Ezra 3:10 where the laying of the temple foundations is celebrated with Levitical singing "according to the directions of King David of Israel." See 2 Chr 7:6; 29:29-30; 35:15; Neh 12:36.

[62] Attributing psalmody to David gave their relatively secondary function status as an institution with as much claim to legitimacy as the sacrificial function of the priests. While the priests offered sacrifices according to the Law of Moses, the

Chronicler portrays a David who appoints Levites to sing certain sections of "his" Psalter, and makes detailed prescriptions for the musical duties of no less than four thousand psalm singers (1 Chr 23:5; 25:1-8). Verses from the "untitled" Pss 105, 96 and 106 are quoted in 1 Chr 16 to represent the implementation by the Levites of David's command to "commemorate," "glorify" and "praise" (1 Chr 16:4).[63] Thus psalms with no לדוד superscript now come under the auspices of David. Appropriately, the Chronicler's version of David's story ends with the culminating liturgy of dedication of gifts for the Temple in which David appears as founder of the Temple, "the sole locus and exclusively valid organization for the worship of the Lord for all Israel."[64] Solomon takes no initiative in this matter; he merely follows his father's instructions. The memory of a David devoted to the worship of God energizes a religious group experiencing oppression and loss of identity, depending utterly, now that the monarchy had failed, on the capacity of its liturgy to offer it a tangible religious world. David is portrayed in Chronicles as "a past reality which is constitutive of what it means to be Israel now."[65]

The Chronicler's presentation of Zerubbabel as a Davidide (1 Chr 3:16-19) is consistent with this view of David. It is essential that Zerubbabel, as Temple builder, be connected with David, but the link which the Chronicler expresses in genealogical terms, is, in reality, an ideological link. It has more to do with David as founder of the Temple than as founder of the dynasty.[66] In this context it is informative to find Ben Sira, writing about 200 years later,[67] remembering Zerubbabel only as builder of the Second Temple and mak-

---

singers offered praise according to the instructions of David. See N. M. Sarna, "The Psalm Superscriptions and the Guilds" in Siegfried Stein & Raphael Loewe (ed.), *Studies in Jewish Religious and Intellectual History Presented to Alexander Altmann* (Alabama: University of Alabama Press, 1979) 281-300.

[63] The three verbs, זכר, ידה and הלל occur in various forms in each of the three selections. See Elieser Slomovic, "Toward an Understanding of the Formation of Historical Titles in the Book of Psalms," *ZAW* 91 (1979) 350-380, at 378-79.

[64] Kenneth E. Pomykala, *The Davidic Dynasty Tradition in Early Judaism: Its History and Significance for Messianism*, (Atlanta: Scholars, 1995) 69-111, at 108.

[65] J. Goldingay, "The Chronicler as Theologian," *BTB* 5 (1975) 99-126, at 113.

[66] Zerubbabel's Davidic lineage rests on very fragile grounds. From his detailed examination of the passages in Haggai and Zechariah which mention Zerubbabel or which are thought to refer to him, Pomykala has found no solid basis for the belief that he was a Davidide and nothing in the language of Hag 2:20-23 that requires it to be read as a prediction of Zerubbabel's imminent reign as a Davidic king. "It may be that the Chronicler has secondarily grafted Zerubbabel, a non-Davidic post-exilic leader, into the davidic family tree to emphasize the continuity between the post-exilic Temple built by Zerubbabel and pre-exilic traditions." See *The Davidic Dynasty Tradition* 45-60, at 46.

[67] The composition of Ben Sira is dated at *ca* 180 BCE with the translation into Greek by the grandson taking place about 50 years later. See A. A. di Lella,

ing no mention of Davidic lineage with regard to him (Sir 49:11-12). Like the Chronicler, Ben Sira envisages David primarily as psalmist and founder of Temple worship, as one who "in all that he did... gave thanks to the Holy One, the Most High, with ascriptions of glory (Sir 47:8-10). Such a portrayal serves to hint at the degree to which, by Ben Sira's time, "David and the psalms are subjects which have been collapsed into each other."[68]

David is portrayed in similar terms in 4Q522 (*4QWork with Place Names*), a Hebrew manuscript, paleographically dated to the mid-first century BCE, with a composition date estimated at roughly 100 years earlier. 4Q522 tells how David was the first to make an offering on the altar which he built on the Rock of Zion. The text consists of fifteen lines. It has required partial reconstruction. The passages relevant to our study are as follows, in the *editio princeps* by Émile Puech:

3 ...un fils est né à Jessé, fils de Pharès, fils de Ju[da, *fils de Jacob. Car/Et c'est lui qui prendra*
4 La Pierre de Sion et il en expulsera tous les Amorites, depuis Jé[rusalem *jusqu'à la mer (?), et qui aura l'idée*]
5 de bâtir le temple de YAHWH, le Dieu d'Israel. Or et argent, [*bronze et fer il preparera, et du bois de*
6 cèdre et de cyprès il fera venir [du] Liban pour sa construction. Mais [c'est] son plus jeune fils *qui bâtira le temple, Cependant lui/David*
7 y officiera le premier, *sa[crifiant sur] cette Pi[erre-ci*...[69]

4Q522 reflects a belief, current around the turn of the era, that the Temple rock was the site of the original altar of sacrifice.[70] From our

---

"Sirach" in Raymond E. Brown, Joseph A. Fitzmyer, Roland E. Murphy (ed.) *The New Jerome Biblical Commentary* (London: Chapman, 1990) 496-509, at 496.

[68] J. L. Mays, "The David of the Psalms." *Int* 40 (1986) 143-55, at 145.

[69] Émile Puech, "La pierre de Sion et l'autel des holocaustes d'après un manuscrit hébreu de la grotte 4 (4Q 522)," *RB* 99 (1992) 676-696, at 696. For ET, see García Martínez, *The Dead Sea Scrolls*, 227.

[70] The publication of this document has contributed significantly to the debate on whether the Temple rock was the traditional foundation for the *debir* or for the altar of holocausts. There is biblical basis for both possibilities. According to 1 Chr 22:1 and 2 Chr 3:1, the threshing floor of Ornan is the site for "the House of the Lord God." 1 Chr 22:1 specifically mentions "the altar of burnt offering for Israel," but cf. "the sanctuary of the Lord God," i.e., the place of rest for the ark of the covenant, in 1 Chr 22:19. In 1 Chr 28:19 David is portrayed as conveying to Solomon the plan for the Temple which he had received "by the writing of the hand of the Lord." The parallel with the desert tabernacle containing the ark (cf. Exod 25:9) is obvious. In Wis 9:8 the *parallelismus membrorum* would suggest that the "holy mountain" is to be understood primarily as the site of the altar. Josephus holds that Arunah's threshing floor is the site of the Temple altar. David "resolved to call that entire place the altar of all the people and to build there a temple to God" (*Ant.* VII, 334). *Ep. Arist* 89-91 supports the "altar" identification. See Margaret Barker, *The Gate of Heaven: The*

perspective, it is of great interest for the emphasis it places on David's foundational role with regard to the sacrificial cult in the Temple on Mount Zion. The final act of David recorded in the Books of Samuel is his vision of the angel of the Lord at the threshing floor of Araunah and his offering of sacrifice on the altar which he has built there (2 Sam 24:18-25). In the view of the editor(s) responsible for the separation of the books of Samuel and Kings, this is clearly the climax of David's life which, after that, "winds down" in an account of his old age and his provision for Solomon's succession (1 Kgs 1-2). In later tradition, 2 Sam 24:18-25 came to be regarded as the founding by David of the Jerusalem Temple and the inauguration of its sacrificial cult. The "seed" of this idea is found in Ps 132 where David's endurance of his hardships is motivated by his desire to establish the Temple. David's zeal for God's house (cf. Ps 69:9) is also evident in the Chronicler's retelling in which David orders Solomon to build the Temple on the site where he built an altar to offer sacrifice (2 Chr 3:1). The Chronicler identifies the place as Mount Moriah (2 Chr 3:1).[71] David says of it, "Here shall be the house of the Lord God and here the altar of burnt offering for Israel" (1 Chr 22:1). In later tradition, this site is known as the Rock of Zion, the bare rock itself being envisaged as the actual threshing area of the earlier story. The climax of David's life, according to the Chronicler, is his prayer and sacrifice in thanksgiving for being able to provide the materials for the construction of the Temple (1 Chr 29:10-22).

A similar concern to show that David is the Temple founder and Solomon, its builder only as an "extension" of David, is evident in a Septuagintal addition to 2 Sam 24:25 explaining how Solomon extended David's original altar "because it was little at first."[72] We en-

---

History and Symbolism of the Temple in Jerusalem (London: SPCK, 1991), 18. It will emerge from our analysis of the Johannine usage of the "Temple Rock" imagery that the Fourth Evangelist probably regarded it as the site of the altar.

[71] James R. Davila, "Moriah" in Freedman (ed.), *ABD* IV, 905, explains that the Chronicler either wants to impart to the Temple and Jerusalem a more ancient sanctity, or that at some time after the Chronicler and before the LXX, the Gen 22:2 location was suppressed in order to associate Abraham with the Jerusalem Temple. Puech notes that 4Q 522.4 may offer an explanation for this tradition. Its reference to the presence of Amorites in Jerusalem possibly reflects a tradition which may account for the localization, by homophony, of the Rock of Zion as Mount Moriah. The identification is clear in Jubilees 18:13—"And Abraham called that place 'The Lord has seen,' so that it is said, 'in the mountain the Lord has seen.' It is Mount Zion." Cf. Jos. *Ant.* I, 224, VIII, 333-34. See Puech, "La Pierre de Sion," 681. The Moriah identifcation is significant for our study, in view of the possibility of Isaac typology in John 1:36.

[72] ...καὶ προσέθηκεν Σαλωμων ἐπὶ τὸ θυσιαστήριον ἐπ' ἐσχάτῳ, ὅτι μικρὸν ἦν ἐν πρώτοις (2 Sam 24:25).

counter here what William M. Schniedewind has identified as a pro-Temple *Tendenz* in the Greek text of Samuel-Kings. Schniedewind discerns the same ideological undercurrent in several other Septuagintal instances of translator's bias.[73] What interests us in these ideological changes is what they imply about the Greek translators' view of David. In their concern to authenticate the Temple and its cult, they appeal not to Moses whose Law ordained the sacrificial system, but to David as Temple founder and as author of the psalms sung in the Temple liturgy. 4Q522 finds an echo in a passage in Eupolemus where David, desiring to build the Temple, asks God to indicate the location for the altar.[74] There is also evidence in four Targum passages that, on the analogy of David remembered as temple builder, the Messiah is expected to build the eschatological temple.[75] Josephus too agrees with the author of 4Q522 that the site of the altar was revealed to David.[76]

4QFlorilegium (4Q174),[77] contains a messianic *relecture* of Nathan's oracle which omits 2 Sam 7:13a "He will build a house for my name." According to 4QFlor, God is to build the eschatological temple in fulfilment of Amos' prophecy, "I will raise up the tent of

---

[73] E.g., in 2 Sam (LXX 2 Kingdoms) 7:11, instead of a promise that God will build a house (i.e., a dynasty) for David, we find a promise that David will build a house (i.e., a temple) for God—...καὶ ἀπαγγελεῖ σοι κύριος ὅτι οἶκον οἰκοδομήσεις αὐτῷ. In LXX 2 Kingdoms 7:5-7, God, instead of querying the whole enterprise as in MT 2 Sam 7, tells David that he is not the one to build the Temple—Οὐ σὺ οἰκοδομήσεις μοι οἶκον τοῦ κατοικῆσαί με·." See William M. Schniedewind, "Notes and Observations, Textual Criticism and Theological Interpretation: The Pro-Temple Tendenz in the Greek Text of Samuel-Kings" in *HTR* 87 (1994), 107-16.

[74] Eupolemus is believed to have written in the mid-first century BCE. Fragments of his writings, as reported by Alexander Polyhistor, are found in Eusebius of Caesarea. See *Praeparatio Evangelica* IX, 30, 5 in Edouard des Places (trans.), Eusèbe de Césarée: *La Preparation Évangélique, Livres VIII-IX-X*, (Paris: Les Editions du Cerf, 1991) 311.

[75] "He will build the house for my name" (Tg 2 Sam 7:13-14); "He will build for me the temple for my name" (Tg 1Chr 17:12-13); "This man, Messiah is his name ... he will build the temple of the Lord (Tg Zech 6:12); "He will build the temple which was profaned because of our transgressions and delivered up for our sins" (Tg Isa 53:5). These are quoted in the translation of Donald Juel who discusses them in his *Messiah and Temple: The Trial of Jesus in the Gospel of Mark* (Missoula: Scholars, 1977) 181-89. As Juel readily admits, however, the value of these texts for NT study is fairly limited, as they did not reach their final form until the 7th cent. CE.

[76] See *Ant.* VII, 334. Josephus' David, even if not actually the Temple builder, is the instigator of the project and the designer of a building which can bear comparison with any of the great examples of Greek or Roman architecture. See *Ant.* VII, 10,75-79; *Ant.* VIII, 2,63 - 3,100.

[77] 4QFlor is a 1st cent. CE pesher-style midrash on the last days. It is the only Qumran document which contains the word מדרש and the word פשר in relation one to the other. See George J. Brooke, *Exegesis at Qumran: 4QFlorilegium in its Jewish Context*, JSOT Supplement Series 29 (Sheffield: JSOT Press, 1985) 38.

David that is fallen" (Amos 9:11).[78] The commentary turns on the double meaning intended in Nathan's oracle for the word בית as both Temple and dynasty (2 Sam 7:4.11). The "House" is the place where God will reign for ever and ever (Exod 15:18). Since the "House" is both Temple and dynasty, this reign of God, through which God's glory is revealed (4QFlor 5), is experienced both in the worship of the Qumran community and in the anticipated rule of David's descendant.

According to 4QFlor 6-7, The Lord "promised to build for himself a sanctuary of men, for there to be in it smoking offerings before him, works of thanksgiving."[79] The Qumran sectarians regarded the worship of their community as an offering of the incense of praise (cf. Ps 141:2).[80] They evaded the theological dilemma in which their withdrawal from the Jerusalem cult placed them, by contending that until the restoration of the corrupt Temple in Jerusalem, the only true worship was being offered in their assembly which was a proleptic representation of the eschatological Temple to be built by God.[81] In this "Temple," the psalms of David, the prayer that formerly accompanied their sacrifices in the Jerusalem Temple, now replaced those sacrifices.[82] From various Qumran documents, notably the Qumran *Hodayoth* (1QH), we learn that the "offering of the lips" was held in high regard as the true means of offering sacrifice.[83]

---

[78] 4QFlor mentions the "Branch of David," designated as God's son on the basis of 2 Sam 7:14 for whom God (apparently) will build the temple. The text is fragmentary, but a citation from Exod 15:17 ("the sanctuary of the Lord which thy hands have established) suggests that 4QFlor is within the tradition, exemplified in Ps 78:69, that God established the Temple. Juel, *Messiah and Temple*, 179, sees the subordination of the Messiah to a priestly Messiah in 4QFlor as "a conscious correction of a traditional view according to which the Messiah was expected to build the Temple."

[79] Translation by Brooke, *Exegesis at Qumran*, 92.

[80] 4QFlor 1:6-7 describes the "offerings" of the community as "like the smoke of incense."

[81] Brooke, *Exegesis at Qumran*, 144. Cf. 1QS 8:4-7; CD 3:18-4:10; 1QpHab 12:3-4.

[82] "They shall atone for guilty rebellion and for sins of unfaithfulness that they may obtain loving kindness for the Land without the flesh of holocausts and the fat of sacrifice. And prayer rightly offered shall be as an acceptable fragrance of righteousness, and perfection of way as a delectable free-will offering."1QS IX, 4-5, in GezaVermes, *The Dead Sea Scrolls, in English* (London: Penguin, 3rd Edition, 1986) 74. Cf. 1QS VIII, 8-9.

[83] The expression "offering of the lips" alludes to Hos 14:3. It occurs frequently in 1QH (e.g., I, 28; XI, 33-34). There are several other expressions found frequently in 1QH which correspond to it, notably "the reply of the tongue," alluding to Prov 16:1 (e.g., 1QH XI, 34; XVI, 6; XVII, 17). According to the "Community Rule," the leader blesses God with the "offering of the lips" (1QS X, 1. 8. 14. 22). It has a biblical background in texts such as Ps 40:6-8 and Hos 6:6. It is mentioned in TLevi 3:6. The idea is likely to have received an impetus from the emergence of the neo-Platonic idea of rational sacrifice (λογικὴ θυσία). According to this doctrine,

The *Hodayoth* themselves exemplify this form of worship. Their extensive literary dependence on the canonical Psalter indicates that David, as "author" of their paradigm and quarry, was held in high regard as the great teacher of true worship.[84] There is also the fact that "there were undoubtedly more copies of psalms in the Qumran library than of any other biblical writings."[85] At Qumran, therefore, David has a foundational role with regard to the eschatological Temple arising not only from his status as founder of the original Temple, but from his role as psalmist.

In Second Temple Judaism, therefore, against the "historical" evidence, David becomes in Israelite memory and imagination, the "builder"—certainly the founder—of the Temple. It was this perception of David that was to flow into the expectation that the Messiah will rebuild the Temple.[86]

E. *The "Autobiographical" David: the Historical Superscript Tradition*

In contrast to other more triumphal portrayals, 2 Sam 9-20 and 1 Kgs 1-2 presents a vulnerable David who suffers bereavement, disloyalty, conspiracy.[87] In this he becomes a model of Israelite piety,

---

there are appropriate forms of worship for each of the various types of gods: wordless interior praise for the highest god, hymn singing for the intellectual gods, offering of the fruits of the earth for the heavenly gods (planets, stars etc.) and animal sacrifice for the demons. The influence of this notion on Jewish thought is seen in Philo's allegorization of the sacrificial rites. In *Spec. Leg.* I, 272, e.g., he describes worshippers as offering themselves and their noble living "as they honour their benefactor and Saviour with hymns and thanksgivings, sometimes with the organs of speech, sometimes without tongue or lips when within the soul alone their minds recite or cry out." See E. Ferguson, "Spiritual Sacrifice in Early Christianity and its Environment" in *Aufstieg und Niedergang der Römischen Welt*, II Principat 23.2. (Berlin & New York: De Gruyter, 1980) 1151-87, at 1159-60.

[84] Eugene H. Merrill has noted the evidence the *Hodayoth* provide of "deliberate patterning of thought and style on biblical antecedents." See *Qumran and Predestination: A Theological Study of the Thanksgiving Hymns* (Leiden: Brill, 1975) 11. Foremost among these antecedents is the Psalter, with the "Servant Songs" coming second. See J. Carmignac, "Les Citations de l'Ancien Testament et spécialement des poèmes du Serviteur dans les Hymnes de Qumrân," *RevQum* 2 (1959-60) 357-94. As we have already seen, a density of allusion to the Psalter is a characteristic of the 11QPs^a extra-canonical psalms. It is also evident in other Qumran prayer texts, the psalm which concludes the Community Rule (1QS X-XI), being just one example. From a study of the Hebrew of this poem, P. Wernberg-Møller, *The Manual of Discipline*, (Leiden: Brill, 1957) 69, has concluded that Ps 104 is the "biblical context which has played the greatest role" in the composition of its opening sequence.

[85] Sanders, *The Dead Sea Psalms Scroll*, 9. Fragments of the biblical Psalter have been found in Caves 1, 2, 3, 4, 5, 6, 8 and 11.

[86] See Juel, *Messiah and Temple*, 181-89.

[87] This narrative block, Rost's "Succession Narrative" has more recently been termed "The Court History of David." See J. W. Flanagan, "Court History or

emerging, above all in the story of Absalom's rebellion, as a man of extraordinary faith in God. While there is no explicit reference to David's psalm composition, it is in this strand of the tradition that the one reference to David praying in time of distress occurs (2 Sam 15:31). It is this scene, where David is portrayed as spontaneously praying, that would contribute more than any other in the Deuteronomistic history to the development of the historical superscripts. David's prayer—"O Lord, I pray you, turn the counsel of Ahithophel into foolishness."—opened the way for an exegetical development in which later editors of the Psalter would pinpoint incidents in David's experience as the occasions on which he had prayed particular psalms. Certainly the David of this narrative who could say, "Let the Lord do to me what seems good to him" (2 Sam 15:26) or, "It may be that the Lord will look upon my affliction and repay me with good" (2 Sam 16:12), could also quite plausibly be credited in Israel's imagination with authorship of the psalms.

The reception of the psalms as "autobiographical" utterances of David is already evident in 2 Sam 22-23.[88] Psalm 18 occurs in 2 Sam 22 as spoken by David "on the day when the Lord delivered him from the hand of all his enemies and from the hand of Saul."[89] As the reader appraises David's whole career in the light of this psalm, the psalm itself becomes, in the words of J. L. Mays, "a hermeneutical door in the narrative for the use of the psalms in general as a context for reading the David story." Mays explains—

> ...the song establishes in the canon a Davidic view of the Psalms. It is the earliest literary evidence of a connection between David and the Psalms, and the only specific witness in the David story to that relationship. The song appears as Psalm 18 in the Book of Psalms, with the narrative introduction composed for its setting in Samuel. Its earliest extant literary use is in the story, but the narrator who put it in its place must have known it as "Davidic. "...As one of the psalms in

---

Succession Document? A Study of 2 Samuel 9-20" and 1 Kings 1-2," *JBL* 91 (1972) 172-81 and P. Kyle McCarter, "Plots, True or False: The Succession Narrative as Court Apologetic." *Interpretation* 35 (1981) 355 - 67.

[88] McCarter, following Noth, sees 2 Sam 22 (=Ps 18) and 2 Sam 23:1-7 ("The Last Words of David") as a post-Deuteronomistic History appendix, inserted "so that David, like Moses, might end his life with a hymn of vindication (See Deut 32:1-43) and a testimony (cf. Deut 33). See his Anchor Bible Commentary, *2 Samuel* (New York: Doubleday, 1984) 475 and 19.

[89] At the very least, the placing of Ps 18 in 2 Sam 22 tells us that this poem had already been attributed to David at the time of the final editing of the books of Samuel. In fact, the early monarchic period is suggested as a date for the composition of a primitive form of this psalm by several archaic features in both its orthography and content, e.g., the reference to fighting on foot (v. 33). See Sabourin, *The Psalms*, 343, 346, and Weiser, *Psalms*, 186.

the growing canonical collection, this psalm inevitably pointed to a narrative setting in David's life for other *lᵉ dawîd* psalms, and may have given some impetus to the production of other different settings of psalms in the narrative of Samuel.⁹⁰

The mention of David's name in five psalms (Pss 18, 78, 89, 132, 144) would also have functioned as "an inner textual code for reading the other psalms in which David is not mentioned."⁹¹ Consequently, the great symbols surrounding the royal ideal—king, anointed, servant, Temple, Zion, etc.—would have put readers in mind of David so that what the psalms originally said about "the king," was received as referring to David.

Seventy three psalms in the MT have the superscript לדוד.⁹² It appears that as the Psalter gradually took shape, individual psalms or smaller collections of psalms were gradually being taken within the ambit of supposed Davidic authorship.⁹³ This authorship was understood in a progressively more developed sense.⁹⁴ The rationale behind it must be sought in what Talmon has called "the gamut of connotations that attach to such a basic term as כתב in biblical and in post-biblical rabbinic literature."⁹⁵ In contrast to our modern differentiation of the diverse procedures involved in the production of a text: creation, preservation, transmission, etc., the verb כתב had, for the ancients, sufficient elasticity to encompass retrospective ascription and pseudonymity.⁹⁶ The "Davidicization" process was still ongoing when

---

⁹⁰ J. L. Mays, "The David of the Psalms," *Interpretation* 40 (1986) 143-155, at 148.

⁹¹ Mays, "The David of the Psalms,"150.

⁹² Pss 3-9, 11-32, 34-41, 51-65, 68-70, 86, 101, 103, 108-110, 122, 124, 131, 133, 138-145.

⁹³ Like the Asaphite and Koraite psalms, the Davidic psalms tended to occur in "song cycles," which would suggest that the ascriptions were originally envisaged as some form of classification. There is a sense in which the assignment of psalms to Korah, Asaph, Jeduthun, Ethan and Heman also amounts to Davidic attribution. These were all appointees of David who served as singers and liturgists under his patronage. See Gerald T. Sheppard, "Theology and the Book of Psalms," *Int* 46 (1992) 143-155, at 147. Even psalms with no ascriptive title could be regarded as Davidic. E.g., in 1 Chr 16 a choir led by Asaph sings, at David's behest, Pss 105, 96, 107 and 96, none of which, as we have seen, appears in the canonical Psalter with either a Davidic or an Asaphite ascription. It could be that Asaph is the performer and David, the composer or patron of the psalmody. See Sarna, "The Psalm Superscripts and the Guilds," 285.

⁹⁴ H. Cazelles suggests that לדוד began to be interpreted as an indication of authorship when what was originally intended as a *lamed* of attribution or classification, transmitting a tradition about the circles in which these compositions originated, came to be understood as a *lamed auctoris*. See, "La question du Lamed Auctoris," *RB* 56 (1949) 93-101.

⁹⁵ Talmon, *Textual Study*, 337.

⁹⁶ The Talmud defines by the term כתב Moses' authoring of the Torah, the Balaam pericope and Job, the compilation of the book of Psalms by David with the help of (or transmitted by) ten sages of old, as well as the transmission or the can-

the psalms came to be translated into Greek, with fourteen further psalms coming under Davidic attribution.[97] The fluctuation between genitive and dative renderings of the MT Davidic superscripts shows that the LXX translators did not take the notion of "authorship" absolutely literally.[98] Further expansion of David's "authorship occurs in the DSS where, as we have seen, psalms with no Davidic superscript in either MT or LXX are attributed to David. It is generally agreed that a careful scholarly study of Scripture, going far beyond the mere noticing of obvious allusions lies behind this tradition. It seems that a technique similar to rabbinic midrash was employed in the creation of the titles.[99] This involved the identification of verbal and thematic affinities between psalms and specific episodes in the narrative traditions, in particular, similarities between the diction of the Psalter and the direct speech of David.[100]

The ascription of psalms to David led naturally to the association of particular psalms with incidents in his career. Thirteen of the seventy three לדוד psalms in the MT had acquired "historical" expansions of

---

onization of Isaiah, Proverbs, Song of Songs and Ecclesiastes by Hezekiah and his college. See *Baba Bathra* 14b-15a, as quoted by Talmon in *Textual Study*, 337.

[97] LXX Pss 9, 32,42,70,90,92-98, 103 & 136. In one case this appears "accidental" in that the Septuagintal treatment of MT Pss 9 and 10 as one psalm has the effect of bringing MT Ps 10 under the Davidic superscript for Ps 9. The supernumerary Ps 151 brings the total number of psalms formally attributed to David in the LXX to 88 as compared to 73 in the Hebrew text. There is also the possibility that LXX Ps 71 should also be considered as attributed, by implication, to David. LXX Ps 71, which concludes οἱ ὕμνοι Δαυιδ τοῦ υἱοῦ Ιεσσαι, has the superscript Εἰς Σαλωμων. This unique rendering of the prepositional *lamed* has the effect of transforming the LXX version into a prayer of David <u>for</u> his son Solomon as he ascends the throne.

[98] They seem to have favoured the *lamed* of attribution, rendering לדוד by the dative τῷ Δαυίδ. The genitive, τοῦ Δαυίδ, occurs in rare cases: LXX Pss 16, 25, 26, 27 & 36. Compare Ps 16, Προσευχὴ τοῦ Δαυίδ with Ps 85, Προσευχὴ τῷ Δαυιδ. Albert Pietersma has demonstrated from the manuscript evidence that in the process of textual transmission of the LXX the notion of a Davidic Psalter was gaining momentum. Since none of the several instances of τοῦ Δαυίδ is uncontested in the witnesses, he is convinced of the originality of the dative rendering of לדוד and of the secondary character of the occasional genitive renderings as "an inner Greek expansion of the direct authorship of David." See "David in the Greek Psalms," *VT* 30 (1980), 213-226.

[99] See Slomovic, "Toward an Understanding," 350-80.

[100] V. 4 of the לדוד Ps 8 recalls the discourse of the Deuteronomistic David, e.g., "Who am I and who are my kinsfolk and my father's family that I should be son-in-law to the king?" (1 Sam 18:18); "Who am I, O Lord God, and what is my house that you have brought me thus far?" (2 Sam 7:8). Those responsible for the addition of the superscript לדוד to Ps 8 would appear to have discerned a parallel between David, raised from lowliness to kingship, and humankind, created from dust and "crowned with glory and honour" (Ps 8:5). The correlation between the David narratives and the "J" narratives in Gen 2-11 are discussed by Breuggemann in "David and His Theologian," *CBQ* 30 (1968) 156-81.

their Davidic superscripts by the time the MT Psalter had reached its present form.[101] They seem to have been in place in the Proto-Masoretic text by a late post-exilic date. They have a close parallel in the superscripts to the prayers of Hezekiah (Isa 38) and Habakkuk (Hab 3:1-19). Brevard Childs believes that the Chronicler would surely have shown an awareness of the superscript tradition if it had been available to him. He would, therefore assign the historical superscripts a *terminus a quo* after the time of the Chronicler's activity. It could be argued, however, that it is unlikely that titles drawing attention to David's "weaker" moments would have appealed to the Chronicler. Childs suggests that a *terminus ad quem* is provided by 11QPs[a] (*ca* 30-50 CE) which, he believes, gives clear evidence that "the technique was fully developed."[102] Unfortunately, the opening of Ps 142, the only one of the 13 psalms with expanded superscripts in the MT which is found in 11QPs[a], is missing. Child's *terminus ad quem* must therefore be based on the historical titles to the extra-canonical psalms of David found in 11QPs[a]. He extrapolates from the way in which the 11QPs[a] superscripts imitate the biblical historical superscripts an already established superscript tradition. This intuition is confirmed by the presence of historical superscripts in other DSS Psalter fragments.[103]

Like the לדוד ascriptions, the historical superscripts are the result of an inner biblical exegesis. They provide important data about the perceptions of the character of David and of his role in Israel's life of faith held by those who composed them. What is noticeable is that every one of the 13 לדוד psalms with historical titles in the MT refers to a situation of distress. As with the ascriptions, this tradition of linking psalms to events in David's career was ongoing in the 3rd-2nd centuries BCE, as shown by some further examples found in the LXX where they function in several different ways. There are "historical" titles linking psalms with events in David's life, quite similar to those in the Hebrew. For example, Ps (142)143 becomes in the LXX "A Psalm of David when his son pursued him," i.e., a prayer of David at the time of Absalom's revolt (2 Sam 15-18).[104] There are two LXX superscripts which refer in a more general way to a state of mind expe-

---

[101] Pss 3, 7, 18, 34, 51, 52, 54, 56, 57, 59, 60, 63 and 142.
[102] See "Psalm Titles and Midrashic Exegesis," *JSS* 16 (1971), 137-150.
[103] E.g., 1QpPs 57 contains the words—[שאול מלפני בורחו] ב *(DJD*, I, 81). Similarly, it is possible to decipher the words נתן הנביא and בת־שבע on the poorly preserved fragments of 4QPs[c] (= 4Q85) which contains Ps 51:1-5. See photo #43.156 in Emmanuel Tov, with the collaboration of Stephen J. Pfann, *The Dead Sea Scrolls on Microfiches* (Leiden: Brill, 1993).
[104] See also LXX Ps 26. Τοῦ Δαυιδ· πρὸ τοῦ χρισθῆναι. (See 1 Sam 16); Ps 142. Ψαλμὸς τῷ Δαυιδ, ὅτε αὐτὸν ὁ υἱὸς καταδιώκει. (See 2 Sam 17:1); Ps 143. Τῷ Δαυιδ,

rienced by David and are thus less obviously connected with a specific incident.[105] There are what we might call "national" titles. Some make a connection between David as psalmist and events in Israel's later experience, notably the Babylonian Exile, the recovery of the land of Israel and the rebuilding of the Temple.[106] In others, a "national" reference seems to be superimposed on the "historical" reference to an event in David's life.[107] This tendency towards a collective reading of the psalms of David is perhaps most dramatically exemplified in LXX Ps 136, one of the psalms which has no superscript in the Hebrew, but is Τῷ Δαυιδ in the LXX. Here we have a psalm obviously composed after 587 BCE, but attributed to David nonetheless in the LXX. Here the people as a whole speak through David's "voice," especially since his psalms, "the hymns of Zion" which they cannot bear to sing in a foreign land, are, in a real sense, the vehicle for their self expression as God's people, Israel. While this national identity functions at the collective level, it is lived out in the individual piety of those who learn from David's prayerful response to all that befell him what it means to live in covenant with God.

The Septuagintal superscripts applying David's psalms to events in Israel's history show a consciousness of the interpretive problem that Davidic authorship created with regard to psalms spoken in the first person plural. A reading of the psalms as spoken by David in the name of nation overcame this.[108] The Septuagintal examples of this "corporate" understanding of David exemplify a dynamic which is characteristic of the *relecture* of the Davidic dynasty traditions in exilic and post-exilic writings, the re-working of David as a representa-

πρὸς τὸν Γολιαδ. (1 Sam 17). Ps 151. Οὗτος ὁ ψαλμὸς ἰδιόγραφος εἰς Δαυιδ καὶ ἔξωθεν τοῦ ἀριθμοῦ· ὅτε ἐμονομάχησεν τῷ Γολιαδ (See 1 Sam 17).

[105] LXX Ps 30,...ψαλμὸς τῷ Δαυιδ· ἐκστάσεως, and LXX Ps 69,...τῷ Δαυιδ εἰς ἀνάμνησιν, εἰς τὸ σῶσαί με κύριον.

[106] LXX Ps 95, Ὅτε ὁ οἶκος ᾠκοδομεῖτο μετὰ τὴν αἰχμαλωσίαν· ᾠδὴ τῷ Δαυιδ, and LXX Ps 96, Τῷ Δαυιδ, ὅτε ἡ γῆ αὐτοῦ καθίσταται.

[107] LXX Ps 55,...ὑπὲρ τοῦ λαοῦ τοῦ ἀπὸ τῶν ἁγίων μεμακρυμμένου· τῷ Δαυιδ εἰς στηλογραφίαν, ὁπότε ἐκράτησαν αὐτὸν οἱ ἀλλόφυλοι ἐν Γεθ, and LXX Ps 70. Τῷ Δαυιδ· υἱῶν Ιωναδαβ καὶ τῶν πρώτων αἰχμαλωτισθέντων.

[108] The "problem" persists even up to the Talmudic period. According to a saying attributed to R. Eliezer (fl. ca 90 CE), David composed all the songs and hymns in the Book of Psalms about himself. Another theory preserved in the name of Eliezer's contemporary, R. Jehoshua, states that the psalms are about the nation. According to the scholars, the psalms in the singular were about David, the ones in the plural were about the community. See *b. Pesah.* 117a. A different tradition, preserved in *Midr. Teh.* 1:6, explains that ten people actually wrote the psalms, but that David's name is put over the whole Psalter because he is the best singer. References to Braude (ed.) *The Midrash on Psalms* employ Braude's enumeration. The first number refers to the psalm being commented upon; the second, to a sub-section of the commentary.

tive figure for Israel and a symbol of what God will do for Israel in the time to come.[109] We will interrupt our discussion of the superscript tradition in order to explore briefly this aspect of David's "literary future." This short digression is important for our study, since the only Deutero-Isaian mention of David by name—Isa 55:3—occurs in a context which seems to have had a particular appeal for the Fourth Evangelist.[110]

In the style of the wisdom literature, Isa 55 invites people of all nations who hunger and thirst to come to Israel's God, to eat good things, and thereby to find life. This free invitation to all people heralds the imminent arrival of the blessings promised to David in 2 Sam 7. It is to this fulfilment that David is appointed by God to bear witness: Ἰδοὺ, μαρτύριον ἐν ἔθνεσιν ἔδωκα αὐτόν (Isa 55:4). Isa 55 continues in v. 3 with the promise, addressed to the exiled people (as indicated by the plural verbs and pronoun in v. 3 ab) of—

"an everlasting covenant,
my sure steadfast-love (pl.) for David" (חסדי דוד הנ אמנים).

This is a clear reference to Nathan's oracle (2 Sam 7:15-16) or to some derivative form of it, perhaps, as the plural of חסד suggests, Psalm 89:49, part of a liturgical reflection on Nathan's oracle and its implications for a situation where God appears to have renounced the covenant with David.[111] Clearly the Davidic ideology is being radically re-visioned.[112] Whether it is now being transferred from David to the nation,[113] or whether the realization has dawned that it

---

[109] See Joachim Becker, "Die kollektive Deutung der Königspsalmen" in Ursula Struppe (ed.) *Studien Zum Messiasbild im Alten Testament* (Stuttgart: Katholisches Bibelwerke, 1989) 291-318.

[110] V. 1 most probably provided the background for Jesus' invitation in John 7:37 Ἐάν τις διψᾷ ἐρχέσθω πρός με καὶ πινέτω. Jesus' urging of the people not to labour for the food which perishes in John 6:27 is strongly reminiscent of v. 2. It has also been suggested that Isa 55:10-11 may have contributed to the Johannine notion of the Λόγος proceeding from God, accomplishing what it was sent to do and returning. See J. V. Dahms, "Isaiah 55:11 and the Gospel of John," *EvangQuart* 53 (1981) 78-88.

[111] For the close connection between Isa 55:3-5 and Ps 89 see O. Eissfeldt, "The Promises of Grace to David in Isaiah 55:1-5" in B. W. Anderson and W. Harrelson (ed.) *Israel's Prophetic Heritage* (London: Harper & Brothers, 1962) 197-201. A similar allusion to Ps 89, including the plural of חסד occurs in 2 Chr 6:42.

[112] J. M. Roberts suggests that the way in which God's commitments to David are directed to the nation may indicate a renunciation or even an opposition to the expectation of a new David. See "The Old Testament's Contribution to Messianic Expectations" in James H. Charlesworth (ed.), *The Messiah: Developments in Earliest Judaism and Christianity. The First Princeton Symposium on Judaism and Christian Origins* (Minneapolis: Augsburg Fortress, 1992) 39-51, at 51.

[113] See Gerhard von Rad, *Old Testament Theology* (New York: Harper and Row,

had always included blessing and promise for all nations,[114] the eternal covenant promise is being interpreted in a new non-dynastic sense as a privilege granted by God through David to the entire nation and through the nation to the world.

The reworking of Davidic ideology evident in Isa 55 is indicative of a major development in the reception of David's "autobiographical" psalms. For example, in the psalm attributed to him in 2 Sam 22 (= Ps 18), David testifies through his victories to God's presence and power in the world.

> You delivered me from strife with the peoples;
> you made me the head of the nations;
> people whom I had not known served me
> As soon as they heard of me, they obeyed me;
> foreigners came cringing to me   (Ps 18:43-44 = 2 Sam 22:44-45).

The author of Isa 55, by means of an unmistakable intertextual echo of these lines, shows that David's role as witness belongs to Israel as a whole:

> Behold, you shall call nations that you know not,
> and nations that knew you not shall run to you,
> because of the Lord your God,
> and of the Holy One of Israel, for he has glorified you   (Isa 55:4-5).

This Dt-Isaian passage thus makes of Ps 18 a further "hermeneutical door," this time for the collective reading of David's psalms as referring to the nation.[115] This is important for our study because there is a strong possibility that the presentation of David both as witness and as chief or commander to the peoples in Isa 55 forms part of the OT background to the Johannine idea that being king means bearing witness (John 18:37).[116] The bestowal of the title, ὁ μάρτυς ὁ πιστός, on Jesus, in Rev 1:5; 3:14 (cf. 19:11) would suggest that David's role as witness was well established in the NT period.[117] It was to develop further in early Judaism with particular reference to David's role as psalmist.[118] We return, therefore to our discussion of the his-

---

1965) 240 and W. A. M. Beuken, "Isaiah 55, 3-5: The Reinterpretation of David," *Bijdragen* 35 (1974) 49-64.

[114] See Walter C. Kaiser Jr, "The Unfailing Kindnesses Promised to David: Isaiah 55:3," *JSOT* 45 (1989) 91-98, at 96-97.

[115] See E. W. Conrad, "The Community as King in Second Isaiah" in J. T. Butler a.o. (ed.), *Understanding the Word* (Sheffield: JSOT Press, 1986) 99-112.

[116] See J. Duncan M. Derrett, "Christ, King and Witness (John 18,37)" in *BeO* 31 (1989) 189-98, and Brown, *Death of the Messiah*, 752.

[117] Both Hebrew and Greek of Ps (88)89:38 in which the moon symbolizes the permanence of David's line, permit a reading which would make the expected descendant of David the "faithful witness in the heavens."

[118] In traditions cited by the rabbis, David's role as witness or, more precisely, as

torical superscript tradition conscious of the likelihood that many of David's "autobiographical" utterances were received in a collective sense as spoken in the name of Israel.

Pietersma has concluded from a study of the Greek expanded superscripts that, since they frequently violate the principle of translational consistency, they must come from a later hand than that responsible for the Greek of the psalms themselves.[119] Thus, as clauses added to the original translation of the Hebrew superscripts, they bear witness to a continuing desire to concretize the connection of particular psalms with David. The LXX superscript to Ps (142)143 concerning Absalom's rebellion, testifies to the ongoing development of the David/Ahithophel reading of certain psalms. This finds further expression in the Pešiṭtā where there is a proliferation of non-biblical historical superscripts. In the Eastern (Nestorian) tradition, for example, non-biblical "historical" titles are provided for Pss 11-20 and 61-70. While many are obviously Christian glosses, they are within a direct line of tradition flowing from the Hebrew Bible, via the Septuagint, into early Christianity.[120] Further expanded Davidic superscripts are found in an apocryphal Hebrew work, "The Words of Gad the Seer," which may date from the end of first or early second century CE. Here Pss 144 and 145 appear with narrative introductions similar to the biblical superscripts.[121]

---

himself the living testimony, is regularly explained in terms of his role as psalmist. In a comment on Ps (39:4)40:3, for example, the *Midr. Teh.* has David explain the new song put in his mouth as the commission to be a witness to the peoples given to him by God who lifted him up in repentance even as he was going down into the pit of destruction through his sin. A similar use of Isa 55:4 is found in the comment on Ps (50)51 where God gives the repentant David as a witness to the nations to testify to God's readiness to forgive. See *Midr. Teh.* 40:2, 51:3.

[119] E.g., the superscripts use ὅτε where ὁπότε would have been more "normal." The originality of αἶνος in the superscripts to Pss 90, 92 & 94 is "not above suspicion." Αἴνεσις would have been more in harmony with the LXX Psalter vocabulary. See Pietersma, "David in the Greek Psalms," 221.

[120] From a study of the Syriac superscripts by J.-M. Vosté, we cite two examples (superscripts to "Fourth Gospel" psalms)—for Ps (21)22: *Dictus a Davide orationis vice cum persecutionis pateretur ab Absalom;* for Ps (40)41: *Dictus a Davide de Ezechia et quae fuerint ab amicis eius tempore infirmitatis eius.* Vosté's source is a 6th century CE copy of a Syriac Psalter, probably compiled at Edessa in the late 5th century CE. See "Sur les titres des psaumes dans la Pesitta surtout d'après la recension orientale," *Bib* 25 (1944) 210-235.

[121] For Ps 144: "These are the prayers of David praising the Lord on the day Elhanan son of Ya'ir smote Lehumi, brother of Goliath of Gat and (when) Jehonatan son of Shim'a (smote) the man of Middah and he said..."; for Ps 145: "At that time David said this praise saying..." The recent research of Meir Bar-Ilan has revealed linguistic evidence and affinities with the Book of Revelation which suggest that "The Words of Gad the Seer," is not, as has been thought, a medieval work. Bar-Ilan believes it is "another example of the vast pseudepigrapha, some works of

The historical superscript tradition allowed the Psalter to supplement the narrative material as a source for the details of David's life. The addition of a superscript allowed Psalm 52, for example, to supply for a perceived lacuna in 1 Sam, the absence of any mention of retribution for Doeg's treachery. The contribution of the psalm achieved in later transmission of the story an equal status with details of the 1 Sam narrative. Eventually, Ps-Philo would confidently report on Doeg's terrible end.[122]

The historical superscript tradition gave rise to a further expansion of David's role as psalmist. Now, instead of newly imagined settings in David's life for pre-existing psalms, there are new "Psalms of David" which expand on the narrative traditions in order to disclose David's state of mind at various key moments in his life. The manifestly autobiographical character of these compositions is utterly foreign to the Psalter. As John Strugnell once wryly commented, "In his canonical writings David practised a greater modesty!"[123] Yet it is clear that the interpretive tradition which gave rise to the historical superscripts is the major generative influence. In these pretended "autobiographical" psalms, the intent to claim Davidic authorship is the controlling force in the actual composition. Thus Ps 151, for example, intentionally corresponds to the narratives in 1 Sam 16-17 while attributing to the young David a poetic style which is recognizably similar to that of his "later works," the canonical psalms. The David who speaks in Ps 151 is the youngest of his family.[124] He is a shepherd who could kill a lion or a wolf to save his flock. He has been anointed and made ruler of God's people. Ps 151 is but one of several compositions which have titles imitating the biblical "historical" superscripts and a content determined by their connection with episodes in the David narratives, e.g., "By David, When He Alone Fought Against Goliath," or, "At the Beginning of David's Power After the Prophet of God Anointed Him."[125]

---

which became known to the scholarly world only relatively recently." See "The Date of *The Words of Gad the Seer*," *JBL* 109 (1990) 475-92, at 478.

[122] *LAB* 63:4. There is a similar use of two psalms with regard to Judas in Acts 1:20. This midrashic technique is seen in a work roughly contemporary with the psalm titles, the Prayer of Manasseh. Here the "problem" of the long life and prosperity of the wicked king Manasseh is confronted. While one tradition reports Manasseh's repentance (2 Chr 33:12-13), another provides the "evidence," Manasseh's "own" psalm which is strikingly imitative of David's psalm of repentance, Ps 51.

[123] "More Psalms of 'David,'" 216.

[124] "The author of 11QPs^a 151 may have borrowed the epithet צעיר from Mic 5:1, correctly identifying David as its object." See Talmon, *The World of Qumran*, 253-4.

[125] The titles of Ps 151A (5 ApocSyrPs 1a) and Ps 151B (11QPs^a 151), as translated by Charlesworth and Sanders, "More Psalms of David," *OTP* II, 614-15.

We referred above to the psalm sung by the newly anointed young David in Ps-Philo's re-telling of 1 Sam 16 (*LAB* 59:4).[126] Emanating as it does from a milieu where David's "authorship" of the psalms was taken for granted, it is not surprising that it should use recognizably psalmic diction and clearly allude to several psalms.[127] Allusions are not confined to לדוד psalms. An allusion to Ps (26)27:10 is perhaps the most interesting.

> Quoniam fratres mei zelaverunt me,
> et <u>pater meus et mater mea neglexerunt me</u>,   Cf. Ps (26)27:10
> et cum veniret propheta non clamaverunt ad me,
> et quando nominatus est christus Domini obliti sunt mei.

It shows that Ps-Philo knew of the tradition represented by the LXX which gives Ps 26 a title linking it with the occasion of David's anointing by Samuel, Τοῦ Δαυιδ· πρὸ τοῦ χρισθῆναι. Later in Ps-Philo's text, David says, *Minimus enim inter fratres meos fui pascens oves* (*LAB* 62:5). This is very similar to the opening of Ps 151—

> I was the smallest among my brothers
> and the youngest among the sons of my father.

Either Ps-Philo knew Ps 151, or he was familiar with the interpretive traditions which lie behind it.[128] David's words (in an extra-canonical psalm) have become as much part of his story as the elements which have a basis in the biblical narratives.

The fact that early versions of Pss 151-155 are extant in Hebrew, Syriac and Greek would suggest that there was quite a "demand" for psalmodic expansions on David's story in early Judaism. This raises the question of their intended purpose. David Flusser sees them as simply part of a "pseudepigraphic autobiographical sequence" inspired by the biblical psalm superscripts and intended for

---

[126] *LAB* is punctuated by literary expansions in the form of prayers attributed to such figures as Moses, Joshua, Deborah, Phinehas, Hannah and David. In this, Ps-Philo can be compared with the authors of the Greek additions to Esther and Daniel. We mentioned Ps-Philo's other "psalm of David," *psalmus quem psallebat in Saulem ut recederat ab eo spiritus iniquus*, in our discussion of Ps (90)91. See p. 62-63 above.

[127] While the detection of allusions in a Latin text which translates a Greek version of a Hebrew original cannot be the most exact of sciences, there appear to be echoes of Ps (26)27:4. 10, Ps (60)61:3, Ps (117)118:15-16, Ps (90)91:11 and Ps (120)121:5.

[128] For example, the tradition (based on 1 Sam 16:1) preserved in The Psalms Targum where the line referring to the anointing of David, "I have exalted one chosen from the people" is rendered *Secrevi iuvenem de populo* (Tg. Ps 89:19 in Walton's version). The Targum version used by Perrot and Bogaert reads, *J'ai séparé le plus jeune des fils de mon peuple*. See C. Perrot & P. M. Bogaert, *Pseudo-Philon, Les Antiquités Bibliques, Tome II, Introduction Litteraire, Commentaire et Index*, SC 230 (Paris: Les Editions du Cerf, 1976) 239.

instruction and edification."¹²⁹ Roger T. Beckwith proposes that those found at Qumran complemented the canonical psalms in order to provide the community with a full sequence of daily psalms modelled after the daily psalmody assigned to the twenty four courses of Levitical singers in the liturgy of the Second Temple.¹³⁰ Talmon believes that the "historical" character of so many of these apocryphal psalms of David indicates that some form of the scribal convention of the inner-sentence caesura, known as *Pisqah Be'emṣa' Pasuq* was in place at the time of their composition.¹³¹

Childs has described the editorial addition of the psalm titles as "surely the most far-reaching alteration with which the collector shaped the canonical Psalter."¹³² In what amounted to a radical hermeneutical shift, psalms which had functioned within a cultic setting would now be re-read as giving individual Israelites a highly personal access to David, not merely as a kingly figure, but in all of his humanity.¹³³ His reaction to victory, failure, exultation, fear, persecution, deliverance, as expressed in the psalms, would model the appropriate response of a faithful Jew in similar circumstances. This does not mean that David evaporates and in his stead emerges "Everyman."¹³⁴ Rather, as the prologue to the Psalter (Pss 1-2) makes clear, David, the anointed king, is the paradigmatic Israelite.

In one of the most moving testimonies to the contribution of David and "his" psalms to Jewish piety around the turn of the era, 4 Macc 18:15 tells of a mother who encourages her children to under-

---

¹²⁹ David Flusser, "Psalms, Hymns and Prayers," *CRINT*, Section 2, Vol. II, 551-577, at 562.

¹³⁰ See "The Courses of Levites and the Eccentric Psalms Scrolls from Qumran," *RevQum* 11 (1982-84) 499-524.

¹³¹ According to this convention, blank spaces were left within a verse of the Hebrew text to indicate to the synagogue reader where extra-textual insertions were to be made. A synagogue reading of 2 Sam 7, e.g., would proceed as far as "But that same night" in v. 4. Then a blank space would indicate that Ps 132 was to be inserted. The psalm would function as a homiletic expansion on David's desire to build a house for the Lord, as just stated in the previous verses (2 Sam 7:2). See Talmon, *Pisqah be 'emsa pasuq*, 11-20 and *The World of Qumran*, 264-72. This practice is in a direct line of continuity with biblical tradition. See, primarily, the insertion of Ps 18 as a prayer of David in 2 Sam 22, but also 2 Chr 6:41-42, where verses from Ps 132 form part of Solomon's prayer at the dedication of the Temple.

¹³² *Introduction to the Old Testament as Scripture* (Philadelphia: Fortress, 1979) 520.

¹³³ Ben Sira emphasizes David's intimacy with God who always heard his appeals for help (Sir 47:5). Cf. 1 Macc 2: 57 where David is cited as an example that none who put their trust in God will lack strength: Δαυὶδ ἐν τῷ ἐλέῳ αὐτοῦ, ἐκληρονόμησε θρόνον βασιλείας εἰς αἰῶνα αἰῶνος.

¹³⁴ So, Roland E. Murphy, commenting on Child's exposition in "Reflections on Contextual Interpretation of the Psalms," McCann (ed.), *The Shape and Shaping*, 21-28, at 27.

go martyrdom by reminding them that their father had taught them about all the great suffering figures in Israel's past. She recalls how he used sing to his children "the psalm of David which says, *Many are the afflictions of the righteous*, "i.e., Ps (33)34—one of the psalms quoted in the Fourth Gospel.

F. *David the Prophet*

An important premise for the NT reception of David's psalms is his status as prophet. The primitive notion of prophecy as an ecstatic state involving musical activity under the influence of the spirit of the Lord (1 Sam 10:6-7) was an important factor in the development of such a perception of David. Psalmody and prophecy would appear to have been long inter-related, as the traces of prophetic oracles discernible in the Psalter show. A distinctly prophetic utterance, "the spirit of the Lord speaks by me," is put on David's lips in a context which refers to his poetic output (2 Sam 23:2).[135] As late as the Chronicler's period, the choral singing of psalms to instrumental accompaniment was still being designated as "prophesying" (1 Chr 25:1).[136] *A fortiori*, David's presumed poetic creativity would have been so understood.

G. Ben Zion Wacholder has found support for the connection between psalmody and prophecy in the subtle manner in which 2 Sam 23:1 is modelled on Num 24:3-4, a text which celebrates the Davidic dynasty—

Num 24:3-4	2 Sam 23:2.1
And the Spirit of God came upon him and he took up his discourse and said, "The oracle of Balaam the son of Beor, the oracle of the man whose eye is opened, the oracle of him who hears the words of God, who sees the vision of the Almighty...	"The Spirit of the Lord speaks by me, his word is upon my tongue..." The oracle of David the son of Jesse, the oracle of the man who was raised on high, the anointed of the God of Jacob, the sweet psalmist (?) of Israel.

---

[135] Cf. Num 11:29 where to be a prophet is to have been given the spirit of the Lord. In 1 Kgs 22:5-8, possession of the spirit of the Lord is claimed (falsely) as proof of the genuineness of prophecy.

[136] According to 2 Chr 29:30, Asaph the Temple singer is a seer, as are Heman (1 Chr 25:5) and Jeduthun (2 Chr 35:15). According to 1 Chr 25:1, David appoints lyrists, harpists and cymbalists to "prophesy." Chronicles reflects a situation where "earlier prophetic guilds ... have been converted into choirs or musical guilds and, as such, have been (*or* are being) merged with other Levitical orders." See Aubrey R. Johnson, *The Cultic Prophet in Ancient Israel* (Cardiff: University of Wales Press, 2nd

From 1 Sam 9:9 we learn that ראה was an earlier term for נביא. David is as much a prophet as the gentile seer. He is even superior to him.[137]

There is also a long-standing correlation between anointing and prophecy. Samuel anoints David and the Spirit leaps (ἐφήλατο) on him (1 Sam 16:13). Similarly, Elijah anoints Elisha as prophet (1 Kgs 19:16). The prophet as anointed and thereby endowed with God's spirit, appears in Isa 61:1 (cf. Joel 3:1). In Ps 105:15 the term "my anointed" occurs in parallelism with "my prophets." 1QM 11:7 refers to the biblical prophets as God's "anointed ones, the seers of things determined." In 2 Sam 23:1 David the psalmist introduces himself as "the anointed of the God of Jacob" (cf. Ps 18:51 =2 Sam 22:15) and the next verse continues: "The spirit of the Lord speaks by me, his word is on my tongue." Being anointed and speaking God's word are clearly connected.

11QPs^aDavComp (quoted in full on p. 70) concludes, "All these he (David) uttered through prophecy (בנבואה) which was given him from before the Most High." This is not an isolated case of the association of נבואה with David, and by extension with the psalms, in Jewish literature around the turn of the era. Several of the authors we have already cited in this chapter make precisely this connection. Josephus, for example, tells of the newly anointed David beginning to prophesy.[138] As we have seen, it is at that precise moment that Ps-Philo imagines David singing a psalm. Josephus praises David's prophetic foresight in referring to Arunah's threshing floor as the Temple.[139] Philo too shares this view of David, reporting In *Heres.* 290 that τις προφητικὸς ἀνὴρ said he would rather live a single day with virtue than ten thousand years in the shadow of death. As we have found, it is the allusion to Ps 83 that identifies τις προφητικὸς ἀνὴρ as David. Philo's *Agr.* 50-54 contains a commentary on Ps 22(23)[140] which states that the authority for the description of God as a shepherd is no ordinary one,

---

ed. 1962) 69-72, at 72. "The expression for 'making music' and 'prophesying' was often identical in ancient tongues. So too, the Greeks called a prophet Χρησμῳδός, and the Hebrew word *Naba* signifies not only 'to prophesy' but also 'to make music.'" See Johannes Quasten, *Music and Worship in Pagan and Christian Antiquity*, trans. Boniface Ramsey (Washington D.C.: National Association of Pastoral Musicians, 1983) 39.

[137] See Wacholder, "David's Eschatological Psalter," 31-2.
[138] *Ant* VI, 166.
[139] *Ant.* VII, 334. Cf. *Ant.* VIII, 109 where Josephus makes an oblique reference to David's prophetic powers: Solomon speaks of future events that God had "revealed" to David. 1Kgs 8:15 has "promised."
[140] This passage tells how God set his true Word and firstborn Son over the universe. John Dillon notes that its language is "strangely anticipatory of the gospels." See "Logos and Trinity: Patterns of Platonist Influence on Early Christianity," in

...ἀλλὰ προφήτης ἐστίν ᾧ καλὸν πιστεύειν, ὁ τὰς ὑμνῳδίας ἀναγράψας.[141]

The fact that the narratives about David were received in Second Temple Judaism as part of "the Former Prophets" also enhanced David's reputation as a prophet. Another influential factor was the practice of interpolating psalmody into the synagogue reading of the narrative traditions about David. The effect of such interpolations was that texts which were, strictly speaking, part of "The Writings" functioned as, and somehow became assimilated to "The Former Prophets," at least in terms of reception.[142] It is important to recall that access to the written Scriptures was extremely limited and that public reading was the means by which all but a privileged few could come to know the Scriptures. Inevitably, the distinction between words of David from 1-2 Sam read in the synagogue *haftarah* and words of David from the psalms quoted in a *Pisqah Be'emṣa' Pasuq* insertion would have become, in practice, somewhat blurred. A similar conflation of narrative and psalmodic David traditions must also have occurred in synagogue homilies, the *petihtah* form of homily, in particular, when employed on occasions when the *haftarah* was from the David cycle and a passage from the psalms was used as the starting point.[143] It is against the background of this reception tradition that the Johannine presentation of psalm citations as part of the Law (Jn 10:34; 15:25) becomes understandable. David's status as a prophet is thus well established in the Judaism contemporary with the NT and persists into later Jewish writings.[144]

Godfrey Vesey (ed.), *The Philosophy in Christianity* (Cambridge: University Press, 1989) 1-13, at 3-4.

[141] As with the designation of David as a disciple of Moses, there is nothing exceptional, for Philo, in regarding David as a prophet. In *Her.* 259-60 he explains that all the wise and the virtuous are in fact prophets. "The name of prophet only befits the wise, since he alone is the vocal instrument of God, smitten and played by his invisible hand." In spite of the musical imagery, Philo's list of prophets in this particular context (Noah, Abraham, Isaac, Jacob and especially Moses) does not include David, presumably because he does not appear in the Pentateuch.

[142] In a similar development, the book of Daniel, originally belonging to "The Writings," was included among the former Prophets in the LXX.

[143] The function of the *petihtah* homily was to stress the unity of the three parts of the Scriptures (Law, Prophets, Writings). The homilist was expected to show "that there is nothing in the prophets and the Hagiographa that could not be found in the Torah, that all three parts are but one and the same expressed in various forms, various modes of the same substance." See D. Patte, *Early Jewish Hermeneutic in Palestine* (Chico CA: Scholars, 1975) 38. In the *Petihtah* homily, a passage from the Hagiographa is taken as a starting point. See I. Sonne, "Synagogue," in George A. Buttrick (ed.), *The Interpreters' Dictionary of the Bible: An Illustrated Encyclopedia* (4 vols). New York/Nashville: Abingdon, 1962, Vol. 4, 476-91. See also P. Grelot, *Homélies sur l'écriture à l'époque apostolique* (Tournai: Desclée, 1989) 40-43.

[144] E.g., the Mishnah asserts that "When the first prophets died, Urim and Thummim ceased" (*m. Sota* 9:12). R. Jonathan is remembered as having held that

David's prophetic status was a crucial support to the early Christian usage of the psalms for preaching and apologetic. David, *qua* psalmist, is mentioned by name as speaking prophetically—ἐν πνεύ-'ματι, in Matt 22:43 and ἐν τῷ πνεύματι τῷ ἁγίῳ in Mark 12:36, but the idea is frequently used in Acts. The Lucan Peter claims that Ps (68)69 was "spoken beforehand" (προεῖπεν) by the Holy Spirit through the mouth of David (Acts 1:16). Furthermore, since David was a prophet (Acts 2:30),[145] he did not speak about himself. Rather Pss (15)16 and (109)110, in which David speaks in the first person, are actually about Jesus (Acts 2:25.29.34). In Acts 13:36 the same claim is made in a speech of Paul. Similarly Luke's Jerusalem believers quote Ps 2 as spoken in the spirit by David (Acts 4:25). In the Pauline writings, David speaks prophetically of the "stumbling" of Israel (Rom 11:9-10, quoting Ps (68)69:22-23). The author of Hebrews too specifically links David with Samuel and the prophets in a list of those who lived by faith.[146]

G. *The Sapientialized David*

The placing of the sapiential Ps 1 at the beginning of the Psalter[147] and the five-fold division of the whole collection indicate an understanding of the Five Books of David as analogous to the Torah. This is an important clue to its editors' perception of David as the bearer of instruction from God. There has been a significant transition in Israel's reception of the Psalter, a shift from interpretation in view of a specific setting to interpretation as a timeless corpus of teaching.[148]

---

the first prophets were Samuel and David (*y. Sota* 9:12). R. Huna is cited as having said that they were David, Samuel and Solomon (*b. Sota* 48b).

[145] The difficulties experienced by J. FitzMyer in finding a Jewish precedent for the Lucan designation of David as a prophet in Ac 2:30 are inexplicable. For FitzMyer, "there seems to be little in the O.T. story of David that would serve as a springboard for it" and "the traditional attribution of the Psalter to David...can scarcely be cited as the basis for (it)." See "David, 'Being Therefore a Prophet...' (Acts 2:30)," *CBQ* 34 (1972) 332-39.

[146] ...ἐπιλείψει με γὰρ διηγούμενον ὁ χρόνος περὶ Γεδεών, Βαράκ, Σαμψών, Ἰεφθάε, Δαυίδ τε καὶ Σαμουὴλ καὶ τῶν προφητῶν,...(Heb 11:32). This passage is significant in that among the deed. of the great figures in Israel's past, the memory that they shut the mouths of lions is chosen for special mention (ἔφραξαν στόματα λεόντων). Of all the heroes of faith listed thus far, David is the only one who has any association with lions. This is another example of the 1 Sam 17:34-36 scene emerging as the salient episode of David's story.

[147] Ps 1 provided a perspective from which the whole Psalter could be read. It may have formed an inclusion with Ps (118)119 at a stage when this long Torah psalm concluded the collection. See Childs, *Introduction to the Old Testament as Scripture* 513-14 and Mays, "The Place of the Torah-Psalms in the Psalter," *JBL* 106 (1987) 3-12, at 9.

[148] See Wilson, *Editing*, 207.

This process is perhaps most aptly described as "sapientialization."[149]

This development presupposes a view of David such as that found in 11QPsªDavComp. We recall the opening lines of this important text—

> And David, the son of Jesse, was wise, and a light like the light of the sun, and literate, and discerning and perfect in all his ways before God and men. And the Lord gave him a discerning spirit...

The description of David as wise (חכם) follows on 2 Sam 23:2 which seems to have been quoted immediately before it, just as that of David as "a light" follows on 2 Sam 23:4. The association of wisdom with David, has already been made in the scroll by means of several extracanonical psalms. We will look briefly at two samples.

Ps 154 (col. xviii, 1-6) is one of the pseudepigraphical psalms in 11QPsª which, although not overtly "autobiographical" are so close to the Psalter in style and diction as to appear "Davidic."[150] As received in Qumran, this sapiential invitatory hymn in which Wisdom is personified, portrays David as a teacher and worship leader who inculcates a belief dear to the sectarians, the superiority of vocal praise over animal sacrifice. In Ps 1, the prologue to his canonical psalms, David has taught that the good should delight in the Law of God and meditate on it day and night. The "pure ones" to whom this psalm is addressed, fulfil this injunction through their life of Torah study and worship—

> Their meditation is on the Law of the Most High;
> their words to announce his power.[151]

11QPsªSirach (col. xxi,11-17) is probably the earlier version of a composition attributed to Ben Sira in Alexandria (LXX Sir 51:13-30). In this poem a teacher sings of his youthful search for Wisdom who is personified in feminine terms similar to those of Wis 7:7-14.

> I was a young man before I had erred
>   when I looked for her.

---

[149] See the subtitle of Sheppard's book, *Wisdom as a Hermeneutical Construct: A Study of the Sapientializing of the Old Testament*.

[150] Ps 154 has been dated by Charlesworth as "first, or better the second century BC." See "More Psalms of David," 617. Sanders, *DJD* IV, 70, believes that it must have been regarded as considerably older in Qumran for it to have been included in the 11QPsª scroll which was considered as Davidic. It is extant in Syriac as 5 ApocSyrPs 2.

[151] Ps 154:14, alluding to Ps 1:2. Cf. 1QS VI.7-8—"And in the place in which the ten assemble there should not be missing a man to interpret the law day and night, always, each man relieving his fellow. And the Many shall be on the watch together for a third of each night of the year in order to read the book, explain the regulation, and bless together." García Martínez, *The Dead Sea Scrolls*, 9.

> She came to me in her beauty
> when finally I sought her out...[152]

The fact that at Qumran this poem was apparently regarded as an "autobiographical" psalm of David offers a fascinating insight into first century CE Jewish views of him. It becomes quite plausible as "a psalm of David," if received against the background of biblical,[153] and Hellenistic[154] traditions associating wisdom with kingship.

11QPs^aDavComp also describes David as literate (סופר). This motif too is consistent with the biblical teaching on kingship. Deut 17:18-20, for example, portrays the king as writing out his own copy of the Law. In view of the Qumran tendency to transfer the legislative role of the king to a priestly figure,[155] the designation of David as סופר in 11QPs^a most probably refers to his psalmody. By the late Second Temple period, the terms חכם and סופר had acquired the additional new referents, "sage" and "scribe."[156] Thus col. xxvii, 2-3 is validly translated by A. Dupont-Sommer—

---

[152] Sanders, *The Dead Sea Psalms Scroll*, 115.

[153] E.g., when Solomon, at his accession to the throne, prays for the ability to rule like his father David, God responds by granting him "a wise and discerning mind" (1 Kgs 3:6-9. 12). Like David's, we are presumably to suppose. Later tradition recasts Solomon's request, construing it as a prayer for the coming of a wisdom figure, now personified as a royal "consort" by whom "kings reign and rulers decree what is just...by whom princes rule and nobles govern the earth" (Prov 8:15; Cf. Wis 9:1-18).

[154] In Stoic and Cynic thought, for example, ruling is a favourite metaphor for the achievement of virtue: it is only the wise who are truly kings. See *Probus* 19 where Philo quotes Diogenes Laertius' dictum that not only are the wise free, but they are also kings. See Plato, *Pol.* IV, 6.

[155] E.g., according to the Temple Scroll version of Deut 17:18-20 (11QT, 56:20-21), it is the Levitical priests who write out the Law for the king and "sit with him" to supervise his administration of justice. " See Johann Maier (ed.) *The Temple Scroll: An Introduction, Translation and Commentary* (Sheffield: JSOT Press, 1985) 49. See also the "correction" of Isa 11:3 in 4Q 161 where the "Branch of David" judges not by appearances, but "by what the priests teach him." The subordination of the king to the priest is evident even in the sect's ritual anticipations of the eschatological banquet, e.g., 1QSa II, 12-21; 1QS VI. For the deference of the Messiah of Israel to the Messiah of Aaron at the eschatological banquet, see 4QpIsa VIII- XI.

[156] The noun חכם had developed the technical sense of "sage" recalling the Greek σόφοι with their schools, pupils, discipline, principles and collections of wisdom. The word סופר had come to mean a "scribe" in the sense of one learned in the Law and qualified to teach its precepts. See F. Brown, S. R. Driver and A. Briggs, *A Hebrew and English Lexicon of the Old Testament* (Oxford: Clarendon, 1979) 315; 708. We cannot know to what extent the scribe of 11QPs^a was conscious of these possible meanings of חכם and סופר, but certainly the David of this prose passage appears to be well on the way towards becoming the "Rabbi David" of later Judaism. See Jacob Neusner, *Messiah in Context: Israel's History and Destiny in Formative Judaism* (Philadelphia: Fortress, 1984), 88-90.

David, fils de Jessé, fut un sage, et une lumière semblable à la lumière du soleil, et un scribe, et un homme intelligent et parfait en toutes ses voies devant Dieu et les hommes.¹⁵⁷

The reference in 11QPsᵃ to David's God-given "spirit of discernment" (רוח נבונה) and its characterization of David as "discerning" (נבון) allude to the report given by one of Saul's servants in response to Saul's quest for a musician (1 Sam 16:18). The servant describes the young man whose performance he has heard, as נבון דבר.¹⁵⁸ As we saw with regard to the Chronicler's portrayal, this account of the young shepherd's musicianship was understood, in later readings, as referring specifically to his role as psalmist.¹⁵⁹

A sapientialized future descendant of David appears in The Psalms of Solomon.¹⁶⁰ PsSol 17 provides our earliest evidence for a specifically messianic *relecture* of Scripture, particularly of the psalms. In fact, PsSol 17-18 are the earliest known texts in which the term "Messiah" is used absolutely.¹⁶¹ In contrast to more militant interpretations, e.g., in the Pseudo-Jonathan Targum to Gen 49:11, the Psalms of Solomon exemplify the type of Scripture study practised in circles of pious Jews whose hope for a future redeemer figure was part of their faith in the God of Israel.¹⁶² The Lord Messiah whom

---

¹⁵⁷ See A. Dupont-Sommer and M. Philonenko (ed.), *La Bible: Ecrits Intertestamentaires* (Paris: Gallimard, 1987) 330-31. Vermes, *The Dead Sea Scrolls in English*, 213, also renders סופר as "a scribe."

¹⁵⁸ See Sanders, *DJD* IV, 92.

¹⁵⁹ It may also recall 2 Sam 14:17 where the woman of Tekoa praises David as "like an angel of God" in his ability to understand good and evil, but set within the 11QPsᵃ context, it is more likely to refer to David's psalmodic output.

¹⁶⁰ The composition of the Psalms of Solomon is dated *ca* 40-50 BCE on the basis of the references to Pompey's invasion of Jerusalem and desecration of the Temple in 63 BCE. "First Baruch, an original Greek composition which quotes the Psalms of Solomon, antedates the end of the first century A.D. because of its testimony to the destruction of the Temple and the extensive quotations from First Baruch by Irenaeus. First Baruch's use of the Psalms of Solomon would suggest that the Greek translation was available by the mid first century A. D." See R. B. Wright, "Psalms of Solomon: A New Translation and Introduction" in Charlesworth (ed.), *OTP*, II, 639-50, at 640.

¹⁶¹ Wright, "Psalms of Solomon," 647. 667, note z, favours the reading, found in several Greek and Syriac Mss, Χριστός Κύριος, which he renders, "The Lord Messiah." In line with this, he renders PsSol 18:6a χριστου κυριου by "(under the rod) of the Lord Messiah." De Jonge, "The Expectation of the Future," 95, prefers the reading, "The Lord's Messiah." An agent of divine deliverance whom God calls, "My Son, The Messiah" (probably against a Ps 2 background) also appears in 4 Ezra (2 Esdras) 12:32-34 which, although dated to the late first century CE, probably reflects earlier traditions. The same can, no doubt, be said for the Syriac Apocalypse of Baruch (2 Bar), dated 200-220 CE. In this text we read of the glorious reign of an Anointed One which is connected with a resurrection of the dead (2 Bar 30:1).

¹⁶² See M. de Jonge, "The Expectation of the Future in the Psalms of Solomon," *Neot* 23 (1989) 93-117, at 96.

they envisaged (PsSol 17:32) would rule a holy people in a cleansed and restored Jerusalem (PsSol 17:30) to which the dispersed would return (PsSol 17:31) and to which all the nations would be attracted. In PsSol 17, the purification of the Temple is to be the prerogative of this messianic figure. In this poem the illegitimate Hasmonean kings are characterised as those who did not fulfil the primary task of kingship: glorifying God's name (PsSol 17:5). The psalm describes a situation where the possibility of temple worship has been denied to the faithful. It promises a new Davidic king who will purge Jerusalem and drive out sinners from "the inheritance" by the strength of his word (PsSol 17:21-22.36). He himself is to lead the people in worship in the restored Temple (PsSol 17:30b). While the establishment of his rule presumably involves the expulsion of the Romans, his anticipated reign is viewed from an entirely theocratic perspective, as M. de Jonge explains:

> Although the expectation has national, political and even military facets, it is concerned primarily with theocracy, the realisation of God's rule over all peoples, groups and nations...The poet of Psalm 17 describes the king, not in the first place as a fighter or a ruler, but as an ideal scribe, a wise man par excellence as Solomon, the hero of the circles in which these psalms originated. There is in reality only one reference in this psalm to violent action against the enemies. This is, however, a traditional motif taken from Psalm 2:9.[163]

PsSol 17-18 provides valuable insight into how the sapientialization of the remembered David produced an imagined David who in turn shaped the expected David.

H. *David as Compared and Contrasted with Moses*

The concrete experience of Jews living in NT times was that the Torah (written and oral) shaped their lives and the Psalter shaped their worship. So it is not surprising that in their writings David is often paralleled and even contrasted with Moses.[164] This is important as background to the study of a gospel where a representative believer is taunted for being a disciple of "that one" (ἐκεῖνος), as dis-

---

[163] De Jonge, "The Expectation of the Future," 102, referring to PsSol 17:22. For another non-violent messianic interpretation of Ps 2, see Acts 4:24-31, especially vv. 29-30.

[164] The tendency to link Moses and David, whether for comparison or contrast, has biblical roots. In 2 Chr 23:18, which is an expansion of 2 Kgs 11:18, there is a description of Temple liturgy where burnt offerings are performed according to the Law of Moses, while rejoicing and singing takes place according to the order of David. See also Ezra 3: 2.10 for a similar parallel.

tinct from being a disciple of Moses (John 9:28). As Martyn perceives it, "This statement...recognizes discipleship to Jesus not only as antithetical, but also as somehow comparable to discipleship to Moses."[165]

With the destruction of the Temple, the sacrifices of Moses were discontinued. All that was left was the psalmody of David which used to accompany them and which now somehow represented them. As the *Midrash Tehillim* would later explain, "When sacrifices, temple and altar were laid waste, nothing was left but prayer."[166] This is just a step away from the Christian idea that David's hymns have replaced Moses' sacrifices, found in early Christian writings.[167]

A connection or, perhaps, a contrast between David and Moses is already implied in the biblical arrangement of the psalms in five books, a fact that did not go unnoticed by the rabbis who relate it to the Pentateuch.

> As Moses gave five books of laws to Israel, so David gave five books of psalms to Israel: the book of psalms entitled *Blessed is the man* (Ps 1:1), the book entitled *For the leader: Maschil* (Ps 42:1), the book entitled *A Psalm of Asaph* (Ps 73:1), the book, *A Prayer of Moses* (Ps 90:1) and the book *Let the redeemed of the Lord say* (Ps 107:2).[168]

The texts presented above which delineate David's foundational role with regard to the sacrificial cult in the Temple on Mount Zion, also imply a comparison with Moses. As Temple founder, David is privileged with a vision of God, a pre-requisite for the creation of a cultic locale.[169] He erects the altar, thus inaugurating the Temple building project which his son Solomon will complete according to his instructions. These instructions he has received in detail from the hand of God (1 Chr 28:11-19), just as Moses was instructed by God on the building of the desert tabernacle. Finally David performs the priestly function of offering sacrifice on the altar. The Chronicler's view of David's position with regard to Moses is explained by W. Riley—

---

[165] *History and Theology*, 39.
[166] *Midr. Teh.* 5:4 .
[167] See Eusebius of Caesarea, *Commentaria in Psalmos* (GCS Vol. I, 136) PG, Vol. 23, Col. 76A.
[168] *Midr. Teh.* 1. 5. Davidic authorship for all 150 psalms is accepted in principle in later Jewish writings. See *b. Pesah.* 117a. Davidic authorship is not limited to psalms with Davidic superscripts. In *Midr. Teh.* 72, 1 the commentator carefully explains that the subscript to Ps 72, "The prayers of David the son of Jesse are ended," does not amount to a denial of Davidic authorship for the rest of the Psalter. The rabbis argue from David's supposed composition of all the psalms under divine inspiration, that his whole life must have been one of unceasing praise and thanksgiving to God, "nothing more than a context for all the psalms." See *b. Bat.* 14b.
[169] Gen 12:6-7; 26:24-25; 28;18.

On the one hand, David is shown as one who is careful to implement the Law given by Moses; on the other hand, David is portrayed as one who is also a receiver of revelation and therefore entitled to introduce authoritatively new elements into the religious life of Israel. David is, therefore, a faithful observer of the Mosaic Law; he is also, according to the Chronicler, a cultic legislator and founder in his own right.[170]

For readers who received the Psalter as Davidic, certain features of the David which it projected were quite reminiscent of the biblical portrayal of Moses. Thus the privilege that the David of the psalms enjoyed in being able to gaze on the beauty of God, thereby replenishing himself with glorious strength (Ps 27:4, 63:2. Cf. Ps 34:5), is not unlike the way Moses came out from God's presence with a radiant face (Exod 34:35). Like Moses (Num 11:17), David was aided by God's spirit in the exercise of his authority (Ps 51:10-13. Cf. 1 Sam 16:13; 2 Sam 23:2). The fate of David's enemies (Ps 55:15) was to be like that which befell those who challenged Moses (Num 16:31-35). Both Moses and David are teachers. But whereas Moses directs his teaching to the people of Israel, David has a world-wide commission to speak words of wisdom to all peoples and their rulers (Ps 49:1-3. Ps 2:10). At the time of the Exodus, Moses led the people in the Song at the Sea (Exod 15:1), but David has led Israel in the singing of praise through his psalms.[171] The singing women who come out to welcome David after his victory (1 Sam 18:7) pointedly recall Miriam and the women of Israel singing their victory song, subsequently remembered as the "Song of Moses" (Cf. Exod 15:20-21).[172] For the rabbis, the contrast persists, even into "the world to come." At the eschatological banquet, God offers a wine cup to Abraham, Isaac, Jacob, Moses and Joshua. Each declares himself unworthy to recite the blessing, but David accepts the offer.[173] In

---

[170] W. Riley, *King and Cultus in Chronicles*, 62.

[171] David's "answer" to the Song of Moses may even turn out to be retrievable in the "Song of the Lamb" (Rev 15:3), as postulated by J. C. De Moor and E. Van Staalduine-Sulman in "The Aramaic Song of the Lamb," *JSJ* 24 (1993) 226-279. It may well be that the "Song of the Lamb" originated as an apocryphal expansion of 1 Sam 18:7, along the lines of the many other compositions of the Second Temple Period which "imagined" the prayers or hymns mentioned in biblical narratives. If this is the case, we find a further strengthening of the lines of comparison drawn between Moses and David.

[172] It has been suggested that the duplication in Exod 15 at vv. 1 and 21 may be the telltale sign that Miriam's initiative in performing the prophetic function of leading Israel in a song of praise has been suppressed. See J. Gerald Jansen, "Song of Moses, Song of Miriam: Who Is Seconding Whom?" *CBQ* 54 (1992) 211-20. If this is so, the comparison between Moses and David extends to the memory that the mighty deed. of both were celebrated in song by the women of Israel.

[173] *Beth-ha-Midrash* 5. 167-8, 6. 25-26

this tradition, eschatologically at least, David, as the only great figure from Israel's past who is worthy, seems to occupy a position superior to Moses.

Jouette M. Bassler has noted the connections which rabbinical texts frequently make between David, the just and righteous lover of Torah, and Moses, the great legislator of Israel.

> Both, for example, are hailed as good administrators (*b. Yoma* 86b), both having been trained for this role through their activity as shepherds (*Exod. R.* 2.2-3). Both were concerned with the Law, Moses delivering it and David clarifying it (*Exod. R.* 15.22). "You will find," said R. Isaac, "that the two immortals, David and Moses, could never have enough of the commandments (Deut R. 2.26-27). The parallels between the two are enumerated in one text that ends with the claim, "Whatever Moses did, David did" (*Midr. Ps.* 1.2).[174]

An awareness of the similarities between Moses and David, as perceived in early Judaism, and of the way in which the two figures are frequently juxtaposed for purposes of comparison or contrast is important for the study of the Fourth Gospel. Many of the features of the Johannine Jesus which are frequently presented as "Mosaic"—notably closeness to God, access to God's presence, and even some form of divine status—can just as convincingly be shown to be "Davidic." To see these features as "Mosaic" requires a "Philonic" reading of the biblical text, as Wayne Meeks' has demonstrated.[175] To see them as "Davidic," one need not go beyond the Psalter and the ideology surrounding Davidic kingship. While there are obviously significant convergences between Johannine thought and Hellenistic Judaism, these should not be exaggerated to the detriment of the Gospel's Jewishness. Philo, after all, develops a portrait of Moses as king which has numerous "Davidic" features.[176] Ashton sees in the Evangelist's handling of Mosaic themes "his conscious substitution of this tradition by the story of Jesus...the deliberate replacement of one founder-figure by another."[177] It is a contention of this study that a model for this replacement was already in place in the Jewish tendency to draw comparisons between Moses and David. If Jesus was to replace Moses, he would do so as "David." In

---

[174] See "A Man for All Seasons: David in Rabbinic and New Testament Literature," *Int* 40 (1986) 156-169, at 162.

[175] See Meeks, *The Prophet King*, 107-17 and "Moses as God and King," in J. Neusner (ed.) *Religions in Antiquity: Essays in Memory of E. R. Goodenough* (Leiden: Brill, 1968) 354-71.

[176] See *Mos.* I, 27; I, 61 (as quoted on p. 2 above), I, 158. Philo sees Moses' period as a shepherd as his apprenticeship for kingship, since the only perfect king is one skilled in shepherding (*Mos.* I, XI, 60; See Jos. *Ant.* 4. 302-06).

[177] Ashton, *Understanding*, 473.

the light of this, it seems quite possible that a contrast between Moses and David may lie behind Jn 1:17. As Breuggemann has proposed, if we refer to the Hebrew behind the Greek ἡ χάρις καὶ ἡ ἀλήθεια, we find a formula which sounds very Davidic and is present in 2 Sam 7:14-16 concerning David—חסד and אמת.[178]

I. *David as Psalmist in the Johannine View*

In claiming that the Fourth Evangelist shared the presupposition that David wrote the psalms, we are immediately confronted with the inescapable fact that there is no mention of David as psalmist in the Fourth Gospel. This is in marked contrast to the synoptic writers who all indicate that they take the superscript Τῷ Δαυιδ ψαλμός quite literally as a reference to David's authorship.[179] David appears as psalmist also in Acts 1:16 (Ps 68 & 108) Acts 2:25 (Pss 15 & 109), Acts 4:25 (Ps 2), Rom 4:6-8 (Ps 31) and Heb 4:7 (Ps 94). All the psalms explicitly attributed to him in these passages have Davidic superscripts in the LXX, except Ps 2, for which Luke obviously presumes Davidic authorship by "internal evidence," the re-statement of Nathan's oracle in v. 7.[180] Of all the NT authors, Luke is the most explicit about David's role as psalmist, understanding it principally in terms of his role as prophet.[181] He also exemplifies the principle that whatever can be gleaned about David from "his" psalms has the same "historical" status as the biblical narratives about him.[182] The absence of any such indications in the Fourth Gospel seems to suggest that David as presumed "author" of the psalms is not important to the Evangelist, not as important as, for example, Isaiah who saw Jesus' glory (John 12:41) or Moses who wrote of Jesus (John 5:46).

---

[178] *David's Truth*, 115.

[179] The fundamental presupposition of Davidic authorship of Ps (109)110 clearly underlies the *Davidssohnfrage* (Mark 12:35-37; Matt 22:41-46; Luke 20:41-44). The synoptic Jesus not only "starts from the belief of his time that David composed the Book of Psalms," but his argument "rests on the popular image of David as psalmist." Chilton, *A Galilean Rabbi*, 168-69. C. F. D. Moule, *The Birth of the New Testament* (London: Adam and Charles Black, 1962) 64-65, notes in this passage "the suggestive quality of words in the context of certain assumptions and presuppositions...entertained by (Jesus') hearers and probably also by him."

[180] See Sheppard, *Wisdom as a Hermeneutical Construct*, 139.

[181] Luke 24:44; Acts 1:16-20; 2:25-36.

[182] In Acts 7:46, Stephen tells of David's desire to build the Temple:...καὶ ᾐτήσατο εὑρεῖν σκήνωμα τῷ οἴκῳ Ἰακώβ. The language here alludes, not to the narrative sources (2 Sam 7:2-16, 1 Kgs 8:17-18, 1 Chr 17:1-14, 2 Chr 6:7-8), but to Ps 131:5 where David says he will not rest or be satisfied—ἕως οὗ εὕρω τόπον τῷ κυρίῳ, σκήνωμα τῷ θεῷ Ιακωβ. Similarly, the Lucan Paul uses Ps 88:21 to supplement his retelling of 1 Sam 16, the account of David's anointing as king in Acts 13:22—Εὗρον Δαυὶδ τὸν τοῦ Ἰεσσαί ...

It also seems that David *per se* is not important to John. In the Fourth Gospel, Jesus is neither presented as a descendant of David,[183] nor ever addressed as "Son of David."[184] In fact, the Fourth Evangelist mentions David by name only once, in John 7:42, and then in a discussion of questions about Jesus' earthly origin which, in the author's opinion, are immaterial and even misdirected. In this passage, expectations surrounding the Davidic promise are recalled by some of the people as a warrant for rejecting Jesus' messianic claim.[185] The "qualifications" for Messiahship—Davidic ancestry and birth at Bethlehem—would seem to be of no significance to an Evangelist who is preoccupied with Jesus' heavenly origin and divine descent.

John's silence on Davidic authorship of the psalms needs to be assessed in terms of his quotation style.[186] Of the fourteen formulae of

---

[183] This is in marked contrast to the synoptics. Matthew begins his Βίβλος γενέσεως Ἰησοῦ Χριστοῦ υἱοῦ Δαυὶδ υἱοῦ Ἀβραάμ with a genealogy structured to highlight the significance of the Davidic title (Matt 1:2-17) and introduces Jesus' legal father as a "son of David" (Matt 1:20). Luke's infancy narrative contains no less than four references to Jesus' Davidic lineage (Luke 1:27. 32. 69, 2:4.) and a genealogy which stresses his Davidic descent (Luke 3:31).

[184] In the synoptics, "Son of David" occurs mainly in healing stories (Mark 10:47-48, Matt 9:27; 12:23; 15:22; 20:30.31; Luke 18:38-39). Matthew also imparts a "Davidic" colouring to the "Hosanna" acclamation from Ps (117)118 (Matt 21:9), reiterated in 21:15 as the cause of the chief priests' and scribes' indignation. Mark's crowd amplifies the psalm verse with the words—Εὐλογημένη ἡ ἐρχομένη βασιλεία τοῦ πατρὸς ἡμῶν Δαυὶδ (Mark 11:9). Although Luke does not mention David's name at this point, his insertion of ὁ βασιλεύς into the psalm quotation strengthens the Davidic overtones.

[185] Some see irony here, presuming that the traditions concerning Jesus' birth at Bethlehem (Matt 2:1, Luke 2:4) would have been known to the author and original readers, e.g., R. Alan Culpepper, *The Anatomy of the Fourth Gospel: A Study in Literary Design* (Philadelphia: Fortress, 1983) 170; John Painter, "Theology, Eschatology and the Prologue of John," *SJT* 46 (1993) 27-42, at 27; F. J. Moloney, "The Fourth Gospel's Presentation of Jesus as 'The Christ' and J. A. T. Robinson's *Redating*," *DRev* 95 (1977) 239-53, at 248. Meeks, "The Man From Heaven in Johannine Sectarianism" in Ashton (ed.), *The Interpretation*, 141-73, at 154, sees this passage as "a choice example of the evangelist's irony," in view of several other passages in the Gospel which turn on the issue of knowing or not knowing where Jesus is from, especially John 9:29 and 19:9. However John 7:40-43 seems to indicate ignorance of Jesus' Davidic descent, or even perhaps a denial of it. Whether such ignorance or denial is to be attributed to the Evangelist or to his characters in the narrative is not clear (The earliest instance of explicit denial of Jesus' Davidic lineage is found in *Ep. Barn.* 12:10-11.). Ashton, *Understanding*, 302, considers two possibilities: the author "either did not know of or else was uninterested in any claim that Jesus was actually a linear descendant of David." The second of these probably comes nearest to explaining the Evangelist's intent. For John, the issue is irrelevant. As M. de Jonge notes, *Stranger From Heaven*, 55, "John, whether knowing about Jesus' birth at Bethlehem or not, does not record it and does not show himself interested in the question of Jesus' earthly origin at all." For a survey of the various interpretations of John 7:40-44, see Meeks, "Galilee and Judea in the Fourth Gospel," *JBL* 85 (1966) 159-69, at 161-3.

[186] The Fourth Evangelist's quotation style is quite conventional, as Joseph A.

quotation in the Fourth Gospel, only three mention an author, Isaiah, quoted in 1:23, 12:38 and 12:40.[187] A fourth formula introducing another quotation from Isaiah reads: ἔστιν γεγραμμένον ἐν τοῖς προφήταις (John 6:45). The only other readily identifiable biblical author formally quoted by John is Zechariah. There is no mention of his name in the formulae introducing the two quotations from his prophecy in the Gospel: καθώς ἐστιν γεγραμμένον (12:15) and καὶ πάλιν ἑτέρα γραφὴ λέγει (19:37). Therefore, the fact that John does not directly mention David as author of the psalms needs to be evaluated in the light of his over-all pattern of scriptural reference. As this chapter has demonstrated, there is sufficient evidence in the literature of early Judaism and in the NT to allow us presume that the Fourth Evangelist would have shared the commonly held belief that David "wrote" the psalms, just as he shared the belief that Moses "wrote" the Pentateuch (John 1:45; 5:46).

We are still confronted with the undeniable lack of reference to David *per se* in the Fourth Gospel. In seeking to assess this, we need to take into account the fact that even in the synoptics, there is evidence of a certain reserve towards the presentation of Jesus as "Son of David." The two Evangelists who connect Jesus with David through linear descent record, nevertheless, his questioning of the apparently widespread practice of referring to the Christ as David's son (Matt 22:41-46; Luke 20:41-44). The *Davidssohnfrage* has been the object of extensive study. Most of it has arrived at some form of the following explanation: Jesus accepts that David is addressing the Messiah in Ps (109)110, but he reasons that David would hardly call his son, "My Lord" and that therefore the titles "Messiah" and "Son of David" are not co-extensive.[188] Whatever the precise interpreta-

---

Fitzmyer has shown in "The Use of Explicit O.T. Quotations in the Qumran Literature and the N.T.," *NTS* 7 (1960-61) 297-333. John's introductory formulae such as καθώς ἐστιν γεγραμμένον (6:31), or καθὼς εἶπεν ἡ γραφή (7:38) are similar to those used in the DSS, the Mishnah and elsewhere in the NT. The formula "When the word will come true which is written..." (CD VII;10-11 and CD XIX:7) would represent the nearest the Qumran documents come to NT "fulfilment formulae" such as ἵνα ἡ γραφὴ πληρωθῇ (John 19:24). See also Metzger, "The Formulas Introducing Quotations of Scripture in the NT and the Mishnah," *JBL* 70 (1951) 297-307, and C. A. Evans, "On the Quotation Formulas in the Fourth Gospel," *BZ* 26 (1982) 79-83.

[187] Menken identifies particular reasons for these three exceptions—"The prophet's name in 1,23, in connection with the quotation from Isa 40,3, comes from the tradition.... In 12:41 John puts Isaiah upon the stage as someone who, in his call-vision (Isaiah 6), saw Jesus' glory, and spoke about him. No wonder then that when he quotes from this prophet in what immediately precedes, he mentions him by name..." *Old Testament Quotations*, 71.

[188] Bruce Chilton, "Jesus *ben David*: Reflections on the Davidssohnfrage" *NTS* 14 (1982) 88-112, at 98, suggests that the messianic colouring of the title was being cor-

tion of the pericope, it is clear that there was considerable ambivalence in early Christianity towards the application to Jesus of the title "Son of David" and a concern to point out that, while appropriate to Jesus, it in no way exhausted his significance. Inherent in this reticence towards the title, there seems also to be a hint that its appropriateness to Jesus would depend on its being radically revised and freed of national-political overtones.[189] Thus, even for the synoptics, there is a certain wariness of the associations David has with a particular "strain" of messianism.[190]

In assessing the Fourth Evangelist's apparent avoidance of Davidic motifs, we need also to remember that Jesus' Davidic descent is a *theo-*

---

rected in favour of a Solomonic interpretation with overtones of wisdom and therapeutic skill. This healing aspect is emphasized by Klaus Berger, "Die Königlichen Messiastraditionen des Neuen Testaments," *NTS* 20 (1973) 1-44, who draws on traditions about Solomon's therapeutic and magical powers (e.g., TSol 1:1-7; 20:1). Dennis C. Duling shows that TSol, the crucial text for Berger's argument, is dependent on the NT. See "Solomon, Exorcism and the Son of David," *HTR* 68 (1975) 235-52. Juel contends that the implied solution to the "contradiction" within the scriptures is provided by events the readers know will soon follow: Jesus' resurrection and enthronement. See *Messianic Exegesis*, 144. Juel acknowledges his debt for this solution to Evald Loevestam's article "Die Davidssohnsfrage," *SEÅ* 27 (1962) 72-82. James M. Gibbs, "Purpose and Pattern in Matthew's use of the Title 'son of David,' " *NTS* 10 (1963-64) 464, believes Matthew regards the title "Son of David," as inadequate in the face of recognition of Jesus as Son of God." According to David Hay, *Glory at the Right Hand*, 111-12, Jesus declares the popular opinion misleading, because the Messiah's kingdom will not be a mere renewal of David's militaristic rule. Jack Dean Kingsbury, "The Title 'son of David' in Matthew's Gospel," *JBL* 95 (1976) 592, sees the title as one that Matthew's community has outgrown and thus as secondary to the title "Son of God." Brown, *Death of the Messiah*, 467, believes this pericope shows "that Christians knew that the Messiah could not be adequately described as Son of David."

[189] "Throughout his ministry Jesus seems to have regularly discouraged hopes that he would exercise political or military power akin to that which David or the Hasmoneans wielded. His words in this pericope may therefore carry a deliberate rejection of the mundane interpretation of Ps 110 favoured by Hasmoneans and other post-exilic Jews." Hay, *Glory at the Right Hand*, 111.

[190] It is important to remember that there was no one coherent or normative messianic theory. Messianic ideas were fluid and varied. As the famous Mishnaic passage about presumption and dearth increasing with "the footsteps of the Messiah" shows, there were circles in early Judaism where messianism was even regarded as an aberration. See *M. Sota* 9:9-15 as discussed by Jacob Neusner in *Messiah in Context*, 25. It follows from this that messianic motifs in the literature of the late Second Temple period are not necessarily or exclusively Davidic. One might think of the pre-existent heavenly Messiah in 1 Enoch, e.g., or the dyarchic messianism of both the DSS and the Testaments of the Twelve Patriarchs. Even though the literary evidence is later than the NT period, one might also include the Samaritan expectation of a Moses *redivivus*, the *Taheb*. See Talmon, "Types of Messianic Expectation at the Turn of the Era," in his *King, Cult and Calendar in Ancient Israel: Collected Studies*, (Jerusalem: Magnes, 1986) 202-24, at 207-9 and Marinus de Jonge, "Jewish Expectations about the 'Messiah' according to the Fourth Gospel," *NTS* 19 (1972-73) 246-270.

logoumenon, rather than merely, or even necessarily, a genealogical reference.[191] The point of the affirmation that Jesus is descended from David is "that in Jesus God fulfilled the promise made in 2 Sam 7."[192] This is what Dennis C. Duling has called, David's "point of entry into early Christianity." The actual acceptance of "Son of David" as a title for Jesus "appears on both historical and redaction critical grounds to be relatively late."[193] It is not surprising, therefore, that all the gospels preserve recollections of the debate that it engendered.

The reserve shown by the synoptics towards the title "Son of David" becomes in the Fourth Gospel a patent avoidance. The absence of reference (by the narrator or by any character in the Gospel) to Jesus as "Son of David" is usually seen as indicating John's lack of interest in, or even resistance to, a Davidic Christology.[194] Instead of a birth narrative or genealogy, there is the Prologue introducing Jesus as the pre-existent Word. The stress on Jesus' origin "from above" is sustained from the Prologue, through the whole Gospel (e.g., 3:31; 8:14. 23; 17:14) to the original ending (20:31). Yet, as John 20:31 states, the Gospel is written—ἵνα πιστεύ[σ]ητε ὅτι Ἰησοῦς ἐστιν ὁ Χριστὸς ὁ υἱὸς τοῦ θεοῦ, καὶ ἵνα πιστεύοντες ζωὴν ἔχητε ἐν τῷ ὀνόματι αὐτοῦ. The confession of Jesus as ὁ Χριστὸς is basic to Johannine faith (11:27). In fact, it is this confession that has caused the rift between John's readers and the synagogue (9:22). It is only in the Fourth Gospel that Jesus lays claim to the title ὁ Χριστὸς, and thus to the role of Messiah, on his own initiative (4:26).[195] Not only is the term "Messiah" used only in the Fourth

---

[191] The Hebrew and Aramaic terms for "son" (בן and בר) point to character as well as to genealogy. "In the Semitic sense, the term 'son of David' connotes 'one with the nature of David, or with Davidic character' as well as 'one of the family of David.' " See Cleon L. Rogers, Jr, "The Davidic Covenant in the Gospels," *BSac* 150 (1993) 458-78, at 463-64.

[192] Meier, *Marginal Jew*, 1, 218.

[193] The affirmation that in Jesus God fulfilled the promise made in 2 Sam 7 underlies the pre-Pauline confessional formulae, notably Rom 1:3-4. The tradition founded on the promises to David enters Christianity in connection with the application of these promises to Jesus' resurrection, apart from the title "Son of David" itself, a title whose acceptance and adaptation in early Christianity appears on both historical and redaction critical grounds to be relatively late. See Dennis C. Duling, "The Promises to David and their Entrance into Christianity—Nailing Down a Likely Hypothesis." *NTS* 19 (1974-75) 55-77, at 68.

[194] Edwin D. Freed, *Old Testament Quotations in the Gospel of John* (Leiden: Brill, 1965) 74, holds that John never uses the words "Son of David" of Jesus "because they do not fit his unique view of Jesus as king." Schuchard, *Scripture Within Scripture*, 54, speaks of the "apparent muting of a Davidic Christology (which itself is so heavily saturated with the issue of earthly origins) in John's portrait of Jesus."

[195] Within the logic of the plot, one would have to suppose that what the Samaritan woman meant by the title ὁ Χριστὸς was "something other than the

Gospel, but it is both transliterated and translated (1:41; 4:25).[196]

Various explanations have been offered for this paradox. F. J. Moloney sees behind it the predicament of the Johannine community. "A community forcibly repudiated by its Jewish roots finds itself in the syncretistic world of Asia Minor, aggressively claims that Jesus is the Christ, but in a non-Jewish world has to show that he is more than the Christ."[197] Moloney thinks, therefore, in terms of a new content for an inadequate ancient title. As the "explanatory note" in John 17:3 makes clear, Jesus is not the Christ of current messianic expectation. He is "the Christ" only as the Revealer of the only God.[198]

George MacRae has suggested that the Fourth Evangelist may have tried deliberately to incorporate a diversity of backgrounds into one gospel message precisely to emphasize the universality of Jesus. Thus MacRae would regard "the heaping up of Christological titles" in John 1 as an incorporation into the understanding of Jesus of whatever Christological labels are current in the Evangelist's milieu. In that case, an interpretation of Jesus in terms of Davidic messianism would be one of several Christologies introduced into the Gospel "to express his universality and assert that he transcends any such labelling."[199]

Ashton sees the vindication of Jesus' messianic status as an important feature of the Johannine circle's insistence that the heritage of Israel belongs to them. The conviction that they are the rightful heirs of the whole biblical tradition is something which they share with early Christianity in general.

> But it is of particular importance in the Fourth Gospel, for there the dominant impression is of an alien Christ moving among the Jews as a stranger. In overemphasising this impression or in isolating it from the data within the Gospel that confirm Jesus' essential Jewishness, one can cut the ties which keep the Johannine Christ pinned down to the ground and allow him to drift off in the direction of docetism.

---

anointed king of the house of David, perhaps a Moses-like figure as we find in the later-attested Samaritan belief in the Taheb," as Brown has suggested. See *Death of the Messiah*, I, 475-6 and *John I-XII*, 172. At story level, the woman and the townsfolk whom she leads to Jesus represent the Samaritan element within the Johannine circle. Looking at the Gospel as a whole, one would suspect that these Christians, whose traditions did not include the idealisation of the Davidic monarchy, have contributed significantly to Johannine Christology.

[196] "But the important point to notice is that (John) is not satisfied merely to employ the translation alone. He emphatically uses the term itself, and he makes clear that he wants it to bear its full titular force." Martyn, *History and Theology*, 92.

[197] "The Fourth Gospel's Presentation," 246.

[198] "The Fourth Gospel's Presentation," 251-52.

[199] "The Fourth Gospel & Religionsgeschichte," 18-19.

> Some members of the community appear to have done precisely this, so provoking the alarm and hostility of the author of the Johannine letters. Yet much of the Fourth Gospel is concerned to vindicate messianic claims, and if, as I believe, most of this material stems from a signs source, taken over by the evangelist, it was nevertheless assumed into his Gospel and, although modified, never repudiated. So if one is to preserve a proper balance, this material must be accorded its due weight.[200]

Thus, according to Ashton, the theme of messianic fulfilment is part of the Fourth Gospel's rootedness in the Jewish heritage which provides a necessary balance to "the ideas of strangeness, alienation and unbridgeable distance that have to be included in any complete account of Johannine christology."[201] Without it, the proclamation of Jesus as "Son of God" would have appeared to Gentiles as just another mystery cult. Without it, one might also add, Johannine Jewish Christians, expelled from the synagogue, would have been effectively cut off from their biblical inheritance. As it was, their conviction that Jesus was the Christ meant not only that they had a claim to that inheritance, but that they, who could see in the Scriptures a witness to Jesus' messiahship, were the only ones capable of understanding and receiving them fully. This last explanation would account for the importance which, as this study will show, the Evangelist does, in fact, attach to David. In the pages which follow, we will attempt to accord "due weight" to David, particularly in view of the high profile of his psalms in the Fourth Gospel, and thus to show that in John, Davidic Christology, although modified, is not repudiated.

In the Judaism contemporary with Johannine Christianity the memory of David was highly evocative of an expected messianic figure. From the Fourth Gospel itself (John 7:41-42; 12:34), we know that Johannine Christianity was in debate with Jewish speculation concerning this figure. Recourse to messianic interpretations of the David materials in the early attempts of Christians to express their understanding of Jesus seems to have aroused serious misgivings within the Johannine circle, to the point where the Evangelist has decided to avoid reference to David. Thus Jesus is never called "Son of David" in the Fourth Gospel. As we will see, the Fourth Evangelist has his own way of affirming that Jesus' resurrection, viewed as exaltation in the manner of royal enthronement, is the fulfilment of the promises to David.

---

[200] Ashton, *Understanding*, 242.
[201] Ashton, *Understanding*, 242-244.

The capacity to envisage David in other ways than as a founder of a dynasty or as a cipher for messianism is amply demonstrated in the writings of several of the authors we have cited in this chapter. The Chronicler, for example, shows no interest in David as dynastic progenitor.[202] Neither do the dynastic dimension of the David materials particularly appeal to Ben Sira.[203] Perhaps the most striking feature of Josephus' portrayal of David is his silence on David's status as ancestor of the Messiah.[204] Josephus presumably shares a common perception of his time that popular messianic movements had led to the disaster of 70 CE. He is clearly at pains to avoid anything that might be deemed subversive by his patrons, the Romans.[205] Ps-Philo displays a decided lack of interest in the messianic aspect of David.[206] The abrupt ending of his *LAB* at the death of Saul, which

---

[202] E. Ben Zvi, "The Authority of 1-2 Chronicles in the Late Second Temple Period," *JSP* 3 (1988) 59-80, has demonstrated that there is no evidence in early Jewish interpreters of Chronicles that its author was understood as envisaging a future for the monarchy, whether royalist or messianic.

[203] Brief references to the Davidic covenant (45:25, 47:11), are somewhat overshadowed by references to covenants made with Moses (45:5), Phineas (45:24) and particularly Aaron (45:7.15), in whose priestly line Ben Sira is obviously much more interested. His verdict on all the kings of Judah, except three, is that they sinned. The three whom he regards worthy of remembrance, David, Hezekiah and Josiah, were all devoted patrons and promoters and reformers of Temple worship (Sir 49:4). David is the great giver of thanks to the Holy One (Sir 47:8) and what commends Hezekiah and Josiah is that they walked in David's ways (See 2 Kgs 18:3, 22:2).

[204] Josephus' version of Nathan's oracle, for example, is considerably toned down. There is no promise of an everlasting dynasty: David simply rejoices that his house is to become glorious and renowned (*Ant.* VII, 94). In an earlier mention of David as the grandson of Obed, Josephus states that the dynasty lasted for 21 generations and makes no mention of any expected renewal of the Davidic line (*Ant.* V, 336). See Feldman, "Josephus' Portrait of David," 129-174.

[205] E.g., in *Wars* VI, 311-13, Josephus says that an ambiguous oracle in the Jewish scriptures stating that "one from their country" would rule the world signified the sovereignty of Vespasian, who was proclaimed emperor on Jewish soil." In *Wars* IV, 9.7, he ignores the clear parallels between the rise of his contemporary Simon Bar Giora and that of David. These parallels are identified by Richard A. Horsley in "Messianic Movements in Judaism," *ABD*, V, 791-97, at 794. See also Louis H. Feldman, "Use, Authority, and Exegesis of Mikra in the Writings of Josephus," in Jan Mulder and Harry Sysling (ed.) *Mikra: Text, Translation, Reading and Interpretation of the Hebrew Bible in Ancient Judaism and Early Christianity*, CRINT 2.1 (Assen: Van Gorcum, 1988) 455-518, at 470-471.

[206] Doron Mendels attributes this to Ps-Philo's opposition to contemporary messianic movements as untimely. Thus in *LAB* 56:2, Samuel criticizes the people's demand for a king—"Ecce nunc video, quoniam non est adhuc tempus regnandi nobis in sempiterno et edificare domum Domini Dei nostri, petentibus regem ante tempus." We note in this passage the linking of kingship and temple-building. See "Pseudo-Philo's Biblical Antiquities, the 'Fourth Philosophy,' and the Political Messianism of the First Century C. E.," in Charlesworth (ed.) *The Messiah*, 261-75, at 268-69.

fulfils Samuel's prophecy (*LAB* 56:3), seems to make the point that the institution of kingship in Israel has been fraught with ambiguity, even from its origins.²⁰⁷ There is almost nothing in Philo relating to the dynastic aspect of David.²⁰⁸ In fact, Philo appears intent on neutralizing texts which he must have received as "messianically" associated with David.²⁰⁹ He never actually calls David king. For Philo "the only real king was God and the only human approximation was the sage. Real kings did not really count."²¹⁰ Philo never mentions the term Χριστός. His only reference to an eschatological saviour figure, in *Praem* 95, is quite vague.

As the material we have surveyed has demonstrated, David is a much modified figure. Certainly by the Second Temple period he represented, particularly in his *persona* as psalmist, far more than a cipher for messianic ideology. The ongoing facetting of the David figure, right into NT times, the burden of this chapter, was to become an important resource for the Fourth Evangelist in the particular articulation of Davidic ideology which his portrayal of Jesus required.

J. *Conclusion*

The earliest clear cut Jewish statements of Davidic authorship of the Psalter postdate the NT period.²¹¹ However, the material pre-

---

²⁰⁷ This is the view of Mendels. Alternatively, Harrington, "Pseudo-Philo,", 298, attributes the abrupt ending to the loss of the original ending. In J. C. O'Neill's opinion, this world history from Adam to the threshold of David's reign is "compiled for a people who should be preparing themselves for the Messiah." See "The Question of Messianic Expectation in Pseudo-Philo's Biblical Antiquities," *JHC* 1 (1994) 85-93, at 86.

²⁰⁸ His idealization of Tamar does, perhaps, show some recognition of the importance of the forebears of the historical David. She deserts to the camp of piety at the risk of her life, wanting to be "the servant and suppliant of the one great cause" (τὴν θεραπείαν καὶ ἱκεσίαν τοῦ ἑνὸς αἰτίου), i.e., to become the matriarch of David's family. See *Virt.* IX, 220-222.

²⁰⁹ E.g., Isa 11:6-8, is "spiritualized" as a description of the establishment of harmony between humankind and the animals in *Praem* 85-87, and the raging of the nations against the king of Ps 2 is transformed into an abstract, idealized bloodless conflict in *Praem* 94. See Richard D. Hecht, "Philo and Messiah" in J. Neusner, W. S. Green and E. S. Fredrichs (ed.), *Judaisms and their Messiahs at the Turn of the Christian Era* (Cambridge: University Press, 1987) 139-68 and Burton Mack, "Wisdom and Apocalyptic in Philo," in Runia, Hay and Winston (ed.), *Heirs of the Septuagint*, 21-39.

²¹⁰ Mack, "The Christ and Jewish Wisdom," in Charlesworth (ed.), *The Messiah*, 192-221, at 208.

²¹¹ "As Moses gave five books of laws to Israel, so David gave five books of psalms to Israel" (*Midr. Teh.* 1.5). David composed all 150 psalms under divine inspiration (*b. Pesah.* 117a). His whole life was one of unceasing praise and thanksgiving to God, "nothing more than a context for all the psalms" (*b. Bat.* 14b). Whenever he found

sented in this chapter indicates that the supposed Davidic authorship of the psalms was universally accepted by the time the Fourth Gospel was written. As a presupposition shared by its author and intended readers, it is an issue not only relevant but even essential to a study of the Johannine reception of the psalms. Having reviewed this material, we are now in a better position to envisage the "author" of the psalms as he might plausibly have been imagined by Johannine Christians. In light of the reception of the historical superscript tradition, it is inconceivable that some of the psalm references in the Gospel would not have carried for the original readers resonances of David and his story. This is especially true of references to "laments of the individual" such as Ps (21)22 or Ps (68)69 which could easily be envisaged as actual utterances of David. But it also applies, albeit in a different way, to psalm references which function as words from Scripture, for example, "He gave them bread from heaven to eat."[212]

In delineating the figure of David as remembered and imagined, we have sought to reconstruct an important feature of the horizon of expectations against which the psalms were received by the Johannine Community. To express it in the terminology of contemporary literary theory: we have been considering prior texts as contributions to the code which makes possible the particular effect of signification which the psalms produce in the Fourth Gospel. At the heart of Jauss' aesthetics of reception is the insight that "a literary work is not an object which stands by itself and which offers the same face to each reader in each period," but that it is more like a musical score which is experienced differently in each performance. Reception is thus a process of production."[213] Applying this insight to the psalms, we might say that Johannine Christians "heard" them as "performed" by the David that they knew. Having sought to reconstruct this David figure, who is himself the product of various literary works, we are now better able to picture the "face" that he offered to Johannine Christians and to allow its lineaments a role in the reconstruction of their reception of the psalms.

Writing on Johannine psalm usage, under the heading "Great David's Greater Son Also in Suffering and Betrayal," L. P. Trudinger remarks:

---

himself in distress, David prayed a psalm (*Midr. Teh.* 63.1).

[212] John 6:31, quoting Ps (77)78:24) with the quotation formula, "as it is written."
[213] See "Literary History as a Challenge," 14. Jauss draws on Barthes' theory that, "The goal of literary work is to make the reader no longer a consumer, but a producer of the text." See Barthes, *S/Z*, 4.

> It is most instructive, I think, to take note of the fact that it is not concerning David in his role of majesty, pomp and power as 'king' only that John understands Jesus as a successor to David. It is precisely in references to moments of deep humility in David's life story; to incidents relating to David's betrayal by close members of his entourage, indeed, of his own family; incidents connected with the ending of David's 'kingship.'[214]

To express this insight in terms of our reconstruction of the figure of David in this chapter, we might say that the connections which the Fourth Evangelist makes between Jesus and David are manyfaceted. The Gospel indicates that for the group behind the Johannine text, David was not only a glorious figure: the shepherd king *par excellence*, the anointed royal "Son of God," but also, and especially, the king who, through his filial communion with God, maintained his serenity in the face of the apparently definitive loss of his sovereignty. In this he was a prophet of Jesus.[215] The nadir of David's decline, when he discovered the complicity of Ahithophel, was actually his great moment of closeness to God, the one occasion in the 2 Sam narrative when he is shown at prayer (2 Sam 15:31). This prayer of David opened the way into a Davidic reading of the psalms and the consequent development of the historical superscript tradition. As we will see, the connections which the Fourth Gospel makes between David and Jesus presuppose a capacity of the religious imagination that must surely have been cultivated through exposure to such a reading.

As we proceed now to a detailed examination of the ten explicit psalm citations in the Fourth Gospel, we will be alert to indications that the psalms quoted in the Gospel were regarded as "compositions" of David—either as prayers uttered by David or as part of his poetic output. A major concern of the next two chapters will be to reconstruct imaginatively the effect of supposed Davidic "authorship" on the Johannine reception of these psalm passages, in other words, to gain access to that "cave of resonant signification" within

---

[214] Trudinger, "Hosanna to the Son of David!: St John's Perspective," *DRev* 109 (1991) 297-301, at 297. Trudinger's summarization of 2 Sam 15-19 as "the ending of David's 'kingship'" is geared towards his extraordinary contention, expressed later in the article, that the Johannine Passion Narrative "does not portray Jesus as a kingly figure." Rather than "the ending" it would be more accurate to speak of the apparent loss of David's kingship out of which was to come a new confirmation of his sovereignty. While Trudinger's appraisal of both narratives is open to question, his basic insight remains valid.

[215] Awareness of David's prophetic status in Judaism can be an important corrective to the tendency in Johannine studies to assume that every "prophetic" feature of Jesus is an indication that he is the "Prophet-like Moses."

which author and ideal reader of the Fourth Gospel heard the psalms. In the process of reconstituting this recital we will encounter several instances where the David narratives or passages in the latter prophets referring to him function like Hollander's "harmonic partials," entering the text as tonal quality and shaping the particular timbre of David's song.[216] Thus we will experience the Fourth Gospel as polyphony, or even as polytextuality, in which the *cantus firmus* of each psalm quotation is heard against the accompanying counterpoint of other passages from David's *oeuvre* and of incidents from his story.[217]

---

[216] Hollander, *The Figure of Echo*, 64.
[217] Polytextuality is a technique used in Renaissance choral music where several liturgically related texts and sometimes even secular songs are sung simultaneously.

CHAPTER THREE

THE PSALMS QUOTED IN THE BOOK OF SIGNS[1]

A. *Introduction*

In this and the next chapter we discuss the psalm quotations, in the order in which they occur in the Fourth Gospel narrative. To this end, the division of the Gospel into two major parts, the first ending with Ch. 12, and the second beginning at Ch. 13, will be used as a framework.[2]

Many commentators have observed that this division corresponds to vv. 11-12 of the Prologue. The Book of Signs, corresponding to εἰς τὰ ἴδια ἦλθεν, καὶ οἱ ἴδιοι αὐτὸν οὐ παρέλαβον, deals with "The public ministry of Jesus where in sign and word he shows himself to his own people, only to be rejected." The Book of Glory, corresponding to ὅσοι δὲ ἔλαβον αὐτόν, ἔδωκεν αὐτοῖς ἐξουσίαν τέκνα θεοῦ γενέσθαι..., tells of how "To those who accept him Jesus shows his glory by returning to the Father in 'the hour' of his crucifixion, resurrection and ascension. Fully glorified, he communicates the Spirit of life."[3] While the synoptics, especially Mark, show traces of the

---

[1] This and the next chapter are entitled "The Psalms Quoted..." rather than "The Psalm Quotations..." This is because the presence of the psalms in the Gospel text is not always confined to the moment when they are explicitly cited. In these chapters, therefore, as well as dealing with the explicit citations, we will explore the possibility that the Evangelist did not merely extract an appropriate verse, but was aware of the total psalm. We will also find that the quotations and allusions to the seven quoted psalms frequently create "sympathetic vibrations" in other analogous psalm passages. We will simply draw attention to these inter-textual links with other passages in the complete *Opus* of David, reserving fuller discussion of their significance to Ch. 5.

[2] For Dodd, the division at this juncture is suggested by the Gospel itself and corresponds to the point in the synoptics where the account of the ministry ends and the Passion Narrative begins. See *The Interpretation on the Fourth Gospel* (Cambridge: Cambridge University Press, 1953), Part III: "Argument and Structure," 289-443, at 289. See also Brown, *John, I-XII*, cxl-cxli and *John, XIII-XXI*, 545-47. For MacRae, "the existence of this natural division need. no demonstration." It corresponds to Mark's division of his Gospel into the pre- and post-Caesarea Philippi sequences which are similarly exoteric and esoteric. See "Fourth Gospel and Religionsgeschichte," 20.

[3] Brown, *John I-XII*, cxxxviii. See Dodd, *The Interpretation* 402-3. Similarly, R. Bultmann, *The Gospel of John: A Commentary* (Oxford: Blackwell, 1971) 48, sees the Prologue as illustrating the two "books": John 1:5.9-11 representing the struggle of light with darkness and John 1:12-18, the victory of light. In Meeks' view, "The

passion story's origin as an independent narrative,[4] the Johannine passion-resurrection sequence is remarkable for its literary, thematic and theological fusion with the rest of the Gospel. The fact that reference to the psalms is far less confined to the Passion Narrative in John than it is in the synoptics is an aspect of this continuity.

In order to see exactly how and where the psalm quotations fit into what Dodd calls "the argument and structure" of the Gospel, we will begin this and the next chapter by situating them within the pattern which he discerned.[5] According to Dodd's analysis, the Gospel begins with a Proem consisting of the Prologue (1:1-1:18) and the sequence of testimonies to Jesus (1:19-51). Then follows the Book of Signs consisting of seven episodes. In the first of these, "The New Beginning" (2:1-4:42), Jesus encounters representatives of different "Judaisms" in various geographical locations: Cana, Jerusalem, Samaria. This first episode contains four scenes: the wedding at Cana (inauguration of a new order in religion) the Temple scene (replacement of the cultic system), the dialogue with Nicodemus (confrontation with a representative of the old order; new birth into a new level of existence), the scene with the Samaritan woman (living water symbolizing the newness of the life that Jesus gives).[6] It is in the second scene of this episode, set in the Temple, that the first psalm quotation occurs: **Ps (68:10)69:9 in John 2:17**—"Zeal for your house will consume me." This utterance of David functions as a programmatic "Scripture" interpreting Jesus' behaviour in the Temple as portending the events of the "hour" which are to result in the replacement of the Jewish cultic system.[7]

Man from Heaven," 141, the Book of Signs tells of the mission of Jesus whose testimony to his descent from heaven and the relationship to God which this implies, constitutes a κρίσις for the world. The pivotal phrase—...εἰδὼς ὅτι...ἀπὸ θεοῦ ἐξῆλθεν καὶ πρὸς τὸν θεὸν ὑπάγει...(John 13:3)—at the opening of the Book of Glory signals the ascent of Jesus, with its implications for his unique relationship with God. Equally this ascent constitutes a κρίσις for the world. For Culpepper, *The Anatomy*, 87, vv. 11-12 are "a summary of the plot."

[4] E.g., the original ending of Mark (13:37), Matthew's typical redactional link (26:1) and the Lukan summary/suture (21:37-38).

[5] We will also keep in mind the slightly different analysis of the structure of the Gospel, although agreeing in general thrust with Dodd, which is offered by Brown in *John I-XII*, cxl-cxli and *John XIII-XXI*, 545-547.

[6] For Brown, the testimony sequence (1:19-51) which tells of the opening days of the revelation of Jesus, opens the Book of Signs. The event in the Temple is the second scene in a "From Cana to Cana" sequence (2:1-4:54) which presents various responses to Jesus' ministry in the different sections of Palestine.

[7] Our use of the term "programmatic" derives from "programme music" (as distinct from "absolute music") in which a pre-existing narrative structure dictates the form and shape of a composition.

Continuing to follow Dodd's analysis, we find that in the Second Episode, "The Life-Giving Word" (4:46-5:47), two healing narratives and a dialogue portray Jesus as conferring life and exercising God's power to judge. In this episode Jesus appears as increasingly provocative to the Jews and their leaders. The Third Episode, "The Bread of Life" (6:1-71), consists of Jesus' feeding of the multitude, their attempt to make him king, the walking on the water, the Bread of Life discourse, the division which Jesus' self-revelation provokes, the desertion by some of his disciples and the forecast of the betrayal. The quotation of **Ps (77)78:24 in John 6:31**—"He gave them bread from heaven to eat."—functions as a word from Scripture. Misused by hecklers in the crowd who repeat their forebears' sin of putting God to the test (Exod 16:2-3), it becomes the catalyst for the revelatory discourse of Jesus which forms the bulk of this episode.

In Dodd's fourth and central episode of the Book of Signs, "Light and Life: Manifestation and Rejection" (7:1-8:59), an atmosphere of controversy is particularly marked and sustained. The narrative, which mainly recounts debates with or about Jesus, is punctuated by references to the threat to his life. It is in this episode that Jesus promises the gift of the waters of life in a second word from Scripture, quoted from the previously cited psalm: **Ps (77)78:16.20 in John 7:38**—"Out of his heart shall flow rivers of living water." This and the previous psalm quotation belong together, not merely because they come from the same psalm, but, more importantly, because they both employ "Exodus" motifs to explain the meaning of Jesus: the manna in John 6:31 and the water from the rock in John 7:37b-38.

The next Psalm quotation occurs in Dodd's Episode Five, "Judgement by the Light" (9:1-10:42). This contains the story of the man born blind which leads into an interrogation scene, in which those who set themselves up as judges end up being judged themselves. The Shepherd Discourse which follows meets with the hearers' incomprehension. With the dialogue in the Portico of Solomon, this incomprehension turns to hostility and determination to kill Jesus. It is at the height of this controversy that the next psalm quotation occurs, another word of Scripture: **Ps (81)82:6 in John 10:34**—"I said, you are gods."

Dodd's sixth episode, "The Victory of Life over Death" (11:1-53), tells of the raising of Lazarus. Jesus' life-giving action provokes the decision for his death which will conclude the episode. Jesus is thus "manifested as Resurrection and Life by virtue of his self-sacrifice."[8]

---

[8] Dodd, *The Interpretation*, 368.

Several verses telling of the threat to Jesus' life form a link to Dodd's Episode Seven, "Life through Death: The Meaning of the Cross" (12:1-36). This final episode of the Book of Signs contains two narratives: the anointing at Bethany, 'a σημεῖον of the burial of Jesus, and the triumphal entry into Jerusalem, a σημεῖον of his "universal sovereignty...as Conqueror of death and Lord of life."[9] It is in the second narrative, the account of Jesus riding into Jerusalem to his death, a scene which points to the meaning of his crucifixion as royal enthronement, that we find the quotation of **Ps (117)118:26 in John 12:13**—"Blessed is he who comes in the name of the Lord." The episode concludes with discourses interpretive of Jesus' approaching hour which form an epilogue to the entire Book of Signs.

From this outline situating Johannine reference to the Psalter within a conspectus of the whole "Book of Signs," we now proceed to a more detailed examination of each of these quotations, conscious of their role in the unfolding of the Evangelist's argument and alert to the particular overtones with which their supposed Davidic "authorship" would have invested them.

B. *Psalm (68:10)69:9 in John 2:17*[10]

In this first of several occurrences of Ps (68)69 in the Fourth Gospel the disciples are described as recalling a line of the psalm on the occasion of Jesus' disruption of the trade in the Temple area—

Ἐμνήσθησαν οἱ μαθηταὶ αὐτοῦ ὅτι γεγραμμένον ἐστίν, Ὁ ζῆλος τοῦ οἴκου σου καταφάγεταί με (John 2:17).

His disciples remembered that it was written, "Zeal for your house will consume me."

This occurs in a story from the tradition. It has, however, all the appearances of having been inserted into the traditional materials by the Fourth Evangelist.[11] This first explicit citation from the Psalter in the Gospel alerts us to the way in which we should interpret the other nine. Two features stand out.

---

[9] Dodd, *The Interpretation*, 370-71.
[10] From now on, the LXX numbering of the psalms will be used in the body of our text.
[11] Menken notes that John 2:17 "displays two characteristics of Johannine style: *asyndeton epicum* (omission of the connecting particle) and John's preferred expression, γεγραμμένον ἐστίν. See *Old Testament Quotations*, 38. Menken's essay on the quotation in John 2:17 was originally published as "De ijver voor uw huis zal mij verteren: Het citaat uit Psalm 69,10 in Johannes 2,17" in D. Akerboom a.o. (ed.), *Broeder Jehosjoea: Festschrift for B. Hemelsoet* (Kampen: Kok, 1994) 157-64.

First, the remembering on the part of the disciples operates on two levels of understanding, what John Ashton calls "the plain and the esoteric."[12] The first or "plain" level of meaning is the degree of insight that could conceivably be achieved by the disciples present at the event. The second or "esoteric" level is the deeper insight that can be achieved only by John and his readers. These two levels correspond to the notions of "story" and "discourse" in contemporary narrative analysis.[13]

At the first level, that of "story," Jesus' angry outburst in the Temple, interpreted by the disciples as zeal, provokes their spontaneous recollection of the words, "Zeal for your house will consume me." In view of the context from which they recall this line, where the psalmist's sufferings have brought him to the point of death, it could also be that the disciples sense that Jesus' uncompromising zeal may well cost him his life. At the second level, that of "discourse," the remembering after Jesus' resurrection, the interpretation of the incident is affected by the Johannine view of Jesus' death as fulfilment of the Scriptures. This is especially important, since, as the Gospel unfolds, the Psalter, and this psalm in particular, will figure prominently among the Scriptures that bear witness to Jesus (John 5:39). At the level of "story," the psalm text illuminates Jesus' action for the disciples. At the level of "discourse," the psalm is understood in a way which would not have been available to those first disciples. It is at the level of this post-resurrectional, Paraclete-taught remembering, that the psalm text functions fully in terms of the author's overall stated intention—a bringing of the reader to full faith in Jesus (John 20:31).[14] However, the story level is equally the creation of an author writing from a post-resurrectional perspective. It too has an important function—to convince John's readers of their privileged standing as those who believe without seeing (John 20:29).

---

[12] *Understanding*, 415-16.

[13] The French literary theorists use the terms "histoire" and "récit." Culler, *The Pursuit of Signs*, 169-74, defines "story" as "a sequence of actions or events, conceived as independent of their manifestation in discourse." He then defines "discourse" as "the discursive presentation or narration of events."

[14] In John 7:39 and 20:9 there are similar references to the community's post-resurrectional understanding. See Lindars, *Gospel of John*, 140. The distinction between the two modes of remembering, as described in John 2:17 and 22, has been well expressed by Wolfgang Iser—"Whenever something is remembered, it changes according to the circumstances under which it is remembered, but the resultant change in the past becomes a past itself which, in turn, can be remembered and changed again." See *The Implied Reader: Patterns of Communication in Prose Fiction from Bunyan to Beckett* (Baltimore: John Hopkins University Press, 1974) 144. The appropriateness of this model to the Fourth Gospel has been noted by Culpepper in *The Anatomy*, 29.

The realization that their insight into the meaning of Jesus far exceeds that of Jesus' first disciples will confirm them in their faith and console them in the loss of their status within Judaism.

At the level of story, the disciples are presented in John 2:17 as possessing a sufficiently advanced knowledge of the Scriptures to be able to recall on impulse an extremely apt and somewhat *recherché* biblical passage.[15] Yet later in the Gospel, the Evangelist will say of these same disciples that they did not know the Scripture (20:9; cf. 12:16). This seeming contradiction serves to emphasize further the contrast between "plain" remembering and "esoteric" remembering. For the Evangelist, the only true knowledge and understanding of the Scripture is that which underpins full Johannine faith.

The second feature is evident in the two interventions of the omniscient author telling us what the disciples remembered—a word of Scripture (v. 17) and a saying of Jesus (v. 22)—and the outcome of this twofold remembering—καὶ ἐπίστευσαν τῇ γραφῇ καὶ τῷ λόγῳ ὃν εἶπεν ὁ Ἰησοῦς (v. 22). The linking of the word of Jesus with ἡ γραφή as object of belief is a vital clue for the reader as to the author's intention and vision. The word of Jesus and the word of God as cited in Scripture are on a par. This equivalence, while not unique to the Fourth Gospel,[16] is particularly developed in John. It makes complete sense when viewed from within a circle that could produce a statement such as ὃν γὰρ ἀπέστειλεν ὁ θεὸς τὰ ῥήματα τοῦ θεοῦ λαλεῖ

---

[15] From what we know of Jewish educational practice in the first century CE, familiarity with the Writings would indicate a knowledge of the scriptures beyond the general basic instruction in Torah acquired in regular schooling. Gerhardssohn has shown that in the curriculum of 1st cent. CE elementary schools in the towns of Palestine the Pentateuch was given priority, followed by the Prophets, with the Writings definitely last in importance. See *Memory and Manuscript*, 61. More recently Gerhardsson's reconstruction of first century Jewish educational practice has been criticized as too dependent on later rabbinic texts to be reliable. The reality was probably far less developed. On this see Meier, *A Marginal Jew*, 271-273. Such a consideration would only strengthen the point made here that a spontaneous recollection of Ps (68:10)69:9 indicates a knowledge of scripture beyond that imparted to the average first century Jewish youth. Familiarity with a psalm such as Ps (68)69, which was not one of the more "popular" psalms such as the Songs of Ascents (Pss 120-134), the Hallel (Pss 113-118), the Great Hallel (Ps 136) or The Praises (Pss 146-150), would thus indicate a level of biblical education beyond the ordinary. For the various liturgical settings in which Jews of the late Second Temple Period would have encountered the psalms, see Michael Maher, "The Psalms in Jewish Worship," *PIBA* 17 (1994) 9-36. Whatever about the "historical" setting, the Johannine community seems to have been well-educated and *au fait* with the finer points of Jewish exegesis.

[16] M. Wilcox has shown how in the synoptic passion predictions Jesus' predictive word takes on "the force of Scripture" and has a similar role to that of Scripture in the development of the passion scenes. See "The Denial Sequence in Mk XIV. 26-31, 66-72," *NTS* 17 (1970-71) 426-36.

(3:34). In fact, all the words of Jesus have a scriptural status. So it is not surprising to find that in John 18:9 a saying of Jesus is introduced by exactly the type of quotation formula that is associated with scriptural citations elsewhere in the Gospel.[17] Just as Jesus' speech is, in some sense, Scripture, so Scripture is, in a very real sense, his speech.[18]

It is not clear whether the remembered Scripture is Ps 68:10 or, perhaps, on the analogy of John 20:9, the OT in general as a source of testimonies to Jesus. There is nothing, however, in the text to prevent the psalm quotation being taken as a possible referent of ἡ γραφή.[19] Neither would this be incompatible with a reference to the Scriptures in general.[20] However, since the context clearly indicates that the remembered word of Jesus is Λύσατε τὸν ναὸν τοῦτον καὶ ἐν τρισὶν ἡμέραις ἐγερῶ αὐτόν, it seems consistent and logical to seek a referent for "the Scripture" within the pericope as well. The fact that the most immediate referent for ἡ γραφή in 2:22 is the psalm text only adds to the importance of this opening episode for our study. If the author has the psalms in mind here and David as their author, then there is at least the hint that Jesus and David are related, and that presumably other words of Jesus will equally echo other words of David.[21]

---

[17] "Since Jesus' words are indeed the words of God (3:34; 5:19), they stand together with the words of God in the Old Testament as equal in authority and significance (18:9. 32). Consequently, only those who are obedient to the older words of God can be obedient to the new words of God uttered by Jesus (8:46)." See Aune, *The Cultic Setting*, 70.

[18] "In John's view (17:8) Jesus' words have been given him by God and have the same divine authority as the scriptures of Israel." Brown, *Death of the Messiah*, I, 290, 599. For Adele Reinhartz, the idea that as divine revelation Jesus' words have the same status as Scripture is linked with Jesus' prophetic role. The Johannine Jesus is "not only the prophet, but the prophesied, not only the mouthpiece for the divine word, but the content of the message itself." See "Jesus as Prophet: Predictive Prolepses in the Fourth Gospel," *JSNT* 36 (1989) 3-16, at 10. Ashton, following Borgen, traces the idea back to the diplomatic convention of agency according to which a royal emissary was to be treated as the king's equal. He sees this as capable of generating the high Christology according to which hearing Jesus is hearing the voice of God. See *Understanding*, 312-17 and P. Borgen, "God's Agent in the Fourth Gospel," in Ashton (ed.), *The Interpretation*, 67-78. For J. Suggit, the equivalence between Jesus' word and scripture is explained by his status as the Logos, as understood in a circle where the language of meditation on Torah, such as that found in Ps (118)119, was referred to Jesus. See "John XVII.17: ὁ λόγος ὁ σὸς ἀλήθειά ἐστιν," *JTS* 35 (1984) 104-17.

[19] So Rudolph Schnackenburg, *The Gospel According to St John*, 3 vols., (London: Burns and Oates, 1980, 1982) I, 353; Lindars *Gospel of John*, 144.

[20] See Fortna, *The Fourth Gospel and Its Predecessor*, 126.

[21] This comes close to the Lukan idea that David did not actually write the psalms about himself, but that, since he was a prophet, what he wrote was intended to find its true expression eventually on the lips of his descendant, Jesus (Acts 2:30-

Our first task in dealing with the quotation itself is to situate it in context by noting the distinctiveness of the Johannine rendering of Jesus' action in the Temple. The placing of this event at the beginning of Jesus' ministry is unique to John, but we will see that he preserves, in his own way, the memory, recorded in the synoptics, that it led to Jesus' death. What is conspicuously absent, compared with the synoptics, is any charge of greed or corruption, of making the Father's "house of prayer" into "a den of thieves."[22] The real issue is more radical than critique of mercantile activity in the Temple area and of profiteering from religious requirements. It has to do with the obsolescence of the whole cultic structure represented by the Temple, now that the consummation of the eschatological reality present in Jesus is imminent.

The reader has already been alerted to the significance of the location by two instances of temple imagery being applied to Jesus. In him, God has pitched a tent among humankind. Jesus is the new tabernacle where the divine glory dwells and is visible—Καὶ ὁ λόγος σὰρξ ἐγένετο καὶ ἐσκήνωσεν ἐν ἡμῖν, καὶ ἐθεασάμεθα τὴν δόξαν αὐτοῦ ...(1:14).[23] In the opening sequence of the Gospel, John appears to link the idea of a vision of the heavenly Son of Man, derived from Daniel, to Jacob's dream (Gen 28:12). The precise point at which John is drawing the comparison is not clear in the text and has been the object of much speculation. At the least, John 1:51 suggests a new בית־אל, that "Jesus as Son of Man has become the locus of the divine glory, the point of contact between heaven and earth."[24]

---

31). There is, however, an important difference. Luke's rationale relies on Jesus' earthly origins, while John's hinges on the claim that Jesus, as the one sent by God, speaks the words of God (John 3:34).

[22] Cf. the composite allusion to Isa 56:7 and Jer 7:11 found in Mark 11:17, Matt 21:13 and Luke 19:46.

[23] The verb σκηνοῦν (used in the NT only here and in Rev 7:15, 12:12, 13:6 & 21:3) recalls the "tent of meeting" of the wilderness years where God's presence was localized (Exod 33:7-11) and God's glory became visible in the form of the cloud which covered it (Exod 40:34). This theophanic aspect of the tent motif overflows into the next phrase: καὶ ἐθεασάμεθα τὴν δόξαν αὐτοῦ. John's verb σκηνοῦν may also allude to Sir 24:8-10 where Wisdom pitches her tent (σκηνή) and dwells (κατασκηνοῦν) in Israel making God known through the Temple worship and the Scriptures. It may also be intended to suggest the Hebrew "Shekinah." See Brown, *John I-XII*, 34; Lindars, *Gospel of John*, 94.

[24] Brown, *John I-XII*, 90. Dodd, *The Interpretation*, 245, suggests that John probably depends on an exegesis, possible for the Hebrew text of Genesis, where the angels are on Jacob, not the ladder. For Lindars, *Gospel of John*, 121-122, the point of John's allusion to Jacob's ladder is "that Jesus is on earth, and the revelation of his glory as the Son of Man does not have to wait for his exaltation to heaven." The popular identification of the Jerusalem Temple as the site of Jacob's vision may also have been known to the Evangelist. See Jerome H. Neyrey, "Jacob Traditions and the Interpretation of John 4:10-26," *CBQ* 41 (1979) 419-37 at 428. Cf. C. Rowland,

Several OT passages dealing with purification of the Temple have been suggested as a background to the event portrayed in John 2:13-16. Jesus recalls the zealous fervour of Nehemiah (Neh 13:15-22). He fulfils Malachi's prophecy about the Lord suddenly coming into his Temple (Mal 3:1b-5). His reaction resembles that of Ezekiel to the desecration of the Temple (Ezek 8:1-18). Even the placing of this pericope at the beginning of Jesus' ministry in John may be guided by Ezekiel's vision of God's judgement being executed on Jerusalem "beginning with the sanctuary" (Ezek 9:6).[25] In view of numerous links between the Fourth Gospel and Zechariah,[26] and of the emphasis John places on the role of the traders in his narrative, it is likely that the final verse of the prophet Zechariah (Zech 14:21) may be the principal influence on John 2:16.[27] If so, Jesus' action inaugurates "that day" when there shall no longer be a trader in the house of the Lord of hosts.[28] As Lindars explains: because of the holiness which will attend the whole city when the new age dawns, special arrangements for the sanctification of sacrifices in the Temple will be unnecessary.[29] Jesus thus ushers in the final age when the holiness proper to the Temple and its officiants will be accessible to all in the Temple which, according to the Johannine author, is Jesus' body.[30]

"John 1,51, Jewish Apocalyptic and Targumic Tradition," *NTS* 30 (1984) 498-507.

[25] So, Schuchard, *Scripture Within Scripture*, 25.

[26] Zechariah provides two of John's scripture citations Μὴ φοβοῦ, θυγάτηρ Σιών... in John 12:15 and Ὄψονται εἰς ὃν ἐξεκέντησαν in John 19:37. Zech is also a significant influence on several important Johannine motifs, notably, the "living water" (John 7:37-39; cf. Zech 13:1.8), the "worthless shepherd who deserts the flock" (John 10:13; cf. Zech 11:17) and the scattering of the disciples (John 16:32; cf. Zech 13:7). For the importance of Zech to the Fourth Evangelist, see Brown, *Death of the Messiah*, 128-30.

[27] The case for Zech 14:21 is strengthened by the fact that the final verse of a biblical book, or even of a synagogue lection, was regarded as especially memorable and thus very significant. See Guilding, *The Fourth Gospel and Jewish Worship*, 22.

[28] John does not follow the LXX in rendering the כנעני of MT Zech 14:21 with χαναναῖος. Aquila has μετάβολος (Vg. *mercator*). The reading which John appears to be following is supported by Targ. Zech. In a note to his translation of Targ. Zech 14:21, R. P. Gordon refers to *b.Pes* 50a which indicates that there were circles in which כנעני was understood in the sense of "trader." Apparently this came about when the rabbis, balking at the statement in Gen 38:2 that Judah married the daughter of a Canaanite, adduced Hos 12:7 and Isa 23:8 to show that he really married the daughter of a trader. See K. J. Cathcart & R. P. Gordon (ed.), *The Targum of the Minor Prophets* (Edinburgh: T & T Clark, 1989) 226.

[29] Lindars, *The Gospel of John*, 139.

[30] Although the Fourth Evangelist is not renowned for social concern, he may have regarded the trade in the Temple as symptomatic of the denial of access "without charge" to communion with God in the Temple (cf. the Isa 55:1 background to John 7:37). Perhaps this is why the Johannine Jesus singles out the pigeon sellers. They were reinforcing social distinctions by selling the offering of the poor. As Son, Jesus wants to give all people the freedom of the Father's house (John 8:35).

John's *Vorlage* for the quotation in 2:17 appears to be the LXX of Ps 68:10—ὅτι ὁ ζῆλος τοῦ οἴκου σου κατέφαγέν με. The most obvious feature of the quotation is that the verb καταφάγεται is in the future middle voice, where one might have expected the aorist of the LXX which translates a Hebrew perfect.[31] If this is an intentional adaptation of Ps 68:10 made by the Evangelist, rather than a recollection of a particular textual tradition, this change may be the key to the function of the quotation in the narrative.[32] For the community remembering this Scripture after Jesus has been glorified (John 12:16), Ps 68:10 describes that consuming commitment to all that the Temple represented which was, in fact, to cost Jesus his life. At the level of narrative this has still to happen, so the verb points to the future. The opposition that will lead to his being devoured by death is already mobilized. The Jews demand to see his credentials. Already his trial is under way. The issue of the destruction and rebuilding of the Temple, which belongs to the trial scene in the synoptic tradition, is already being taken up within a context of conflict.[33]

We find in this modification of the verbal form of the citation an indication that the so-called "order"—story, discourse (or *histoire, récit*)—is being subverted so that the "story" is actually being produced by the "discourse," the event by the discursive forces. In the case of the Fourth Gospel, the most productive of these discursive forces is reflection on Scripture. Culpepper writes of the particular way the Fourth Gospel blends narrative memory and Scripture: "Memory provokes interpretation of Scripture, and the latter overlays memory and gives it a new focus so that the story the narrator tells us is set in a perspective no 'on the scene' reporter would have

---

For Lindars, *Gospel of John*, 133, Jesus "brings a new and better way of access to God."

[31] The suggestion has been made that a variant of LXX Ps 118:39 (ἐξέτηξέν με ὁ ζῆλος τοῦ οἴκου σου LXX Bא) may indicate John's source, but it is recognized that John may have influenced copyists of the LXX. See Freed, *Old Testament Quotations*, 9-10.

[32] According to Schuchard, *Scripture Within Scripture*, 21-22, two variant Mss (B and א) which have the aorist, most likely betray the influence of John 2:17. The two Hebrew verbs in v. 10 are both perfects and both are rendered by the aorist in the LXX. In support of this we might note that in Rom 15:3, which quotes Ps 68:10b, the second of these verbs is rendered with an aorist.

[33] As we saw in our discussion of 4Q522 (See p. 75-77 above), the issue of the (re-) building of the Temple was charged with messianic nuances. John has adapted here an element from the tradition: that the charge was made against Jesus that he would destroy and rebuild the Temple. In Juel's view, *Messiah and Temple*, 206-8, the function of the Temple charge is "that it identifies Jesus as the Messiah who will build the Temple at the end of days." The report that Jesus claimed he would destroy the Temple is false testimony, but it is also ironic in that it makes the point that with Jesus' death the old religious order comes to an end.

had."[34] As we will see, this "subversion" is particularly evident with regard to the psalm citations in the Gospel. In this first example, it is the Paraclete-inspired reflection on the part of a community, remembering and believing the Scripture after Jesus has been glorified that has led to the inclusion of the psalm quotation in John's account. The "story" requires the future tense, so it has shaped the verbal form of the citation. For the author, knowledge of the eventual consequences of Jesus' action and their victorious outcome has provoked a more figurative reading of the psalm verse. In its turn, this more figurative reading has coloured the "discourse."

Why, though, might this particular psalm verse have suggested itself?[35] If, as most commentators suggest, it points towards the death of Jesus, why is this described as a being devoured or consumed? This does not appear, at first sight, to be a characteristically Johannine way of seeing the death of Jesus. In fact, the suggestion inherent in the image that Jesus is to fall victim to a force stronger than himself is difficult to reconcile with Johannine thought.

The only NT usage of the verb κατεσθίω coming anywhere near John 2:17 in intent, (Rev 12:4, where the apocalyptic dragon stands before the woman ἵνα ὅταν τέκῃ τὸ τέκνον αὐτῆς καταφάγῃ) is not helpful. As for a ζῆλος which consumes, the NT is equally lacking in helpful parallels.[36] Turning to the LXX, we find that enemies (e.g., Ps 13:4; 78:7), worms (e.g., Deut 28:39), plagues (e.g., Ps 77:45; 104:35) and the sword (e.g., 2 Sam 2:26, Isa 31:8, Jer 2:30) can all devour. The verb κατεσθίω is frequently used, however, of fire and often of a destructive fire blazing forth from God on sinners and on Israel's enemies.[37] There is, however, another kind of divine fire

---

[34] *The Anatomy*, 29.

[35] Lindars, *Gospel of John*, 139-40, believes that it was actually the key word "house" in a psalm already quarried for quotations by several NT writers, that made it possible for John to connect the Temple scene with the "Passion" and to show how Jesus' zeal for the house of God precipitated the plot against him. This does not, however, explain the "zeal."

[36] The image is found in T. Sim 4:9, but in that context it refers to envy. The verb ἐσθίω is used figuratively in Heb 10:27 with reference to a fire about to devour enemies. The intensive form, κατεσθίω occurs in its literal sense—"eat up" or "devour"—in Mark 4:4 (cf. Matt 13:4, Luke 8:5) where the birds devour the seed on the path. See Bauer, *Greek-English Lexicon*, 422; J. P. Louw and E. Nida *Greek-English Lexicon, of the New Testament Based on Semantic Domains* (New York: United Bible Societies, 1989) I, 233. Then, by figurative extension, κατεσθίω has several other senses in the NT: The prodigal son devours his living (Luke 15:30). The scribes devour widows' houses (Mark 12:40. cf. Matt 23:13, Luke 20:47), and the feuding Christians in Galatia risk devouring each other (Gal 5:15).

[37] Dahood, *The Psalms 51-100*, 158, renders the Hebrew אכלתני of Ps 69:9, "has eaten me up." He explains: "Like a devouring flame, since 'akal in both Ugaritic

which is a manifestation of the divine good pleasure (e.g., Gen 15:7-21). A frequent sense in which the verb κατεσθίω is used is where God indicates acceptance of a sacrifice by sending down fire to consume the offering, e.g., the sacrifice of Aaron (Lev 9:24), of Solomon (2 Chr 7:1) and of Elijah (1 Kgs 18:38 cf., Sir 48:3).

The Elijah story was read at Hanukkah, recalling the lighting of the altar fires in 445 BCE (in the days of Nehemiah) and 167 BCE (by Judas Maccabeus). The fire symbolized the return of the God's glory, the restoration of the Temple and the reuniting of the scattered nation.[38] Apart from the obvious links between this liturgical *relecture* and Johannine themes, the Elijah tradition itself may also be important for our investigation. It has a key word in common with our psalm citation, the word ζῆλος. Zeal is the great characteristic of Elijah (1 Kgs 19:10, Sir 48:2). For his zeal, he found that the Israelites were "seeking (his) life to take it away" (1 Kgs 19:14). There are several indications in the Fourth Gospel that Jesus has certain Elijah-like traits.[39] In view of this, it may well be that at some stage in the process of reflection on Ps 68, which must account for its high profile in the Fourth Gospel, v. 10 carried resonances of Elijah and his costly zeal. Certainly, the contacts between the Elijah traditions and the Fourth Gospel, taken with the fact that both spatially and temporally John 2:13-22 is set in a cultic locale would suggest that the sacrificial sense of the verb κατεσθίω which we are suggesting might be the more appropriate meaning to pursue.

If this is the case, a further and more profound layer of meaning for the citation, Ὁ ζῆλος τοῦ οἴκου σου καταφάγεταί με, comes into view. As we have seen, it refers at one level to Jesus' consuming commitment and at a second level towards the death that will devour him. We posit a third and more figurative level at which it would point to the Father's acceptance of that death as a perfect sacrifice. While the sacrificial aspect may not be central to the Johannine view of Jesus' death, it is, nevertheless an important ele-

---

and Hebrew is frequently predicated of fire." For the destructive fire of God's judgement, see, e.g., Num 11:1, Ezek 23:25, Ps 20:10. The imagery occurs metaleptically in Exod 15:7 where God's wrath devours the Egyptians like stubble. To add a few examples of the LXX usage of κατεσθίω—fire comes from the Lord to devour the two sons of Aaron (Lev 10:2) and the murmurers (Num 11:1; 16:35). According to Deut 32:22, God's wrath is a consuming fire. The prophetic word of Jeremiah is a fire, while the people are the timber it is about to consume (Jer 5:14). Fire from God is a judgement on the unfaithful (Jer 17:27).

[38] For the tradition of the miraculous fire (2 Macc 1:18-36) associated with this feast, see J. C. VanderKam, "Dedication, Feast of," *ABD* II, 123-25, at 124.

[39] See J. L. Martyn, *The Gospel of John in Christian History* (New York: Paulist, 1978) 12-28. 38.

ment received from the tradition. The traces that show through, as it were, at various junctures of the Gospel indicate a definite assimilation and transformation of the idea.⁴⁰ It is our belief that the form of the psalm quotation in John 2:17 is one of the more significant of these outcroppings of sacrificial imagery.

At the dedication of the first temple, as recounted by the Chronicler, the fire from heaven that consumed the sacrifice was both a sign of God's approval and a theophany.

> When Solomon had ended his prayer, fire came down from heaven and consumed (κατέφαγε) the burnt offering and the sacrifices, and the glory of the Lord filled the temple (2 Chr 7:1).

At the meeting of the Sanhedrin (John 11:47-53) Jesus is "formally devoted to death"⁴¹ by the high priest who delivers his sentence in strikingly sacrificial terms: one man is to die for (ὑπέρ) the people.⁴² Driven by fear that the Temple might be destroyed, he decides on the destruction of Jesus. Like the consumption of the Temple dedication sacrifice by fire from heaven, the "devouring" of Jesus is a manifestation of God's presence. As Jesus consecrates himself (John 17:19), the death that consumes him is also the means by which he receives the Father's approbation (cf. John 6:27), and God's glory fills the new temple of his body. Jesus' sacrificial death is God's judgement in his favour (John 12:31), revealing his union with the Father, and thereby revealing his glory in an epiphany of the Godhead (cf. John 12:28; 17:2).⁴³ John has

---

⁴⁰ Dodd, *The Interpretation*, 437, sees sacrificial resonances in Jesus' last word, Τετέλεσται, the verb τελεῖν having a special liturgical sense "of the due performance of religious rites, such as sacrifices or initiations." He also notes the liturgical quality of the term ἁγιάζειν used of Jesus' death in 17:19, as does Schnackenburg, *The Gospel III*, 187. As evidence for the presence of a sacrificial interpretation of the death of Jesus in the Gospel, Ashton cites: the Good Shepherd laying down his life (10:11), Caiphas' prophecy (11:50-52), the saying about the grain of corn (12:24-26), Jesus' determination to "consecrate himself" (17:19) and the washing of the feet (13:1-15). See *Understanding*, 490-91. Schuchard, *Scripture Within Scripture*, 82, mentions "the sacrificial character of Jesus' anointing" (12:1-8). Menken suggests that the title ὁ ἅγιος τοῦ θεοῦ (6:69) could be connected with 10:36 and 17:19, characterizing Jesus as consecrated to death. Thus the Father sanctifies the Son, sending him to death, and the Son continues this act in sanctifying himself by his death. See "John 6, 51c-58: Eucharist or Christology?" in *Bib* 74 (1993) 1-26, at 26. B. H. Grigsby sees the Evangelist as having "conceived of an expiatory rationale, however "johannized," behind Christ's death." See "The Cross as Expiatory Sacrifice in the Fourth Gospel," *JSNT* 15 (1982) 51-80, at 52.
⁴¹ Dodd, *Interpretation*, 367.
⁴² For F. J. Matera, the sacrificial aspect is conveyed by the idea of Jesus' freely given life on behalf of others. It is expressed particularly by the use of the word ὑπέρ, e.g., in 6:51, 10:11, 11:50 and 17:19. See "'On Behalf of Others,' 'Cleansing,' and 'Return:' Johannine Images for Jesus' Death" in *LS* (1988) 161-178, at 164-69.
⁴³ Recalling our earlier discussion of the story of David's sacrifice on Arunah's

not abandoned the sacrificial aspect of the early Christian tradition regarding the death of Jesus for a gnosticising revelatory paradigm, as is sometimes said, but rather has deepened the understanding of sacrifice by giving it a context of manifestation. This is especially so *if* the Johannine title for Jesus, ὁ ἀμνὸς τοῦ θεοῦ (John 1:29.36) is intended to show that he is the lamb that God will provide for the burnt offering (cf. Gen 22:8).[44]

Psalm 68, as received by Johannine Christians, bore the superscript τῷ Δαυιδ. It comes from Book 1 of the Psalter, a collection identified as the תפלות of David the son of Jesse (Ps (71)72:20). How might the belief that this was a psalm of David have affected their hearing of the citation, Ὁ ζῆλος τοῦ οἴκου σου καταφάγεταί με? Firstly, we should recall that the first psalm quotation follows on the opening sequence of the Gospel in which a series of messianic titles have been applied to Jesus as expressions of incipient faith. The recognition (at the level of "story") of Jesus as one to whom David's words are applicable flows from this. As Menken explains:

> In all probability, then, John wants to say in 2:17 that at the cleansing of the temple the disciples reached the insight that the words of Ps 69:10a, which they took to mean that the Messiah, Son of David, is involved in a potentially fatal conflict, in fact applied to Jesus, whom they had already recognized as the Davidic Messiah.[45]

The remembering (at the level of "discourse") which grasps the full meaning of the Scripture will involve post-Easter disciples in interpreting that title in a new direction, as a subsequent psalm quotation in the Gospel will make clear.

Secondly, the Temple setting would have functioned as "a cave of resonant signification" within which the disciples could hear strong Davidic overtones. As we have seen, the Temple is David's project. It is the sign of God's goodness to David (1 Kgs 8:66). Zeal for the Temple and for the cult which it housed is the outstanding characteristic of David. He endured his many hardships that he might es-

---

threshing floor (2 Sam 24:16-25) as interpreted in 4Q522 (See p. 75-77 above) we note that the Temple Rock, the place of sacrifice, is also the place of theophany where David beheld a vision of God. Furthermore, since it was there that God had appeared threatening destruction and the threat had been averted, it was the place of judgement. The author of 4Q522, apparently aware of this last aspect, alludes several times to Ps (121)122, the psalm in which the "House of God" in Jerusalem appears as the place where "the thrones for judgement," "the thrones of the house of David" are set.

[44] In support of the suggestion that there may be an "akedah" background to this title, we recall the popular identification of the Temple site as Mount Moriah, the place of Abraham's sacrifice as mentioned in our discussion of 4Q522. See p. 76 above.

[45] Menken, *Old Testament Quotations*, 44.

tablish it (Ps [131]132:1). Since the purging and re-founding of the Temple is part of the scenario for a future ideal king like David,[46] maybe even the word οἶκος in the citation might have reminded them of Nathan's oracle (2 Sam 7:11) and of the word-play on "house" as both Temple and dynasty. Certainly for Johannine readers, the psalm citation would have been a hint to the solution of the riddle posed by Jesus' enigmatic words justifying his action in the Temple, Λύσατε τὸν ναὸν τοῦτον καὶ ἐν τρισὶν ἡμέραις ἐγερῶ αὐτόν (John 2:19). If the words of a psalm of David are fulfilled on the lips of Jesus, then there is a suggestion that David as Temple builder/founder is also prophetic of Jesus. As our study unfolds, we will discover the fuller implications of this hint.

Apart from the actual quotation, resonances of the wider psalm context can be detected in the Gospel. For example, in the lines directly preceding the quoted line, the psalmist laments that he has become a stranger to his brothers and an alien to his mother's sons (Ps 68:9). The Evangelist has just noted in 2:12, immediately preceding the Temple scene, that Jesus has been with his mother and brothers in Capernaum. It appears that he leaves them to go to Jerusalem. This is a strong resonance, textually in close proximity to the actual citation.[47] At a further remove (7:5), we read that Jesus does actually become a stranger to his brothers because of their unbelief, οὐδὲ γὰρ οἱ ἀδελφοὶ αὐτοῦ ἐπίστευον εἰς αὐτόν, a fainter resonance, but equally suggestive of a special intertextual relationship between Ps 68 and the Fourth Gospel. In fact, these echoes of the psalm touch on an issue by no means peripheral to Johannine thought, that of how the new "family" of Jesus is formed at his "lifting up," when the grain is no longer alone as the community of believers is created.[48] The sug-

---

[46] See our discussion of PsSol 17-18 on p. 97-98 above. We might also recall that this association of a new David with the building of the Temple is evident in Mark 14:61, where a claim by Jesus that he would rebuild the Temple prompts the high priest to ask him if he is the Christ. As James D. G. Dunn notes, "it was precisely this association of ideas which the messianic prophecy (4QFlor 1:10-13) of 2 Sam 7:13-14 would suggest—the son of David (royal messiah) who would build the temple and who would be God's son." See "Messianic Ideas and their Influence on the Jesus of History" in Charlesworth (ed.), *The Messiah*, 365-81, at 373.

[47] Brown, *John I-XII*, 123-24.

[48] See Meeks, *Man from Heaven*, 157. As Brown has shown, *Death of the Messiah*, II, 1025, the two scenes where the mother of Jesus appears represent a Johannine equivalent to the synoptic texts dealing with the issue of how Jesus' natural family was related to the new family created through discipleship. At Cana the mother learns that she has no claim on Jesus arising from fleshly ties. Only considerations related to the "hour" can set Jesus' *agendum* (John 2:3-5). On Golgotha the natural brothers who do not become disciples are replaced by the beloved disciple who by becoming her son, becomes Jesus' brother.

gestion that Ps 68:9 has contributed to the elaboration of this motif is supported by the fact that there are possibly two further quotations from the psalm in the Gospel. One of them, as we will discover, is closely connected with the Golgotha scene. Even from what we have seen so far, it is evident that the actual verbal citation from the text of the psalm, the "fundamental note," receives its particular timbre from the resonances it stimulates in the wider context of the psalm. When these "overtones" are raised to audibility, the psalm's influence or presence can be discerned, even at moments when none of its words is actually "spoken."

In summary, Ps 68:10 is to be viewed from a twofold temporal perspective. It is, to use Mark W. Stibbe's metaphor, the "filter" through which the event in the Temple is first remembered and later understood.[49] The narrative setting of the citation illustrates the Fourth Evangelist's penchant for equating the word of Jesus with the word of Scripture. The citation occurs in a distinctively Johannine setting against a theologically rich background of OT allusion to the Temple and its purification. Its particular textual form lays it open to figurative interpretation: the use of the future tense allowing it to point to Jesus' death, and the metaphorical connotations of the verb κατεσθίω suggesting an interpretation of that death as sacrifice, as divine approbation of Jesus and as manifestation of God's glory. Thus we are told by means of this programmatic Scripture not merely "that Jesus' end is both inevitable and acceptable,"[50] but that it is to be an awesomely revelatory moment. The Temple atmosphere of the whole pericope, suggests that the psalm's Davidic "authorship" would have been significant for Johannine Christians. If, as E. P. Sanders has proposed, this pericope is, at its most basic level, "an interpretation of the memory that Jesus predicted or threatened the destruction of the Temple," then David, as remembered and as expected, necessarily surfaces.[51]

The presence of Psalm 68 in the Gospel is by no means confined to explicit citation; John 2:17 is one of three occasions when a psalm that frequently functions subliminally is momentarily brought to the surface of the text. On this occasion the psalm underlines two aspects of the meaning of Jesus' action in the Temple which are defining features of Johannine Christology. Firstly, Jesus is the sacrificial victim, so "in his presence sheep and oxen are superfluous."[52] Secondly, the

---

[49] Mark W. Stibbe, *John* (Sheffield: JSOT Press, 1993) 51.
[50] Fortna, *The Fourth Gospel and Its Predecessor*, 267.
[51] E. P. Sanders, *Jesus and Judaism* (London: SCM, 1985) 72.
[52] See J. Duncan M. Derrett, "The Zeal of the House and the Cleansing of the Temple," *DRev* 95 (1977) 79-94 at 90.

"hour" of his self-offering to which the psalm quotation points is the great moment of revelation, when Jesus will become "the place where God can be encountered in a new and never-to-be destroyed Temple."[53] The psalm citation thus fulfils an important role in the Gospel's articulation of the Johannine church's belief.

C. *Psalm (77)78:24 in John 6:31*

Our second psalm citation occurs in Dodd's "Episode 3, The Bread of Life." It is connected with the one miracle of Jesus recorded in all four gospels, the feeding of the five thousand. John 6:31 contains the first of two OT citations which are unparalleled in the other gospel accounts of the feeding.[54] Having eaten their fill, the people recall the manna miracle as recounted in Scripture and demand that Jesus impress them with an equally compelling sign which will persuade them to believe in him:

> οἱ πατέρες ἡμῶν τὸ μάννα ἔφαγον ἐν τῇ ἐρήμῳ, καθώς ἐστιν γεγραμμένον, Ἄρτον ἐκ τοῦ οὐρανοῦ ἔδωκεν αὐτοῖς φαγεῖν.
>
> Our fathers ate the manna in the wilderness; as it is written, "He gave them bread from heaven to eat."

Of course, the reader who is aware of the biblical tradition foresees the outcome: these people will no more believe as a result of this sign than their fathers did as a result of the manna miracle.

The introductory formula for the quotation is unique in that, with characteristic irony, the narrator puts the Scripture on the lips of people who do not actually regard it as having any application to Jesus. All the other OT quotations in the Fourth Gospel, whether spoken by Jesus or by the narrator, represent the perspective of faith. From the narrative point of view, this quotation from Ps 77 is a challenge hurled at Jesus, from the standpoint of unbelief. A demand for a sign is a characteristic indication of unbelief in the Fourth Gospel (See John

---

[53] F. J. Moloney, "Reading John 2:13-22; The Purification of the Temple," *RB* 97 (1990) 432-51, at 450.

[54] The other is the quotation in John 6:45, Καὶ ἔσονται πάντες διδακτοὶ θεοῦ. There is no unanimity about the source of this quotation. It is most usually attributed to Isa 54:13, though sometimes Jer 31:33-34 is adduced as either source or contributor to a composite citation of both texts. Other texts about God's eschatological teaching which are suggested as part of a composite source are Jer 24:7, Joel 2:27 and Hab 2:14. No known version of the LXX adequately explains the textual form of the citation which is most probably attributable to Johannine redaction. See Menken, *Old Testament Quotations*, 67-78. Menken's chapter on the quotation in John 6:45 was originally published as "The Old Testament Quotation in John 6,45," *ETL* 64 (1988) 164-72.

2:18; 4:48). However, as so often happens in the Fourth Gospel, the spoken word can have a sense unsuspected by those who utter it.[55]

In order to situate the quotation in its context, we need first to define our approach to the "Bread of Life Discourse."[56] Clearly Jesus is portrayed in John 6 as using language evoking the wisdom literature in which the metaphor of eating and drinking refers to the acquiring of wisdom from God. There may also be reference to the eucharist, although this is not universally accepted.[57] Some think the eucharistic theme is secondary in the more "sapiential" section (vv. 26-51b) and comes to the fore in vv. 51c-58,[58] a passage which is sometimes identified as a redactional unit of teaching on the eucharist.[59] Others discern a metaphorical use of eucharistic terminology throughout a homogeneous sapiential discourse.[60] The general consensus is that the intent of the whole discourse is Christological, with, at the least, eucharistic undertones.[61]

---

[55] Meeks, *The Man from Heaven*, 152, notes: "The irony in vv. 30-31 is very heavy, for precisely the "sign" which they request—one analogous to the manna which Moses gave—has already been provided for the "men who saw" (v. 14)...The irony is now carried yet farther by the identification of the "bread from heaven" not with the bread of the miracle but with the Son of Man."

[56] The literature on John 6 from 1900 to 1994 has been collated and summarized in several articles by Michel Roberge to which I am indebted for my own summary of the *status quaestionis*—"Le discours sur le pain de vie: Jean 6, 22-59," *LTP*, 38 (1982) 265-99; "La composition de Jean 6, 22-59 dans l'exégèse recente," *LTP* 40 (1984) 91-123; "La Composition de Jean 6, 25b-34," *LTP* 50 (1994) 171-186.

[57] Hugo Odeberg regards hearing the discourse eucharistically as comparable to Nicodemus' mistake (John 3:1-15). See *The Fourth Gospel Interpreted in its Relation to Contemporary Religious Currents and the Hellenistic-Oriental World* (Amsterdam: B. R. Grüner, 1968) 239.

[58] E.g., Brown, *John I-XII*, 272-75 and 284-85. Lindars believes that "the eucharistic interpretation is latent beneath the sapiential section (35-50) and the sapiential continues without any diminution in the eucharistic section (51-58)." See *The Gospel of John*, 251 and "Word and Sacrament in the Fourth Gospel," *SJT* 29 (1976) 49-63, at 60.

[59] According to Bultmann, vv. 51c-58 are a secondary eucharistic interpretation of the Bread of Life "employing the language and style of the foregoing discussion." See *The Gospel of John*, 234. Among those who regard both sections as Johannine, some suggest that they reflect different stages of theological development within the Johannine circle, e.g., M.-É. Boismard and A. Lamouille, with the collaboration of G. Rochais, *L'Évangile de Jean*, Vol. III of *Synopse des quatre évangiles en français* (Paris: Les Éditions du Cerf, 1977) 204-05.

[60] E.g., Dodd, *The Interpretation*, 335, and Barrett, *The Gospel*, 283-84. Dunn, "John VI—A Eucharistic Discourse?" *NTS* 17 (1970-71) 328-38, at 331-33, sees the eating and drinking as a metaphor for the reception of the Spirit. De Jonge, *Stranger from Heaven*, 208, believes vv. 51c-58 use eucharistic terminology to define the unity between believers and Jesus. For John Painter, the shift at v. 51c is not from sapiential to eucharistic terminology, but from "belief in the person of Jesus as the emissary of God...to belief in the saving efficacy of his death." See his "Tradition and Interpretation in John 6" *NTS* 35 (1989) 421-50, at 444-45.

[61] Menken makes the helpful suggestion that the so-called eucharistic language in

The Scripture quoted in John 6:31 is most likely Ps 77:24—

καὶ ἔβρεξεν αὐτοῖς μαννα φαγεῖν
καὶ ἄρτον οὐρανοῦ ἔδωκεν αὐτοῖς.

The other major "contender" is Exod 16:4,15.[62] A strong argument for the psalm as source is the fact that nowhere else in the OT is דגן rendered by ἄρτος rather than the usual σῖτος.[63] In support of Ps 77:24, Freed also notes that the whole psalm verse combines the words manna and bread, both of which John needs for his argument.[64] Also in favour of Ps 77:24 as the primary source, we note that in the extant biblical *relecture* of the late Second Temple period, there are several examples of Pentateuchal stories being recalled *via* their poetic recital in the psalms.[65]

The impetus for the φαγεῖν in the quotation may have been provided by Exod 16:15, but it could also come from the first line of the parallel pair in the psalm.[66] While Ps 77 has ἄρτον οὐρανοῦ the Fourth Gospel quotation has ἄρτον ἐκ τοῦ οὐρανοῦ. There is the possibility that the psalm quotation may be coloured at this point by a recollection of Exod 16:4 where the phrase ἐκ τοῦ οὐρανοῦ occurs with reference to the manna. Another explanation of the ἐκ could be that Ps 77:26 was influential: ἀπῆρεν νότον ἐξ οὐρανοῦ, said with reference to the gift of the quails.[67] Neh 9:15 might also be an influence: Καὶ ἄρτον ἐξ οὐρανοῦ ἔδωκας αὐτοις εἰς σιτοδοτίαν αὐτῶν.[68]

John 6 might best be understood on the analogy of Ignatius of Antioch's description of his expected martyrdom as eucharistic communion with Christ (See *IgRom* 7.3). For Menken, Ignatius' text is "comparable to the way the Fourth Evangelist uses eucharistic language to make Christological statements." See "John 6, 51c-58," 8.

[62] See Borgen, *Bread from Heaven*, 40-41; Reim, *Studien*, 13-14.

[63] See Menken, *Old Testament Quotations*, 49. Menken's chapter on the quotation in John 6:31 was originally published as "The Provenance and Meaning of the Old Testament Quotation in John 6:31," *NovT* 30 (1988) 39-56.

[64] Freed, *Old Testament Quotations*, 15.

[65] There may even be an example in Ps-Philo of the manna story being remembered as told in Ps 77:24. The words, *pluit illis de celo panem*...(Cf. *LAB* X, 7) appear closer to Ps (77)78:24—

"...and he rained down upon them manna to eat
and gave them the grain of heaven."

—than to the Pentateuchal account (Exod 16:4). However, in the absence of the original Hebrew, we cannot claim certainty. We will see in the discussion of our next quotation that John also recalls the story of the water-flowing rock in the Ps 77 re-telling.

[66] There is a similar conflation of synonymously parallel lines in the quotation of Isa 40:3 in John 1:23. Menken, *Old Testament Quotations*, 52-53, refers to the rabbinical rule (the 22nd of the 32 *middot* of R. Eliezer b. Jose ha-Gelili) which allows an exegete to supply what is missing in one line from its parallel line. Menken adduces evidence that this rule was in use in the 2nd century CE.

[67] Menken, *Old Testament Quotations*, 52.

[68] Arguing for the influence of Neh 9:20 on John 6:31, Barrett, *The Gospel*, 239,

Whatever its source, whether the influence of other "Scriptures" or simply Johannine redaction, the Fourth Gospel's slight departure from the psalm text is telling. To suit the author's purpose, the Scripture should speak not just of "bread of heaven," but of "bread which comes down from/out of heaven." As John 6:33 explains—ὁ γὰρ ἄρτος τοῦ θεοῦ ἐστιν ὁ καταβαίνων ἐκ τοῦ οὐρανοῦ.[69] The psalm quotation is thus fortified with the Johannine "ἐκ of origin" referring to the source of Jesus' being and life (John 1:1-5). It is thus enabled to carry a precise connotation: Jesus is ἐκ τῶν ἄνω (8:23). He has issued ἐκ τοῦ θεου (8:42) and has come down into the world.[70]

When we come to assess the contribution of the quotation to the unfolding of the Bread of Life Discourse, we are confronted with an array of theories concerning the composition of John 6. Our view of the quotation's role will depend largely on which theory we decide to follow. Roberge comments on his extensive review of 20th century research into this aspect: "on retrouve presque autant de plans que d'auteurs."[71] The approaches to the problem tend to follow two major trends: analysis according to thematic structures[72] and analysis based on what is known of Jewish liturgical preaching.[73] The most fruitful compositional analyses for the purposes of this study have proved to be those taking a homiletic interpretation of the discourse as a basis.

The discourse in John 6 is presented by the Evangelist as Jesus' teaching in the synagogue (John 6:59). This has led many commentators to analyse its structure with reference to Jewish homiletic forms. The whole Bread of Life discourse has been convincingly explained as an extended exegesis of the quotation in the form of a dialogue.[74] Although various proposals have been made concerning

---

notes that it brings together three Johannine terms: spirit, manna and water. For another example of a possible instance of Nehemiah's influence on the Fourth Gospel, cf. the mention of the Sheep Gate in John 5:2 in the context of controversy about Sabbath breaking with Neh 13:19.

[69] Schnackenburg *The Gospel I*, 122. Cf. John 6:38, 41-42, 50-51, 58.

[70] Dodd, *The Interpretation*, 259-60.

[71] "La composition de Jean 6, 22-59," 91.

[72] Brown, *John I-XII*, 287-89; Lindars, *The Gospel*, 231-70; Schnackenburg, *The Gospel II*, 31-32; X. Léon-Dufour, "Trois chiasmes johanniques," *NTS* 7 (1960-61), 249-55. Roberge himself regards vv. 30-31 as the centre point of 'un dialogue dont les étapes conduisent à la déclaration solenelle: "Je suis le pain de vie" (v. 35a).' The first part of this dialogue (vv. 26-29, dealing with the gift) is elaborated in vv. 48-58 of the discourse. The second part (vv. 30-33, dealing with the giver), in vv. 36-47. See "La composition de Jean 6, 25b-34," 171, 177, 184-85.

[73] Notably, Borgen, *Bread from Heaven*.

[74] See Severino Pancaro, *The Law in the Fourth Gospel: The Torah and the Gospel, Moses and Jesus, Judaism and Christianity According to John* (Leiden: Brill, 1975) 462.

the structure of this exposition,[75] it is agreed that the elaboration of the psalm quotation proceeds by the accepted methods of early Jewish hermeneutic, in particular by allusion to analogous Scripture passages. Apart from the manna background, there is, of course, in John 6 intertextual reference across a wide spectrum of the Jewish Scriptures, notably the Wisdom literature and Isaiah.[76] The input of the Psalter too is not limited to the verse formally cited. Snatches from elsewhere in the complete *Opus* of David, in particular from Pss 21, 22, 71 and 105, can be caught throughout. The effect that all these biblical resonances create is a remarkably polytextual recital of the quotation, Ἄρτον ἐκ τοῦ οὐρανοῦ ἔδωκεν αὐτοῖς φαγεῖν.

The belief that the structure of the entire discourse is homiletic has, in its turn, affected the assignment of a source for the quotation. Thus, while admitting that Ps 77:24 has had an impact on the formulation, Borgen favours as primary source a "pericopal" text that would have been the subject of a synagogue homily, that is, a Pentateuchal passage. He is concerned to demonstrate that the whole discourse follows the structure of a synagogue liturgy in which Exod 16 is the *seder* and Isa 54, quoted in John 6:45, is the *haftarah*. He thus concludes that John 6:31 contains not a psalm quotation but rather an echo of the whole manna pericope in an allusion to Exod 16:4-5 coloured by Ps (77)78:24. There is, however, as we have seen, another form of homily, the *petihtah* homily. In this, a "proemial" text from the Prophets or the Hagiographa, chosen to throw light on the Pentateuchal pericope of the day, opens the exposition.[77] Ps 77:24 could be such an opening text, especially since there appears to be a reprise of it at the end of the homily (cf. John 6:58).[78]

Turning now to the meaning of the psalm quotation in its Johannine context, we find that Jesus' reply to the quotation takes up the

---

[75] Borgen, *Bread from Heaven*, 28-68, especially 61-65, has discerned two sections: vv. 32-48 paraphrasing Ἄρτον ἐκ τοῦ οὐρανοῦ ἔδωκεν αὐτοῖς, and vv. 49-57 paraphrasing φαγεῖν. He also mentions a variant of this theory, that the dialogue falls into three sections: vv. 32-40 elaborating on ἄρτον..... ἔδωκεν, vv. 41-51 on ἐκ τοῦ οὐρανοῦ, and vv. 52-58 on φαγεῖν. The twofold division was earlier proposed by E. J. Kilmartin in his "The Formation of the Bread of Life Discourse (John 6)," *Scr* 12 (1960), 75-78. Kilmartin also suggested an influence on the composition of the ritual questions at the Passover Meal. See his "Liturgical Influence on John 6," *CBQ* 22 (1960) 183-91. Alternatively, Meeks, *The Man from Heaven*, 152, suggests that the two scripture citations in vv. 31 and 45 organize the discourse.

[76] E.g., Sir 24:19-21; Prov 9:5: Isa 25:6; 54:13 (quoted in John 6:45); 55:2.

[77] See Borgen, *Bread from Heaven*, 53-54.

[78] This is the suggestion of A. Finkel, *The Pharisees and the Teacher of Nazareth* (Leiden: E. J. Brill, 1964) 149-59.

crowd's reference to the manna story: Ἀμὴν ἀμὴν λέγω ὑμῖν, οὐ Μωϋσῆς δέδωκεν ὑμῖν τὸν ἄρτον ἐκ τοῦ οὐρανοῦ, ἀλλ' ὁ πατήρ μου δίδωσιν ὑμῖν τὸν ἄρτον ἐκ τοῦ οὐρανοῦ τὸν ἀληθινόν. It is generally agreed that there is a contrast here between Moses and Jesus. There are, however, varying views on the actual point of comparison.[79] Meeks, for example, italicises for emphasis the word "Moses" in his translation of this verse.[80] Roberge envisages Jesus' reply as contrasting Moses who gave in the past and the Father who is giving the bread now.[81] For Menken, the contrast should be understood along the lines of other contrasts in the Gospel drawn between great figures from Israel's past—Jacob (4:12), Abraham (8:53).

> Jesus' claim to be the Son of Man, giver of abiding food, implies that he is greater than Moses, who gave the manna, and such a claim should be substantiated by means of a sign. The remark in 6,31 is tantamount to the question: "Are you greater than Moses, who gave our fathers the bread from heaven to eat?", and, just as in the parallels adduced, a negative answer is expected.[82]

Although it is not expressly stated, the crowd evidently envisages Moses as the subject of the verb ἔδωκεν in the quotation. Menken remarks that the psalm lends itself to such a reading, because the subject (God or Moses?) is not specified. He notes that taking advantage of a syntactic feature such as a pronoun whose referent is not immediately clear is a common exegetical technique of the period.[83] This reading is in conflict with all the biblical accounts of the manna where God is the giver of the manna. It seems, however, to be compatible with views of Moses current among Jews in the milieu of the Fourth Evangelist. It could even be that the psalm itself suggested

---

[79] The difficulty in pinpointing the actual contrast is shown by Pancaro, *The Law in the Fourth Gospel*, 462.

[80] "It is not *Moses* who gave you the bread from heaven, but my father is giving you the real bread from heaven." See *The Prophet-King*, 91-2.

[81] "Le Père qui donne, opposé à Moïse qui a donné." See "La Composition de Jean 6," 178.

[82] Menken, "Some Remarks on the Course of the Dialogue: John 6,25-34," *Bijdr* 48 (1987) 139-49, at 145-46. Schuchard, on the other hand, seems perplexed that neither in the psalm nor in the OT is Moses ever regarded as performer of the manna miracle. He believes that by identifying himself as the given, Jesus is ruling out any hope in himself as a second Moses. See *Scripture Within Scripture*, 41-44.

[83] This is one of the indications which convince Menken that the quotation is from Ps 77:24. See *Old Testament Quotations*, 63-64. Subsequently he writes *re* John 19:37: "We have an example in John 6:31 where Moses, not God, is supposed to be the subject of Ps 78[77]:24b and thus the giver of the manna (see the correction in 6:32); there are other examples of this exegetical device." See *Old Testament Quotations*, 178. Menken's chapter on the quotation in John 19:37 was originally published as "The Textual Form and Meaning of the Quotation from Zech 12:10 in John 19:37," *CBQ* 55 (1993) 494-511.

this to the Evangelist as in vv. 15-16 God is depicted as striking the rock, whereas in the Pentateuchal accounts it is actually Moses who does so.

Jesus' response to the psalm quotation appears to be a correction of current interpretations of the manna story on three scores.[84]

The crowd	Jesus
Μωϋσῆς (i.e., their presupposition)	ὁ πατήρ μου
ἔδωκεν	δίδωσιν
Ἄρτον ἐκ τοῦ οὐρανοῦ	τὸν ἄρτον ἐκ τοῦ οὐρανοῦ τὸν ἀληθινόν·

Thus Jesus' counters the crowd's claim that Moses gave the bread from heaven with his revelation that his Father is (now) giving the true bread from heaven. This reading fits well with the general tendency in the Fourth Gospel to counter a Jewish piety in which Moses had a central position, even to the point of being divinized.[85]

The full *parallelismus membrorum* of Ps 77:24 and the continuation in v. 25 throw considerable light on John's quotation:

καὶ ἔβρεξεν αὐτοῖς μαννα φαγεῖν
καὶ ἄρτον οὐρανοῦ ἔδωκεν αὐτοῖς·
ἄρτον ἀγγέλων ἔφαγεν ἄνθρωπος...

We have already noted Freed's point that the whole psalm verse combines the words manna and bread, both of which John needs for his argument.[86] The Targum of these lines may well preserve an interpretive tradition which contributed to John 6—

---

[84] Jewish views of Moses and of the manna miracle which the Evangelist seems to be representing and possibly correcting here can be detected in the writings of Philo. There is, for example, the idea that in saying "Stand here with me," to Moses (Deut 5:31), God invites him to share the divinity (*Sacr.* 8; *Post.* 28; *Gig.* 49). The idea is even more explicit in Philo's reading of Exod 7:1, "See, I have made you a god to Pharaoh" (*Somn.* 2, 189; *Sacr.* 9; *Mos.* 1, 158). While Philo stops short of saying that Moses actually gave the manna, the view of Moses as in some sense divine to which he attests would have made such a belief a logical supposition. See Borgen, "Some Jewish Exegetical Traditions as Background for Son of Man Sayings in John's Gospel (Jn 3, 13-14 and context)," in M. de Jonge (ed.) *L'Évangile de Jean: Sources, rédaction, théologie* (Leuven: Gembloux/ Leuven University Press, 1977) 243-258, at 243-48; Meeks, *The Prophet King*, 100-31, and "Moses as God and King," in J. Neusner (ed.), *Religions in Antiquity: Essays in Memory of E. R. Goodenough* (Leiden: Brill, 1968) 354-71.

[85] For direct references to Moses, see John 5:45; 9:28-29. For possible Johannine ripostes to Jewish beliefs that Moses ascended into heaven and saw God (attested in Philo *Mos.* 1, 158, Josephus, *Ant.* 3, 88.96 and Ps-Philo *LAB* 12,1) see John 1:18; 3:13; 6:46.

[86] Freed, *Old Testament Quotations*, 15.

Et descendere fecit super illos manna ut manducarent
et triticum caeli dedit eis.
<u>Cibum qui descendit</u> de habitaculo angelorum comederunt homines.

Both MT and LXX of Ps (77)78 refer to the manna being "rained down," as does Exod 16:4. By developing the idea of the manna "coming down," probably attributable to Num 11:9 and influenced by the "descent of Wisdom" background (cf. Wis 9:10; Bar 3:36-4:4; Sir 24:7-22), the tradition preserved in the Targum opens the way for a personification of the bread such as that found in John 6:33—ὁ γὰρ ἄρτος τοῦ θεοῦ ἐστιν ὁ καταβαίνων ἐκ τοῦ οὐρανοῦ καὶ ζωὴν διδοὺς τῷ κόσμῳ.[87]

We come now to ask whether this quotation and the psalm from which it is taken have any particular connection with David. Firstly we should note that this quotation functions quite differently to that from Ps (68)69 in John 2:17 which would readily have been received as an utterance of David. Ps (77)78:24 functions in John 6:31 as a word from Scripture. We must, therefore, ask, if its perceived provenance—the Psalms of David—would have had any impact on its reception within the Johannine circle.

In Second Temple Judaism, the end time, in which a David-like figure would play an important part, was envisaged as a new Exodus. This line of thought can be traced back to the "Latter Prophets."[88] As it was progressively elaborated, it created the expectation that at the close of the age, the manna would fall again. The earliest extant evidence we have for this belief is a passage in 2 Bar dating from the early 2nd century CE—"And it will happen at that time that the treasury of manna will come down again from on high, and they will eat of it in those years because these are they who will have arrived at the consummation of time."[89] A further example post-dates even further the NT period. We quote this passage at some length, nevertheless, as it contains several parallels between Moses and the Messiah which, judging by their similarity to early Christian appeals to Scripture, appear to reflect quite old traditions:

> As the first redeemer was, so shall the latter Redeemer be. What is stated of the former redeemer? And Moses took his wife and his sons, and set them upon an ass (Ex. IV,20). Similarly will it be with the lat-

---

[87] It is possible that Ps 71:6—

> May he be like rain that falls on the mown grass,
> like showers that water the earth.

—has also contributed to this development.

[88] See our earlier discussion of Isa 11-12, p. 71 above.

[89] 2 Bar 29:8. See A. F. J. Klijn, "2 (Syriac Apocalypse of) Baruch: A New Translation and Introduction" in Charlesworth (ed.), *OTP* I, 615-52, at 631.

ter Redeemer, as it is stated, Lowly and riding upon an ass (Zech. IX, 9). As the former redeemer caused manna to descend, as it is stated, Behold, I will cause to rain bread from heaven for you (Ex. XVI,4), so will the latter Redeemer cause manna to descend, as it is stated, May he be as a rich cornfield in the land (Ps. 72:16). As the former redeemer made a well to rise, so will the latter Redeemer bring up water, As it is stated, And a fountain shall come forth of the house of the Lord, and shall water the valley of Shittim. (Joel IV,18).[90]

Which direction the influence worked, we do not know. We certainly cannot ignore the possibility of Christian (or even Johannine) influence on a Jewish text. However, the passage is extremely valuable for several reasons. It portrays a Messiah who does Moses-like deeds, but who, in some sense, replaces Moses. That this "latter Redeemer" is envisaged as "my servant David (who) shall feed them and be their shepherd" (cf. Ezek 34:23) is clear from the use of Ps 72, the conclusion of Book 1 of the Psalter, the תפלות of David. Actually, it is the possible influence of the Fourth Gospel which makes this text so significant for us. It would then attest to a reading of the Fourth Gospel which understood the Evangelist's project accurately: an authentication of the concrete experience of Jewish Christians, that faith in Jesus the Messiah had replaced devotion to Moses.

In view of the Passover time frame (John 6:4), it is also important to remember that the interpretation of the Passover meal involved an eschatological *relecture* of the manna story in terms of the "Messianic Banquet." In the Midrash on the Song of Songs (1:18) there is a comment on the unleavened bread of Passover attributed to R. Eliezer ben Hyrcanus (fl. c. 90 CE). R. Eliezer represents God as saying, "From this (sc. the unleavened bread) you may learn what I shall do for them subsequently in the End, and so it is written, 'There shall be abundance of corn in the land' (Ps 72.16)."[91] Note that this is a quotation from a psalm received in Second Temple Judaism as David's prayer for Solomon as he ascends the throne.[92]

Finally, with reference to David, an important motif connected with the Messianic Banquet theme is the idea of eating sacred food

---

[90] This saying is attributed to R. Isaac , fl. 3rd cent. CE. See *Qoh. Rab.* 1, 9, 1[23] trans. A. Cohen in H. Freedman and M. Simon (ed.) *The Midrash Rabbah, Translated into English*, 9 vols (London: Soncino Press, 1939, 1977), Vol. 8, 33. Also, according to the Sibylline Oracles, parts of which may date back to the 2nd cent. CE, the people of the age to come will eat "the dewy manna." See *Sib. Or.* 7, Charlesworth (ed.), *OTP* I, 148-49.

[91] Quoted by Joachim Jeremias in: *The Eucharistic Words of Jesus* (London: SCM, 1966) 59.

[92] See p. 82 above.

which confers life. In the biblical tradition, this motif finds its most familiar expression in the image of the "Tree of Life."[93] In the Second Temple, the "Tree of Life" was represented by the *menorah*, a lampstand in the form of a stylized tree, standing in an architectural space designed on the "model" of Paradise.[94] In earlier traditions, the *menorah* was the royal "lamp" symbolizing the continuation of the dynasty which was believed to assure God's presence with Israel.[95] In later writings, the "Tree of Life" would come to be identified with Wisdom (Prov 3:18) and with *Torah* (Sir 24:12-22)[96] The attributes of David, as listed in 11QPs^aDavComp ("wise," "a light," "literate," "discerning" and "perfect in all his ways"), would suggest that he was remembered as "a light" in line with this particular development of the "Tree of Life" motif. By the NT period, the "light" aspect of the *Menorah* seems to have become paramount with the "tree" aspect reduced to a relatively vestigial status.[97] Nevertheless, an appreciation of how David can, in some sense, be a "tree" which is at the same time a "light" can, perhaps, contribute something to our understanding of how the Johannine Jesus is both Light (John 8:12) and Vine (John 15:1).[98]

---

[93] See D. E. Smith, "Messianic Banquet," *ABD*, Vol. 4, 788-91, at 788.

[94] In the longer recension of 2 Enoch (first century CE) the author describes a great tree in Paradise which was "gold-looking and crimson with the form of fire" (2 En 8:4). The shorter recension of this passage refers to "another tree near it, an olive, flowing with oil continually," thus suggesting an identification of this burning "Tree of Life" with the *menorah* described in Zech 4:12. See "2 (Slavonic Apocalypse of) Enoch" translated by F. I. Anderson in Charlesworth (ed.), *OTP*, I, 91-221. A similar association of the menorah with the Tree of life is found in Philo's *Quaest Gen* 1.10, where he applies the same astronomical symbolism to both. For early Christian iconographical examples where the images of tree and lamp are combined, see L. Yarden, *The Tree of Light*, (London: Horovitz, 1971) 20.

[95] In biblical tradition David's royal house is represented as a tree out of which a "Branch" is to grow (Isa 4:2; 11:1; Zech 3:8; 6:12, Jer 23:5; 33:15). Note too that even the ancient parable about monarchy in Judges 9 is a story about trees. See Barker, The *Gate of Heaven*, 94.

[96] Ben Sira's Wisdom compares herself to a tree, planted in the Temple, possessing the most delightful feature of every tree on earth, and bearing sweet fruit which all are invited to taste. The strong likelihood of an intertextual relationship between Wisdom's invitation in Sir 24:21 and Jesus' words in John 6:35 should be borne in mind.

[97] See Carol L. Meyers, *The Tabernacle Menorah: A Synthetic Study of a Symbol from the Biblical Cult* (Missoula, Montana: Scholars, 1976) 95-202.

[98] See Barker, *The Gate of Heaven*, 95. In Sir 24, Wisdom as "Tree of Life" possesses the attributes of the cedar, cypress, palm, rose, olive, plane, cassia, myrrh, terebinth and grape vine. Yarden, *The Tree of Light*, 40, writes, concerning the *menorah*, that "Late Jewish tradition and the art of succeeding ages think of it as a vine (thus presumably the golden vine in the Temple) palm or other tree. " See also the portrayal of Jesus in arborescent terms found in early Syriac hymnody (e.g., Ephraim's *De Ecclesia*), as described by R. Murray in his *Symbols of Church and*

In view of this clustering around the figure of David of several images eventually applied to Jesus by the Fourth Evangelist, it seems no coincidence that the Bread of Life Discourse alludes several times to the Tree of Life story in Genesis.

Gen 3:3	John 6:50
You shall not eat of the fruit of the tree...lest you die.	...that a man may eat of it and not die.
Gen 3:22	John 6:51
...lest he...take also of the tree of life, and eat, and live for ever...	...if anyone eats of this bread, he will live for ever.
Gen 3:24	John 6:37
...he drove out the man...	...and him who comes to me I will not cast out.

In the Johannine perspective, the believer who eats the bread of life obtains the eternal life denied to humankind when they were barred from access to the Tree of Life (Gen 3:22.24).[99] If, as these Johannine echoes of Genesis suggest, the Bread of Life, the revelation that Jesus brings, is comparable to the eternal life bestowed by the Tree of Life, then we might think of the identification of the tree with Wisdom and Torah and the connection of this image with David through his association with wisdom and through the biblical use of arborescent imagery to symbolize his royal line.

All of this has implications for our reading of the quotation in John 6:31. In the Fourth Gospel, the people react to the feeding sign by attempting to make Jesus king (John 6:15). In view of the reference to "the prophet" in v. 14 and the prominence of Moses generally in John 6, most commentators explain this in terms of the view of Moses as king which developed in Hellenistic Judaism, with the corollary that Jesus is the "prophet-like-Moses."[100] Valid though this may be, it should not be allowed to eclipse a more obvious and far more directly biblical explanation in terms of David as king with the corollary that Jesus is the Christ.[101] Within the world of the narra-

---

Kingdom: A Study in Early Syriac Tradition (Cambridge: Cambridge University Press, 1975) 113-14. As Murray shows, the vine is one of several "trees" employed in early Christian writings to carry the "Tree of Life" symbolism.

[99] See Guilding, *The Fourth Gospel and Jewish Worship*, 62, Brown, *John I-XII*, 279, and Pancaro, *The Law in the Fourth Gospel*, 457.

[100] E.g., according to Martyn, *History and Theology*, 111, "John is alone in explicitly interpreting the feeding as a repetition of the manna miracle and therefore as a transparent witness to Jesus as the Mosaic Prophet. "

[101] This does not necessarily involve a denial of the Mosaic traits of the Johannine Jesus. One could speak of a fusion of Moses and David in Johannine thought

tive, the people want to make Jesus king (6:15). The feeding has clearly surfaced a particular memory, that of David as the ideal ANE king, the provident shepherd providing lavishly for his people (2 Sam 6:19; 1 Chr 16:3.).[102] Schnackenburg has noted that John's description of the people sitting on the grass (John 6:10, possibly an allusion to Ps 71:6), "eliminates a reminiscence of Israel's camp in the wilderness and the division of the people."[103] We thus have here "a very potent mix of messianic ideas."[104]

For Brown, looking at John 6:14-15, "the seeming identification of the Prophet and the (messianic) king is difficult."[105] The paradox disappears, however, if we recall that tendency which we noticed in Second Temple Judaism for David and Moses to be contrasted and even for David to somehow replace Moses.[106] As we have seen, it is possible that this Moses/David dialectic lies behind John 1:17. In view of the programmatic nature of the Johannine prologue, it is only to be expected that the contrast would surface elsewhere in the Gospel text, as it does, for example in 3:14-15 and, clearly, here in 6:31-33. Attentiveness to the David-like traits of the Johannine Jesus alerts us to the sense in which he fulfils the expectation for a saviour figure who would, as it were, take Moses' place.[107] As we have seen, this makes complete sense in a *Sitz im Leben* where discipleship to Jesus is perceived by some as "not only as antithetical, but also as somehow comparable to discipleship to Moses."[108] This has further

---

whereby the "Mosaic" and "Davidic" strands are incorporated into the understanding of Jesus to express his fulfilment and his transcendence of the expectations which both figures raise. See MacRae, "The Fourth Gospel and Religionsgeschichte," 19. However, in view of the motivation behind the Gospel (John 20:31), the "Davidic" strand is more central than the comparatively peripheral "Prophet-like Moses" motif. See Ashton, *Understanding*, 100.

[102] Cf. 2 Sam 6:19; 1 Kgs 8:65-66; 1 Chr 29:22. The Johannine feeding scene recalls the Chronicler's account of the banquet on the occasion of David's anointing as king of all Israel at Hebron, when thousands of his followers ate and drank with him for three days (1 Chr 12:38-40), a scene which lent itself readily to messianic *relecture* and was probably quite influential in the delineation of the Qumran vision of an eschatological banquet celebrated in the presence of the Messiah(s) of which the sect's community meals were proleptic representations. See Dunn, *Messianic Ideas*, 374 and Smith, "Messianic Banquet," 790.

[103] Schnackenburg, *The Gospel*, II, 16.
[104] Dunn, "Messianic Ideas," 374.
[105] Brown, *John I-XII*, 235.
[106] See p. 48-102 above.
[107] Recognition of the Johannine Jesus' David-likeness is not, of course, a denial of his Mosaic features, or, for that matter, of his fulfilment of many other OT motifs in the feeding story and discourse of Ch. 6. For example, the reference to barley loaves in John 6:9 may be intended to recall Elisha (2 Kgs 4:42-44). See G. W. Buchanan, "The Samaritan Origin of the Gospel of John," in J. Neusner (ed.), *Religions in Antiquity*, 149-75, at 169.
[108] Martyn, *History and Theology*, 39.

implications for our understanding of the function of the quotation in John 6:31. Since the Bread of Life Discourse is primarily "sapiential," then the conception of David as a wisdom figure is surely significant. In Jewish thought contemporary with the Fourth Gospel, the Law of Moses was regarded as the fruit of the tree of life, procuring, for those who observed its precepts, the life of the world to come. In Johannine thought, it is Jesus/David's bread that bestows, even in this world, the life of the world to come—"eternal life."[109]

In resumé of this section: while not excluding other possible texts (in particular, Exod 16:15), we find the textual arguments for Ps 77:24 as the primary source of the quotation in John 6:31 convincing. We also regard the proposal that a homiletical schema structures the discourse as having considerable merit, especially since the Evangelist himself offers us a hint to that effect (6:59). We therefore regard the quotation as the catalyst for an extended dialogue in which Jesus discloses himself in revelatory speech and his hearers become increasingly divided over whether or not to accept him.

Within the logic of the narrative, the quotation is part of the demand for a sign, a challenge to Jesus—"Are you greater than Moses who gave us the bread from heaven?" (cf. John 4:12). Jesus replies, nuancing and expounding the quotation, that he himself is the sign, especially as he will be seen at "the hour" when his body is given in death for the life of the world. The crowd seek to verify his authority by determining whether he measures up to Moses. Clearly, they accept that there is "some kind of typological relationship between Moses and the Messiah."[110] We recall that in early Judaism David is regarded, "eschatologically at least," as occupying a superior position to Moses.[111] The Johannine church has reached this conviction by its own route: Jesus/David is "greater than Moses."

John 6 thus reflects an appropriation, or even an arrogation, of the manna tradition by Johannine Christianity in which the "bread from heaven" is reinterpreted as a prefiguration of Jesus. A figurative re-reading of the manna story is no novelty.[112] This, however, is

---

[109] As our study unfolds, we will find that the "bread" of Jesus' teaching may even be compared to David's instruction, particularly his teaching on knowledge of God and closeness to God through "his" psalms.

[110] Martyn, *History and Theology*, 105-6.

[111] See pp. 100-01 above.

[112] See Deut 8:3-4; Neh 9:20; Wis 16:26. For Philo, the manna is "the word of God, the heavenly incorruptible food of the soul" (*Heres*. 79. Cf. *Leg. All.* III, 169-70). It is "heavenly wisdom sent from above on souls who yearn for virtue" (*Mut.* 259-60). It is also the logos—τὸν πρεσβύτατον τῶν ὄντων λόγον θεῖον (*Deter*. 118).

a particularly partisan reading, emanating from a situation of conflict. The quotation functions as a vehicle for Johannine "replacement theology." The reception of the psalms, exemplified here, is all of a piece with the way the Jesus of the Fourth Gospel nullifies and replaces the Jewish liturgical institutions that the Johannine church has lost in its divorce from the synagogue.[113] In this case, he is presented as relegating the unequivocal referent of the text (the manna) to the realm of prefiguration in favour of the "true" interpretation. Thus the Johannine Jesus demonstrates that the Scriptures are fully understood only by those who believe in him.

As our next citation is also from Ps (77)78, we will defer until the end of Section D a short *excursus* on the psalm itself, its provenance, its "Davidic" features and its currency within the Johannine circle. This will also serve to bring out the connection between John's two "words from Scripture" quoted from this psalm, which refer to two great Exodus images: the manna and the water from the rock. In John 6:35, Jesus promises satisfaction of both the hunger and the thirst of those who come to him. Having seen how the Johannnine Jesus is ὁ ἄρτος ἐκ τοῦ οὐρανου, we now consider him as the source of ποταμοὶ...ὕδατος ζῶντος.

D. *Ps (77)78: 16. 20 in John 7:38*

On the seventh day of the feast of Tabernacles, Jesus stands in the Temple and cries out, inviting all who thirst to come to him and drink. All who do this in faith will experience the reality of what the Scripture has said, ποταμοὶ ἐκ τῆς κοιλίας αὐτοῦ ῥεύσουσιν ὕδατος ζῶντος. We cite the immediate context of the quotation in full.

> Ἐν δὲ τῇ ἐσχάτῃ ἡμέρᾳ τῇ μεγάλῃ τῆς ἑορτῆς εἱστήκει ὁ Ἰησοῦς καὶ ἔκραξεν λέγων, Ἐάν τις διψᾷ ἐρχέσθω πρός με καὶ πινέτω. ὁ πιστεύων εἰς ἐμέ, καθὼς εἶπεν ἡ γραφή, ποταμοὶ ἐκ τῆς κοιλίας αὐτοῦ ῥεύσουσιν ὕδατος ζῶντος.
>
> On the last day of the feast, the great day, Jesus stood up and proclaimed, "If any one thirst, let him come to me and drink. He who believes in me, as the scripture has said, 'Out of his heart shall flow rivers of living water.'" (John 7:37-38)

Figurative interpretations of the manna are relatively rare in the NT—apart from John 6, only 1 Cor 10:3 and Rev 2:17.

[113] See Gale A. Yee, *Jewish Feasts and the Gospel of John*, (Wilmington: Glazier, 1989) 27. For an explanation of how symbols from Judaism are re-interpreted in the Fourth Gospel "in order that they might retain their viability and provide continuity in a context of profound crisis and change," see Culpepper, *The Anatomy*, 184.

For at least three reasons, this is, perhaps, the most enigmatic "Scripture" in the Fourth Gospel. Firstly, there is the question of the punctuation: should the phrase ὁ πιστεύων εἰς ἐμέ be regarded as the beginning of a new sentence, as above, or should it be treated as the subject of πινέτω? Secondly, there is the uncertainty with regard to the antecedent for the αὐτοῦ: the text does not make clear whether αὐτοῦ refers to Jesus or to the believer. Thirdly, there is the problem of the identification of ἡ γραφή: this "Scripture" corresponds fully to no single biblical passage.[114] Our evaluation of the quotation within the general framework of Johannine thought will depend on the position we adopt with regard to these three questions.

In the history of the interpretation of this passage, the fundamental question seems to have been the punctuation. This then affected the way in which the αὐτοῦ was read, that is, whether the rivers of living water were understood as flowing from within the believer or from within Jesus. The answer given to this question affected, in its turn, the quest for the source of the quotation. We will therefore begin our analysis by comparing the two possible ways of dividing the text into sense lines.

In the reading followed by Origen, which predominates among the Fathers, the sense break comes after πινέτω, the phrase ὁ πιστεύων εἰς ἐμέ is read as a *nominativus pendens*. Our full quotation above follows this punctuation.[115] In the alternative reading, the sense break occurs as follows:

Ἐάν τις διψᾷ ἐρχέσθω πρός με
καὶ πινέτω ὁ πιστεύων εἰς ἐμέ,
καθὼς εἶπεν ἡ γραφή, ποταμοὶ ἐκ τῆς κοιλίας
αὐτοῦ ῥεύσουσιν ὕδατος ζῶντος.

---

[114] The difficulty in identifying the biblical source has even suggested to some that the "Scripture," possibly Isa 55:1-3, might be found in the words preceding the quotation formula, Ἐάν τις διψᾷ ἐρχέσθω πρός με καὶ πινέτω ὁ πιστεύων εἰς ἐμέ. See Germain Bienaimé, citing A. Pinto da Silva, in "L'annonce des fleuves d'eau vive en Jean 7, 37-39," Part I, *RTL* 21 (1990) 281-310, Part II: 417-454, at 288-89. While there is obviously a high degree of biblical allusion in Jesus' invitation (especially of Isa 55:1) the Evangelist's usual procedure is that formal scripture citations follow the introductory formula. For Reim, *Studien*, 56-88, the quotation consists of ὁ πιστεύων εἰς ἐμέ, a citation of Isa 28:16. Why this familiar expression in the Gospel should be raised to the status of a formal citation in this one passage, however, remains a problem.

[115] See Nestle-Aland, *Novum Testamentum Graece*, 27th edition revised (Stuttgart: Deutsche Bibelgesellschaft, 1993). For other instances of the pendent nominative in the Fourth Gospel, see John 1:12, 6:39 and 15:2. In all of these examples the pendent nominative is resumed by a personal pronoun in an oblique case. For examples from ancient Greek literature where the person indicated by the pendent nominative is not the same as the person referred to in the resumptive word in the main clause, see Menken, *Old Testament Quotations*, 193. Menken's chapter on the quotation in John 7:38 was originally published as "The Origin of the Old Testament Quotation in John 7:38," *NovT* 38 (1996) 160-75.

"If anyone thirsts, let him come to me
and let him who believes in me drink.
As the scripture has said, 'Out of his heart will flow rivers of living water.'"

The resulting chiasm would be unique in John, but is not, so the adherents of this punctuation claim, a drastic departure from the Evangelist's style.[116]

The scholarly σχίσμα over whether the αὐτοῦ refers to Jesus or to the believer may also be traced back to the patristic commentators.[117] As we have seen, the answer to this question tended to follow from whichever punctuation was accepted. Origen's reading, which predominated in the patristic period, lent itself to an interpretation of the living water as flowing from within the believer. The alternative punctuation tended to facilitate a reading of the αὐτοῦ as referring to Jesus. As might be expected, this Christological reading did not find favour in an Eastern Christianity vehemently opposed to its inherent suggestion of a "procession" of the Spirit from the Son. It has, nevertheless, considerable patristic support. There are several allusions to John 7:38 in Justin which provide an early interpretation of ἡ γραφή as the story of the water-giving rock in the desert.[118] The earliest firm attestation to the Christological reading of the αὐτοῦ is found in Hippolytus' commentary on Daniel, written *ca* 204-6 CE, from which we quote in the French translation:

> Le Christ, qui est le fleuve, est annoncé dans le monde entier par le quadruple évangile. Il arrose toute la terre et sanctifie tous ceux qui croient en lui, selon la parole du prophète: *Des fleuves sortent de son corps*.[119]

---

[116] Among the modern commentators who defend the "alternative" punctuation (with sense break after ἐμέ) are Dodd, *The Interpretation*, 349; Brown, *John I - XII*, 319; Ashton, *Understanding*, 422; Bienaimé, "L'annonce des fleuves," 304-7.

[117] For a concise synopsis of this division of opinion, see Schnackenburg, *The Gospel II*, 153.

[118] Justin, *Dial.* 114, extols the willingness of Christians to die gladly "for the name of that noble Rock (διὰ τὸ ὄνομα τὸ τῆς καλῆς πέτρας) whence gushes forth living water." Later, in *Dial.* 135, he refers to Christians as "hewn" from the κοιλία of Jesus, ἐκ τῆς κοιλίας τοῦ Χριστοῦ λατομηθέντες. In another possible allusion to John 7:38 (*Dial.* 69), Justin also refers to Christ as "the fountain of living water which gushed forth from God upon a land devoid of the knowledge of God." See J. C. D. Otto (ed.), *S. Justini Philosophi et Martyris Opera* (Jena: F. Mauke, 1843) Vol. II, 444-46. English translation from Thomas B. Falls (ed.) *Saint Justin Martyr*, (Washington D. C.: Catholic University of America Press, 1948) 325; 357.

[119] G. Bardy & M. Lefèvre (ed.), *Hippolyte: Commentaire sur Daniel*, SC 14, I, XVII (Paris: Les Editions du Cerf, 1947) 86. The evocation of the paradise theme in this passage (cf. Gen 2:10) has a significance which will become clear as our discussion progresses.

There may be another witness to the Christological interpretation in a second century Coptic text, the Gospel of Thomas.[120] Further possible evidence for the Christological reading comes from Tg. Ps-Jonathan.[121]

By the first half of this century we find the matter of the referent for the αὐτοῦ still unresolved.[122] By 1971 Schnackenburg could report that reference to the believer was "losing ground."

> There are much stronger grounds for applying the image to Jesus: (1) The parallels in 4:10, 14a and 6:35; (2) The Old Testament themes of water flowing from the rock, or from the temple in the eschatological Jerusalem; (3) The probable connection between this scene and 19:34; (4) Jesus' giving of the Spirit (20:22). On all these grounds, we may regard the application to Jesus as certain.[123]

Schnackenburg also reached the conviction that, as regards the division of the sentence, we do not in fact have to choose, that either reading will support the application of the "Scripture" to Jesus. Menken concurs in regarding ἐκ τῆς κοιλίας αὐτοῦ ῥεύσουσιν ὕδατος ζῶντος as a statement about Jesus and not about the believer.[124] He favours reading ὁ πιστεύων εἰς ἐμέ as a *nominativus pendens* and sees no conflict between this and the Christological interpretation of αὐτοῦ.

---

[120] "Jesus said: I am not your master, because (ἐπεί) you drank (and) became drunken from the bubbling spring which I have measured out." *Gos. Thom.* 13. See Bruce M. Metzger (trans.), "The Gospel of Thomas," in Kurt Aland, *Synopsis Quattuor Evangeliorum* (Stuttgart: Deutsche Bibelgesellschaft, 1985) 517-30, at 519.

[121] In Tg. Ps-Jonathan Num 20:11, Moses' two blows to the rock in the desert yielded blood first and then water. The relatively late dating of this Targum (definitive redaction *ca* 6th cent. CE) and the fact that this reading is not confirmed by the Palestinian Targum immediately arouses a suspicion of anti-Christian polemic. Even if this is the case, the Targum still provides valuable indirect attestation to the Christological reading of John 7:38 as a reference to the water-flowing rock, and to its interpretation in the light of John 19:34. See M.-E. Boismard, "De son ventre couleront des fleuves d'eau: Jo., VII, 38," *RB* 65 (1958) 523-46, at 539.

[122] E. C. Hoskyns, *The Fourth Gospel*, (London: Faber, 1947) 322, was able to show that both readings are "wholly Johannine." R. H. Lightfoot, *Saint John's Gospel: A Commentary* (Oxford: Oxford University Press, 1957), 183, opted for the water flowing from within the believer. H. Odeberg, *The Fourth Gospel Interpreted in its Relation to Contemporary Religious Currents and the Hellenistic-Oriental World*. (Amsterdam: Grüner, 1968) 284, held that ἐκ τῆς κοιλίας αὐτοῦ "naturally refers to the spiritual organism of the spiritually born." Favouring the sense break after εἰς ἐμέ, Brown, *John I - XII*, 321, however, saw "little reason for supposing that the 'him' of the citation is the believer."

[123] Schnackenburg, *The Gospel II*, 153-54.

[124] Menken gives five reasons: (1) for John, Jesus is the source of salvation, (2) the whole ch. 7-8 context indicates self-disclosure by Jesus, (3) v. 39 interprets the water as the Spirit and for John it is Jesus who gives the Spirit to believers, (4) in John, invitations to faith are consistently combined with statements of Jesus' soteriological identity, (5) the "scripture" points forward to John 19:34. See *Old Testament Quotations*, 192-93.

The meaning-effect of this reading may be conveyed by the following paraphrase:

> The one who believes in me—for that person, as Scripture has said, rivers of living water shall flow from within him (sc. Jesus).

This seems to be the primary sense. The application to the believer may perhaps be best understood as operating in a derived sense. Indeed, Ashton has suggested not only leaving the punctuation question open to both readings, but also leaving the question of the αὐτοῦ unresolved. In his opinion, the Christological reading is "marginally more likely," but he thinks it conceivable that both meanings are intended.[125]

We come now to the question of the biblical source for John's "Scripture," ποταμοὶ ἐκ τῆς κοιλίας αὐτοῦ ῥεύσουσιν ὕδατος ζῶντος.[126] The introductory formula, καθὼς εἶπεν ἡ γραφή, would lead us to expect a readily identifiable Scripture quotation. As we have seen, in the history of the interpretation of this passage, the particular "Scripture" proposed as source has depended on the reading adopted, that is, whether the αὐτοῦ was taken as referring to the believer or to Jesus.[127] Thus Freed, a proponent of reference to the believer, suggests Isa 58:11; Jer 2:13; 17:13 and Prov 18:4, venturing that perhaps John's is a composite citation from some of them.[128] Charles Goodwin, who also favours the believer as referent, regards Isa 55:1, Prov 18:4 and Cant 4:15 as "the least inconceivable" possible sources. He thinks that John may have used a text which he supposed to be Scripture because of its Semitic idiom.[129]

---

[125] As Ashton explains, *Understanding*, 422, "Before the advent of the Spirit, it is Jesus alone who is the source of revelation; subsequently any believer, sent by him as he was sent by the Father, can be the spring from which others may drink the life-giving waters of revelation."

[126] For recent surveys of the suggestions made, see Bienaimé, "L'annonce des fleuves," 289-90, 307-10, 417-20 and Hanson, *The Prophetic Gospel*, 99-115.

[127] Thus Boismard, presenting the *status quaestionis* in 1958, could show that interpreters favouring the view that the waters flow from within the believer suggested mainly Isa 58:11, Zech 14:8 and Prov 5:15 (cf. Prov 4:23), while those who preferred the Christological reading thought in terms of Exod 17:1-7, Isa 48:21 and Ps 78:15-16. See "De son ventre couleront des fleuves d'eau: Jo., VII, 38," *RB* 65 (1958) 523- 46, at 543.

[128] Freed, *Old Testament Quotations*, 21-38.

[129] Goodwin, "How did John treat his Sources?" 65, envisages a text which had some relationship with Odes Sol. 30:1-3a or 36:7, persuaded, no doubt, that the Odes are Jewish. A better hypothesis may have been 1 Enoch 48:1 where all the thirsty drink of the fountain and become filled with wisdom. Cf. also the tradition preserved in *Midr. Teh.* 1.18 which comments on Ps 1:3 in the light of Isa 55:1—"*He is like a tree planted by the rivers of water*—One day a man learns one law, the next day another law, until brimming with wisdom he wells forth like a fountain."

The most obvious referent for the quotation, if it is understood Christologically, is the story of the rock that provided water in the desert. However, the verbal parallels between John 7:38 and the accounts in Exod 17:1-7 and Num 20:2-13 do not seem sufficient to warrant a designation of the citation as ἡ γραφή.[130] The Tabernacles background has been consistently seen as providing a clue to the source. Thus Dodd is guided by the most frequently occurring citations in rabbinic authorities with reference to the water libations at Tabernacles, when he suggests Isa 12:3, Ezek 47:1-14 and Zech 14:8 as possible sources.[131] Lightfoot agrees with Dodd that the quotation is "perhaps a paraphrase" of Zech 14:8 with resonances of Ezek 47:1-11. He also thinks it possible that the Evangelist, rather than quoting any one text, is "collecting the sense" of various Old Testament passages, such as Num 20, Isa 43:20, 55:1.[132] Boismard sees a composite reference to Ps 77:16 and Isa 48:21-22.[133] P. Grelot, having earlier held that Ps 77:16 was the primary source, has more recently become convinced that the quotation is from Zech 14:8 with an implied background of Ezek 47 and with Ps (77)78:16 supplying the "rivers."[134] Schnackenburg adds to these Zech 13:1 and Ps (77)78:16.20, venturing that an unknown Aramaic source has influenced ἐκ τῆς κοιλίας αὐτοῦ.[135] Odeberg sees two possibilities: either John freely mixes together several passages or the quotation is from a lost (apocryphal) writing.[136] For Bienaimé, the citation is from Exod 17:6 *et ses harmoniques:* Zech 14:8, Ps 78:20, Ps 104:41, Isa 48:21, *etc.*[137] According to Brown and Menken, the strongest case, in terms of verbal links, seems to be that for LXX Ps 77:16.20.[138] We adopt this position.

Even though the citation straddles several verses of Ps 77, they do create a literary unit dealing with the water from the rock. In fact,

---

[130] Thus, for Hoskyns, *The Fourth Gospel,* 323, John 7:38 is not a quotation of either of these texts, but a "Christian midrash" bringing out "the prophetic significance of the Mosaic miracle."

[131] Dodd, *The Interpretation,* 350.

[132] Lightfoot, *St John's Gospel,* 183.

[133] Boismard, "De son ventre," 545.

[134] P. Grelot, "De son ventre couleront des fleuves d'eau: la citation scriptuaire de Jean, VII, 38." *RB* 66 (1959) 369-74, at 370, and "Jean VII, 38: Eau du rocher ou source du Temple?" *RB* 70 (1963) 43-51, at 48.

[135] Schnackenburg, *The Gospel I,* 122-23.

[136] Odeberg, *The Fourth Gospel,* 284.

[137] Bienaimé, "L'annonce des fleuves," 431.

[138] Brown, *John I - XII,* 322 and Menken, "The Origin of the OT Quotation in John 7:38," 170-71. Schnackenburg's view and Grelot's 1963 position are, in fact, quite similar. We note, however, that Brown seems to have modified his position more recently in favour of Num 20:11 as primary source. See *Death of the Messiah,* 1181.

they form what we might call a double *parallelismus membrorum*. In the following quotation of the verses in question, the key words which the Evangelist appears to have recalled and woven together are underlined.[139]

> Ps 77:16
> καὶ ἐξήγαγεν ὕδωρ ἐκ πέτρας
> καὶ κατήγαγεν ὡς ποταμοὺς ὕδατα.
>
> Ps 77:20 ab
> ἐπεὶ ἐπάταξεν πέτραν καὶ ἐρρύησαν ὕδατα
> καὶ χείμαρροι κατεκλύσθησαν,

Another strong contender for possible source may be LXX Ps 104:41—

> διέρρηξεν πέτραν, καὶ ἐρρύησαν ὕδατα,
> ἐπορεύθησαν ἐν ἀνύδροις ποταμοί.[140]

—particularly in view of ποταμοί. However, three details may tip the balance in favour of Ps 77: first, the fact that John has already quoted from it in 6:31; second, the reference in v. 15 of the psalm to God giving the people to drink (ἐπότισεν αὐτούς) which may be echoed in Jesus' word, πινέτω (John 7:37); third, the Hebrew of Ps (77)78:16 can explain the expression ποταμοὶ...ὕδατος.[141]

So far we have accounted for ποταμοὶ...ῥεύσουσιν ὕδατος. We now turn to the term ζῶντος which qualifies ὕδατος. Is it simply part of the Evangelist's vocabulary, or does it have a precise biblical source? If it does, this will widen the scope of our exploration to a veritable web of other "Scriptures" from which the quotation from Ps 77 cannot easily be disentangled. Menken is, no doubt, correct in his assessment "that the basic quotation has been influenced by one or more other OT passages, or that it has been manipulated otherwise in agreement with extant exegetical devices in such a way that the final result is adapted to the evangelist's christological ideas."[142] The most likely source for ζῶντος is Zech 14:8—καὶ ἐν τῇ ἡρέμᾳ ἐκείνῃ ἐξελεύσεται ὕδωρ ζῶν ἐξ Ιερουσαλήμ, especially in view of John's

---

[139] In a similar way, the Evangelist has already conflated two lines of the psalm for the quotation in John 6:31.

[140] Ps 104 covers much the same historical ground as Ps 77. We noted it as a possible source for the scripture in John 6:31, on the basis of the line immediately preceding the reference to the rock, καὶ ἄρτον οὐρανοῦ ἐνέπλησεν αὐτούς. (LXX Ps 104:40 b).

[141] Ps 78:16 reads, "He caused to flow down waters like rivers." Depending on the vocalisation, כנהרות מים can be read as "water like rivers" or (with נהר in the construct) as "like rivers of water."

[142] Old Testament Quotations, 189.

predilection for Zech 9-14. In the Tabernacles setting, Zech 14:8 was interpreted by means of the water flowing from the eschatological Temple in Ezek 47:1-2. Such a reading suits John's theological schema perfectly: the true Temple is Jesus' body. The quotation from Ps 77, with resonances of Zech 14:8 and Ezek 47:1-2, is thus made to point forward to John 19:34.[143]

The phrase ἐκ τῆς κοιλίας αὐτοῦ appears to correspond to the phrase ἐκ πέτρας in v. 16 of the psalm. Various possible backgrounds have been offered for this phrase, in particular, LXX Ps 39:9—καὶ τὸν νόμον σου ἐν μέσῳ τῆς κοιλίας μου.[144] The unsatisfactory nature of the explanations offered for the phrase has even led some to posit an Aramaic influence or the use of a hypothetical Targum.[145]

In Menken's view, the "missing link" which explains the expression ἐκ τῆς κοιλίας αὐτου is another psalm passage dealing with the water-flowing rock, Ps (113)114:8, which, as part of the *Hallel*, would also have had associations with Tabernacles. The psalmist calls on the whole earth to tremble at the presence of God—

> ...who turns the rock into a pool of water,
> the flint into a spring of water.

As Menken explains,

> Now, Ps 114:8 makes clear, by means of two parallel lines, that God made the rock into a spring. This "divine equation" of rock and spring made it legitimate for an ancient interpreter of the OT to replace in the Hebrew text of Ps 78:16, the word סלע "rock," by the word מעין "spring."...It seems, then, that we can explain the word κοιλία in John 7:38 as a substitute of πέτρα in Ps. 77:16 LXX by supposing the following exegetical steps: (1) on the basis of Ps. 114:8, the rock of Ps 78:16 is equated with a מעין, a spring; (2) by means of a different vocalization, this word gets the meaning "inside," and it is accordingly translated by κοιλία.[146]

---

[143] The water from Siloam, fed by the Gihon Spring, which was used in the Tabernacles libations, was regarded as living water. See Bruce H. Grigsby, "Washing in the Pool of Siloam—A Thematic Anticipation of the Johannine Cross," *NovT* 28 (1985) 227-35, at 228-29.

[144] Since, as Brown believes, the living water is capable of a sapiential interpretation, the "law" in Jesus' midst (Ps 39:9—καὶ τὸν νόμον σου ἐν μέσῳ τῆς κοιλίας μου) could be understood, in the light of Sir 24: 23-29, as divine Wisdom communicated to humankind, flowing abundantly like a river. See *John I-XII*, 328. In support of his claim for Ps 39:9 as source, Hanson draws attention to echoes of Ps 39:9 which he sees in John 17:17-24. See *The Living Utterances*, 120.

[145] See Boismard, "Les citations targumiques dans le quatrième évangile," *RB* 66 (1959) 374-78.

[146] By way of summary of Menken's technical details: the Hebrew for a "spring," מַעְיָן, if vocalized as מָעְיָן, can be read as an Aramaic equivalent of the Hebrew word for "intestines, inside," מֵעִים. If vocalized as מְעִין or as מֵעִין, it becomes a Tannaitic Hebrew equivalent. See *Old Testament Quotations*, 200-01.

Menken notes that both these exegetical steps stay within the bounds of early Jewish and early Christian exegesis as known to us from the exegetical rules of Hillel.[147] If Menken is correct, it may well be that the basic quotation from Ps 77 carries resonances of the two other passages from the Psalter which we have mentioned—Ps 104:41 and Ps 114:8. Even without recourse to Hillel's *middoth*, we can see from what we established in our previous chapter concerning the "textualization" of the Psalter as a unified *oeuvre*, that various elements from several different psalms could form as valid a citation as one which drew upon and condensed several lines of the same psalm. One thing is certainly clear from the textual form of the citation in John 7:38. As with the citation in John 6:31, the recollection of the Pentateuchal story has come to the Evangelist via the poetic recital found in the Psalter.

In the citation, the Evangelist has changed the tense of the verb ῥέω to the future, ῥεύσουσιν. This is not unlike the tense change in John 2:17 where the Scripture is adapted to make it point forward prophetically to Jesus' death. As we have seen, here it points forward to John 19:34. The future is, however, not just the "hour," still to come (at the level of *histoire*), but the eschatological era which that "hour" will inaugurate. It is likely that Zech 14:8—καὶ ἐν τῇ ἡρέμα ἐκείνῃ ἐξελεύσεται ὕδωρ ζῶν ἐξ Ἰερουσαλήμ—lies behind the tense change. Another possible influence would be Dt-Isa. We might note, especially in view of its use of the future tense and its presentation of the future deliverance as a new Exodus, the LXX of Isa 48:21—

> Καὶ ἐὰν διψήσωσι, δι᾽ ἐρήμου ἄξει αὐτοὺς,
> ὕδωρ ἐκ πέτρας ἐξάξει αὐτοῖς·
> σχισθήσεται πέτρα, καὶ ῥυήσεται ὕδωρ,
> καὶ πίεται ὁ λαός μου.
>
> And if they thirst, he shall lead them through the desert;
> he shall bring out water for them from the rock.
> The rock will be torn and the water will flow
> and my people will drink.

Isa 44:3, occurring in a lection for Tabernacles, may well have been another of the strands woven into the texture of Ps 77:16.20.[148]

---

[147] The exegetical technique involved in the replacement of "rock" by "spring" was later codified in Hillel's list of *middoth* as *binyan av*, "the founding of a family." On the *middoth*, see R. Kasher, "The Interpretation of Scripture in Rabbinic Literature," in Mulder & Sysling (ed.), *Mikra*, 547-94. According to the rule *binyan av*, an element found in one text could be applied to other related texts. See also E. Earle Ellis, "Biblical Interpretation in the New Testament Church," in *Mikra*, 691-726, at 699-700.

[148] See Guilding, *The Fourth Gospel and Jewish Worship*, 105; Schnackenburg, *The Gospel II*, 155.

> For I will pour water on the thirsty land,
> and streams on the dry ground;
> I will pour my Spirit on your descendants,
> and my blessing on your offspring.

The analogy it draws between an outpouring of miraculous water and an expected future outpouring of God's spirit certainly elucidates the Evangelist's commentary on Jesus' Scripture citation, τοῦτο δὲ εἶπεν περὶ τοῦ πνεύματος...(John 7:39).[149]

While it is evident from 1 Cor 10:4 that the Fourth Evangelist is using early Christian tradition in his presentation of Jesus as the "rock," the quotation is extremely well integrated into the flow of the Gospel, particularly in its continuity with the previous psalm quotation (from the same psalm), presenting Jesus as the new "manna," and its anticipation of John 19:34. Even the verb κράζειν which introduces it, gives the sense of a solemn public proclamation and draws attention to the revelatory character of Jesus' utterance on the greatest day of the festival.[150] The "Scripture" in John 7:38, in its relationship to so many other texts, activates the biblical resonances connected with a major rite in the feast of Tabernacles, the water libation. For John, this rite, symbolically anticipating the outpouring of God's spirit in the end time, not only explains Jesus, but is fulfilled and even replaced by him.[151]

Against this background, there is a logic in the way "the Scripture" as cited in Jesus' invitation immediately provokes a debate among the people as to whether Jesus might possibly be "the prophet" or "the Christ" (John 7:40-41). Commentators on the por-

---

[149] An outpouring of God's Spirit was an expected feature of the eschatological era (Joel 2:28). This belief is evident in a commentary on Isa 12:3 ("With joy you will draw water from the wells of salvation.") as sung during the ritual drawing of water at Tabernacles. The Talmud preserves a teaching attributed to R. Jehoshua ben Levi (fl. ca 250 CE) who recalls the rite and explains its meaning. "They drew the holy spirit according to the word, "With joy you will draw water..." See *b. Sukk.* 5:55a.

[150] Κράζειν is used of Jesus in the Fourth Gospel here, in 7:28 and in 12:44, and of John the Baptist's witness to Jesus in 1:15. The Johannine use of κράζειν corresponds to the use of κηρύσσειν in the other NT writings. Both verbs render the Hebrew קרא in the LXX. In John, κράζειν does not carry the sense of urgent emotional utterance that it has in the synoptics (e.g., Mark 3:11; 10:47; etc.). Neither, as John 12:44 illustrates, does it necessarily refer to any particular occasion on which Jesus uttered the direct speech which follows it in the text. For Bultmann, *The Gospel of John*, 302, the verb suggests inspired speech in the wisdom tradition—"The words Ἰησοῦς δὲ ἔκραξεν...mean rather, 'This is the content of the κήρυγμα of Jesus.' " See Dodd, *Interpretation*, 382; Schnackenburg, *The Gospel II*, 146-147. Ashton, *Understanding*, 182, would align the Johannine use of the verb κράζειν with the introductory "Amen" to certain sayings of Jesus as indicating the activity of cultic prophets who spoke in the name of Jesus during Johannine community worship.

[151] Similarly, the illuminations, recalled by Jesus' claim to be "the light of the

trayal of Jesus in terms of the water-giving rock in the desert tend to confine their attention to its implications for a "Mosaic" presentation of Jesus.[152] There is, however, as the ensuing dialogue in John 7:40-42 makes clear, a "Davidic" aspect to this *pericope* as well. So this brings us to the question we raised with regard to John 6:31—whether the perceived provenance of this "word from Scripture"—the Psalms of David—would have impacted on its reception within the Johannine circle.

According to John 7:40-42, the impact of "the Scripture" on the people is to make them ask, not only whether Jesus might be "the prophet" of Deut 18:18, but also, at more length and in more searching terms, whether he might be "the Christ," and whether, if he is the Christ, this would necessarily involve genealogical descent from David. The phrase, ἀκούσαντες τῶν λόγων τούτων...(7:40) and the Evangelist's intervention in v. 39 direct us to see the debate as a reaction to Jesus' promise of the gift of the Spirit. Possession of the divine spirit was associated with Moses (Num 11:16-30) and therefore expected of "the Prophet." However, the evident influence of the "hidden Messiah" tradition on the crowd's speculation about Jesus' identity and origins (John 7:41-42) alerts us to another possibility, that, on the basis of 1 Sam 16:13 (cf. Isa 11:2), the Evangelist is showing that Jesus' unique possession of the Spirit marks him out as the Davidic Messiah. There is a sense in which the debate in John 7:40-44 is the converse of John 1:33 where the Baptist's Samuel-like recognition of Jesus' David-like identity hinges on his discernment of Jesus' possession of the Spirit. The people in John 7 verge on that insight, but never quite reach it.

There is an even more profound level of reference to David in the Johannine handling of the "Scripture," ποταμοὶ ἐκ τῆς κοιλίας αὐτοῦ ῥεύσουσιν ὕδατος ζῶντος—an implied claim that Moses has been re-

---

world" (John 8:12), anticipated the end time when there would be no more night. See Bultmann, *The Gospel of John*, 305.

[152] Fairly typical would be the estimate of F. F. Bruce that what is involved here and in 6:14, is "the conception of the Messiah as a second Moses, supplying his people with bread and water." See *1 and 2 Corinthians*, NCB, (London: Oliphants, 1971) 91. For John Ashton, *Understanding*, 303, "It is easy to see in this pronouncement, especially if one remembers the particular quality of the Feast of Tabernacles and its ritual, an implicit claim on Jesus' part to be a new Moses, less easy, perhaps, to read it as a claim to be the Davidic Messiah." It is striking that Boismard, writing in a vein which might have called for a certain emphasis on the Mosaic dimension, stresses the complementarity of the two identities proposed by the crowd for Jesus: the prophet and the Christ. He sees this as underlined in the analogous wording of the confessions of faith in Jesus as ὁ προφήτης ὁ ἐρχόμενος εἰς τὸν κόσμον (John 6:14) and as ὁ Χριστὸς ὁ υἱὸς τοῦ θεοῦ ὁ εἰς τὸν κόσμον ἐρχόμενος (11:27). See Boismard, *Moïse ou Jésus*, 7-9.

placed by Jesus, the new David. We recall again, as we did in our exploration of the citation in John 6:31, the way in which the David of early Judaism is frequently compared with Moses and how at times he even seems to occupy a position superior to Moses. The psalm quotation in John 7:37b-38 is yet another illustration.

In order to appreciate this, we need to trace the *survie* of the desert rock. In the biblical tradition, the story of Moses striking the rock appears twice: in Exod 17:1-7 and in Num 20:10-11. This, apparently, led early interpreters to envisage the rock as travelling with the people during the desert journey, since God was believed to have provided for Israel during the whole desert sojourn. In a further development, the rock became assimilated to the well at Beer (Num 21:16-18) also known as the well of Miriam. Paul's reference to "the Rock that followed them" in 1 Cor 10:4 provides a valuable first century CE attestation to the tradition that the rock travelled with the people. The legend is also found in *LAB* 10:7—

> Populum autem suum deduxit in heremum, quadraginta annis pluit illis de celo panem et ortigometram adduxit eis de mari, et <u>puteum aque consequentis</u> eduxit eis.[153]

A second reference to the rock which followed the people occurs in Ps-Philo's account of how God gave the Law to Moses (*LAB* 11:15)—

> ...et ostendit ei lignum vite de quo absidit et accepit et misit in Myrram, et dulcis facta est aqua Myrre. Et sequebatur eos in heremo annis quadraginta, et ascendit in montem cum eis et descendit in campos.

Ps-Philo's account then proceeds with God's instructions for the building of the sanctuary, which, of course, retroject into the desert period features of the Second Temple. In the *Targumim*, the water-flowing rock is described as travelling with the people throughout the desert journey over the mountains and down to the plains.[154] It is striking that for Ps-Philo the water of Marah follows the people for forty years in the desert and then ascends the mountain (singular) with them, from which it then descends into the plains. In *LAB*, the mountain is apparently the rock of Sion, which is, of course, the ul-

---

[153] The underlined words are translated "a well of water to follow them" by Harrington, "Pseudo-Philo," 317, and "un puits d'eau qui les suivait" by Perrot & Bogaert, *Pseudo-Philon*, 119. Interestingly, the very next line in Ps-Philo is a quotation from Ps 78:14. Like the Fourth Evangelist, Ps-Philo recalls the story in the poetic account found in this psalm.

[154] See Martin McNamara, *Targum Neofiti 1: Numbers* and Ernest G. Clarke, *Targum Pseudo-Jonathan: Numbers* (Edinburgh: Clark, 1995) 120; 249. Also *t. Sukk* 3:11-13 as cited by Grelot, "Jean, VII, 38: Eau du rocher," 46.

timate destination of the Exodus journey, even in Exod 15:17. Obviously Ps-Philo was in contact with a tradition which identified the waters of the desert rock with the waters flowing from under the Temple rock down to the plains in life-giving streams (Ezek 47:1-12; Zech 14:8-10). His reference to the Tree of Life suggests that he may also have known the tradition identifying these waters with the four rivers in Paradise. *LAB* has therefore preserved important first century CE evidence for the assimilation of the desert rock to the rock of Sion and to its interpretation in the light of passages which, as we have already seen, were particularly associated with Tabernacles.

We recall part of the quotation from *Qoheleth Rabbah* which we quoted above with reference to the expected renewal of the manna miracle.[155] Expounding the preacher's dictum that there is nothing new under the sun, the midrashist comments—

> As the former redeemer made a well to rise, so will the latter Redeemer bring up water, As it is stated, And a fountain shall come forth of the house of the Lord, and shall water the valley of Shittim. (Joel IV,18).[156]

On the analogy of the manna reference, we might have expected that the second Redeemer would renew the gift of the water from the desert rock. What we find instead is an expectation centred on the Temple rock, to which the desert rock has apparently been assimilated. In view of the late dating of *Qoh. Rab.*, Bienaimé is cautious about attributing the fully metamorphosed form of the belief to the Fourth Evangelist.

> L'intégration plus ou moins réussie du puits futur et de la source du Sanctuaire, telle que nous la lisons dans les recueils rabbiniques, est de loin postérieure à la rédaction johannique. Mais elle suggère que la mentalité aggadique ne répugne pas à un certain amalgame des deux cycles de traditions. Il en résulte pour Jn 7, 38c que, sur le plan de la sensibilité midrashique, une référence à un renouvellement du prodige de l'exode et, conjointement, à la venue de l'eau eschatologique du Temple ne serait pas nécessairement perçue comme insolite.[157]

An awareness of the Jewish capacity to superimpose layers of meaning would encourage us to be a little more daring. As Grelot has shown, the way in which the lections for Tabernacles superimpose an anticipation of the eschatological time on an actualisation of the desert time help us to see how John 7:38 can refer, without any con-

---

[155] See p. 139 above.
[156] *Qoh. Rab.* 1, 9, 1[23]
[157] Bienaimé, "L'annonce des fleuves d'eau vive," II, 446-7.

flict, to both the desert rock and the Temple rock.[158] In Jewish thought the two have been assimilated, or rather, in the light of what we have learned about David's tendency to supplant Moses, we might say that Moses' rock has now become David's rock, the foundation of the Temple.

With regard to the "Rock of Sion," there is a rich tradition of the superimposition of various meanings. As we saw in our discussion of 4Q 522, the Temple rock was believed to be the threshing floor of Araunah (2 Sam 24:18) and that it was also identified with the land of Moriah (2 Chr 3:1), thus becoming the site of Abraham's sacrifice.[159] The Samaritan transfer of the place of Abraham's sacrifice to Mount Gerizim presupposes this identification of the Jerusalem site.[160] Targum Pseudo-Jonathan situates Adam's banishment at Mount Moriah.[161] According to *LAB* 16:2 the Rock of Zion is the location for the murder of Abel by Cain.

The natural springs underneath the altar were believed to be the primeval waters which God had subdued at the creation, the Temple rock itself being the first area of dry land to emerge from the watery chaos.[162] The site of the Temple was the place where humankind was created.[163] God's presence in the Temple was that of the Lord "enthroned over the flood" (Ps 29:10; cf. Ps 93). The Temple area was thus identified with the site of Paradise, a belief at-

---

[158] Grelot, "John ,VII, 38: Eau du Rocher?" 46. See also Brown, *John, I-XII*, 323, who asks, "In searching for the background of Jesus as the source of living water, must one choose between the rock of the desert and the apocalyptic passages of Zechariah and Ezekiel with their eschatological rivers of living water flowing out of Jerusalem and the Temple?"

[159] See p. 75-76 above

[160] Similarly the site of Jacob's Gen 28 vision was believed by the Samaritans to be Gerizim and by the Judeans to be the Jerusalem Temple. See Neyrey, "Jacob Traditions," 428.

[161] Michael Maher, *Targum Pseudo-Jonathan: Genesis, Translated with Introduction and Notes* (Edinburgh: Clark, 1992) 53. See also *Midr. Teh.* 92.6, where Mount Moriah, to which Adam is banished, is described as "the place where the Temple was to stand."

[162] See *b. Yoma* 54 a. The identification of the water from the desert rock with the primeval waters under the Temple rock at the centre of creation is borne out by the Targum to Ps 78:15.
  Rupit montes virga Mosseh praeceptoris eorum in deserto
  et potum dedit eis veluti ex abyssis magnis.
Even though this Targum post-dates the NT period, an early dating for this reading is confirmed by its similarity to the LXX.

[163] According to Tg. Ps.-J Gen 2:7, God used "dust from the site of the sanctuary" to create the first man. Tg. Ps.-J. Gen 2:15 tells how God took Adam "from the mountain of worship, the place where he had been created." This location is identified as Mount Moriah in Tg. Ps.-J Gen 3:23. See Maher (ed.),*Targum Pseudo-Jonathan: Genesis*, 22-23. 30. For Mount Zion as the navel of the earth, see Jub 8:19.

tested by its architectural and decorative features as well as in numerous writings of the Second Temple period,[164] and reflected in the design of the Temple. The two great *menoroth* were Eden's two trees, for example. The "bronze sea" represented the primeval waters over which God sat enthroned (Ps 29:10).[165]

The impression made on Aristeas by the sight and sound of the Temple's subterranean water system makes this belief understandable.

> There is an uninterrupted supply not only of water, just as if there were a plentiful spring rising from within, but also of indescribably wonderful underground reservoirs, which within a radius of five stades from the foundation of the Temple revealed innumerable channels for each of them, the streams joining together on each side... They conducted me more than four stades outside the city, and told me to bend down at a certain spot and listen to the noise at the meeting of the waters. The result was that the size of the conduits became clear to me.[166]

A story attributed to the third century Rabbi Johannan, preserved in the Babylonian Talmud, tells of David's role in controlling these subterranean waters so that enough would be released to ensure fertility for the earth, but not so much as to overwhelm the world with a flood.[167] While the legend itself is obviously a rabbinical construction, it testifies to an imaginative expansion of David's association with the "Rock of Sion" as the various layers of interpretation were superimposed upon it.

The description of the Second Temple in *The Letter of Aristeas* describes the channels under the altar of holocausts for draining off the water used for washing away the blood of the sacrifices.[168] Aristeas'

---

[164] E.g., in a Qumran commentary on Isa 5:1-7 (4Q500), the Temple mount is portrayed as the Lord's vineyard of Isa 5:1-5 in which flow the four streams of Paradise. See J. M. Baumgarten, "4Q500 and the Ancient Conception of the Lord's Vineyard," *JJS* 40 (1989) 1 - 6. See Hippolytus, *Commentary on Daniel* 1:17 quoted above and *b. Sukk.* 53b. See also 2 En 8:4-6; T. Dan 5:12; Jub 8:19 where Eden is identified with "the holy of holies;" ApocMos 22:3, where Eden is the location of God's throne.

[165] Tg. Ps.-J. Gen 2:15, where "the place of creation" is "the mountain of worship," presumes an identification between Eden and the Temple complex. This identification must also underlie several passages in Revelation, notably Rev 22:1-5. See Barker, *The Older Testament: The Survival of Themes from the Ancient Royal Cult in Sectarian Judaism and Early Christianity* (London: SPCK, 1987) 241-45 and *The Gate of Heaven*, 62-88.

[166] *The Letter of Aristeas (Ep. Arist.)*, 89, 91, translated by R. J. H. Shutt, *OTP* II, 7-34, at 18-19. Shutt proposes a dating of around 170 BCE for its composition.

[167] *b. Sukk.* 53b.

[168] *Ep. Arist.* 88.

account is confirmed by *m. Yoma* 5:6 which mentions the blood being washed away into the Kidron. It is this water mixed with sacrificial blood, flowing from the Rock into the subterranean springs, there, as it were, becoming the "rivers" flowing from the Temple to water the whole earth, that would appear to have been the inspiration for John 19:34. For the Fourth Evangelist, Jesus is the Temple Rock from which, in Ezekiel's imagery, the river that is the source of life flows. If Jesus is the new Rock, he is also the builder/founder of the new Temple. As his sacrificial blood flows from the pierced "rock" of his body, his self-offering (cf. John 17:19) inaugurates the new worship (cf. John 4:21-24). Even the point that Jesus' sacrificial death takes place on a rock (John 19:17), is probably significant.[169] It is, therefore, as a new "David" that he declares he will rebuild the temple of his body (cf. John 2:19). Indeed, it is only in the light of this understanding of John 7:38 that the full extent of the aptness to Jesus of David's words, Ὁ ζῆλος τοῦ οἴκου σου καταφάγεταί με (John 2:17), becomes apparent.

There are two further aspects to the "Rock" which we should also take into account: its role as a representation of God and its symbolic role vis à vis the Law/Wisdom.

According to a midrash on Exod 17:6, God was the rock from which the water came. This rock was always present to Israel's need, because God went wherever Israel went.[170] In biblical thought, the word "Rock" frequently functions as an epithet for God.[171] The Fourth Evangelist, therefore, in presenting Jesus as the Rock, is actually hinting at his divine status.

With regard to the Rock as a symbol of divine Wisdom, light is cast on both the Pauline and Johannine usage of the desert rock motif by two passages in the writings of Philo. In one of these, he describes the soul as a prey to the passions—

---

[169] The popular etymology of Golgotha, "the place of the skull" may be a reference to its rock-like appearance and terrain.

[170] See W. Forr & J. A. Walther, *1 Corinthians*. (New York: Doubleday, 1976) n. 4, 245.

[171] The key passage is Moses' address to God as "The Rock" (הצור) in Deut 32:4. David calls God his "Rock" in 2 Sam 22:2.47 (=Ps (17)18:1.46). The LXX rendering of this psalm displays the tendency, encountered throughout the Greek Psalter, to replace the Hebrew צור (or less frequently, סלע as in Ps 18:2a) with other addresses—principally θεός (Ps 17:46; 94:1; 30:2; 61:2), but also στερέωμα (Ps 17:2), βοηθός (Ps 17:2) and φύλαξ in the 2 Sam 22:47 version of Ps 17:46. The LXX translators clearly wish to avoid any suggestion of idolatry, particularly of the worship of stone images. Their alternative images of God as firm support, helper and guardian are of great value as indicators of the interpretation of the "Rock" metaphor current at the time of the translation of the scriptures into Greek.

...until God send forth the stream from His strong wisdom and quench with unfailing health the thirst of the soul that had turned from Him. For the flinty rock (ἡ γὰρ ἀκρότομος πέτρα) is the wisdom of God, which he marked off highest and chiefest from His powers, and from which he satisfies the thirsty souls that love God. And when they have been given water to drink, they are filled also with the manna...[172]

Similarly, in *Deter.* 115-18, Philo explains that Moses "uses the word 'rock' to express the solid and indestructible wisdom of God which feeds and nurses and rears to sturdiness all who yearn after imperishable substance." Developing the image of the rock as a nursing mother, he then describes it as "the fountain of the divine wisdom." Finally, he shows that this nourishing rock is, in fact, synonymous with the manna which is "the divine word." Philo is here continuing a tradition of interpretation which sees the waters, (whether the rivers of paradise, the water from the rock or the waters flowing from the Temple, or all three "superimposed") as symbolizing the Wisdom of God, especially as expressed in the Law.[173] From a Fourth Gospel point of view, Philo's juxtaposition of the manna which satisfies hunger with the water from the rock and his eventual identification of the two is significant. We find hunger-satisfying eating similarly connected with and equivalent to thirst-quenching drinking in John 6:35.

We recapitulate our exploration of "the Scripture" in John 7:38. Notoriously difficult to identify, it is clearly a reference to the rock struck by Moses in the desert. It is most likely to be a citation from the account of this event in Ps (77)78 with resonances of Ezek 47 and Zech 14:8. In Jewish tradition, several layers of meaning have been superimposed on this rock. To its Mosaic significance has been added its perceived identity as the Rock of Sion, the place of theophany, sacrifice and judgement (2 Sam 24:18-25), designated by David as the site for the Temple. The Temple rock is then envisaged as the source of the four rivers of Paradise and, in eschatological speculation, of the river in Ezek 47 and Zech 14:8.

---

[172] Philo, *Leg. All.* II, 21, 86. Philo's designation of the desert rock as the ἀκρότομος πέτρα probably comes from Deut 8:15. The cognate noun occurs in LXX Ps 113:8 rendering the "flint" which becomes a spring. As we have seen, the Hebrew and Aramaic "behind" ἀκρότομος in this psalm may explain the word κοιλία in John 7:38.

[173] See Sir 24:23-31 and the identification of the well of Num 21:18 as the Law in CD VI, 3-11. Given Paul's presentation of Jesus as the Wisdom of God in 1 Cor 1:24, it may well be that he came to the conviction that Christ was "the rock that followed them" through contact with the "wisdom" reading of the story. See Orr & Walther, *1 Corinthians*, 245.

We have already had occasion to refer to the messianic overtones with which the paradise motif resonated because of the "royal" background to the Tree of Life image and the use of arborescent terminology in messianic speculation on the "shoot of David" and the "branch."[174] Against that background, we have also drawn attention to several paradisial allusions in John 6 which effected a parallel between the fruit of the Tree of Life and the bread that Jesus offers, suggesting a presentation of Jesus in wisdom/Torah terms as the new Tree of Life.

The whole dialogue in which the citation in John 7:37b-38 is set reflects these developments. Jesus' invitation to the thirsty suggests to some that he is "the prophet" (like Moses) of Deut 18:18. They see in his words the possibility of a repetition of the "water from the rock" provided by Moses. It appears to others, however, that Jesus is the Christ. They see in his words evoking Isa 55:1, Ἐάν τις διψᾷ ἐρχέσθω πρός με καὶ πινέτω., the possibility that the covenant with David is somehow at issue. This impression is confirmed by other "David" hints: the citation from the Psalter with its evocation of the Temple Rock, and the "Tabernacles" ambience pointing back to the dedication of the original Temple (1 Kgs 8:2. 65) and forward to the great celebration of the feast "on that day" when "there shall no longer be a trader in the house of the Lord (Zech 14:21)."[175] The form of the citation is thus profoundly affected by messianic expectation of a repetition of the Exodus which would also involve a paradisial renewal. At the heart of this continuity with biblical and midrashic reflection on the "rock," however, there is a decisive break with Jewish tradition.

> De Jésus s'écoulent à nouveau les fleuves jaillis du rocher et, dans le prolongement de la symbolique juive, cette eau représente la révélation messianique. Mais à l'intérieur de cette continuité, un contraste est marqué: c'est l'eau dispensée par le Christ qui détient la qualité paradisiaque de procurer la vie.[176]

Excursus: The Johannine Reception of Ps (77)78

The quotations in John 6:31 and 7:38 are both "words from Scripture" drawn from a didactic psalm presenting an interpretation of Israel's history which is noticeably pro-David and which includes

---

[174] See pp. 139-41 above.
[175] See John J. Castelot and A. Cody, "Religious Institutions of Israel," in *NJBC* 1253-83, at 1279 (76:133).
[176] Bienaimé, "L'annonce des fleuves," 453.

several pejorative references to places, people and events in Samaritan history. The psalm contains numerous references to Samaritan topography and history: Jacob (vv. 5, 21), Ephraim (vv. 9, 67), Joseph (v. 67), Shiloh (v. 60). The people referred to as οἱ πατέρες ἡμῶν (αὐτῶν), mentioned five times in the psalm (vv. 3. 5. 8. 12. 57) and, no doubt, alluded to in John 6:31, are the ancestors of the Samaritans. These "proto-Samaritan" fathers bear much of the blame for Israel's failure to keep the covenant. Their major sin is unbelief (v. 22). Even extraordinary wonders worked by God on their behalf do not produce the desired result of faith (v. 32). On the other hand, according to Ps (77)78 Jerusalem is most definitely the place where God is to be worshipped (v. 67-8). Its sanctuary is built by God and is established for ever. Moreover, there is in this psalm a view of David as a figure standing at the culmination of the recounted events, not unlike that found in Chronicles. Because of God's choice of Judah, Zion and David, the temple of God and the throne of the house of David are inextricably linked. They stand together, established by God for ever (v. 69, cf. Ps 122:1-5).

As we have seen, the Fourth Evangelist recalls the stories of the manna and the water from the rock as told in the Ps 77(78) version, rather than the Pentateuch. Obviously poetry, of its nature, has various mnemonic features, but there seems to be a definite intentionality about the Fourth Evangelist's use of ths psalm. In fact, Ps (77)78 seems to have had quite a currency in late Second Temple Judaism.[177] It has been suggested that it may have provided a "framework" for John 6. According to Georg Geiger, there are significant verbal, thematic and theological echoes of the psalm throughout John 6 which suggest that the Evangelist saw in the psalm's reference to the "turning back" of the Ephraimites an analogy to the abandonment of Jesus by many of his disciples. The Johannine use of the psalm represents an appeal to these not to be like their fathers (Ps 77:8), but to return to faith in Jesus.[178] This cre-

---

[177] The Qumran version of Ps 151 may allude to v. 70—"But he sent and took me from behind the flock." Ps-Philo's retelling of the manna story *(LAB X, 7)* is coloured by it.

[178] Among the common features of the psalm and John 6 identified by Geiger are: signs and wonders, the work(s) of God, eating and being satisfied, (from) heaven, not believing, flesh to eat, turning back, being like (the) fathers. In over-all structure, both the psalm and John 6 move from "signs and wonders," to discourse to a decision-making question resulting in a split. See Georg Geiger, "Aufruf am Rückkehrende Zum des Zitats von Ps 78, 24b in Joh 6,31," *Bib* 65 (1984) 449-64. This type of psalm influence is not unique to the Fourth Gospel. Hamish Swanston, *The Community Witness: An Exploration of the Influences at Work in the New Testament*

ates the impression that the audience for such an appeal included Samaritan believers, now wavering in their new-found faith.

The reasons for the Samaritan repudiation of the three-fold canon are particularly evident in Ps (77)78.[179] It could only, therefore, have been acceptable in a circle which included Samaritans, if understood in terms of a radically re-thought Davidic ideology, or, more precisely a Davidic ideology freed from any insistence on Judean hegemony.[180] A key to this is surely the association of David in Israel's memory and imagination with the hope for a re-unification of the twelve tribes under one shepherd and in worship at one sanctuary, a theme which, as we saw in our previous chapter, has influenced the editing of the Psalter.[181] The David of Ps (77)78, the shepherd who tends "Jacob/Israel" (all twelve tribes) with upright heart and skilful hand (vv. 71-72) is the pattern for a new David who would make the old divisions between Jews and Samaritans obsolete. In him, the permanence of both Temple and dynasty is assured. This David is not a Judean king in the popular messianic sense, but one whose zeal for God's worship is such that he will himself be the new Temple, divinely built, where God will dwell among humankind (cf. Ps 77:60 σκήνωμα αὐτοῦ, οὗ κατεσκήνωσεν ἐν ἀνθρώποις.). The Johannine reception of this psalm, therefore, brings much light to bear on Jesus' statement, ἡ σωτηρία ἐκ τῶν Ἰουδαίων ἐστίν (John 4:22). In fact, Geiger's suggestion could be taken further by extending the "plot" of Ps 77 to John 7 where, especially in the citation we have just explored, Jesus, the replacement Temple, fulfils the aspirations of the Feast of Tabernacles (cf. Ps 77:68-69). Significantly, it is in the debate which this development provokes that Jesus is called a Galilean and a Samaritan (John 7:41.52; 8:48).

Community and its Writings (London: Burns and Oates, 1967) 57-59, has noted a similar structural impact of Ps (105)106 on the Lucan order of the temptations of Jesus.

[179] After the destruction of Samaria by John Hyrcanus in 120 BCE, the Samaritans rejected the Prophets and the Writings "because of the recognition these books give to the Jerusalem Temple and their denunciation of the sins of Ephraim." See Roger T. Beckwith, "Formation of the Hebrew Bible," in Mulder (ed.), *Mikra*, 39-86, at 85.

[180] Since John 4 indicates acceptance of the idea of Samaritans joining the Johannine group, any appeal to Ps 77 as part of the community's self understanding would have to be couched in such a way that unbelieving Ἰουδαῖοι also incurred the psalm's promise of rejection and that all who accepted Jesus as saviour, whether Samaritan or Jew, shared in the redemption it promises.

[181] The prayer, "Gather us from among the nations," brings Book IV to its conclusion and Ps (106)107, referring to the ingathering as accomplished, opens Book V.

E. *Ps (81)82:6 in John 10:34*

The next formal psalm quotation in the Fourth Gospel occurs in the series of confrontational debates between Jesus and "the Jews," immediately following the Shepherd Discourse which may originally have formed the end of the Book of Signs.¹⁸² The actual scene in which the quotation occurs is set against the backdrop of τὰ ἐγκαίνια, the festival of Hanukkah commemorating the re-consecration of the Temple by Judas Maccabeus in 165 BCE, a feast celebrating the renewal of worship in the Temple. Significantly, perhaps, the quotation itself is from one of the psalms sung in the Temple Liturgy.¹⁸³ Jesus, the one whom the Father has consecrated (ἡγίασεν v. 36), is strolling in the portico named for another figure associated with an earlier Temple dedication ritual, David's son, Solomon.¹⁸⁴ Even before any outright conflict develops, there is a certain menace in the way "the Jews" surround Jesus. Threatening forces are closing in on the shepherd who has just declared that he will lay down his life for the sheep (John 10:11). The verb κυκλόω evokes numerous scenes in which the psalmist is encircled by opponents intent on harm.¹⁸⁵ This is no gathering of the sheep around their shepherd at the sound of his voice, such as the earlier part of John 10 might have led us to expect. This is a trial scene. Those "under the illusion that they are the judges"¹⁸⁶ demand that Jesus explain himself. As the scene develops, it will be Jesus' revelatory self-disclosure in response to this demand that will provoke the real κρίσις.

This scene has all the appearances of legal proceedings.¹⁸⁷ It is carefully constructed in two sequences, each involving a challenge

---

¹⁸² Brown, *John I - XII*, 414. 427-29.

¹⁸³ According to *m. Tamid* 7:4, Ps 82 was sung on the third day of the week.

¹⁸⁴ The term ἐνκαινία, literally "renewal," used in Num 7:10-11, I Kgs 8:63, 2 Chr 7:5 and Ezra 6:16 is "somewhat evocative of the consecration of all the houses of God in Israel's history." Brown, *John, I-XII*, 402.

¹⁸⁵ The cluster of verbs κυκλόω, περικυκλόω and περιέχω occur frequently and often in parallel with reference to foes encircling the psalmist, e.g., Pss 16:9, 17:5-6 (= 2 Sam 22:5-6), 21:13.17, 31:7, 87:18, 108:3. We draw attention to Ps 117:10-12 in view of the quotation from this psalm in John 12:13. In 1 Kgs 5:3 Solomon recalls how David was continually surrounded by enemies until the Lord put them under the soles of his feet.

¹⁸⁶ See Bultmann, *The Gospel of John*, 86.

¹⁸⁷ For the forensic terms in which the Fourth Evangelist conceives the conflict between Jesus and "the Jews" as representatives of "the world," see N. A. Dahl, "The Johannine Church and history," in Ashton (ed.), *The Interpretation of John*, 122-140, at 135. For the debates between Jesus and the Jews as forensic proceedings, See Neyrey, "Jesus the Judge: Forensic Process in John 8:21-29," *Bib* 68 (1987) 509-42, and *An Ideology of Revolt: John's Christology in Social-Science Perspective* (Philadelphia: Fortress, 1988) especially Ch. 3 dealing with John 10.

by the "prosecuting" Jews, a "defence" by Jesus in which he calls upon the testimony of witnesses, and an unsuccessful attempt to execute judgement on him. In the first sequence (vv. 24-31) the "prosecution" challenges Jesus' status as the Christ. If he is the Christ, he should say so openly—παρρησία, a word which will appear again in a judicial context (John 18:19-21). In his reply Jesus refers to the testimony of his works and, refusing to fit himself into popular messianic categories, defines his messiahship in terms of his divine sonship.[188] Jesus' hearers judge his words as blasphemous.[189] They react by preparing to carry out the death sentence. In the second sequence (vv. 32-39) there is a strong sense of spiralling confrontation as "the Jews" become more hostile and Jesus becomes more vehement. The "prosecution" challenges his status as Son of God. In his defence Jesus calls on the witness of Scripture as well as the testimony of his works. Again the reaction of "the Jews" is to judge Jesus deserving of condemnation, but their attempt to arrest him fails. It is in the course of his second defence that Jesus adduces a "word from Scripture"—Psalm (81)82:6—

Οὐκ ἔστιν γεγραμμένον ἐν τῷ νόμῳ ὑμῶν ὅτι ἐγὼ εἶπα Θεοί ἐστε;

"Is it not written in your law, 'I said, you are gods'?"

In order to appreciate the full effect of this quotation, we need to uncover the tradition which generated the dialogue into which it is introduced. This scene is one of the narratives in the Fourth Gospel when we can most clearly see the bringing forward of the trial scene into the period of the ministry. It is the first occasion in the Fourth Gospel where Jesus is explicitly charged with blasphemy (10:33. Cf. Mark 14:64). The structuring of the scene in two sequences, one dealing with Jesus as the Christ and the other with Jesus as the Son of God, corresponds to the twofold question of the High priest recorded in the synoptics—Σὺ εἶ ὁ Χριστὸς ὁ υἱὸς τοῦ εὐλογητοῦ; (Mark 14:62).[190] Interestingly, the Lucan version gives evidence of a

---

[188] Ashton explains the Fourth Evangelist's dissatisfaction with a *merely* messianic view of Jesus as follows: "It is not that John no longer subscribes to the traditional belief that 'Jesus is Messiah'; but by the time the Gospel has been composed the twin titles of 'Messiah' and 'son of God' have gathered all the additional significance attached by John to the special relationship between Jesus and the Father." See *Studying John: Approaches to the Fourth Gospel*, (Oxford: Clarendon Press, 1994) 107.

[189] Bultmann, *The Gospel of John*, 245, comments on the similar accusation in John 5:18 that Jesus made himself equal to God: "They can only conceive equality with God as independence from God, whereas for Jesus it means the very opposite, as is brought out immediately in v. 19."

[190] Fourth Gospel declarations of faith in Jesus as the Christ and as the Son of God also seem to echo this traditional sequence. The pattern can be most clearly

development of the tradition not unlike that which has shaped John 10:22-39.[191] It is this forensic character of John 10:22-39 which explains the absence of a Jewish trial from the Johannine Passion Narrative. As Frank J. Matera has demonstrated, apart from the temple charge (found in John 2:19-22) and the condemnation (found in John 11:47-53), the major elements of the synoptic trial tradition can be accounted for in this scene—the messianic question, Jesus' affirmation and the charge of blasphemy.[192] Furthermore, like the synoptic trial scene, John 10:22-39 is a climactic moment of self-disclosure on the part of Jesus.[193] As in the synoptics, that self-disclosure of a Jesus apparently on trial is in reality the judgement of the world.[194]

In the synoptics the portrayal of Jesus as eschatological judge is achieved by means of Jesus' claim that he is to be "seated at the right hand of God," an allusion to Ps 109:1. The Fourth Gospel contains no such allusion. In fact the Evangelist's apparent avoidance of a metaphor belonging to the tradition would suggest that it did not suit the Johannine theological schema. As suggested in our discussion of Ps (109)110,[195] presumably its two-stage application to Jesus in early Christianity (e.g., Rom 1:3-4), suggesting elevation from a lower to a higher status, would not have fitted with Johannine Christology. However, from within the tradition based on a widely attested Christological reading of Ps 109:1, the Fourth Evangelist seems to have developed his own way of subverting the

---

discerned in John 20:31—ταῦτα δὲ γέγραπται ἵνα πιστεύ[σ]ητε ὅτι Ἰησοῦς ἐστιν ὁ Χριστὸς ὁ υἱὸς τοῦ θεοῦ...It is also perceptible in Martha's profession (11:27). Nathaniel's profession too (1:49), Ῥαββί, σὺ εἶ ὁ υἱὸς τοῦ θεοῦ, σὺ βασιλεὺς εἶ τοῦ Ἰσραήλ, merits a reply from Jesus which, on the analogy of Acts 7:56, bears a strong resemblance to the synoptic trial scenes, except that instead of the synoptic reference to Ps 109:1, the Fourth Gospel alludes to Gen 28:12.

[191] Luke has the Jewish leaders assembled in council make two separate interventions: a challenge almost identical with that in John, Εἰ σὺ εἶ ὁ Χριστός, εἰπὸν ἡμῖν and a question, Σὺ οὖν εἶ ὁ υἱὸς τοῦ θεοῦ; (Luke 22:67.70). Jesus' reply to the first challenge is virtually the same as his answer in John 10:25.

[192] See "Jesus before Annas: John 18, 13-14. 19-24," *ETL* 66 (1990) 38-55.

[193] In the diachronic perspective of Fortna, the John 10 trial scene is one of several occasions where the Fourth Gospel "has replicated Jesus' explicit self disclosure, coming only at the end of his life in the source, as an event repeated again and again." See *The Fourth Gospel and its Predecessor*, 159.

[194] Bultmann, *The Gospel*, 86, sees this confrontation between Jesus and "the Jews," which is ongoing throughout the Gospel as a struggle "which reaches its conclusion in the κέκριται 16.11 and the ἐγὼ νενίκηκα τὸν κόσμον 16.33." As Dahl explains, John's view of the Jews as representatives of the world "is based on the Jewish idea, that Israel is the centre of the world." Therefore, "the world's enmity and opposition to God gets its concentrated expression through the Jews." See "The Johannine Church and History," 126.

[195] See p. 54-56 above.

trial proceedings. The unspoken Ps 109:1 "waits in the wings" while on-stage the Johannine Jesus quotes from another psalm very much concerned with judgement, the words ἐγὼ εἶπα Θεοί ἐστε. As we are about to see, the meaning effect of the synoptic quotation from Ps 109 is conveyed, in large part, by John's quotation from Ps 81, with the major difference that in John, the judgement is no future event, but a present reality.

The citation, ἐγὼ εἶπα Θεοί ἐστε, forms part of Jesus' argument from Scripture defending his claim, ἐγὼ καὶ ὁ πατὴρ ἕν ἐσμεν, against the charge of blasphemy. This is the only citation from Ps (81)82 in the NT. Its agreement with the LXX is striking in that only here is the verbal form εἶπα found in the Fourth Gospel. The quotation is introduced by the formula: Οὐκ ἔστιν γεγραμμένον ἐν τῷ νόμῳ ὑμῶν ὅτι...; The ὑμῶν most likely has a purely argumentative function: "the law that even you admit."[196] The wider sense in which the Law is used here as encompassing the whole of Scripture is found elsewhere in the NT.[197] We will encounter it again at John 15:25. The quotation is followed by a commentary, put on the lips of Jesus, in the typical rabbinic style of *a minori ad maius* argument according to the first of Hillel's rules, *Qal wahomer*.[198] The rather literalist phrase, καὶ οὐ δύναται λυθῆναι ἡ γραφή, somewhat uncharacteristic of the Johannine Jesus who "in general...uses Scripture in an allusive, poetic and evocative way" probably exemplifies a style of argumentation used in the debate between the Johannine church and the synagogue.[199]

Who does the Evangelist understand as "those to whom the word of God came" who in the psalm are called "gods"? Are we to take the quoted verse in isolation, as it were, or are we to assume that the

---

[196] Brown, *John, I-XII*, 403, suggests that the omission of the ὑμῶν in some Mss may be a scribal attempt to soften Jesus' apparent dissociation of himself from the Jewish heritage. We will encounter a similarly argumentative use of the possessive pronoun in the formula introducing the quotation from Ps 68:4 in John 15:25.

[197] In 1 Cor 14:21 a quotation from Isaiah is said to be from the Law. In Rom 3:19 Paul, having quoted a psalm, refers back to it as "whatever the Law says." In John 12:34, the text, "the Christ remains for ever," though difficult to identify, is clearly not from the Pentateuch.

[198] For the hermeneutical principles (*middoth*) attributed to Hillel, see *b. Sanh* 7 and the Midrash, *Abot of R. Nathan* 37. See also Kasher, "The Interpretation of Scripture," 584, and Ellis, "Biblical Interpretation," 699, who cites 2 Cor 3:6-11 as an example. F. Manns believes that *Qal Wahomer* reasoning is also evident in John 7:22-23. See "Exégèse rabbinique et exégèse johannique," *RB* 92 (1985) 525-38 at 531. Holladay, *The Psalms through Three Thousand Years*, 128, sees *Qal wahomer* at work in Luke 12:24.

[199] Moule, *The Birth of the New Testament*, 66, notes that Jesus uses a similar style of argument in John 7:23.

"gods" addressed in v. 6 of the psalm are those also mentioned in v. 1. If v. 1 is to be taken into account, then we need to be aware of the fluidity of its textual form. In the LXX, it appears as follows—

> Ὁ θεὸς ἔστη ἐν συναγωγῇ θεῶν,
> ἐν μέσῳ δὲ θεοὺς διακρίνει.

The LXX is the only one of the ancient Greek versions to keep to the original meaning of v. 1a—that God is in a court scene with other gods. It also deliberately mistranslates v. 1b so that God is not in the midst of the gods, but rather, "In the midst he judges gods."[200] Various interpretations found in Jewish sources which may preserve interpretations current at the time of the writing of the Fourth Gospel have suggested equally varied identifications for these "gods," principally that they are (1) angels, (2) the Israelites after their reception of the Law, or (3) judges.[201] We will examine each of these proposals to see if they can help us in our reading of John 10:34.

(1). The 'gods' could be angels. The Psalms Targum reflects this solution to what was, no doubt, a problematic text for monotheists—

> Ego dixi, veluti angeli vos estis reputati
> et tamquam angeli excelsi vos omnes.

The research of J. A. Emerton has revealed that the Pešhittā and several Targumim quite often translate אלהים as "angels" or "sons of angels." Emerton proposes that the Fourth Evangelist understood the "gods" of Ps (81)82 to be superhuman beings appointed to rule each nation, regarded as angels by Jews and as gods by gentiles. He notes that Paul seems to have accepted their existence (1 Cor 8:5). If this is the background to the Johannine Jesus' use of the psalm text, then, Emerton suggests, the charge of blasphemy hinges on a distinction between these beings to whom God has committed authority and Jesus who claims divine authority in his own right.[202] The

---

[200] Cf. Aquila: θεὸς ἔστη ἐν συναγωγῇ ἰσχυρῶν, ἐν ἐγκάτῳ κύριος κρινεῖ, and Symmachus: ὁ θεὸς κατέστη ἐν συνόδῳ θεοῦ, ἐν μέσοις θεὸς κρίνων. R. B. Salters, "Psalm 82,1 and the Septuagint," *ZAW* 103 (1991) 225-39, at 227, believes that the LXX translator is eager to identify the אלהים of v. 1 with the אלהים of vv. 6-7 precisely "because there existed at the time of translation a body of opinion which pressed for an interpretation of verse 1 as referring to a council of human beings, and, perhaps, a separate and unrelated interpretation of vv. 6f."

[201] See J. S. Ackerman, "The Rabbinic Interpretation of Ps 82 and the Gospel of John," in *HTR* 59 (1966) 186-91. For a convenient summary of these three proposals, see Schuchard, *Scripture Within Scripture*, 62-63.

[202] J. A. Emerton, "Some New Testament Notes, I: The Interpretation of Ps 82 and John 10," *JTS* 11 (1960) 329-36. Emerton's view of Ps (81)82:1 was confirmed with the publication of 11QMelch. See his "Melchizedek and the Gods: Fresh

"gods" would thus be angelic beings or spirits such as those encountered in 11QMelch.²⁰³ Ashton believes that an explanation along these lines is the only one of the three proposals "strong enough to suit the context." Only a claim on the part of Jesus to be superior to these heavenly beings would be "strong enough to warrant the response he receives."²⁰⁴ The main problem with the "angels" proposal is that it is difficult to see how it fits with Jesus' reference to the "gods" as those πρὸς οὓς ὁ λόγος τοῦ θεοῦ ἐγένετο (John 10:35).

(2). In another Jewish interpretation, the "gods" addressed in the psalm are the people of Israel after their reception of the Law. A tradition preserved in the name of R. Jose (fl. *ca* 250 CE) comments on Ps (81)82:6 as follows:

> The Israelites accepted the Torah only so that the Angel of Death should have no dominion over them, as it is said, "I SAID YE ARE GODS AND ALL OF YOU SONS OF THE MOST HIGH" (Ps 82:6). Now that you have spoilt your deeds, "YE SHALL DIE LIKE MORTALS" (Ps 82:7).²⁰⁵

If they had kept the Law, they would not have died. After the golden calf episode, they "will die like men" (cf. Ps 82: 7).²⁰⁶ This identification of "those to whom the word of God came" (John 10:35), leads some to think of a contrast between the giving of the Law as word of God and the coming of Jesus as the Word made flesh. Thus, if those addressed by the word of God in the Law can be called gods, the title "Son of God" can certainly be applied to Jesus. This interpretation is espoused by Dahl.²⁰⁷ Hanson offers a variant of it:

Evidence for the Jewish Background of John X. 34-6," *JTS* 17 (1966) 399-401. M. de Jonge and A. S. van der Woude agree that Emerton's suggestion receives support from 11QMelch, although they prefer to think in terms of (human) "heavenly beings" rather than angels. See their "11QMelchizedek and the New Testament," *NTS*, 12 (1966), 301-26.

²⁰³ According to this document, an eschatological Melchizedek figure, referred to as Elohim or El, will judge his demonic counterpart, Belial and his minions, who as punishment have become mortal beings, subject to death. Melchizedek will execute judgement, as it is written concerning him in the Songs of David, who said, 'ELOHIM has taken his place in the divine council; in the midst of the gods he holds judgement.'

²⁰⁴ Ashton, *Understanding*, 147-50, acknowledges that such a reading is "a long way from the strict monotheism of the Jews who are Jesus' adversaries in the Fourth Gospel," but points out that there is a considerable variety of angelological vocabulary in some Qumran texts, e.g., 11QMelch and 4Q400-404 (4Q ShirShab).

²⁰⁵ *b. Abod. Zar.* 5a, trans. I. Epstein, *The Babylonian Talmud* (London: Soncino Press, 1935) 19.

²⁰⁶ *Midr. Rab. Exod* 32:7. *Midr. Teh.* 82, 3 preserves a similar tradition according to which Adam was "like God" and "a son of the Most High," but having sinned, received God's sentence as found in Ps (81)82:7—"You shall die like Adam and fall like one of the princes."

²⁰⁷ "The Johannine Church and History," 130. Also in favour are Barrett, *The*

the Law was addressed to Israel by the pre-existent Word. If this address, mediated by Moses (and in the case of the psalm, David) justified human beings in being called "gods," far more are we justified in applying the title "Son of God" to the bearer of the pre-existent Word, sent by the Father in unmediated and direct presence.[208] J. Neyrey, who also accepts the interpretation of the "gods" as Israel at Sinai, understands the notion of Israel's deathlessness on receipt of the Law as a restoration of Adam's privilege in sharing God's imperishability (Wisd 2:23). He connects this with Jesus' claim that he gives his sheep eternal life (John 10:28).[209]

This second interpretation, particularly in Neyrey's "version," does have the advantage of situating the quotation in the Johannine context and may, therefore, be of some help to us. There is also a tannaitic adaptation of this interpretation which has a certain affinity with the Fourth Gospel. In it the "gods" are those who do Torah and the will of their Father in heaven, while those who will "die like men" (Ps 82:7) are those who reject Torah.[210] However, as Boismard has warned, there is the problem that Jesus refers to the "gods" as "those to whom the word of God came." The phrase "the word (singular) of God" is not used as a designation for the Law in the Judaism contemporary with the writing of the Fourth Gospel. Rather, the biblical stock phrase, "the word of God came to..." consistently refers to individuals who are called to speak and act on God's behalf, and especially to prophets.[211]

(3). In a third Jewish interpretation of the psalm, the "gods" are judges.[212] Having failed to judge in line with God's justice, they

---

Gospel, 384-85; Schnackenburg, *The Gospel II*, 310-11; Pancaro, *The Law in the Fourth Gospel*, 177-85; Ackerman, "The Rabbinic Interpretation of Ps 82," 186-91.

[208] Hanson, "John's Citation of Psalm LXXXII: John X. 33-36." *NTS* 11 (1964-1965) 158-62, at 161. Hanson later modified his position after the publication of 11QMelch. See "John's Citation of Psalm LXXXII Reconsidered." *NTS* 13 (1966-1967) 363-67.

[209] Neyrey admits, however, that the Evangelist does not make full use of this interpretive tradition which was available to him. He also acknowledges that the midrashic tradition on which this argument depends reached written form considerably later than the Fourth Gospel did. Consequently, he confines his conclusions to the modest claim that John 10:34-36 "might be the earliest extant witness of that tradition, although not the most complete example." See Neyrey, "I Said: You Are Gods: Psalm 82:6 and John 10." *JBL* 108 (1989), 647-63 and *An Ideology of Revolt*, 221-224.

[210] *Sifrei Deut.* 306 as quoted by S. Safrai. in "Oral Torah," S. Safrai (ed.), *The Literature of the Sages*, CRINT 2, 3 (Assen/Philadelphia: Van Gorcum/Fortress, 1897) 35-120, at 113.

[211] Boismard has furthermore demonstrated an impressive similarity between John 10:35-6 and the account of the prophetic vocation in Jer 4:10 which in its turn is modelled on the Prophet like Moses in Deut 18:18. See *Moïse ou Jésus*, 2 and 114.

[212] This interpretation is found in *b. Sanh.* 6b-7a, *b. Sota* 47b, *b. Ber.* 6a and in

themselves fall under the judgement of God who upbraids them in the psalm. This line of thought seems, to a good number of scholars, to best explain Jesus' citation from the psalm.[213]

Many who follow this explanation tend to understand John 10:34 in terms of Jesus' role as the eschatological Prophet-like-Moses. The idea that the "gods" are judges recalls Moses the original judge and the great prophet conveying God's words to the people (Exod 18:15-16). The psalm verse is applicable to Moses (and by extension to the select group of tribal leaders with whom he shared his judicial and prophetic role) because Moses was "like God,"[214] and in Hellenistic Judaism was even regarded as somehow divine.[215] Thus Schuchard, for example, would see the point of the quotation as follows—If Moses and even his successors, the judges, could be called gods, how much more justifiably can Jesus, the Prophet-like-Moses who incomparably surpasses Moses, be called Son of God.[216] The weakness of this explanation is that it drifts somewhat from the core issue in the pericope: εἰ σὺ εἶ ὁ Χριστός, εἰπὲ ἡμῖν παρρησίᾳ. Jesus' messiahship is at issue here no less than in the synoptic trial scenes to which, as we have seen, John 10:22-39 corresponds. Nevertheless, the idea that the "gods" are judges fits well with the forensic character of John's scene. It may yield fruit, if taken in a slightly different direction.

A sounder approach would be to take account of Jesus' reference to those addressed as "gods" as those πρὸς οὓς ὁ λόγος τοῦ θεοῦ ἐγένετο (John 10:35). If we understand this as analogous to the biblical commissioning formula, "the word of God came to N.," then we can think in terms of various individuals called to leadership—whether judges, kings, prophets, or even, by extension, those who hold authority in virtue of their knowledge of the Law. The contrast in John 10 would then appear as one between those commissioned to act in

---

Midr. Teh. 82.1. A tradition preserved in *m. Abot* 3:6 uses the notion of God judging among the judges (who must always be a minimum of three) as a proof that the Shekinah rests even among only three men sitting together occupied with Torah. We mentioned this interpretation in connection with Matt 18:20 (See p. 45 above). The same Mishnah passage also claims, on the basis of the previous line of the psalm—"God stands in the congregation of God"—that the Shekinah rests with ten. This is the minimum number of a congregation according to *m. Sanh.* 1:6.

[213] E.g., Brown, *John I-XII*, 409-11; Reim, *Studien*, 23; Lindars, *The Gospel of John*, 374.

[214] This idea comes from Exod 4:16 where Moses is to be "like God" to Aaron, and Exod 7:1—"See, I make you as God to Pharaoh."

[215] According to *Mos.* I, 27, the young Moses' developing mind was both divine and human. *Mos.* I, XXVIII, 155 states that God gave the whole world into the hands of Moses, his heir, who as prophet and friend of God shared God's possessions entered into the divine darkness (Exod 20:21). Moses was named "God" for his partnership with God and was called "God and king of the whole nation."

[216] Schuchard, *Scripture within Scripture*, 67-68.

God's name, especially to judge, and Jesus who is uniquely commissioned by the Father—ὃν ὁ πατὴρ ἡγίασεν καὶ ἀπέστειλεν εἰς τὸν κόσμον (John 10:36), also especially to judge.

We need also to maintain the close connection between the disputation in which the citation occurs (vv. 22-39) and the Shepherd Discourse which immediately precedes it.[217] The earlier part of John 10 has touched on several themes evocative of David as ideal shepherd and in response to the demand for clarity, Jesus has spoken as shepherd in words reminiscent of Αἶνος ᾠδῆς τῷ Δαυιδ, Psalm 94.[218] The Ezek 34 background to the Shepherd Discourse also highlights the contrast between those commissioned by God to shepherd Israel who failed in their responsibility and the expected ideal shepherd (David, according to Ezek 34:23) through whom God himself will shepherd Israel (Ezek 34:11), judging between sheep and sheep (Ezek 34:22).[219] All of this shepherd imagery spills over, as it were, into the confrontation between Jesus and "the Jews," especially into vv. 26-27. Thus, when Jesus quotes Ps (81)82, he is still speaking in the "shepherd/king" mode.

One of the major facets of Israelite kingship ideology was the belief that the king's justice in judgement embodied God's kingly reign. The Chronicler's assessment of David's reign is that "he administered justice and equity to all his people" (1 Chr 18:14). Commissioned by God, the king bore the title "Son of God" (2 Sam 7:14, Ps 2:7). He is even addressed as "god" in Psalm 44:7, and this within a context which stresses his commitment to justice in his judgements, for which he has been anointed by God. A new king of David's line is called "Mighty God" in Isa 9:6. The expression "like God" is used of David's line, in a context which, as we have already seen, was important for the Fourth Evangelist; the MT of Zech 12:8 reads—"....the feeblest among them on that day shall be like David, and the house of David shall be like God (כֵּאלֹהִים)."[220] There is also

---

[217] This suggestion presupposes a synchronic view of the text. In fact, a diachronic reading which recognizes 10:1-21 as inserted in a sequence which originally moved from Ch 9 directly to the scene in Solomon's Portico. Ashton, *Studying John*, 122-25, would support the interpretation we are suggesting for John 10:34.

[218] See pp. 308-09 below.

[219] Other OT "shepherd" passages echoed in John 10 include Isa 40:11, Ezek 37:24; Ps (22)23:1-3 and Ps (94)95:7. See Johannes Beutler, "Der Alttestamentlich-jüdischer Hintergrund der Hirtenrede," in J. Beutler and R. T. Fortna (ed.), *The Shepherd Discourse of John 10 and its Context* (Cambridge: University Press, 1991) 18-32, at 25.

[220] Even though the LXX adjusts the text in deference to monotheistic sensibilities (ὁ δὲ οἶκος Δαυὶδ ὡς οἶκος Θεοῦ), the analogy between the Davidic king and God not only remains, but opens up a further link, that between the Temple and the Davidic dynasty.

the fact that both David and Solomon are among those "to whom the word of God came" (cf. 1 Chron 22:8; 1 Kgs 6:11).

All of this suggests that the interpretation of Ps 81:6 in which the "gods" are judges was probably uppermost in the Evangelist's mind and that he understood the "judges" in the psalm as those commissioned to rule God's people. If these leaders of Israel, these "shepherds," bearers of the title "Son of God" could be called "gods," how much more appropriately is ὁ ποιμὴν ὁ καλός, Jesus the Christ, called, in a unique sense, "Son of God." In view of the influence of Ezekiel's "one shepherd" (Ezek 34:23; 37:24) on John 10:16, it could also be that Ezekiel's idea that both God and David will shepherd Israel (Ezek 34:16.23) has strengthened the Johannine Jesus' biblical warrant for claiming: ὅτι ἐν ἐμοὶ ὁ πατὴρ κἀγὼ ἐν τῷ πατρί (John 10:38). Certainly, Jesus as shepherd takes over what Ezekiel regards as God's role. The great advantage of such a reading is that it explains the quotation in terms of Jesus' messianic claim. This is important since, as John Painter has pointed out, the Fourth Evangelist is constructing in this disputation "a defence, not only against the Jewish charge of ditheism, but also against the charge laid by Christian Jews that this (*sc.* Johannine) christology is not true to Jesus' messianic status and role."[221]

It is surprising that the second half of the psalm verse, which one would have thought would greatly strengthen the argument, is not quoted. But it is certain that readers familiar with the Psalter would, in fact, have "heard" the whole verse:

ἐγὼ εἶπα Θεοί ἐστε
καὶ υἱοὶ ὑψίστου πάντες·

The second line can certainly be glimpsed behind Jesus' claim: Υἱὸς τοῦ θεοῦ εἰμι. It is actually in the complete parallelism that we find the two designations "god" and "son of God" treated as identical.[222] The whole psalm verse thus facilitates that momentous theological shift whereby the originally messianic title "son of God," now understood as the equivalent of the title "God," can be made to carry the full weight of Johannine Christology.

Another indication that the Evangelist understands the Θεοί as "judges" is his apparent consciousness of the whole psalm context.

---

[221] John Painter, "Tradition, History and Interpretation in John 10," in Beutler & Fortna (ed.), *The Shepherd Discourse of John 10 and its Context*, 53-74. For Dodd, *The Interpretation*, 361, the reply "I and the Father are one" to the question "Are you the Christ?" indicates a re-interpretation of Messianic categories "for a wider, non-Jewish public."

[222] Boismard, *Moïse ou Jesus*, 114.

The *incipit* of the psalm describes a judgement scene:

Ὁ θεὸς ἔστη ἐν συναγωγῇ θεῶν,
ἐν μέσῳ δὲ θεοὺς διακρίνει...

As the Johannine scene unfolds, it begins to look uncannily like the Ps (81)82 scene. In fact, an extremely ironic situation develops. Those who encircle Jesus to judge him resemble the "circle" of "gods" in the psalm with Ὁ θεὸς standing in their midst. Viewed through the lens of the psalm, Jesus appears as the divine judge standing in the midst of Israel's judges accusing them of not judging "with right judgement" (cf. John 7:24). They themselves enact v. 5 of the psalm—

οὐκ ἔγνωσαν οὐδὲ συνῆκαν,
ἐν σκότει διαπορεύονται·

In fact the exact words, οὐκ ἔγνωσαν, have already been used of them (John 10:6). Furthermore, their unwillingness to believe in Jesus puts them in the category of those who prefer to walk in darkness (John 1:9-11, 3:19, 9:39-41). Regarding Jesus as a sinner, guilty of blasphemy, their intent is to kill him, but it is they who will die. Verse 7 of the psalm, ὑμεῖς δὲ ὡς ἄνθρωποι ἀποθνήσκετε, might even be echoed in John 8:21—καὶ ἐν τῇ ἁμαρτίᾳ ὑμῶν ἀποθανεῖσθε.

The Jewish interpretation of Ps (81)82:6 which refers to Israel at the giving of the Law may also help us to appreciate the irony of the situation in John 10:22-39. By refusing to accept Jesus, "the Jews" show their true colours. They are no longer "those to whom the word of God came." They have therefore relinquished their status as "gods," as "immortals" who find eternal life in the Law (John 5:39). It is the Johannine Christians who have accepted Jesus who have eternal life. They are the "gods," or, as the psalm itself explains that term, υἱοὶ ὑψίστου, or, again, as the Fourth Evangelist calls them, τέκνα θεοῦ (John 1:12). To Jewish opponents, the quotation is a retort, in words from their own Law, that there was no blasphemy in Jesus' claim to be Son of God. For Johannine Christians, the quotation speaks of Jesus' right to the title "Son of God" not only in view of his role as judge, but also in view of his role as bestower of life (John 5:21-24).[223] It also speaks of their right, as those who welcomed the Word when he came among them, to be called children of God.[224] The "undersong" of the whole psalm thus provides a bril-

---

[223] As Ashton, *Understanding*, 139, has shown, Jesus insists on his equality with God by claiming that God associates him with himself in the divine work of judgement and bestowal of life.

[224] Pancaro, *The Law in the Fourth Gospel*, 188-9.

liantly ironic commentary reinforcing the sense of scriptural fulfilment at a juncture in the Fourth Gospel when the confrontation between Jesus and "the Jews" is intensifying. The ironic dimension to the theme of judgement is in continuity with Chs 7-8 and anticipates the final judgement scene before Pilate.

In conclusion, Ps 81:6 is quoted in a narrative which portrays the ongoing confrontation between Jesus and "the Jews" as a trial scene. Structured according to a definite pattern found in the synoptic accounts of the trial of Jesus, this scene is the Johannine equivalent of the high priest's question in the synoptics, "Are you the Christ, the Son of God?" The designation ὁ υἱὸς τοῦ θεοῦ, as understood within the Johannine circle, has become a qualifying term, defining the sense in which Jesus is ὁ Χριστός. To those who want him to tell them plainly if he is the Christ, Jesus' affirmative reply takes the form of an explanation of his sonship: that he does the works of his Father (John 10:37), and is one with the Father (John 10:30). This nuancing of the title ὁ Χριστός exemplifies John's capacity to transform and redefine a received tradition, to modify without repudiating.

The choice of Ps (81)82 is most appropriate because of the close connection it makes between the idea of judgement and that of God's universal kingship. The "gods" of the psalm, whom Jesus identifies as "those to whom the word of God came," are probably best understood as those commissioned by God to judge, particularly the kings in their responsibility to execute the judgements of God. The narrative setting of the quotation, following directly on the Shepherd Discourse alerts the reader to resonances of OT shepherd imagery, notably Ezek 34 with its contrast between the failed leaders of Israel and the expected ideal judge-king-shepherd, "David." The setting of the confrontation in the Portico of Solomon, son of David, recalls the theme of wisdom in judgement (1 Kgs 3:9). The fact that the quotation comes from the Temple liturgy devised by David also seems to be an important hint, especially in view of the carefully constructed Temple ambience for the scene. All contribute to an impression that the special authority with which Davidic "authorship" invests the psalm is significant. As Trudinger notes—

> John...treats of the significance of Jesus's life and death by subtle references to that "messiah" *par excellence*, David, whom he would have accepted, I believe, as the writer of Psalm 82, which he has Jesus quote favourably in support of his claim to be the Son of God (John 10:34-36).[225]

---

[225] Trudinger, "Hosanna," 297.

So, once again we find that the perceived provenance of this "word of Scripture"—the Psalms of David—has profoundly affected its reception within the Johannine circle.

In the light of all this, the argument of the quotation appears to be as follows. Judgement is ultimately God's and is therefore most appropriately delivered by those familiar with the holy sphere, those who hear the divine counsel.[226] In Israel's past there have been divinely commissioned judges-kings-shepherds, notably David. If God addresses these as "gods," or, in the case of David, as "my son," how much more appropriately, then, is Jesus, who "is not merely a human messenger, but comes from the divine side of reality into the world,"[227] addressed as "the Son of God." It is the unspoken second half of the verse which shows the alert Johannine reader that, applied to Jesus, "Son of God" is no mere messianic title to be understood figuratively. It is to be taken in its deepened Johannine sense as the equivalent of the title "God."

As we have found with regard to other psalm quotations, the quotation of Ps 81:6 has its own constellation of allusions and echoes. Viewing the Johannine scene as an enactment of the complete psalm brings out the irony of the situation. While the would-be judges of Jesus have come under condemnation, those who have accepted him have become τέκνα θεοῦ (John 1:12). Unlike those who would put Jesus on trial, believers in Jesus have professed their faith in him as the Christ and as the Son of God. There is thus a very real sense in which the psalm can give expression to the judgement already pronounced in their favour—Θεοί ἐστε καὶ υἱοὶ ὑψίστου πάντες.

F. *Ps (117)118:26 in John 12:13*

The cry addressed to the Johannine Jesus as he enters Jerusalem—

Ὡσαννά· εὐλογημένος ὁ ἐρχόμενος ἐν ὀνόματι κυρίου, [καὶ] ὁ βασιλεὺς τοῦ Ἰσραήλ.

"Hosanna! Blessed is he who comes in the name of the Lord, (and) the King of Israel!"

draws on Ps 117:25-26. This acclamation cites the only psalm passage that is found *verbatim* in all four gospels: the line, εὐλογημένος ὁ ἐρχόμενος ἐν ὀνόματι κυρίου.[228] While regarding it as an explicit

---

[226] See J. H. Eaton, *Kingship and the Psalms* (Sheffield: JSOT Press, 1986), 177.
[227] Painter, "Tradition, History and Interpretation in John 10," 71.
[228] As we have seen, the dividing of the garments and the giving of vinegar to drink, both motifs drawn from the Psalter, are common to all four gospels. Ps (117)118:26, however, is the only case of substantial verbal congruence among all four Evangelists in a reference to the Psalter.

psalm quotation for the purposes of this study, we note that it is "the only direct quotation in John not introduced or followed by a formula."[229] In both Matt 21:9 and Mark 11:9 it is quoted as it stands in the LXX. In the Lucan version (Luke 19:38) an interpretive gloss, ὁ βασιλεύς, has been inserted. John leaves the citation intact, but appends the words, [καὶ] ὁ βασιλεὺς τοῦ Ἰσραήλ.

Examining the wider narrative context, we find that the solemn entry into Jerusalem occurs within the final sequence of events in the Book of Signs, Dodd's Episode 7, "Life through Death: The Meaning of the Cross" (12:1-36). This episode includes the anointing, the solemn entry and some discourses interpretive of Jesus' approaching hour. The Evangelist makes a point of linking the solemn entry with the raising of Lazarus (John 12:10.17). The Lazarus miracle is a σημεῖον of Jesus' victory over death; the anointing at Bethany, 'a σημεῖον of his burial, and the triumphal entry into Jerusalem, a σημεῖον of his "universal sovereignty...as Conqueror of death and Lord of life."[230] The paradoxical nature of Jesus' arrival in Jerusalem both anticipates and illustrates the great paradox of his ultimate crucifixion as the King of the Jews.

If we look at the more immediate narrative setting of the citation, we find that, characteristically, the Fourth Gospel goes its own way "in every point where it is possible to differ in relating the same event."[231] In the synoptics, Jesus, already riding on the donkey, is greeted by the people singing their "Hosannas." They lay branches and their garments down at Jesus' feet. The narrative in all three recalls Zech 9:9 and there is a formal quotation of this text in Matthew. The sequence of events is quite different in John. Jesus is apparently approaching Jerusalem on foot. The crowds swarm out to meet him, waving palm branches and singing a chant based on Ps 117:26. Jesus' response to the crowd's greeting is to find an ass and sit on it.[232] His action is at once an affirmation and a critique of the crowd's acclamation of him as "King of Israel."[233] The Fourth

---

[229] Freed, "The Entry into Jerusalem in the Gospel of John," *JBL* 80 (1961) 329-38, at 332.

[230] Dodd, *The Interpretation*, 370-71.

[231] See Dodd, *Historical Tradition in the Fourth Gospel* (Cambridge: Cambridge University Press, 1963) 155; D. Moody Smith, *Johannine Christianity: Essays on its Setting, Sources, and Theology* (Edinburgh: Clark, 1984) 97-105; Brown, *John I-XII*, 459-61; K. Tsuchido, "Tradition and Redaction in John 12.1-43," *NTS* 30 (1984) 609-19, at 615.

[232] Typically, the Johannine Jesus takes the initiative. Cf. Luke 19:35, where Jesus' innocence of political messianic pretentions is stressed by having the disciples seat Jesus on the colt.

[233] "Jesus chooses to ride a donkey's colt as a corrective to the crowd's nationalism.

Evangelist alerts the reader to the fulfilment of Zech 9:9. Jesus' action is, therefore, an interpretation of the psalm text, εὐλογημένος ὁ ἐρχόμενος ἐν ὀνόματι κυρίου.

"Jesus' actions are presented as an attempt to affirm yet inform the crowd's reference to him as ὁ βασιλεὺς τοῦ Ἰσραήλ."[234] Various explanations have been offered for this addition to the psalm quotation. It may allude to Zeph 3:15, where the prophet tells Jerusalem that Βασιλεὺς Ἰσραὴλ Κύριος is in her midst.[235] This royal acclamation of Jesus towards the end of his manifestation to the world recalls Nathaniel's confession of Jesus as ὁ βασιλεὺς τοῦ Ἰσραήλ at the beginning.[236] If this Johannine addition echoes v. 2 of Isa 44, the only place in the LXX where ὁ βασιλεὺς τοῦ Ἰσραήλ occurs, it may reveal the context which prompted the Evangelist to open the Zech quotation with Μὴ φοβοῦ.[237] A particularly helpful explanation for our purposes is offered by F. Manns. The reason for the gloss, ὁ βασιλεὺς τοῦ Ἰσραήλ, as proposed by Manns, is that the Evangelist is using here the Jewish exegetical technique, *gezerah shawah* ("identical category," another of Hillel's *middoth*), the bringing together of two texts so that one may colour the reading of the other.[238] We have already mentioned the bringing together of two Scripture texts at the level of the narrative—The crowd chants Ps 117:26, believing it to be an appropriate acclamation to Jesus. Jesus enacts Zech 9:9 in order to correct their understanding, that is, in order to make Zech 9:9 colour their reception of Ps 117:26. This is effected at the level of text by the quotations from Ps 117:26 and Zech 9:9. Both have the verb "to come" in common (ἐρχόμενος in Ps 117:26 ; ἔρχεται in Zech 9:9). John amplifies the Ps 117 quotation with the gloss, ὁ βασιλεὺς τοῦ Ἰσραήλ in order to show that ὁ ἐρχόμενος is to be un-

---

He is a king, yes, but not the kind of king they are expecting." Stibbe, *John*, 133-34.

[234] Schuchard, *Scripture within Scripture*, 78.

[235] Brown, *John I-XII*, 458.

[236] Meeks, *The Prophet-King*, 83. A. S. Geyser sees the use of the sacral title "Israel" as important, in view of this inclusion with the confession of the "true Israelite" in John 1:49. It also proclaims that with Jesus' coming, the expected ingathering of the tribes into the restored kingdom of David is taking place. See "Israel in the Fourth Gospel," *Neot* 20 (1986) 13-20, at 13 and 15.

[237] So suggests Schuchard, *Scripture within Scripture*, 76-79. Μὴ φοβοῦ, is more usually traced to Zeph 3:16, e.g., by Lindars, *New Testament Apologetic*, 113; Brown, *John I-XII*, 458; Freed, *Old Testament Quotations*, 78. Others see it as also alluding to Isa 40:9, e.g., Reim, *Studien*, 29-31; Menken, *Old Testament Quotations*, 84.

[238] *Gezera shawa* involves using a part of one text as a substitute for part of another analogous text or adding in a phrase from an analogous passage to a text. The analogy is established by means of at least one word in common and often there is a similarity in content between the two passages. See Menken, *Old Testament Quotations*, 52-53. For the use of this technique in Philo and Qumran see Brooke, *Exegesis at Qumran*, 22-24, 166, 294-8, 306-8, 319.

derstood as the king described in Zech 9:9. The gloss, ὁ βασιλεὺς τοῦ Ἰσραήλ, reinforces the *gezerah shawah*.[239]

The acclamation, Ὡσαννά, also used by Mark and Matthew, is a transliteration of the Hebrew and Aramaic הושיעה נא which the LXX of Ps 117:25 translates as σῶσον δή. It may thus be regarded as part of the citation. Its appearance in three of the gospels does not necessarily suggest a Hebrew *Vorlage*. From what we know of the early stages of the development of the *Piyyut*, it appears that "Hosanna" was a popular festal refrain to a liturgical adaptation of Ps (117)118.[240] By NT times, its original supplicatory meaning had probably been forgotten and it was regarded as an acclamation of joyful praise.[241] Retention of Hebrew or Aramaic words is characteristic of the conservative nature of liturgical usage, as the retention of the word "Hosanna" in the Christian liturgy shows (See *Didache* 10.6).

John is the only Evangelist to specify that the branches were from palm trees. The waving of palm branches in John 12:13 is generally thought to be indicative of the crowd's messianic understanding of Jesus.[242] The palm tree had strong messianic associations. Coins minted by the insurgents during the revolts against Rome in 66-70 and 135 CE bear the inscription, "For the redemption of Sion" (לגאלת ציון), and the image of a palm tree, a symbol associated, no doubt, with memories of the Maccabean struggle for Jewish identity and independence.[243]

---

[239] See Manns, "Exégèse rabbinique," 533. According to J. Cazeau, the peaceful king of Zech 9:9-10, divested of all the usual trappings of royalty reflects a non-militant re-interpretation of Jacob's blessing for the tribe of Judah (Gen 49:8-12). See "'Toi, bethléem, n'est-tu pas le parent pauvre des clans de juda?' le theme du roi dans l'évangile de jean." *LumVie* 35 (1986) 69-88, at 80.

[240] The acclamation of the populace at Jesus' entry into Jerusalem may owe as much to predecessors of the *Piyyut* as it does to Ps (117)118. The *Piyyut* is a simple, litany-style, rhythmic chant, intended to encourage popular participation. Each line ends with a primitive form of rhyme produced by identical suffixes and the people respond with a simple refrain. See Joseph Heinemann, *Prayer in the Talmud: Forms and Patterns*. (Berlin/New York: Walter de Gruyter, 1977) 139.

[241] Freed, "The Entry into Jerusalem," 330. According to M. H. Pope, as an acclamation, "Hosanna" represents a Christian misapprehension of an intercessory term. See "Hosanna," ABD III, 290-91. However, Sanders has drawn attention to the biblical use of "Hosanna" as "the cry of the litigant as he or she entered the presence of the king sitting in judgement" (e.g., 2 Sam 14:4, 2 Kgs 6:26). This background would illuminate the acclamation as an address to the king whose "hour," about to be inaugurated, is the judgement of the world (John 12:31). See "A New Testament Hermeneutic Fabric: Psalm 118 in the Entrance Narrative," in C. A. Evans and W. F. Stinespring (ed.), *Early Jewish and Christian Exegesis: Studies in Honour of William Hugh Brownlee* (Atlanta: Scholars, 1987) 177-90, at 186.

[242] Freed, "The Entry," 334.

[243] Triumphal processions into Jerusalem with singing and waving of palm branches are recalled in 1 Macc 13:51 and 2 Macc 10:7. See H. St J. Hart, "The Palm Branches in John 12:13," *JTS* 3 (1952) 62-63.

In John, the people do not lay the branches down in homage at Jesus' feet, as in the synoptics, but rather they wave them. This has struck many as more evocative of the festival of Tabernacles than purely messianic in intent,[244] In view of the citation of Ps (117)118, we should probably see the waving of the branches which accompanied the crowd's acclamation as "inspired" by the liturgical application of v. 27bc of the psalm in the לולב ceremony of Tabernacles.[245] The ritual for the feast called for the waving of palm branches during the singing of Ps (117)118 which includes the verse—

συστήσασθε ἑορτὴν ἐν τοῖς πυκάζουσιν
ἕως τῶν κεράτων τοῦ θυσιαστηρίου.[246]

There are problems with the "Tabernacles" suggestion, since John has told us that Passover is just six days away (John 12:1). Perhaps John's "corrective" citation from Zechariah (and even, perhaps the Zechariah quotation in 19:37) points to the resolution of this apparent contradiction. In Zechariah, the eschatological day when a fountain will be opened for the house of David, when "living waters will flow out from Jerusalem ... and when the Lord will be king over all the earth," is a great feast of Tabernacles (Zech 13:1; 14:8-9.16). The first psalm quotation in the Gospel (John 2:17) pointed towards "that day," or, in Johannine terms, "the hour," which Jesus was already inaugurating in his attack on the traders (Zech 14:21). Tabernacles was, of course, a great Temple feast, especially since it was remembered as the occasion of Solomon's transfer of the ark and dedication of the newly built Temple (1 Kgs 8:2. 65). As we have seen, the Temple was the great sign of God's goodness to David, and that goodness was, in fact, God's goodness to the whole people (1 Kgs 8:66). The Temple was thus, as Hamish Swanston has described it, "the developing sign of what God is doing for the people."[247] It was, therefore, the covenant with David, understood

---

[244] E.g., Barrett, *The Gospel*, 347-48; Schnackenburg, *The Gospel 2*, 374. It has been shown that Tabernacles was significant for the Jewish revolt. See H. Lapin, "Palm Fronds and Citrons: Notes on Two Letters from Bar Kosiba's Administration," *HUCA* 64 (1993) 111-135.

[245] "Every day of the first six days of Tabernacles they circled about the altar once saying *We beseech you, O Lord, make us now to prosper* [Ps. 118:25]." *Midr. Teh*, 17:5. See 26:5, quoting *m. Sukkah* 4:5.

[246] This verse is a notorious *crux*. Oesterley, *The Psalms*, 482, translates the LXX:

"Set in order the procession with leafy (branches)
Unto the horns of the altar.

For the justification of his rendering "leafy" (*lit.* 'thick") and supplying of "branches," see "boughs of leafy trees" (RSV) in Lev 23:40.

[247] *The Community Witness*, 108.

afresh in the light of Zechariah's prophecy, that the people were celebrating when they waved their palms and greeted Jesus with their song from Ps (117)118.

This brings us to the connection of the psalm itself with David. It does not have a "Davidic" superscript in either the Hebrew or the Greek, but its reception history in late Second Temple Judaism abounds in examples of "Davidic" readings. The psalm's character as a liturgy of entrance to the Temple, for example, would have recalled David. As the final psalm in the "Egyptian Hallel," Ps (117)118 was sung at the conclusion of the paschal meal, in which Israel prayed for the coming of the Messiah. The extensive NT messianic usage of the psalm, especially of "the stone rejected" (v. 22) clearly stems from a reading that was current in the contemporary Judaism.[248] The psalm's association with David in Jewish exegesis is attested by a tradition preserved in the Targum which allocates various lines from vv. 22-29 to the characters in the 1 Sam 16 scene where the boy David is anointed as king.

> Puerum despexerunt aedificatores qui fuit inter filios Issai et meruit constitui rex et dominator.
> A conspectu Domini hoc extitit, dixerunt aedificatores:
> hoc mirabile est in conspectu nostro, dixerunt filii Issai.
> Haec diem fecit Dominus, dixit aedificatores,
> exultemus et laetemur in ea, dixerunt filii Issai.
> Obsecramus te, Domine, [confer salutem] nunc dixerunt aedificatores:
> obsecramus te, Domine, prosperare nunc, dixit Issai et uxor eius.
> Benedictus qui venit in nomine verbi Domini, dixit aedificatores.
> Benedicant vobis de domo sanctuarii Domini, dixit David.
> Deus Dominus illuxit nobis, dixit tribus domus Jehudae...
> Deus meus es tu et confitebor coram te;
> Deus meus, laudabo te, dixit David.
> Respondit Samuel et dixit: Laudate, ecclesia Israel, confitemini coram Domino, quoniam bonus,
> quoniam in aeternum benignitas eius.[249]

Like the NT messianic usage of Ps (117)118, this dramatized *relecture* of the psalm hinges on the identification of David as "the stone rejected" which has become the cornerstone.

Among various interpretations of Ps (117)118 preserved in the *Midrash Tehillim*, is the following comment on v. 23 which would appear to be in the same line of interpretive tradition as the Targum quoted above—

---

[248] E.g., Mark 12:10-12; Luke 20:17; Acts 4:11. Juel, *Messiah and Temple*, 54, believes that the verb ἀποδοκιμασθῆναι in the synoptic passion predictions should also be regarded as an allusion to Ps 117:22.
[249] Walton, *Biblia Sacra Polyglotta*.

This is the Lord's doing alludes to King David, king of Israel, who at one moment was keeping his father's sheep, and in the very next moment was made king, so that everyone exclaimed: One moment David keeps sheep, and the next he is king. And he replied: You wonder at me! Verily I wonder at myself more than you do. But the Holy Spirit replied: *This is the Lord's doing.*[250]

Late though these examples are, they clearly are in continuity with the earlier traditions about David which, as we proposed in Ch. 2, would have formed part of the "horizon of expectations" against which the Fourth Evangelist and his intended readers viewed the psalms.

For Johannine Christians, the decisive factor in terms of their reception of Ps (117)118 was probably the presence in the psalm of first-person-singular lament features. In hearing the "I" in the psalm as David, they would have thought not so much of the David of messianic expectation, but of the king who suffered distress, who was surrounded by enemies, and who was exalted by God. In their belief, this is the David who "wrote" of Jesus (cf. John 5:46), as is borne out by the many references to his psalms in the Passion Narrative.

In our General Introduction, we made the point that quotations, even if lexically they appear to be faithful representations of the cited text, are still radical reinterpretations of the original voice that generate new signification. This is certainly the case with John's citation of Ps 117:26. It contains two expressions, equivalents of which are frequently found in the Fourth Gospel: ὁ ἐρχόμενος and ἐν ὀνόματι κυρίου. Once introduced into their new setting, these expressions take on the meaning that their verbal and thematic equivalents have in that setting. This "new signification" can be inferred from the Gospel itself, as we will now discover.

In the Judaism contemporary with the NT, the term ὁ ἐρχόμενος was a technical term for the expected "Messiah."[251] In the Fourth Evangelist's view, the designation of Jesus as ὁ ἐρχόμενος is a solemn testimony to Jesus on the part of John the Baptist (John 1:15). The

---

[250] *Midr. Teh.* 118:21. In *Midr. Teh.* 11:1 and 63:1 verses from Ps (117)118 are taken as spoken by David. In *Midr. Teh.* 78:5 David is described as 'speaking for Israel' when he utters Ps (117)118:5.

[251] See Moloney, "The Fourth Gospel's Presentation," 249. Amid the variants in Jewish expectation, the term ὁ ἐρχόμενος had many different connotations. It carried suggestions of the mysterious figure of Dan 7:13, ὡς υἱὸς ἀνθρώπου ἐρχόμενος, of the cry Ἰδοὺ ἔρχεται which was to greet the sudden coming of the Lord to his Temple (Mal 3:1), of the promise that ὁ ἐρχόμενος ἥξει καὶ οὐ χρονίσει (Hab 2:3 LXX. See Heb 10:37). In the early episodes of all four gospels John the Baptist speaks to his followers of ὁ ἐρχόμενος, the one coming after him (John 1:15.27.30; Mark 1:7-8; Matt 3:11; Luke 3:16. See Matt 3:11 and 11:3).

messianic sense of the designation, ὁ ἐρχόμενος is elaborated extensively in the Fourth Gospel. Characters in the narrative use it to give expression to various expectations concerning "one who is to come." The Samaritan woman, for example, declares, Οἶδα ὅτι Μεσσίας ἔρχεται ὁ λεγόμενος Χριστός (4:25). Those who eat the bread are in no doubt that Jesus is ὁ προφήτης ὁ ἐρχόμενος εἰς τὸν κόσμον (6:14). The debate among the people of Jerusalem in 7:25-31 provides a fascinating insight into the Johannine handling of popular messianic beliefs. According to these beliefs, the Messiah is certainly ὁ ἐρχόμενος, but in such a mysterious way that, as the people say, ὁ δὲ Χριστὸς ὅταν ἔρχηται οὐδεὶς γινώσκει πόθεν ἐστίν (7:27). Jesus' clarification of the sense in which he is ὁ ἐρχόμενος challenges his hearers to discern, by the evidence of his words and his works, not just that he is "the one who was to come," but, more importantly, where he comes from. It is therefore on the lips of Jesus that the Johannine usage of ὁ ἐρχόμενος diverges from the purely messianic sense.

According to the Fourth Gospel, Jesus comes "from above" (8:23). The function of his being ὁ ἐρχόμενος is "for judgement" (9:39), "as a light for the world" (12:46), "to bear witness to the truth" (18:37), to do the Father's will (6:38).[252] The extension of ὁ ἐρχόμενος to the Paraclete (15:26; 16:7; 16:13) is a further instance of the uniqueness of the Johannine handling of this motif. For the disciples facing the onslaught of "the hour," Jesus becomes "the one who is to come" in yet a further sense (14:3. 18. 23. 28.). This corresponds to the eschatological interpretation of εὐλογημένος ὁ ἐρχόμενος ἐν ὀνόματι κυρίου, as found in Matthew's second citation of Ps 117:26 (Matt 23:39), mentioned in our introductory discussion of the transformative power of quotation.[253] For the Fourth Evangelist, this eschatological event is already happening.

We now come to the second expression from the psalm quotation which takes on the meaning of its equivalents in the Fourth Gospel, ἐν ὀνόματι (κυρίου). For the Fourth Evangelist, Jesus' coming ἐν ὀνόματι κυρίου is the theological equivalent of his coming from God—ἐγὼ ἐλήλυθα ἐν τῷ ὀνόματι τοῦ πατρός μου (5:43). Jesus is ὁ ἄνωθεν ἐρχόμενος (3:31. cf. 7:29). Thus Martha professes a full Johannine faith in Jesus as ὁ Χριστὸς ὁ υἱὸς τοῦ θεοῦ ὁ εἰς τὸν κόσμον ἐρχόμενος (11:27). De Jonge, commenting on this profession, says,

> The title ὁ Χριστὸς and the use of the verb ἔρχεσθαι in connection with it are well-known features of Jewish statements in John...But the

---

[252] John 6:38 seems to reflect the early Christian reception of Ps 39:7-9—envisaged as spoken by Jesus at his coming into the world—exemplified by Heb 10:5-9.
[253] See p. 11 above.

Christian confession ὁ Χριστὸς is interpreted by the addition ὁ υἱὸς τοῦ θεου. This is also the case in XX.30, 31, the well-known 'first ending' of the gospel.[254]

As Bultmann comments, here the messianic title, ὁ ἐρχόμενος, has been transformed into the most significant of the three eschatological titles which Martha's confession attributes to Jesus, "because ὁ εἰς τὸν κόσμον ἐρχόμενος most plainly affirms the inbreaking of the beyond into this life."[255]

The idea that Jesus comes ἐν ὀνόματι κυρίου has struck many commentators as having particular resonances within the Johannine ambience.[256] This is perhaps best understood within the framework of John's emissary Christology, which, as Borgen has shown, is moulded on Jewish rules for agency according to which the emissary, even if not in fact the king's equal, is in law entitled to be treated with the deference due to the king.[257] In the high Christology of John's gospel there is evidence of "a profound reflection upon the theological principle of the law of agency."[258] In particular, the Gospel maintains a fine balance between the two apparent opposites: the sender is greater than the one sent (John 13:16), yet the one sent is the sender's equal (John 12:45).[259] In the Johannine perspective, when Jesus, who comes ἐν ὀνόματι κυρίου, is praised as ὁ βασιλεὺς τοῦ Ἰσραήλ, he is praised as the Christ, the Son of God, equal to God and one with the Father. Jesus' status as ὁ Χριστὸς ὁ υἱὸς τοῦ θεου is the outcome of his union with the Father, as concretely expressed by his performance of what the Father intends; τὰ ἔργα ἃ ἐγὼ ποιῶ ἐν τῷ ὀνόματι τοῦ πατρός μου ταῦτα μαρτυρεῖ περὶ ἐμοῦ (John 10:25; cf. 5:19). Because of this, he can say to God, Ἐφανέρωσά σου τὸ ὄνομα (John 17:6). The idea that Jesus comes ἐν ὀνόματι κυρίου is thus intimately related to his role as Revealer.

---

[254] De Jonge, "Jewish Expectations," 251. Moloney does not regard Martha's profession as "full Johannine Faith" because she subsequently refers to Jesus as "the Teacher" (John 11:28), a title which Jesus corrects by his use of the title "Son of Man" in John 3:13-14 See *The Johannine Son of Man* (Rome: Las-Libreria Ateneo Salesiano, 1978) 210. The *histoire* / *récit* distinction may solve this apparent conflict.

[255] Bultmann, *The Gospel*, 404.

[256] E.g., on the analogy of Matt 10:41, which speaks of the reward due to one who welcomes a prophet "in the name of a prophet," i.e., because he is a prophet, Dodd, *Historical Tradition*, 154, proposed that to early Christian readers the Ps 117:26 citation might have suggested the meaning, "May the coming one be praised as Κύριος." Alternatively, according to Brown, *John I-XII*, 457, the words ἐν ὀνόματι κυρίου have special significance "since according to xvii 11-12 the Father has given Jesus the divine name (ego eimi?)."

[257] Borgen, "God's Agent," 67-78.

[258] Ashton, *Understanding*, 314.

[259] Ashton, *Understanding*, 314.

Manifesting God's name recalls the biblical tradition, especially the psalms, where the name of the Lord "expresses all the mystery and wonder of revelation ...'In Judah God is known, his name is great in Israel' (Ps 76:1)."[260] The Fourth Evangelist has thus utilized to the full the potential in this "Scripture" from the tradition for portraying the one who comes as divine. It is therefore appropriate that the greeting Ὡσαννά, originally a prayer to God for salvation, should now be addressed to Jesus, since it invokes him as "the Saviour of the world" (cf. John 4:42).

The Johannine Jesus is not proclaimed "Son of David" as in Matthew. While he is indeed "the king of Israel," his rule is not acclaimed as ἡ ἐρχομένη βασιλεία τοῦ πατρὸς ἡμῶν Δαυίδ as in Mark 11:4. John appears determined to avoid any reference to David.[261] Yet, for the attentive reader, the Jesus who comes in the name of his Father (John 5:43) recalls the David who comes "in the name of the Lord" against Goliath (1 Sam 17:45).[262] Moreover, the biblical sources the Evangelist mines in this pericope are such that recollections of David are inevitable. Looking at the Zechariah citation, in the light of which the Evangelist intends the Ps 117:26 acclamation to be understood, we find that John has given it a "Davidic" colouring in three significant ways.

Firstly, he has pared it down to the simple statement that the approaching king is sitting on an ass's colt. The verb καθήμενος, not found in Zech 9:9, is a royal motif (1 Kgs 1:35; Isa 14:13; Ps 113:8 [263]). In fact, it echoes 1 Kgs 1:38.44 where, on the instruction of David, Solomon sits (ἐπικαθίζω) on David's mule and rides to the Gihon spring, publicly declaring his right be appointed king of Israel and Judah in David's stead and to sit on David's throne (1 Kgs 1:35).[264] The echo is reinforced by the realization that this story has obviously served as a model for the portrayal of Jesus as the messianic king riding "on the king's mule" (cf. 1 Kgs 1:38) into Jerusalem to rule forever over a united Israel.

---

[260] Kraus, *Theology of the Psalms*, 20.

[261] For Freed, a reference to Jesus as "Son of David" would not fit John's unique view of Jesus as king." See "The Entry into Jerusalem in the Gospel of John," *JBL* 80 (1961) 329-38, at 332-33. Schuchard, *Scripture within Scripture*, 54, n. 46 and 82, remarks that John "stops short of suggesting that Jesus is to be recognized as the Son of David." This "apparent muting of a Davidic Christology in John's portrait of Jesus" arises out of his desire to stress Jesus' heavenly origins."

[262] This echo is noted by Eaton in *Kingship and the Psalms*, 62; cf. also 156.

[263] For further instances, see Menken, *Old Testament Quotations*, 92-93. Menken's chapter on John 12:15 was originally published as "Die Redaktion des Zitates aus Sach 9,9 in Joh 12,15." *ZNW* 80 (1989) 193-209.

[264] Menken, *Old Testament Quotations*, 92-95; Marie de Mérode, "L'acceuil triomphal de Jésus selon Jean, 11-12," *RTL* 13 (1982) 49-62, at 56.

Secondly, the Johannine reference to Jesus' mount, ἐπὶ πῶλον ὄνου, also not found in Zech 9:9, may echo Jacob's blessing of Judah in Gen 49:10-11, of which Zech 9:9 is a *relecture*.[265] Both passages were frequently read in conjunction with each other and were interpreted messianically.[266]

Thirdly, although Zechariah's king is not explicitly said to belong to David's family, there is a strongly evocative allusion in the immediate context (Zech 9:10) to v. 8 of Ps (71)72, the psalm "for Solomon" which ends Book I of the Psalter, "the prayers of David, the Son of Jesse." The psalm allusion describes the peaceful king as one whose "dominion shall be from sea to sea, from the River to the ends of the earth." This identifies him as the one for whom David prayed, "O God give your judgement to the king, to the king's son your justice" (Ps 71:1). Thus the immediate context of the citation from Ps 117:26 reverberates with messianic resonances.

The scene in which the citation occurs concludes with an authorial comment on the remembering of the disciples (John 12:16), very similar to that which we found in John 2:22—

> ...ταῦτα οὐκ ἔγνωσαν αὐτοῦ οἱ μαθηταὶ τὸ πρῶτον, ἀλλ' ὅτε ἐδοξάσθη Ἰησοῦς τότε ἐμνήσθησαν ὅτι ταῦτα ἦν ἐπ' αὐτῷ γεγραμμένα καὶ ταῦτα ἐποίησαν αὐτῷ.
>
> His disciples did not understand this at first; but when Jesus was glorified, then they remembered that this had been written of him and had been done to him.

There is here, what appears at first sight to be quite an un-Johannine reference to what was done to Jesus. This is usually taken to refer to Jesus' action of riding on the donkey.[267] Its uncharacteristic note of passivity on the part of Jesus has been explained as an un-

---

[265] To summarize part of an article by Cazeau, in Gen 49, Jacob speaks of a noble and proud prince which the pro-David tradition interpreted, at least going by the conduct of the kings of Israel, as a potentate. Zechariah portrays a shepherd king who is to deprive unworthy leaders of their tyranny (cf. John 9). The palm episode (John 12:12-19) "sert de jalon." See Cazeau, "Toi, bethléem," 80.

[266] See Schnackenburg, *The Gospel* 2, 376; D. J. Derrett, "Law in the New Testament: The Palm Sunday Colt," *NovT* 13 (1971) 241-58, at 255; Freed, *Old Testament Quotations*, 78; Menken, "Die Redaktion des Zitates aus Sach 9,9," mentions *Tg. Ps.-J.* and *Tg. Neof.* Gen 49:10, *b. San.* 98b, Justin, *Apol.* I,32; 54; *Dial.* 52-54 and *T. Jud.* 22:3 as examples of the messianic reading of Gen 49:10-11. For the connection with Zech 9:9 in Jewish exegesis, see also Douglas J. Moo, *The Old Testament in the Gospel Passion Narratives* (Sheffield: Almond, 1983) 182. For an early Christian reference to both Gen 49:10-11 and Zech 9:9, see Justin, *Dial.* 53,3.

[267] E.g., Bultmann, *The Gospel*, 418—"it is not till after the glorification of Jesus that the disciples gained an insight into the fact that the entry of Jesus into Jerusalem fulfilled the Zechariah prophecy."

conscious recollection of the tradition reflected in the synoptics where the disciples take the initiative and bring the colt to Jesus (and, in Luke, seat him upon it).[268] Viewed in this way, it certainly conflicts with the Evangelist's statement that the Johannine Jesus took the initiative in finding the colt and sitting on it. In John, the only thing done to Jesus is the singing of Ὡσαννά· εὐλογημένος ὁ ἐρχόμενος ἐν ὀνόματι κυρίου, [καὶ] ὁ βασιλεὺς τοῦ Ἰσραήλ to the accompaniment of waving palm branches. This means that what the disciples did not at first understand and what they remembered after the resurrection as written about Jesus is the acclamation based on Ps 117:26. The implications of this are brought out by Marie de Mérode.

> A mon avis cependant, it faut rapporter ταῦτα à l'acclamation de la foule: les disciples ne réalisent pas immédiatement la portée de cette acclamation qu'ils comprendront plus tard comme une anticipation de la gloire de la résurrection. Notons...que la foule, au v. 17, est dite "rendre témoinage", verbe très important chez Jean...Si donc nous prenons au sérieux ce "témoinage" de la foule chez Jean, nous y voyons une anticipation de la glorification, anticipation que Jésus reconnaît et accepte, anticipation due au miracle que Jésus vient d'accomplir en Lazare.[269]

We have shown in this section that John received the psalm quotation as part of the tradition of Jesus' solemn entry into Jerusalem. His modification of the narrative sequence and the way in which ὁ ἐρχόμενος ἐν ὀνόματι κυρίου must be understood when received within the context of his Gospel make of this citation a true "creation" of the Evangelist, even though verbally it appears to be the same as the synoptic versions. John's interpretive gloss appended to the citation reinforces its connection with Zech 9:9, also quoted in this narrative and the royal/Davidic texts of which Zech 9:9 is a *relecture*. Even though the Evangelist appears to downplay the strictly messianic elements in the traditional story (notably by avoiding the title "Son of David"), he stresses Jesus' royalty. In Jewish exegesis, Ps (117)118 has a strong association with David and the Temple. We believe that this association, which was not limited to messianic interpretation, contributed significantly to the remembering of the "Scripture" after Jesus was glorified (John 12:16). Those who recalled the event saw in the people's shout an acclamation of Jesus as one who had come from God, who acted in the name of God and who, in his triumphant royal enthronement on the cross, returned to God.

---

[268] Brown, *John I-XII*, 458.
[269] De Mérode, "L'acceuil triomphal," 53.

G. *Over-View of the Five Citations in the Book of Signs*

Ps 68:10, in the context of Jesus' visit to the Temple, a text recalled by the disciples both at the event and later, functions programmatically within the whole Gospel of John. It anticipates "the hour" and points the discerning reader to a true understanding of the person of Jesus and the significance of the sacrifice of his life, by situating his ministry against the backdrop of God's restored Temple and the glory revealed in it. Ps 77:24, put, with characteristic Johannine irony, on the lips of the unbelieving crowd, introduces the different levels of understanding which Jesus' self revelation is to encounter. There is a link between the first two citations: both occur within a context where a sign is demanded of Jesus. In John 2, the sign is the Temple of Jesus' body destroyed and rebuilt. In John 6, it is Jesus' body, given for the life of the world and raised from the dead. The third quotation, Ps 77:16.20, cited by Jesus himself, extends his self-revelation and raises further questions for the crowd about his true identity. It is linked to the previous citation, also from Ps 77. Both "Scriptures" are bearers of Jesus' self revelation in terms of the two great Exodus motifs: the manna and the water from the rock. The Fourth citation, Ps 81:6 comes in the "trial" scene where Jesus insists that his messiahship must be understood as divine sonship. Here the misunderstanding and questioning of Jesus escalate into hostility and even an attempt to kill him. Finally, Ps 117:26 forms an inclusion with Ps 68:10, both "Scriptures" being the object of the "two-stage remembering" on the part of the disciples. The psalm verse conveys the crowd's acceptance of Jesus as Messiah. Understood by the disciples later, in the light of Jesus' resurrection, it testifies to the true nature of his messiahship, his status as "Son of God."

CHAPTER FOUR

THE PSALMS QUOTED IN THE BOOK OF GLORY

A. *Introduction*

As we did for the "Book of Signs," we begin by situating each citation in the Book of Glory[1] within the flow of the Johannine "argument," using Dodd's analysis as a framework.

The first citation in the Book of Glory, **Ps (40:10)41:9 in John 13:18**—"He who ate my bread has lifted his heel against me."—occurs in the first episode, the supper scene during which Jesus is instructing "his own" by action and word (John 13:1-30). Like the first psalm quotation in the Book of Signs, it has a programmatic function. The treachery of which it speaks is to be perpetrated in the events of the hour. The significance of this treachery as fulfilment of Scripture is to emerge as the revelatory character of these events becomes clear.

In Dodd's analysis, the supper scene is followed by a first cycle of discourse (13:31-14:31) a monologue of Jesus (15:1-16:33) and the prayer of Jesus (17:1-26) all represented as addressed to "his own." The next psalm quotation occurs in the monologue. Just as John's first psalm quotation in the Book of Glory employed the motif of Scripture fulfilment as a key to understanding Jesus' sovereign and serene command over all the events of the hour, the second quotation, **Ps (68:5)69:4 in John 15:25**—"They hated me without a cause."—extends this strategy to disciples undergoing persecution in the years following these events. It encourages them to see their suffering as a means of communion with their Lord who was also hated by the world.[2]

The next two psalm quotations occur in the crucifixion scene itself. The programmatic psalm quotations at the beginning of each Book of the Gospel have prepared the reader to recognize in the events of the hour the fulfilment of what is written in the psalms.

---

[1] Since the term "Passion" is really a misnomer for what, in John's perspective, is the great action of a Jesus who takes all the initiatives in the laying down of his life, Brown's title, "The Book of Glory" will be used here in preference to Dodd's "The Book of the Passion."

[2] Dodd, *The Interpretation*, 413.

Now what is written actually takes place: **Ps (21:19)22:18 in John 19:24**—"They parted my garments among them, and for my clothing they cast lots."—as the executioners share out Jesus' garments among themselves, **Ps (68:22)69:21 in John 19:28**—"I thirst."—as Jesus cries out and someone offers him vinegar to drink. Brown has discerned a seven-episode chiastic structure in the crucifixion scene. Within this pattern, the central episode is the address of Jesus to his mother and the beloved disciple, in which is seen "the fulfilment of the Prologue's stated purpose for the word becoming flesh" (cf. John 1:12-13).[3] The importance of the Psalter to the Evangelist is underlined by the fact that this centrepiece is framed by a psalm citation and narrative of its fulfilment both before and after.

The final psalm citation, **Ps (33:21)34:20 in John 19:36**—"Not a bone of him shall be broken."—is enacted as a soldier decides that it is unnecessary to break Jesus' legs. Together with the citation from Zechariah in John 19:37, this forms the last explicitly cited "Scripture" in the Gospel. Its climactic character is heightened by the solemn invitation challenging the reader to faith. Thus the whole presentation of the passion sequence as Scripture fulfilment is geared towards the final sequence in the Book of Glory, the appearances of the Risen Lord. At the end of this, the author will invite the reader to respond in a faith which knows the Scripture, ὅτι δεῖ αὐτὸν ἐκ νεκρῶν ἀναστῆναι (John 20:9). As our statistical analysis in Ch. 1 has suggested, it would seem that even a cursory analysis of the theological structure of the work confirms that the psalms predominate in this scriptural witness to Jesus.

We found that the psalm citations in the Book of Signs functioned at a symbolic level in keeping with the stress on Jesus' revelatory self-disclosure which is characteristic of the first half of the Gospel. With regard to the citations in the Book of Glory, it is important to remember that John is using the fulfilment mode of Scripture reference which he has inherited from the tradition. In his reference to the Psalter, therefore, he envisages David principally, although not

---

[3] The seven episodes are as follows:

A. Elevation of Jesus on the cross	A¹. Deposition of Jesus from the cross

B. Inscription about Jesus kingship
   Pilate's refusal of the Jews' request
	B¹. Flow of blood and water
	   Pilate's granting of the Jews' request

C. the fulfilment of Ps 21:19	C¹. the fulfilment of Ps 68:5
D. Jesus' mother and the beloved disciple	

Whether the intended audience would actually hear chiasms remains a question, but the centrality of episode D is well founded and points to the importance of the episodes before and after when what is foretold in the psalms actually happens. See Brown, *John XIII-XXI*, 911 and *Death of the Messiah*, 1071.

exclusively, as prophet. The first three citations in the Book of Glory all have synoptic parallels (These are allusions, however, not quotations). As this chapter will show, John transforms this received pattern of Scripture reference, highlighting it through explicit citation and enhancing it with the revelatory dimension, just as he transforms the passion tradition itself into an account of how Jesus shows his glory by returning to the Father.

B. *Ps (40:10)41:9 in Jn 13:18*

We now come to the first psalm quotation in the Book of Glory. Here John's handling of the tradition is "wholly dominated by his preoccupation with the theme of discipleship."[4] The foot-washing scene, in which the citation occurs, falls into two sections, vv. 1-11 and vv. 12-20 which are thought to be two interpretations of Jesus' symbolic action, the first presents it as a sign of Jesus' death, the second, as an example to be followed.[5] The psalm quotation occurs in the second of these sections. Addressing his disciples, having washed their feet, Jesus tells them how they will participate in his suffering. He adds that what he is saying does not refer to all of them (13:18). One of those whom he has chosen is about to betray him (13:21), but this is to fulfil the Scripture:

ὁ τρώγων μου τὸν ἄρτον ἐπῆρεν ἐπ' ἐμὲ τὴν πτέρναν αὐτοῦ.

"He who ate my bread has lifted his heel against me."

The whole point of the quotation is that when the denials, betrayals, and the death of Jesus have been perpetrated, the disciples will remember what Jesus said and come to belief in him as ἐγώ εἰμι.[6] Like the Scriptures in John 2:17 and 12:13, therefore, Ps 40:10 has a revelatory function which will become fully operative only in the future which is, of course, the "now" of the reader.

The Scripture here is universally accepted to be Psalm 40:10 (41:9), but the quotation differs considerably from the LXX:

ὁ ἐσθίων ἄρτους μου, ἐμεγάλυνεν ἐπ' ἐμὲ πτερνισμόν.

---

[4] Lindars, *The Gospel*, 441-42.
[5] Brown, *John XIII-XXI*, 555-60. 562; Moloney, *The Johannine Son of Man*, 193. Lindars, *The Gospel*, 447, disputes the division into two units, believing it "disregards John's methods of building on traditional material, expanding it with dialogue, and often singling out a particular person."
[6] Moloney, "A Sacramental Reading of John 13:1-38," *CBQ* 53 (1991) 237-56, at 247.

There is a different verb "to eat." The word "bread" is in the singular in John. The main clause in John 13:18 ("has lifted up his heel against me") diverges substantially from the LXX ("has magnified craft against me"). There is no possessive pronoun in the LXX main clause. Looking at the Hebrew version—

אוכל לחמי הגדיל עלי עקב

("... who ate of my bread, has made great the heel against me."[7]

—we find that the Fourth Gospel citation is actually closer to it than to the Septuagint in two respects. The word "bread" is in the singular, corresponding to the Hebrew, לחמי (my bread). The Fourth Gospel's πτέρναν is an accurate rendering of the Hebrew עקב (heel), compared with the LXX, πτερνισμόν ("craft").[8] These two features suggest a Hebrew *Vorlage* for John 13:18, but even if this were the case, it would still not explain why the Fourth Gospel diverges so much from both LXX and MT.[9]

The word order of the relative clause in the LXX is, ὁ ἐσθίων ἄρτους μου. In the Fourth Gospel citation, it is slightly different: ὁ τρώγων μου τὸν ἄρτον. At first sight, this appears to be simply a matter of Johannine style, as the possessive pronoun is found in this position elsewhere in the Gospel.[10] However, the fact that three examples (John 6:54. 56. 58) occur in a reference to eating bread, the "bread" of Jesus' flesh, is hardly without significance. John has a different verb "to eat," the verb τρώγειν which is used four times in John 6.[11] This alerts us to the possibility that John's other departures from the LXX in this citation might be at least as suggestive. Foremost among these is his choice of the verb ἐπαίρω, "lift up" rather than the LXX verb,

---

[7] Cf. the exact translation of the Hebrew in Aquila and Theodotion: κατεμεγαλύνθη μου πτέρνα.

[8] For a detailed explanation of how the use of the word πτερνισμόν "made it possible for the LXX translator to combine a minimum of comprehensibility of the Greek with a maximum of literal translation from the Hebrew," see Menken, *Old Testament Quotations*, 130-131. Menken's chapter on the quotation in John 13:18 was originally published as "The Translation of Psalm 41.10 in John 13.18," *JSNT* 40 (1990) 61-79.

[9] Among those who believe the citation is in John's own translation of the Hebrew are: Freed, *Old Testament Quotations*, 89; Brown, *John XIII-XXI*, 571; Reim, *Studien*, 40; Schnackenburg, *The Gospel 3*, 26; Moo, *Old Testament Quotations*, 237.

[10] Menken, *Old Testament Quotations*, 129 calls it "a minor Johannine stylistic peculiarity."

[11] See C. Spicq, "Τρώγειν: Est-il synonyme de φαγεῖν et d'ἐσθίειν dans le Nouveau Testament?" *NTS* 26 (1979-80) 414-19. According to Menken, *Old Testament Quotations*, 129, "The use of τρώγειν is a recognized Johannine stylistic trait." For Borgen, *Bread from Heaven*, 93, the agreements between John 6:51-58 and 13:18 indicate that the word τρώγειν comes from eucharistic traditions.

μεγαλύνω, "make great" (which accurately translates the Hebrew הגדיל). This must have been made for a reason.[12]

In view of the similar use of Ps 40:10 in the synoptics, some have explained the Johannine wording by the likelihood that the quotation found its way into the Gospel as a *testimonium*.[13] Oral transmission and quoting from memory would thus account for the discrepancies between John's version and both Greek and Hebrew. Barrett believed the author was "probably rewriting freely."[14] Lindars thought it was "a pesher text already established in the apologetic."[15] Several, noticing that John's rendering of the second phrase is a grammatical improvement on the LXX, and realising that a literal translation of the Hebrew would have resulted in clumsy Greek, have thought in terms of changes to a received text intended as "improvements for the Greek reader."[16] In view of what we have already seen of the Evangelist's intentionality in these matters, none of these theories seems adequate. It is far more likely that the unusual form of the quotation is the product of Johannine redaction. Menken suggests that there are two clues to the solution of this puzzle. Firstly, as we have seen, John most likely had good reason for not using the LXX as it stands. Secondly, in adapting it to his theological purposes, he most probably worked within the confines of current exegetical methods.

Menken explains that John could not possibly use the LXX translation of Ps. 40:10, because it would be at variance with his ideas about Jesus' omniscience.[17] The LXX has introduced a note of trickery by its substitution of "craft" for "heel."[18] Certainly, the idea that Judas "made great craft," implying the cunning deception of an unsuspecting Jesus, would be utterly inappropriate.

In order to appreciate Menken's second clue to the puzzle of the form of the citation, we need first to look at the relationship between

---

[12] An interesting illustrative parallel to John's citation is found in a passage based on this same verse in the 1QH XIII 23-24—

[Even all those who e]at my bread
have raised their heel against me.

The Qumran hymn presents quite a literal paraphrase of the Hebrew. See García Martínez, *The Dead Sea Scrolls*, 338.

[13] Dodd, *Historical Tradition*, 37; Lindars, *New Testament Apologetic*, 98
[14] Barrett, *The Gospel*, 371. See also Freed, *Old Testament Quotations*, 92.
[15] Lindars, *New Testament Apologetic*, 98.
[16] So, Schnackenburg, *The Gospel III*, 26. See also Dodd, *Historical Tradition*, 36-37; Barrett, *The Gospel*, 370.
[17] Menken, *Old Testament Quotations*, 137.
[18] The introduction of a note of beguilement is also evident in the Targum: *qui comedebat panem meam, magnificavit se super me astute.*

John's cited text and another very similar psalm passage. Ps (54)55:13-14. Apart from the obvious analogy in terms of content, both passages, when read in the Hebrew, have the crucial word הגדיל (literally, "makes great") in common. We present both texts, as translated in the RSV, with the translation of הגדיל underlined.

Ps (40:10)41:9	Ps (54:14-15)55:13-14
Even my bosom friend in whom I trusted, who ate of my bread, <u>has lifted</u> his heel against me.	It is not an adversary who <u>deals insolently</u> with me … But it is you, my equal, my companion, my familiar friend.

Clearly the analogy is based not only on the verb in common, but on a general similarity in content.[19]

Apart from the verbal analogies, there is also the fact that both psalms come from Book 1 of the Psalter, the תפלות of David the son of Jesse (Ps (71)72:20) and have a Davidic superscript in the Hebrew. Several Jewish sources show that Ps (54)55 was envisaged as a prayer of David confronted with Absalom's revolt and that the passage about the disloyalty of an intimate friend was applied to Ahithophel, the king's counsellor, of whom David had thought so highly that he regarded his advice as nothing less than an oracle of God (2 Sam 16:23). We have seen how the moment when the treachery of Ahithophel is unmasked, the only occasion in the David narratives that he is represented as praying out of his distress and fear (2 Sam 15:31), became the catalyst for the development of the "historical" Davidic superscripts to the psalms.[20] Later Jewish exegetes were drawing on this tradition, when they "found" allusions to Absalom's rebellion and the treachery of Ahithophel in the actual "text" of the psalm. The Targum to Psalm 55:14, for example, reads:

> Et tu Achitophel homo similis mihi,
> praeceptor qui docuisti me ac notam reddis me sapientiam…[21]

The Mishnah confirms the application of this verse to Ahithophel as well as the notion that he was David's teacher.

---

[19] The LXX rendering of Ps 54:15 would suggest that these two passages were regarded as analogous at the time of their translation into Greek. According to the LXX, the intimate friend sweetened food in companionship with the psalmist: ὃς ἐπὶ τὸ αὐτό μοι ἐγλύκανας ἐδέσματα. The meaning effect of this translation is very similar to the ὁ ἐσθίων ἄρτους μου of Ps 40:10.

[20] See pp. 79-80 above.

[21] The Targum also mentions Ahithophel in verse 17, along with another of David's enemies who also features in the psalm superscripts:…*et sententiam feret malorum adversum ipsos Doeg et Achitophel.*

> David, king of Israel...learned only two things from Achitophel, but called him his teacher, his companion and his familiar friend; for it is written, "But it was thou, a man mine equal, my companion and my familiar friend."[22]

The *Midrash Tehillim* commentary on Ps 55 also reflects this exegetical tradition:

> David had no greater friend than Achitophel, whom David made chief of his prosecutors, and who was the king's counsellor in all his affairs, as it is said 'Achitophel was the king's counsellor' (1 Chron 27:33)...David was not afraid of any man except Achitophel. Hence David said: Give ear, O God to my prayer; and hide not Thyself from my supplication...[23]

What David said is actually Ps (54)55—identified by its *incipit*.

Although these sources post-date the NT period they are clearly within a much earlier line of tradition. It is on the basis of such a reading of Ps (54)55:13-14 that Menken argues that a similar reading of Ps (40:10)41:9 allowed the Evangelist to understand it as "originally" spoken by David in the context of Absalom's revolt and Ahithophel's treachery. This perceived *Sitz im Leben* for the psalm then allowed him to make a *gezerah sawa* ("identical category") connection between it and a text which referred to those events, 2 Sam 18:28. Menken suggests that the verb ἐπαίρειν found its way into the Johannine rendering of Ps (40:10)41:9 under the influence of an analogous expression in 2 Sam 18:28. In this passage Ahimaz, bringing the good news of the suppression of Absalom's revolt to King David says, "Blessed be the Lord your God who has delivered up the men who <u>raised their hand</u> against my lord the king."[24] Foremost among these men was, of course, Ahithophel. The particular idiomatic expression for acting insolently, "raising one's hand against someone" is found only here and in 2 Sam 20:21 which also concerns a rebellion against David. It is an analogous idiom to that in Ps (40)41, "making great one's heel against someone," also a reference to rebellion against David, once the psalm is read from within the interpretive tradition that gave rise to the his-

---

[22] *m. Abot* 6:3, Danby, *The Mishnah*, 459.

[23] *Midr. Teh.* 55,1. The Midrash on Psalm 3, "a psalm of David when he fled from Absalom his son," also applies this same Ps 55 passage to Ahithophel. Cf. *Midr. Teh.* 3,4. The Ahithophelian connection may also account for the note of cleverness and beguilment introduced into Tg. Ps 41:19, quoted in note 18 above.

[24] The connection can only be established with the Hebrew נשאו את־ידם and not with the LXX of 2 Sam 18:28 which has the men "hating (μισοῦντας) their hand..." There is, of course, the possibility that John had a corrected Greek text. Early witnesses offer the variant readings, ἐπαραμένους and ἀντάραντας. See Menken, *Old Testament Quotations*, 133-34.

torical superscripts. So the metaphor from one passage, 2 Sam 18:28, can throw light on the other corresponding passage, Ps (40:10)41:9.

The question of intentionality on the part of the Johannine author must arise. Whether this is really a case of conscious application of *gezera shawa* or rather of spontaneous and perhaps even unconscious recollection of the wording of an analogous passage, it is impossible to say. Even if his use of the 2 Sam 18:28 expression was spontaneous, it could still have been due to his perception of Jesus as prefigured in David.[25] His reference to Judas as "the son of perdition" (John 17:12) may also be an allusion to traditions about Ahithophel, and, if so, a further indication that the Evangelist saw in Ahithophel's betrayal of David a prefiguraton of Judas' betrayal of Jesus.[26] What is evident is that the supposed Davidic authorship of the psalm, with the hermeneutical implications that follow from this, appear to have affected the form of the quotation. As we will see, these factors may also have affected its role in the narrative.

As we saw in Ch. 1, the application of this psalm verse to Judas' betrayal of Jesus is not confined to the Fourth Gospel. In Mark 14:18 Jesus makes an oblique reference to his betrayer by means of a verbal allusion to the psalm: Ἀμὴν λέγω ὑμῖν ὅτι εἷς ἐξ ὑμῶν παραδώσει με ὁ ἐσθίων μετ' ἐμοῦ. Jesus then shows that the scriptural prophecy is being fulfilled in that one of the twelve who are now sharing the meal with him is his betrayer.[27] The Scripture fulfilment motif is underlined by Jesus' statement, immediately following, that he goes to his death "as it is written of him" (Mark 14:21). These three elements, the reference to betrayal, the mention of the betrayer's table fellowship with Jesus and the Scripture fulfilment motif, are found in both the Matthean and Lukan parallels. The psalm verse is represented in Matt 26:23 by Jesus' designation of the betrayer as: Ὁ ἐμβάψας μετ' ἐμοῦ τὴν χεῖρα ἐν τῷ τρυβλίῳ and has inspired in Luke 22:21 a thematic allusion which does not require of the reader a knowledge of Jewish table customs:...πλὴν ἰδοὺ ἡ χεὶρ τοῦ παραδιδόντος με μετ' ἐμοῦ ἐπὶ τῆς τραπέζης. This is followed immediately by Luke's version of the scriptural fulfilment motif:...ὅτι ὁ υἱὸς μὲν τοῦ ἀνθρώπου κατὰ τὸ ὡρισμένον πορεύεται...(v. 22).

---

[25] Glasson, "Davidic Links with the Betrayal of Jesus." *ExpTim* 85 (1973-1974), 118-19, at 118, argues purely from the Davidic superscript to Ps (40)41 that Judas' perfidy would have been seen as a reference to Ahithophel.

[26] The earliest evidence for the belief that Ahithophel has no share in the world to come is *m Sanh.* 10:2. The tradition is also preserved in *Midr. Teh.* 5, 9.

[27] Mark uses here an idiomatic expression, ὁ ἐμβαπτόμενος μετ' ἐμοῦ εἰς τὸ τρύβλιον. This refers to the dipping of food in a sauce, and means "to share a meal with someone. "Louw & Nida, *Greek-English Lexicon*, I, 70.

The three features present in the synoptic treatment of Ps 40:10 —the reference to betrayal, an "acting out" of the psalm verse and the Scripture fulfilment motif—are also present in John. Yet his handling of the psalm is distinctive in several important ways. Firstly, as regards the Scripture fulfilment motif, John exhibits his preference for formal citation. Then, in John 13:26-27, Jesus engages Judas in an enactment of Ps 40:10 by dipping a ψωμίον and handing it to him. There are three uniquely Johannine features here. (1) In John, the enactment of the psalm is Jesus' way of identifying the betrayer to Peter. In Mark and Luke, Jesus does not appear to know which of the twelve is his betrayer is. In Matthew, it is not clear, since Judas' question—Μήτι ἐγώ εἰμι, ῥαββί;—and Jesus' reply—Σὺ εἶπας—could be understood as indicating that his guilty behaviour identified him to Jesus as the betrayer. (2) In John, Jesus' takes the initiative in fulfilling the Scripture. This is in marked contrast to the synoptics where the reference to the dipping of food by all the participants in the meal is simply a metaphor for table fellowship. (3) In John, the food which Jesus dips and hands to Judas is definitely bread.[28] The unspecified food being dipped in Mark 14:20 and Matt 26:23 could be either the bitter herbs or the unleavened bread of the Passover meal. The synoptics do not make it clear.[29]

The greater precision in the Johannine use of the word ψωμίον is in accord with the use of the singular ἄρτον in the citation. Both have an important function. Jesus' act of giving (John 13:26—δίδωσιν) the morsel of bread recalls the feeding miracle when he gave (John 6:11—διέδωκεν) the miraculous bread.[30] The singular ἄρτον in the quotation recalls the earlier citation from Ps 77:24, Ἄρτον ἐκ τοῦ οὐρανοῦ ἔδωκεν αὐτοῖς φαγεῖν. Thus both quotation and dramatisation of the psalm passage form a link to the Bread of Life Discourse where, significantly, the first mention of Judas as betrayer occurs (John 6:64.70-71). Probably, this also explains why John has

---

[28] The word ψωμίον is the diminutive of ψωμός, a piece of bread. See Bauer, *Greek-English Lexicon*, 894; Louw & Nida, *Greek-English Lexicon*, 49.

[29] In the Fourth Gospel the supper is not a Passover meal, although it is set in the context of Passover. See J. Jeremias, *The Eucharistic Words*, 82-83; Brown, *John XIII-XXI*, 555-56; Moloney, *The Johannine Son of Man*, 190. The presence of the food-dipping motif, could be explained either as characteristically Johannine evocation of an Exodus motif—the Passover meal, or as a vestige of a pre-Johannine account of the supper which can be derived by synoptic analogy. See Fortna, *The Fourth Gospel and Its Predecessor*, 148-9. Lindars, *The Gospel*, 446, attributes the confusion over whether or not the supper is a Passover meal to the Evangelist's tendency to be inconsistent!

[30] Another significant point of contrast with the synoptics—in Mark 6:41, Matt 14:19 and Luke 9:16, the disciples give the bread to the people.

used the verb τρώγειν in the quotation.³¹ We mentioned above that John's word order—genitive personal pronoun preceding the article and noun (*sc.* μου τὸν ἄρτον)—differs from the LXX. Again we cannot avoid the impression that we are being emphatically reminded of John 6:54.56—

ὁ τρώγων μου τὴν σάρκα καὶ πίνων μου τὸ αἷμα ἔχει ζωὴν αἰώνιον…

…ὁ τρώγων μου τὴν σάρκα καὶ πίνων μου τὸ αἷμα ἐν ἐμοὶ μένει κἀγὼ ἐν αὐτῷ…

The Johannine Jesus' initiative in giving the bread, and thus setting in motion the process that will lead to his own death, points to the giving of the true bread for the life of the world (John 6:32-33). For Culpepper, there is irony here: "Judas refused to eat the true bread; the bread he ate had no power to give life."³²

This brings us to a further level of understanding. If the bread is to be understood primarily in a "sapiential" sense (as we saw in our discussion of John 6:31) it symbolizes Jesus' self-revelation. If the presence of eucharistic "overtones" in John 6 is acknowledged, then they too must be taken into account in an understanding of John 13:18. Two important considerations flow from this. Firstly, there is the late Second Temple period conception of David as a wisdom figure. Secondly, there follows from that sapiential understanding a portrayal of Judas which is totally different from that in the synoptics.

The "wisdom" portrayal of David is particularly significant for the Fourth Gospel in view of its presentation of Jesus as incarnate Wisdom. We recall that the David of Israel's memory and imagination was sapientialized with particular reference to his role as psalmist. In the *Midrash Tehillim* there is a comment on Ps (40:10) 41:9 which has several points of contact with John 6. In this interpretation, David explains the lifting up of the heel against himself by those who ate his bread as follows:

---

³¹ Τρώγειν is used in John 6:54. 56.57.58. Brown, *John XII-XXI*, 571, supposes that τρώγειν in John 13:18 might be one of several indications that the "eucharistic" verses (John 6:51-58) once stood in the same context as John 13:12-20. If, as is frequently suggested, John 6:51c-58 is redactional, the question of the direction in which the influence worked must be asked. In a synchronic study such as this, we take it that the author/editor who gave us the text as it is now stands intended the citation in John 13:18 to remind the reader of the Bread of Life Discourse.

³² See *The Anatomy*, 197. We cannot agree with Lindars, *The Gospel*, 453, that the giving of the morsel is "a last appeal by Jesus to him (Judas) to reconsider his intentions."

Even my disciples turned on me with kicks. How so? When they entered the house of study, they entered my presence gentle as kids; but when they left my presence, they became like goats goring with their horns. By *bread* David meant words of Torah, as in the verse *Wisdom...saith...Come eat of my bread* (Prov 9:5).[33]

This David, a wisdom teacher suffering rejection by the disciples to whom he offers the bread of his instruction is not unlike the Jesus of John 6. Of course, the characterization of David as a rabbinical sage indicates a late dating for this particular comment. However, as our reconstruction of David's "literary future" has shown, this is the outcome of a gradual re-shaping of his memory, developing principally out of his role as psalmist, which was well under way in the NT period. From the form and function of Ps 40:10 in the Fourth Gospel, therefore, we can infer its attribution to a David figure positioned somewhere along the trajectory traversed by the David of Israel's imagination and memory which was to lead to his eventual installation in the *Beth Ha Midrash* as "Rabbi David."[34]

We come now to explore the implications of the sapiential understanding for Johannine perceptions of Judas. If the disciples have been made clean by the word Jesus has spoken to them (John 15:3), the reason why Judas is not clean (13:11) is because he has refused that word. He appears, therefore, as an ex-disciple who initially received Jesus, but subsequently rejected him.[35] Again, a reminder of the reaction to the Bread of Life Discourse: Ἐκ τούτου πολλοὶ [ἐκ] τῶν μαθητῶν αὐτοῦ ἀπῆλθον εἰς τὰ ὀπίσω καὶ οὐκέτι μετ' αὐτοῦ περιεπάτουν (John 6:66). Judas departs into the night (13:30), a potent Johannine symbol of the blind refusal to believe (3:19). Judas, however, does more than merely walk away from Jesus, he leaves the supper to inform the Jewish authorities of Jesus' whereabouts. Such a Judas must surely have been a familiar figure to Johannine Christians living the experience of denunciation to the authorities, possibly even by defectors from among their number.[36] In going so far as to say that Jesus' chose Judas that the Scripture might be ful-

---

[33] *Midr. Teh.* 41:7 (Braude I, 439).
[34] For David as a "rabbi," see Neusner, *Messiah in Context*, 88-90.
[35] See Schuchard, *Scripture within Scripture*, 111.
[36] In making this suggestion we assume the scenario painted by Martyn in his study of the separation between Church and Synagogue which forms the background to the Fourth Gospel. See *History and Theology in the Fourth Gospel*. See also Culpepper's character analysis of Judas, *The Anatomy*, 125: "Judas does not betray Jesus for the money—the silver is not mentioned in John ... so John strips Judas of psychologically plausible motivations. What matters to him is that Judas is the representative defector ... Judas represents *the disciple* who betrays Jesus."

filled (John 6:70),[37] the Evangelist reassures his readers that their persecutors are equally the instruments of Scripture fulfilment and have no more power over them than Judas had over Jesus. The eucharistic overtones in John 6 serve only to reinforce the impression that John intends the application of Ps 40:10 to ex-Johannine Christians who have shared in the eucharistic meal and have now apostasized. If John 6 is the eucharistic institution narrative transposed, then it is probable that traces of it—literary and/or thematic—will show through in the supper scene, the point in John's narrative where the eucharistic institution might have been expected.[38]

This brings us again to the Davidic "authorship" of the psalm and the effect that this might possibly have had on the Johannine reception of the quotation. There are three levels at which the psalm can be interpreted: as spoken by—

1 David, experiencing betrayal by Ahithophel
2 Jesus, experiencing betrayal by Judas
3 Johannine Christians experiencing betrayal by defectors/denouncers.

We recall the testimony of 4 Macc 18:15 to the consolation which the psalms of David brought to the persecuted: how a mother reminded her children as they faced martyrdom of how their father used sing to them "the psalm of David which says, "Many are the afflictions of the righteous." The NT leaves us in no doubt of Jesus' own sharing in a similar access to the Psalter. In their persecution, even unto death in some cases (John 16:2), Johannine Christians see Jesus as the "David" who speaks in the psalm, but they also share in Jesus' experience of interiorizing the psalm in this way. The quotation in John 13:18 helps Jesus' "own" to interpret his death, but it is also directed towards their life situation, as is appropriate for a "Scripture" occurring in the last discourse. As we will see, this "third level" of interpretation is sustained in the next psalm quotation.

In summary, a comparison with the synoptics shows that the Fourth Evangelist has gone his own way with the citation of Ps 40:10. The basic function of Ps 40:10, in the tradition, is to show

---

[37] Menken, "The Translation of Ps 41:10," 61, draws attention to the elliptical use of ἀλλ' ἵνα in John 13:18 which allows for the translation, "I know whom I have chosen; but [I chose Judas] that the scripture may be fulfilled ..." See also Brown, *John XIII-XXI*, 553.

[38] Brown's hypothesis concerning John 6 is "that the backbone of vss 51-58 is made up of material from the Johannine narrative of the institution of the Eucharist which was located in the Last Supper scene and that this material has been recast into a duplicate of the Bread of Life Discourse." See *John I-XII*, 287. Lindars, *The Gospel*, 443-44, compares the eucharistic institution narrative to the "agony" tradition which is absent from John 18, yet found in another form in John 12:27-28.

that Judas' betrayal was in fulfilment of the Scripture. John fully accepts this, emphasizing it by presenting the Scripture as a formal citation. However, he also brings the reception of the psalm quotation to an entirely new level of understanding.[39] In accordance with his view of Jesus' omniscience and sovereign control of the events of "the hour," he adapts the text to remove any suggestion that Judas' betrayal was trickery of an unsuspecting Jesus. The verbal form of the quotation (the product of either *gezerah shawa* exegesis or of spontaneous association, attributable to John's acceptance of Davidic authorship of the psalm) indicates that John understands the psalm as spoken by David on the particular occasion of Ahithophel's treachery. The comparison thus implied between David and Jesus means that ἵνα ἡ γραφὴ πληρωθῇ actually refers to David's story, as mediated through the psalm quotation. At a further level of interpretation, John brings out the connection with the Bread of Life Discourse, understood in terms of Jesus' sapiential role (for which David is also a model). The verbal and thematic links with John 6, which are highly significant in view of the supper setting, indicate that the "bread" is not only a Wisdom/Jesus' self revelation, but is also the bread of the eucharist. At a third level of interpretation, in the "now" of the Johannine readers, the time of the *récit*, the psalm speaks of their experience of denials, betrayals and denouncements, and shows them that it is through this that they will participate in Jesus' triumphant death.

C. *Ps (68:5)69:4 in John 15:25*

Our next psalm quotation occurs in the farewell discourses in which, as Dodd has shown, Jesus addresses the community in the post-Easter situation—

> ...the whole series of discourses, including dialogues, monologues and the prayer in which it all culminates, is conceived as taking place within the moment of fulfilment. It is true that the dramatic setting is that of 'the night in which He was betrayed', with the crucifixion in prospect. Yet in a real sense it is the risen and glorified Christ who speaks.[40]

---

[39] This level is missed by many commentators. Cf. Bultmann's understanding of the citation as merely intended "to warn the disciple against any false assurance," *The Gospel*, 477-78. Cf. Lindars' assessment, *The Gospel*, 442,—"all the emphasis goes on the enormity of betrayal of trust involved in the breach of table fellowship." Cf. also Moo's statement, *The OT in the Gospel Passion Narratives*, 236, that "Ps 41:9 is cited as explanatory of the fact that Jesus has chosen his betrayer as a disciple."

[40] Dodd, *The Interpretation*, 397. See also Culpepper, *The Anatomy*, 37; G. R. O'Day, "I have Overcome the World: Narrative Time in John 13-17," *Semeia* 53 (1991) 153-166.

Reflecting with his disciples on the hostility of "the Jews" who, having heard him speak and having seen his works, persecute him, Jesus speaks of a hatred of both himself and his Father which, strange as this may seem,[41] fulfils the Scripture:

> ...ἀλλ᾽ ἵνα πληρωθῇ ὁ λόγος ὁ ἐν τῷ νόμῳ αὐτῶν γεγραμμένος ὅτι Ἐμίσησάν με δωρεάν.
>
> "It is to fulfil the word that is written in their law, 'They hated me without a cause.'"

The quotation occurs in a unit of discourse (15:18-16:4a) in which Jesus warns his disciples about the hatred which they are to encounter. Those who have been with him from the beginning and have accepted his progressive self-revelation as the one who is ἐκ τοῦ θεοῦ and thus "not of the world" have themselves become "not of the world."[42] Jesus has chosen them out of the world (15:19; 17:14). They are the ones the Father gave him out of the world (17:6). There is thus a real sense in which they too are ἐκ τοῦ θεοῦ. Consequently, the world will react to them as it did to Jesus (17:14). The "Scripture," Ἐμίσησάν με δωρεάν refers to the great sin of those who have rejected Jesus: their unbelief, in spite of the revelatory works he has done among them.

This rather terse quotation is unique to the Fourth Gospel, although an example of similar recourse to the Psalter by an oppressed group is found in PsSol 7:1—

> Do not move away from us, O God,
> lest those who hate us without cause (οἳ ἐμίσησαν ἡμᾶς δωρεάν) should attack us.

John's quotation is also difficult to identify as there is no passage in the OT with exactly this wording. The most frequently suggested candidate for the Scripture in question is Ps. (68:5)69:4, in which the psalmist refers to enemies as οἱ μισοῦντές με δωρεάν. On textual grounds, an equally good case can be made for Ps (34)35:19 which

---

[41] In Bultmann's reading, *The Gospel*, 551, it is the unexpressed thought which connects vv. 24 and 25 that explains the ἀλλά—"such a reaction is indeed inconceivable, but ..."

[42] As Meeks makes clear, *The Man From Heaven*, 161, this is not to be understood in an ontological sense, but in a conferred sense. Looking from a social science perspective at the alienation of the Johannine circle, Neyrey remarks that in the earlier stages of the community's existence the world was "a place to be catechized, a place deserving of God's benevolent attention, and a place in which the Word seemed willing to pitch his tent. But as opposition to Jesus culminated in excommunication from the synagogue, this world became a hateful place (15:18-25), a place from which one should flee (13:1-3; 17:5), a place of exile." See *An Ideology of Revolt*, 143-44.

contains exactly the same phrase.⁴³ Another possibility, however, is Ps (108)109:3.⁴⁴ Here the psalmist complains of the lying tongues that speak against him:

...καὶ λόγοις μίσους ἐκύκλωσάν με
καὶ ἐπολέμησάν με δωρεάν.

Not only is the word δωρεάν in common, but the "hateful words" could have suggested the verb ἐμίσησάν. Moreover, we have already found Jesus "surrounded" (John 10:24). A further suggestion as a source for the quotation in John 15:25 is Ps (118)119:161— Ἄρχοντες κατεδίωξάν με δωρεάν.⁴⁵ In favour of this, it might be argued that Jesus' interlocutors are, in fact, the ἄρχοντες of the Jews and that Jesus has just warned his disciples concerning them, εἰ ἐμὲ ἐδίωξαν, καὶ ὑμᾶς διώξουσιν (John 15:20 cf. John 3:1; 7:26, 48; 12:42). In view of the high profile of Ps (68)69 in the NT generally and in the Fourth Gospel, Ps (68:5)69:4, the most likely primary source for the quotation, seems a good "working hypothesis."⁴⁶

According to Schuchard, who agrees that the four sources which we have mentioned are possible solutions to the problem of the citation's provenance,—

> ... no one solution emerges as the preferred solution. Whether a particular textual tradition is recalled is similarly uncertain. Any of the above solutions, however, would result in an essentially equivalent understanding of the purpose of this citation. The hatred of the Jews signals the fulfillment of Old Testament prophecy and the approaching consummation of Jesus' work in the world.⁴⁷

We believe that it is possible to be a little more precise. It is noteworthy that all four passages most frequently suggested as sources for John 15:25 are from the psalms. Moreover, Ps 68 is one of the תפלות of David the son of Jesse collected in Book 1 of the Psalter (Ps (71)72:20). Given the Johannine tendency to allude simultaneously to several passages, and in view of the then accepted perception of the Psalter as a unit, we could fruitfully allow the other three psalms to "colour" Ἐμίσησάν με δωρεάν. It would then appear, not just as

---

⁴³ Among those accepting both as possible sources are Bultmann, *The Gospel*, 551, n. 7; Schnackenburg, *The Gospel 3*, 117; Freed, *OT Quotations*, 94-95; Pancaro, *The Law in the Fourth Gospel*, 330; Moo, *The OT in the Gospel Passion Narratives*, 243; Holladay, *The Psalms through Three Thousand Years*, 689.
⁴⁴ Schnackenburg, *The Gospel 3*, 117.
⁴⁵ Schnackenburg, *The Gospel 3*, 117.
⁴⁶ This is the view of Dodd, *According to the Scriptures*, 58; *Historical Tradition*, 38-39. Brown, *John XIII-XXI*, 698, believes that the context of Ps (68)69 is "better for the meaning that John gives to the citation."
⁴⁷ Schuchard, *Scripture within Scripture*, 123.

fulfilment of (unspecified) OT prophecy, but as a familiar phrase of David, which finds its true significance on the lips of Jesus. Read in this way, the words Ἐμίσησάν με δωρεάν would conjure up memories of the groundless harassment of David with which Jonathan reproached Saul: καὶ ἱνατί ἁμαρτάνεις εἰς αἷμα ἀθῶν θανατῶσαι τὸν Δαυὶδ δωρεάν; (1 Sam 19:5).[48]

As we have seen, the Evangelist is quite uninhibited when it comes to curtailing and changing the biblical text. Taking the phrase, "Who hate me without cause," a participle functioning as a noun in both the Hebrew and the LXX of the psalm, he converts it into an independent clause: "They hated me without cause." The formula of quotation is most likely elliptical, requiring the reader to supply "this is."[49] It has been suggested that it could also be translated as an imperative: "Let the text in their law be fulfilled."[50] This is the longest quotation formula in John and perhaps in the whole NT.[51] The usage of νόμος as a reference to the tripartite canon as a whole has already been encountered at John 10:34 "where a similarly remarkable and isolated scriptural text is cited."[52]

Looking more closely at how the quotation fits into its immediate context, we find that the literary unit in which it occurs falls into two parts, 15:18-25 (re the world's hatred of both Jesus and the disciples) and 15:26-16:4a (re the Paraclete and the disciples' witness to Jesus). The quotation concludes the first part. The verb μισέω occurs five times in the verses immediately preceding the quotation. The cumulative effect of this repetition greatly strengthens the impact of the verb's sixth appearance in the quotation itself. Ἐμίσησάν με δωρεάν then recalls, by means of an inclusion, the opening verse of the unit —Εἰ ὁ κόσμος ὑμᾶς μισεῖ, γινώσκετε ὅτι ἐμὲ πρῶτον ὑμῶν μεμίσηκεν. The effect of this is to emphasize that the world's hatred of the disciples is as much a fulfilment of what is written in the Law as its hatred of Jesus was. The introduction of the Paraclete theme in the

---

[48] This does not, of course, exclude the possibility of seeing, as Brown does, the world's rejection and hatred of Jesus as the antithesis of the respect God demands for the "prophet-like-Moses" (Deut 18:18-19). See *John XII-XXI*, 697.

[49] Bultmann, *The Gospel*, 551, draws attention to the similar ellipse in 13:18. See also John 9:25

[50] Brown, *John XIII-XXI*, 688, suggests that the usage identified by Max Zerwick as "Ἵνα *in exhortatione independente* may be in operation here. In his explanation of this usage of ἵνα, Zerwick quotes Mark 14:49, ἀλλ' ἵνα πληρωθῶσιν αἱ γραφαί where the sense is undoubtedly imperative. His only Johannine example is John 13:34. See *Graecitas Biblica: Novi Testamenti Exemplis Illustratur* (Rome: Pontifical Biblical Institute, 1966) #415, p. 141.

[51] Freed, *Old Testament Quotations*, 94.
[52] Schnackenburg, *The Gospel III*, 117.

second part of the literary unit, immediately after the quotation is by no means extraneous. The Paraclete comes to the disciples, "not in the first place to comfort them by predicting that hatred and to strengthen their faith,...but rather to encourage them to proclaim the word and bear witness in the world."[53] As well as having the forensic role of pointing out the world's guilt (16:8-11), the Paraclete reminds them of the Scripture (14:26). The psalm quotation is to be remembered by the disciples when the "hour" comes (16:2) for the world's hatred to be unleashed on them, just as they were enabled by the Spirit to remember and understand the Scripture in the light of Jesus' hour (2:22; 12:16).

One of the striking features of John 15:18-16:4a is the compression of time. In the narrative Jesus speaks proleptically of the life situation of the Johannine author and implied readers. Within *histoire* / "story" time he warns his disciples of future persecution and offers them a scriptural resource with which to interpret it. In *récit* / "discourse" time, this persecution has already happened in the implied readers' experience.[54] By setting their experience within the story of Jesus' hour, the Gospel gives the readers a frame of reference within which they can make sense of what is happening to them and take hope for a similarly glorious outcome. The effect of the psalm allusion is to draw the reader further into the circle of those who "know the Scripture" (12:16, 20:9). The resulting sense of being "insiders" over against the "outsiders" who know neither the Scripture (5:39), nor Jesus (3:10, 8:43, 10:6), nor the Father (8:55, 15:21. 16:3), is a powerful support to a beleaguered community. This is especially welcome when the "outsiders" have a certain prestige. For the "insiders," the psalm speaks of the hatred of God which manifested itself in hostility to their master and which now takes the form of persecution of his servants (John 15:20). As Jesus himself warned them, ταῦτα ποιήσουσιν ὅτι οὐκ ἔγνωσαν τὸν πατέρα οὐδὲ ἐμέ (John 16:3).

Within the narrative structure of the Gospel, the quotation serves to heighten the sense of mounting hostility towards Jesus and to stress his serenity in the face of his impending death. The fact that this "hatred without cause" will lead to Jesus' death is equally ἵνα πληρωθῇ ὁ λόγος ὁ ἐν τῷ νόμῳ αὐτῶν γεγραμμένος (John 15:25). The quotation has an analogous function with regard to the situation of

---

[53] Schnackenburg, *The Gospel III*, 114.
[54] We encounter here what Martyn called "the essential *integrity* of the *einmalig* drama of Jesus' earthly life and the contemporary drama in which the Risen Lord acts through his servants." See *History and Theology*, 89.

its Johannine readers who are being expelled from the synagogue and who even face the threat of death. If they are hated, it can only be because they too do not belong to the world. It reassures them that they are most truly ἐκ τοῦ θεου when they bear the brunt of that hatred which is the mark of those who are ἐκ τοῦ κόσμου. The function of the quotation is thus to keep them from falling away (John 16:1), to motivate and form their reaction to the experience of persecution.[55]

For Johannine Christians, Ps (68)69 carries two strong reminders of Jesus: of the zeal which consumed him (John 2:17) and of his thirst on the cross (John 19:28). As we saw, there may also be echoes of the psalm in John's reference to the unbelief of Jesus' brothers (John 7:5). Furthermore, the psalmist's imprecation against those who hate him without cause, σκοτισθήτωσαν οἱ ὀφθαλμοὶ αὐτῶν τοῦ μὴ βλέπειν (v. 24) is strongly reminiscent of Jesus' verdict on the forerunners of those who would persecute his disciples—Εἰς κρίμα ἐγὼ εἰς τὸν κόσμον τοῦτον ἦλθον, ἵνα...οἱ βλέποντες τυφλοὶ γένωνται (John 9:39). It is quite possible that Johannine Christians putting the words ὁ ζῆλος τοῦ οἴκου σου κατέφαγέν με on the lips of Jesus would also have understood the very next line—καὶ οἱ ὀνειδισμοὶ τῶν ὀνειδιζόντων σε ἐπέπεσαν ἐπ' ἐμέ—in the same way. It certainly resonates with the thought of John 15:18-25 and, in fact, with several scenes in the Gospel where the attack on Jesus is directed against a representative-disciple figure (for example, John 5:10; 9:34; 12:10). We know too from Rom 15:3 that it was applied to Jesus in early Christianity. In his discussion of dualism in the Fourth Gospel, John Ashton writes of the "pithy oppositions that typify the Evangelist's style—light/dark, above/below, sight/blindness. "Sometimes," he notes, citing John 15:25 as an example, "the intended contrast is left to be inferred."[56] If we were to attempt to spell out what John infers here, envisaging the whole psalm, and in particular v. 10b, as received within the Johannine circle at the three levels which we posited for Ps (40:10)41:9 in the previous section, we might come up with an interpretive scheme such as the following—

---

[55] This type of psalm usage is not unique to the Fourth Gospel. E.g., the words of consolation addressed in 1 Pet 4:14 to those suffering reproach for the name of Christ allude, by means of the phrase—εἰ ὀνειδίζεσθε ἐν ὀνόματι Χριστου, to the ὀνειδιζμός inflicted on the Lord's anointed, as lamented in Ps (88:51-52)89:50-51. As with Ps (68)69 in the Fourth Gospel, so in 1 Pet, the Christological interpretation of the psalm offers comfort to a community suffering persecution and provides an interpretation of their distress which makes it bearable and even a reason for joy.

[56] Ashton, *Understanding*, 312.

1. David rules in God's name; therefore he bears the brunt of the hatred of those opposed to God—οἱ ὀνειδισμοὶ τῶν ὀνειδιζόντων σε ἐπέπεσαν ἐπ᾽ ἐμέ (Ps 68:10b).
2. Jesus comes in God's name; therefore those opposed to God will hate him—ὁ ἐμὲ μισῶν καὶ τὸν πατέρα μου μισεῖ (John 15:23).
3. Johannine Christians are sent in Jesus' name, so they will encounter the hatred that was vented on him—εἰ ἐμὲ ἐδίωξαν, καὶ ὑμᾶς διώξουσιν (John 15:20).

It is surely no accident that one of the Gospel's clearest articulations of the "third-level" interpretation—καὶ ὅπου εἰμὶ ἐγὼ ἐκεῖ καὶ ὁ διάκονος ὁ ἐμὸς ἔσται (John 12:26)—echoes Ittai the Gittite's pledge of loyalty to David (2 Sam 15:21). If we imagine οἱ ὀνειδισμοὶ τῶν ὀνειδιζόντων σε ἐπέπεσαν ἐπ᾽ ἐμέ as received at this "third level," it becomes, to borrow J. L. Mays' term, a "hermeneutical door" into the reading of the psalm as an address of the believer to Jesus. This is our first encounter with an important aspect of the Johannine reception of the psalms which we will discuss in our next chapter: the role of certain psalms as prayers addressed to Jesus. In this usage, the Psalter provides the Johannine Christian with the words to worship Jesus as Ὁ κύριός μου καὶ ὁ θεός μου (John 20:28, alluding to LXX Ps 34:23). It is significant that one of the earliest examples of a Christian prayer to Christ, which identifies the glorified Jesus as the Κύριος addressed in the psalms, is also situated in a context of persecution—Stephen's dying prayer (Acts 7:59, alluding to LXX Ps 30:6). It is also significant that we have touched on this issue in the context of the tension between Jesus' disciples and "the world." There is an important connection between this Christological development and the *Sitz im Leben* in which we have placed the Johannine reception of this and the previous psalm citations. The evolution of Johannine Christology to the point where Jesus is seen as a divine figure is in direct correlation with the spiralling of conflict to the point where strained relations between Johannine Christianity and Judaism become outright hatred.[57]

To recapitulate this section, the quotation in John 15:25 occurs on the lips of Jesus in his "Farewell Discourses" which refer proleptically to the life situation of Johannine Christians. The recourse to a scriptural antecedent is intended to encourage a community now experiencing persecution to see a parallel between their situation and the events of Jesus' hour which were also foretold in Scripture. It

---

[57] For Neyrey's assessment of the social locations of the three successive Christologies which he believes are reflected in the Fourth Gospel (1. Jesus as prophet and king; 2. Jesus as replacement of Judaism; 3. Jesus as equal to God), see *An Ideology*, 148-50.

does this by giving them a sense of having a superior insight into the Scriptures to that of their opponents and an entitlement to claim as their own the heritage which their persecutors would wish to deny them. Their resilience in the face of hatred is born of their belief in the Scripture and in the word of Jesus (John 2:22): Εἰ ὁ κόσμος ὑμᾶς μισεῖ, γινώσκετε ὅτι ἐμὲ πρῶτον ὑμῶν μεμίσηκεν (John 15:18).

From the literary standpoint, the quotation forms the peak of a unit of discourse in which there is a carefully orchestrated crescendo of references to hatred. This is no "ordinary" hatred. It is cosmic in its scale, being the outcome of the diametrical opposition of "the world" to Jesus. The fact that the four possible sources for the quotation are all psalms, indicates a view of this hostility as prefigured in David's experience of being hated without cause, in particular his persecution by Saul, the great opponent of his God-given entitlement to the kingship. As we discovered with regard to the first citation of this psalm in the Gospel, the explicit citation creates "sympathetic vibrations" which extend its influence far beyond its immediate context. The fact that Ps (68)69 is formally cited three times in the Fourth Gospel and the widespread usage of this psalm in the NT generally, would suggest that, in the Johannine view, the psalm as a whole was "about Jesus." The psalmist's lament that the reproaches of those who reproached God fall on him corresponds exactly to the experience of Jesus and, eventually, of his disciples as described in John 15:18-25. By imaginatively articulating the implied usage of v. 10b as an address of the Johannine Christian to Jesus, we gain an insight into the role that the psalms played in the development of the Gospel's high Christology.

D. *Ps (21:19)22:18 in John 19:24*

The next quotation is connected with the following one (Ps 68:22 in John 19:38) in that both are instances of Jesus' active fulfilment of the psalms in the passion narrative. Both form a "frame" for the central episode of the crucifixion scene where Jesus speaks to his mother and the beloved disciple.

The synoptics tell of the casting of lots by the soldiers in order to divide Jesus' garments among themselves (Mark 15:24; Matt 27:35; Luke 23:34) in words that allude clearly to Ps (21:19)22:18—

> ...διεμερίσαντο τὰ ἱμάτιά μου ἑαυτοῖς
> καὶ ἐπὶ τὸν ἱματισμόν μου ἔβαλον κλῆρον.
>
> They parted my garments among them,
> and for my clothing they cast lots.

The Fourth Gospel parallel is distinctive in several ways. Firstly, there is John's selectivity in his utilisation of elements from Ps (21)22 belonging to the passion tradition. The synoptic references to Ps 21:19 are immediately followed by strong verbal allusions to other verses of the psalm in the account of the mockery of the bystanders. In Mark and Matthew, moreover, the psalm's *incipit* is used to portray the dying Jesus' sense of abandonment by God. The Fourth Gospel "corrects" both these applications of the psalm to Jesus.[58] In contrast to the strident atmosphere of mockery and shouting recorded by the synoptics, there is a profoundly reverent stillness about the Johannine crucifixion scene.[59] Far from experiencing forsakenness, the Johannine Jesus remains assured that the Father is with him (See John 8:29; 16:32). There is already a hint, then, in the Evangelist's selectivity with regard to Ps 21 that he must have been able to interpret the one verse he does choose to use in line with his view of the crucifixion as the most complete manifestation of Jesus' glory.

Turning our attention to the Johannine reference to Ps 21:19, we find that the treatment of this element from the tradition is marked by two distinctive features. Firstly, the Fourth Gospel describes two separate actions by which the psalm verse is enacted: the sharing out of the garments among four soldiers and the casting of lots over the tunic. Secondly, it appends a formal quotation of the psalm.

The first feature has been accounted for in various ways. Barrett saw it as "arising out of a failure to understand that in the parallel form of Hebrew verse ἱμάτιά and ἱματισμός (בגדי and לבושי) are to be regarded as synonyms and not to be distinguished."[60] Dodd thought it indicated a secondary stage in the use of testimonies.[61] Like Dodd, Schnackenburg held that it represented a "more extensive reflection based on the word of Scripture."[62] Certainly it is quite conceivable that the plural ἱμάτιά and the collective singular ἱματισμός, probably most accurately rendered by a word such as "raiment" or "vesture," could have inspired a midrashic expansion such as that found in the Fourth Gospel. Brown mentions that the Targum of the psalm, which

---

[58] See Kraus, *Theology of the Psalms*, 189-90.

[59] See James McPolin, *John* (Dublin: Veritas & Wilmington: Glazier, 1979) 244.

[60] Barrett, *The Gospel*, 458. A similar case is found in Matt 21:5-7 where the ὄνος and the πῶλος of Zech 9:9 are taken as two separate animals. Interestingly, the Fourth Gospel parallel (John 12:14) mentions one animal, so its author would appear to understand Hebrew parallelism.

[61] Dodd, *Historical Tradition*, 40; See also Jean Daniélou, *Études d'exégèse judeo-chrétienne: Les Testimonia* (Paris: Beauchesne et ses fils, 1966) 31.

[62] Schnackenburg, *The Gospel III*, 272-73.

has "clothes" and "cloak," could have provided the basis for the Johannine handling of the text.[63]

Various attempts have been made to discern the Johannine author's deeper purpose in highlighting the tunic of Jesus. The suggestion of High Priestly symbolism, "much in favour at the beginning of this century, is being abandoned more and more because of the absence of exegetical foundation."[64] The theory that the seamless tunic is a symbol of the unity of the Church has continued to find adherents.[65] Schnackenburg's objection against both the "High Priest" and the "Unity of the Church" theories, "that Jesus is *deprived* of his tunic," may have some validity, although Jesus' laying down and taking up of his life is symbolized in the laying aside and taking up of his garments in John 13:4.12.[66] Schnackenburg's point that the soldiers share the clothes among themselves is also well taken. His preferred explanation is that the utter degradation and despoliation of Jesus' "unclothing" is still an indication of God's protection, because his tunic is not destroyed. He connects this with the preservation of Jesus' body from the breaking of the bones.[67] To us, this seems to point in the right direction, locating the quotation within John's over-all project in the Book of Glory: to show that the apparent defeat of Jesus' death was actually his victory.

In the course of his exposition of John 19:24 in terms of the unity of the church, de la Potterie refers in passing to 1 Kgs 11:29-31 as a context where the tearing of a garment symbolizes division. The prophet Ahija tears his garment into twelve pieces and gives ten to Jeroboam saying, "Thus says the Lord, the God of Israel, 'Behold I am about to tear the kingdom from the hand of Solomon and will give you ten tribes...'" While it is true that the tearing of the garment symbolizes the division of the land of Israel, it also betokens the diminishment of Solomon's kingly status. The new (that is, valu-

---

[63] Brown, *John XIII-XXII*, 920. Subsequently, Brown has come to regard this suggestion as problematic because of the difficulties involved in dating the Targumim. See *The Death of the Messiah*, 954, n. 41.

[64] Ignace de la Potterie, *The Hour of Jesus: The Passion and the Resurrection of Jesus According to John*. Trans. Gregory Murray (New York: Alba House, 1989) 99. See also de la Potterie's article opposing the "unity of the Church" interpretation, "La tunique sans couture, symbole du Christ grand-prêtre?" *Bib* 60 (1979) 255-269.

[65] See De la Potterie, *The Hour of Jesus*, 100-4. A variant of it has recently been offered by Schuchard, *Scripture within Scripture*, 129-30. The distribution of the garments among the soldiers means that the gentiles too are to be allotted (λαγχάνω, John 19:24) a share (μέρος, John 19:23) in "an indivisible inheritance which, in turn, engenders a corresponding wholeness for those who receive Jesus."

[66] See Bultmann, *The Gospel*, 384-85.

[67] Schnackenburg, *The Gospel III*, 272-4; 457, n. 30.

able) garment worn by the prophet represents the king's royal robe, the symbol of his sovereignty,[68] about to be drastically reduced. The son of David is no longer to be "ruler over Israel and over Judah" (1 Kgs 1:35). He is, however left with the tribe of Judah, "for David's sake" (1 Kgs 11:32.36). There are echoes here of the story of the tearing of Saul's cloak by David in the cave at En-gedi (1 Sam 24:1-22), a portent both of Saul's eventual failure as king and of David's ascendancy. This, in its turn, recalls another significant occasion in biblical lore when a garment is torn—

> As Samuel turned to go away, Saul laid hold upon the skirt of his robe, and it tore. And Samuel said to him, "The Lord has torn the kingdom of Israel from you this day, and has given it to a neighbour of yours, who is better than you" (1 Sam 15:27-28).

The RSV, quoted here, clarifies the sense by adding in the name, Saul, just as the LXX has done, so that it is the prophet's robe that is torn (as in 1 Kgs 11:29-31). Thus Samuel turns and *he* (*sc.* Saul) lays hold of *Samuel's* robe. In the Hebrew text, however, it is not clear whose robe is being torn, Samuel's or Saul's. The ambiguity is also retained in the Targum.[69]

The following version of this incident preserved in the *Midrash Tehillim* takes full advantage of the ambiguity in the Hebrew text to emphasize the symbolic import of the tearing of the robe—

> ...and as Samuel turned to go away, he rent Saul's robe, as it is said, *And as Samuel turned about to go away, he laid hold upon the skirt of his robe, and it rent. And Samuel said unto him: "The Lord hath rent the kingdom of Israel from thee this day, and hath given it to a neighbour of thine, that is better than thou."* Saul asked, "And who is this neighbour of mine who is better than I, and who will rule instead of me?" Samuel answered, "I shall give thee a clue: he who rends thy robe shall take away thy kingship." And when Saul entered into the cave, and David cut off the skirt of his robe, Saul remembered at once what Samuel had told him. Thereupon Saul said, "*I know that as king thou wilt rule* (1 Sam 24:20): Thou wilt be *king* in this world, and *thou wilt rule* in the world-to-come," for it is said *And my servant David shall be king* (Ezek 37:24).[70]

Obviously traditions found in the *Midrash Tehillim* cannot be guaranteed to pre-date the Fourth Gospel. On the other hand, this interpretation depends completely on biblical texts which were available in

---

[68] For David's robe, see 2 Sam 6:14; Ps (44)45: 8. See also Isa 22:21-22—"...and I will put on him (Eliakim) thy (Shebna's) robe and I will grant him thy crown with power...and I will give him the glory of David..."

[69] "And Samuel turned around to go, and he took hold of the edge of his robe, and it was torn." Tg. 1 Sam 15:27, Harrington & Saldarini (ed.). *Targum Jonathan of the Former Prophets*. 130.

[70] *Midr. Teh.* 57.3 (Braude I, 501).

the NT period and the Johannine community seems to have been heir to similar modes of interpretation, as we have already seen more than once.[71] This reworking of 1 Sam 15:27-28 follows a reading of the text which the LXX translator seems to have encountered and decided to "correct." As a reading preserved in an exegetical collection, it is the product of a pervasively oral/aural culture which stressed the importance of memorization and ensured an effective "filtering" of the Scriptures through interpretive tradition. The interpretation is haggadic, not halakhic, therefore "much less subject to fluctuation" and "more apt to conserve extremely ancient traditions."[72]

Supposing that this tradition did influence the Fourth Evangelist, how would it have functioned in terms of the Evangelist's over-all purpose in the "Book of Glory"? In view of the prominence that the Fourth Gospel passion narrative gives to Jesus' kingship, and the fact that the dividing of the garments immediately follows the account of Pilate's "royal inscription," it could well be that the tunic of Jesus which is not torn is intended to symbolize his royal status which remains intact. The tunic without seam is a costly garment and thus, perhaps, another hint at Jesus' royalty.[73] There is also the implication in the Gospel that the Johannine Jesus goes to his death robed in royal purple,[74] a striking instance of the Evangelist's capacity for "wringing every ounce of irony out of the situation."[75] Certainly, Jesus' garments, laid aside and taken up again (John 13:4.12) have particular symbolic value for the Fourth Evangelist. Possibly the strongest argument in favour of this "royal" understanding of Jesus' un-torn tunic is that it harmonizes so well with the Johannine perspective. As we have seen, the Evangelist has omitted several other

---

[71] It is interesting to find that a 20th century Jew, commenting on Ps (21)22, uses 1 Sam 15:27-28 to show that the garments are a figurative representation of the psalmist's rank and authority. See Jonathan Magonet, *A Rabbi Reads the Psalms* (London: SCM, 1994) 106.

[72] See Bloch, "Methodological Note," 54. That this is true of the *Midrash Tehillim* is borne out by several of the sources cited in this study, e.g., the reading of Ps (54)55:12-13 as a reference to Ahithophel in *Midr. Teh.* confirmed by *m. Abot* 6:3 and the NT.

[73] In an article which presents descriptions and illustrations of ancient weaving techniques, N. Primentas has shown that the seamless tunic, not knitted, but woven, was a costly and precious garment. See "'Ο Ἄρραφος Χιτώνας: Τεχνολογική και Ερμηνευτική Προσέγγιση" ("The Tunic without Seam: Technological and Hermeneutical Approach") *DeltBibMel* 10 (1991) 38-50.

[74] In Mark 15:20 and Matt 27:31 the imitation royal regalia in which Jesus is mocked is subsequently removed. In John there is no mention of its removal, although, of course, one could argue with Brown, *Death of the Messiah*, 848, that neither is there any report that Jesus continues to wear it.

[75] Lindars, *The Gospel*, 441.

elements from Ps 21 used in the passion tradition. We can only surmise that the one he keeps and emphasizes in both narrative enactment and formal citation must, in his view, portray Jesus in the light in which he sees him—as reigning triumphantly on the cross.

This "royal" interpretation of John 19:23-24 can also include the idea of the seamless robe as a symbol of unity. Caiphas prophesied that Jesus would die, ὑπὲρ τοῦ ἔθνους, καὶ οὐχ ὑπὲρ τοῦ ἔθνους μόνον ἀλλ' ἵνα καὶ τὰ τέκνα τοῦ θεοῦ τὰ διεσκορπισμένα συναγάγῃ εἰς ἕν (John 11:51-52). Who exactly the scattered children of God are is a matter of debate.[76] What is clear is that the Johannine view of Jesus as lifted up, drawing all to himself (John 12:32), is inspired by the prophetic vision of an ideal king, ruling over all Israel and Judah now restored to unity as in the days of David.[77] Understood in this way, the tunic that is not torn (σχίζω) is indeed a symbol of unity.[78] The ingathering of all the tribes is of world significance, since Jesus, the temple rock from which flow the rivers of living water, has taken over the Jerusalem Temple's prerogative as the centre of the earth. A reading such as this renders the "undersong" of Nathan's oracle audible at the very moment when its promise is being fulfilled in such an unexpected way—"I will establish the throne of his kingdom for ever...I will not take my steadfast love from him as I took it from Saul" (2 Sam 7:15).[79] Read in this way, John's citation of Ps

---

[76] E.g., John 11:52 represents a broadening of the old image of the gathering of the scattered Israelites to include Gentile believers in Jesus—Schnackenburg, *The Gospel 2*, 350. They are the reconstituted Israel—Geyser, "Israel in the Fourth Gospel," 19. They are "the gentiles destined to believe in Jesus"—Brown, *John I-XII*, 440. They are not Gentiles, but neither are they necessarily only Judean Jews; they could include other Christian Jewish groups—Ashton, *Understanding*, 106. They are Jews, Samaritans and Gentiles—Neyrey, *An Ideology*, 125.

[77] According to Geyser, "Israel in the Fourth Gospel," 13, the Gospel "reaches out to the remnants of the lost tribes in the persons of those marginal Jews, the Samaritans, the Galileans and the diaspora Jews, rejected, or at best tolerated by the "pure" Judean Jews. It proclaimed to these that with Jesus' coming had started the ingathering of the tribes into the restored kingdom of David as promised by the prophets since Moses."

[78] Brown sees a parallel with the net that is not torn (21:11, the only other Johannine occurrence of the verb σχίζω). While unbelief produces σχίσμα (7:43; 9:16; 10:19), faith in Jesus gathers into unity (10:16; 11:52; 17:21-22). "The idea, then, would be that the Roman soldiers...did not tear apart what belonged to Jesus." See *Death of the Messiah*, 957.

[79] Schnackenburg's objection that Jesus was deprived of his tunic could perhaps be levelled at this interpretation. However, Jesus freely lays aside his garment (John 13:4) and besides, Nicodemus' lavish provision ensures that the linen cloths in which Jesus is buried are fragrant with myrrh and aloes (19:39) as befits the robes of a king. Cf. LXX Ps 44:9— ...σμύρνα καὶ στακτὴ καὶ κασία ἀπὸ τῶν ἱματίων σου. Many commentators take a negative view of this action of Nicodemus, thus missing its importance as a feature of the Johannine understanding of the "lifting up" of Jesus as his most kingly moment.

21:19 exemplifies the principle that what is said is always heard against the background of the vast "unsaid." To quote Roland Barthes—

> Alongside each utterance one might say that off-stage voices can be heard: they are the *codes:* in their interweaving, these voices (whose origin is "lost" in the vast perspective of the *already written*) de-originate the utterance: the convergence of the voices (of the codes) becomes *writing*, a stereographic space where the ... codes and the ... voices intersect.[80]

There is the possibility that other verses of the psalm have contributed to the Johannine Passion Narrative. For example, one of several candidates for "the Scripture" which the thirst of the crucified Jesus fulfils is Ps 21:16—

...ἐξηράνθη ὡς ὄστρακον ἡ ἰσχύς μου,
καὶ ἡ γλῶσσά μου κεκόλληται τῷ λάρυγγί μου...[81]

As we are about to see, the Johannine handling of this motif from the passion tradition involves multi-layered scriptural reference of which Ps 21:16 is almost certainly one component. The Johannine reference to the wounds in Jesus' hands too (20:25) may owe as much, perhaps, to Ps 21:17—ὤρυξαν χεῖράς μου καὶ πόδας—as it does to historical reminiscence.[82] Such synoptic-type references to the psalm would be in line with the recourse to Psalter phraseology to describe affliction or persecution which is common in Jewish Literature of the Second Temple Period.[83] In fact, Ps 21 is used in this way quite frequently in the NT.[84] The extensive use of the psalm in the passion

---

[80] Roland Barthes, *S/Z*, 21. Barthes speaks of five codes: empirics, science, truth, the person and symbol. Under science, he includes the cultural codes of knowledge and wisdom which give the discourse its authority. In the case of the Fourth Gospel, the biblical tradition would be such a cultural code.

[81] For this suggestion, see Kraus, *Theology of the Psalms*, 190.

[82] *Gos. Pet.* 21 agrees with the Fourth Gospel in its reference to wounds in Jesus' hands. Luke 24:40 possibly implies that there were wounds in Jesus' hands and feet. Justin, *Dial.*, 97:3 clearly states that there were, alluding to Ps 21:17. Both Luke and Justin are indicative of a tendency to read back into the passion narrative elements from the psalm. See Jean Daniélou, *Études d'exégèse judeo-chrétienne*, 29.

[83] It appears that Ps (21)22 was a familiar psalm that reassured pious Jews in times of affliction. There are several clear allusions to Ps (21)22 in the Qumran *Hodayoth*, although not to the verses employed in the gospels. E.g., 1QH IV, 33-34, "...all my bones are broken; my heart dissolves like wax before the fire and my knees are like water pouring down a steep place," alludes to Ps 22:14; 1QH V,11 refers to enemies "opening their mouths" at the poet (cf. Ps 22:13); in 1QH VI, 34 he describes himself as "the worm of men" (cf. Ps 22:6) and in 1QH XV, 15 as "established from the womb" (cf. Ps 22:9).

[84] For example, there is an apparently spontaneous (humorous?) structural echo of Ps 21:17 in Paul's warning against the activities of his Judaizing opponents in

tradition, suggests that its application to Jesus was widespread in early Christianity and that out of this developed an application by extension to all who followed him in his sufferings. This would be in line with the Fourth Gospel usage of Ps 68.

There are, however, several places outside the passion narrative where the Fourth Evangelist's consciousness of Ps 21 is sensed. We already mentioned that the input of the Psalter to John 6 is not limited to the passage formally cited in v. 31. In fact, it is possible that Ps 21:27 (φάγονται πένητες καὶ ἐμπλησθήσονται) has inspired the verb ἐμπίμπλημι in John 6:12. The phrase ὡς δὲ ἐνεπλήσθησαν (John 6:12) has attracted some attention because of the verb ἐμπίμπλημι, not only a divergence from the synoptics' χορτάζω, but a *hapax* in the Fourth Gospel itself. John appears to have received the verb χορτάζω in the tradition, as represented by the synoptic parallels, since he uses it in a retrospective reference to the eating of the bread in 6:36.[85] So why has he chosen this unexpected verb for v. 12? Dodd has suggested that this *hapax* may go back to a directive for the celebration of the eucharist preserved in the *Didache*.[86] A more readily verifiable source, definitely known to the Evangelist, because explicitly cited later in the Gospel, would be Ps 21. Verse 27 actually has several points of contact (underlined) with John 6—

> φάγονται πένητες καὶ ἐμπλησθήσονται,
> καὶ αἰνέσουσιν κύριον οἱ ἐκζητοῦντες αὐτόν·
> ζήσονται αἱ καρδίαι αὐτῶν εἰς αἰῶνα αἰῶνος.

Having eaten their fill—ὡς δὲ ἐνεπλήσθησαν (John 6:12)—the people come ζητοῦντες τὸν Ἰησοῦν (6:24). In words which echo Isa 55:2, Jesus directs their thoughts beyond their physical hunger and its satisfaction to the food which will enable them to live εἰς ζωὴν αἰώνιον (John 6:27). Allowing Ps 21, which functions primarily in the Fourth Gospel as a passion testimony, to lend its overtones to John 6 leads the reader to

---

Phil 3:2. The reference in 2 Tim 4:17 to being rescued ἐκ στόματος λέοντος is strongly reminiscent of Ps 21:22—σῶσόν με ἐκ στόματος λέοντος. As in the psalm, the outcome of the rescue is witness to God's greatness. Several echoes of Ps 21 in Revelation suggest an identification on the part of persecuted believers with their Lord whose sufferings they perceived as depicted in the psalm, e.g., Rev 11:15; 19:5-6 (alluding to Ps (21:29)22:28.

[85] Mark 6:42, Matt 15:37, Luke 9:17. Χορτάζω is the more usual translation of שׂבע in analogous contexts such as Ps 36:19, Ps 80:17 and Ps 131:15.

[86] *Didache* X,1.—μετὰ τὸ ἐμπλησθῆναι οὕτως εὐχαριστήσατε...Dodd notes several 'Johannisms' in this part of the *Didache*. The κλάσματα (cf. John 6:12) and the ποτήριον (cf. John 18:11) are both symbols of the πνευματικὴ τροφή τε καὶ ποτὸς καὶ ζωὴ αἰώνιος given through Jesus. Dodd would, however, be the first to admit that the use of ἐμπίμπλημι in the *Didache* could equally go back to the Fourth Gospel. See *Historical Tradition*, 207.

think of the ἄρτος ἐκ τοῦ οὐρανοῦ as the bread given, in Jesus' death, ὑπὲρ τῆς τοῦ κόσμου ζωῆς (John 6:31.51). This echo of Ps 21 functions, in effect, as a proleptic reference to "the hour," the moment when the bread which is Jesus' flesh is "given for the life of the world" (6:51).

We also referred briefly to a citation of Ps 21:23 in Heb 2:12 where the line in the psalm which marks the passage from affliction to vindication (v. 23a)—διηγήσομαι τὸ ὄνομά σου τοῖς ἀδελφοῖς μου— is envisaged as spoken by Jesus after his resurrection.[87] This line is sometimes suggested as a background to Jesus' declaration at his passing from this world to the Father—Ἐφανέρωσά σου τὸ ὄνομα τοῖς ἀνθρώποις οὓς ἔδωκάς μοι ἐκ τοῦ κόσμου (John 17:6). After his resurrection, Jesus does, in fact refer to those the Father has given him as his "brothers" (John 20: 17; cf. John 1:12).[88] This touches on a theme which, as we saw in our discussion of the Johannine reception of Ps (68)69, is important for the Fourth Evangelist: the status of believers as Jesus' new family of brothers (and sisters).[89] If, as we suggest, Ps 21:23 has been influential here, as in Hebrews, this marks a significant development in the early Christian reception of the psalm. As Daniélou explains with reference to Heb 2:12, but with equal applicability to John 17:6,

> L'interêt de ce passage, c'est d'une part qu'il ne s'arrête pas seulement aux détails anecdotiques, comme les outrages ou les vêtements partagés, mais que c'est la signification théologique de la Passion du Christ qui est exprimée au moyen du Psaume. C'est ensuite que ce n'est pas seulement un passage du Psaume, mais c'est l'ensemble de celui-ci qui est considéré comme exprimant le mystère pascal.[90]

If the Evangelist thought of the psalm in this way—as an "ensemble," rather than simply a source for anecdotal "passion" details— then the interpretation we have suggested for John 19:23-24 gives us an important lead. It indicates that the Evangelist's main purpose in citing Ps 21 is that the reader should see the fulfilment in Jesus of a psalm in which David bears witness to God's vindication of him at the very moment of his most abject humiliation. We have already seen that David's role as witness is an important aspect of his *persona* as psalmist.[91] Testimony is, after all, one of the most frequently en-

---

[87] See p. 40 above.
[88] This could also be an allusion to Gen 45:4. The selling of Joseph into Egypt (Gen 37:26-28) and Joseph's eventual salvation of his brothers was an influential story in the development of the passion tradition. See Brown, *Death of the Messiah*, 1447. In LXX Gen 37:3, Joseph's garment is a χιτών.
[89] See pp. 129-30 above.
[90] Daniélou, *Exégèse Judéo-Chrétienne*, 34.
[91] See p. 85-86 above.

countered literary forms in the Psalter, Ps 21:23-32 being a prime example. We found this aspect of David delineated in Isa 55, a reworking of Davidic ideology which apparently appealed to the Fourth Evangelist and has had a considerable influence on his presentation of Jesus. As Derrett has suggested, David, confirmed as king for ever and appointed to speak as "a witness to the peoples"—Ἰδοὺ, μαρτύριον ἐν ἔθνεσιν ἔδωκα αὐτὸν (Isa 55:4)—provided the Evangelist with a model for the unique combination of the roles of king and witness in his presentation of Jesus.[92] In the Fourth Gospel it is Jesus' role as witness, testifying to the truth, which in fact defines the nature of his kingship—

Σὺ λέγεις ὅτι βασιλεύς εἰμι. ἐγὼ εἰς τοῦτο γεγέννημαι καὶ εἰς τοῦτο ἐλήλυθα εἰς τὸν κόσμον, ἵνα μαρτυρήσω τῇ ἀληθείᾳ (John 18:37).[93]

It is the fact that God has glorified David—ἕνεκεν Κυρίου τοῦ Θεοῦ σου τοῦ ἁγίου Ἰσραὴλ, ὅτι ἐδόξασέ σε (Isa 55:5)—that assures his universal sovereignty. Similarly, throughout the account of "the hour" of Jesus' glorification, his universal kingship is persistently underlined.

In the light of this, it is permissible bring Isa 55, as part of the Evangelist's general repertoire, into intertextual play with Ps 21, the source of the verse quoted and enacted in the pericope of the dividing of Jesus' garments. In the psalm, the line, διηγήσομαι τὸ ὄνομά σου τοῖς ἀδελφοῖς μου (Ps 21:23) functions as a kind of "hinge." Spoken out of utter degradation and despoliation, it points to the victory which assures the continuance of David's reign. It thus

---

[92] Derrett mentions several biblical sources for the idea that the Messiah is a witness which he believes illuminate the notion of truth in the Fourth Gospel—Isa 43:10, Isa 55:4 and the Hebrew of Ps (88)89:37-38 which can be read as the psalmist (traditionally David) stating "that David's descendant (the Messiah?) shall be a reliable witness in the clouds—meaning in the heavenly courts, though he is obviously functioning on earth." See, "Christ, King and Witness," 192-95.

[93] Cf. John 3:11.32; 8:14.17. On the subject of "truth" in the Fourth Gospel, De la Potterie has shown that it is not quite the same as the OT *emet*, "God's faithfulness." Neither is it adequately explained in gnostic (Bultmann) or Platonic (Dodd) terms. Rather, it should be understood within the literary milieu to which John is closest (wisdom/apocalyptic traditions in Judaism), as the revelation Jesus comes to impart. See "The Truth in Saint John," in J. Ashton (ed.) *The Interpretation*, 53-66. Meeks, "The Man from Heaven," 151-54, explains that the sole object of the Johannine Jesus' testimony is himself, and that this witness is virtually reduced to the statement of the "descent-ascent" and of the relationship to God which that pattern implies. As the Gospel unfolds, Jesus' prophetic *martyria* is progressively identified with his knowledge of his own origins and destiny which demonstrates his unique relation to the Father. See P. Moulon Beernaert, "La Verité au sens biblique: approche de saint Jean," *LumVit* 46 (1991) 287-300 and Dennis R. Lindsay, "What Is Truth?' Αλήθεια in the Gospel of John," *ResQ* 35 (1993) 129-45.

marks the turning point not only for him, but for the nation and for all peoples to whom he bears witness. It is surely no accident that the Johannine Jesus' echoes these words as he enters upon his "hour" (John 17:6; cf. 20:17), this time of suffering which is also the moment when the promised everlasting kingship of David is assured. This confirmation of the promise to David will benefit all the scattered children of God (John 11:52; 12:32; cf. Isa 55:5). Lifted up that he might declare God's name (John 8:28; cf. Ps 21:23), the glorified Jesus is himself the testimony that God is true (cf. John 7:28). Against this background, the full force of Pilate's question in John 18:37—Οὐκοῦν βασιλεὺς εἶ σύ;—becomes apparent. He is the unwitting agent of the real drama. The implication of his οὐκοῦν is that an affirmative answer is required. As with his title for the cross (19:19), Pilate unwittingly confirms that Jesus is indeed ὁ βασιλεὺς τοῦ Ἰσραήλ.[94]

To summarize: The Fourth Evangelist's usage of Ps (21)22 is distinctively corrective of the passion tradition as we might infer it from the synoptics. He highlights only v. 19, presenting the *parallelismus membrorum* in a two-action narrative and formally quoting it. In biblical lore, prophetic garment-tearing symbolizes the loss of the kingship (Saul) or the division of the kingdom with concomitant diminishment of the king's sovereignty (Ahijah). Set against this background, the Johannine insistence that Jesus' tunic was not torn is a declaration that, in spite of the utter despoliation that he willingly suffered, Jesus' royal status remained intact and undiminished. "The hour" thus emerges as the definitive moment when the 2 Sam 7 promise to David of everlasting kingship is realized. This royal interpretation of the psalm enactment and citation can also include the notion of unity. The ingathering of the tribes, however, is now seen within the Johannine view of Jesus as having taken over the Jerusalem Temple's position at the centre of the world.

There are several echoes of Ps (21)22 elsewhere in the Gospel, the presence of which suggests that the Evangelist is conscious of the psalm as a whole and sees its progression from suffering to witness as

---

[94] When used as an interrogative, the adverb οὐκοῦν has inferential force. See Bauer, *Greek-English Lexicon*, 592. Zerwick, *Analysis Philologica*, 247, sees its usage in John 18:37 (a NT *hapax*) as comparable to the Latin "nonne," used when an affirmative answer is expected. Brown, *John XIII-XXI*, 853, draws attention to its function of "returning the subject to the main theme after a parenthesis." Pilate is, therefore, asking Jesus, with the expectation of an affirmative reply being the truth, if he is the King of the Jews (John 18:33). He uses the terminology of the non-Jew (also in 19:19) as distinct from the sacral and honorific title, "King of Israel" used by Jews in 1:49 and 12:13.

prophetic of Jesus. He seems to hear David's testimony in the psalm to God's fidelity at his hour of greatest need against the accompanying counterpoint of Isa 55:1-5, where a "corporate" David testifies to the world that God has glorified him. Viewed in this way, Ps (21)22 becomes the testimony to the truth of a Jesus whose garments were shared out, but whose tunic was not torn, a king who suffered pain and humiliation and yet whose everlasting sovereignty, guaranteed by God, was to bring life to the whole world.

E. *Ps (68:22)69:21 in John 19:28*

Our next citation is similar in function to the previous one. Both together form a "frame" for the central episode in the crucifixion sequence where Jesus speaks to his mother and the beloved disciple. Both exemplify David's role as prophet through the fulfilment of his psalms in the events of Jesus' passion. In fact, this is "the last explicit example of Jesus' active fulfilment of the Scriptures in John's Gospel."[95] As such, it forms an inclusion with the first example, Ὁ ζῆλος τοῦ οἴκου σου καταφάγεταί με (John 2:17), also from Ps (68)69.

The single word, Διψῶ ("I thirst.") is spoken by the crucified Jesus. In view of the vinegar given in response, most see here an allusion to Ps 68:22—

καὶ ἔδωκαν εἰς τὸ βρῶμά μου χολὴν
καὶ εἰς τὴν δίψαν μου ἐπότισάν με ὄξος.[96]

The synoptic parallels confirm the existence of a tradition associating this psalm verse with the bitter drink offered to Jesus shortly before he died. Mark's account contains a strong verbal reminiscence of LXX Ps 68:22b—δραμὼν δέ τις [καὶ] γεμίσας σπόγγον ὄξους περιθεὶς καλάμῳ ἐπότιζεν αὐτόν (Mark 15:36). In Luke, the soldiers' offer of vinegar forms part of the mockery sequence (Luke 23:36). In Matthew, there may even be a recollection of both parallel lines of the psalm verse: the gall (χολή) mixed with the wine offered to Jesus on his arrival at the place of crucifixion recalling the first (Matt 27:34), and the sponge soaked in vinegar (ὄξος) offered by a bystander corresponding to the second (Matt 27:48).[97] There is a char-

---

[95] Moo, *The OT in the Gospel Passion Narratives*, 278.
[96] Among those who accept Ps 68:22 as ἡ γραφή of John 19:28 are Reim, *Studien*, 94; Barrett, *The Gospel*, 459; Lindars, *NT Apologetic*, 100; Schnackenburg, *The Gospel 3*, 283 ; Freed, *OT Quotations*, 105; Hanson, *The Prophetic Gospel*, 212-13; Moo, *The OT in the Gospel Passion Narratives*, 277.
[97] If so, this would be another example of an NT author reading the *parallelismus membrorum* as two separate actions. Cf. John 19:23-24; Matt 21:5-7.

acteristic twist to the handling of this motif from the passion tradition in the Fourth Gospel. The giving of the vinegar to drink is neither a reaction to a cry of dereliction (as in Mark and Matthew), nor an initiative taken by the mocking soldiers (as in Luke). Jesus himself intentionally sets the fulfilment of the Scripture in motion with his unparalleled statement, "I thirst." It is not until he gives the biblical cue that the "script" of Ps 68:22 can be acted out. In contrast to the synoptics, the Fourth Gospel makes it clear that Jesus drinks the vinegar. Only after doing this does he finally and freely lay down his life.

The incident is introduced by a solemn indication of its final and culminant nature—Μετὰ τοῦτο εἰδὼς ὁ Ἰησοῦς ὅτι ἤδη πάντα τετέλεσται ἵνα τελειωθῇ ἡ γραφή λέγει...It is not clear from the text whether the conjunction ἵνα is connected to λέγει or to τετέλεσται.[98] Consequently, the fulfilment of Scripture could refer either to what has gone before, or to what is to follow, depending on the reading one accepts. Perhaps there is deliberate ambiguity here and, as Brown suggests, "the two possibilities should not be sharply separated."[99] As G. Bampfylde has shown, however, there is a strong theological and philological case for connecting the ἵνα clause with Jesus' knowledge: Jesus knows that everything has now been completed in order to bring the Scripture to fruition.[100] Read in this way, the text would repeat a pattern which Roland Bergmeier has detected elsewhere in the Gospel: a reference to Jesus' knowledge, followed by a ὅτι clause and then a ἵνα clause—

6:15	13:1	19:28
Ἰησοῦς οὖν γνοὺς	εἰδὼς ὁ Ἰησοῦς	Μετὰ τοῦτο εἰδὼς ὁ Ἰησοῦς
ὅτι μέλλουσιν ἔρχεσθαι καὶ ἁρπάζειν αὐτὸν	ὅτι ἦλθεν αὐτοῦ ἡ ὥρα	ὅτι ἤδη πάντα τετέλεσται,
ἵνα ποιήσωσιν βασιλέα...	ἵνα μεταβῇ ἐκ τοῦ κόσμου τούτου πρὸς τὸν πατέρα...	ἵνα τελειωθῇ ἡ γραφή...

---

[98] With the ἵνα connected to λέγει: "Jesus, knowing that all was now finished, said, to fulfil the scripture, 'I thirst.'" With the ἵνα connected to τετέλεσται: "Jesus, knowing that all was now finished to fulfil the scripture, said, 'I thirst.'" For the purposes of this discussion, we ignore the parenthetical commas around the ἵνα clause, as found in the Greek NT of both Nestle-Aland and the United Bible Societies.

[99] Brown, *John XIII-XXI*, 908; *Death of the Messiah*, 1071-72.

[100] G. Bampfylde, "John XIX 28: A Case for a Different Translation," *NovT* 11 (1969), 247-260. Bampfylde's case is built on several considerations among which are the lack of a formal quotation, the problem of a suggestion, inherent in the usual translation, that Jesus deliberately sets out to fulfil prophecies (cf. 12:16), and

In Bergmeier's view, τετέλεσται refers to the realization of the Scriptures as foreseen by a Jesus who knew all that was to befall him (cf. John 18:4).[101]

According to the more widely accepted reading, the clause ἵνα τελειωθῇ ἡ γραφή is part of the formula of quotation introducing Διψῶ.[102] Whatever reading one prefers, it remains true that the appearance of ἵνα τελειωθῇ...where one might have expected the more usual formula, ἵνα πληρωθῇ ἡ γραφή, intensifies the sense of consummation.[103] The verb τελειόω points forward to the use of its cognate, τελέω, for Jesus' last word, Τετέλεσται (John 19:30) and back to the opening of the Book of Glory—εἰς τέλος ἠγάπησεν αὐτούς. It reaches even further back via Jesus' declaration in 17:4—τὸ ἔργον τελειώσας ὃ δέδωκάς μοι ἵνα ποιήσω·—to 4:34 and 5:36 where Jesus has already used the verb τελειόω to convey his intent with regard to the work the Father has given him to do.[104] Similarly, by way of inclusion, the reference to Jesus' knowledge in 19:28 recalls εἰδὼς ὁ Ἰησοῦς ὅτι ἦλθεν αὐτοῦ ἡ ὥρα...(13:1).

If ἵνα τελειωθῇ ἡ γραφή goes with λέγει as an introductory formula, it is surprising that ἡ γραφή, which is to find complete and final fulfilment at this climactic moment, is quoted with far less precision than other texts cited in the Fourth Gospel. Still, it could certainly be claimed that the real evocation of the psalm is not so much the word Διψῶ as the narrative account of a threefold action: Jesus' declaration, the giving of a drink and Jesus' drinking. This would then correspond to the three elements of the Psalm text: εἰς τὴν δίψαν μου / ὄξος / ἐπότισάν με.[105] Since the fulfilment is in the unfolding of the event, it is logical that the psalm's εἰς τὴν δίψαν μου should be reformulated by the author as direct speech of Jesus, thus Διψῶ. Nonetheless, the questions have persisted: whether the precise verbal form used in John 19:28 might be better explained by the influence of some other scriptural passage; whether it refers not to any particular passage, but rather to the "total witness" of Scripture,[106] whether "although John

---

the absence of any precedent in John for translating τελειόω in the same way as πληρόω. Bampfylde's thesis is accepted by de la Potterie, *The Hour of Jesus*, 109.

[101] Roland Bergmeier, "ΤΕΤΕΛΕΣΤΑΙ Joh 19:30," *ZNW* 79 (1988) 282-90.

[102] Schnackenburg, *The Gospel 3*, 283.

[103] See E. Haenchen, *John 2: A Commentary on the Gospel of John, Chapters 7-21* (Philadelphia: Fortress, 1984) 193. The phrase ἵνα πληρωθῇ ἡ γραφή is used in 12:38; 13:18; 15:25; 17:12; 19:24, 36.

[104] Bultmann, *The Gospel*, 673, n. 6.

[105] We recall the possible influence on John's composition of a similar division of a scripture quotation into its constitutive elements—Ἄρτον ἔδωκεν αὐτοῖς / ἐκ τοῦ οὐρανοῦ / φαγεῖν. See p. 135 above.

[106] Brown, *John XIII-XXI*, 929.

19:28-29 induces readers to recall Psalm 69, it also teases them with the paradox of an absent complement—the Scripture is missing,"[107] whether the Evangelist even intended to cite Scripture at all.[108]

We have seen that Jesus' thirst could be a thematic echo of Ps 21:16, particularly in view of this psalm's prevalence in the passion tradition.[109] As another possible source, Dodd proposes Psalm (41)42:2 —ἐδίψησεν ἡ ψυχή μου πρὸς τὸν θεὸν τὸν ζῶντα. He notes that Pss (21)22 and (41)42 both share "the same sense of the absence of God," and wonders if the thirst of the crucified is perhaps the Johannine equivalent of the cry of dereliction in Mark and Matthew.[110] An allusion to Ps (41)42 would, therefore, represent a Johannine adaptation of a motif from Ps (21)22 inherited by the Fourth Evangelist from the passion tradition and transformed in line with his perspective. Dodd's intuition of another source which opens up a further level of meaning is most valuable. At this more figurative level, Διψῶ could be envisioned as an expression of Jesus' longing to return to his Father. The continuation of the psalm—πότε ἥξω καὶ ὀφθήσομαι τῷ προσώπῳ τοῦ θεοῦ;—undoubtedly lends itself to such a reading. There is another passage where the psalmist thirsts for God, Ps (62)63:1. In the Johannine context, Διψῶ could also be an allusion to ἐδίψησέν σοι ἡ ψυχή μου, understood like Ps 41:2, as an expression of Jesus' desire to come to the Father.[111] Either psalm source would fulfil this function. The fact that Pss 41-42 played an important part in the development of the passion tradition may perhaps "tip the balance" in its favour.[112]

---

[107] Robert L. Brawley, "An Absent Complement and Intertextuality in John 19:28-29," *JBL* 112 (1993) 427-43, at 443.

[108] Schuchard, *Scripture within Scripture*, does not count John 19:28 among the explicit Old Testament Citations in the Gospel of John.

[109] Brown, *John XIII-XXI*, 929, suggests this, but ultimately favours Ps 68:22.

[110] Dodd, *Historical Tradition*, 41-42. Dodd sees the role of Ps 41:2 in John 19:28 in terms of "the thirst of the righteous sufferer" (Dodd uses here the category "Psalms of the Righteous Sufferer" from the psalm study of his day which dismissed Davidic "authorship" of the psalms as unreliable on historical and text-critical grounds.). Johannes Beutler sees John 19:28 as one of several allusions to Ps 41-42 in the Fourth Gospel. He hears Jesus' Διψῶ "als Gebet des scheidenden Offenbarers in der Sehnsucht nach Gottes heiligen Bezirk und Gottes Antlitz." See "Psalm 42/43 im Johannesevangelium," *NTS* 25 (1978) 33 - 57, at 57.

[111] T. Boman, "Das Letzte Wort Jesu," *ST* 17 (1963), 103-119, argued that Ps (62)63:1, "You are my God ... for you I thirst" was John's biblical explanation for the Aramaic cry of Jesus in the tradition, *Eli atta* (Ps 118:28), misunderstood by the crowd as *Elija ta*. Schnackenburg, *The Gospel*, 3, 460, n. 67, finds Boman's theory attractive but unlikely, especially since it ignores the drinking of vinegar. Other authors accepting the possibility of allusion to Ps 41:2 or Ps 62:1, expressing Jesus' longing to return to his Father, are Hoskyns, *The Fourth Gospel*, 531; Beutler, "Psalm 42/43 im Johannesevangelium," 56; L. Th. Witkamp, "Jezus' laatste woorden volgens Johannes 19:28-30," *NedTT* 43 (1989) 11-20.

[112] For Johannine indebtedness to Ps 41-42, see p. 253-58 below.

On the other hand, as we shall see, the Davidic "historical" superscript to Ps (62)63 may argue for its presence "behind" John 19:28.

It is not necessary to see the Ps 41:2/Ps 62:1 allusion as replacing a tradition about the physical thirst suffered by Jesus, which John regards as theologically "niet acceptabel."[113] It may rather be a case of an allusion superimposed on the Ps 68 quotation/enactment in John 19:28-29 bringing it to a figurative level of understanding more in keeping with John's theological schema.[114] As we have already seen, transformative citation is a distinguishing feature of the Johannine reception of the psalms. A reference of some sort to Ps 68 is indisputable in view of the narrative development of it in v. 29. However, there is no reason why Ps 41:2 and 62:1 might not be considered as a complementary pre-text to John 19:28, drawn from the same source, the psalms of David. While Ps 68 is enacted, Ps 41/62 functions at a more figurative level at which thirst is a symbol of longing for God. The further intertextual link thus admits new dimensions of meaning. In support of such a claim, we might also note that the form of the verb in Ps 41:2 and 62:1—ἐδίψησεν—is closer to the Fourth Gospel's Διψῶ than εἰς τὴν δίψαν μου of Ps 68:22.

There is a further aspect of the thirst motif which lends support to the figurative reading of Διψῶ proposed here. In John 18:11 Jesus responds to his disciples' futile attempt to prevent his arrest with the words: τὸ ποτήριον ὃ δέδωκέν μοι ὁ πατὴρ οὐ μὴ πίω αὐτό; Here again, there is a particular Johannine bias in the treatment of a motif from the passion tradition. In the synoptics Jesus refers to his passion as a ποτήριον, a cup of suffering which the Father wills that he should drink.[115] The formative influence there is the OT theme of the cup of the terrible judgements of God which evil doers have to drink.[116] The synoptic stress in the use of this image is on the suffering for sin endured by the innocent one (Luke 23:47) who gives his life "as a ransom for many." In contrast, the Johannine handling of the ποτήριον image is similar to the way the image of food functions in the Fourth Gospel. In John 4:34, for example, Jesus speaks of his delight in doing the Father's will—Ἐμὸν βρῶμά ἐστιν ἵνα ποιήσω τὸ θέλημα τοῦ πέμψαντός με καὶ τελειώσω αὐτοῦ τὸ ἔργον. Here the for-

---

[113] For this view, see L. Th. Witkamp, "Jezus' laatste woorden," 17
[114] For another example of a figurative reading of Ps (68)69, see 1QH XII, 11—
They have denied the drink of knowledge to the thirsty,
in their thirst they have given them vinegar to drink.
García Martínez, *The Dead Sea Scrolls*, 334.
[115] Mark 10:38-39, 14:36; Matt 20:22-23, 26:39; Luke 22:42.
[116] See Isa 51:17.22, Jer 32:1-17 (LXX 25:15-31), Lam 4:21, Ps 10:6; 75:8-9. Texts such as these have provided the background for Rev 14:10, 15:7, 16:19, etc.

mative influence is the theme of God's word as food as developed particularly in the wisdom literature and the psalms.[117] The verb τελειόω in John 4:34, by pointing towards the hour when Jesus will complete the Father's work (19:28), brings out the complementarity of the two images, food and drink. It is the food of doing the Father's will that sustains Jesus. It is the food of completing that work that will finally and fully satisfy his hunger. It is the draining to the last of the cup given him that will finally and fully satisfy his thirst for union with the Father.[118]

Allowing Jesus' word, Διψῶ, to evoke Ps 41:2/62:1 opens up a whole new level of meaning. Those who offer him vinegar misunderstand this word, taking it as no more than the plaint of a dying man tortured by thirst, and yet their response unwittingly fulfils a scriptural prophecy, Ps 68:22.[119] Yet this is only an "elementary" level of Scripture fulfilment, comparable to the plot-time "plain" remembering of the Scripture in John 2:17. There is a more "advanced" level of "esoteric remembering," reached only by those who view the scene from the post-resurrection perspective. Jesus' real thirst is his longing to drink the cup the Father has given him (John 18:11), and thus to come to the Father (John 13:1). John 19:28 is not the first time in the Gospel that a request for a drink on the part of Jesus has been the occasion of misunderstanding.[120] On the earlier occasion too, "it was about the sixth hour" (cf. 4:6 and 19:14).[121] Jesus asks for a drink, but he is the giver of living water. If they had known the gift of God, they would have asked him for a drink, because this is "the hour" in which he is to be glorified and the Spirit is to be given.[122] Jesus thirsts for that Spirit to become in himself a

---

[117] The starting point for this development is the gift of the manna, interpreted as showing that the real food by which humankind lives is everything that comes from the mouth of God (Deut 8:3). In Sirach 24:19-21 we find the food offered by Wisdom tasting sweeter than honey. Cf. Pss (18:11)19:10 and (118)119:103. In Wis 16:24-26 this evolves into the idea that the manna appealed to each individual's taste.

[118] Schnackenburg, *The Gospel 3*, 283.

[119] The irony here is characteristically Johannine. Cf. John 11:49-52 where an enemy fulfils the real purpose of the text at a deeper level.

[120] Cf. John 4:7-15. Note too in 4:31-34 a similar misunderstanding with regard to food.

[121] Brown's dismissal of this linkage as "interpreters' accommodation" is motivated by his concern to stress the paschal lamb symbolism at this point. See *Death of the Messiah*, 847. We do not regard the two interpretations as exclusive of each other. The Evangelist's intention of evoking Passover/Exodus themes is evident in his reference to the hyssop in 19:29 and, as we are about to see, in the underlying imagery of the desert rock.

[122] See the proleptic references to the giving of the Spirit in John 19:30. 34. In this context, the Johannine expression for Jesus' expiry, παρέδωκεν τὸ πνεῦμα (John

river of living water (John 7:37b-38). Now lifted up, he is inundated with that torrent which then flows in a stream from his pierced side into all the world.

This reading of the text finds support from Bampfylde who arrives at basically the same conclusion by a different route. She believes that the Scripture brought to fruition at this important moment is that mentioned in 7:37b-38—Zech 14:8, understood in conjunction with the Ezek 47 vision of water flowing from the Temple.

> The Scripture here is Zech. XIV 8, but in place of the Temple built with hands from which flows terrestrial water, Jesus speaks of the Temple of his body in which the Holy Spirit dwells and flows out as the life-giving water from a spring or well. This Scripture, quoted by Jesus at Tabernacles, is the one spoken of in XIX 28. To bring it to fruition was the purpose of His Passion.[123]

Although we regard Ps 77:16.20 as the source of the Scripture in John 7:37b-38, we do agree that both Zech 14:8 and Ezek 47 are highly influential. So again we find the Fourth Evangelist "wringing every ounce of irony out of the situation."[124] Jesus asks for a drink, but his body is the water-giving desert rock, which has become assimilated to the Temple rock. Now that Jesus is glorified, ποταμοὶ ἐκ τῆς κοιλίας αὐτοῦ ῥεύσουσιν ὕδατος ζῶντος.

As we have found with the other quotations, reference to the Psalter often opens up the Gospel text to the influence of the David narratives in ways that are fruitful for our appreciation of the Johannine project. We come now, therefore, to enquire whether in the case of the "Scripture" in John 19:28 the commonly accepted Davidic authorship of the Psalter might have anything to contribute to our understanding.[125]

There do not appear to be any extant early Jewish exegetical traditions associating Ps (68)69 or Pss (41-42)42-43 with particular events in David's life. Ps (62)63, however, is linked by its MT and

---

19:30), with its openness to interpretation at a deeper level as a giving of the Spirit, is in marked and significant contrast to its synoptic equivalents. Cf. ἐξέπνευσεν (Mark 15:37; Luke 23:46) and ἀφῆκεν τὸ πνεῦμα (Matt 27:50).

[123] Bampfylde, "John XIX 28," 253. Hoskyns, *The Fourth Gospel*, 532, also believes that the Scripture fulfilled in 19:28 is that mentioned in 7:37-39.

[124] Lindars' expression; see *The Gospel*, 441.

[125] Pss 68 and 62 are τῷ Δαυιδ. The appearance in the LXX of Ps 42 (Koraite in the MT), as Ψαλμὸς τῷ Δαυιδ, would suggest that the placement of Pss 41-42 within the Davidic Book 1 of the Psalter was the over-riding consideration. Therefore, reception of the Psalter as "Davidic" included the belief that David was given a vinegary drink at a time of distressful thirst (at least in a figurative sense) and that twice in his psalms he described his longing for God as thirst.

LXX superscript with David's period of hiding in the wilderness of Judah. On the basis of the psalm's content, we would take this to be a reference to the time of Absalom's rebellion, a phase of David's career which, as we have seen, is particularly influential in the Johannine passion narrative.[126] In this incident, which later exegesis connects, by means of a "historical" superscript, with Ps (62)63, David and the people with him suffer thirst (2 Sam 17:29). The portrayal of this thirst in terms that unmistakably evoke Israel's Exodus journey serves to heighten the import of the events that are unfolding and to identify David as the rightful King of Israel. Viewed through the "lens" of the psalm, David's thirst in the wilderness becomes a thirst for the privilege of beholding the ark in God's habitation (cf. 2 Sam 15:25), a thirst to see God's glory in God's dwelling (cf. Ps [62]63:1-2).

In a second incident where David thirsts, he is portrayed as longing to drink the water from the spring in his native Bethlehem.[127] As the context makes clear, what David actually longs for is to have returned in triumph after a successful campaign, to the place of his birth. The image used is a familiar biblical motif: the satisfaction of thirst as a symbol of victory.[128] As we have seen, the idealization of David in Second Temple Judaism was such that all his struggles to gain, maintain and increase the prestige of the throne were seen as motivated by his desire to build the Temple (See Ps [131]132). Johannine readers hearing resonances of Ps 62:1 in Jesus' cry, would have recognized the lineaments of this David in the Gospel's portrayal of Jesus. His David-like thirst would have reminded them that

---

[126] Stuhlmueller, *Psalms 1*, 287, believes the historical superscript to Ps(62)63 refers to the period of Saul's persecution of David (1 Sam 23:14; 24:2). It is more likely, however, to refer to David's sojourn in the wilderness during Absalom's rebellion (2 Sam 15:23) as this story specifically mentions David's experience of thirst (2 Sam 17:29). As well as the desert location (cf. Ps [62]63:2d) which presumably was the main impetus for the assignment of the superscript, this narrative has another important point of contact with Ps (62)63: reference to the ark (Ps [62]63:2; cf. 2 Sam 15:24-29). The midrash on Ps (62)63 connects it with Ps 3—"A psalm of David when he fled from Absalom his son." See *Midr. Teh.* 63:1 (Braude, I, 524).

[127] 2 Sam 23:13-17. This is one of the "flattering" stories about David that the Chronicler chooses to record (1 Chr 11:15-19).

[128] See Judg 15:18-19; 2 Kgs 3:16-17; The motif of miraculous satisfaction of thirst by God is found frequently in Isaiah, e.g., 25:4 (LXX); 41:17-18; 43:20; 49:10, and is ultimately to be traced back to the desert rock of Exod 17. This symbolic understanding of the quenching of thirst helps explain the reference to drinking in v. 7 of the poem for a royal enthronement, Ps (109)110. 1 Kgs 1:33 indicates that the ritual slaking of the king's thirst at the Gihon spring was part of an early enthronement rite. See S. Mowinckel, *He that Cometh*, trans. G. W. Anderson, (Oxford: Basil Blackwell, 1959) 63-64, and Kraus, *Worship in Israel*, trans. G. Buswell (Richmond: John Knox Press, 1966) 222-23.

he was the rightful King of Israel, now apparently dispossessed, but assured of the triumph that would bring him into the presence of the God for whom he thirsted. In such an understanding, the bitter vinegary potion which Jesus drinks is, in reality, his "victory drink" in celebration of the royal enthronement by which he returns to his own realm. Like David's thirst in the wilderness, Jesus' thirst has Exodus overtones, reinforced by the mention of the "hyssop."[129] Just as the people thirsted in the desert before entering the land (Exod 17:3), Jesus thirsts before entering the house of the Father.[130]

If we allow both the "water-flowing rock" background and the David resonances full play, we can hear Jesus' cry, as the *cantus firmus* in a many-voiced polytextual rendering of psalmody. Jesus' thirst is traced back to the "vinegar "motif from Ps 68, but is also allowed to "visit" Pss 42/62 and other allusions to David's thirst with which it intersects to form a rich intertextual complex. The evocation of the Temple reminds us that this is the moment when Jesus' zeal for God's house will, in fact, consume him—the inclusion with the first psalm citation, also from Ps 68. If Jesus' body, from which the living waters flow, is the "new" Desert Rock, it is also the Temple Rock, the site of David's Temple-founding sacrifice. Even Jesus' last word, Τετέλεσται, has sacrificial overtones.[131] As Jesus receives and even welcomes (ἔλαβεν in John 19:30) the cup which the Father has given him (18:11), the liturgy of his death replaces the water libation of Tabernacles, definitively re-actualizing the Exodus rock miracle and signifying the arrival of "that day" when living waters will flow from the Temple to bring life to the whole earth. Jesus' death is not only

---

[129] "Noting the impossibility of hyssop supporting a sponge, Brawley," An Absent Complement," 433, comments—"This conflict with normal reality creates an inconsistency that drives interpretation to a metaphorical level. ... Though "hyssop" is but a single term, it is so unusual and conspicuous as to recall the Passover ritual in Exod 12:2 and the divine deliverance of the people of Israel from oppressors." F. G. and P. A. Beetham point out that while hyssop would have reminded readers of Passover, it would also have recalled other sacrificial rites in which it was used, such as cleansing from leprosy (cf. Lev 14:4-5) and the sacrifice of the red heifer (cf. Num 19:6). They note that *Barn.* 8 connects a Jewish purification rite similar to the red heifer rite with the crucifixion and that the author of Hebrews inserts "hyssop" into his re-telling of Exod 24:8. See "A Note on John 19:29," *JTS* 44 (1993) 163-69. To this we might add, in view of the currency of Ps (50)51 in early Christianity, that it mentions hyssop in v. 9 (quoted in 1 Clem 18) and that this verse is the particular object of early Christian *relecture*, as shown by an early Egyptian text of Ps 50:9 with a Christian gloss—ραντιεις με υσσωπω <u>απω του αιματος του ξυλου</u>. See Rahlfs, *Psalmi Cum Odis*, Gottinger LXX 10, (Göttingen: Vandenhoeck & Ruprecht, 1979) 31.

[130] Freed links Exod 17:2 ("Give us water to drink...") with John 4:15 ("Give me this water..."). See "Psalm 42/43 in John's Gospel," *NTS* 29 (1982) 62-73, at 71.

[131] See note 40, p. 127 above.

sacrifice, but theophany. As his thirst to return to the Father is satisfied, he is glorified with the glory he had before the world was made (John 17:5.24). Now, those who look to him to satisfy their thirst can see in him the glory of God revealed.[132] An understanding of the thirst of the Johannine Jesus such as this might well have inspired the words of Ignatius of Antioch, martyred during the reign of Trajan (98-117 CE), who longed to imitate the passion of Jesus by his own death: "...there is in me...only water living and speaking in me and saying to me from within, 'Come to the Father.'"[133]

In summary, the primary reference of Διψῶ in John 19:28 is to Ps (68:22)69:21, as attested by the synoptic parallels. The narrative evocation of Ps 68:22 in John 19:28-30 is the "said." The recovery of the "unsaid" is left to the reader—echoes of David's experience of thirst and of that thirst re-interpreted as thirst for God by means of the attribution of Ps 41:2/62:1 to him; links with other passages in the Gospel where the images of food and drink portray Jesus' delight in union with the Father, as expressed in his readiness to do the will of the one who sent him. These intertextual and intratextual resonances overlay the reference to Ps 68 from the tradition, making of Jesus' declaration, Διψῶ, an expression of his longing to return to the Father. His reception of the vinegar then appears as a manifestation of his willingness to drink the cup that the Father has given him. The word Διψῶ, therefore, marks the bringing to fulfilment of the Scripture quoted in John 7:38. Jesus thirsts to be inundated with the waters of the Spirit which will then flow out from the Temple of his

---

[132] It is possible that Jesus' prayer that his disciples might see his glory (John 17:24 —ἵνα θεωρῶσιν τὴν δόξαν τὴν ἐμήν) echoes Ps 62:3—

οὕτως ἐν τῷ ἁγίῳ ὤφθην σοι
τοῦ ἰδεῖν τὴν δύναμίν σου καὶ τὴν δόξαν σου.

If this is the case, it would indicate a reading of Ps 62 as an address to Jesus which fits exceptionally well with Johannine theology. Believers would thus worship the Risen Jesus as God, their God (cf. John 20:28) for whom they thirst (cf. John 7:37), whose glory they long to behold (cf. John 17:24).

[133] ...ὕδωρ δὲ ζῶν καὶ λαλοῦν ἐν ἐμοί ἔσωθέν μοι λέγον Δεῦρο πρὸς τὸν πατέρα. See *IgRom* VII, 2, trans. Kirsopp Lake, LCL, *The Apostolic Fathers* (London: Heineman & New York: MacMillan, 1912) I, 234-35. It is generally held that Ignatius did not make use of the Fourth Gospel. See, for example, Walter Schmithals' introduction to the ET of Bultmann, *The Gospel*, 12. However, the fact that Ignatius nowhere explicitly quotes the Fourth Gospel while he does quote Paul does not necessarily mean that he did not know his writings, as E. Haenchen points out. See *John 1: A Commentary on the Gospel of John Chapters 1-6* (Philadelphia: Fortress, 1984) 7-8. There are certainly contacts between Ignatius and Johannine thought, of which *IgRom* VII, 2 is surely evidence. See also the reference to ὁ ἄρχων τοῦ αἰῶνος τούτου in *IgRom* VII, 1 (cf. ὁ ἄρχων τοῦ κόσμου τούτου in John 12:31 and 16:11) and *IgRom* VII, 3— ἄρτον θεοῦ θέλω, ὅ ἐστιν σάρξ Ἰησοῦ Χριστοῦ, τοῦ ἐκ σπέρματος Δαυείδ (cf. John 6: 52-57 and ἐκ τοῦ σπέρματος Δαυίδ in John 7:42).

body to bring salvation to the world. The lightness of the Fourth Gospel allusion to Ps 68:22 does not tie the text exclusively to this one psalm, but allows other echoes to resound. It is through its evocation of other thirsts that the Johannine account of the final action of Jesus can so deftly encapsulate in just one word so much of the meaning of "the Hour."

F. *Ps (33:21)34:20 in John 19:36*

We come now to the last psalm citation in the Gospel. Having told of Jesus' death, the author records a final violence contemplated against him by "the Jews"—the breaking of his legs.[134] He tells of how this intended violation of Jesus' corpse was thwarted by the soldiers, who decided instead to verify his death by piercing his side,[135] and of how a flow of blood and water came out of Jesus' body. He then pauses in his narrative to address the readers, defending the validity of his eyewitness testimony (v. 35). His apologia functions as an extended formula of quotation introducing two Scripture passages which, in his view, have just been fulfilled—

> ... ἐγένετο γὰρ ταῦτα ἵνα ἡ γραφὴ πληρωθῇ, Ὀστοῦν οὐ συντριβήσεται αὐτοῦ καὶ πάλιν ἑτέρα γραφὴ λέγει, Ὄψονται εἰς ὃν ἐξεκέντησαν.

> For these things took place that the scripture might be fulfilled, "Not a bone of him shall be broken." And again another scripture says, "They shall look on him whom they have pierced."

The author's defence in v. 35 is connected to the quotation formula proper, ἵνα ἡ γραφὴ πληρωθῇ, by the conjunction γάρ. It refers, therefore, not only to his record of the events, but to his claim that these events fulfil the Scriptures. V. 35, even if originally a redactional anti-docetic interpolation,[136] functions now, as it stands in the text, as an elaborated "intonation," a prelude to the final instance of explicit Scripture citation in the Gospel. Coming at this climactic moment, it also looks back over the whole Gospel, highlighting the role played by ἡ γραφή in the author's persuasion of the readers to share his understanding of Jesus—ἵνα καὶ ὑμεῖς πιστεύ[σ]ητε (John 19:35).

---

[134] Whether this was a mercy or a punishment is debated. According to Jacquet, *Les Psaumes*, I, 722, Jesus is spared "le supplice du crurifragium." Brown, *Death of the Messiah*, 1176, thinks it possible that in requesting the leg-breaking, the Jews "ask that one final act of suffering be imposed." In *Gos. Pet.* 4:14, however, one of the criminals crucified with Jesus defends Jesus' innocence, thereby angering the Jews who order that he be left with unbroken legs so that he might die in torment. This suggests that the leg-breaking was a termination of the crucifixion punishment.

[135] Brown, *John I-XII*, 935.

[136] So Lindars, *The Gospel*, 589.

Obviously, just as the two components of the narrative (the not-breaking and the piercing) are interdependent, the two Scriptures are connected in the author's mind and not merely because they correspond to two consecutive narrative elements in his text.[137] Our interest is in the first one—Ὀστοῦν οὐ συντριβήσεται αὐτοῦ, but we will find that, in order to appreciate it, we must take account of its "companion," a quotation from Zech 12:10.

Unparalleled elsewhere in the NT, the "Scripture," Ὀστοῦν οὐ συντριβήσεται αὐτοῦ, has proved notoriously difficult to identify precisely. Two possible sources are generally suggested. It may refer to the prescriptions prohibiting the breaking of the bones of the paschal lamb in either Exod 12:10.46 or Num 9:12, both of which contain a similar phrase—

> καὶ ὀστοῦν οὐ συντρίψετε ἀπ' αὐτοῦ
> ...and you shall not break a bone of it (Exod 12:10.46).
>
> καὶ ὀστοῦν οὐ συντρίψουσιν ἀπ' αὐτοῦ...
> ...and they shall not break a bone of it Num 9:12).[138]

Alternatively, Ps (33:21)34:20—

> κύριος φυλάσσει πάντα τὰ ὀστᾶ αὐτῶν,
> ἓν ἐξ αὐτῶν οὐ συντριβήσεται.
>
> The Lord will guard all their bones;
> not one of them will be broken.

—may be its source.[139] The verbal similarity between the Fourth Gospel citation and the paschal Lamb texts makes them an attractive possibility. In order to render them applicable to Jesus, the Evangelist would have had to construe the neuter αὐτοῦ in the biblical source as masculine, so that instead of "not a bone of it" the reader understands "not a bone of him." This is a relatively minor adaptation of the Scripture, by no means in excess of John's usual procedure. The fact that the prepositional phrase ἀπ' αὐτοῦ lends itself to being understood in a personal possessive sense has simply fa-

---

[137] For Schnackenburg, *The Gospel 3*, 287, there is an irony here. "The Jews press for the completion of the execution, Jesus is to disappear from the cross and no longer to be proclaimed as 'King of the Jews' (cf. 19:20f). But God directs it differently: they are to look on him whom they have pierced (v. 37)."

[138] Reim, *Studien*, 52, regards Num 9:12 as the source. For Freed, *OT Quotations*, 113, and Brown, *John XIII-XXI*, 937, it is Exod 12:10. Cf. also Moo, *The OT in the Gospel Passion Narratives*, 315.

[139] Cf. Dodd, *The Interpretation*, 233-34; Jacquet, *Les Psaumes I*, 722; Jaak Seynaeve, "Les citations scriptuaires en Jn., 19, 36-37: une preuve en faveur de la typologie de l'agneau pascal?" *RevAT* 1 (1977) 67-76.

cilitated his *relecture*. Receiving Ὀστοῦν οὐ συντριβήσεται αὐτοῦ as a citation of Ps 33:21 also requires allowing for adaptation of the LXX by the Evangelist: a change of the plural personal pronoun to the singular.[140] This change is quite minimal, since the psalm's adjectival pronoun (αὐτῶν) corresponds more precisely to John's αὐτοῦ. Ps 33:21 also has exactly the same verbal form as that in John 19:36—συντριβήσεται. Instead of ἓν ἐξ αὐτῶν (referring to πάντα τὰ ὀστᾶ) he writes Ὀστοῦν, a logical and obvious way of combining two lines of the psalm into one.[141] So, from the verbal angle, the citation in John 19:36 is, perhaps, marginally closer, to Ps 33:21 than to the paschal lamb texts.

Viewing the problem from the thematic standpoint, we find that accepting Exod 12:10, Exod 12:46 or Num 9:12 as source, involves seeing Jesus as the paschal lamb, an early Christian typology used well before the date of composition of the Fourth Gospel (See 1 Cor 5:7). The case for this interpretation is usually argued on the basis of the Baptist's designation of Jesus as ὁ ἀμνὸς τοῦ θεοῦ (1:29.36)[142] and the frequent occurrence of "Passover" imagery in the passion narrative.[143] There are, however, other ways of looking at some of the evidence brought forward to establish this claim.[144] Besides, the word ἀμνός is not used for the paschal victim in the OT.[145]

The title ὁ ἀμνὸς τοῦ θεοῦ is quite an enigma. While it could suggest that Jesus is the paschal lamb, there are several other possible explanations. It could evoke the lamb led to slaughter of Isa 53:7,[146]

---

[140] The need for this adaptation would not arise if he used a Hebrew *Vorlage*, as the Hebrew refers to a single righteous person.

[141] Cf. John 7:37b-38 where the Evangelist also contracts more than one line of the source text to form a citation.

[142] There is the problem that the purpose of the paschal lamb in Jewish tradition is "apotropaic and commemorative, but not expiatory." See Barrett, "The OT in the Fourth Gospel," 155. However, the phrase ὁ αἴρων τὴν ἁμαρτίαν τοῦ κόσμου in John 1:29 is generally regarded as a redactional assimilation to 1 John 3:5. See Brown, *John I - XII*, 56; Ashton, *Understanding*, 491.

[143] E.g., the inauguration of "the hour" just before Passover, the condemnation to death at "the sixth hour," the hour of the slaughter of the paschal lambs (19:14), the mention of hyssop (19:29), the reference to "the day of Preparation" (19:31) and, possibly, the haste to remove Jesus' body so that the slain paschal lamb will not remain until the next day (John 19:31.38. cf. Exod 12:10). See Grigsby, "The Cross as Expiatory Sacrifice," 53-59.

[144] The reference to "the sixth hour" (19:14), e.g., could be intended to bring out the connection between the promise of living water to the Samaritan woman scene (John 4:6) and the fulfilment of that promise in the death of Jesus.

[145] In Exod 12:10, the paschal lamb is a πρόβατον; in Exod 12:46 and Num 9:12, it is called τὸ πάσχα, as in the Fourth Gospel. Cf. John 18:28—ἵνα μὴ μιανθῶσιν ἀλλὰ φάγωσιν τὸ πάσχα.

[146] For Stibbe, *John*, 197, there is an irony in the soldiers' decision not to break Jesus' legs. It is their "unconscious testimony to the blamelessness of Jesus as the

although this suggestion may depend too heavily on prior assumptions about pre-Christian Jewish interpretation of the "Servant Songs."[147] It could, as well, reflect an understanding of Jesus' death in terms of the *Akedah*, God's beloved son (cf. Gen 22:2) being the sacrificial lamb that God promised to provide instead of Isaac (cf. Gen 22:8). The echo of Gen 22:2 in John 3:16, the Isaac-like way in which Jesus carries his own cross (John 19:17; cf. Gen 22:6) and the application of the term μονογενής to Jesus in John 1:14.18, 3:16[148] are sometimes cited in connection with this suggestion.[149] The belief that the Temple rock was the site of Abraham's sacrifice would also support this "Isaac" identification of Jesus.

The title ὁ ἀμνὸς τοῦ θεοῦ could also express Jesus' Messiahship by recalling the victorious lamb of Jewish apocalyptic thought. In 1 Enoch, a book of great importance for Christian origins,[150] the eponymous author records, from his antediluvian perspective, a dream vision he has received of the whole history of Israel in which various symbolic animals represent the characters, for example, a

---

supreme Lamb of God." For Brown, *Death of the Messiah*, 416, ὁ ἀμνὸς τοῦ θεου as a title for Jesus is "a polyvalent symbol pointing not only to elements of the paschal lamb in his death but also to his role as a servant who goes to his death as a lamb led to slaughter (Isa 53:7).

[147] Juel, *Messianic Exegesis*, 127, has warned that we cannot assume "the Suffering Servant" or "the Servant of the Lord" represents a distinct conception in postbiblical Judaism or that Jews understood the servant passages in Isaiah to refer to the Messiah. "Even where such interpretation can be found, there is no indication that prior to Christianity the Messiah was expected to suffer after installation to office or that his suffering was viewed as atoning in light of Isaiah 53."

[148] Μονογενής, is thought to be analogous to πρωτότοκος. See Bauer, *Greek-English Lexicon*, 527. According to Brown, *John I - XII*, 13-14, it reflects the Hebrew יחיד (solitary one, only one, OL *unicus*) used of Abraham's "one and only," in the sense of "precious," son Isaac (cf. Gen 22:2, 12, 16). The LXX of Gen 22, however, uses not μονογενής, but a more explanatory equivalent, ἀγαπητός. We depend on Heb 11:17 for an instance of μονογενής being used for Abraham's יחיד, Isaac. On Jesus as an Isaac figure, see Grigsby, "The Cross as Expiatory Sacrifice," 59-61. Μονογενής is also used of David, however. It occurs in LXX Ps 24:16 where it portrays him as uniquely precious to God and therefore deserving of God's protection. In view of its etymological connection with πρωτότοκος, it also carries resonances of David's royal status as "son of God." Cf. πρωτότοκος in LXX Ps 88:27, applied to Jesus in Rev 1:5.

[149] F.-M. Braun, "Le Sacrifice d'Isaac dans le quatrième évangile d'après le Targum," *NRT* 101 (1979) 481-497, mentions also Abraham's vision of the glory of Jesus (John 8:56) and the contrast between son and slave (John 8:35-36) as "Isaac" motifs in the Fourth Gospel. As Trudinger suggests, "Hosanna," 297, the Baptist's declaration, Ἴδε ὁ ἀμνὸς τοῦ θεοῦ (John 1:29), may be the answer to Isaac's question in Gen 22:7. See also Barrett, "The Old Testament," 155-56.

[150] "Few other apocryphal books so indelibly marked the religious history and thought at the time of Jesus." See E. Isaac, "1 (Ethiopic Apocalypse of) Enoch," 8. 10.

flock of sheep for the nation, wild beasts and birds of prey for Israel's enemies. The image of the lamb symbolizes David's rise from obscurity to the status of judge and leader of the people. David appears as a lamb which the Lord of the sheep promotes to become a ram to lead the flock instead of that other ram, Saul, who, having taken to attacking the sheep and trampling on them, has abandoned his own glory (1 Enoch 89:45). In a subsequent sequence of Enoch's zoomorphic dream vision, a passage dealing with the establishment of the messianic kingdom, the ram grows a single horn which his adversaries try without success to smash (1 En 90:9-17). The title "Lamb," as a Christological epithet, is found in the Book of Revelation.[151] Keeping in mind the ease with which the Fourth Evangelist handles polyvalence, we will find, as Dodd who first proposed this solution found, that accepting the "messianic" interpretation in no way obliges us to dismiss other possibilities.[152]

The Jewish capacity for the overlaying of different interpretations, as exemplified by the various traditional identifications of the Temple rock, gives us a hint as to how we might contend with all these conflicting opinions. It teaches us that arguments for other interpretations of ὁ ἀμνὸς τοῦ θεοῦ are not necessarily arguments against the case for paschal lamb symbolism. It is part of the Jewishness of John's Gospel that Jesus, ὁ ἀμνὸς τοῦ θεοῦ, can be the Paschal Lamb and "Isaac," as well as the individual who speaks in Ps (33)34. Not only that: there is a sense in which the Jesus who is greater than Abraham, Jacob and so many other figures in Israel's history, "is" Moses, or "is" Elijah or "is" David, since he fulfils, completes and replaces the total witness of the

---

[151] The Fourth Gospel uses ἀμνός and Revelation has ἀρνίον, but both words designate a young ram. The fact that the Pešhittā translates both by the word '*mr*' would indicate that the difference between them cannot have been particularly significant. Certainly, the Lamb in the Book of Revelation, who is identified as the "Root of David" and who becomes a lion, the "Lion of Judah" (Rev 5:5) is the product of similar interpretive traditions to those preserved in 1 Enoch. According to Dodd, *The Interpretation*, 232, Revelation reflects an early Christian fusion of the messianic lamb with the lamb of sacrifice. Recent studies of the Tosephta-Targum to 1 Sam 17 have yielded a "new" text which elucidates the image of the Lamb as used in Revelation. See De Moor and Van Staalduine-Sulman, "The Aramaic Song of the Lamb," 226-279.

[152] Dodd's contention, *The Interpretation*, 234, 236- 38 (1953), that the messianic reading is the correct understanding of ὁ ἀμνὸς τοῦ θεοῦ met with a certain scepticism. For the arguments against, see Brown, *John I - XII*, 59-60. With our more recent recognition of the importance for NT study of the OT Pseudepigrapha, Dodd's theory has received more attention. Ashton, *Understanding*, 257-58, for example, thinks Dodd's case for a messianic derivation "marginally more probable than either of the other two leading candidates, Suffering Servant and Paschal Lamb." See also D. B. Sandy, "John the Baptist's 'Lamb of God' Affirmation in its Canonical and Apocalyptic Milieu," *JETS* 34 (1991)447-60, at 453.

Scriptures.¹⁵³ Jesus fulfils, completes and replaces the whole Temple cult, so his death is at least Passover and Tabernacles, if not the whole Jewish festal calendar summed up in "the hour." He himself is offerer, victim, altar (rock) and Temple. Thus, Ὀστοῦν οὐ συντριβήσεται αὐτοῦ " can still be "*the* place in his gospel where John would have the reader finally see that Jesus is without a doubt the Paschal Lamb,"¹⁵⁴ without excluding a simultaneous reference to Ps 33:21. As Grelot sees it, John 19:36 is—"une actualisation d'Ex., XII, 46 (l'agneau pascal) effectué à l'aide du Ps XXXIV, 21 (le Juste protégé par Dieu), sur la base d'une rencontre verbale."¹⁵⁵

Our focus now is on Ὀστοῦν οὐ συντριβήσεται αὐτοῦ, received as a citation of Ps (33:21)34:20. Here a vividly graphic image is used to convey the idea that God redeems the lives of his servants: God preserves their bones from being broken.¹⁵⁶ Ancient ideas about the connection between the bones and the innermost core of a person's being underlie numerous psalm passages where the bones appear as synonymous with the person's most profound level of being.¹⁵⁷

---

¹⁵³ In a similar way, the fact that the hyssop symbol is not confined to Passover but evokes various other sacrificial rituals allows it to underline the sacrificial efficacy of Jesus' death, with reference to other aspects of its cultic character, e.g., the purificatory dimension. See Beetham, "A Note on John 19:29," and the discussion of Jesus as "cleansing fountain" in Grigsby, "The Cross as Expiatory Sacrifice," 61-2.

¹⁵⁴ Schuchard, *Scripture within Scripture*, 136.

¹⁵⁵ Grelot, "Jean VII, 38: Eau du rocher?" 50; Schuchard, *Scripture within Scripture*, 139-40, favours the 'Paschal Lamb' source, but sees the verb συντριβήσεται as evidence that John recalls Ps (33)34, even while quoting Exod 12:10 or 12:46; Brown, *Death of the Messiah*, 1185-89 favours the paschal lamb as the primary reference with echoes of the psalm as well; Menken, *Old Testament Quotations*, 152, sees "the peculiar textual form" of John's citation (i.e, the position of the αὐτοῦ at the end of the clause, where one might have expected Ὀστοῦν αὐτοῦ οὐ συντριβήσεται) as best explained by a combination of elements from Ps 33 and the Pentateuchal texts. Menken's chapter on the quotation in John 19:36 was originally pubished as "The Old Testament Quotation in John 19:36: Sources, Redaction, Background" in F. van Segbroeck et al. (ed.), *The Four Gospels, 1992, Festschrift: F. Neirynck* (Leuven: Peeters, 1992) 2101-18. Others who opt for the double reference are Barrett, "The OT in the Fourth Gospel," 157; Lindars, *The Gospel*, 590; Hanson, *The Prophetic Gospel*, 222.

¹⁵⁶ From elsewhere in the Psalter, e.g., Pss 2:9; (52:6)53:5; (140)141:7, we learn that the worst possible fate that Israelites could wish on their enemies was that their shattered bones should be strewn on the ground, in other words, that they should be completely annihilated.

¹⁵⁷ In Pss 6:3 and (30:11)31:10, e.g., distress is depicted as a disturbance (verb, ταράσσω) of the bones. In Ps 6:3 τὰ ὀστᾶ μου parallels ἡ ψυχή μου. Similarly in Ps (34)35:10 the exultation and delight of the Psalmist's ψυχή in the experience of salvation finds expression in the cry of his bones in praise of God. Cf. Ps (50:10)51:8. Jacquet explains, *Les Psaumes*, I, 721-22, "En gardants intacts leur os, c'est-à-dire ce que nomades et arabes de tous temps considéront comme le support de l'âme, Dieu leur assure invulnerabilité et survie."

There is a hint that the reality which the bones symbolize might somehow continue to exist even after death in the story of the dead man who came to life when his corpse touched the bones of Elisha (2 Kgs 13:20-21). This idea is found in a more developed form in Sir 49:10—"May the bones of the twelve prophets revive from where they lie." From his study of later Jewish sources, David Daube has found that beliefs about the resurrection of the dead, inspired by the Ezekiel 37 "dry bones," included the idea that broken bones would prevent resurrection. This would explain why rabbinic interpretation of Ps 34:20 (33:21) sees in this verse a promise of resurrection of the body, quoting it in a prayer for the deceased.[158] It is, therefore, quite possible that the preservation of Jesus' body from the violation of the *crurifragium* would have been regarded by early Christian readers as a pledge of his resurrection.

In Ps (33)34, the psalmist speaks as a wisdom teacher inviting disciples, "children," to come to him and learn from his experience of God's care for the righteous, willingness to hear their prayer, and readiness to deliver them. In the immediate context from which Ὀστοῦν οὐ συντριβήσεται αὐτοῦ is drawn (vv. 20-23 of the psalm) the central issue is death. While the death of the wicked is something evil, the death of God's servants, the righteous, demonstrates that their trust in God has not been misplaced. The didactic sequence in the psalm begins with the statement in v. 16 that God's ears are open to the prayer of the righteous. This is a recurrent motif in the Psalter, whether in this form, or as the obverse principle, that God does not listen to the wicked, stated in an analogous passage to the context from which Ὀστοῦν οὐ συντριβήσεται αὐτοῦ has been drawn, Ps (65)66:16-19.[159] There, the psalmist's victory over life-threatening danger is presented as evidence of his righteousness—"If I had cherished iniquity in my heart, God would not have listened." Against the background of the wider Psalter context, therefore, the Jesus whose bones God preserves so that not one of them is broken appears as a righteous fearer of God to whose prayers God's ears are open —

ὀφθαλμοὶ κυρίου ἐπὶ δικαίους,
καὶ ὦτα αὐτοῦ εἰς δέησιν αὐτῶν   (Ps 33:16).

---

[158] See Daube, *The New Testament and Rabbinic Judaism*, 309. We refer here, of course, to reception, not to the original intent of the psalm. As Oesterly, *The Psalms*, 215, points out, the psalmist's view that the reward for the godly is a long life indicates that he does not hold any belief in a future life.

[159] A Christian addition, dated by Rahlfs, *Septuaginta*, 2, 66, to 1st-2nd cent. CE, of the word ἀναστάσεως to the title of Ps 65 testifies to a very early Christological *relecture* of this psalm as spoken by Jesus after his resurrection.

The issue of God hearing Jesus' prayer surfaces several times in the Fourth Gospel (3:2; 9:31-32; 11:41). In fact, there may even be in the words of the man born blind—οἴδαμεν ὅτι ἁμαρτωλῶν ὁ θεὸς οὐκ ἀκούει, ἀλλ' ἐάν τις θεοσεβὴς ᾖ καὶ τὸ θέλημα αὐτοῦ ποιῇ τούτου ἀκούει —an echo of Ps 33:16 and/or the analogous passage in Ps 65:16-19. What is really at issue here is the credibility of Jesus. How could he do the signs that he does were he not the emissary of God that he claims to be? Yet there are those who think he is a sinner. The great sin of which Jesus is accused is, of course, the supposed blasphemy of claiming to be the Christ, the Son of God in a sense which makes him the equal of God. At the "hour," as it becomes clear who is the righteous and who is the sinner, Jesus is given a sign of God's special protection from the evil planned against him by "the Jews," οἱ μισοῦντες τὸν δίκαιον (Ps 33:22; cf. John 15:25). This fulfilment of Ps 33:21, is full of promise that God will vindicate Jesus' claim by listening to his prayer, Δόξασόν σου τὸν υἱόν (John 17:1).[160]

The reading of Ὀστοῦν οὐ συντριβήσεται αὐτοῦ as a citation of Ps 33:21 fits well with a pattern we have already noticed in the Johannine passion narrative. Jesus is executed as a messianic pretender, but he is still declared "King of the Jews." He is despoiled of his clothes, but his tunic is not torn. The Father gives him the bitter cup to drink (18:11), but at the same time he satisfies his thirst to return to his heavenly home. He suffers a cruel death, but not a bone of him is broken.[161] The idea in the psalm that, despite all his suffering, not one of the psalmist's bones were broken has a parallel in Jewish interpretations of the prescriptions concerning the paschal lamb where the intact bones symbolize Israel's hope of a glorious future. Daube thinks it probable that this idea was well known in the Judaism contemporary with the Fourth Gospel.[162] A reference to the unbroken bones of the paschal lamb in Jub 49:13 reads: "They shall roast it in fire without breaking any of its bones within it because no bone of the children of Israel will be broken."[163] Menken has drawn

---

[160] Menken, *Old Testament Quotations*, 158, sees in the psalm's reference to the sinners whose death will be evil (Ps 33:22) a parallel with "the Johannine idea that unbelievers will die in their sin(s) (Jn 8,21.24; cf. 16,9)."

[161] Brawley, "An Absent Complement," 434, speaks of the repetition of a pattern where senselessness becomes significant—"The notice that none of Jesus' bones were broken actually conjures up a non-event that ordinarily would draw no attention. Scripture gives meaning to something that did not happen."

[162] Daube, *The New Testament and Rabbinic Judaism*, 309. For a post-biblical interpretation of the sprinkling with hyssop in the Passover ritual as ensuring that death will pass Israel by, see Ezekiel the Tragedian (2nd cent. BC), *Exag.* 188-92.

[163] Trans. O. S. Wintermute, "Jubilees: A New Translation and Introduction" in Charlesworth (ed.), *OTP* 2, 35-142, at 141.

attention to the influence of Ps (33)34 on this passage which he believes is particularly evident in the Ethiopic version.[164] If this is so, we have in Jub 49:13 a valuable pre-Christian Jewish example of an interpretation of the bones of the paschal lamb as expressing the hope of the nation and as distinctly recalling the statement in Ps (33)34 that not one of the bones of the righteous will be broken. This would suggest that the Johannine double reference in John 19:36 is inspired by a familiar Jewish *gezera shawa* exegesis of the biblical prescriptions about the paschal lamb which referred to Ps (33:21)34:20.

Ps (33)34 not only occurs among the תפלות דוד בן־ישי (Book 1 of the Psalter) but has a historical Davidic superscript associating it with the occasion during David's persecution by Saul when he feigned madness to hide his identity (1 Sam 21:13).[165] As we have seen, there was evidently a hermeneutical rationale behind the "historical superscripts." In the case of Ps (33)34, the Jewish exegesis preserved in *Midr. Teh.* 34, 1 explains that David is depicted as feigning madness out of fear that he was doomed to destruction. The psalm praises God for delivering its author from all his fears (Ps 34:4). Various modern commentators have made other suggestions for the connection which the composer of the historical superscript saw between the Achish incident and the psalm.[166] Unlike the other two psalms quoted in the passion narrative—Pss (68)69 and (21)22—Ps (33)34 has no lament features. Any "flashbacks" to the psalmist's experience of distress are presented in the context of praise. Heard as David's, the psalm presents his role as witness in a sapiential mode. David appears

---

[164] In a literal translation of the Ethiopic by L. Van Rompay it reads: "... and there is no breaking of bone from the middle of it [the paschal lamb], not a single one, because not will be broken from the children of Israel a single bone." In the Latin, the only other extant early version, it reads: *et non erit quod frangatur ex omnibus ossibus eius, et non erit tribulatio in filiis Israhel in die hac.*—quoted in Menken, *Old Testament Quotations*, 161-62.

[165] Obvious to all commentators is that, according to 1 Sam 21:11-16, David feigned madness in the presence of Achish, not Abimelech. Sabourin, *The Psalms*, 285, attributes the reference to Abimelech to scribal error whereby אכיש מלך גת was shortened to אכיש מלך and then to אבימלך.

[166] Childs, *Psalm Titles and Midrashic Exegesis*, 144.147, has noticed that Ps 34 has a reference to the psalmist's fear from which he is rescued (Ps 34:4) and that the only explicit reference to David's fear is in the account of this incident with Achish King of Gath (1 Sam 21:10-16) which is mentioned in the superscript. Sabourin, *The Psalms*, 285, and Stuhlmueller, *Psalms 1*, 192, identify a subtle wordplay which they believe a scribe has employed in order to give the psalm a Davidic reference. The verbs טעמו ("taste") and תהלל ("make a boast") found at vv. 8 and 2 respectively of the psalm also occur in the Achish incident. There they have completely different meanings: טעמ means "change one's behaviour" (literally, change one's taste) and תהלל means "feign madness." For "an imaginative reading of the text that listens for David's voice," see K. H. Richards, "Psalm 34," *Int* 40 (1986) 175-80.

in the psalm as a wisdom teacher (cf. v. 12) instructing his disciples. In the course of his "lesson" he shows them how Israel's faith that God will keep its "bones" intact is verified by his own experience of divine deliverance.

It is quite possible, therefore, that Johannine Christians would have "heard" David as alluding to their understanding of the symbolism of the "paschal" bones when he spoke in his psalm of God preserving intact the bones of the righteous. Allowing Ὀστοῦν οὐ συντριβήσεται αὐτοῦ to resonate with Passover echoes enables the text to bring other motifs to expression. These may be sacrifical motifs, reminding the reader that Jesus is ὁ ἀμνὸς τοῦ θεοῦ and thereby evoking Isaac typology, for example, or the "consuming" of the sacrificial victim (cf. John 2:17). They may be Exodus motifs, alerting the reader to Jesus' role as the paschal journeyer passing from this world to the Father on Passover day.[167] This overlaying of image upon image is indicative of what Stibbe has called "the vast increase in discernible intertextuality in John's narration of the crucifixion."[168]

Our study of the Fourth Evangelist's psalm usage has taught us to be alert to the implications of Davidic authorship. In the case of John 19:36, viewed as a citation of Ps 33:21, they are particularly important. Those who argue for the psalm citation in John 19:36, tend to think in terms of a presentation of Jesus as one of the δίκαιοι depicted in the psalm.[169] Jesus is certainly this, but he is also much more. The tendency to see the role of the psalms in the passion narratives in terms of the "righteous sufferer" tradition has been incisively criticized by Hengel, Dahl and Juel. With reference to Mark's gospel, but with obvious implications for the Fourth Gospel, Hengel, for example, insists that the psalms are used in the passion story to speak of Jesus as king and that even where features from the suffering righteous tradition do appear, "they are also in a messianic key."[170] Taking as his starting point "the irreducible historicity" of the title, ὁ βασιλεὺς τῶν Ἰουδαίων (John 19:19), Juel

---

[167] See Boismard, *Moïse ou Jésus*, 22.
[168] Stibbe, *John*, 196.
[169] Schuchard, *Scripture within Scripture*, 139-40, sees a reference to Jesus as "one of the 'righteous' " which prepares the reader for the next citation in which Jesus is described as "the one whom they have pierced..." Menken, *Old Testament Quotations*, 157, sees 19:36 as another instance of Johannine identification of Jesus with "the righteous sufferer who will be vindicated by God." For Seynaeve, "Les citations scriptuaires," 76, Ps 33:21, as cited in John 19:36 evokes the figure of the "suffering servant."
[170] Hengel, *The Atonement*, 41.

too holds that "the Psalms...are enlisted to tell the story of the death of Jesus, the King of the Jews. They do not provide an alternative view of Jesus, e.g., as a paradigmatic righteous sufferer."[171] In making this claim, we do not depend on evidence that the psalms quoted in the passion narratives were read as messianic in pre-Christian Judaism. Rather, the critical factor, as Juel points out, "is the reconstruction of a midrashic logic that can explain how these psalms came to narrate the story of the King of the Jews."[172] It is the contention of this study that the exegetical warrant for regarding a psalm quotation such as Ὀστοῦν οὐ συντριβήσεται αὐτου as spoken about Jesus the Messiah is to be found in the supposed Davidic authorship of the Psalter. According to the midrashic logic which this warrant permits, Jesus is to be recognized by his David-likeness (not, John would say, by linear descent from David) as the king in whose name King David prophetically composed this psalm. Thus John's psalm citation portrays Jesus not as "righteous," but as royal.[173]

Allowing the Davidic superscript its full role, in terms of reception, produces quite a different reading to the "righteous sufferer" reading which is typical of those who accept Ps (33)34 as a source of John 19:36. The fact that the reference to the δίκαιοι is plural in the Greek leads commentators to see v. 21 as a sapiential axiom with a general application to a category of people, "the suffering righteous" among whom they then include Jesus. In order to hear the psalm citation with the Johannine Christians as τῷ Δαυιδ, we need to think in terms of a single "righteous" person, as in the Hebrew, and as in the Johannine reception. David then emerges from the psalm as "this poor man" (Heb v. 6: זה עני; LXX v. 7: οὗτος ὁ πτωχὸς) who cried out to the Lord and was heard, who was crushed and afflicted, but none of whose bones was broken. David's words, with their echoes of Passover lamb symbolism, are fulfilled in Jesus' deliverance from death. In our exploration of David's "literary future," we found that from the Latter Prophets onwards he becomes primarily a symbol of

---

[171] John's usage of Ps 33 is much more pointedly Christological than, e.g., that of the author of 2 Tim who follows in the line of interpretation exemplified by 4 Macc 18:13-14. See 2 Tim 3:11.

[172] Juel, *Messianic Exegesis*, 103

[173] Ps 33:21 may have a long line of ancestry in ANE royal burial customs. In an article on a possible background for the psalm passage quoted in John 19:36, G. A. Barton refers to an inscription found on an Egyptian royal tomb dating from the third millennium BCE. It tells of the heavenly life of the Pharaoh Pepi II, describing his ascent to the sky to take his place with the other gods. Included in the inscription are the words, "Not broken is a bone of Pepi II." See "'A Bone of Him Shall Not Be Broken,' John 19:36," *JBL* 49 (1930), 12-18.

what God will do for Israel in the time to come.[174] So it is the Passover hope of Israel that death would pass it by, celebrated by means of the paschal lamb, and confirmed by David's testimony that not one of his bones was broken, that is fulfilled in Jesus' "passing over" to the Father.

It is the hearing of Ὀστοῦν οὐ συντριβήσεται αὐτοῦ as a psalm citation that facilitates the shift from ritual prescription concerning "it" to personal reference concerning "him," thus effecting a smooth transition to Ὄψονται εἰς ὃν ἐξεκέντησαν. The Zechariah context from which John draws this second citation is very much concerned with the royal House of David (See Zech 12:7. 8. 10. 12).[175] If, as we have seen, the Scriptures in John 7:38 and 19:28 are both prophecies of the opening of a fountain for this House of David and the inhabitants of Jerusalem (Zech 13:1) from which living waters will flow out (Zech 14:8), then "that day" has arrived when the Lord will become king over all the earth (Zech 14:9).[176] Received as a psalm quotation, Ὀστοῦν οὐ συντριβήσεται αὐτοῦ identifies Jesus as that king.

In summary: The Scripture in John 19:36 is inseparable from Zech 12:10, quoted in 19:37, both being introduced under the one formula of quotation, including the narrator's address to the reader in v. 35. Ὀστοῦν οὐ συντριβήσεται αὐτοῦ is a double reference to the prescriptions concerning the paschal lamb and to Ps (33:21)34:20. The two sources complement each other: the paschal lamb reference pointing to the sacrificial efficacy of Jesus' death, the testimony of David pointing to the vindication of Jesus, not merely as "righteous," but as royal—as ὁ Χριστὸς ὁ υἱὸς τοῦ θεοῦ. This royal portrayal of Jesus facilitates the recognition of the pierced one (Zech 12:10) as the one in whom ἔσται Κύριος εἰς βασιλέα ἐπὶ πᾶσαν τὴν γῆν (Zech 14:9).

---

[174] See pp. 85-86 above.

[175] Exactly how the Davidic traditions are being used in these passages is a much debated question. Having outlined and assessed a bewildering variety of hypotheses, Pomykala, *Davidic Dynasty Tradition*, 113-26, concludes that the "House of David" in Zech 12 is a large clan group, in genealogical continuity with the former royal family, now holding no official office, but enjoying social prominence. From Zech 12:8-9 it emerges that the designation, "House of David" refers to the great and powerful among the inhabitants of Jerusalem, as distinct from the least, "the feeblest among them."

[176] As we have seen, there is a veritable web of intertextual connections between Zechariah and the Fourth Gospel. The Zechariah quotation in John 19:37 effects an inclusion between the Johannine 'hour' and the Temple scene in John 2:13-22 by evoking a prophetic oracle which concludes with: 'And there shall no longer be a trader in the house of the Lord of Hosts on that day.' This, of course, serves to recall the citation from Ps 68:10—Ὁ ζῆλος τοῦ οἴκου σου καταφάγεταί με—at the very moment in the text when its deeper significance is being revealed.

G. *Overview of the Five Citations in the Book of Glory*

The five psalm citations keep apace with the unfolding argument of the "Book of Glory." The first two, from Ps (40)41 and Ps (68)69, are connected, in that they both occur in Jesus' Farewell Discourses. Both point to the fulfilment of the Scriptures in Jesus' hour, but also open up for readers, living in the time after he had risen from the dead, the possibility of seeing the Scriptures fulfilled in their experience of betrayal and hatred. The next two citations from Ps (21)22 and (68)69 come at the centre of the crucifixion scene. They fit into the pattern of Scripture reference in the actual passion narrative where what was foretold in prophecy now actually happens. The second of these citations represents the last incidence of Scripture fulfilment before Jesus' death. Since it comes from Ps (68)69, the first psalm cited in the Gospel, it reminds the reader of the programmatic nature of that first citation which pointed to Jesus death. Unlike the other psalms cited in the passion narrative, Ps (33)34, is a psalm of uninterrupted praise. As cited in John 19:36, it underlines the Johannine conception of Jesus' death as his triumphant royal enthronement.

It is particularly significant that the double Scripture citation in John 19:36-37 is introduced by the author's rationale for Scripture usage in the Gospel generally—ἵνα καὶ ὑμεῖς πιστεύ[σ]ητε (John 19:35). This final instance of formal Scripture citation in the Gospel, combining an Exodus allusion from the Law, a vision from the Prophets and a psalm of David from the Writings, encapsulates and exemplifies the function of Scripture reference in the Gospel generally—ἵνα πιστεύ[σ]ητε ὅτι Ἰησοῦς ἐστιν ὁ Χριστὸς ὁ υἱὸς τοῦ θεοῦ, καὶ ἵνα πιστεύοντες ζωὴν ἔχητε ἐν τῷ ὀνόματι αὐτοῦ (John 20: 31).

So far in this study we have seen how the Evangelists' usage of the psalms is not confined to isolated phrases which seem pertinent to Jesus, but extends, at least in some cases, to the psalm as a whole.[177] We have also continually encountered the impossibility of treating even a whole psalm in isolation. In order to understand a reference to one psalm, we invariably found ourselves referring to several others. In trying to reconstruct the reception which first century readers might have afforded the Psalter, we found ourselves being drawn into their intuition of the inter-relatedness of psalm with psalm. Our experience bore out the validity of what had emerged in our second

---

[177] An earlier generation of scholars saw a parallel to this in the *pesher* method of line by line exegesis, known from the Qumran documents. See especially Lindars, *New Testament Apologetic*, 15.

chapter, that in late Second Temple Judaism, the Psalter was regarded as a unified work with its own internal logic, and that the major factor in its reception as a unified work was its association with David.

CHAPTER FIVE

OTHER PSALMS PRESENT IN THE FOURTH GOSPEL THROUGH ALLUSION AND ECHO

A. *Introduction*

In the two preceding chapters dealing with the ten psalm citations in the Fourth Gospel, we found that seven psalms are quoted, two of them more than once. We also detected, in some cases, an influence of these psalms on the composition which goes far beyond the impact of the actual lines cited. In other words, we found that several of the quoted psalms also function in the text through allusion and echo. This chapter explores such a presence, through allusion and echo, of psalms not explicitly quoted in the Fourth Gospel.

In our introductory discussion of intertextuality, we noted that non-explicit reference to an earlier work can range from verbal allusions, where there is a readily recognizable reminiscence of the source text, to echoes which "constitute a kind of underground cipher message...or perhaps a private melody or undersong hummed during composition."[1] In this chapter, therefore, we are dealing with a much more covert, faint, blurred and subliminal form of intertextual reference which often consists of no more than a single word, a turn of phrase, or even a hidden influence generating the sequence of thought. It need not necessarily be intentional on the author's part, but may be simply the product of the cultural conventions and presuppositions which have conditioned the author's approach to his text. In the case of the Fourth Gospel, one of the factors which have conditioned the Evangelist's approach has been his own profound familiarity with the language and imagery of the Psalter. As we will see, this has left a deep imprint on the work which he has produced.

As we found in Ch. 1, the play of allusion and echo is not statistically quantifiable. The more subtle forms of intertextual reference are difficult to pin down, as there is always the possibility of different and competing voices. Writing on John 14:1-9. 27, but with an application to the whole question of John's sources, Edwin D. Freed states—

---

[1] Hollander, *The Figure of Echo*, ix, as discussed on pp. 10-13 above.

> ...the writer used traditional Jewish language and imagery. However, his composition reveals a lot of creative work in adapting that language and imagery to his unique conceptions of Christ. And behind and in that creative work are many sources of various kinds, so many, in fact, that it is impossible to determine which ones were the most influential.[2]

The difficulty is compounded by the danger of the commentator's subjectivity, of believing that what is uppermost in one's own mind corresponds to the Evangelist's preoccupations. This chapter, therefore, calls for quite a different approach to that taken in Chs 3 and 4. Without claiming to provide an exhaustive survey, we propose some samples of Fourth Gospel allusion to the Psalter, ranging from instances which border on explicit citation, to others where the verbal indications are minimal and yet the influence of a psalm is still keenly sensed. This chapter will demonstrate, therefore, how the various modes of intertextual reference function on that "sliding scale" of decreasing visibility on the surface of the text which we described in the Introduction to this study. We look first at some examples of substantial verbal allusion to the Psalter.[3] We then explore less overt modes of the Psalter's presence. Finally, we ask whether there may be an intertextual relationship between the Psalter and the over-all structure of the Gospel. Our purpose, in this chapter, is not to document every possible psalm allusion and echo in the Fourth Gospel—an impossible task anyway, but rather to convey a sense of the high regard in which the Evangelist held the Psalter as Scripture that bears witness to Jesus (John 5:39).

In exploring Fourth Gospel allusions to "un-quoted" psalms, we bring to audibility, as it were, the "harmonics" which account for the colour and timbre of the Johannine rendering of David's "praises" in the explicit citations. In this chapter, therefore, we attempt to hear the unexpressed psalm reference in the Gospel, the "unsaid" which forms the background to what is said.

> Texts, as language, not only say what they say but evoke a world of the unsaid that might well become articulate under different circumstances of interpretation. This unspoken range of meaning waits in the wings even as the spoken acts its part upon the stage of discourse. The cue for its appearance needs only to be whispered.[4]

---

[2] Freed, "Psalm 42/43 in John's Gospel," *NTS* 29 (1982) 62-73, at 71.

[3] The term "substantial" refers to the volume of the allusion (i.e., a sentence or a phrase, not just a word) which is a clear indication of intentionality on the Evangelist's part. It does not imply, however, that the precise source of the allusion is beyond dispute.

[4] Schneiders, *The Revelatory Text*, 139, following Hans-Georg. Gadamer, *Truth and Method*, 2d rev. ed., translated and revised by J. Weinsheimer and D. G. Marshall (New York: Crossroad, 1989) 65-78.

The psalms not explicitly quoted in the Fourth Gospel are an important aspect of its intertextuality, revealing an author and a community steeped in the thought and diction of David the psalmist.

While many of the intertextual links discussed in this chapter have been noted by others, there does not appear to have been an attempt to bring them together, to appraise them in light of the explicit psalm citations in the Gospel, and to draw out the implications of their supposed Davidic "authorship." Hollander, speaking of the way the re-appearance of elements from an earlier text in a later work has long been acknowledged in critical apparatus such as footnotes and indices of sources, comments that "the tendency of annotators, employing the genially open 'cf.,' has been to shun the caves of ambience and the chambers of meaning."[5] In this chapter, we invite David, in his capacity as psalmist, to lead us into those caves of ambience and those chambers of meaning. In that acoustical environment, which has been formed by the interpretive traditions of Second Temple Judaism which we explored in Ch. 2, we may be able to come some way towards hearing Fourth Gospel psalm allusions and echoes as they might have been heard by Johannine Christians.

B. *Substantial Allusion: Ps (88)89*

We begin with two allusions which border on explicit citation. The first appears in the course of the debate among the people which ensues when Jesus promises the gift of the Spirit, quoting from Ps (77)78:16.20. A suggestion that he might be the Christ raises the following question—

> ...οὐχ ἡ γραφὴ εἶπεν ὅτι ἐκ τοῦ σπέρματος Δαυὶδ καὶ ἀπὸ Βηθλέεμ τῆς κώμης ὅπου ἦν Δαυίδ, ἔρχεται ὁ Χριστός; (John 7:42).
>
> "Has not the scripture said that the Christ is descended from David, and comes from Bethlehem?"

There are actually two "Scriptures" here: one stating that the Christ comes from Bethlehem,[6] the other, which concerns us here, stating that the Christ is "of the seed of David." The second allusion which we will be considering occurs in John 12:34, where the crowd declares:

---

[5] Hollander, *The Figure of Echo*, 88
[6] Commentators agree on Mic 5:2 as the source of the "Bethlehem" Scripture. Schnackenburg, *The Gospel*, 158, and Reim, *Jochanan*, 156, also mention 1 Sam 20:6.

Ἡμεῖς ἠκούσαμεν ἐκ τοῦ νόμου ὅτι ὁ Χριστὸς μένει εἰς τὸν αἰῶνα…
"We have heard from the Law that the Christ remains for ever."

As we have learned from John 10:34 and 15:25, the Fourth Evangelist regards the psalms as part of "the Law." Obviously, these appeals to Scripture are more a reflection of the crowd's presuppositions than a representation of the Evangelist's own point of view.[7] However, as we have learned, Johannine characters often unwittingly utter a truth which, although quite beyond their comprehension, is patently clear to the informed reader. The primary reference in both passages is to the part of Nathan's oracle (2 Sam 7:12-13), where God promises—

…ἀναστήσω τὸ σπέρμα σου μετὰ σέ…καὶ ἀνορθώσω τὸν θρόνον αὐτοῦ ἕως εἰς τὸν αἰῶνα.

I will raise up your seed afer you…and I will set up his throne for ever.

The textual form of ἡ γραφή in John 7:42 leads commentators to propose as its source various biblical restatements of this oracle.[8] Of these, the source that is generally felt to come closest verbally to John 7:42 is Ps (88)89 where there are two derivative forms of the promise to David concerning his "seed"—

Ἕως τοῦ αἰῶνος ἑτοιμάσω τὸ σπέρμα σου
καὶ οἰκοδομήσω εἰς γενεὰν καὶ γενεὰν τὸν θρόνον σου (Ps 88:5).

I will establish your seed for ever
and build up your throne to all generations.

Τὸ σπέρμα αὐτοῦ εἰς τὸν αἰῶνα μενεῖ…(Ps 88:37).

His seed will endure for ever.

The second of these texts may account for the idea that "the Christ remains for ever" in John 12:34.

---

[7] The opinions expressed in these two gospel passages concerning the Messiah and his connection with David are not necessarily those of the Johannine circle. De Jonge has warned, "Jewish Expectations," 247, "We cannot use the Johannine material without taking into account that the Jews whose opinion is expressed in the Gospel appear on a scene set by a Christian evangelist. They are portrayed as 'representative Jews' and are obviously introduced into the Gospel because it was important to compare John's views on Jesus the Christ with Jewish expectations concerning the Messiah."

[8] Re the source of ἐκ τοῦ σπέρματος Δαυίδ … ἔρχεται ὁ Χριστός, Bultmann, *The Gospel*, 305, n. 5, suggests 2 Sam 7:12-13, Isa 11:1 and Jer 23:5; Lindars, *The Gospel*, 303, suggests Isa 7:13-14 and Ps 17:51; Schnackenburg, *The Gospel*, 2, 158, notes that ἐκ τοῦ σπέρματος Δαυίδ is found nowhere in Scripture, but that 2 Sam 7:12-16, Ps 17:51, Isa 11:1. 10, Jer 23:5 and Ps 88:3-4. 35-37 presuppose it. Brown, *John I-XII*, 324, limits his proposals to Mic 5:2 as the source for ἀπὸ Βηθλέεμ τῆς κώμης ὅπου ἦν Δαυίδ.

The lack of any biblical passage with exactly the wording in John 12:34 has led several to search the *Targumim* for the source.[9] The problem with positing a Targum, though, is that nowhere in the Fourth Gospel is there clear verbal evidence that the Evangelist quotes from the *Targumim*.[10] Moreover, the Targum sources proposed do not approximate John's "Scripture" any more nearly than Ps 88:37. For others, the answer is to be found in a different text from the Psalter, e.g., Ps (60)61:7-8.[11] While various other texts have been proposed as the source of ὁ Χριστὸς μένει εἰς τὸν αἰῶνα, Ps 88:37 has the advantage of containing the verb μενεῖ. There is also the fact, observed by W. C. Van Unnik, that the psalm mentions God's χριστός in v. 52.[12] If Ps 88:37 (or even Ps 60:7-8) is the source of ὅτι ὁ Χριστὸς μένει εἰς τὸν αἰῶνα, this would mean that the quotation from "the Law" which the crowd cites in unwitting testimony to Jesus' pre-existence and ongoing life as Lord and God comes, not from "Moses," but from "David."

Perhaps, the deciding factor in tracing the "Scripture" in John 12:34 back to Ps (88)89 is the context in which the word χριστός appears. The psalm is a poetic evocation of Nathan's oracle (2 Sam 7) fraught, particularly in its final section, with all the urgency which the apparent extinguishment of the Davidic dynasty must have engendered. In its position within the purposeful ordering of "The Five Books of David," Ps (88)89 tackles a serious problem: God's covenant with David appears

---

[9] For Bruce Chilton, the Targum to Isa 52:13 offers the best solution. In it the servant is said to be the Messiah and the Targumic development of the "lifting up" theme seems to fit well with the continuation of the crowd's speech—καὶ πῶς λέγεις σὺ ὅτι δεῖ ὑψωθῆναι τὸν υἱὸν τοῦ ἀνθρώπου; τίς ἐστιν οὗτος ὁ υἱὸς τοῦ ἀνθρώπου; See "John xii 34 and the Targum Isaiah lii 13," *NovT* 22 (1980) 176-78. The Targum of Isa 9:5, which refers to the Messiah as "He who lives for ever," has also been proposed by Brian McNeil in "The Quotation at John XII 34," *NovT* 19 (1977) 22-33.

[10] This is the conclusion of Menken, *Old Tstament Quotations*, 199, reached after detailed study of Scripture citations in the Fourth Gospel.

[11] Bampfylde, "More Light on John XII 34," *JSNT* 17 (1983) 87-89, points out that Ps (60)61:7-8 contains the three elements found in the quotation: ὁ Χριστός (implied by βασιλεύς), μένει and εἰς τὸν αἰῶνα. Among the several reasons which she presents in favour of Ps (60)61, are its Davidic superscript, its status as a prophecy in view of David's role as prophet, and its character as a royal psalm lending itself to messianic interpretation.

[12] Van Unnik states the "case" for Ps 88:37 in his "The Quotation from the Old Testament in John 12:34," *NovT* 3 (1959) 174-79. Other proposals are as follows—Bultmann, *The Gospel*, 355, n. 2, suggests 1 Kgs 8:25; 9:5, Ezek 37:25, Isa 9:6, Ps (71)72:5 and Ps (109)110:4. As well as Ps 88:37, Lindars, *The Gospel*, 434, suggests Ps 109:4, Isa 9:6-7 and Ezek 37:25; Schnackenburg opts for Ps 88:37. Brown stresses the difficulty of finding a precise passage, but suggests as possibilities Ps 88:5, Ps 109:4, Isa 9:7 and Ezek 37:25. He also believes that, in view of the identification of the Messiah and the Son of Man in John 12:34, Dan 7:14 could also be the source of the idea that the Christ remains for ever.

to have come to nothing. This raises the very issue that is the occasion for the Scripture citation in John 12:34, the contradiction in terms involved in the very idea of a suffering "Anointed." The real question in John 12 is whether the crucified one can be identified with the Messiah/Son of Man.[13] This raises the issue which Ps (88)89 has already confronted. Poised at the end of Book 3 of the Psalter, it recalls and celebrates the promises to David in a situation where, to all intents and purposes, they appear to have failed. According to the psalm, "a serious defeat...has not only jeopardized God's promises to David, but the entire universe is liable to fall apart and creation be undone."[14] The great point of issue on which the psalm concludes—If the king is humiliated (v. 51) is not God's promise to David put into question?—finds an echo in the query of the Johannine ὄχλος as to whether the crucified one can be identified as the Messiah/Son of Man. For those who know the Scriptures (John 20:9), Ps (88)89 provides the key. In the over-all plan of the Psalter, the seeming inconsistency between a defeated "David" and God's promise to him of eternal rule is finally resolved in Book 5 where David glorifies God for ever. The irony of the Scripture in John 12:34 is that the crowd refers to the very psalm which could have enabled them to reconcile the apparently contradictory and to see Jesus' death as his glorification.

As we have found with so many of the other psalms used in the Fourth Gospel, the moment of "visibility" in the text is merely the most obvious of several occasions when the presence of the psalm is sensed. For example, it is, perhaps, in his constant reference to God as "my father," that the Johannine Jesus appears most clearly as the "David" of Ps (88)89. A comparison of Ps 88:27 with John 20:17 suggests the possibility of an important intertextual relationship.[15]

John 20:17	Ps 88:27
Ἀναβαίνω πρὸς τὸν πατέρα μου καὶ πατέρα ὑμῶν καὶ θεόν μου καὶ θεὸν ὑμῶν.	...αὐτὸς ἐπικαλέσεταί με Πατήρ μου εἶ σύ, θεός μου καὶ ἀντιλήμπτωρ τῆς σωτηρίας μου·
"I am ascending to my Father and your Father, to my God and your God.	...He will say to me, "You are my Father, my God and the helper of my salvation."

---

[13] So, Lindars, *The Gospel*, 434-35.

[14] Stuhlmueller, *Psalms 2*, 62. Ps (88)89 has been described by Wilson, "The Shape of the Book of Psalms," 140, as "the clearest articulation of the crisis of identity and faith that precipitates the theological response one finds in the final form of the Psalter."

[15] Boismard, *Moïse ou Jésus*, 112, sees here "une discrète allusion à la royauté de Jésus, solidement établie malgré les apparences."

This crucial allusion to Ps 88 reveals the Johannine Jesus as the πρωτότοκος, spoken of in the very next line of the psalm—κἀγὼ πρωτότοκον θήσομαι αὐτόν (Ps 88:28a). In Ps (88:28)89:27 God bestows the title בכור (first-born) on David and, by extension, on each succeeding king of his line. The title refers to to the king's unique and privileged covenantal relationship to God.[16] In the LXX, בכור is rendered by πρωτότοκος. Evidently, a certain exegetical ingenuity was required in order to explain how David could be appointed firstborn by God. The *Midrash Tehillim* no doubt depends on this interpretive labour when it comments on Ps (88:28)89:27—

> When Scripture says, *I will appoint him first-born, the highest of the kings of the earth* (Ps 89:27), does it really mean that David was the first-born? Is it not said of him *And David was the youngest* (1 Sam 17:14)? Why then does Scripture speak of him as *first-born?* Because like the firstborn who takes a double portion of an inheritance, so David inherited a double portion of kingship: one portion in this world, and the other in the world-to-come.[17]

The Fourth Evangelist's insight thus concurs with that of the author of Revelation that Jesus is ὁ πρωτότοκος and ὁ ἄρχων τῶν βασιλέων τῆς γῆς (Rev 1:5, quoting Ps 88:28).[18] In fact, we even find in the psalm passage "behind" the second of these titles—(θήσομαι αὐτὸν) ὑψηλὸν παρὰ τοῖς βασιλεῦσιν τῆς γῆς—an expression distinctly reminiscent of the specialized Johannine usage of the verb ὑψόω.[19]

In view of the widespread use of Ps (88)89 in the NT, and since it is quite possible that John 7:42 and 12:34 actually refer to it, we are justified in supposing that the psalm as a whole was familar to the

---

[16] See Kraus, *Theology of the Psalms*, 113-14.

[17] Cf. *Midr. Teh.* 5.4. If the general lines of this interpretation go back to the first century, it could have contributed to the idea that Jesus' kingdom is "not of this world" (John 18:36). On the other hand, it is noticeable that the Midrash takes "advantage" of the Hebrew in which בכור has no pronominal suffix, interpreting it in terms of God's reversal of David's position as the youngest of Jesse's sons. This seems strange when the immediate context of the verse (especially, "He shall cry to me, You are my father") and its background in Israelite kingship ideology indicate that David is God's firstborn. It may, perhaps, indicate a Jewish anxiety to disprove Christian claims and hence, a reading post-dating the NT period.

[18] The author of Revelation interprets Jesus' "firstborn" status as that of ὁ πρωτότοκος τῶν νεκρῶν (Rev 1:5). The term πρωτότοκος and the immediately preceding reference to Jesus as ὁ μάρτυς ὁ πιστός both come from Ps 88:28. As mentioned in connection with Jesus' role as witness (See P. 217, note 92) the Hebrew of this verse can be read as a statement "that David's descendant (the Messiah?) shall be a reliable witness in the clouds." See, Derrett, "Christ, King and Witness," 192-95.

[19] The adjectival form used in the psalm, ὑψηλός, a cognate of the verb ὑψόω, does not occur in the Fourth Gospel. It is found in Heb 7:26 with reference to Jesus' role as high priest lifted up above the heavens, ὑψηλότερος τῶν οὐρανῶν γενόμενος.

Fourth Evangelist. We may, therefore, realistically posit an "input" from the psalm to the Gospel in the form of fleeting echoes or turns of phrase. Recalling the composite quotation in Acts 13:22, based on Ps 88:21, εὗρον Δαυιδ τὸν δοῦλόν μου, we might ask if, perhaps, Andrew's words to Peter, Εὑρήκαμεν τὸν Μεσσίαν and the authorial note, ὅ ἐστιν μεθερμηνευόμενον Χριστός (John 1:41), both with their resonances of the "hidden Messiah" tradition, may echo Ps 88:21—

εὗρον Δαυιδ τὸν δοῦλόν μου,
ἐν ἐλαίῳ ἁγίῳ μου ἔχρισα αὐτόν.[20]

"I have found David my servant;
With my holy oil I have anointed him."

Perhaps too John 8:51 is another moment when the psalm's phraseology has come quite spontaneously to the Evangelist's pen.

JOHN 8:51	Ps 88:49
...ἐάν τις τὸν ἐμὸν λόγον τηρήσῃ, θάνατον οὐ μὴ θεωρήσῃ εἰς τὸν αἰῶνα.	...τίς ἐστιν ἄνθρωπος, ὃς ζήσεται καὶ οὐκ ὄψεται θάνατον;
"...if any one keeps my word, he will never see death."	...who is the man who will live and not see death?

John 12:34 is indicative of an interpretation of the "Scripture," ὅτι ὁ Χριστὸς μένει εἰς τὸν αἰῶνα..., as a basis for the belief in the eternal life of the Messiah. The notion of David's continued life through his dynasty was to develop, in later tradition, into belief in his own continued existence with God, in the eternal life of his descendant, the Messiah, and even in that descendant's pre-existence.[21] Clear textual

---

[20] The finding of Jesus the Messiah is an important motif. In Martyn's view, the verb εὑρίσκειν "serves as the means by which the witness-chain is continuously extended from John the Baptist outwards (vss. 41 and 45; cf. vss 35ff)." Martyn explains the breaking of this chain in v. 43, where Jesus "finds," as an *aporia* caused by the redactor who is also responsible for the three finite verbs (ἠθέλησεν, εὑρίσκει and λέγει) with no subject named. See "Glimpses into the History of the Johannine Community," in M. de Jonge (ed.) *L'Évangile de Jean: Sources, rédaction, théologie* (Leuven: Leuven University Press / Gembloux: Duculot, 1977) 149-75.

[21] The pre-existence of the Son of Man/Messiah figure seems presupposed, e.g., in 1 En 48:2-3 where he is apparently in God's presence even before creation. Charlesworth considers that the Parables of Enoch force us to rethink the assumption that the Son of Man and the Messiah should be distinguished. Both may be identified in the 1 En 48:10 passage (clearly influenced by Ps 2), "They have denied the Lord of Spirits and his Messiah." See Charlesworth, "From Messianology to Christology: Problems and Prospects," in Charlesworth (ed.) *The Messiah*, 3-35, at 31.

evidence for the belief in the eternal life of the Messiah postdates 70 CE, but the tradition out of which it arose is much older.[22] It is to such a belief that the Fourth Gospel alludes in the claim of the crowd that the Christ is to remain for ever (John 12:34). The contribution of this belief to the Johannine doctrine of the pre-existence of the Word (John 1:1-18) would have to be recognized. The Gospel's evidence for the awareness of this belief in the Johannine circle permits us to see in certain later Jewish readings of the psalms the traces of much earlier interpretations. For example, the distinction some of these interpretations make between the earthly and heavenly rule of the Messiah may help to explain Jesus' kingship that is "not of this world" (John 18:36) and perhaps may even elucidate, to some extent, the Johannine distinction between earthly things and heavenly things (John 3:12).[23]

In this exploratory look at two substantial allusions to Ps (88)89, we have found it impossible to speak of the actual allusion without referring to the psalm as a whole. The more closely one looks at the intertextual relationship between the Fourth Gospel and the Psalter, the more one becomes conscious of a whole mesh of connections within psalms and with various psalms which are themselves interconnected with each other. The metaphor from the craft of weaving at the Latin root of our word" text" (*texere;* to weave) is extremely apt to the Fourth Gospel. The unifying factor which allowed the early Christian writers to exploit what we would see as "so many different psalms" was their view of the Psalter as an integrated whole. This aspect of their reception of the psalms is, of course, intimately bound up with their perception of the Psalter as "the five books of David."

C. *More Transitory Allusion*

The two allusions to Ps (88)89 which we have just discussed could almost be regarded as citations. We move on now to examine some examples of a less obvious form of intertextual reference in which

---

[22] L. Ginzberg, *The Legends of the Jews*, I,22; V,33; VI,351, records a tradition in which the Messiah was taken from paradise after the fall and is to be protected by God until the end of time. An early form of this tradition would appear to underlie Acts 3:19-20. Depending on how one understands the verb ἀνάξει, PsSol 18:5 may be a reference to the day when God "brings back" the Messiah. According to 4 Ezra 7:28, 12:32 (late first century CE), the Messiah has been kept hidden by the Most High for many ages. According to 2 Bar 30:1 (ca 200-220 CE), the Messiah returns from heaven.

[23] E.g., *Midr. Teh.* 5, 4 (quoted on p. 249 above) where David receives kingship in this world and in the world to come; *Midr. Teh.* 57, 3 (quoted on p. 211 above) where Saul says to David, "Thou wilt be king in this world and thou wilt rule in the world to come."

1. *Ps (39)40*
The Johannine insistence on Jesus' readiness to do the Father's will is strongly reminiscent of Ps 39:8-9—

> τότε εἶπον Ἰδοὺ ἥκω,
> ἐν κεφαλίδι βιβλίου γέγραπται περὶ ἐμοῦ·
> τοῦ ποιῆσαι τὸ θέλημά σου, ὁ θεός μου, ἐβουλήθην
> καὶ τὸν νόμον σου ἐν μέσῳ τῆς κοιλίας μου.
>
> Then I said, Behold I come:
> In the volume of the book it is written concerning me,
> I desired to do your will, O my God,
> and your law in the midst of my heart.

Ps 39:8-9 is explicitly cited, as applied to Jesus, in a work which has many affinities with the Fourth Gospel, the Letter to the Hebrews (Heb 10:5-7). There are several moments in the Fourth Gospel when the phraseology of this passage is heard in Jesus' articulation of his desire to do the will of the Father, for example—

> ...ἵνα ποιήσω τὸ θέλημα τοῦ πέμψαντός με...
> (John 4:34)
> ...to do the will of him who sent me.

> ...οὐχ ἵνα ποιῶ τὸ θέλημα τὸ ἐμὸν ἀλλὰ τὸ θέλημα τοῦ πέμψαντός με
> (John 6:38)
> ...not to do my own will, but the will of him who sent me.

Equivalent expressions occur frequently throughout the Gospel, e.g., "I seek the will of the one who sent me (5:30; cf. 7:17. 28).

Two other passages from Ps 39 appear to be operative in the Fourth Gospel. First, the moment when those who come to arrest Jesus fall backwards (εἰς τὰ ὀπίσω John 18:6) might be seen as an "answer" to David's prayer that his enemies might be turned back in Ps 39:15...ἀποστραφείησαν εἰς τὰ ὀπίσω καὶ ἐντραπείησαν οἱ θέλοντές μοι κακά.[24] Second, it is difficult to avoid hearing in Jesus' defence before the high priest that he has always spoken openly, teaching in synagogues and in the Temple where all Jews come together (John 18:19), an echo of Ps (39)40—

---

[24] Obviously, reference to other psalms of David, e.g., Pss (34)35:4 or Ps (55:10) 56:9, is also possible. Since the Fourth Gospel phrase εἰς τὰ ὀπίσω, which occurs in these psalms, is an unnecessarily long way of saying ὀπίσω, the case for allusion to the Psalter is strong.

εὐηγγελισάμην δικαιοσύνην ἐν ἐκκλησίᾳ μεγάλῃ·
ἰδοὺ τὰ χείλη μου οὐ μὴ κωλύσω·
κύριε, σὺ ἔγνως.
τὴν δικαιοσύνην σου οὐκ ἔκρυψα ἐν τῇ καρδίᾳ μου,
τὴν ἀλήθειάν σου καὶ τὸ σωτήριόν σου εἶπα,
οὐκ ἔκρυψα τὸ ἔλεός σου καὶ τὴν ἀλήθειάν σου ἀπὸ συναγωγῆς πολλῆς.

I have announced righteousness in the great congregation.
I will not close my lips;
Lord, you know.
I have not hidden your truth within my heart,
I have declared your salvation.
I have not hidden your love and your truth from the great assembly
(Ps 39:10-11. cf. Prov 1:20).

The Jesus who might be imagined as the speaker of this and the Ἰδοὺ ἥκω passage may best be described in Johannine terms, as saying, Εἰς τοῦτο ἐλήλυθα εἰς τὸν κόσμον, ἵνα μαρτυρήσω τῇ ἀληθείᾳ (18:37). Jesus' kingship consists in bearing witness to the truth. According to Ps (39)40, coming to do God's will involves declaring and not hiding God's truth.

All of this would suggest that the Fourth Evangelist encountered an early Christian interpretation of Ps 39:7-9 similar to that which inspired Heb 10:5-7. The declaration, Ἰδοὺ ἥκω...τοῦ ποιῆσαι τὸ θέλημά σου, ὁ θεός μου, in this τῷ Δαυιδ ψαλμός, was understood in light of the idealized portrayal of David as "the man after God's heart" (1 Sam 13:14) who would do all God's will (Acts 13:22) which developed in Second Temple Judaism. As a prophetic intimation of Jesus' coming to do the will of the Father, it coloured the Johannine understanding of Jesus as ὁ ἐρχόμενος ἐν ὀνόματι κυρίου (John 12:13).

2. *Pss (41-42)42-43*

As another sample of the more fleeting type of verbal allusion to the psalms, we look now at the Fourth Gospel usage of Ps (41-42)42-43. This provides us with a paradigmatic instance of an interpretation received in the passion tradition which John has anticipated in earlier sequences of his narrative.

It would appear from the synoptic concentration of psalm usage in the Passion Narrative that this was the earliest form of Christian *relecture* of details in the Psalter as prophetic of Jesus' sufferings.[25] The

---

[25] Cf. the pre-Pauline formula, κατὰ τὰς γραφάς, in 1 Cor 15:3-4. The prominence of Ps 109 in early Christianity would suggest that perhaps the interpretation of Jesus' resurrection as an enthronement at God's right hand was the original impetus for the mining of the Psalter for anecdotal details to amplify the passion tradition. See Juel, *Messianic Exegesis*, 136.

psalms in which a distraught David prayed in the first person singular (i.e., to use the *Gattungsforschung* terminology, the "laments of the individual") with their constant shift from prayer in distress to praise for God's deliverance, were seen as a prophecy of Jesus' death and resurrection. Through a process of imaginatively envisaging Jesus as the speaker in these psalms which told of his sufferings and vindication, Johannine Christians developed their own Christological reading of the Psalter which is, in many ways, quite unique in NT Christianity. As we have seen, the Fourth Evangelist has, as it were, advanced the psalm usage into his account of the ministry, in keeping with his bringing forward of aspects of the Passion narrative, for example, the trial of Jesus. We will begin, therefore, by looking briefly at the role of Ps 41-42 in the passion tradition.

In his study of the origin of the Passion Narratives, *The Passion as Liturgy*, Etienne Trocmé explains how—

> ...an early church that constantly read the Psalms of David was influenced by some of them in the process of elaboration of a tradition telling the story of the Passion, to the extent of structuring some episodes or enlarging some after models found in the Psalms.[26]

We have already seen how the Johannine treatment of single psalm verses exemplifies this process (for example, Ps 21:19 enacted in the two-action dividing of Jesus' garments in John 19:24). Here we are concerned with a structural influence of a whole psalm, Ps 41-42.[27] Trocmé suggests that this psalm may have had a role in shaping the passion tradition—

> ...the words of Jesus speaking to his disciples in Gethsemane (Mark 14.34 and Matt 26.38) before he goes aside to pray are clearly reminiscent of Pss. 42.6, 12 and 43.5, a hymn of despair and hope in God which may have helped to mould the Markan story around three prayers of Jesus.[28]

It is precisely the ternary form of this episode that Trocmé thinks may have something to do with its literary dependence on Ps 41-42 with its thrice-repeated refrain. This may indicate a liturgical *Sitz im Leben* for the archetypal Passion Narrative. The inter-textual links operate firstly at the level of verbal contacts between Jesus' words and the text of the psalm—

---

[26] Trocmé, *The Passion as Liturgy*, 59.
[27] That these two psalms form one poem is clear from the refrain they share. See Dahood, Psalms I, 255; Sabourin, *The Psalms*, 239. Stuhlmueller, *Psalms 1*, 226, notes the lack of a title for Ps (42)43 in the Hebrew and the fact that some very early Hebrew MSs indicate no break between the two. The LXX provides the untitled "third stanza" of Pss 41-42, i.e., LXX Ps 42, with the superscript τῳ Δαυιδ.
[28] Trocmé, *The Passion as Liturgy*, 59.

Ps 41:6	Mark 14:34; Matt 26:38
ἵνα τί <u>περίλυπος</u> εἶ, <u>ψυχή</u>, καὶ ἵνα τί <u>συνταράσσεις με</u>;	<u>Περίλυπός</u> ἐστιν <u>ἡ ψυχή</u> μου ἕως θανάτου·

At another level, they connect the ternary structure of the scene—three times Jesus withdraws to pray and returns to find the disciples sleeping—with the three-stanza form of the psalm with its thrice-repeated refrain portraying, in a Christological reading, the dynamic of Jesus' prayer in its movement from desolation to trust in God—

> ἵνα τί περίλυπος εἶ, ψυχή, καὶ ἵνα τί συνταράσσεις με;
> ἔλπισον ἐπὶ τὸν θεόν, ὅτι ἐξομολογήσομαι αὐτῷ·
> σωτήριον τοῦ προσώπου μου ὁ θεός μου.[29]
>
> Why are you very sad, my soul and why do you trouble me?
> Hope in God, for I will give thanks to him,
> the salvation of my countenance, my God.

In a major article which appeared in 1978, Johannes Beutler has suggested that Ps 41-42 is of considerable importance in the Fourth Gospel.[30] In his opinion, two Johannine passages, John 12:27 and 13:21 contain indications of Fourth Gospel dependence on the Gethsemane tradition, from which the Mark 14:34 allusion to Ps 41-42 stems. The verbal aspect of their intertextual relationship to Ps 41-42 is presented in the following table—

(1) John 12:27	Ps 41:7
Νῦν <u>ἡ ψυχή μου τετάρακται</u>, καὶ τί εἴπω;	πρὸς ἐμαυτὸν <u>ἡ ψυχή μου ἐταράχθη</u>·
	Ps 41-42 (refrain x 3)
Πάτερ, <u>σῶσόν</u> με ἐκ τῆς ὥρας ταύτης;	ἵνα τί περίλυπος εἶ, ψυχή, καὶ ἵνα τί συνταράσσεις με; ...<u>σωτήριον</u> τοῦ προσώπου μου ὁ θεός μου.
(2) John 13:21	Ps 41:7
Ταῦτα εἰπὼν [ὁ] Ἰησοῦς <u>ἐταράχθη</u> τῷ πνεύματι...	πρὸς ἐμαυτὸν <u>ἡ ψυχή μου ἐταράχθη</u>·

---

[29] These lines appear three times, at LXX Ps 41:6, 41:12 and 42:5. We will refer to them as the Ps 41-42 refrain.

[30] Johannes Beutler, "Psalm 42/43 im Johannesevangelium," 33-57.

John 12:27 and 13:21 have frequently been explained as the Johannine equivalent of the synoptic Gethsemane scene.[31]

> John clearly experienced some difficulty, even embarrassment, in adapting this particular prayer to fit his own conviction of Jesus' absolute control over his own destiny: Jesus openly wonders whether he should pray in the way that tradition demanded, and then decides that he should not" 'And what shall I say? "Father, save me from this hour"? No, for this purpose I have come to this hour' (12:27).[32]

We encounter in this scene not just an eloquent silence with regard to psalm allusions received in the tradition, but a conscious independence from the tradition, highlighted for the reader by means of a negative assessment of that tradition put on the lips of Jesus himself. Jesus refuses to pray the psalms! Still, for all the Evangelist's care, the indelible traces of the tradition show through elsewhere in his work.

Beutler is not the first to notice the link with Ps 41-42.[33] His particular contribution, however, is his insight that the reading of Ps 41-42, learned from the passion tradition, has had wider repercussions in the Gospel. In positing the link between Ps 41:7 and John 13:21, he notes that ψυχή corresponds to πνεῦμα (used with ταράσσω in John 11:33) and καρδία (used with ταράσσω in John 14:1), all three being Septuagintal renderings of נפש. This leads him to see a reflection of Ps 41-42 in the distress of Jesus when confronted with the death of Lazarus and in the grief of the disciples at the prospect of Jesus' death.

John 11:33	Ps 41-42 refrain
Ἰησοῦς...ἐνεβριμήσατο τῷ πνεύματι καὶ <u>ἐτάραξεν</u> ἑαυτόν...	ἵνα τί περίλυπος εἶ, ψυχή, καὶ ἵνα τί <u>συνταράσσεις</u> με;
John 14:1	
Μὴ <u>ταρασσέσθω</u> ὑμῶν ἡ καρδία·	ἵνα τί περίλυπος εἶ, ψυχή, καὶ ἵνα τί <u>συνταράσσεις</u> με;
<u>πιστεύετε εἰς τὸν θεόν</u> καὶ εἰς ἐμὲ πιστεύετε.	<u>ἔλπισον ἐπὶ τὸν θεόν</u>...
John 14:27	Ps 41-42 refrain
μὴ <u>ταρασσέσθω</u> ὑμῶν ἡ καρδία μηδὲ δειλιάτω.	ἵνα τί περίλυπος εἶ, ψυχή, καὶ ἵνα τί <u>συνταράσσεις</u> με;

---

[31] Ashton notes, *Understanding*, 36, concerning the Gethsemane scene, "This is not found as such in the Fourth Gospel, but 12:27-33 clearly depends upon the same tradition." See Brown, *John I - XII*, 475 and Schnackenburg, *The Gospel*, II, 386.

[32] Ashton, *Understanding*, 327.

[33] Beutler is particularly influenced by Dodd's testimony theory. See Dodd, *Historical Tradition*, 37-38, 42, 53-71.

Beutler believes that there is a connection between the weeping of Jesus in the Lazarus story (John 11:35) and the Gethsemani tradition, especially as reflected in Heb 5:7 which mentions Jesus' tears.[34] Building upon his perception of verbal contacts between John 14:1 and the psalm, he notes that the words of Jesus in John 14:2 also have their correspondences in Ps 41-42—

John 14:2	Ps 41:5
ἐν τῇ οἰκίᾳ τοῦ πατρός μου μοναὶ πολλαί εἰσιν	ὅτι διελεύσομαι ἐν τόπῳ σκηνῆς θαυμαστῆς ἕως τοῦ οἴκου τοῦ θεοῦ (Ps 41:5).[35]

While it is possible to find many of the phrases which Beutler uses elsewhere in the Psalter,[36] Beutler's proposal benefits from the added "weight" of the role played by Ps 41-42 in the formation of the Passion Narrative. Still, it is significant that the alternatives which have been proposed are all psalms.

If Ps (41-42)42-43 is, in fact, as influential as Beutler believes, then there has been a progression in the reception of the psalm analogous to the way in which Ps (68)69 has been appropriated in the Johannine circle. Ps (68)69 would appear to have entered Johannine consciousness as a passion testimony (the reference to the vinegary drink), but the quotation in John 15:25 shows how it has enabled the community to see their own predicament as, in some sense, a repetition of Jesus' experience of distress and therefore, as also full of the promise of a glorious outcome.[37]

There is another way in which the Johannine reception of Ps (68)69 helps us appreciate the full significance for John of Ps (41-42)42-43. We have seen that Ps (68:22)69:21 occurs in the Johannine passion narrative as enacted rather than as explicitly cited. While the "vinegar to drink" motif from the passion tradition was

---

[31] Beutler sees John's verb δακρύω (a *hapax* in the NT) instead of the more usual κλαίω (used twice of Lazarus' mourners in John 11:33), as a verbal allusion to Ps 41:4—ἐγενήθη μοι τὰ δάκρυά μου ἄρτος ἡμέρας καὶ νυκτός. The connection with Hebrews is also brought out by Brown, *Death of the Messiah*, 227-233.

[35] Beutler explains, "Psalm 42/43 im Johannesevangelium," 49, that "My Father's house" is *johanneisch* for the OT "House of God" and that the μοναί correspond to the Hebrew שׁכן. Moreover, he adds, Ps 41:5 is the only psalm passage where the terms οἶκος and σκηνή occur together.

[36] In a response to Beutler's article, Freed, "Psalm 42/43 in John's Gospel," 62-73, holds that most of what Beutler claimed for Ps (41-42)42-43 could also be said of passages in other psalms: Ps (54)55, Ps (85)86, Ps (142)143 and, especially, Ps 6.

[37] Such an appropriation of the psalms is not unique to Johannine Christianity. The same dynamic underlies Luke's use of Ps (30)31 in Luke 23:46 and Acts 7:59.

certainly the catalyst for Jesus' cry of thirst, the actual word Διψῶ, is not tied to Ps 68:22, but opens up the text to other possibilities. The intertextuality thus experienced has the effect of "untying the text."[38] Beutler is among those who believe that there may be an allusion in John 19:28 to either Ps 41:3 or Ps 62:1. His recognition of the role of Ps 41-42 in the portrayal of the disciples' longing to be with Jesus in the Father's house (cf. John 14:1) contributes to a better understanding of Jesus' cry of thirst on the cross as an allusion to Pss 41:3 and 62:1. The depiction of the disciples' ταραχή illuminates Jesus' distress in the face of death, both his own (John 12:27; 13:21) and that of Lazarus (John 11:33). Its resolution in confident longing for the Father's house is modelled on Jesus' desire "to depart out of this world to the Father" (John 13:1), an outcome which he earnestly desires for his disciples (John 17:24). Thus, according to Beutler, John has discovered in Ps 41-42 "the prayer of the departing Revealer, yearning for God's holy realm and God's countenance."[39]

3. *Ps (22)23 and Ps (94)95*

Allusion to the Psalter has contributed significantly to the Johannine portrayal of Jesus as Davidic and divine shepherd. Jesus self designation as ideal shepherd (John 10:11.14) is a moment which Fischer identifies as a classic example of the Christologization of the psalms.[40] As we have seen, shepherding is a Davidic role in Jewish tradition,[41] a role in which David, as remembered and as expected, mirrors God's relationship with Israel.[42] The whole dynamic of the Shepherd Discourse and the ensuing altercation climaxing in Jesus' statement, ἐγὼ καὶ ὁ πατὴρ ἕν ἐσμεν (John 10:30), makes it clear that Jesus' claim to a divine prerogative is the issue in dispute. In fact, as we will see, this moment turns out to be another exceedingly apt "hermeneutical door," this time, into a Christological reading of the Psalter in which expressions of worship addressed to God are interpreted as addressed to Jesus.

In the Fourth Gospel Jesus declares, Ἐγώ εἰμι ὁ ποιμὴν ὁ καλός (John 10:11.14). This is one of several ἐγώ εἰμι sayings in the Fourth

---

[38] See the title of Robert Young's book, *Untying the Text*.
[39] Beutler, "Psalm 42/43 im Johannesevangelium," 57.
[40] "Christological Interpretation," 232.
[41] Of course, we do not exclude the idea that Moses was Israel's shepherd/king, current in formative Judaism. This, however, is an aspect of the "Davidicisation" of Moses. See Philo, *Mos.* XI, 60; Jos. *Ant.* 4.302-06; Ps-Philo, *LAB* 19:3. 9.
[42] See Ezek 34 where both God (v. 15) and David (v. 23) are to shepherd Israel and where the people's experience of David's shepherding is an experience God's presence (v. 30-31).

Gospel where the predicate is an adaptation of an OT symbol for God's relations with Israel.⁴³ As such, it may reflect the Johannine reception of Ps (22)23:1, Κύριος ποιμαίνει με, to which it possibly alludes thematically.⁴⁴ Following Hollander's example, we seek now to go beyond "the genial 'cf.'" and to gain entrance to "the caves of ambience and the chambers of meaning."⁴⁵ There is an implication inherent in the suggestion of a reference to Ps (22)23:1 in John 10:11.14 that Jesus is to be identified with the Κύριος of the psalm, that he is somehow speaking as God.⁴⁶ Indeed, because of its Ἐγώ εἰμι formulation, Jesus' statement lends itself to interpretation in terms of his role as heavenly Revealer.⁴⁷ A sense of how the Fourth Evangelist might have arrived at such a position may help us appreciate the *relecture* which Ps (22)23 and the psalms generally have undergone in the Johannine milieu.

Looked at from what we might call the intertextual perspective, Ἐγώ εἰμι ὁ ποιμὴν ὁ καλός might evoke the Deuteronomistic description of the young shepherd anointed by Samuel—

> ...καὶ οὗτος πυρράκης μετὰ κάλλους ὀφθαλμῶν καὶ ἀγαθὸς ὁράσει κυρίῳ· καὶ εἶπεν κύριος πρὸς Σαμουηλ Ἀνάστα καὶ χρῖσον τὸν Δαυιδ, ὅτι οὗτος ἀγαθός ἐστιν (1 Sam 16:12).
>
> ...and he was ruddy, with beauty of eyes, and good in the sight of the Lord, and the Lord said to Samuel, "Arise and anoint David, for he is good."

---

⁴³ See Brown, *John I-XII*, Appendix 4, 533-38, at 534.

⁴⁴ This is suggested in Reim, *Studien*, 160. See also *Greek NT* (United Bible Societies), 906. Obviously, Ps (22) is only one of many psalm passages where God is depicted as Israel's shepherd, e.g., Ps (73)74:1, Ps (78)79:13, Ps (94)95:7, Ps (99)100:3, mentioned by Barrett, *The Gospel*, 310, as background to John 10:11. Ps (22)23:1 is a particularly direct statement of God's role as shepherd.

⁴⁵ Hollander. *The Figure of Echo*, 88.

⁴⁶ For Aune, *The Cultic Setting*, 72, the origin of the ἐγώ εἰμι sayings "can only be adequately accounted for by considering them the products of Christian prophecy, whereby the risen Lord speaks in the first person singular through inspired Christian prophets within a cultic setting."

⁴⁷ In the Fourth Gospel, there are two main categories of ἐγώ εἰμι sayings—absolute (John 8:24. 28. 58; 13:19) and predicative (e.g., 6:35; 11:25; 14:6). In the absolute sayings, Jesus claims the right to echo God's self-revelation in his own self-disclosure, a claim which his interlocutors find blasphemous. The predicative sayings have been described by Ashton, *Understanding*, 186, as "miniature gospels," invitations to believe and find life in Jesus' name (John 20:31) which are then explained in the subsequent discourse. While the two categories are to be distinguished, their relation should not be neglected. As Ashton has shown, *Understanding*, 184-89, both have their roots in an understanding of Jesus' relationship with his Father based on the analogy of the ANE concept of agency. The Revealer can claim God's name because he is endowed with the authority of the one who sent him. In the predicative ἐγώ εἰμι sayings Jesus explains the purpose of his mission, thereby identifying himself as the emissary of God who bears the authority of God's name. See Borgen, "God's Agent," 67-78.

A connection between the substantive, κάλλος (used in the physical sense in 1 Sam 16:12) and the adjective καλός (used in the moral sense in John 10:11.14) might suggest itself. True, in light of the re-imagining of David in Second Temple Judaism, the physical description would have been received figuratively as referring to moral beauty. However, the real link may be that between ἀγαθὸς and καλός. As Brown, who translates Ἐγώ εἰμι ὁ ποιμὴν ὁ καλός as "I am the model shepherd," explains,—

> Greek *kalos* means "beautiful" in the sense of an ideal model of perfection; we saw it used in the "choice wine" of ii 10. Philo (*Agric*, 6, 10) speaks of a good (*agathos*) shepherd...In the Midrash Rabbah II 12 on Exod iii 1, David who was the great shepherd of the OT is described as *yafeh ro'eh*, literally "the handsome shepherd" (see 1 Sam xvi 12).[48]

The connection with David is particularly strong in view of the contacts between Jesus' self-portrayal in the Shepherd Discourse and the biblical portrayal of David—not only the remembered David, but also the expected David of the future.[49]

The shepherd is, of course, a universal image of the king in the ancient world, one which emphasizes his leadership and his provision for the needs of his subjects. In the Israelite view, the king rules in the name of God. He is subject to God. He is assessed according to his fidelity to God's commandments.[50] He is a "good shepherd," (ἀγαθός, καλός), to the extent that God's shepherding of Israel is reflected in his exercise of kingship. David's rule, as idealized in Israel's imagination and memory, is a reflection of God's kingship. David is "a man after God's heart" (1 Sam 13:14), referred to by God as "a king for myself" (1 Sam 16:1). In the psalm with which the Deuteronomistic history sums up his life, David declares, "I have kept the ways of the Lord" (Ps 18:21 = 2 Sam 22:22). This perception of him is implied in his charge to Solomon to follow his example of obedience to God's commandments.[51] It is also implied in the biblical summary of the reign of Hezekiah, who "did what is right in the eyes of the Lord, according to all that David his Father had done" (2 Kgs 18:3). Thus, at this intertextual level of interpretation,

---

[48] Brown, *John I - XII*, 386.

[49] As envisaged, e.g., in Isa 40:11, Ezek 34:23; 37:21-24, texts mentioned as background to John 10 by Beutler, "Der Alttestamentlich-jüdischer Hintergrund der Hirtenrede," 25.

[50] See the references to whether or not the kings of Israel "did what is right in the eyes of the Lord" throughout 2 Kgs, e.g., 2 Kgs 12:2; 14:3. 24; 15:3, etc.

[51] 1 Kgs 2:3. Cf. 1 Kgs 3:14; 9:4.6; 11:38. Just as Saul lost the kingship for not keeping God's commandments (1 Sam 15:10), so part of the kingdom will be torn from Solomon's hand for a similar failure on his part (1 Kgs 11:10-11).

informed by the resonances we have mentioned, the reader hears Jesus' statement, Ἐγώ εἰμι ὁ ποιμὴν ὁ καλός, as a claim to be the full realization of the ideal of kingship associated with David.

There is, however, a deeper, theological sense in which the Johannine Jesus is ὁ ποιμὴν ὁ καλός. With Jesus, kingship in the name of God takes on a wholly new meaning. Every feature of ideal kingship in Israel is present in Jesus to a surpassing degree. For example, the idea that the king reflects God's kingship to the extent that he obeys God's commandments, has flowed into the Johannine conception that Jesus' laying down of his life is his willing response to a command which he has received from God, his Father (John 10:17-18). In fact, it may even help to explain the Johannine Jesus' reference to his "word" which his disciples are to keep as his "commandments" (John 13:34; 14:15.21; 15:10. 12). In trying to make sense of what might otherwise appear as "an unnecessarily roundabout and even a clumsy and obscure way of emphasizing the need for faith," Ashton has proposed "two alternative, possibly complementary answers"—the "new Moses" motif—that Jesus' commandments are a new Law, and the influence of the testament and commission genres in which the departing person gives commandments to those being left behind.[52] A third proposal, along the lines of the second of these, might add even more light—the "new David" motif.

Both the Deuteronomist and the Chronicler portray David, towards the end of his life, as bidding Solomon farewell and giving him a commission. In summing up David's career, the Deuteronomist thinks mainly in terms of his military exploits, from his risking of his life to fight Goliath until his defeat of all his enemies (2 Sam 22:1). The commission to Solomon in 1 Kgs 2:5-9 is thus in a similar vein. For the Chronicler, David's principal achievement is his provision for the building of the Temple. So the Chronicler's version of David's commission to Solomon, therefore, reflects this preoccupation (1 Chr 28:8-21). Both traditions also show David making a prayer of thanksgiving in which he declares that he has accomplished what God has commanded him to do (2 Sam 22 = Ps [17]18; 1 Chr 29:10-19). The Deuteronomistic prayer, Ps 18, is particularly relevant to our concerns, as David stresses in it that he has kept God's commandments (2 Sam 22:21-24 = Ps (17)18:21-23).[53]

---

[52] Ashton, *Understanding*, 458-59.
[53] Ashton, *Understanding*, 448-49, has drawn attention to the Deuteronomistic version of David's final testament (1 Kgs 2:1-9), "one of the earliest examples of the farewell discourse form in the Bible," as a biblical precedent for the combination of farewell (testament) and commission found in John 13-17.

In the laying down his life, Jesus is seen as the king who keeps the command of God (John 10:18; 14:31). In his prayer, he too declares that he has kept God's command, accomplishing the work God gave him to do (John 17:4). He passes on the command of God to him as a commission from himself to "his own" (John 15:12-13), a point well taken by the earliest commentator on the Fourth Gospel (See 1 John 3:16). It is surely no accident that the Johannine understanding of Jesus' death reflects the two perspectives found in the two traditions of David's last testament and final prayer: David as shepherd "laying down" his life to protect God's flock from marauding beasts (John 10:11, the "Vézelay David") and David as "Temple-builder/founder" (John 2:19-21).

Looked at from the "intertextual" perspective, therefore, the "hour" when Jesus reaches his complete fulfilment of the Father's command appears as his most David-like moment—ὁ ποιμὴν ὁ καλὸς τὴν ψυχὴν αὐτοῦ τίθησιν ὑπὲρ τῶν προβάτων (John 10:11; cf. 1 Sam 17:34-36). Looked at from the "theological" angle, it is the great revelatory moment when Jesus' kingship so powerfully reflects God's that it reveals him as ruling, as shepherding, in God's name and therefore, as possessing the authority to define himself in terms which echo God's self-revelation. Bringing both perspectives together, we can see how Jesus can conceivably be identified both as "David" and as the Κύριος of Ps (22)23:1.

Another possible allusion to Ps (22)23 in the Fourth Gospel may help to clarify this notion. We return again to John 6, keeping in mind the memories and expectations which the plentiful food provided by Jesus would have stirred. As we saw in our discussion of John 6:31, the provision of lavish banquets on special occasions was part of the king's role as provident shepherd.[54] Ps 22:2—εἰς τόπον χλόης, ἐκεῖ με κατεσκήνωσεν—is proposed by Schnackenburg as a background to the χόρτος πολύς (John 6:10). He sees this, coupled with the absence of the Marcan and Lukan division of the crowd into groups, as distinguishing John's account from the synoptic reminiscence of Israel's camp in the wilderness.

> The evangelist is not interested in presenting a 'wilderness scene.' He is interested in the saving time of Passsover (cf. v.4). The 'much' grass gives the feeding a festive character. Jesus, the messianic shepherd, is leading his people—no longer the old Israel, but the universal people of God—in green pastures (cf. Ps 23:2) and provides them with rich nourishment in the meadows, the food of life (cf. 10:9-10).[55]

---

[54] See p. 141-142 above.
[55] Schnackenburg, *The Gospel*, II, 16.

If this is so, the portrayal of Jesus as ὁ ποιμὴν ὁ καλός (John 10:11.14), feeding his flock forges a further intertextual link with Ps (77)78, as quoted in John 6:31. In Ps (77)78:20 the fathers voice their doubt that God is going to be able to give his people bread, to prepare a table for them in the desert. In a surprising reversal of the old story of Israel putting God to the test, Jesus tests Philip. Does he believe that Jesus can "prepare a table" and provide bread for the crowd? The reader familiar with the Psalter, appreciates the irony, knowing that the words of Ps (22)23:5, ἡτοίμασας ἐνώπιόν μου τράπεζαν, are most appropriately addressed to Jesus. For such a reader, the psalm would also have struck resonances with the theme of David as shepherd/king with which it concludes. Against this background, it is clear that, in Johannine thought, Ἐγώ εἰμι ὁ ποιμὴν ὁ καλός is a revelatory declaration by Jesus of his identity with the Lord who is depicted as shepherd in Ps 22.

This identification is carried through in the subsequent unfolding of the "Shepherd Discourse." Of particular significance are several striking parallels with Ps (94)95—

John 10:28	Ps 94:7ABC
καὶ οὐχ ἁρπάσει τις αὐτὰ ἐκ τῆς χειρός μου.....	ὅτι αὐτός ἐστιν ὁ θεὸς ἡμῶν, καὶ ἡμεῖς λαὸς νομῆς αὐτοῦ καὶ πρόβατα χειρὸς αὐτοῦ.
John 10:29	
...καὶ οὐδεὶς δύναται ἁρπάζειν ἐκ τῆς χειρὸς τοῦ πατρός	" "
John 10:3-4	Ps 94:7D
καὶ τὰ πρόβατα τῆς φωνῆς αὐτοῦ ἀκούει...καὶ τὰ πρόβατα αὐτῷ ἀκολουθεῖ, ὅτι οἴδασιν τὴν φωνὴν αὐτοῦ·	...σήμερον, ἐὰν τῆς φωνῆς αὐτοῦ ἀκούσητε,
John 10:37-38	Ps 94:9
...εἰ οὐ ποιῶ τὰ ἔργα τοῦ πατρός μου, μὴ πιστεύετέ μοι· εἰ δὲ ποιῶ, κἂν ἐμοὶ μὴ πιστεύητε, τοῖς ἔργοις πιστεύετε,	...οὗ ἐπείρασαν οἱ πατέρες ὑμῶν, ἐδοκίμασαν καὶ εἴδοσαν τὰ ἔργα μου.

We begin with the allusion in John 10:28 to Ps 94:7, which is, perhaps, the most obvious.[56] In the Gospel, Jesus gives the assurance that his sheep will not be snatched out of (ἐκ) his hand. Being in Jesus' hand means being one of "his own"—ὁ πατὴρ ἀγαπᾷ τὸν υἱόν, καὶ πάντα δέδωκεν ἐν τῇ χειρὶ αὐτοῦ (John 3:35). The background is the idea that the king holds the people that God has given him in his hand.[57] The shepherd context would suggest that this is correct. In the deft move from ἐκ τῆς χειρός μου to ἐκ τῆς χειρὸς τοῦ πατρός, a shift mirroring that from intertextual to theological perspective, the Evangelist hints at the identity between Jesus and the divine shepherd of Ps 94.[58]

Once this identity is established, the reader can hear in Jesus' claim that his sheep recognize and listen to his voice an echo of the psalmist's plea, σήμερον, ἐὰν τῆς φωνῆς αὐτοῦ ἀκούσητε (Ps 94:7).[59] If they listen with faith they will hear the voice of God—ὃν γὰρ ἀπέστειλεν ὁ θεὸς τὰ ῥήματα τοῦ θεοῦ λαλεῖ (John 3:34). The echoes of Ps 94 produce the effect of aligning those who refuse to listen to Jesus with "the fathers" who tested God in the desert, in spite of having seen God's works. As in John 6, they repeat the pattern of their ancestors' unbelief.

---

[56] This is the only allusion to Ps 94 mentioned by Beutler in his "Der Alttestamentlich-jüdischer Hintergrund."

[57] Ashton, *Understanding*, 321-22, arguing for the importance of the sender/agent image in the Gospel, refers to the phrase "to give into the hand (of)" as "a formal expression signifying the transmission of authority." The Midrashic examples cited by Ashton in support of this are all stories about kings. 1 Kgs 11:29-31 tells of ten tribes being torn from the hand of Solomon. The king's hand may also lead rather than actually hold the people, as in the reference to David in Ps (77)78:72—καὶ ἐν ταῖς συνέσεσι τῶν χειρῶν αὐτοῦ ὡδήγησεν αὐτούς.

[58] Günter Reim, "Späte Entdeckung: Psalm 95 als Darstellungsprinzip für das Wirken des johanneischen Jesus," in *Jochanan: Erweiterte Studien zum Alttestamentlichen Hintergrund des Johannesevangeliums* (Hessdorf-Hannberg: Verl. der Ev.-Luth. Mission, 1995) 369-88, refers to several rabbinical interpretations of this verse where "He" (the Messiah) is "our God" and we are the people of his pasture." Whether Reim's examples, which are all Talmudic, can be relied on as true reflections of 1st cent. CE exegesis of the psalm remains a question.

[59] In the view of Günter Reim, Ps 94 functions *als Darstellungsprinzip für das Wirken des johanneischen Jesus*. Reim sees the "today" of the psalm as echoed in the Johannine concept of "the hour." Thus the σήμερον of the psalm becomes in Johannine thought, "the hour" of which Jesus says, ἀμὴν ἀμὴν λέγω ὑμῖν ὅτι ἔρχεται ὥρα καὶ νῦν ἐστιν... (John 5:25). In this "today," the eschatological sabbath, the dead will hear the voice of the Son of God and live, "eternal life" being the Johannine equivalent of the psalm's "rest;" The Johannine νῦν, seen, for example in John 13:31—Νῦν ἐδοξάσθη ὁ υἱὸς τοῦ ἀνθρώπου—is, therefore, in Reim's view, a reflection of the psalm's σήμερον. The Gospel's call to faith invites the reader to hear God's voice in Jesus—σήμερον, ἐὰν τῆς φωνῆς αὐτοῦ ἀκούσητε (Ps 94:7). Cf. *Jochanan*, 369-88.

4. Allusion to David's Psalms and the Shaping of Johannine Christology

So far, we have found that there are numerous examples in the Fourth Gospel of the unfolding of the story of Jesus in "Davidic" terms—through evocation of οἱ ὕμνοι Δαυιδ τοῦ υἱοῦ Ιεσσαι (Ps 71:20). We have also found that there is a different type of allusion which leads the reader to identify Jesus as the κύριος addressed in the psalm. Sometimes one psalm is used in both these ways. To give a further example, a fleeting reminiscence of Ps 26, Τοῦ Δαυιδ πρὸ τοῦ χρισθῆναι,[60] in John 18:6 follows the fulfilment pattern which we observed in the explicit citations in the Passion Narrative.

Ps 26:2	JOHN 18:6
...οἱ θλίβοντές με καὶ οἱ ἐχθροί μου αὐτοὶ ἠσθένησαν καὶ ἔπεσαν·	...ὡς οὖν εἶπεν αὐτοῖς, Ἐγώ εἰμι, ἀπῆλθον εἰς τὰ ὀπίσω καὶ ἔπεσαν χαμαί.

As evildoers, intent on devouring Jesus (cf. the verb καταφαγεῖν in John 2:17), draw near, they fall backwards.[61] Yet there is another quite different type of allusion to this psalm. On the analogy of the contribution of Ps 22:1 to Ἐγώ εἰμι ὁ ποιμὴν ὁ καλός (John 10:11.14), Ps 26:1, Κύριος φωτισμός μου, has probably influenced the saying in John 8:12, Ἐγώ εἰμι τὸ φῶς τοῦ κόσμου.[62] In this form of psalm allusion, Jesus claims for himself what the psalm states as a divine prerogative. This claim is underlined by Jesus' use of the Ἐγώ εἰμι formulation.[63]

Günter Reim believes that the Evangelist found crucial scriptural support for such an understanding of Jesus in Ps 44:7-8, where the king is addressed as ὁ θεός. He believes that the confession of Jesus as God in the Fourth Gospel stems from a pre-Christian messianic

---

[60] The LXX superscript most likely refers to the anointing by Samuel (1 Sam 16:1-13), since we know from *LAB* 59:4 that an interpretation of Ps 26:10 was current according to which the line "My father and mother have forsaken me" referred to Jesse's underestimation of his youngest son.

[61] Even the phrase εἰς τὰ ὀπίσω in John 18:6 is found in three other Τῷ Δαυιδ psalms with reference to David's triumph over his enemies—LXX Ps 34:4; 39:15 and 55:10. All three psalms are alluded to elsewhere in the Fourth Gospel. Ps 34:19 contains the phrase οἱ μισοῦντές με δωρεάν, often mentioned as a potential source for the scripture in John 15:25. The address to God in Ps 34:23, ὁ θεός μου καὶ ὁ κύριός μου, may also have influenced John 20:28. The light that is life, of Ps 55:14, may have contributed to John 1:4 and 8:12.

[62] In using φωτισμός rather than φῶς, the LXX does not render the Hebrew literally, perhaps fearing a Persian-style identification of God with impersonal light.

[63] As Brown, *John I - XII*, 537, explains: John draws attention to the implications of divinity in the use of *ego eimi* by Jesus. "After the use in viii 58, the Jews try to stone Jesus; after the use in xviii 5, those who hear it fall to the ground."

understanding of Ps. (44)45 known in Johannine circles.⁶⁴ In Jewish exegesis, Ps (44)45 was understood as referring to the King Messiah, particularly since it portrays him as God's anointed.⁶⁵ In the Targum, v. 2 reads:

> Pulchritudo tua, O rex christe, praestantior est filiorum hominum datus est spiritus prophetiae in labiis tuis.

An early date for this reading may be indicated by the fact that the author of Hebrews, who uses Ps (44:7)45:6 to the same purpose, is the only other NT writer, apart from the Fourth Evangelist, who directly states that Jesus is God (Heb 1:8-9). Although there is no direct evidence of the influence of Ps (44)45 in the Fourth Gospel, it does present a king whose δικαιοσύνη is principally evident in his judicial pronouncements (cf. John 5:30; 8:16).⁶⁶ Certainly, its exhortation to the king, βασίλευε ἕνεκεν ἀληθείας καὶ πραΰτητος καὶ δικαιοσύνης (v. 5), its "programme" for kingship in the name of God, is fully implemented by the Johannine Jesus whose kingship consists of bearing witness to the truth (John 18:37).

A recurring refrain of this chapter has been the role which the Psalter seems to have played in the delineation of Johannine Christology, In considering this possibility, it is important to remember that other quite different strands of thought, both Jewish and non-Jewish, have also played their part in reinforcing the Johannine conviction that Jesus can appropriately be called θεός.⁶⁷ In particular, we should allow for the influence of the currents of thought in Hellenistic Judaism which are reflected in the Philonic use of the epithet θεός for Moses. It seems, though, that the contribution of David as psalmist to this development is far greater than has, perhaps, been recognized.

At two critical junctures in the Fourth Gospel, the word θεός appears as a designation for Jesus. It is used with reference to his preexistence as the Λόγος in John 1:1 and to his risen state in John 20:28. Both occurrences form an inclusion, especially if John 20:30

---

⁶⁴ Reim, "Jesus as God in the Fourth Gospel: The Old Testament Background," *NTS* 30 (1984) 158-60, reprinted in Reim, *Jochanan*, 348-51.

⁶⁵ *Gen. Rab* 99 (63b), for example, connects the reference to the sceptre not departing from Judah (Gen 49:10) with Ps 45:7.

⁶⁶ Reim finds support for his thesis of the influence of Ps 44 on the Fourth Gospel in several passages where Justin uses Ps 44 Christologically, *Dial.* 38:1, 43:3, 56:14, 86:3. See "Jesus as God," 159-60.

⁶⁷ See Meeks, "Equal to God," in R. T. Fortna and B. T. Gaventa (ed.), *The Conversation Continues: Studies in Paul and John in Honour of J. Louis Martyn* (Nashville: Scholars, 1990) 309-21.

represents an earlier ending of the Gospel.⁶⁸ The second occurrence take the form of an allusion to Ps 34:23—ὁ θεός μου καὶ ὁ κύριός μου. As we have seen, the earliest example we have of a Christian prayer to Christ, Stephen's prayer in Acts 7:59, also identifies the glorified Jesus as the Κύριος addressed in the psalms.⁶⁹ It is possible that Ὁ κύριός μου καὶ ὁ θεός μου (John 20:28) may reflect a Christian reaction against the imperial cult under Domitian.⁷⁰ It is unlikely though, given the extent to which the Fourth Gospel is rooted in the Jewish Scriptures, that this address to Jesus is merely a parody of the pagan title without any foundation in the biblical tradition.⁷¹

In suggesting that the psalm passages mentioned in this section could possibly have furnished a rationale for the attribution of the title θεός to Jesus, we are not ignoring the address, ὁ θεός μου καὶ ὁ κύριός μου in Ps (34)35. Obviously, this bears an impressively strong verbal resemblance to Thomas' confession in John 20:28 and could very well have provided the words, Ὁ κύριός μου καὶ ὁ θεός μου. Ps 34:23 could thus be the clue to John 20:28 from the perspective of its precise literary dependence on the Psalter text. What the broader allusiveness to the Psalter, which we have posited, would have provided for the Evangelist was biblical authority for putting these words on Thomas' lips as an address to the risen Jesus. This authority is not, of course, limited to any particular text and not even to the Psalter. It arises out of the whole portrayal of Jesus in biblical terms which have hitherto been associated only with God. As Neyrey has shown, the acclamation of Jesus as "Lord and God" in John 20:28 is based largely on material in John 8, 10 and 11 where Jesus claims equality with God, the divine power to bestow life, the right to execute judgement, entitlement to the honour due to God, the power to raise the dead, and the possession of life in himself.⁷²

In this section, we encountered several revelatory moments in the

---

⁶⁸ A third possible occurrence is in John 1:18, if one accepts the reading, μονογενὴς θεός. In this case, the title would refer to Jesus' earthly life viewed from the perspective of his role as Revealer.

⁶⁹ See Adalbert Hamman, "La prière chrétienne et la prière paienne: formes et différences," in Wolfgang Haase (ed.), *Aufstieg und Niedergang der Römischen Welt*, II Principat, 23. 2 (Berlin: De Gruyter, 1980) 1190-1246, at 1238.

⁷⁰ See Swanston, *The Community Witness*, 23, and B. A. Mastin, "A Neglected Feature of the Christology of the Fourth Gospel," *NTS* 22 (1976) 32 - 52, at 44. Suetonius records that Domitian was addressed as "Dominus et Deus Noster" (*Domitianus* xiii, 2).

⁷¹ Schnackenburg, *The Gospel*, 3, 333, disagrees that Domitian's title influenced John. Hengel explains that *Dominus et Deus* was not an official title for Domitian. See his "Christological Titles in Early Christianity," in Charlesworth (ed.), *The Messiah*, 425-448, at 431.

⁷² See Neyrey, " 'My Lord and my God," 158.

Fourth Gospel where Jesus exhibits characteristics or uses ways of speaking which, according to the psalms, are divine prerogatives. We thus saw that allusion to David's psalms has played an important part in the development of a Christology which would regard θεός as a fitting title for Jesus. We do not claim that the Psalter was solely responsible for this development, nor do we claim that such a usage of the Psalter is exclusive to John.[73] While with agree with Aune that the Fourth Gospel is "the product of the worship and piety of the Johannine Community,"[74] we are wary of assuming that any role that the Psalter may have played in this development necessarily involves a liturgical *Sitz im Leben* for the *relecture*.[75] We are convinced, though, that the Psalter, as received in the Johannine circle, was an important component of the biblical authorization for the theological development whereby Jesus came to be regarded as "God."[76] Johannine Christians regarded Jesus' equality with God as consistent with Jewish monotheism. The Johannine Jesus even echoes the *Shema* (Deut 6:4-5) when he addresses God as τὸν μόνον ἀληθινὸν θεόν (John 17:3). His divine status must therefore, in their view, have had a sound basis in Judaism's Scriptures. The identification of the Κύριος addressed in the psalms as the risen Jesus is one of several possible backgrounds in the biblical and pseudepigraphical writings which have been proposed: the notion of the appearing

---

[73] The phrase, ὅταν ἔλθῃ ἐνδοξασθῆναι ἐν τοῖς ἁγίοις αὐτοῦ, in 2 Thess 1:10, e.g., shows that in Pauline circles, Jesus is expected to be manifested as ὁ θεὸς ἐνδοξαζόμενος ἐν βουλῇ ἁγίων of Ps (67:36)68:35.

[74] In Aune's view, the three elements which have gone into the depiction of the Johannine Jesus are (1) traditions about the historical Jesus, (2) elements of traditional Christologies, (3) "the current experience of the living Jesus as the mediator of salvific benefits and the object of cultic worship within the Johannine Community." See *The Cultic Setting*, 76.

[75] According to Hengel, "the unfolding of the titles of divine dignity of the Crucified one ... occurred not so much in the prose of theoretical speculation or missionary preaching, as in the poetic, inspired language of hymn and confession, i.e., they had their place in the *worship service*. " See "Christological Titles," 429. It is frequently inferred from statements such as this that Jewish-Christians would have been especially familiar with the psalms from their synagogue worship. This is not necessarily the case. The extensive use of the Psalter in liturgical prayer is a third century CE Christian development. As historians of Christian liturgy such as Joseph Jungmann have long since demonstrated, for the first two hundred years of Christianity, the Jewish tradition was retained in which the Psalter was part of the lectionary rather than a hymnal—*nicht Gesangbuch, sondern nur Lesebuch*. See *Missarum Solemnia* (Vienna: Herder, 1949) I, 540, n. 9.

[76] This involved a re-interpretation of the originally royal/messianic title, "Son of God." Apparently, the bestowal of the title "Son of God" on a human being was not outside the realm of possibility in Palestinian Judaism since it did not necessarily carry any connotation of divinity. 4Q246, e.g., contains the words, "He shall be hailed (as) the Son of God and they shall call him the Son of the Most High." See Fitzmyer, "The Aramaic Language," 14.

deity (See the references to the theophanies to Jacob, Abraham and Isaiah in John 1:51; 8:56; 12:41),[77] the Jewish notion of royal agency,[78] and Jewish angelology.[79]

In assessing the contribution of the Psalter, it is important to be aware of the way the Johannine reception of the psalms fluctuates between two different, but complementary, readings. Particularly in the psalm citations coming from the pre-Gospel tradition, Jesus appears to be the "David" who prays to his Lord in the psalm. At other times, particularly in the uniquely Johannine allusions to the psalms, Jesus appears to be the Κύριος addressed in the psalm.[80] We are required to make a shift in perspective very similar to that which John Ashton finds demanded by the biblical and pseudepigraphical angelological texts which he proposes as authorizing the claim of Jesus' divinity—

> ...the perplexingly rapid shift of perspective demanded ... is matched very clearly...by a similar oscillation between the claims attributed to Jesus in the Fourth Gospel, where we experience the same difficulty in saying whether Jesus is claiming divinity with the Father or acknowledging his complete dependence. The pendulum swings back and forth between the two poles in such a way that we cannot arrest it at either pole, or indeed at any point in between, without radically misrepresenting the evidence.[81]

We would thus say that the Johannine reception of the psalms, as exemplified by the more transitory allusions we have been discussing, oscillates between the Christian and Christological readings.[82] The reminiscence of David's career not only shows the reader that Jesus is the Christ (the Christian reading), but leads that reader to the further insight that being ὁ Χριστός is inextricably

---

[77] Neyrey, "'My Lord and my God': The Divinity of Jesus in John's Gospel," in K. Richards (ed.) *1986 SBL Seminar Papers* (Atlanta: Scholars, 1986) 152-71, at 152-54.

[78] See Borgen, "God's Agent," 67-78, and Meeks, "Equal to God," 309-22.

[79] Ashton proposes as background to the Johannine confession of Jesus as "God" features of Jewish angelology such as the biblical "angel of the Lord" who is frequently indistinguishable from God (e.g., Gen 21:17), the angel of the Exodus (Exod 23:20), the *Angelus Interpres* (e.g., Dan 10:5; Ezek 8:2). See *Studying John*, Ch. 3, "Bridging Ambiguities," 71-89.

[80] We have already seen that when John takes a psalm reference from the tradition, he shows a preference for formal citation. Reim, *Jochanan*, 371, has found that, in contrast to the direct citation characteristic of the Evangelist's use of traditional material, when he crosses over into his own *Sprechweise*, the use of scripture is much less immediately obvious, as it lacks introductory formulae and is frequently adapted.

[81] Ashton, *Studying John*, 87-88.

[82] Fischer, "Le Christ dans les Psaumes," *La Maison-Dieu*, 27 (1951) 86-113, at 94 & 100, shows that this oscillation continues into the Patristic period. See also Daniélou, *Études d'exégèse judéo-chrétienne*, 141-42.

bound up with being ὁ υἱὸς τοῦ θεοῦ. Jesus is so completely "one" with the Father that he is actually to be identified and worshipped as the Κύριος and θεός addressed in the psalms (the Christological reading).

This two-directional reading reflects an interpretation of the Psalter at the very point where messianism becomes Christology. The Johannine allusions to the psalms indicate what was undoubtedly a significant hermeneutical event, a radically transformative reception of the source text. The oscillation "back" to the "David" (Christian) reading ensured the continuity with Jewish tradition, while the forward movement of the Christological *relecture* conveyed the essential newness of the Johannine Jesus' claim of equality with God.

D. *Echo: Ps (109)110 and Ps 8*

In order to illustrate this extremely subtle form of intertextual reference, we will use Ps (109)110. We will also refer to Ps 8 which, as we saw in Ch. 1, tends to be connected with Ps (109)110 in the early Christian reception.[83] We commented there that the apparent absence of Ps (109)110 from the Fourth Gospel is, at first glance, surprising, given the psalm's importance in early Christian tradition. The Evangelist can hardly have been unaware of its Christological interpretation, particularly of the idea it engendered that the risen Jesus is seated at God's right hand (cf. Ps 109:1). The Fourth Gospel thus confronts us with an apparent authorial decision against citing this verse. We suggest that the Fourth Gospel's "silence" on a psalm so vocal in the NT may turn out to be just as eloquent as its citation of others.

To begin our search for traces of Ps (109)110 which may be suggestive of its influence on the Fourth Gospel, we return to the scene in the Portico of Solomon (John 10:22-39), the context for the Fourth Gospel citation of Ps (81)82:6. We recall the literary dependence of this scene on the synoptic trial narratives.[84] The synoptic accounts record Jesus' reply to his interrogators that he is to be "seated at the right hand of God." This claim amounts to a total subversion of the trial proceedings. Those who would judge Jesus are confronted with the prospect of his eventual elevation to the divine realm and his role as eschatological judge. The image used in the synoptics to convey this notion comes from Ps 109:1—

---

[83] See p. 54 above.
[84] See p. 165-66 above.

Εἶπεν ὁ κύριος τῷ κυρίῳ μου Κάθου ἐκ δεξιῶν μου,
ἕως ἂν θῶ τοὺς ἐχθρούς σου ὑποπόδιον τῶν ποδῶν σου.

As we have suggested already, the absence of any reference to this verse in the Fourth Gospel is probably to be explained theologically. Its inherent implication that Jesus was raised from a lower to a higher status would not have been acceptable in a circle where Jesus is believed to be "equal with God" (John 5:18). However, the early Christian reflection on Ps (109)110:1 to which the synoptics bear witness seems to have inspired the Fourth Evangelist to develop his own way of presenting Jesus as subverting the trial proceedings. In this way, the Evangelist confronts the opponents of Johannine Christianity with the spectre of the eschatological judgement already present in the division provoked by Jesus. As we saw in Ch. 3, the scene in the Portico of Solomon follows closely the pattern of the synoptic trial narratives. One cannot avoid the impression that the received tradition on which the Fourth Evangelist based his scene would also have contained the reference to Ps 109:1. In order to appreciate how the Fourth Evangelist has modified this tradition in keeping with his Christology, we will need to trace the long and rather complex exegetical tradition which was to facilitate the application of Ps (109)110:1 to Jesus' heavenly enthronement.

There is evidence of several interpretations of Ps (109)110:1 in post-biblical literature,[85] but by far the most well attested interpretation is a messianic reading which interprets the psalm in light of Dan 7:13. This reading has roots in OT kingship ideology. It was the belief of ancient Israel that it was God who actually set the king on the throne of Israel (1 Kgs 10:9). In the work of the Chronicler, we can see the metamorphosis of this belief already in progress. Under the impact of the royal ideology expressed in Ps (109)110, it developed into the idea that God placed the king on the heavenly throne to rule for the Lord his God and to execute the divine justice (2 Chron 9:8). The later rabbinical development of this theme is exemplified by R. Akiba's claim that David sat on a throne adjacent to God's (cf. *b. Sanh.* 38b), although the possible impact of Christian claims cannot be ruled out. Ps (109)110:1 is frequently associated in early Jewish exegesis with Dan 7:13.[86] The connection was made

---

[85] E.g., *T. Job* 33:3, where a throne at the right hand of God appears to be the reward for a righteous sufferer, and *T. Levi* 8:3 which is influenced by the court propaganda of the Hasmoneans who used Ps (109)110 and its reference to Melchizedek to justify their claim to priestly and royal prerogatives. See Hay, *Glory at the Right Hand*, 23-24; Juel, *Messianic Exegesis*, 137.

[86] For a convenient survey of the relevant material, see Ashton, *Understanding*, 358-61.

through Dan 7:9 in which heavenly thrones are placed and the Ancient of Days takes his seat. It was deduced from the psalm that there are two heavenly thrones, one for God and a second intended for the enthronement of the mysterious Son of Man to whom God would grant dominion. All of this was deemed to have been prophetically foretold by David when he wrote, "The Lord said to my Lord, sit at my right." The outcome of this exegetical tradition is evident in 1 Enoch 61:8—"He placed the Elect one on the throne of glory; and he shall judge all the works of the holy ones in heaven above, weighing in the balance their deeds." We find the same pairing of exaltation to divine status and appointment as eschatological judge in 1 En 62:3—"On the day of judgement, all...shall see and recognize him, how he sits on the throne of glory."[87] The reference in 1 Enoch 48:10 and 52:4, to this figure as "the Messiah of the Lord of Spirits" would indicate a coalescence of the roles of Messiah and "Son of Man" which is very important for an understanding of the Johannine Son of Man.[88] This is because the Danielic Son of Man, as connected with the Ps (109)110 tradition of exaltation to God's right hand, is the taproot of the Johannine Son of Man sayings.[89] Norman Perrin proposed, some years ago, that an early Christian pesher-style tradition linked not only Ps (109)110:1 and Dan 7:13, but also Zech 12:10, quoted in John 19:37.[90] More re-

---

[87] 1 Enoch, therefore, shows that the tradition preserved in *Midr. Teh.* 18.29, according to which Ps (109)110 is understood as referring to "the time to come, when the Holy One, blessed be he, seats the Lord Messiah at his right hand" may well date back to the 1st cent. CE. *Midr. Teh.* 2.9, also preserves a commentary on Ps 2:7 ('You are my son') understood as addressed to the nation, in which Ps (109)110:1 is linked to Dan 7:13.14. In Acts 7:55-58, we find a 1st cent, CE author depicting a Jewish audience as extremely alert to the implications of this linkage as applied to Jesus.

[88] The late 1st cent. CE text, 4 Ezra also speaks of a figure flying on the clouds of heaven (4 Ezra 13:3) who has earlier been identified as "My Son, the Messiah" (4 Ezra 7:29). The coalescence of the Messiah with the Danielic Son of Man also underlies the teaching attributed to R. Aqiba, that the two thrones were for God and for David (*b. Ḥag.* 14a).

[89] In this we follow Ashton, *Understanding*, 340, in preference to the interpretation of the title as referring to the historical presence of Jesus as a human figure held by Moloney, *The Johannine Son of Man*, 208-20, and Thomas L. Brodie, *The Gospel According to John: A Literary and Theological Commentary* (New York/Oxford: Oxford University Press, 1993) 58, 353.

[90] Perrin believes that in the process which produced Mark 14:62, there were two separate strands of Christian pesher tradition: one an interpretation of Dan 7:13 combined with Ps (109)110:1, the other of Zech 12:10. Rev 1:7 combines elements from each of these: the looking on the pierced one from Zech 12:10, the coming on the clouds from Dan 7:13. According to Perrin, these two pesher traditions are reflected in Mark 13:26 and 14:62, where the "seeing" motif reflects Zech 12:10, the sitting at the right hand of God reflects Ps (109)110:1 and the coming on the clouds reflects Dan 7:13. They are the basis for further theologizing in John

cently, Matthew Black has suggested that passages such as these may stem from a midrash on Ps (109)110 in circulation in NT times which influenced both the Enoch material and the gospels.[91] Jesus' claim in the synoptics that he is to be seated at the right hand of the Father amounts to a definition of his messianic status in terms of his eventual heavenly exaltation and appointment as eschatological judge. Mark and Matthew both add to their Ps (109)110 allusion—καὶ ὄψεσθε τὸν υἱὸν τοῦ ἀνθρώπου ἐκ δεξιῶν καθήμενον τῆς δυνάμεως—the clause inspired by the phrase in Dan 7:13—καὶ ἐρχόμενον μετὰ τῶν νεφελῶν τοῦ οὐρανοῦ.[92]

From the synoptics, we know that, at least in some circles, the Davidic superscript of Ps (109)110 was taken quite literally in NT times, and that David was believed to have referred in this psalm, under divine inspiration, to the Messiah as his Lord. We saw, in Ch. 1, that Ps 109:1 is frequently conflated with Ps 8:7 to form what amounts to an early Christian variant of Ps 109:1.[93] This was no doubt encouraged by the presence of the expression υἱὸς ἀνθρώπου in Ps 8:5. Some even see this as the "missing link" explaining the connection between Ps 109 and Dan 7.[94] Perhaps, though, a more potent influence was the Davidic reading of both Ps 8 and Ps (109)110.

An example of a Davidic reading of Ps 8 is preserved in the *Midrash Tehillim*—

> In saying *Thou puttest all things under his feet* (Ps 8:7), they were referring to David, all of whose enemies fell before him, so that he said: "Then did I beat them small as the dust of the earth: (2 Sam 22:43).[95]

Late though the dating of the Midrash is, there is nothing in this interpretation which could not have been gleaned from the Scripture itself by an earlier interpreter versed in the traditions which we explored in Ch. 2 above. For example, Jacquet has drawn attention to the similarity between v. 4 of the לדוד Ps 8—

1:51. See "Mark XIV.62: The End Product of a Christian Pesher Tradition?" *NTS* 13 (1966) 150-55, at 150-51.

[91] See "The Messianism of the Parables of Enoch: Their date and contribution to Christological Origins," in Charlesworth (ed.), *The Messiah*, 145-68, at 153-54.

[92] While Luke does not use Dan 7:13 at precisely this point, he alludes to it in a similar vein in 18:8 and 21:36.

[93] See p. 54 above.

[94] So, W. D. Walker, "The Origin of the Son of Man Concept as Applied to Jesus," *JBL* 91 (1972) 482-90.

[95] *Midr. Teh.* 8.7. Another reading preserved in *Midr. Teh.* 18.32 interprets Ps (109)110:1 as a reference to Goliath falling on his face at David's feet (1 Sam 17:49).

> ...what is man that you are mindful of him
> and the son of man that you care for him?

—and the Deuteronomistic presentation of David as a man insignificant in his origins and exalted by God. In 1 Sam 18:18, for example, David says to Saul, "Who am I and who are my kinsfolk and my father's family that I should be son-in-law to the king?" In 2 Sam 7:8, David says to God, "Who am I, O Lord God, and what is my house that you have brought me thus far?"[96] In our discussion of the "Davidic" superscripts in Ch. 2, we saw that those responsible for the addition of the superscript לדוד to Ps 8 would appear to have discerned a parallel between David, raised from lowliness to kingship, and humankind, created from dust and "crowned with glory and honour" (Ps 8:5).[97] The David of Ps (17)18:38 (=2 Sam 22:39) boasts of how his enemies always fell under his feet. Not only Ps (109)110, but also the narrative traditions refer to David's enemies surrounding him "until the Lord put them all under the soles of his feet" (1 Kings 5:3). Therefore, what we perceive as a conflation of Ps 8:7 and Ps (109)110:1 in the above-mentioned NT texts could equally be explained, by means of the Davidic authorship of the psalms, as a direct throwback to the narrative traditions about David. Imaginative expansion of the "until" motif in light of the narrative traditions is a feature of Jewish exegesis of Ps (109)110, as is shown by a Davidic reading of Ps (109)110:1 preserved in the Psalms Targum—

> Dixit Dominus in verbo suo, se constiturum me dominum totius Israelis, sed dixit mihi denuo opperire vero Saulem qui est de tribu Benjamin <u>donec</u> moriatur
>   quia non convenit regno cum socio
> et postea ponam inimicos tuos suppedaneum pedum tuorum.

The basic midrashic technique employed here is one which we have encountered frequently in this study: the exegesis of the psalm in the light of the David narratives. The particular form which it takes in this case, the imaginative expansion of the "until," is a feature of another first century CE reading of the same verse, Paul's Christian reading in 1 Cor 15:25-27. Jesus is to reign—ἄχρι οὗ θῇ πάντας τοὺς

---

[96] Jacquet, *Les Psaumes*, I, 304.
[97] This shows that, even at quite an early stage in the transmission of the Psalter, David had acquired a collective significance, a paradigmatic role with regard to Israel (and even with regard to humankind) as a whole. Jacquet's insight is confirmed by Brueggemann who has discerned a correlation between the David narratives and Gen 2 - 11. See "David and His Theologian," *CBQ* 30 (1968), 156-81 and "From Dust to Kingship" 1-18.

ἐχθροὺς ὑπὸ τοὺς πόδας αὐτοῦ (Ps 109:1 conflated with Ps 8:7). For Paul, Christians live in the "until" period, awaiting the subjection of authorities, powers and ultimately death itself to their Lord.

This brief tradition history of Ps (109)110:1 shows how readily its portrayal of David's ideal kingship, as remembered and as expected in the future, was able to provide for various groups in early Christianity a conceptual model for describing the divine status of the risen Jesus as messianic king and eschatological judge. Given the NT evidence for such a widespread use of Ps (109)110:1 in early Christianity, we can expect that it would have made some impact on Johannine thought, even as a motif that the Fourth Evangelist might have regarded as in need of major recasting.

In Schnackenburg's opinion—

> ...it cannot be doubted that the Johannine concept of the "exaltation" takes up the synoptic "sitting at the right hand of God"...though it does not treat it as a second stage following the "humiliation" of the Cross, but rather understands the Crucifixion itself as "exaltation."

In our discussion of the quotation from Ps (81)82 in John 10:34, we referred briefly to Nathaniel's profession—Ῥαββί, σὺ εἶ ὁ υἱὸς τοῦ θεοῦ, σὺ βασιλεὺς εἶ τοῦ Ἰσραήλ—and showed how it follows the structure of the questioning of Jesus in the synoptic trial—"Are you the Christ?" "Are you the Son of God?"[98] On the analogy of Acts 7:56, Jesus' reply to Nathaniel bears a strong resemblance to the synoptic trial references to Jesus as eschatological judge at the right hand of God—

> Ἀμὴν ἀμὴν λέγω ὑμῖν, ὄψεσθε τὸν οὐρανὸν ἀνεῳγότα καὶ τοὺς ἀγγέλους τοῦ θεοῦ ἀναβαίνοντας καὶ καταβαίνοντας ἐπὶ τὸν υἱὸν τοῦ ἀνθρώπου (John 1:51).[99]
>
> "Truly, truly, I say to you, you will see heaven opened, and the angels of God ascending and descending upon the Son of man."

Not surprisingly though, John avoids any reference to Ps (109)110:1, preferring to combine his Dan 7:13-14 allusion with Gen 28:12.[100]

Might we not also see in the idea that the Father has given Jesus authority to exercise judgement because he is the Son of Man (John 5:27), a reflection of the psalm as interpreted along the lines we have described—the echo of Ps (109)110 referring to the judicial role of

---

[98] See p. 165-66 above.
[99] Cf. Mark 14:62, Matt 26:64, Luke 22:69.
[100] Hay, *Glory at the Right Hand*, 69, sees a similarity between this "faith vision" promised to Nathaniel and the Lucan idea that believers such as Stephen (Acts 7:55-56) may be granted such visions even before the second coming of Jesus. Hay's insight would confirm the contribution to John 1:51 of the *relecture* of Ps (109)110 reflected in the synoptic trial scenes.

the Messiah, and the title "Son of Man" alluding to Jesus' heavenly origin? Certainly, the reception we have posited for the psalm illuminates a passage such as John 5:22-23—

> ...οὐδὲ γὰρ ὁ πατὴρ κρίνει οὐδένα, ἀλλὰ τὴν κρίσιν πᾶσαν δέδωκεν τῷ υἱῷ, ἵνα πάντες τιμῶσι τὸν υἱὸν καθὼς τιμῶσι τὸν πατέρα.
>
> ...the Father judges no one, but has given all judgement to the Son, that all may honour the Son, even as they honour the Father.

John adopts the apocalyptic idea that at the end of the age, the Messiah or "Son of Man" will exercise the office of judgement alongside or in place of God. He adapts it, however, in accordance with his view that the eschatological judgement is *now*. Thus Ps (109)110:1 has contributed significantly, even if not overtly, to the development of a major theme in the Fourth Gospel, that of judgement.[101] As we have proposed, its hidden influence is particularly strong in John 10:22-39. Perhaps the Evangelist gives us a hint of this by setting this scene in the portico named after Solomon, the king whom God seated on the heavenly throne and endowed with wisdom to judge (cf. Wis 9:3.5.7.12).

There are several other indications in the Fourth Gospel that early Christian reflection on Ps 109 as applied to Jesus has flowed into Johannine thought. The particular Johannine use of the verb ὑψόω is a case in point. It may owe something to Ps (109)110:7—

> ...ἐκ χειμάρρου ἐν ὁδῷ πίεται·
> διὰ τοῦτο <u>ὑψώσει</u> κεφαλήν.[102]
>
> From the brook on the way he shall drink
> therefore he will lift up (his) head.

It was suggested by Dodd that διὰ τοῦτο ὑψώσει κεφαλήν influenced John 8:28—Ὅταν ὑψώσητε τὸν υἱὸν τοῦ ἀνθρώπου, τότε γνώσεσθε ὅτι ἐγώ εἰμι.[103] This would be especially significant if, as we proposed in our discussion of Jesus' thirst, the rather mysterious reference to the hero of the psalm drinking from a spring at his moment of victory forms part of the background to John 19:28-30.[104] The strong tradi-

---

[101] Hay, *Glory at the Right Hand*, 81, would trace the idea that the reign of Jesus "consists mainly or exclusively in judgement" ultimately back to Ps (109)110.

[102] This does not, of course, exclude other potential antecedents for the Johannine ὑψοῦν, notably Isa 33:10—Νῦν ἀναστήσομαι, λέγει Κύριος, νῦν δοξασθήσομαι, νῦν ὑψωθήσομαι.

[103] *Historical Tradition*, 89. For Dodd, John 8:28 is a theological equivalent of Mark 14:62. Both texts draw upon Ps (109)110:1 (and Dan 7:13-14) in order to describe a heavenly enthronement of Jesus which is to be manifested to those about to put him to death. While Mark alludes to Κάθου ἐκ δεξιῶν μου, John opts for the verb ὑψοῦν.

[104] See p. 226 above.

tion of a Davidic/messianic interpretation of Ps (109)110 would allow that v. 4, Σὺ εἶ ἱερεὺς εἰς τὸν αἰῶνα, could be one aspect of the background to the popular belief expressed in John 12:34 that the Christ is to remain for ever. Then, there is the psalmist's reference to the king as "my Lord" which may account, at least in part, for Thomas' address to Jesus, (John 20:28). "My Lord" is frequently found in the Deuteronomistic History as the form of address from the royal protocol of the Davidic court.[105] Ps (109)110, interpreted, as we have shown, in terms of exalted heavenly beings, helps us to understand the "quantum leap" from Ὁ κύριός μου, understood as a deferential form of address to a king, to Ὁ κύριός μου used "in the same breath" as ὁ θεός μου. In the light of the correspondence between Ps 109:1 and Ps 8:7 in Jewish and early Christian exegesis, we might also see a possible background to Jesus' claim in John 17:2 that the Father has given him power over all flesh (... καθὼς ἔδωκας αὐτῷ ἐξουσίαν πάσης σαρκός ...) in Ps 8:7—

... καὶ κατέστησας αὐτὸν ἐπὶ τὰ ἔργα τῶν χειρῶν σου,
πάντα ὑπέταξας ὑποκάτω τῶν ποδῶν αὐτοῦ...

In view of the reception of Ps 8, which sees a parallel between humankind, created from dust and "crowned with glory and honour" (Ps 8:5), and David, raised from lowliness to kingship, such an allusion would contribute significantly to the royal character of Jesus' prayer for those the Father has given to him.

Finally, since, in the Johannine perspective, heavenly enthronement is not a position that Jesus assumes after his resurrection, but is his prerogative as the pre-existent Word, we would have to ask if Ps (109)110 might somehow have flowed into the concept of the μονογενὴς θεὸς ὁ ὢν εἰς τὸν κόλπον τοῦ πατρὸς (John 1:18).[106] There are no verbal indications of dictional dependence on Ps 109. However, it is quite possible that *thematically* Johannine pre-existence theology represents the terminus of an ongoing transformative reception of Ps 109 which drew from its scriptural witness to Jesus' heavenly en-

---

[105] Its plural variant "our Lord" refers to David in 1 Kgs 1:11.43.47 but is directed only to God in post-exilic literature, e.g., Neh 10:29; Ps 8:1; Ps 134:5. It was to form the early prayer of the Aramaic-speaking church, Μαρανα θα: Our Lord, come (1 Cor 16:22).

[106] Hay, *Glory at the Right Hand*, 56-57, cites *Gosp. Bart.* 1.32 ("Even when I taught among you, I sat at the right hand of the Father...") as exemplifying the early Christian tendency to project the session at God's right hand back into the period of Jesus' earthly life. He suggests that the reading, ὁ ὢν ἐν τῷ οὐρανῷ, at John 3:13 may be the product of similar theological reflection stemming from Ps (109)110. This would resonate with the "Davidic" overtones which we suggest would have been carried by the word μονογενὴς, if viewed as equivalent to πρωτότοκος in, for example, Ps 88:28. See p. 249 above.

thronement the implication that since οὗτος ἦν ἐν ἀρχῇ πρὸς τὸν θεόν (John 1:2), his heavenly enthronement was a return to where he had been before (John 6:62 cf. 3:13).[107] This would represent the most radical aspect of the transformation wrought on Ps 109:1 through its absorption into the texture of the Fourth Gospel.

In attempting to hear the echoes of Ps (109)110 and to define its role in the Fourth Gospel, we might recall the characteristics of the biblical text as language, as articulated by Schneiders in the passage quoted in the Introduction to this chapter – "... language, what is said, stands always against *the background of the vast unsaid* to which it is related."[108] Applying this principle, we might regard Ps 81:6, cited in John 10:34, for example, as the "said" which is more fully appreciated against the background of the "unsaid" Ps (109)110:1. As we have seen, an attentiveness to the hidden presence of the "unsaid" Ps (109)110 in other passages of the Gospel uncovers for us some of the "raw material" with which the Fourth Evangelist has worked.

E. *Johannine Resonances of Ps 1-2: An Intertextual Relationship?*

The last speech of Jesus in the Fourth Gospel is the beatitude, μακάριοι οἱ μὴ ἰδόντες καὶ πιστεύσαντες (John 20:29). A key to its importance is the way it leads directly into the conclusion where the Evangelist states his purpose in writing the Gospel. While it could possibly show the influence of Sir 48:11,[109] its particular significance for this study is that it is strongly reminiscent of the beatitude which forms the last line of Ps 2—

> ... μακάριοι πάντες οἱ πεποιθότες ἐπ᾽ αὐτῷ.[110]
> Blessed are all who trust/believe in him.

---

[107] Meeks, *The Prophet-King*, 296-97, confronted with the problem that the Johannine exaltation of the Son of Man has little in common with the legends of Moses' ascension, turns to the Mandaean writings and their "enthronement of the returning messenger in the upper world" as a closer analogy to the Fourth Gospel. Our proposals concerning David's Ps (109)110 would undermine what Meeks regards as the strongest support for his hypothesis, "that the Johannine christology is connected with gnostic mythology."

[108] Schneiders, *The Revelatory Text*, 138.

[109] An allusion to Μακάριοι οἱ ἰδόντες σε, a reference to the blessedness of those who were privileged to be contemporaries of the timebound Elijah, would point up the transcendent superiority of the risen Jesus. There are indications in the Fourth Gospel of a concern to challenge Jewish expectations surrounding the figure of Elijah. Notably, John 3:13 "corrects" the notion of heavenly ascent associated with him.

[110] In the literature of early Christianity, the verb πειθώ with which the LXX renders the Hebrew חסה (take refuge in) of Ps 2:11 can have the meaning "depend on, trust in, put one's confidence in," e.g., the taunting of the crucified Jesus in Matt

The slight ambiguity of LXX version suits John's context perfectly. In contrast to the Hebrew which proclaims the blessedness of those who trust in God, the Greek speaks of trust in "him," thus permitting a Christian reading of the macarism as referring to faith in Jesus, which is actually, in the Johannine reception, faith in God.

In exploring the effect of Davidic attribution on the final editing of the Psalter, we noted briefly the character of Pss 1-2 as a programmatic prologue, by means of which "the entire Psalter ... is made to stand theologically in association with David as a source of guidance for the way of the righteous."[111] It is to this prologue that we now turn.

Pss 1-2 may have originally prefaced just Book 1 of the Psalter, or perhaps the תפלות of David" (Pss 3-72, that is, Books 1-2). By NT times, Pss 1-2 appear to have been received as a preface to the entire Psalter.[112] There are literary connections between them—the inclusion formed by the "beatitudes" at the opening of Ps 1 and the end of Ps 2, the theme of "the two ways" with its characteristic terms, אבד and דרך, found together in both psalms—"...but the way of the wicked shall perish (Ps 1:6)" and "...lest he be angry and you perish in the way (Ps 2:11)."[113] To some, these convergences suggest a compositional unity. E. Lipinsky, for example, believes that Ps 2 was inserted into Ps 1 as an interpretation of the way of the

---

27:43 where πέποιθεν ἐπὶ τὸν θεόν reflects Ἤλπισεν ἐπὶ κύριον of Ps 21:9. This is a sense which πειθώ frequently approximates in the LXX, where, for example, in the Psalter it expresses David's faith in God (e.g., Ps 10:1; 24:2; 56:2; 117:8; 124:1) as contrasted with misdirected faith in idols (Ps 113:16; 134:18), men (Ps 117:8), or princes (Ps 117:8; 145:3). In Ps 117:8-9 πεποιθέναι is clearly the equivalent of ἐλπίζειν. Πειθώ can also mean "be convinced, come to believe, believe," as in a passage somewhat akin to John 20:29, Luke 16:31—Εἰ Μωϋσέως καὶ τῶν προφητῶν οὐκ ἀκούουσιν, οὐδ' ἐάν τις ἐκ νεκρῶν ἀναστῇ πεισθήσονται. See Bauer, *Greek-English Lexicon*, 639. Πειθώ is not used in the Fourth Gospel, but its LXX usage, particularly in the Psalter, would readily permit the designation, οἱ πιστεύσαντες in John 20:29 (aorist participle of πιστεύω, John's preferred verb for references to faith) to be regarded as the dynamic equivalent of οἱ πεποιθότες in Ps 2:12.

[111] Sheppard, *Wisdom as a Hermeneutical Construct*, 142, as quoted on p. 67 above.

[112] Several factors combine to create this impression. The absence of a superscript to Ps 2 is unusual for Book 1 where only Pss 10 and 33 lack a superscript. See Patrick D. Miller, "The Beginning of the Psalter," in McCann, *The Shape and Shaping*, 83-92, at 84. In the Western text of Acts 13:33 (*Codex Bezae*), the Lucan Paul presents Υἱός μου εἶ σύ, ἐγὼ σήμερον γεγέννηκά σε (Ps 2:7) as ἐν τῷ πρώτῳ ψαλμῷ γέγραπται (Cf. also *b. Ber.* 9b, where Ps 19 in the Hebrew numbering is given as Ps 18.). This could mean that Ps 1 was still unnumbered. See Wilson, "The Shape of the Book of Psalms," *Int* 46 (1992) 129-42, at 132. Alternatively, what we know as Pss 1 and 2 may have formed "the first psalm." See E. Lipinsky, "Macarismes et Psaumes de Congratulation," *RB* 75 (1968) 321-67, at 331-32.

[113] For "the two ways," see Deut 11:26-28; 30:15-20; Jer 21:8; Prov 12:28; 14:2; 1QS 3.13-4.26. *Didache* I - VI, 1 contrasts the way of the Law with the way of death. Cf. *Ep. Barn.* 18.1-2.

wicked as revolt against the Lord's anointed. This had the effect that the last part of Ps 1, the wisdom injunction concluding with the macarism, became the conclusion to Ps 2.[114] Whatever its literary development may have been, the prologue, as received under David's sponsorship of the Psalter, tells of how the way of the wicked will perish when God sends the Messiah.[115] Already, sympathetic vibrations within the Fourth Gospel begin to stir, but before we direct our attention to them to them, we need to discover more about the reception of Pss 1-2 in Second Temple Judaism.

The treatment of Pss 1-2 in 4QFlor is illustrative of the "Davidic" reception which we have been suggesting. Here, explanations of verses from Pss 1 & 2 follow immediately on citations from 2 Sam 7. The blessedness of those who do not walk in the counsel of the wicked (Ps 1:1) is taken as a description of the present Qumran community. Then Ps 2 refers to a future time of trial when the nations will take counsel together against the Lord and his Anointed.[116] There is ample evidence elsewhere in the DSS that the community saw their way of life as achieving the blessedness which Ps 1 promises to those who meditate day and night on the Law.[117] The 4QFlor *pesher* on Ps 2 describes the time of trial for the community when the sons of Belial "devise against them plots of wickedness" (4QFlor 8). As Brooke explains, "...the intention of the midrash on Psalms 1 and 2 is to identify the good parties in those psalms with the community and to suggest that it is the community who is the remnant that is to survive the trial of the latter days, the period that also looks beyond that testing to a time when the understanding of the wise

---

[114] See "Macarismes et Psaumes," 331-32. For a more reserved treatment of the possibility of compositional unity of the two psalms, see J. Willis, "Psalm 1—An Entity," *ZAW* 9 (1979) 381-401, and Wilson, *The Editing*, 205-6.

[115] Lipinsky, "Macarismes et Psaumes," 331-32.

[116] This *pesher* on Pss 1-2 is a paradigm for the reading of the whole Psalter as illuminating the community's life experience, as is borne out by the interpretations of Pss 37, 45 and 60 in the "*Pesher* on Psalms," 4QPs^a (4Q171). E.g., the conflict between the Teacher of Righteousness and the Wicked Priest is read into the dichotomy these psalms make between the just and the wicked. The "little while" of Ps 37:10 is read as the 40 years to be endured before the defeat of the sect's enemies. The "meek" who will possess the land (Ps 37:10) are the Qumran community under the designation, "the congregation of the poor." See Devorah Dimant, "Qumran Sectarian Literature" in Stone (ed.), *Jewish Writings of the Second Temple Period*, 483-550, at 512-13.

[117] The psalm which concludes the Community Rule (1QS X, 6), e.g., develops the theme of "the fruit of praise" which is "the portion of the lips" in a passage echoing Deut 6:7—"Before I move hands and feet I will bless his Name. I will praise him before I go out or enter, or sit or rise, and whilst I lie on the couch of my bed." 1QS VI shows the lengths to which they went to ensure continuous Torah study, even throughout the night.

will be vindicated."[118] Again, a comparison with the Johannine community suggests itself. Although obviously nuanced according to their own preoccupations, the Qumran sectarians' interpretation would be in line with the reception of Pss 1-2 as a prologue to the Psalter in their contemporary Judaism.

> Psalms 1 and 2 together elevate the paired topics of Torah and kingship of the Lord. This introduction opens a book which with its five sections is itself a kind of Torah. It introduces themes which occupy much of the book—the questions of how individual life and historical destiny are to turn out.[119]

Since Pss 1-2 were received as a programmatic prelude, their dualism functioned as an interpretive framework for the reading of the rest of the Psalter.

> "There is some sense in which human community is broken up into these two groups, though at times they are given other names, such as fool and wise, or evil-doers and those who fear the Lord. But how these two groups act, the way they go—whether one means their path of life or their ultimate fate—is very much the subject of the psalms."[120]

Thus there is a complementarity of content in Pss 1-2. What Ps 1 sets forth as wisdom teaching, is modelled in concrete historical terms in Ps 2.[121]

As an example of this, we recall PsSol 17, mentioned in our discussion of David as a wisdom figure.[122] This is an illuminating example of a reception of Ps 2 from late Second Temple Judaism which shows the "sapientializing" influence of Ps 1. According to PsSol 17:23, the expected king will implement the psalmic scenario for the ideal Davidic king: smashing the arrogance of sinners like a potter's jar. There is a political dimension—the desired expulsion of the Romans—but, as the context makes clear, the king's implementation of Ps 2 is to be interpreted in a metaphorical sense. His rule will be that of the sort of person proclaimed blessed in Ps 1—"an ideal scribe, a wise man par excellence," devoted to the way of *Torah*.[123]

Is there anything corresponding to this reading of Pss 1-2 in our

---

[118] Brooke, *Exegesis at Qumran*, 159.
[119] J. L. Mays, "The Question of Context in Psalm Interpretation," in McCann (ed.), *The Shape and Shaping*, 14-20, at 16. For a similar view, see Sheppard, *Wisdom as a Hermeneutical Construct*, 142 and Miller, "The Beginning of the Psalter," 85. 86.
[120] Miller, "The Beginning of the Psalter," 85.
[121] Sheppard, *Wisdom as a Hermeneutical Construct*, 140.
[122] See p. 97-98 above.
[123] See De Jonge, "The Expectation of the Future," 102, referring to PsSol 17:22.

early Christian writings? We do find a non-violent messianic interpretation of Ps 2, in Acts 4:24-31, especially vv. 29-30. A "programmatic" role of Ps 2 has been convincingly demonstrated, with reference to Luke/Acts, by W. J. C. Weren. According to his theory, the similarity between the *kerygma* (as found in 1 Cor 15:3b-5, for example) and the outline of Ps 2 suggests that the interpretation of Ps 2 by the early Christian community has influenced their preaching of the passion of Jesus.[124] Weren sees seven elements of the psalm reflected in the *kerygma*, but, for our purposes, it is sufficient to distinguish three main phases in the psalm, each of which have their counterpart in the Christian proclamation—

PHASE 1

Ps 2:1-3 (e.g., Acts 2:23)
the plot against the Lord and his anointed You had him put to death.

PHASE 2

Ps 2:4-9 (e.g., Acts 2:24)
God's intervention in establishing the king God raised him.

PHASE 3

vv. 10-12 (e.g., Acts 2:38)
the submission of the former plotters. The hearers' response of faith.[125]

Some of the synoptic allusions to Ps 2 would be assigned, in this theory, to Phase 1, e.g., the gathering together against Jesus (Matt 26:3)[126] and the connivance of Herod and Pilate (Luke 23:6-12; Acts 4:27). Obviously, proclamation of the resurrection would correspond to Phase 2, e.g., Acts 13:33, quoting Ps 2:7—Κύριος εἶπεν πρός με Υἱός μου εἶ σύ. There would also be proleptic references to Phase 2 in the allusions to Ps 2:7 in the synoptic baptism and transfiguration narratives. Phase 3 is reflected in the summons to faith which concludes the proclamation, e.g., in Acts 13:38-41.

---

[124] Weren, "Psalm 2 in Luke/Acts," 189-203. Weren actually attributes this theory to his teacher Bas van Iersel.

[125] This early Christian *relecture* of Ps 2 is reflected in two Syriac superscripts to Ps 2: *In secundo psalmo beatus David prophetans narrat omnia quae a Iudaeis passionis tempore impleta sunt*, and *Prophetat omnia quae in passione Domini a Judaeis facta sunt*. See Vosté, "Sur les titres des psaumes dans la Pesitta," 223.

[126] A comparison of Mk 14:1 with Matt 26:3-5 shows how Ps 2 has provided Matthew with the means of elaboration.

If we move beyond Weren's area of interest, the Lucan writings, we find that our three-phase version of his theory throws considerable light on allusions to Ps 2 in other NT writings. A particular echo of Ps 2 which Weren sees in Luke's gospel sensitizes us to highly refined forms of the psalm's presence elsewhere in the NT, alerting us to the possibility of similar instances in the Fourth Gospel. In Luke's little parable within the parable of the pounds (Luke 19:14.27), the citizens send a message after the king designate, Οὐ θέλομεν τοῦτον βασιλεῦσαι ἐφ᾽ ἡμᾶς (Luke 19:14). If this is understood as a Phase 1 echo of Ps 2, the strangely violent reaction of the king on his return (Luke 19:27) is immediately explained—the newly appointed king is acting out the script for Phase 2, of the psalm, shattering his enemies with a rod of iron (Ps 2:9).[127] The cry, Οὐ θέλομεν τοῦτον βασιλεῦσαι ἐφ᾽ ἡμᾶς cannot but remind us of John 19:15—

...λέγει αὐτοῖς ὁ Πιλᾶτος, Τὸν βασιλέα ὑμῶν σταυρώσω; ἀπεκρίθησαν οἱ ἀρχιερεῖς, Οὐκ ἔχομεν βασιλέα εἰ μὴ Καίσαρα.

Hearing in this passage an echo of Ps 2 intensifies the irony of the situation; a gentile, dragged unwilling into the plot against the Lord and the Lord's Anointed, goads Israel into denying its Jewish faith. Caesar, not God, is their king (John 19:15). Pilate's title, bearing witness to Jesus' kingship, stands in for "the Scripture" which the Jews have repudiated. While the pagan ruler concurs with God's judgement in favour of Jesus by declaring him king, the Jews act out the role of the gentiles in Ps 2. By refusing to accept Jesus' messiahship, they act κατὰ τοῦ κυρίου καὶ κατὰ τοῦ χριστοῦ αὐτοῦ (Ps 2:2).

The presence of this admittedly faint echo opens up John's whole passion/resurrection narrative to the possibility of reading it against the Ps 2 background which seems to have been so formative of the pre-gospel passion tradition. There is no verbal linkage with Phase 1, but its general atmosphere is sensed in the gathering of the chief priests and Pharisees to plot Jesus' death. John 11:47-53 would correspond to the precise moment in the pre-gospel passion tradition where the Ps 2 terminology occurs. Again with thematic rather than verbal linkage, Phase 2 would correspond to the whole portrayal of Jesus' passion and death as "the hour" when his kingship, understood as divine sonship, is vindicated as he overcomes "the world" (John 16:33). The "hour" thus becomes the σήμερον in the psalm, when God declares to Jesus, Υἱός μου εἶ σύ (Ps 2:7),[128] the moment

---

[127] Cf. PsSol 17:23 where the "Son of David" is "to shatter the arrogance of sinners like a potter's jar" (alluding to Ps 2:9).
[128] There is the possibility that the σήμερον of Ps 2:7 which early Christianity saw

when Jesus royalty is most apparent.¹²⁹ The allusion to the last line of the psalm at the (original) last line of the Johannine narrative may well be an echo of Phase 3. If so, this is the only incidence of actual verbal alusion. It could well be the moment in the Johannine passion narrative when we can glimpse something of the larger "raw material" with which the Fourth Evangelist has worked—

JOHN 20:29	Ps 2:12D
μακάριοι οἱ μὴ ἰδόντες καὶ πιστεύσαντες.	μακάριοι πάντες οἱ πεποιθότες ἐπ᾽ αὐτῷ.

Jesus blessing for believers would thus be the Johannine equivalent of the call to faith in Phase 3 of the early Christian reception of Ps 2. Several other NT allusions to Ps 2 confirm this impression, notably, Phil 2:12—μετὰ φόβου καὶ τρόμου τὴν ἑαυτῶν σωτηρίαν κατεργάζεσθε —and Eph 6:5—Οἱ δοῦλοι, ὑπακούετε τοῖς κατὰ σάρκα κυρίοις μετὰ φόβου καὶ τρόμου ἐν ἁπλότητι τῆς καρδίας ὑμῶν ὡς τῷ Χριστῷ ... It is evident from these echoes of Ps 2 that v. 11—

δουλεύσατε τῷ κυρίῳ ἐν φόβῳ
καὶ ἀγαλλιᾶσθε αὐτῷ ἐν τρόμῳ.

—was received in early Christian circles as a "programme" for the life of Christian faith.

The suggestion of a covert and subtle influence of Ps 2 on the Book of Glory raises the question—If, as appears evident, Pss 1-2 were received in NT times as a unit introducing the Psalter, could Ps 1 have had a similar role in the Book of Signs? If Ps 1 is about humanity divided into two groups—one accepting God's Law and finding life, the other rejecting it and perishing—is it not rather similar to the Book of Signs? If the issues raised in Ps 1-2 are "very much the subject of the psalms,"¹³⁰ is it not to be expected that they will permeate a Gospel which refers to the psalms as frequently as we have shown? This must remain a question which the

---

as fulfilled in Jesus' resurrection may have been seminal in the development of the Johannine notion of "the hour." Reim's idea, *Jochanan*, 369-88, that the σήμερον of Ps 94:7 becomes in Johannine thought, "the hour" of which Jesus says, ἀμὴν ἀμὴν λέγω ὑμῖν ὅτι ἔρχεται ὥρα καὶ νῦν ἐστιν ... (John 5:25) would be more convincing if argued on the basis of Ps 2:7.

¹²⁹ In the royal installation protocol which has left its traces in Ps 2, the "today" was the moment when the king was declared to be Son of God. See J. H. Hayes, "The Resurrection as Enthronement and the Earliest Church Christology," *Int* 22 (1968) 333-45.

¹³⁰ See Miller, "The Beginning of the Psalter," 85, as quoted on p. 281 above.

present study certainly does not attempt to answer definitively. Several features of Ps 1, however, go against the outright dismissal of the idea.

Ps 1 is about the two "ways," the division/judgement which separates those open to the word from those who reject it. We know from Qumran (See especially 1QS III,13 - IV,26) that this dualism was extensively developed in Judaism as a contrast between truth and falsehood, light and darkness, righteousness and iniquity. It is clear that this dualism was taken up from Judaism by several early Christian authors.[131] In the Johannine understanding, those receptive to the "Law," as fulfilled in Jesus, receive the life-giving water and bear fruit (Ps 1:3; cf. John 15:2), while those who refuse perish. Just as the way of the wicked leads to death—καὶ ὁδὸς ἀσεβῶν ἀπολεῖται (Ps 1:6), so those who reject Jesus as "the way" die in their sin (John 8:21). Like John's "Book of Signs" (See John 12:36-43), Ps 1 ends on a note of failure and refusal. Discovering the Johannine Christians as readers of Ps 1, allows us to hear it as resonating in "sympathetic vibrations" with the Book of Signs. The psalm highlights John's challenge to the reader to "choose life" now, in the σήμερον while the light still shines, "the moment of decision concerning life and death."[132]

Ps 2, the background to the title "Son of God" in the initial phase of Christological reflection, collects much larger connotations when received in Johannine Christianity. In a presentation of Jesus where the correct answer to the question, "Are you the Messiah?" is "I and the Father are one,"[133] Ps 2 has clearly undergone transformation. Yet, the psalm, as understood in 4QFlor, for example, with all its resonances of 2 Sam 7:14 and Ps 88:26-27, is equally a "Scripture" fulfilled in the events of "the Hour." As a promise in the context of the Davidic history, it brings out the Davidic colouring in John's portrayal of Jesus, a colouring which is by no means a "messianic" monochrome, as this study has shown. Received as a prophecy of the enthronement of the Son of God (Ps 2:7), it points to Jesus who has overcome the world (John 16:33) and declares, μακάριοι πάντες οἱ πεποιθότες ἐπ' αὐτῷ.

---

[131] E.g., the opening of the *Didache*—Ὁδοὶ δύο εἰσί, μία τῆς ζωῆς καὶ μία τοῦ θανάτου—introduces a wisdom discourse contrasting ἡ ὁδὸς τῆς ζωῆς, the way of Torah as interpreted by Jesus, with ἡ τοῦ θανάτου ὁδος (*Did.* 1-6). Cf. also *Barn.* 18, 1-21. For the influence on these texts of Jewish dualism, see W. Rordorf and A. Tuilier (ed.) *La Doctrine Des Douze Apôtres (Didachè)*, SC 248 (Paris: Les Editions du Cerf, 1978) 22-34.

[132] See the comment of Bultmann on John 12:34-36, *The Gospel*, 355-56.

[133] Ashton, *Understanding*, 180, n. 39.

In light of this, it is significant that John 15:1-9 appears to take up imagery common to the wisdom Ps 1 and the presentation of a sapientialized David in 2 Sam 23. According to "The Last Words of David" (2 Sam 23:1-7), those loyal to him experience his reign as growth-producing sunlight and rain. While they flourish, David's opponents are thorny weeds which shrivel in the heat and are fit only to be burned (John 15:6).[134] Again, the echo, if such there be, is fleeting, covert, subliminal, but we have the distinct impression that David as "a model of the obedient life in the manner of the wisdom tradition,"[135] is not far from the Evangelist's mind as he sets about his portrayal of Wisdom incarnate in Jesus. The dualism of David's Ps 1 clearly resonates with the provocation of κρίσις[136] which characterizes the Book of Signs, just as the royal protocol of David's Ps 2 does with John's account of the enthronement of the King who is Son of God. If there is an intertextual relationship between the Psalter Prologue and the Fourth Gospel, it would represent a particularly dramatic example of *relecture* as transformative reception.

So we conclude this section by asking—Was the pattern of thought found in the Pss 1-2 "diptych," an influence (even an unconsious one) on the Fourth Evangelist as he created his "Book of Signs" and "Book of Glory" structure?[137]

F. *Overview of Fourth Gospel Allusions to the Psalter*

We began our study of allusions by suggesting that the Psalter may be the source of the two "Scriptures" in John 7:42 and 12:34. Our discussion of what we regard as substantial allusions to Ps (88)89 in

---

[134] Cf. the opening of 1QH VIII on which Ps 1 is an important influence and where several of the biblical images that cluster around the figure of Jesus in the Fourth Gospel appear.

[I give you thanks, Lord]
because you have set me in the source of streams in a dry land ...

As the poem progresses, there is a metamorphosis of the tree planted by running water (from Ps 1) into the Everlasting Plant. This in turn is described in vine imagery from Ps 80 and then appears as the "root out of dry ground" (Isa 53:2) and the "Tree of Life" (Gen 3:22). See García Martínez, *The Dead Sea Scrolls*, 345.

[135] Sheppard, *Wisdom as a Hermeneutical Construct*, 158.

[136] Ashton, *Understanding*, 211.

[137] Various such influences have been suggested for the Fourth Gospel. Douglas K. Clark, e.g., believes that the *relecture* of the Exodus story in Wis 11 - 19 has dictated the sequence for John's seven signs. See "Signs in Wisdom and John," *CBQ* 45 (1983) 201 - 209. More recently, Mark Kiley has proposed what he calls "a psalmic backbone" to the Book of Signs, consisting of Ps 22 and part of Ps 26. See "The Exegesis of God: Jesus' Signs in John 1-11," in *SBL 1988: Seminar Papers*, ed. David J. Lull (Atlanta: Scholars, 1988) 555-69.

these passages led us to other moments in the Gospel when this psalm seems to be subliminally operative. We then examined some less immediately obvious examples of John's literary dependence on "David." In the course of this, we encountered several psalm passages where references or addresses to God lent themselves to being applied to the glorified Jesus. This opened up the whole question of the contribution of the Psalter to the Johannine confession of Jesus as God.

As we moved to a less explicit form of intertextual reference, we found that hearing the harmonics and noting the sympathetic vibrations which certain combinations of texts set in motion requires attuning the ear to what is often no more than a single word or a particular turn of phrase. We saw that Fourth Gospel allusion to the Scriptures is frequently thematic, rather than dictional. Thus we found that verbal allusions to the psalms can be quite fragmentary and elusive.

We then discerned the latent presence in the Fourth Gospel of Ps (109)110, an influential psalm in early Christianity, and yet, it would appear at first sight, ignored or even purposely avoided by the Fourth Evangelist. In looking at this and other "un-quoted" psalms, we were able to learn from their role in the pre-Gospel tradition, inasmuch as this can be gleaned from the synoptics, how to recognize their influence on the Fourth Gospel. Similarly, an awareness of the Jewish reception of certain psalms alerted us to the particular "tributaries" by which they appear to have flowed into Johannine thought. Finally, we asked whether the two-part structure of the Gospel might have some form of intertextual relationship with the two-psalm prologue to the Psalter.

There are two possibilities with regard to the psalm allusions and echoes in the Fourth Gospel. Either, they are the means by which the Evangelist hints at Jesus true identity, presupposing in the reader a familiarity with the Psalter which will illuminate the intertextual subtleties. Or, the Evangelist spontaneously and even inadvertently slips into the language and patterns of thought he has absorbed during his Jewish education and which he has been steeped in while delving into the Scriptures which, as he has come to believe, bear witness to Jesus. It is impossible and unnecessary to decide between the two. Probably the truth lies in a mixture of both.

Our intuition that David as "writer" and as "written about," is subliminally influential in the Gospel does not lead us to claim that his is the only voice. However, there is no doubt that the book of ἡ γραφή which the Fourth Evangelist favours most as a witness to Jesus has exerted a profound influence on his entire composition.

CHAPTER SIX

SHADES OF DAVID IN THE JOHANNINE PRESENTATION OF JESUS

A. *Introduction*

Having established that the Book of Psalms has played an important role in the theological argument of the Johannine author, we now ask whether the figure of David might have played a more significant role in the narrative presentation of the Johannine Jesus than is sometimes acknowledged. The question becomes more pressing since in our exploration of psalm citations and allusions we have frequently sensed the presence and influence of David. Sometimes it seemed that the Fourth Evangelist was receiving a psalm as an "autobiographical" utterance of David. At other moments, the intertextual play of motifs associated with David's roles as king, cultic founder, poet, wisdom figure, could be heard in counterpoint with "his" psalms. This chapter suggests that the biblical David materials—the Deuteronomistic History, Chronicles and "the Latter Prophets"—have contributed to the Johannine presentation of Jesus. It suggests that the figure of David himself, as portrayed in narrative and prophetic traditions, has a significant part to play in the Fourth Gospel. If this claim can be sustained, it would prove to be a corroboration of the over-all claims of this study.

B. *The Synoptic Presentation of Jesus in Terms Reminiscent of David*

As we found with the question of psalm usage, it will be useful to look briefly at echoes of David's story in the synoptic presentation of Jesus so that the distinctiveness of the Johannine allusions might emerge more clearly. The contribution of features from Davidic covenant theology to the portrayal of Jesus are particularly pronounced in Matthew, as has been shown by Brian M. Nolan.[1] Our

---

[1] These would include, for example, Jesus' divine sonship proclaimed in the baptism and transfiguration narratives, his kingly and filial wisdom tested in the temptation narrative, his status as shepherd of the twelve tribes and his role as judge and expounder of the *Torah*. See *The Royal Son of God: The Christology of Matthew 1-2 in the Setting of the Gospel* (Göttingen: Vandenhoeck und Ruprecht, 1979) 201-15 for the infancy narratives, 170-200 for the rest of the gospel.

interest here, however, is in a more explicit type of allusion to David—occasions in all three synoptics when the narrative evokes memories of his career. At these moments, aspects of David other than his role as progenitor of the Messiah are brought into play.

The synoptic allusions to the David narratives refer mainly to the hardships which David endured. In the Deuteronomistic history these sufferings are recounted in two sequences, the persecution of David by Saul (1 Sam 18-31) and the conspiracy of Absalom (2 Sam 15-18). The synoptic echoes of these parts of David's story are concentrated mainly in the Passion Narrative, a tendency which we also noted with regard to synoptic psalm usage. These reminiscences invite the reader, by means of the similarity (or perhaps the dissimilarity) between Jesus and David to draw interpretive conclusions.

For example, Matthew's detail that Judas went out and hanged himself serves to cast him in the role of David's betrayer, Ahithophel, and thus to hint at a parallel between David and Jesus. A comparison of the two relevant passages reveals striking verbal and syntactical similarities.

2 Sam 17:23	Matt 27:3-5
καὶ Αχιτοφελ εἶδεν ὅτι οὐκ ἐγενήθη ἡ βουλὴ αὐτοῦ,...καὶ ἀπήγξατο καὶ ἀπέθανεν...	Τότε ἰδὼν Ἰούδας ὁ παραδιδοὺς αὐτὸν ὅτι κατεκρίθη,...ἀπελθὼν ἀπήγξατο.
And Ahithophel saw that his counsel was not followed...and he hanged himself and died.	When Judas, his betrayer, saw that he (Jesus) was condemned,...he went and hanged himself.

The memory of David's story is clearly influential.[2]

This is one of several similarities between the synoptic Passion Narratives and the story of the plot of Absalom against David, "the

---

[2] Matthew is the only Evangelist who mentions Judas' suicide. According to Glasson, "Davidic Links," 118-19, the suicide element in Matthew's account is suspect. Not only is it not endorsed by Luke, who also recounts Judas' death, but the strong similarity to 2 Sam 17:23 suggests that the point of the story is to make the connection between Ahithophel and Judas. Glasson has found that Matt 27:5 is the only place in the NT and 2 Sam 17:23 is the only place in the LXX where the word ἀπήγξατο occurs (except in the deuterocanonical Tob 3:10). Ahithophel's is the only suicide in the OT (outside a situation of war), just as Judas' is the only suicide in the NT. Luke also draws the lines of comparison by means of David, but he uses David's supposed authorship of imprecatory psalm passages which he has Peter quote against Judas. See Acts 1:18-20 quoting Pss (68)69 and (108)109, both of which have Davidic superscripts.

most desperate moment of David's life."³ The theme of betrayal by a confidant is common to both narratives (2 Sam 15:31, 16:23; Matt 26:20-25; Mark 14:17-21; Luke 22:21-23). Like Ahithophel who plots to take King David at night (2 Sam 17:1), Judas arranges for the arrest of Jesus by night (Mark 14:17.30; Matt 26:31; Luke 22:53.66). The announcement of the defection of the disciples and of Peter's denial and their protestations of loyalty on the way to the Mount of Olives (Mark 14:29-31; Matt 26:30-35; Luke 22:33) has a parallel in 2 Sam 15. There, walking sorrowfully towards the Mount of Olives (2 Sam 15:30), aware of the defection of those close to him, David receives professions of loyalty from his faithful servants (2 Sam 15:15.21). Both Jesus and David pray in sorrow and distress at a location on the Mount of Olives (2 Sam 15:30-31; cf. Matt 26:36-39, Mark 14:32-33, Luke 22:39-43). In the light of these links, the impetus for the quotation from Zech 13:7, Πατάξω τὸν ποιμένα, καὶ διασκορπισθήσονται τὰ πρόβατα τῆς ποίμνης, in Mark 14:27 and Matt 26:31 would certainly seem to have come *via* the influence of 2 Sam 17:2—... καὶ ἐκστήσω αὐτόν, καὶ φεύξεται πᾶς ὁ λαὸς ὁ μετ' αὐτοῦ, καὶ πατάξω τὸν βασιλέα μονώτατον.⁴

All of these synoptic reminiscences of David occur in the Passion Narratives.⁵ There is just one occasion in the synoptic accounts of the ministry where an explicit connection is made between David and Jesus. It is the controversy story found in Matt 12:1-8, Mark 2:23-28 and Luke 6:1-5.⁶ Jesus himself is portrayed as making the

---

³ Brown, *Death of the Messiah*, II, 1448. Attention has been drawn to several of these similarities in the following studies: L. P. Trudinger, "Davidic Links with the Betrayal of Jesus: Some Further Observations" *ExpTim* 86 (1974-75) 278-79, written in response to Glasson's article mentioned above, and "Hosanna to the Son of David!: St John's Perspective," *DRev* 109 (1991) 297-301; Bassler, "A Man for All Seasons," 168-169; Menken, *Old Testament Quotations*, 134-35; Brown, *The Death of the Messiah* I, 125. 291.

⁴ In what may be an interesting Qumran parallel to the NT usage of the Absalom story, 1QpHab V, 9-12 states that "the House of Absalom" gave no help to the Teacher of Righteousness against the "Liar." However, the reference may be to a certain Absalom, an ambassador of Judas Maccabeus, who is mentioned in 2 Macc 11:17. See Vermes, *The Dead Sea Scrolls in English*, 32.

⁵ There may, perhaps, be a reminiscence of David, independent of the Passion Narrative, in Luke 3:23 where we read that when he bgan his ministry, Jesus was about thirty years of age. A reader familiar with the Deuteronomistic History would be reminded that David was thirty years old when he began to reign over all Israel in Jerusalem (2 Sam 4:4). Such a connection would be in keeping with Luke's interest in showing how the restoration of the kingdom to Israel comes about as the message of Jesus radiates out from Jerusalem to the ends of the earth (Acts 1:6-8).

⁶ Alan Richardson held that this is the only *pericope* in all four gospels which sets Jesus forth as "the new David." See *An Introduction to the Theology of the New Testament* (London: SCM, 1958) 126.

comparison with 1 Sam 21:1-7 in order to justify his own action in allowing his disciples to pluck grain on the Sabbath for the relief of their hunger.[7] For some, this is simply a *kal wahomer* argument.[8] The conclusion which Jesus draws from the analogy, ὥστε κύριός ἐστιν ὁ υἱὸς τοῦ ἀνθρώπου καὶ τοῦ σαββάτου (Mark 2:28; cf. Matt 12:8, Luke 6:5), would indicate that there is much more involved here than the subjection of *Torah* observance to human need. It should probably be read against the background of certain aspects of the figure of David as it had developed in Second Temple Judaism, notably David's justice in administering the Law (cf. 1 Sam 30:21-25), the analogy drawn between him and Moses in Chronicles, and his role as a prophet. This background allows us to see in the *pericope* an evocation of David as just judge (2 Sam 23:1-7) which carries the inherent implication that Jesus is the expected just ruler who is to sit on David's throne (Isa 16:5).[9]

C. *Echoes of David's Story in the Johannine Passion Narrative*

As with the synoptics, there is a concentration of allusions to 2 Sam 15-18 in the Johannine Passion Narrative. The most obvious example is the opening verse where there is a distinct recollection of David's departure from the city of Jerusalem with his loyal followers at the time of Absalom's conspiracy:

---

[7] In both stories forbidden food is eaten by the leader's followers with his approval. While in the OT story David's and his companions' hunger is implied, but not actually mentioned, in all three synoptics Jesus refers to it. The Matthean version is especially interesting in that it mentions the disciples' hunger in the opening of the story. This establishes the "humanitarian" grounds on which it could be argued that the "reaping" is necessary to sustain life and therefore allowed by the Law. See Menahem Kister, "Plucking on the Sabbath and Christian-Jewish Polemic," *Immanuel* 24-25 (1990) 35-51. However, Matthew's mention of the hunger factor could have another important function: it would strengthen the allusion to the story of David and his "young men" in need of sustenance after their three day unprovisioned journey (cf. 1 Sam 21:5).

[8] "David, who received the kingdom from God was blameless when he and those with him violated the Law ... ; the Son of Man who also received a kingdom from God (Dan 7:13f) is equally blameless when those with him violate the Sabbath law in similar circumstances." See Ellis, "Biblical Interpretation in the NT Church," 700-01.

[9] See D. Roure, *Jesús y la figura de David en Mc 2, 23-26: Trasfondo bíblico, intertestamentario y rabínico* (Rome: Pontificio Istituto Biblico, 1990).

2 Sam 15:23	John 18.1
καὶ πᾶς ὁ λαὸς παρεπορεύοντο <u>ἐν τῷ χειμάρρῳ Κεδρων</u>, καὶ ὁ βασιλεὺς διέβη <u>τὸν χειμάρρουν Κεδρων</u>· καὶ πᾶς ὁ λαὸς καὶ ὁ βασιλεὺς παρεπορεύοντο ἐπὶ πρόσωπον ὁδοῦ τὴν ἔρημον.	Ταῦτα εἰπὼν Ἰησοῦς ἐξῆλθεν σὺν τοῖς μαθηταῖς αὐτοῦ πέραν <u>τοῦ χειμάρρου τοῦ Κεδρὼν</u> ὅπου ἦν κῆπος, εἰς ὃν εἰσῆλθεν αὐτὸς καὶ οἱ μαθηταὶ αὐτοῦ.
And all the people passed by over the Kidron valley, and the king passed over the Kidron valley, and all the people and the king passed on towards the way of the wilderness.	When Jesus had spoken these words, he went forth with his disciples across the Kidron valley, where there was a garden, which he and his disciples entered.

Of course, this could be explained (on the analogy of John 5:2 or 19:13.20) simply as an aid for readers unfamiliar with the topography of Jerusalem.[10] Brown suggests that the crossing of the Kidron is mentioned in order to have Jesus inaugurate his "hour" at the Mount of Olives, the scene of the eschatological battle, according to Zech 14:4.[11] However, the strong intertextual link with the David story in the passion tradition, as reflected in the synoptics, strengthens the case for an echo of 2 Sam 15:23. The textual clarity of the echo is particularly persuasive in that the Evangelist refers to the location as the χείμαρρος of the Kidron, that is, the winter-flowing stream bed, rather than calling it simply the Κεδρών.[12] At this crucial point in John's narrative, the echo has the effect of alerting the reader to other points of similarity between the Johannine "Hour" and the "Passion of David."[13]

In the 2 Sam narrative, the crossing of the Kidron follows a scene in which a declaration of loyalty to David is made by Ittai the Gittite. It occurs during David's journey towards the Mount of Olives which, as we saw above, is echoed in the passion tradition reflected in Mark and Matthew. Urged by David to return to Jerusalem and not to feel bound as a foreigner to take David's side, Ittai declares his willingness to accompany his lord the king even if it

---

[10] This is how Culpepper, *Anatomy of the Fourth Gospel*, 217, sees it.

[11] In making this suggestion, Brown notes that the Mount of Olives is the scene for Mark's apocalyptic discourse (Mark 13:3) and Luke's ascension (Acts 1:12). For Jesus' "Hour" as a combat with Satan (John 12:31-32; 13:27.30; 14:30-31), See Boismard, *Moïse ou Jésus*, 21.

[12] Both designations are found in Josephus: τὸν χειμάρρουν Κεδρῶνα in *Ant.* 8:17 and Κεδρών in *Wars* 5, 70; 252. Josephus is the only other contemporaneous author writing in Greek who mentions the Kidron. John 18:1 is the only NT reference to it.

[13] For this designation, see Michael Goulder, *The Prayers of David: Psalms 51-72*. Studies in the Psalter II, (Sheffield: JSOT Press, 1990) 31.

means dying with him. Echoes of his declaration can be heard in Jesus' words warning his disciples that following him will involve losing their life and yet keeping it for eternal life:

2 Sam 15:21	John 12:26
...ζῇ Κύριος καὶ ζῇ ὁ κύριός μου ὁ βασιλεύς, ὅτι εἰς τὸν τόπον οὗ ἐὰν ᾖ ὁ κύριός μου, καὶ ἐὰν εἰς θάνατον καὶ ἐὰν εἰς ζωήν, ὅτι ἐκεῖ ἔσται ὁ δοῦλός σου.	...ἐάν ἐμοί τις διακονῇ, ἐμοὶ ἀκολουθείτω, καὶ ὅπου εἰμὶ ἐγὼ ἐκεῖ καὶ ὁ διάκονος ὁ ἐμὸς ἔσται.
"As the Lord lives, and as my lord the king lives, in whatever place my lord shall be, whether it be for death or life, there shall your servant be."	"If anyone serves me, he must follow me; and where I am, there shall my servant be."

It is as if David's invitation to Ittai, Δεῦρο, καὶ διάβαινε μετ' ἐμοῦ (2 Sam 15:22) is being extended by Jesus to those who would follow him as he crosses the Kidron in the first stage of his passing from this world to the Father.

In the 2 Sam narrative, David's crossing of the Kidron has several similarities with an earlier crossing of another stretch of water, the crossing of the Jordan at Israel's entry into the land. The carrying of the Ark is a feature of both crossings. In both stories too the bearers of the Ark stand still while all the people "pass over."[14] Since the earlier crossing of the Jordan, with its separation of the waters to allow the nation to pass over on dry land, recalls the crossing of the Red Sea, there may actually be two layers of intertextual reference involved. David's sorrowful crossing over (2 Sam 15:23) would thus assume the proportions of the nation's great foundational journey to take possession of the land.[15] This would be, of course, a powerful way of giving expression to the significance of David and his dynasty as a symbol of God's fidelity to Israel. In 2 Sam 15 there is an apparent reversal of the nation's foundational journey; a dispossessed king is forced to leave his royal city. Yet he and those going with

---

[14] Cf. Josh 3:17 and 2 Sam 15:24. The verb διαβαίνω occurs five times in Josh 3. If 2 Sam 15:23 refers to the dry stream bed, there is possibly a further parallel with the crossing of the dry riverbed of the miraculously divided Jordan (Josh 3:17).

[15] In another possible "exodus" reference, David and the people with him, as fugitives in the wilderness, suffer thirst (2 Sam 17:29). We referred to this text in connection with Jesus' thirst on p. 226 above. Cf. also our presentation of the double reference of John's citation in 19:36 (p. 238 above), where we found that the Exodus and David backgrounds were not incompatible, but that, in fact, they dovetailed together.

him into exile, are the true king and the true Israel, not those installed in the city plotting against him. The eventual resolution of the story will show that David is the one that God was with.[16] David's sorrowful crossing of the Kidron will have its "counter-balance" in his ceremonial crossing back over the Jordan as he returns in victory to resume his rule (2 Kgs 19:15-18. 31. 39). For readers alert to these layers of intertextual reference and believing that God was with Jesus (John 3:2), this implies a devastating judgement on the Jerusalem authorities, not only those who persecuted their Lord, but those who are now persecuting and excluding his followers (John 15:20-16:4).

Later in the narrative (2 Sam 17:1-4), Ahithophel undertakes to ensure the return of all the people who have gone after David.[17] He plans to strike the king with terror, expecting that those with him will then flee. John 16:32 perhaps shows traces of the application of Zech 13:7 to Jesus in the pre-gospel passion tradition—"The hour is coming, indeed it has come, when you will be scattered, every man to his home, and will leave me alone." Typically, the Evangelist "corrects" the received tradition by adding—"Yet I am not alone, for the Father is with me." We have already noted the influence of 2 Sam 17:1-4 on the synoptic passion narratives. It is even more pronounced in John. Ahithophel's advice to Absalom and all the elders of Israel to kill only David finds an echo in the words addressed to a later gathering of the elders of Israel, convened to deal with another mass "defection" of the people. Caiphas' recommendation to this assembly is strikingly "Ahithophelian"—

2 Sam 17:3	John 11:50
...πλὴν ψυχὴν ἀνδρὸς ἑνὸς σὺ ζητεῖς, καὶ παντὶ τῷ λαῷ ἔσται εἰρήνη.	...οὐδὲ λογίζεσθε ὅτι συμφέρει ὑμῖν ἵνα εἷς ἄνθρωπος ἀποθάνῃ ὑπὲρ τοῦ λαοῦ καὶ μὴ ὅλον τὸ ἔθνος ἀπόληται.[18]
"You only (need to) seek the life of one man, and all the people shall have peace."	"...you do not understand that it is expedient for you that one man should die for the people, and that the whole nation should not perish."

---

[16] That God was with David is a recurring refrain in the narrative of David's rise: 1 Sam 16:18; 18:14; 18:28; 2 Sam 5:10.

[17] A minor, but interesting point of comparison between 2 Sam and the 4th Gospel here: Ahithophel undertakes to bring the people back to Absalom "as a bride comes home to her husband." The image of the king (albeit here a pretender to the throne) as bridegroom of his people contributes to our understanding of the bridegroom image as applied to Jesus in the Fourth Gospel (John 3:29).

[18] Bultmann, The *Gospel*, 411, sees a parallel to Caiphas' decision in 2 Sam

Another moment in the Fourth Gospel Passion Narrative which gives a strong impression of Davidic influence is when Jesus orders that his disciples are to be let go. The Evangelist explains that this is in fulfilment of Jesus' own word, Οὓς δέδωκάς μοι οὐκ ἀπώλεσα ἐξ αὐτῶν οὐδένα (John 18:8-9).[19] Brown has drawn attention to the illogicality of the fact that Peter, whose act of aggression is subsequently recalled by a relative of his victim (John 18:6), is not seized. Brown's solution is to suggest that "Peter could not be touched because of the protective power of Jesus' word and name." Brown also wonders, however, if "the evangelists' (note the plural) outlook might be shaped" by 2 Sam 17:1-2 where Absalom says, "I will come upon him while he is weary and discouraged...and all the people with him will flee. I will strike down the king only."[20] This could certainly be true of the synoptics, but when it comes to the Fourth Gospel an account of the precise role of 2 Sam at this point needs to be a little more nuanced. As we have seen, there is a strong case for the influence of 2 Sam 17 (via Zech 13:7) on the motif of the aloneness of Jesus at this point. There are however two points of glaring dissimilarity. Firstly, the Johannine Jesus is neither weary nor discouraged. Secondly, his disciples do not flee. Jesus calmly and assertively arranges for their safe departure. The echo at this juncture seems rather to be of 2 Sam 15:25-27 where David tells the priests, Zadok, Abiathar and their sons to return to Jerusalem with the ark. The feature of David that comes through very strongly at this moment is his willingness to trust God: "If I find favour in the eyes of the Lord, he will bring me back and let me see both it (the ark) and his habitation; but if he says, 'I have no pleasure in you,' behold, here I am, let him do to me what seems good to him." As P. Kyle Mc Carter has noted, "In David's attitude towards the disposition of the ark and the chief priests we see a king prepared to submit fully to the divine will."[21] No doubt, this aspect would have furthered the appeal of the 2 Sam 15 scene in a circle where Jesus was remembered as one utterly devoted to his Father's will (John 4:34; 5:30; 6:38).

20:20-22, which concerns the death of Sheba. We think that if the Fourth Evangelist had any part of the story of Sheba's rebellion in mind, it is surely 2 Sam 20:1, "We have no portion in David and we have no inheritance in the son of Jesse," which provides an illuminating background to John 19:15.

[19] We note that Jesus' word is given scriptural status here, as in John 2:22.
[20] Brown, *Death of the Messiah*, I, 291.
[21] McCarter, *II Samuel*, 375.

This is also a moment when David shows a concern for the safety of those loyal to him which is very much in keeping with the protectiveness towards his flock on which he prided himself as a youth.[22] The David of the Deuteronomistic history certainly cares for those who are loyal to him. At an earlier stage of his career, during the persecution by Saul, he reassured the one survivor of the sons of Abimelech in words that would not sound out of place on the lips of the Johannine Jesus—

> Κάθου μετ' ἐμοῦ, μὴ φοβοῦ, ὅτι οὗ ἐὰν ζητῶ τῇ ψυχῇ μου τόπον, ζητήσω καὶ τῇ ψυχῇ σου, ὅτι πεφύλαξαι σὺ παρ' ἐμοί.
>
> Stay with me; fear not, for whever I shall seek a place for my life, I will seek a place for your life, for you are safe with me (1 Sam 22:23. Cf. John 12:26, 14:2, 15:4).

So David, as shepherd-king, ensuring the safety of his flock, could also be a pre-text for John 18:8-9. This would find support in the suggestion of Barnabas Lindars that the "word" of Jesus—"Of those whom you gave me I lost not one."—fulfilled when he arranges for the disciples' departure, is John 10:28 where Jesus says of his sheep, "... I give them eternal life, and they shall never perish, and no one shall snatch them out of my hand." To quote Lindars—

> If John is correcting the earlier tradition of the flight of the disciples, it would be natural for him to think of the Shepherd allegory because of the proof text which belongs to that tradition; 'I will strike the shepherd, and the sheep will be scattered' (Mk 14.27 + Zech. 13.7). John cannot allow that the Good Shepherd should be so careless; indeed it is for the sake of the sheep that he gives his life. Consequently the scattering of the disciples, which is a fixed item of tradition, has to be represented as Jesus' own way of ensuring their safety.[23]

As in the synoptics, there is the motif of betrayal by a confidant (John 13:18; 17:12). Absalom and Judas both leave, under a dishon-

---

[22] Of course, we are dealing here with idealisation. Perhaps something nearer to the historical reality is remembered, e.g, in 1 Chr 22:8 and 28:3 where it is explained that David was not allowed to build the Temple because he was a warrior and had shed much blood. J. Weingreen, "The Rebellion of Absalom," *VT* 19 (1969) 263-66, believes that this is explained by a comment in *Midrash Tanhuma* on Ps 3, "A Psalm of David, when he fled from Absalom his son." On v. 2 ("Many are saying of me, there is no help for him in God"), the midrash comments: "They were saying of David, "How can there be salvation for a man who took the lamb captive and slew the shepherd and who caused Israel to fall by the sword?" Weingreen sees in the third of these deeds of David a reference to his ruthlessness in sacrificing his men's lives in his military campaigns.

[23] Lindars, *Gospel of John*, 542, sees John 6:39 and 17:12 as other possibilities for the 'word' of Jesus in John 18:9. In support of his option for John 10:28 as the primary reference, it might be added that the phrase in 10:29, ὁ πατήρ μου ὃ δέδωκέν μοι, seems to be 'picked up' in the Οὓς δέδωκάς μοι of 18:9.

est pretext, to set their plots in motion with the consent of the one they are about to betray (2 Sam 15:7-9, John 13:27). John's succinct comment on Judas' exit, ἦν δὲ νύξ, which aligns Judas with those who prefer darkness to light (cf. John 3:19), emphasises, even more than the synoptics do, the memories of Ahithophel's plan to strike David at night (2 Sam 17:1). The Johannine Jesus' reference to Judas as ὁ υἱὸς τῆς ἀπωλείας (John 17:12) bears a strong resemblance to designations for David's arch-enemies Doeg and Ahithophel in Jewish exegesis of the David narratives.[24] At the moment of departure from the city, David says to all his servants, Ἀνάστητε καὶ φύγωμεν (2 Sam 15:14). The Johannine Jesus, who lays down his life freely (John 10:18), does not flee from anyone. Nevertheless, the cadences of David's address to his servants are audible in his words as he is about to cross the Kidron, Ἐγείρεσθε, ἄγωμεν ἐντεῦθεν (John 14:31). Peter's attempt to defend Jesus with his sword recalls the request of Abishai to David to be allowed to cut off Shimei's head (2 Sam 16:9). Neither Jesus nor David allow violent reprisals. Each entrusts himself to God.[25]

Like David, the Johannine Jesus has his "servants." His designation of the disciples as his διάκονοι and δοῦλοι serve to underline his royal status.[26] Once "the hour" has come, Jesus calls the disciples no longer δοῦλοι but φίλοι (John 15:15). This is, of course, entirely in keeping with his role as Revealer.[27] However, it also bespeaks his royalty. Far from being a waiver of royal protocol, Jesus' address to the disciples admits them to the status of "friends of the king."[28] As David's servants leave the city, weeping with him, they

---

[24] In *m Sanh.* 10:2 it is stated that Ahithophel has no share in the world to come. This is a valuable earlier witness to a tradition preserved in *Midr. Teh.* 5, 9 according to which Doeg and Ahithophel will not be resurrected nor even permitted to come up for judgement.

[25] See Derrett, "Peter's Sword and Biblical Methodology," *BeO* 32 (1990)180-92, at 184-5.

[26] The Johannine Jesus uses two nouns for the disciples as servants. He speaks of the one who follows him as his διάκονος in 12:26. In 13:16 he tells them, οὐκ ἔστιν δοῦλος μείζων τοῦ κυρίου αὐτοῦ. This he repeats at 15:20. The terms κύριος and δοῦλος/δούλη come from the language of kingship (e.g., 1 Sam 25:24, 2 Sam 8:6, 11:9, 15:21, 19:20 etc).

[27] For Bultmann, *The Gospel of John*, 543, the disciples' status as friends is to be understood in the light of 8:32 as the freedom that comes from knowledge of the truth. For Brown, *John XIII-XXI*, 682-3, John 15:15 recalls God's revelation to Moses as a man speaking to his friend (Exod 33:11); Jesus acts in the manner of divine Wisdom, making people the friends of God (Wis 7:27).

[28] In the Graeco-Roman society contemporary with the Fourth Gospel, the φίλοι of a ruler were groups such as the Roman *amici Augusti*, the senators admitted to the daily *salutatio* who functioned as counsellors, courtiers or ministers. The term "friends" is used in this sense by Nepos (fl. 44 BCE) and Suetonius (ob. 160 CE);

demonstrate an impressive capacity to identify with him in his hardships (2 Sam 15:30). Their declaration, Κατὰ πάντα, ὅσα αἱρεῖται ὁ κύριος ἡμῶν ὁ βασιλεύς, ἰδοὺ οἱ παῖδές σου (2 Sam 15:15) is borne out in their readiness to risk their lives for their king. As David warned an earlier friend, "Who seeks my life seeks yours" (1 Sam 22:23; cf. 1 Sam 22:16). Similarly Jesus warns his disciples, Οὐκ ἔστιν δοῦλος μείζων τοῦ κυρίου αὐτοῦ. εἰ ἐμὲ ἐδίωξαν, καὶ ὑμᾶς διώξουσιν... (John 15:20).

Then there is the royal burial accorded to Jesus. The lavishness of Nicodemus' provision of spices is seen by some as a final example of Johannine "misunderstanding."[29] Others see it as indicating Nicodemus' growth in faith, even if his action "does not display true comprehension of the significance of Jesus."[30] Yet others see it far more positively, as royal homage paid to Jesus, particularly if viewed in the light of Mary's anointing of Jesus in anticipation of his burial (John 12:3.7).[31] Eduardo Huerta, for example, views the enthronement and the burial in a royal sepulchre as a diptych portraying the royalty of Jesus. In the first scene, the title, "King of the Jews" is a statement of his royal dignity. In the second, his royalty is implied by features such as the anointing with perfumes and the garden burial.[32] Brown has drawn attention to significant evidence for the use of large quantities of spices at royal burials which would suggest that

---

references in Charlton T. Lewis and Charles Short, *A Latin Dictionary* (Oxford: Clarendon, 1980), 106. Coins from the reign of Herod Agrippa (37-44 C. E.) bear the inscription, Φιλοκαίσαρ, a title which Philo records was bestowed on him by Flaccus who referred to him as βασιλέα καὶ θίλον Καίσαρος (*Flac.* 6:40). See Brown, *Death of the Messiah*, 843. The doubt cast over Pilate's status as a φίλος τοῦ Καίσαρος in John 19:12 suggests that the Evangelist is aware of this specialized meaning for φίλοι. The related, but somewhat different, designation, "Friend (singular) of the King" is explained on p. 304-05 below.

[29] Wayne Meeks, "The Man from Heaven," 149, thinks that Nicodemus' "ludicrous 'one hundred pounds' of embalming spices indicate clearly enough that he has not understood the 'lifting up' of the Son of Man." A similarly negative view of Nicodemus' action is held by Culpepper, *Anatomy*, 136. "He expresses his grief by bringing expensive spices, but finds no life in Jesus' death." M. Goulder, "Nicodemus," *SJT* 44 (1991) 153-68, regards the Evangelist's attitude to Nicodemus as "solidly negative throughout the Fourth Gospel." For D. D. Sylva, Jesus dissociates himself from Nicodemus' futile actions by shedding the spiced cloths in which he is bound as contrary to his function as "the resurrection and the life." See "Nicodemus and his Spices," *NTS* 34 (1988) 148-151, at 148-49.

[30] John Painter, "Quest and Rejection Stories in John," *JSNT* 36 (1989) 17-46, at 25.

[31] For Jean-Marie Auwers, "La nuit de Nicodème (Jean 3, 2; 19,39) ou l'ombre du langage, " *RB* 97 (1990) 481-503), 494, Nicodemus' spices are "une marque de profonde vénération, qui éveille l'impression d'obsèques royales." See also Stibbe, *John's Gospel*, 197.

[32] E. Huerta, "La realeza de Jesús en el cuarto evangelio," *TyV* 32 (1991) 213-20, at 219.

John intends to show how "one who reigned as a king on the cross receives a burial worthy of his status."[33]

As Huerta suggests, the burial in a garden tomb is a royal motif having strong associations with the Davidic line. In 2 Kgs 21:18.26 there is mention of royal burials "in the garden of Uzza."[34] The LXX of Neh 3:16 tells of repairs being carried out in Jerusalem "as far as the garden of David's sepulchre" (ἕως κήπου τάφου Δαυὶδ). Noting that from Acts 2:29 we know that David's tomb was "popularly familiar in NT times," Brown asks,

> Was the garden burial of Jesus remembered because it was seen as symbolically appropriate for the Son of David? Was the tradition recalled by John in particular because of his emphasis that Jesus of Nazareth on the cross was triumphantly proclaimed as "the King of the Jews"? The evidence for this thesis is not sufficient to establish proof, but such a symbolism would be a most appropriate conclusion to John's PN (Passion Narrative).[35]

Brown suggests that John may have intended the garden of 18:1 to form an inclusion with the garden of Jesus' burial.[36] Stibbe also notes "a certain circularity."[37] It is at least this, and more, if the opening of the Passion Narrative on the Davidic note of the Kidron reference and the royal aspects of the burial are allowed full play.

It is remarkable that so many of the events of the hour take place in a garden setting: the arrest of Jesus (18:1), his death and burial (19:41) and his appearance to Mary Magdalen (20:15). It has long been recognized that the garden references carry overtones of Eden.[38] The paradise motif is, of course, closely connected in biblical

---

[33] Jeremiah, e.g., tells the Davidic king Zedekiah, "As spices were burned for your fathers, the former kings who were before you, so men shall burn spices for you and lament for you" (Jer 34:5). In 2 Chr 16:14 we read of how another Davidic King, Asa, was buried "in the tomb which he had hewn out for himself in the city of David. They laid him on a bier...filled with various kinds of spices prepared by the perfumer's art ..." Josephus too provides evidence for large amounts of spices being used at royal burials. At the burial of Herod the Great, e.g., five hundred servants were needed to carry the spices (Jos. *Wars* 1.33.9; 673). The passages cited in this paragraph have all been suggested as a background to John 19:39-40 by Brown. See *Death of the Messiah*, 1268. 1269-70.

[34] Cf. also "the king's garden" mentioned in 2 Kgs 25:4, Jer 39:4 and 52:7.

[35] Brown, *Death of the Messiah*, 1270.

[36] Brown, *Death of the Messiah*, 1269.

[37] Stibbe, *John's Gospel*, 195.

[38] Two early modern commentators who see paradisial nuances in John's garden references are Hoskyns, *The Fourth Gospel*, ii, 646, and Lightfoot, *St John's Gospel*, 322. Their proposal has not won great acceptance among more recent commentators, however. Brown, e.g., one of the few to refer to it, dismisses the suggestion of a possible Eden reference in John 20:15 as "tenuous." See *John XIII-XXII*, 990.

thought with royal ideology.³⁹ From the reference to the "Fountain Gate" in Neh 3:15-16, we get the impression that the king's garden was near the city's water supply. The fountain is presumably the Gihon which fed the pool of Siloam and which, as we have seen, played an important part in the royal enthronement rituals (1 Kgs 1:33-40.45 and Ps 110:7). Moreover, as we saw in our discussion of the quotation in John 7:38, there is a strong connection between Eden and the Temple.⁴⁰

In the light of all this, it would seem that the garden references in the Johannine passion narrative are not merely topographical, but are profoundly symbolic. These references are redolent of the Davidic palace and temple complex on Mount Sion on which Jewish tradition super-imposes a whole range of images. As Nicolas Wyatt sees it,—

> ... when we come to the use of the garden motif in John's gospel, it is not only futile, but misdirected to attempt to locate it. John has no actual garden in mind, and the synoptics make no mention of it. Rather is John drawing on the garden tradition, and taking advantage of its rich ideological and cultic overtones to make a point about the nature of Jesus.⁴¹

The garden references would not have been wasted on the Gospel's earliest readers. The background we have sketched here was widespread knowledge in their cultural milieu. John's evocation of the royal garden, which is at once Eden and the Temple Mount, would undoubtedly have surfaced memories of David and stirrings of the hope bound up with his memory.

In the Fourth Gospel narrative of "the Hour," there are also what might be called theological echoes of David, as distinct from anecdotal recollections of narrative material. For example, in the Chronicler's version of David's prayer in response to Nathan's oracle, David marvels that God has loved him for ever—τίς εἰμι ἐγὼ Κύριε ὁ Θεός...ὅτι ἠγάπησας με ἕως αἰῶνος; God has exalted him—καὶ ὕψωσάς με—and now he asks how he can glorify God in return —Τί προσθήσει ἔτι Δαυὶδ πρὸς σὲ τοῦ δοξάσαι; (1 Chron 17:16-18). In this context dealing with the establishment of David's eternal rule through the one of whom God says, Ἐγὼ ἔσομαι αὐτῷ εἰς πατέρα, καὶ

---

³⁹ In Ezek 28, e.g., the king is depicted as enthroned both in an Eden-like setting at the cosmological world-centre, the navel of the earth (v. 13) and in a garden on the holy mountain (v. 14). Isa 51:3 envisages the restored Zion as Eden, "the garden of the Lord." Ps (35)36:8-9 draws on the same mythical tradition.
⁴⁰ See p. 157-58 above.
⁴¹ Wyatt, "Supposing Him to be the Gardener," 27-28. 31.

αὐτὸς ἔσται μοι εἰς υἱόν (1 Chr 17:13), we find three verbs in close proximity (underlined above) which are especially associated in the Fourth Gospel with "the hour" when Jesus is most clearly seen as the Father's loved and loving Son (cf. John 14:31).[42]

By way of summary to this section, we borrow from Raymond Brown—

> ...John and the Synoptics echo the same OT traditions but in ways so different that only with great difficulty can one imagine deliberate change of the synoptic account by John. In the independent development of the synoptic and Johannine Gospels an older appeal to II Sam's picture of David has been articulated in different ways.[43]

D. *Reminiscences of David Elsewhere in the Fourth Gospel*

When considering the "shades of David" in the synoptic presentation of Jesus, we found that the lines of comparison are drawn principally with the narrative of Absalom's rebellion and that, apart from the isolated case of the Sabbath controversy story, the connections all occur within the context of the Passion Narrative. With the Fourth Gospel the situation is quite different. As we have seen, intertextual reference to 2 Sam 15-18 is frequent in the Johannine Passion Narrative. This reference is quite extensive, compared with the synoptics, and is expressly articulated in line with the Evangelist's theological concerns. The same can be said of David echoes in the Johannine account of the ministry. Their influence is remarkably pervasive.

There are fleeting moments when the Fourth Gospel evokes memories of David, where the "undersong" of the David materials constitutes what Hollander has called "an underground cipher message."[44] Both David and Jesus are seen by their opponents as potential new kings who pose a threat to political stability (1 Sam 20:31; John 18:33-35). The fear of both David and Jesus on the part of those currently in power is in marked contrast to the high esteem in which they are held by the people (1 Sam 18:6-8. 16. 28; John 7:45-49. 12:19). During Saul's persecution of him, David has to hide himself and dwell in secret (1 Sam 19:2; 23:15). During Absalom's re-

---

[42] See especially John 10:17, 14:31, 15:9 and 17:23. 26 in which the verb ἀγαπᾶν is used, with reference to 'the hour,' for the Father's love of Jesus. For the use of ὑψοῦν with reference to 'the hour,' see John 3:14, 8:28, 12:32. 34. Similarly for the use of δοξάζειν with reference to Jesus' glorification of the Father, see, for example, John 12:28, 13:31-32, 17:1.5.

[43] *Death of the Messiah*, 125-26.

[44] Hollander, *The figure of Echo*, ix.

volt, David and his band of loyal followers take refuge in the "wilderness" outside Jerusalem (2 Sam 17:29). As the persecution of Jesus gathers momentum, he too has to avoid going about openly (John 7:10.25, 11:54). There are even occasions when both David and Jesus find themselves in danger of being stoned (1 Sam 30:6; John 8:59). Having been anointed king at Hebron, David provides a banquet for all the people who have gathered for the installation of the ark, distributing food to them himself (2 Sam 6:19).[45] Like those who came to Hebron to make David king over all Israel (2 Sam 5:1-3, 1 Chr 12:38), the people to whom Jesus distributes food in abundance want to make him king (John 6:11.15).[46]

Two episodes in David's story in particular have shaped the Fourth Gospel presentation of Jesus in ways that are decisively formative of Johannine Christology. Both are scenes from the early life of David: his anointing by Samuel and his youthful career as a shepherd.

1. *David Anointed by Samuel*

The Johannine portrayal of John the Baptist as a prophetic figure who is enabled, by means of a divine communication, to recognize Jesus as the Christ, shows signs of being modelled on that of the prophet Samuel.[47] This is in marked contrast with the synoptics where John the Baptist appears an Elijah figure.[48] In 1 Sam 16:3,

---

[45] According to the Chronicler, David hosts a banquet which lasts for three days on the occasion of his anointing and a further feast to celebrate the arrival of the ark (1 Chron 12:38-40, 16:3).

[46] On the strong messianic and eschatological overtones in these banquet scenes, see Smith, "Messianic Banquet," 788-91.

[47] See Aune, "Christian Prophecy and the Messianic Status of Jesus," in Charlesworth (ed.), *The Messiah*, 404-22, at 414. The suggestion that John 1:29-34 is modelled on 1 Sam 16:1-13 does not, of course, exclude other possible OT background texts. In particular Isa 42:1 should be mentioned in view of the possibility that the text of John 1:34 originally read ὁ ἐκλεκτός and not ὁ υἱὸς τοῦ θεοῦ, a variant most likely due to harmonization with the synoptic accounts of the baptism of Jesus. According to Brown, *John I-XII*, 57, this reading, "found in the original hand of Codex Sinaiticus, OL, OS and some Fathers" and supported by Oxyrhynchus Papyrus 208 (3rd cent.) seems, despite the weaker textual evidence, to be the best. The designation of Jesus as ὁ ἐκλεκτός, the mention of the Spirit and the fact that this scene corresponds to the synoptic baptism scene all contribute to an impression of the influence of Isa 42:1. In actual fact, an allusion to Isa 42:1 would fit well with the 1 Sam 16 background suggested here. Ashton, *Understanding*, 258, (who also favours the reading ὁ ἐκλεκτός) provides several examples of passages where it is a messianic title, notably *Apoc. Abr.* 31:1-2 and 4Q 174. The latter is of special interest in that it refers to the "anointed" of Ps 2:2 as "the elect (pl.) of Israel."

[48] As Martyn has shown, drawing attention to the strong Elijah-like traits in the Fourth Gospel's portrait of Jesus, in the Fourth Gospel it is Jesus, not John the Baptist, who is "Elijah." Martyn also suggests that the Baptist's denial that he is

God tells Samuel, "You shall anoint for me him whom I name to you." Like Samuel, who mistakenly thinks that several of Jesse's other sons are the Lord's anointed (1 Sam 16:6-10), John the Baptist admits, "I myself did not know him," but he too has received a divine communication—"He on whom you see the Spirit descend and remain, this is he who baptizes with the Holy Spirit" (John 1:33). Samuel's moment of recognition also involves a manifestation of the Spirit of God—"and the Spirit of the Lord came mightily upon David from that day forward" (1 Sam 16:13). Much later in the narrative, Samuel will be called upon to testify to God's choice of David, as manifested through his (Samuel's) prophetic action of anointing (1 Sam 28:17). In the Fourth Gospel, the whole *raison d'être* of John the Baptist is his witness to Jesus as the Lord's anointed— "And I have seen and have borne witness that this is the Son of God"(John 1:34).[49] Even his role as "the friend of the bridegroom (John 3:29) is a statement about Jesus' messianic status. It corresponds to the biblical "friend of the king" (שושבין), the "best man" who arranges for the marriage of his lord.[50]

There may also be a Samuel/David background to the Fourth Gospel statement that John was not the light (1:8), but was in some sense a provisional lamp (5:35), shining until the coming of the definitive light (1:9). Samuel appears as a temporary light until the anointing of David in the concluding lines of Hannah's song of thanksgiving for the birth of Samuel, as found in Ps-Philo's *LAB*—

> Et hec sic manent,
> quousque dent cornu christo suo,
> et aderit potentia thronis regis eius.
> Stet autem filius meus hic ministrans,
> quousque fiat lumen genti huic.

Elijah may originally have had its positive counterpart (as the other two denials do) in an affirmation by the disciples that in Jesus they have found "Elijah," just as they have found "the Messiah" (John 1:41) and "the one Moses and the prophets wrote about" (John 1:45). " See *The Gospel of John in Christian History*, 12-28. 38.

[49] Bultmann, *The Gospel of John*, 87, notes 'the cumbrous legal language,' appropriate to the genre of testimony, of the Baptist's confession (John 1:20). Bultmann also points out that the information that John baptized only emerges incidentally at John 1:25 and that for John the Baptist, the imparting of the Spirit is significant only as a sign of recognition. Menken, *Old Testament Quotations*, 31-33, has shown that even the form of the citation which identifies John as the voice in the wilderness is motivated by the desire to present him more as witness than as precursor. Menken's chapter on the quotation in John 1:23 was originally published as "The Quotation from Isa 40:3 in John 1:23," *Biblica* 66 (1985) 190-205. See also Dahl, "The Johannine Church and History," 128.

[50] See the LXX of Gen 26:26 where King Abimelech's "friend" is rendered as ὁ νυμφαγωγὸς αὐτοῦ. Because of the political importance of royal marriages and the frequency with which they were concluded, the role of friend of the king developed

Of particular interest to us is the line *quousque fiat lumen genti huic*. Ps-Philo's Hannah has already exclaimed, *Aut que est filia Batuel, ut pareret lumen populis?* Samuel, her son, is to be "a light to the peoples" (cf. Isa 51:4), but, as she later explains in the passage quoted above, only until the coming of David, the light of Israel.[51] This reading is confirmed by another passage in *LAB* where Samuel's status as a light is intimately bound up with his role as prophet. *Populus illuminabitur a verbis eius ...* (*LAB* 51:3). As "the light from which wisdom is to be born"—*lumen ex quo nascetur sapientia* (*LAB* 51:4)—Samuel paves the way for a "sapientialized" David who, as we have found, appears in 2 Sam 23:4 and *11QPsDavComp* as "a light," particularly in connection with his wisdom.[52] The Johannine Jesus speaks of John's provisional status as a lamp until the coming of "the true light"— "He was a burning and shining lamp, and you were willing to rejoice for a while in his light (John 5:35). Against the Samuel/David background which we have delineated, the Evangelist's estimate of John's role *vis à vis* Jesus emerges with striking clarity—"He was not the light, but came to bear witness to the light. The true light that enlightens every man was coming into the world ..." (John 1:8-9). The Fourth Gospel may thus provide an independent and contemporaneous testimony to the interpretation of David which is reflected in Ps-Philo's work.

We would suggest that two aspects of the image of David as a light have influenced the Fourth Gospel. The light image, as associated with David refers to two aspects of his kingship: his wisdom in judgement and his eternal rule. The portrayal of David as judge in 2

---

from "best man" to personal adviser, to adviser on foreign affairs (e.g., Hushai in 2 Sam 15:37; 16:17 and Zabud in 1 Kgs 4:5). See A. Van Selms, "The Origin of the Title 'The King's Friend'," *JNES* 16 (1957) 118-23. A more recent article has brought out the implications for Jesus' royal messianic status in the Johannine casting of John the Baptist in this role. See R. Infante, "L'amico dello sposo, figura del ministero di Giovanni Battista nel quarto vangelo," *Rivista Biblica* 31 (1983) 3-19.

[51] Such a reading of the text is supported by Perrot and Bogaert, *Pseudo-Philon, I*, 365, who render the last two lines of *LAB* 51:6 as follows:

> *Que mon fils se tienne ici pour (le) servir,*
> *jusqu'à ce que vienne la lumière de cette nation.*

In their commentary, *Pseudo-Philon II*, 220, they note that Samuel is to be *la lumière du peuple en attendant David, la nouvelle lumière*. An alternative rendering is offered by D. J. Harrington, "Pseudo-Philo," 366.

> "And let my son stay here and serve
> until he be made a light for this nation."

While Harrington's reading is grammatically possible, the syntactical structure of the immediate context (particularly the repetition of *quousque*) would seem to favour Perrot and Bogaert's reading.

[52] See p. 95 above.

Sam 23:3-4 is clearly derived from the tradition of the morning as the time for the king to come to the gate of the city and dispense justice (See, for example, 2 Sam 15:2-6). The idea flowed into the psalms where the morning is the time of vindication for the unjustly accused (Ps 17:15; 101:8; 143:8). Thus the portrayal of David as "dawning like the morning light" (2 Sam 23:4) refers, in particular, to his royal prerogative as judge. There is a strong parallel here with the Johannine Jesus who as "the light" brings about judgement (John 3:19). With regard to the second aspect, the promise to David's dynasty is frequently symbolized by the image of an eternal flame, a lamp for God's Anointed (2 Kgs 8:19; Ps 132:17). In his later years, for example, David is urged by his servants not to venture into a dangerous battle lest "the lamp of Israel" be quenched (2 Sam 21:17). Ahijah's prophecy of the division of the kingdom includes God's promise that Solomon's son would keep one tribe— "that David my servant may always have a lamp before me in Jerusalem" (1 Kgs 11:36. See also 1 Kgs 15:4). In our discussion of Johannine allusions to Ps (88)89, we suggested that the notion of David's eternal rule is transformed in the Fourth Gospel into that of Jesus' pre-existence.[53] In John 1:4-5 this is expressed through the imagery of light.

It is often suggested that John the Baptist's inability, at first, to recognise Jesus is connected with idea of the "hidden Messiah."[54] Thus Boismard, for example states, "C'est le thème juif du Messie caché et manifesté, le Baptiste tenant le rôle d'Elie redivivus de la tradition juive."[55] The decidedly Elijan portrayal of John the Baptist in the synoptics seems to indicate a dependence on this belief. In John, however, as we have seen, "Elijah *redivivus*" is one of three identifications which John the Baptist solemnly declines to accept for himself (John 1:20-21).

The Fourth Gospel diverges in another important respect from the "hidden Messiah" background evident in the synoptics, "by insisting *against* the tradition," as John Ashton has pointed out, "that Jesus does know where he comes from." Ashton also mentions that in the Johannine scene corresponding to the synoptic baptism story, "Elijah is replaced by the descent of the Holy Spirit in the form of a dove (1:33)."[56] Judging by the way Jewish tradition tends to project

---

[53] See p. 250-51 above.
[54] The popular belief that the Messiah, even if he is already born, is unrecognised as Messiah, even by himself, until Elijah comes and anoints him, is voiced by Justin's Jewish dialogue partner, Trypho. Cf. Justin *Dial.* 8.4.
[55] *Moïse ou Jésus*, 52.
[56] Ashton, *Understanding*, 305.

features of David on to the expected ideal king, it would seem that it was the story of the recognition and anointing of David by the prophet Samuel that gave rise to the expectation that a "hidden Messiah" would be anointed by the prophet Elijah.[57] The Johannine recognition scene with its resonances of 1 Sam 16:1-13 may thus be more dependent on the story behind the belief than on the belief itself. In that case, the Johannine insistence on the role of the Spirit as indicator of Jesus' identity to John the Baptist would be an echo of the story of David's anointing rather than a point of divergence from a popular belief about the "Hidden Messiah." It does seem from John 7:27 that the Evangelist was aware of the popular belief.[58] At the very least then, we might say that the form in which traces of the "hidden Messiah" tradition appear in John 1:29-34 suggests that the author was aware of that tradition's origin in the story of the anointing of David by Samuel. This awareness has generated a presentation of John the Baptist as Samuel from which flows, by way of corollary, that of Jesus as David.

In view of the Johannine portrayal of the Baptist as "Samuel," it would be natural to expect him to identify Jesus in David-like terms. We therefore believe that of several possible referents for ὁ ἀμνὸς τοῦ θεοῦ (John 1:29) which we discussed,[59] the apocalyptic lamb, is the primary one. We might further note that in the Fourth Gospel, Andrew proceeds, on the basis of the Baptist's second testimony to Jesus as ὁ ἀμνὸς τοῦ θεοῦ, to tell his brother, Simon, Εὑρήκαμεν τὸν Μεσσίαν. As we have seen, the finding of the Messiah is an important motif from Ps (88)89:20—

> "I have found David my servant;
> with my holy oil I have anointed him."

The authorial clarification in John 1:43, ὅ ἐστιν μεθερμηνευόμενον Χριστός, seems intended to emphasize the point that it is as ὁ ἀμνὸς τοῦ θεου that Jesus is recognized as Messiah.

---

[57] E.g., according to Isa 11:2 the spirit of the Lord is to rest on the shoot from the stock of Jesse as it did on David. In Ezek 37:24, the future ideal king is called, "my servant David."

[58] Bultmann, *The Gospel of John 91*, sees the phrase "one whom you do not know" (John 1:26) and also the statement of the crowd, "When the Christ appears no one will know where he comes from" (John 7:27), as allusions to the "hidden Messiah" belief. See also De Jonge, "Jewish Expectations," 246-70.

[59] See p. 231-33 above.

2. David as Shepherd

We have already considered this aspect of David/Jesus in connection with Pss (22)23 and Ps (94)95.[60] Here we are concerned with the input of the narrative traditions about David to the Johannine presentation of Jesus as shepherd. This brings us to the young David's account to King Saul of his shepherding exploits with which this study began. David tells how he has often risked his life to rescue his sheep out of the mouths of wild animals. Within the codes of ANE culture, this amounts to saying that he has already served an apprenticeship for kingship. This, in fact, he demonstrates when he risks his life to fight Goliath to save God's flock from the Philistine threat. As Jonathan later reminds Saul, this act of selfless bravery shows that David is a good man. To kill him without cause (δωρεάν) would be a great sin.[61] An echo of Jonathan's defence of David can be heard in Jesus' own description of his role as ὁ ποιμὴν ὁ καλὸς—

1 SAM 19:5	JOHN 10:11
καὶ ἔθετο τὴν ψυχὴν αὐτοῦ ἐν τῇ χειρὶ αὐτοῦ καὶ ἐπάταξεν τὸν ἀλλόφυλον...	ὁ ποιμὴν ὁ καλὸς τὴν ψυχὴν αὐτοῦ τίθησιν ὑπὲρ τῶν προβάτων·
"...and he put his life in his hand and struck the Philistine."	"The good shepherd lays down his life for the sheep."

The echo is further strengthened by Jesus' refusal to accept the defence of a sword as he goes to lay down his life (John 18:11), just as the young David went to risk his life in combat with Goliath, not with weapons but "in the name of the Lord God" (1 Sam 17:38-39.45).[62] As Jesus will later tell Pilate, his kingship does not involve the use of weapons. (John 18:36).[63] There are several layers of intertextual reference here. Jesus' self description in John 10:11 recalls the young David's defence of his father's flock. This, in its turn, is the model for

---

[60] See p. 258-64 above.
[61] Cf. Ἐμίσησάν με δωρεάν (John 15:25).
[62] In 1 Sam 19:5 the verb τίθημι has the sense of risking one's life, being willing to die even if this does not happen in the event. It thus functions similarly to the idiom παραδίδωμι τὴν ψυχήν in Acts 15:26. According to Bauer, *A Greek-English Lexicon*, 816, τίθημι has, in the Johannine literature, the sense of giving one's life. It is used thus in John 10:11.15.17.18, 13:38. In John 13:4 it is used of Jesus laying aside his garments, a gesture symbolizing the laying down of his life.
[63] Matthew's version of this element from the tradition reflects a pacifist interpretation: "All who take the sword will perish by the sword" (Matt 26:52). In contrast, John uses it to delineate Jesus' kingship as the readiness of the shepherd to face "the wolf" alone, not calling on his servants to fight that he might not be handed over (John 18:36), but willingly laying down his life.

David's stance against Goliath: the Philistine was to fare no better than the wild beasts that David tackled and killed (1 Sam 17:34-37). These two interconnected scenes provide in their turn the model for David's exercise of kingship. In all the hardships he endures (Ps 131:1) until those who pose a threat to his flock are subdued, David is continually risking his life.[64] In a touching moment of tenderness where David refers to the people as οὗτοι τὰ πρόβατα, he even asks God to let him die instead of them (2 Sam 24:17). Jesus loses not one of his Father's flock. He guards them when they are under attack and lays down his life for their sake (John 17:6.12.19; 18:9).

E. *The Johannine Jesus as the Expected "David"*

Finally, and not surprisingly, there are affinities between the Johannine Jesus and the idealised David of the future, especially as the "one shepherd" envisaged by Ezekiel (Ezek 34:23; 37:24) a motif which has clearly influenced the shepherd discourse in John 10.

Ezek 37:22.24.25	John 10:16
... καὶ ἄρχων εἷς ἔσται αὐτῶν ...	... καὶ γενήσονται μία ποίμνη, εἷς ποιμήν.
Καὶ ὁ δοῦλός μου Δαυὶδ ἄρχων ἐν μέσῳ αὐτῶν, ἔσται ποιμὴν εἷς πάντων...	
... καὶ Δαυὶδ ὁ δοῦλός μου ἄρχων εἰς τὸν αἰῶνα.	

Ezekiel exemplifies here that important development in the perception of David which took place in the exilic and post-exilic periods. Faith in the promises to David, which had persisted in spite of two major "setbacks"—the schism between the two kingdoms and the apparent quenching of the "lamp" of David's dynasty in 587 (2 Kgs 25:7; Jer 23:5)—forged the promise to David into a powerful and enabling symbol. In the "Latter Prophets" David, king of "all Israel and Judah" (cf. 2 Sam 5:5), became a sign of hope, that a reunited Israel would again be ruled by one king, as in the days of David.[65] There is a noticeable

---

[64] This can be deduced from the scene where David's servants beg him not to go out to battle (2 Sam 21:17).

[65] In what is obviously a post-exilic addition to the first Isaiah's oracle about the "branch" of Jesse's tree (Isa 11:1-9), this ideal king's reign is described as a new phase in the history of Israel when North and South, Ephraim and Judah, shall no longer harass each other (Isa 11:13). Jeremiah too thought of the future restoration of the integral kingdom as a time when both Israel and Judah would serve the Lord their God and David their king (Jer 30:9. cf. 33:23-26).

tendency in these writings to refer to this future ideal king as "David." "They will seek David, their king" (Hos 3:5). "They shall serve the Lord their God and David their king" (Jer 30:9). "I will set up over them one shepherd, my servant David" (Ezek 34:23. cf. 37:24).[66]

It is significant that none of these texts requires us to assume a Davidic genealogy for this king. He is envisaged as typologically, rather than genealogically, connected with David.[67] In view of the Fourth Evangelist's stance on the question of Jesus' Davidic lineage, it is striking that he apparently regards these non-dynastic references to the expected David such as Ezek 34:23 and 37:24 as particularly appropriate to Jesus.[68] The obvious appeal for the Fourth Evangelist of Isa 55, the only Dt-Isaian passage where David is mentioned by name, is equally notable.[69]

This has important implications for Johannine studies. Much of the hesitation in allowing that David has any role in the Gospel arises from the common assumption that Davidic typology, such as that found in the latter prophets necessarily implies Davidic genealogy for the expected figure.[70] This assumption has been questioned in recent scholarship, and it is now recognized that a Christian preoccupation with Davidic messianism has led to a belief that dynastic concerns are more dominant in these texts than

---

[66] The later reception of such texts is exemplified in the Jerusalem Talmud: "If the Messiah-king comes from the living, his name will be David. If he comes from the dead, he will be King David himself." Cf. *Y. Ber.* 2:3.

[67] Brueggemann sees an example of this development in a phrase from the Davidic dynasty tradition recalled by the author of Lamentations and incorporated into one of his poems.

The steadfast-love (pl.) of the Lord never ceases,
his mercies never come to an end (Lam 3:22).

Within the structure of the lament, it is this derivative form of the 2 Sam 7 covenant formula which marks a complete turnabout from hopelessness to confidence. Thus a mere allusion to the Davidic covenant without even the mention of David's name, let alone king, throne or dynasty, is sufficient to give hope to desperate exiles. See *David's Truth*, 94-5.

[68] The absence of firm evidence that Ezekiel anywhere (with the *possible* exception of Ezek 17:22-24) predicted a revival of the Davidic dynasty would suggest that, in the case of these passages, the David motif points not to the genealogy of the expected king, but rather to the reconstitution of the whole kingdom of Israel as at the time of David's rule. See Pomykala, *The Davidic Dynasty Tradition*, 27-28.

[69] See pp. 85-87 above.

[70] Davidic genealogy is certainly implied in a text such as Mic 5:2-4, although, even there, the promise of a new ruler from Bethlehem Ephratha (Mic 5:2-4) does involve "some kind of genealogical break with the currently ruling line." Pomykala suggests that the ruler may be expected to come from David's family, i.e., from Jesse's stock (Isa 11:1) or merely from the tribe of Judah (Gen 49:10). See *The Davidic Dynasty Tradition*, 18. Jewish expectations based on this text, as reported in John 7:41-42, however, do seem to entail Davidic descent.

in fact they are.⁷¹ We also recognize nowadays that in NT times there was no one coherent or normative messianic theory. Messianic ideas were fluid and varied.⁷² It follows from this that messianic motifs in the literature of the late Second Temple period are not necessarily or exclusively Davidic,⁷³ and that where Davidic motifs do occur, they are not necessarily to be taken as messianic.⁷⁴

The "invention" of a Davidic genealogy for one believed to fulfil "Davidic" expectations was to become a feature of some strands of Jewish thought. The tendency can be detected in the writings of the Second Temple period, even before messianism as such appears, the Chronicler's invention of a Davidic ancestry for Zerubbabel being an obvious example (1 Chr 3:16-19). While there is no history of David's descendants during this period, there is considerable literary evidence that the belief in the restoration of the house of David persisted.⁷⁵ It seems, however, that it had no genealogical base and was not connected with the members of any actual families regarded as descendants of the house of David.⁷⁶ On the other hand, several popular

---

⁷¹ J. D. Levenson, e.g., considers it "a fundamental mistake to see the Davidic Covenant lurking behind all the material relevant to the Judean monarchy." Kingship and the Davidic dynasty were not always synonymous. Davidic covenant ideology was quite localised in certain Judean circles and was therefore less ubiquitous and less influential than the Sinaiatic traditions. See "The Davidic Covenant and its Modern Interpreters," *CBQ* 41 (1979) 205-19 at 216-17. Pomykala, *Davidic Dynasty Tradition*, 67, warns that "to assume that every early Jewish text that speaks of David, the davidic dynasty or covenant, or Israelite kingship entails an expectation for the re-establishment of the davidic monarchy or hope for a davidic messiah is a faulty approach."

⁷² As the famous Mishnaic passage about presumption and dearth increasing with "the footsteps of the Messiah" (*M. Sota* 9:9-15) shows, there were circles in quite early Judaism where messianism was even regarded as an aberration. See Neusner, *Messiah in Context*, 25.

⁷³ One might think of the pre-existent heavenly Messiah in 1 Enoch, or the dyarchic messianism of both the DSS and the Testaments of the Twelve Patriarchs. Even though the literary evidence is later than the NT period, one might also include the Samaritan expectation of a Moses *redivivus*, the *Taheb*. See Talmon, "Types of Messianic Expectation at the Turn of the Era," in his *King, Cult and Calendar in Ancient Israel: Collected Studies*, (Jerusalem: Magnes, 1986) 202-24, at 207-9.

⁷⁴ Thus, for example, none of the 11QPsᵃ "Davidic" pseudepigraphical psalms is messianic. The portrayals of David in Josephus, Philo and Ps-Philo are non-messianic or even, in some cases, as we will see, anti-messianic.

⁷⁵ E.g., Isaac blesses Judah in Jubilees 31:18 (160-140 BCE) saying, "A prince shall you be, you and one of your sons." The Testament of the Twelve Patriarchs (2nd cent. BCE) refers several times to the expectation of a king from the tribe of Judah. According to 1 Macc 2:57 (late second century BCE), "David, because he was merciful, inherited the throne of the kingdom for ever."

⁷⁶ There were, in fact, several Davidic families, but none of their members ever claimed to be the expected "Son of David." In Zech 12:7, the "House of David" appears to be a large clan group, in genealogical continuity with the former royal family, holding no official office, but enjoying social prominence. The students of

"Messiahs" appeared. The fact that they either claimed to be, or were acclaimed as, Sons of David would indicate that their "Davidic" standing was based, not on their genealogy, but on their deeds which were perceived as revealing their "Davidic" status.[77] The acclamation of such leaders as "messiahs" has, perhaps, more to tell us about the first century CE reception of the biblical accounts of David than about genealogical matters.[78] It therefore appears that inasmuch as various historical or expected messianic figures were believed to fulfil the hope arising out the promise to David, they were invested with a "Davidic" allure. One way of doing this was to provide such a figure with a royal genealogy, thus revealing his hidden messianic status. Another perhaps more subtle way was to portray him in terms reminiscent of the biblical traditions surrounding David. Then he would be recognized as the Messiah. It was this latter modification of the dynastic notion that gave rise to the idea of the "hidden Messiah." As Yehezkel Kaufman explains:

> During this period there was a firm belief in the Son-of-David. But this belief was that the Son-of-David will *appear*, that he will become revealed...Being a child of the house of David, was never understood as a mere phrase or a mystical symbol of the eschatological redemption. It was meant to convey a real flesh and blood relationship. In the course of history, the people had lost track of all the children of the Davidic dynasty, and as a result there were families in the line of royalty although no one was aware of it. The revelation of the Messiah revealed also this lost genealogical information...In those days the belief spread that the Son-of-David existed somewhere hidden from the people until the time of his revelation...With the growth of the belief in a redeemer-Son-of David, the flesh and blood relationship became less relevant until it finally lost all importance. The actual work of redemption was a sign of the redeemer's genealogical credentials.[79]

Rabbi Judah the Prince, a member of the House of David, lament his death using the words from Lam 4:20, "The breath of our nostrils, the anointed of the Lord." (Cf. *Y. Shabbath* 16.1). This is a comparatively late text, but it illustrates the possibility of a reference to Davidic lineage being simply a proclamation of noble ancestry with no messianic overtones.

[77] Some of these leaders appear to have themselves fostered specifically messianic hopes inspired by David. Josephus says of two of them, Menahem (*Wars* 2. 433-34, 441-48) and Simon bar-Giora (*Wars* 4. 510 & 575; 7. 229-31), that they had royal aspirations. We know too that the star from Jacob of Num 24 was interpreted messianically by R. Akiba concerning Simon bar Kokhba at the time of the revolt, 132-35 CE (*y. Ta'an* 4.68d).

[78] Popular messianic leaders and their followers were clearly inspired by the narratives about David's period as a bandit chief. The depiction of stringed instruments on coins of the Bar Kokhba period lends weight to the suggestion that David was a powerful symbol for the insurgents and their supporters. It is noteworthy that the principal identifying image of David on these coins refers to his role as psalmist.

[79] Y. Kaufmann, "The Messianic Idea: The Real and the Hidden Son-of-David," *JBQ* 22 (1994) 141-50, at 146-47, 150.

It is surely from a "strain" of messianic expectation akin to this thinking that the Johannine idea that Jesus' works establish his credentials as the Christ arises (John 10:37-38). Within that frame of reference, the "Davidic" qualities of Jesus are important arguments for Jesus' status as the Christ.

A non-dynastic interpretation of Nathan's oracle would allow other motifs from royal ideology to be brought into play, in particular the unity of the Northern and Southern kingdoms as in the days of David, and the renewal of the Temple cult. The tendency towards a *relecture* of the promises to David as made to the nation, which we noted as a feature of the reception of the psalms in the post-exilic period, was part of this development. It was to find expression, for example, in the theocratic perspective from which PsSol 17-18 views the anticipated rule of the Davidic Messiah. This "son of David" (17:21), who is to usher in the eschatological era, is a sapiential figure who will rule a holy people in a cleansed and restored Jerusalem (PsSol 17:30) to which the dispersed will return (PsSol 17:31) and to which all the nations will be attracted (PsSol 17). It was a re-visioned David such as this whose psalms and whose story were to become such an important resource for the Fourth Evangelist in his portrayal of Jesus.

The ruler whom Ezekiel foresees is to be typologically like David, the ideal king who ruled over a united Israel as the Lord's faithful servant. Thus Ezekiel writes of a people gathered into unity under a divinely appointed shepherd, of two 'sticks' becoming one 'staff' in the hand of the king of Judah, that is, of the northern and southern kingdoms being united as in the days of David (Ezek 37:17). For the Fourth Evangelist, those gathered into the one fold of Jesus are held in his hand or in the Father's hand—one and the same reality, as the next verse makes clear, because Jesus and the Father are one (John 10:28-30). Ezekiel presents the future David figure as instrumental in the establishment of a definitive and everlasting Temple (Ezek 37:26-28).[80] A phrase from Ezek 37 may even perhaps "un-

---

[80] There is a constant connection between expectation of a 'David' figure and that of a rebuilding of the Temple. Both are connected in *4QFlor* 10-13, for example. In the synoptic trial narratives too, the accusation that Jesus spoke of destruction/rebuilding of the Temple results in the question, 'Are you the Messiah?' See Dunn, "Messianic Ideas and the Jesus of History," 372. Luke's conflation of Ps 88:21, 1 Sam 13:14 and Isa 44:28 in Acts 13:22 is significant in this regard. The first two source texts (Εὖρον Δαυὶδ and ἄνδρα κατὰ τὴν καρδίαν μου) refer to David, but the third text (... ὃς ποιήσει πάντα τὰ θελήματά μου) refers to Cyrus. The link between David and Cyrus, which has prompted Luke to apply a description of Cyrus to David, may well be that both made provision for the building of the Temple.

derlie" that moment in the Johannine prologue where the first hint is given that Jesus is himself that Temple—

Ezek 37:27	John 1:14
...καὶ ἔσται ἡ <u>κατασκήνωσίς</u> μου ἐν αὐτοῖς...	Καὶ ὁ λόγος σὰρξ ἐγένετο καὶ ἐσκήνωσεν ἐν ἡμῖν
"...and my tabernacle shall be among them..."	And the Word became flesh and dwelt among us...

Finally, it is through "David" the "one shepherd" of Ezekiel's prophecy that God shepherds God's people—

> I myself will be the shepherd of my sheep, and I will make them lie down, says the Lord.... I will feed them in justice (Ezek 34:15-16).

> And I will set up over them one shepherd, my servant David, and he shall feed them... (Ezek 34:23).

Ashton asks, "Is the fourth Evangelist deliberately fusing two figures (Yahweh/Messiah) placed in succession by the prophet?" It could well be that he is. Moreover, the interpretive framework within which such a theological development could be possible has, perhaps, a useful illustrative parallel in another development which Ashton has suggested may have provided a model for the Johannine presentation of Jesus as God: the fusion of "Angel of the Lord" with "the Lord."[81]

Against the background of all we have outlined in this section, particularly the importance of the expected David as a symbol for the ingathering of the tribes, we can understand how the establishment of the eschatological Temple at Jesus' death is his most David-like moment, the "hour" when he lays down his life for his sheep,— "for the nation, and not for the nation only, but to gather into one the children of God who are scattered abroad" (John 11:51-52).

F. *Overview of the Davidic Features in the Johannine Portrayal of Jesus*

Taken individually, any one of the similarities between David and Jesus which we have posited in this chapter might seem insignificant or even tenuous.[82] However, the portrayal of Jesus to which they together contribute is one in which Davidic elements have an undeni-

---

[81] See *Studying John*, 124, n. 20. and Ch. 3, "Bridging Ambiguities," 71-89.

[82] Glasson, for one, *Davidic Links*, 118, does not put much weight on the similarity between Ittai's words in 2 Sam 15:21 and John 12:26. Yet Trudinger, *Hosanna*

able role. The resulting picture might be compared to the art form of graphic collage in which the original nature and function of the constituent elements remains evident even when these elements are transformed by their incorporation into a totally new context. The cumulative effect of these recollections of David is a strong impression of his latent presence in the Fourth Gospel. As we have seen, this in itself is not unique to the Fourth Gospel. What is unique is the way in which the Fourth Gospel appropriates the stories and expectations surrounding David and adapts them in line with his view of Jesus.

David's influence on the Fourth Gospel, therefore, is sensed not only through the high profile of "his" psalms, but also through numerous subtle recollections of the remembered and expected David, which encourage the reader to see analogies between him and Jesus. As has been noted with regard to the use of the psalms in the Gospel, John is selective in his choice of motifs from the David story, not taking up from 2 Sam 15:30-31, for example, David's weeping and his prayer in sorrow and fear. Again, as with the psalm references, the "David" echoes are less confined to the Passion Narrative than those in the synoptics.

In considering David's paradigmatic role in relation to Jesus in the Fourth Gospel, we should bear in mind the particular emphasis which the Fourth Evangelist places on Jesus' kingship, as both correction and complement to other notions of kingship and as closely connected with his role as revealer of God. In discussing the radical re-definition of Jesus' kingship in the Fourth Gospel, De Jonge speaks of the way in which the Jewish technical term ὁ χριστός is interpreted anew in the Fourth Gospel: "it is taken over as worthy of reinterpretation."[83] The literary *persona* of David, as it had evolved by the Second Temple period, as the protagonist of narrative traditions, as "author" of the psalms, and as an idealised symbol of hope for the future, provided the Evangelist with a paradigm and a resource for such reinterpretation.

298, writing seventeen years after his article in response to Glasson, not only finds it hard to believe that John did not have Ittai's declaration in mind, but adds that he believes Peter's bold words of allegiance in John 13:36-37 are also a probable reflection of it.

[83] De Jonge, *Jesus: Stranger from Heaven*, 52. 54.

GENERAL CONCLUSION

In our General Introduction to this study, we referred to T. S. Eliot's reflections on the transformative power of citation, and how the literary past is altered by the present (the later text which cites it) as much as the present is directed by the past. We quoted from his essay, *Tradition and the Individual Talent* (1919), his statement that true individuality lies in those parts of a writer's work "in which the dead poets, his ancestors, assert their immortality most vigorously." In an application of this theory to biblical studies, Michael Fishbane offers an insight which is eminently applicable to the Fourth Gospel as a work in which the "poet" David lives and speaks.

> There is, then, something of the dynamic of "tradition and the individual talent" here—where the tradition sets the agenda of problems which must be creatively resolved or determines the received language which may be imaginatively reworked. The strategies vary from textual annotation, literary allusion, and types of analogical or synthetic reasoning. They include also the ethical, legal or even spiritual transformation of textual content. In all cases the "tradition" maintains its generative and often determinative hierarchical pre-eminence, even as "individual talent" (of an individual in fact, or a school representative) clarifies or transforms tradition in the light of present-day ignorance or other exigencies.[1]

In this study, we have sought to explore the "tradition" enshrined in the Psalter as transformed by the "individual talent" of the Fourth Evangelist. In order to do this, we first had to discover the Evangelist and his circle as readers of that "tradition." In seeking to do this, we found that foremost among the generative and determinative features of the Psalter, as it would have been received by him and his circle, was its supposed Davidic "authorship."

What Gerald T. Sheppard has to say about the biblical presentation of Solomon's wisdom is applicable to the neglect of David's role as psalmist which has been a feature of much modern biblical scholarship:

> Once this presentation became historically discredited by subsequent scholarship, it has been almost entirely overlooked in modern study. Nonetheless, it belongs to the 'literary form of the story' within scrip-

---

[1] Michael Fishbane, "Inner Biblical Exegesis: Types and Strategies of Interpretation in Ancient Israel," in G. H. Hartman and S. Budick (ed.), *Midrash and Literature* (New Haven & London: Yale University Press, 1986) 19-37, at 34.

ture and, therefore, remains an integral feature of both Jewish and Christian claims about 'the truth.' Rather than debunking a naive historical assumption, I will work in the opposite direction, building on the negative historical conclusions of modern scholarship as a heuristic aid for our understanding of the biblical tradition and, ultimately, its theological implications.[2]

At first sight, David's role as a source of psalmody seems of marginal interest to the NT writers, Luke being its principal exponent. But it is important to remember that Davidic "authorship" of the psalms was a "given" so obvious that it did not require reiteration every time a psalm was cited. This presupposition was the basis for the use of the psalms in early Christianity. As J. L. Mays has put it, "The psalms were used and were understood as they were, because of their connection through David with Christ."[3] This idea has been resisted in Johannine scholarship because of the Fourth Evangelist's perceived preoccupation with Jesus' heavenly pre-existence. It has been felt, correctly, that David as genealogical ancestor of the Messiah does not come within the Fourth Evangelist's area of theological concern. However, as this study has shown, there is much more to David than his role as progenitor of the Messiah. He is "the sweet psalmist of Israel" (2 Sam 23:1, RSV) and, as such, he pervades the Gospel as "author" of its most extensively cited biblical book.

In the memory and imagination of Second Temple Judaism, the psalms are filtered through the lens of the narrative traditions about David. Thus they become a story of David's "hardships" (Ps [131]132:1), of the intimate, filial relationship with God which sustained him, of his zeal for the worship of God, and of the glorious vindication with which God rewarded his devotion. This seems to be the story which most frequently sprang to mind when Johannine Christians recalled what Jesus had done and remembered what had been done to him. Jesus had shown a David-like zeal for the Temple and all it stood for (John 2:22); sufferings like David's had been inflicted on him (John 19:24); yet he was preserved from destruction (John 19:36) and assured of the eternal kingship promised to David. Understood in this way, David emerges as a highly significant figure, both as "writer "and as "written about," in the Scriptures which bear witness to Jesus (John 5:39).

David is important in the Fourth Gospel as "author" of the biblical book which the Evangelist cites most extensively, as Scripture brought to completion in Jesus (cf. John 19:28). But this is not all.

---

[2] "The Relation of Solomon's Wisdom to Biblical Prayer," *TJT* 8 (1992) 7-27, at 7.
[3] J. L. Mays, "The David of the Psalms," 146.

The Fourth Evangelist received the memory of David as part of an early Christian interpretive tradition which, like the Psalter itself, set its own agenda of "problems" to be creatively resolved. The language of Davidic Messianism, as received in early Christological reflection would have to be imaginatively reworked if it was to meet the exigencies of John's theological project. In determining how the received tradition could be adapted, he would decide to omit some features and develop others. Thus, while his portrayal of Jesus never refers to him as "Son of David," it draws extensively on the multifaceted richness which the figure of David had acquired in Second Temple Judaism.

In view of this, the findings of our study call for a re-appraisal of the claim that the Fourth Evangelist intentionally dissociates Jesus from David. This claim can often be detected as the presupposition underlying "sightings" of Prophet-like-Moses typology in the Fourth Gospel. For example, in the course of an astute feminist-critical reading of John 4:1-42, Schneiders comments:

> The woman has questioned Jesus on virtually every significant tenet of Samaritan theology. Through this process she has come to suspect that he is the messiah in and through his own self-revelation as the new prophet like Moses (significantly, not a new David), thus vindicating the Samaritan claim to be spiritually a legitimate part of the Chosen People and thus of the New Israel.[4]

Schneiders' assurance that the Johannine Jesus is "not a new David" is of a piece with her later statement, "The path to Christian identity for the Samaritans does not necessarily pass by way of Jerusalem."[5] Such a reading ignores the Johannine Jesus' statement, ὅτι ἡ σωτηρία ἐκ τῶν Ἰουδαίων ἐστίν (John 4:22). It also fails to take into account a whole biblical and pseudepigraphical tradition according to which ἡ σωτηρία, "the redemption," is the longed for gathering of scattered Israel under one shepherd, David, in whom God will be their shepherd, the restoration of the united kingdom of Israel and Judah, as in the days of David. The restored temple, to which the Northern tribes will return, is in the Johannine view, the temple of Jesus' body. This is not to deny that Jesus is the "prophet like Moses." Our insistence that David is an important paradigm for the Johannine portrayal of Jesus does not exclude other biblical figures. An important aspect of the Jewishness of the Fourth Gospel is its portrayal of Jesus as the fulfilment of so many different scriptural "types" or motifs. Just as, in Jewish tradition the Rock of Zion is

---

[4] Schneiders, *The Revelatory Text*, 190.
[5] Schneiders, *The Revelatory Text*, 195.

Paradise, the site of Abraham's sacrifice, Arunah's threshing floor, the original altar of the Temple, so the Johannine Jesus is prophet-like Moses, Isaac, Elijah, and, most especially, David.

The re-working of David which was the burden of Ch. 2 of our study provides a most fruitful analogy to the Johannine re-working of Jesus.[6] The intertextual play between psalms and narrative traditions which resulted in the literary entity of David is analogous to the role of the psalms in the process which produced the Jesus of early Christian imagination and memory. In both processes the psalms fulfil initially a relatively subordinate role *vis à vis* the narrative traditions. Selected psalm verses furnish material for interpretation and amplification of the tradition. Gradually the rest of the psalm from which a verse has been drawn comes to be seen as applicable. Then other psalms with similar motifs begin to cluster around the historical memory. Eventually, the whole Psalter is seen as pertinent to the figure who has by now become a purely literary construct. And all the while, an almost imperceptible shift has been taking place. The psalms have begun to dictate to the narrative, determining its contours. Eventually they so control its course that, by the mature phase of the process, creation and reception of narrative presuppose the "account" given in the psalms. The historical data is selected, modified and interpreted to accord with the psalmic view. A mature phase of this development is represented by the rabbinical writings in the case of David, by the Fourth Gospel and early patristic writings in the case of Jesus.

A "by-product" of this study is the evidence it provides that some interpretive traditions about David found in texts of later Judaism may go back at least to the first century CE. While both the Psalms Targum and, even more so, the *Midrash Tehillim* postdate the Fourth Gospel to such an extent that reference to them in NT studies is seen by some as methodologically unsound, it is not outside the realm of possibility that the NT may attest to the antiquity of interpretive traditions which they contain.

This study also shows how methodologies from contemporary literary theory open up possibilities in biblical study which were unthinkable for earlier scholars. We refer in particular to the notion of intertextuality and the concept of literary echo. Without the benefit

---

[6] Commenting on the "remarkable literary device Martyn discerns in the Fourth Gospel," that John narrates a story which, on the face of it, is about the past but which speaks to current events, Ashton, *Understanding*, 413, draws a parallel with the Chronicler's portrayal of David and Solomon which aims at "inviting his readers to see the Second Temple and its cult as a direct return to the First."

of these approaches, earlier scholars found, for example, that the psalm quotations in the passion narrative, "seem to have no close relation with specifically Johannine theology,"[7] or that in the psalm quotations in the Johannine passion narrative "there is no apparent allusion to ideas specifically Johannine,"[8] or that Ps (81)82 is quoted in John 10:34 "without any regard for the original meaning and context of the verse,"[9] or that there is nothing in the citation from Ps (21:19)22:18 to indicate whether the episode has a particular meaning for the Evangelist.[10]

How do the psalms actually "work" in the Gospel? The genre of the psalms formally cited as fulfilled in the events of "the hour," Pss [68]69, [40]41, [21]22 and [33]34 (first person singular lament, prayer, and testimony) allows the Evangelist to present passages from them as prophetic anticipations of what would actually happen to Jesus: persecution, betrayal, despoliation, thirst, death, preservation from the *crurifragium*.[11] These four psalms all come from Book 1 of the Psalter and have Davidic superscripts. Ps [117]118 also fits into this category in that it includes first person singular passages and has a strong association with David in Jewish tradition. All of these psalms contain words of David which reach their fulfilment on Jesus' lips. In contrast, Ps [77]78 and Ps [81]82, both τῷ Ασαφ, belong to quite different genres and have quite a different purpose in the Gospel. They function principally in terms of Jesus' revelatory self-disclosure. As the formula καθώς ἐστιν γεγραμμένον (John 6:31) indicates, they are part of the scripture or "the Law" which is being continually "searched" for testimony to Jesus (John 5:39).[12] Thus, there are, on the one hand, anecdotal psalm testimonies which John has received in the tradition and from which there have been Johannine outgrowths, notably, the two further citations from Ps [68]69. Then, on the other hand, there is John's own unique psalm usage exemplified in the two quotations from Ps [77]78 and the one from Ps [81]82. These reflect a reception of the Psalter as scripture in which "David," is believed to have written about Jesus in much the same way that Moses wrote of him. Here it is not a question of David's "autobiographical" outpourings finding their fulfilment on the lips of Jesus. Instead the psalm citations are in-

---

[7] Barrett, "The OT in the Fourth Gospel," 168.
[8] Dodd, *Interpretation*, 428.
[9] Bultmann, *The Gospel*, 389.
[10] Bultmann, *The Gospel*, 671.
[11] For the purposes of this discussion we include all three citations from Ps 68 in this category.
[12] Cf. Matt 13:35 where Ps (77)78:2 is cited as an authentication of Jesus' teaching style.

stances of the total witness of Scripture to the whole coming into the world of the Word made flesh.

This interpretation of events in the light of Scripture and the corresponding *relecture* of Scripture is literally a matter of life and death for Johannine Christians. It was crucial that the Scriptures be given new meaning so that they might retain their viability and provide continuity in a time of crisis and change.[13] Intertextual reference to the psalms in the Fourth Gospel, therefore, had an important social function. The psalms helped Johannine Christians to cope with their experience that faith in Jesus meant alienation from Judaism.[14] Firstly, as part of the general Scripture reference in the Gospel, the psalms showed how Jesus fulfils and replaces the great religious institutions of Israel. In that way, they reinforced the legitimacy of the Johannine group's isolation from Judaism. Secondly, the Psalter provided them with the possibility of an intimacy with Jesus comparable with the profound personal access to David which it fostered in Second Temple Judaism. This is just one example of a feature of Jewish piety which has been appropriated and revisioned by Johannine Christians, just as, devotion to the Temple, for example, is taken over and re-interpreted.

This brings us back to our question—whether there might be an intertextual relationship between the two-psalm prologue to the Psalter and the two-book structure of the Gospel. Understood "Johanninely," Ps 1 tells how those who acknowledge Jesus as their "way" find life, while unbelievers go the way of the wicked and perish. Ps 2 tells of the opposition to Jesus, of the hatred he encountered, of God's vindication of his claim to divine sonship and of the blessedness of those who respond to this in faith. Just as the prologue encapsulates the whole Psalter, so too the Psalter "stands" for the whole of scripture. Thus by implementing the script of Pss 1-2, Johannine Christians experience the scripture as fulfilled, and themselves fulfil the purpose for which the Gospel was written: ἵνα πιστεύ[σ]ητε ὅτι Ἰησοῦς ἐστιν ὁ Χριστὸς ὁ υἱὸς τοῦ θεοῦ (the programme of Ps 2) καὶ ἵνα πιστεύοντες ζωὴν ἔχητε ἐν τῷ ὀνόματι αὐτοῦ (the programme of Ps 1).

By far the most significant aspect of this putative Johannine reception of Pss 1-2, however, is its exemplification of the radically interpretive power of citation. The "past" is altered by the "present,"

---

[13] See Dahl, "Messianic Ideas and the Crucifixion of Jesus," in Charlesworth (ed.) *The Messiah*, 382-403, at 384.
[14] See Meeks, *Man From Heaven*, 145

once Johannine Christians open the scroll of the psalms. For John's audience, Jesus is not merely the Lord King declared Son of God in Ps 2, but is the divine Κύριος to whom the response of faith is directed—μακάριοι πάντες οἱ πεποιθότες ἐπ' αὐτῷ (Ps 2:12). As such, he is the Lord whose Law/word brings life (Ps 1:1-3) and, since the reception of the prologue is the model for the reception of the whole Psalter, he is the Lord who loosens from the bonds of death (John 11:44; cf. Ps [115:7]116:16), who breathes his spirit on his disciples (John 20:22; cf. Ps [103]104:30), who teaches his ways which are truth (John 14:26; 16:13; cf. Ps [24:5-11]25:4-10) As the patristic psalm exegesis abundantly shows, once the Christological reading is established, there are endless possibilities for imaginative reworking of the language received in the psalms. The contribution of this study is to show that this is not fanciful accommodation of the text, but is faithful to an exegetical tradition rooted firmly in the Jewishness of the Fourth Gospel.

BIBLIOGRAPHY

Achtemeier, Paul J. "*Omne Verbum Sonat:* The New Testament and the Oral Environment of Late Western Antiquity." *JBL* 109 (1990) 3-27.
Ackerman, J. S. "The Rabbinic Interpretation of Ps 82 and the Gospel of John." *HTR* 59 (1966) 186-91.
Aland, B., K. Aland, J. Karavidopoulos, C. M. Martini and B. M. Metzger (ed.). *The Greek New Testament.* 4th rev. ed. Stuttgart: Deutsche Bibelgesellschaft, 1993.
Aland, Kurt. *Synopsis Quattuor Evangeliorum.* Stuttgart: Deutsche Bibelgesellschaft, 1985.
Alter, Robert and Frank Kermode (ed.). *The Literary Guide to the Bible.* Glasgow: Collins, 1987.
Ashton, John. *Understanding the Fourth Gospel.* Oxford: Clarendon Press, 1991.
———. *Studying John.* Oxford: Clarendon Press, 1994.
Ashton, John (ed.). *The Interpretation of John.* Issues in Religion and Theology 9. Philadelphia; Fortress & London: SPCK, 1986.
Aune, David E. *The Cultic Setting of Realized Eschatology in Early Christianity.* Suppl. *NovT* XXVIII. Leiden: E. J. Brill, 1972.
———. "Christian Prophecy and the Messianic Status of Jesus." In *The Messiah*, ed. J. H. Charlesworth, 404-22. Minneapolis: Augsburg Fortress, 1992.
Auwers, Jean-Marie. "La nuit de Nicodème (Jean 3, 2; 19,39) ou l'ombre du langage." *RB* 97 (1990) 481-503.

Bampfylde, Gillian. "John XIX 28: A Case for a Different Translation." *NovT* 11 (1969) 247-260.
———. "More Light on John XII 34." *JSNT* 17 (1983) 87-89.
Bardy, G. and M. Lefèvre (ed.). *Hippolyte: Commentaire sur Daniel.* SC 14. Paris: Les Éditions du cerf, 1947.
Bar-Ilan, Meir. "The Date of *The Words of Gad the Seer.* " *JBL* 109 (1990) 475-92.
Barker, Margaret. *The Older Testament: The Survival of Themes from the Ancient Royal Cult in Sectarian Judaism and Early Christianity.* London: SPCK, 1987.
———. *The Gate of Heaven: The History and Symbolism of the Temple in Jerusalem.* London: SPCK, 1991.
Barrett, C. K. "The Old Testament in the Fourth Gospel." *JTS* 48 (1947) 155- 69.
———. *St John's Gospel: A Commentary.* London: SPCK, 1956.
Barthélemy, D. and J. T. Milik. *Discoveries in the Judean Desert: Vol. 1, Qumran Cave I.* Oxford: Clarendon Press, 1955.

Barthes, Roland. *Le Plaisir du Texte*. Paris: Les Éditions du Seuil, 1973.

——. *S/Z: A Structuralist Reading of Balzac's "Sarrasine."* Trans. Richard Miller. Oxford: Blackwell, 1990.

——. "The Theory of the Text." In *Untying the Text: A Post Structuralist Reader*, ed. Robert Young, 32-49. Boston, London and Henley: Routledge and Kegan Paul, 1981.

Barton, G. A. " 'A Bone of Him Shall Not Be Broken,' John 19:36." *JBL* 49 (1930) 12-18.

Bassler, Jouette M. "A Man for All Seasons: David in Rabbinic and New Testament Literature." *Int* 40 (1986), 156-169.

Bauer, Walter. *A Greek-English Lexicon of the New Testament*. 2d ed. Trans. William F. Arndt and F. Wilbur Gingrich. Chicago: Chicago University Press, 1979.

Baumgarten, J. M. "4Q 500 and the Ancient Conception of the Lord's Vineyard." *JJS* 40 (1989) 1-6.

Beaucamp, E. *Le Psautier*. 2 vols. Sources Bibliques. Paris: Gabalda, 1976 and 1979.

Becker, Joachim. "Die kollektive Deutung der Königspsalmen." In *Studien Zum Messiasbild im Alten Testament*, ed. Ursula Struppe, 291-318. Stuttgart: Katholisches Bibelwerke, 1989.

Beckwith, Roger T. "The Courses of Levites and the Eccentric Psalms Scrolls from Qumran." *RevQum* 11 (1982-84) 499-524.

Beernaert, P. Moulon. "La Verité au sens biblique: approche de saint Jean." *LumVit* 46 (1991) 287-300.

Beetham, F. G. and P. A. Beetham. "A Note on John 19:29." *JTS* 44 (1993) 163-69.

Berger, Klaus. "Die Koniglichen Messiastraditionen des Neuen Testaments." *NTS* 20 (1973) 1-44.

Bergmeier, Roland. "ΤΕΤΕΛΕΣΤΑΙ: Joh 19:30." *ZNW* 79 (1988) 282-90.

Betz, Otto. "The Qumran Halakhah Text Miqsat Ma'ase Ha-Torah (4QMMT) and Sadducean, Essene, and Early Pharisaic Tradition." In *The Aramaic Bible: Targums in Their Historical Context*, ed. D. R. G. Beattie and M. J. McNamara, 176-202. JSOT Suppl. Series 166. Sheffield: Sheffield Academic Press, 1984.

Beuken, W. A. M. "Isaiah 55, 3-5: The Reinterpretation of David." *Bijdragen* 35 (1974) 49-64.

Beutler, Johannes. "Psalm 42/43 im Johannesevangelium." *NTS* 25 (1978) 33-57.

——. "Der Alttestamentlich-jüdischer Hintergrund der Hirtenrede." In *The Shepherd Discourse of John 10 and its Context*, ed. J. Beutler and R. T. Fortna, 18-32. Cambridge: Cambridge University Press, 1991.

Beutler, Johannes and Robert T. Fortna (ed.). *The Shepherd Discourse of John 10 and its Context*. Cambridge: Cambridge University Press, 1991.

Bienaimé, Germain. "L'annonce des fleuves d'eau vive en Jean 7, 37-39." Part I, *RTL* 21 (1990) 281-310. Part II, 417-54.

Black, Matthew. "The Messianism of the Parables of Enoch." In *The Messiah*, ed. J. H. Charlesworth, 145-68. Minneapolis: Augsburg Fortress, 1992.

Bloch, R. "Methodological Note for the Study of Rabbinic Literature." In *Approaches to Ancient Judaism: Theory and Practice,* ed. W. S. Green. Brown Judaic Studies I. Missoula: Scholars Press, 1978, 51-75.
Bloom, Harold. *The anxiety of Influence: A Theory of Poetry.* London and Oxford, N.Y: Oxford University Press, 1973.
Boismard, M.-É. "De son ventre couleront des fleuves d'eau: Jo., VII, 38." *RB* 65 (1958) 523- 46.
——. "Les citations targumiques dans le quatrième évangile," *RB* 66 (1959) 374-78.
——. *Moïse ou Jésus: Essai de Christologie Johannique.* Leuven: Leuven University Press, 1988.
Boismard, M.-É. and A. Lamouille, with the collaboration of G. Rochais. *L'Évangile de Jean.* Vol. III of *Synopse des quatre évangiles en français.* Paris: Les Éditions du Cerf, 1977.
Boman, T. "Das Letzte Wort Jesu." *ST* 17 (1963) 103-119.
Borgen, Peder. *Bread from Heaven, An Exegetical Study of the Concept of Manna in the Gospel of John and the Writings of Philo.* NovT Suppl. Series 10. Leiden: E. J. Brill, 1965.
——. "Some Jewish Exegetical Traditions as Background for Son of Man Sayings in John's Gospel (Jn 3, 13-14 and context)." In *L'Évangile de Jean: Sources, rédaction, théologie,* ed. M. de Jonge, 243-58. Leuven: Leuven University Press & Gembloux: Duculot, 1977.
——. "God's Agent in the Fourth Gospel." In *The Interpretation of John,* ed. John Ashton, 67-78. Philadelphia: Fortress & London: SPCK, 1986.
——. "Philo of Alexandria." In *The Anchor Bible Dictionary,* ed. D. N. Freedman, Vol 5, 333-42. New York and London: Doubleday, 1992.
Botha, P. J. J. "Living Voice and Lifeless Letters: Reserve towards Writing in the Graeco-Roman World." *HTS* 49 (1993) 742-759.
Braude, William. *The Midrash on Psalms.* Yale Judaica Series XIII, 2 vols. New Haven: Yale University Press, 1959.
Braun, F.-M. "Le Sacrifice d'Isaac dans le quatrième évangile d'après le Targum." *NRT* 101 (1979) 481-497.
Brawley, Robert L. "An Absent Complement and Intertextuality in John 19:28-29." *JBL* 112 (1993) 427-43.
Brettler, Marc and Michael Fishbane (ed.). *Minhah le Nahum: Biblical and Other Studies Presented to Nahum M. Sarna in Honour of His 70th Birthday.* Sheffield: Sheffield Academic Press, 1993.
Brodie, Thomas L. *The Gospel According to John: A Literary and Theological Commentary.* New York and Oxford: Oxford University Press, 1993.
Brooke, George J. *Exegesis at Qumran: 4QFlorilegium in its Jewish Context.* JSOT Supplement Series 29. Sheffield: JSOT Press, 1985.
——. *Biblical Interpretation in the Dead Sea Scrolls.* Presented at the Colloquium, "Qumran and the Dead Sea Scrolls," convoked by the Consultative Committee on Biblical and Near Eastern Texts at the Royal Irish Academy, Dublin, 1993.
Brown, F., S. R. Driver and A. Briggs. *A Hebrew and English Lexicon of the Old Testament.* Oxford: Clarendon, 1979.

Brown, Raymond E. *The Gospel According to John, I-XII*. Anchor Bible 29. Garden City, N.Y.: Doubleday, 1966.
———. *The Gospel According to John, XIII-XXI*. Anchor Bible 29A. Garden City N.Y.: Doubleday, 1970.
———. *The Birth of the Messiah: A Commentary on the Infancy Narratives in the Gospels of Matthew and Luke*. The Anchor Bible Reference Library. London: Chapman, 1993.
———. *The Death of the Messiah*. The Anchor Bible Reference Library. London: Chapman, 1994.
Brown, Raymond E., Joseph A. Fitzmyer and Roland E. Murphy (ed.). *The New Jerome Biblical Commentary*. London: Geoffrey Chapman, 1990.
Bruce, F. F. *1 and 2 Corinthians*. New Century Bible. London: Oliphants, 1971.
Brueggemann, Walter. "David and His Theologian." *CBQ* 30 (1968) 156-81.
———. "From Dust to Kingship." *ZAW* 84 (1972) 1-18.
———. *David's Truth in Israel's Imagination and Memory*. Philadelphia: Fortress, 1985.
———. "Response to James L. Mays, 'The Question of Context'." In *The Shape and Shaping of the Psalter*, ed. J. Clinton McCann, 29-41. JSOT Supplement Series 159. Sheffield: Sheffield Academic Press, 1993.
Buchanan, George W. "The Samaritan Origin of the Gospel of John." In *Religions in Antiquity: Essays in Memory of E. R. Goodenough*, ed. Jacob Neusner, 149-75. Leiden: E. J. Brill, 1968.
Bultmann, Rudolph. "The History of Religions Background of the Prologue to the Gospel of John" (1923). In *The Interpretation of John*, ed. John Ashton. Philadelphia: Fortress & London: SPCK, 1986.
———. *The Gospel of John: A Commentary*. Trans. G. R. Beasley-Murray. Oxford: Blackwell, 1971.
Buttrick, George A. (ed.). *The Interpreter's Dictionary of the Bible: An Illustrated Encyclopedia*. 4 vols. New York and Nashville: Abingdon, 1962.

Carmignac, J. "Les Citations de l'Ancien Testament et spécialement des poèmes du Serviteur dans les Hymnes de Qumrân." *RevQum* 2 (1959-60) 357-94.
Castelot, John J. and Aelred Cody. "Religious Institutions of Israel." In *The New Jerome Biblical Commentary*, ed. R. E. Brown, J. A. Fitzmyer and R. E. Murphy, 1253-83. London: Geoffrey Chapman, 1990.
Cathcart, Kevin J. and Robert P. Gordon. *The Targum of the Minor Prophets: Translated with a Critical Introduction, Apparatus and notes*. The Aramaic Bible. Edinburgh: T. and T. Clark, 1989.
Cazeau, J. "'Toi, bethléem, n'est-tu pas le parent pauvre des clans de juda?' le theme du roi dans l'évangile de jean." *LumVie* 35 (1986) 69-88.
Cazelles, H. "La Question du Lamed Auctoris." *RB* 56 (1949) 93-101.
Charlesworth, James H. (ed.). *The Old Testament Pseudepigrapha*, Vol. I,

London: Darton, Longman and Todd, 1983. Vol. II, New York: Doubleday, 1985.

Charlesworth, J. H. and J. A. Sanders. "More Psalms of David." In *The Old Testament Pseudepigrapha*, ed. J. H. Charlesworth, Vol. II, 611-24. New York: Doubleday, 1985.

——. (ed.). *The Messiah: Developments in Earliest Judaism and Christianity (The First Princeton Symposium on Judaism and Christian Origins)*. Minneapolis: Augsburg Fortress, 1992.

——. "From Messianology to Christology: Problems and Prospects," in Charlesworth (ed.), *The Messiah*, 3-35. Minneapolis: Augsburg Fortress, 1992.

Childs, Brevard. *Introduction to the Old Testament as Scripture*. Philadelphia: Fortress, 1979.

——. "Psalm Titles and Midrashic Exegesis." *JSS* 16 (1971) 137- 50.

Chilton, Bruce. "John xii 34 and the Targum Isaiah lii 13." *NovT* 22 (1980) 176-78.

——. "Jesus *ben David:* Reflections on the Davidssohnfrage." *NTS* 14 (1982) 88-112.

——. *A Galilean Rabbi and His Bible*. Wilmington, DE: Michael Glazier, 1984.

Clark, Douglas C. "Signs in Wisdom and John." *CBQ* 45 (1983) 201-09.

Colson, F. H., G. H. Whitaker and R. Marcus. *Philo*. Loeb Classical Library. Cambridge, MA: Harvard University Press & London: Heinemann, 1962.

Conrad, E. W. "The Community as King in Second Isaiah." In *Understanding the Word*, ed. J. T. Butler, E. W. Conrad and B. C. Ollenburger, 99-112. JSOTSup 37. Sheffield: JSOT Press, 1986.

Cooper, A. M. "The life and times of King David According to the Book of Psalms." In *The Poet and the Historian: Essays in Literary & Historical Biblical Criticism*, ed. R. E. Friedman, 117-31. Chico CA: Scholars, 1983.

Cotterell, Peter and Max Turner. *Linguistics and Biblical Interpretation*. London: SPCK, 1989.

Cross, F. M. and S. Talmon (ed.). *Qumran and the History of the Biblical Text*. Cambridge MA and London: Harvard University Press, 1975.

Culler, Jonathan. *The Pursuit of Signs: Semiotics, Literature, Deconstruction*. London and Henley: Routledge and Kegan Paul, 1981.

Culpepper, R. Alan. *The Anatomy of the Fourth Gospel: A Study in Literary Design*. Philadelphia: Fortress, 1983.

Dahl, Nils. A. "The Johannine Church and History." In *The Interpretation of John*, ed. John Ashton, 122-140. Philadelphia: Fortress & London: SPCK, 1986.

——. "Messianic Ideas and the Crucifixion of Jesus." In *The Messiah*, ed. J. H. Charlesworth, 382-403. Minneapolis: Augsburg Fortress, 1992.

Dahms, J. V. "Isaiah 55:11 and the Gospel of John." *EvangQuart* 53 (1981) 78- 88.

Dahood, Mitchell, *Psalms*. 3 vols. Anchor Bible. New York: Doubleday, 1965.
Danby, Herbert. *The Mishnah: Translated from the Hebrew with Introduction and Brief Explanatory Notes*. Oxford: Oxford University Press, 1933, 1964.
Daniélou, Jean. *Études d'exégèse judeo-chrétienne: Les Testimonia*. Paris: Beauchesne et ses fils, 1966.
Daube, David. *The New Testament and Rabbinic Judaism*. London: Athlone Press, 1956.
Davenport, Gene L. "The 'Anointed of the Lord' in Pss Sol 17." In *Ideal Figures in Ancient Judaism: Profiles and Paradigms*, ed. George W. E. Nickelsburg and John J. Collins, 67-92. Chico CA: Scholars Press, 1980.
Davila, James R. "Moriah." In *The Anchor Bible Dictionary*, ed. D. N. Freedman, Vol. IV, 905. New York and London: Doubleday, 1992.
Derrett, J. Duncan M. "Law in the New Testament: The Palm Sunday Colt." *NovT* 13 (1971) 241-58.
———. "The Zeal of the House and the Cleansing of the Temple." *DRev* 95 (1977) 79-94.
———. "Christ, King and Witness (John 18,37)." *BeO* 31 (1989) 189-98.
———. "Peter's Sword and Biblical Methodology." *BeO* 32 (1990) 180-92.
Dillon, John. *The Middle Platonists: A Study of Platonism 80 B.C. to A.D. 220*. London: Duckworth, 1977.
———. "Logos and Trinity: Patterns of Platonist Influence on Early Christianity." In *The Philosophy in Christianity*, ed. Godfrey Vesey, 1-13. Cambridge: Cambridge University Press, 1989.
Dimant, Devorah. "Qumran Sectarian Writings." In *Jewish Writings of the Second Temple Period: Apocrypha, Pseudepigrapha, Qumran Sectarian Writings, Philo. Josephus*, ed. M. Stone, 483-550. CRINT 2, 2. Assen: Van Gorcum & Philadelphia: Fortress, 1984.
Dix, Gregory. *The Shape of the Liturgy*. London: Dacre Press, Adam and Charles Black, 1945.
Dodd, C. H. *Historical Tradition in the Fourth Gospel*. Cambridge: Cambridge University Press, 1963.
———. *According to the Scriptures: The Substructure of New Testament Theology*. London: Nisbet, 1952 & Fontana, 1965.
———. *The Interpretation on the Fourth Gospel*. Cambridge: Cambridge University Press, 1953.
Draisma, Spike (ed.). *Intertextuality in Biblical Writings: Essays in honour of Bas van Iersel*. Kampen: J. H. Kok, 1989.
Duling, Dennis C. "The Promises to David and their Entrance into Christianity — Nailing Down a Likely Hypothesis." *NTS* 19 (1974-75) 55-77.
———. "Solomon, Exorcism and the Son of David." *HTR* 68 (1975) 235-252.
Dunn, James D. G. "John VI — A Eucharistic Discourse?" *NTS* 17 (1970-71) 328-38.
———. "Messianic Ideas and the Jesus of History" In *The Messiah*, ed. James

H. Charlesworth, 365-81. Minneapolis: Augsburg Fortress, 1992.
Dupont-Sommer, A and M. Philonenko (ed.). *La Bible: Ecrits Intertestamentaires.* Paris: Gallimard, 1987.
Eaton, John. H. *Kingship and the Psalms.* Sheffield: JSOT Press, 1986.
Efird, James M. (ed.). *The Use of the Old Testament in the New: Studies in Honor of William Franklin Stinespring.* Durham, NC: Duke University Press, 1972.
Eissfeldt, O. "The Promises of Grace to David in Isaiah 55:1-5." In *Israel's Prophetic Heritage,* ed. B. W. Anderson and W. Harrelson, 197-201. London: Harper & Brothers, 1962.
Eliot, T. S. *Selected Essays.* London: Faber and Faber, 1932.
Ellis, E. Earle. "Biblical Interpretation in the New Testament Church." In *Mikra: Text, translation, Reading and Interpretation of the Hebrew Bible in Ancient Judaism and Early Christianity,* ed. M. J. Mulder and H. Sysling, 691-726. CRINT 2, 1. Assen, Maastricht: Van Gorcum & Philadelphia: Fortress, 1988.
Emerton, J. A. "Some New Testament Notes, I: The Interpretation of Ps 82 and John 10." *JTS* 11 (1960) 329-36.
——. Melchizedek and the Gods: Fresh Evidence for the Jewish Background of John X. 34-6." *JTS* 17 (1966) 399-401.
Epstein, I. (trans.). *The Babylonian Talmud.* London: Soncino Press, 1935.
Evans, C. A. "On the Quotation Formulas in the Fourth Gospel." *BZ* 26 (1982) 79-83.

Falls, Thomas B. (trans. and ed.) *Saint Justin Martyr.* Washington DC: Catholic University of America Press, 1948.
Farrell, Shannon Elizabeth. "Le rouleau 11QPs^a et le psautier biblique," *LTP* 46 (1990) 353-68.
Feldman, Louis H. "Use, Authority, and Exegesis of Mikra in the Writings of Josephus." In *Mikra: Text, Translation, Reading and Interpretation of the Hebrew Bible in Ancient Judaism and Early Christianity,* ed. Jan Mulder and Harry Sysling, 455-518. CRINT 2, 2. Assen: Van Gorcum & Philadelphia: Fortress, 1988.
——. "Josephus' Portrait of David." *HUCA* 60 (1989) 129-74.
Ferguson, E. "Spiritual Sacrifice in Early Christianity and its Environment." In *Aufstieg und Niedergang der Römischen Welt,* II Principat 23. 2, cd. Wolfgang Haase, 1151-87. Berlin and New York: De Gruyter, 1980.
Feuillet, André. "Souffrance et confiance en Dieu: Commentaire du Psaume XXII." *NRT* (1948) 137-149.
Finkel, A. *The Pharisees and the Teacher of Nazareth.* Leiden: E. J. Brill, 1964.
Fischer, Balthasar. "Le Christ dans les Psaumes." *La Maison-Dieu* 27 (1951) 86-113.
——. "Christological Interpretation of the Psalms Seen in the Mirror of the Liturgy." *Questions Liturgiques* 71 (1990) 227-235.
Fishbane, Michael. "Inner Biblical Exegesis: Types and Strategies of Interpretation in Ancient Israel." In *Midrash and Literature,* ed. G. S.

Hartman and S. Budick, 19-37. New Haven and London: Yale University Press, 1986.
Fitzmyer, Joseph A. "The Use of Explicit O.T. Quotations in the Qumran Literature and the N.T." *NTS* 7 (1960-61) 297-333.
———. "David, 'Being Therefore a Prophet...' (Acts 2:30)." *CBQ* 34 (1972) 332-339.
———. "The Aramaic Language and the Study of the New Testament." *JBL* 99 (1980) 5-21.
Flanagan, James W. "Court History or Succession Document? A Study of 2 Samuel 9-20 and 1 Kings 1-2." *JBL* 91 (1972) 172-81.
———. "Samuel, Book of." In *The Anchor Bible Dictionary*, ed. D. N. Freedman, Vol. 5, 957-65. New York and London: Doubleday, 1992.
Flusser, David. "Psalms, Hymns and Prayers." In *Jewish Writings of the Second Temple Period: Apocrypha, Pseudepigrapha, Qumran Sectarian Writings, Philo, Josephus*, ed. M. Stone, 551-77. CRINT 2, 2. Assen: Van Gorcum & Philadelphia: Fortress, 1984.
Forr, William and J. A. Walther. *1 Corinthians*. Anchor Bible 32. New York: Doubleday, 1976.
Fortna, Robert T. *The Fourth Gospel and its predecessor: From Narrative Source to Present Gospel*. Philadelphia: Fortress, 1988.
Fortna, R. T. and B. T. Gaventa (ed.). *The Conversation Continues: Studies in Paul and John in Honour of J. Louis Martyn*. Nashville: Abingdon, 1990.
Freed, Edwin D. "The Entry into Jerusalem in the Gospel of John." *JBL* 80 (1961) 329-38.
———. *Old Testament Quotations in the Gospel of John*. Supplements to Novum Testamentum XI. Leiden: E. J. Brill, 1965.
———. "Psalm 42/43 in John's Gospel," *NTS* 29 (1982) 62-73.
Freedman, David Noel (Editor-in-Chief). *The Anchor Bible Dictionary*. 6 Vols. New York and London: Doubleday, 1992.
Freedman, H. and M. Simon (ed.). *The Midrash Rabbah, Translated into English*. London and New York: Soncino Press, 1939, 1983.
Friedman, R. E. "Torah (Pentateuch)." In *The Anchor Bible Dictionary*, ed. D. N. Freedman, Vol. VI, 605-22. New York and London: Doubleday, 1992.

Gadamer, Hans-Georg. *Truth and Method*. 2nd rev. ed. Trans. and rev. by J. Weinsheimer and D. G. Marshall. New York: Crossroad, 1989.
García Martínez, Florentino. *The Dead Sea Scrolls Translated: The Qumran Texts in English*. Trans. Wilfred G. E. Watson. Leiden: E. J. Brill & Grand Rapids: Eerdmans, 1994.
Geiger, Georg. "Aufruf an Rückkehrende Zum des Zitats von Ps 78, 24b in Joh 6,31." *Bib* 65 (1984) 449-64.
Gerhardssohn, Birger. *Memory and Manuscript: Oral and Written Transmission in Rabbinic Judaism and Early Christianity*. Copenhagen: G. W. K. Gleerup & Lund: Ejnar Munskgaard, 1961.
Geyser, A. S. "Israel in the Fourth Gospel." *Neot* 20 (1986) 13-20.
Gibbs, James M. "Purpose and Pattern in Matthew's use of the Title 'Son of David.'" *NTS* 10 (1963-64) 446-64.

Ginzberg, Louis. *The Legends of the Jews.* Vol. IV, "Bible Times and Characters from Joshua to Esther." Philadelphia: Jewish Publication Society of America, 1941.

Glasson, T. F. "Davidic Links with the Betrayal of Jesus." *ExpTim* 85 (1973- 1974), 118-19.

——. *Moses in the Fourth Gospel.* London: SCM, 1963.

Goldingay, J. "The Chronicler as Theologian." *BTB* 5 (1975) 99-126.

Goodwin, Charles. "How Did John Treat His Sources?" *JBL* 73 (1954) 61- 75.

Goshen-Gottstein, M. H. "The Psalm Scroll (11QPs^a): a Problem of Canon and Text." *Textus* 5 (1966) 22-33.

Goulder, Michael. *The Prayers of David: Psalms 51-72.* Studies in the Psalter II. JSOT Sup. Series 102. Sheffield: JSOT Press, 1990.

Greenspoon, Leonard. "The Use and Abuse of the Term 'LXX' and Related Terminology in Recent Scholarship." *BIOSCS* 20 (1987) 21-29.

Grelot, Pierre. "De son ventre couleront des fleuves d'eau: la citation scripturaire de Jean, VII, 38." *RB* 66 (1959) 369-74.

——. "Jean, VII, 38: Eau du rocher ou source du Temple?" *RB* 70 (1963) 43-51.

——. *Homélies sur l'écriture à l'époque apostolique.* Introduction à la Bible, édition nouvelle, III, 8. Tournai: Desclée, 1989.

Grigsby, Bruce H. "The Cross as Expiatory Sacrifice in the Fourth Gospel." *JSNT* 15 (1982) 51-80.

——. "Washing in the Pool of Siloam — A Thematic Anticipation of the Johannine Cross." *NovT* 28 (1985) 227-35.

——. " 'If any man thirsts ...': Observations on the Rabbinic Background of John 7, 37-39." *Bib* 67 (1986) 101-8.

Guilding, Aileen. *The Fourth Gospel and Jewish Worship.* Oxford: Clarendon Press, 1960.

Haenchen, E. *John 1: A Commentary on the Gospel of John Chapters 1-6.* Philadelphia: Fortress, 1984.

——. *John 2: A Commentary on the Gospel of John Chapters 7-21.* Philadelphia: Fortress, 1984.

Hamman, Adalbert. "La prière chrétienne et la prière paienne: formes et différences." In *Aufstieg und Niedergang der Römischen Welt,* II Principat, 23.2, ed. Wolfgang Haase, 1190-1246. Berlin: De Gruyter, 1980.

Hanson, Anthony T. "John's Citation of Psalm LXXXII: John X. 33-36." *NTS* 11 (1964-1965) 158-62.

——. "John's Citation of Psalm LXXXII Reconsidered." *NTS* 13 (1966-1967) 363-67.

——. *The Living Utterances of God: The New Testament Exegesis of the Old.* London: Darton, Longman and Todd, 1983.

——. *The Prophetic Gospel: A Study of John and the Old Testament.* Edinburgh: T. and T. Clark, 1991.

Haran, Menahem. "The Two Text Forms of Ps 151." *JJS* 39 (1988) 171-82.

———."11QPsª and the Canonical Book of Psalms." In *Minhah le Nahum: Biblical and Other Studies Presented to Nahum M. Sarna in Honour of His 70th Birthday*, ed. Marc Brettler and Michael Fishbane, 193-201. Sheffield: Sheffield Academic Press, 1993.

Harrington, Daniel J. "The Biblical Text of Pseudo-Philo's 'Liber Antiquitatum Biblicarum.'" *CBQ* 33 (1971) 1-17.

———. (ed.). *Pseudo-Philon. Les Antiquités Bibliques*, Sources Chrétiennes 229. Paris: Les Éditions du Cerf, 1976.

———. "Pseudo-Philo: A New Translation and Introduction." In *The Old Testament Pseudepigrapha*, ed. J. H. Charlesworth, Vol. II, 297-377. New York: Doubleday, 1985.

Harrington D. J. and A. J. Saldarini (trans. and ed.). *Targum Jonathan of the Former Prophets*. The Aramaic Bible, Vol. 10. Wilmington DE: Glazier & Edinburgh: T. and T. Clark, 1987.

Hart, H. St J. "The Palm Branches in John 12:13." *JTS* 3 (1952) 62-63.

Harvey, A. E. *Jesus and the Constraints of History*. Philadelphia: Westminster & London: Duckworth, 1982.

Hay, David M. *Glory at the Right Hand: Psalm 110 in Early Christianity*. SBLMS 18. Nashville: Abingdon, 1973.

———. "Philo's View of Himself as an Exegete: Inspired, but Not Authoritative." In *Heirs of the Septuagint* (Festschrift for Earle Hilgert), ed. David T. Runia, David M. Hay and David Winston, 40-52. Atlanta: Scholars, 1991.

Hayes, J. H. "The Resurrection as Enthronement and the Earliest Church Christology." *Int* 22 (1968) 333-45.

Hays, Richard B. *Echoes of Scripture in the Letters of Paul*. New Haven and London: Yale University Press, 1989.

Hecht, Richard D. "Philo and Messiah." In *Judaisms and their Messiahs at the Turn of the Christian Era*, ed. J. Neusner, W. S. Green and E. S. Fredrichs, 139-68. Cambridge: Cambridge University Press, 1987,

Heinemann, Joseph. *Prayer in the Talmud: Forms and Patterns*. Berlin and New York: Walter de Gruyter, 1977.

Hengel, Martin. *The Atonement: The Origin of the Doctrine in the New Testament*. Philadelphia: Fortress & London: SCM, 1981.

———. "Christological Titles in Early Christianity." In *The Messiah*, ed. J. H. Charlesworth, 425-448. Minneapolis: Augsburg Fortress, 1992.

———. "The Old Testament in the Fourth Gospel," *HBT* 12 (1990) 19-41. A shortened English version, by the author, of the German original "Die Schriftauslegung des 4 Evangeliums auf dem Hintergrund der urchristlichen Exegese," *JBTh* 4 (1989) 249-289.

Holladay, William L. *The Psalms Through Three Thousand Years: Prayerbook of a Cloud of Witnesses*. Minneapolis: Fortress, 1993.

Hollander, John. *The Figure of Echo: A Model of Allusion in Milton and After*. Berkeley: University of California Press, 1981.

Holm-Nielsen, Svend. *Hodayot: Psalms from Qumran*. Copenhagen: Universitetsforlaget I Aarhus, 1960.

Horsley, Richard A. "Messianic Movements in Judaism." In *The Anchor*

Bible Dictionary, ed. D. N. Freedman, Vol. IV, 791-97. New York and London: Doubleday, 1992.

Hoskyns, Edwyn C. *The Fourth Gospel*. 2nd ed. F. N. Davey. London: Faber, 1947.

Howard, David M. Jr. "David." In *The Anchor Bible Dictionary*, ed. D. N. Freedman, Vol. II, 41-49. New York and London: Doubleday, 1992.

———. "Editorial Activity in the Psalter: A State-of-the-field Survey." In *The Shape and Shaping of the Psalter*. JSOT Suppl. Series 159, ed. J. Clinton McCann, 52-70. Sheffield: JSOT Press, 1993.

Huerta, Eduardo. "La realeza de Jesús en el cuarto evangelio," *Teología y Vida* 32 (1991) 213-20.

Hultgård, Anders. "The Ideal 'Levite:' The Davidic Messiah and the Savior Priest in the Testaments of the Twelve Patriarchs." In *Ideal Figures in Ancient Judaism: Profiles and Paradigms*, ed. George W. E. Nickelsburg and John J. Collins, 93-110. Chico CA: Scholars Press, 1980.

Infante, R. "L'amico dello sposo, figura del ministero di Giovanni Battista nel quarto vangelo." *Rivista Biblica* 31 (1983) 3 - 19.

Isaac, E. "1 (Ethiopic Apocalypse of) Enoch." In *The Old Testament Pseudepigrapha*, ed. J. H. Charlesworth, Vol. I, 5-89. London: Darton Longman and Todd, 1983.

Jacquet, Louis. *Les psaumes et le coeur de l'homme: etude textuelle, litteraire et doctrinale*, 3 Vols. Gembloux: Duculot, 1975, 1977 and 1979.

Jansen, J. Gerald. "Song of Moses, Song of Miriam: Who Is Seconding Whom?" *CBQ* 54 (1992) 211-20.

Jauss, Hans Robert. "Literary History as a Challenge to Literary Theory." A translation of Chs 5-12 of "Literaturgeschichte als Provokation der Literaturwissenschaft" (Konstanz: 1967). In *New Directions in Literary History*, ed. Ralph Cohen, 11-36. London: Routledge and Kegan Paul, 1974.

Jeremias, Joachim. *The Eucharistic Words of Jesus*. Trans. Norman Perrin. London: SCM, 1966.

Johnson, Aubrey R. *The Cultic Prophet in Ancient Israel*. Cardiff: University of Wales Press, 1962.

Jonge, M. de and A. S. van der Woude, "11QMelchizedek and the New Testament." *NTS* 12 (1966) 301-26.

Jonge, Marinus de. "Jewish Expectations about the 'Messiah' according to the Fourth Gospel." *NTS* 19 (1972-73) 246-270.

———. *Stranger From Heaven and Son of God: Jesus Christ and the Christians in Johannine Perspective*. Missoula: Scholars Press, 1977.

———. (ed.). *L'Évangile de Jean: Sources, rédaction, théologie.* Leuven: Leuven University Press & Gembloux: Duculot, 1977.

———. "The Expectation of the Future in the Psalms of Solomon." *Neot* 23 (1989) 93-117.

———. "Messiah." In *The Anchor Bible Dictionary*, ed. D. N. Freedman, Vol. IV, 777-788. New York and London: Doubleday, 1992.

Juel, Donald. *Messiah and Temple: The Trial of Jesus in the Gospel of Mark.* SBL Dissertation Series 31. Missoula: Scholars, 1977.

———. *Messianic Exegesis: Christological Interpretation of the Old Testament in Early Christianity.* Philadelphia: Fortress, 1988.

Kaiser, Walter C. Jr. "The Unfailing Kindnesses Promised to David: Isaiah 55:3." *JSOT* 45 (1989) 91-98.

Kasher, Rimon. "The Interpretation of Scripture in Rabbinic Literature." In *Mikra: Text, Translation, Reading and Interpretation of the Hebrew Bible in Ancient Judaism and Early Christianity*, ed. J. Mulder and H. Sysling, 537-94. CRINT 2, 1. Assen: Van Gorcum & Philadelphia: Fortress, 1988.

Kaufmann, Yehezkel. "The Messianic Idea: The Real and the Hidden Son-of- David." *JBQ* 22 (1994) 141-50.

Kee, H. C. "Testaments of the Twelve Patriarchs: A New Translation and Introduction." In *The Old Testament Pseudepigrapha*, ed. J. H. Charlesworth, Vol. I, 775-828. London: Darton Longman and Todd, 1983.

Keel, Othmar. *The Symbolism of the Biblical World.* Trans. T. J. Hallett. London: SPCK, 1978.

Kiley, Mark. "The Exegesis of God: Jesus' Signs in John 1-11." In *SBL 1988: Seminar Papers*, ed. David J. Lull, 555-69. Atlanta: Scholars, 1988.

Kilmartin, E. J. "The Formation of the Bread of Life Discourse (John 6)." *Scr* 12 (1960) 75-78.

———. "Liturgical Influence on John 6." *CBQ* 22 (1960) 183-91.

Kingsbury, Jack Dean. "The Title 'Son of David' in Matthew's Gospel." *JBL* 95 (1976) 591-602.

Kister, Menahem. "Plucking on the Sabbath and Christian-Jewish Polemic." *Immanuel* 24-25 (1990) 35-51.

Klijn, A. F. J. "2 (Syriac Apocalypse of) Baruch: A New Translation and Introduction." In *The Old Testament Pseudepigrapha*, ed. J. H. Charlesworth, Vol. I, 615-52. London: Darton, Longman and Todd, 1983.

Kloppenborg, John S. *Q Parallels: Synopsis, Critical Notes and Concordance.* Sonoma CA: Polebridge Press, 1988.

Knibb, Michael A. *The Qumran Community.* Cambridge Commentaries on Writings of the Jewish and Christian World 200 B.C. to A.D. 200. London: Cambridge University Press, 1987.

Kraus, Hans-Joachim. *Theology of the Psalms: A Continental Commentary.* Trans. Keith Crim. Minneapolis: Fortress, 1992.

———. *Worship in Israel.* Trans. G. Buswell. Richmond: John Knox Press, 1966.

Lapin, H. "Palm Fronds and Citrons: Notes on Two Letters from Bar Kosiba's Administration." *HUCA* 64 (1993) 111-135.

Leclercq, Henri. "Orphée." In *Dictionnaire d'Archéologie Chrétienne et de Liturgie*, ed. F. Cabrol and H. Leclercq, Vol. 12, 2735-55. Paris: Libraire Letouzey et Ané, 1936.

Leclercq, Jean, with C. H. Talbot and H. M. Rochais (ed.). *Sancti Bernardi Opera*. 8 Vols. Rome: Editiones Cistercienses, 1957-77.

Lella, A. A. di. "Sirach." In *The New Jerome Biblical Commentary*, ed. R. E. Brown, J. A. Fitzmyer and R. E. Murphy, 496-509. London: Chapman, 1990.

Léon-Dufour, X. "Trois chiasmes johanniques." *NTS* 7 (1960-61) 249-55.

Levenson, J. D. "The Davidic Covenant and its Modern Interpreters." *CBQ* 41 (1979) 205-19.

Levi, Israel (ed.). *The Hebrew Text of the Book of Ecclesiasticus*. Semitic Studies III. Leiden: E. J. Brill, 1969.

Levine, Lee I. *The Synagogue in Late Antiquity*. Philadelphia: The American Schools of Oriental Research, 1987.

Lewis, Charlton T. and Charles Short. *A Latin Dictionary: Founded on Andrews' Edition of Freund's Latin Dictionary*. Oxford: Clarendon Press, 1980.

Liddell, H. G. and R. Scott, *Greek-English Lexicon*. Revised by H. S. Jones. Oxford: Clarendon Press, 1961.

Lightfoot, R. H. *Saint John's Gospel: A Commentary*. Oxford: Oxford University Press, 1957.

Lindars, Barnabas. *New Testament Apologetic: the Doctrinal Significance of the Old Testament Quotations*. London: SCM, 1961.

———. *Behind the Fourth Gospel*. London: SPCK, 1971.

———. *The Gospel of John*. New Century Bible. London: Oliphants, 1972.

———. "Word and Sacrament in the Fourth Gospel." *SJT* 29 (1976) 49-63.

Lindsay, Dennis R. "What Is Truth?' Ἀλήθεια in the Gospel of John. *ResQ* 35 (1993) 129-45.

Lipinsky, E. "Macarismes et Psaumes de Congratulation." *RB* 75 (1968) 321- 67.

Lohse, E. *A Commentary on the Epistles to the Colossians and to Philemon*. Hermeneia Series. Philadelphia: Fortress, 1971.

Louw, J. P. and E. Nida. *Greek-English Lexicon of the New Testament Based on Semantic Domains*. New York: United Bible Societies, 1989.

Lull, David J. (ed.). *SBL 1988: Seminar Papers*. Atlanta: Scholars, 1988.

Mack, Burton. "The Christ and Jewish Wisdom." In *The Messiah*, ed. J. H. Charlesworth, 192-221. Minneapolis: Augsburg Fortress, 1992.

———. "Wisdom and Apocalyptic in Philo." In *Heirs of the Septuagint: Philo, Hellenistic Judaism and Early Christianity. Festschrift for Earle Hilgert*, ed. David T. Runia, D. M. Hay and D. Winston, 21-39. Studies in Hellenistic Judaism. Brown Judaic Studies, Subseries Studia Philonica. Atlanta: Scholars, 1991.

MacRrae, George. "The Fourth Gospel and Religionsgeschichte." *CBQ* 32 (1970) 13-24.

Magne, Jean. "Orphisme, Pythagorisme, Essenisme dans le texte hebreu du Psaume 151." *RevQum* 8 (1975) 508-45.

———. "Le Verset des trois pierres dans la tradition du Psaume 151." *RevQum* 8 (1975) 565-91.

———. "'Seigneur de l'Univers' ou David-Orphee?" *RevQum* 9 (1977) 189-96.

Magonet, Jonathan. *A Rabbi Reads the Psalms*. London: SCM, 1994.
Maher, Michael (ed.). *Targum Pseudo-Jonathan: Genesis, Translated with Introduction and Notes*. Edinburgh: T. and T. Clark, 1992.
———. "The Psalms in Jewish Worship." *PIBA* 17 (1994) 9 -36.
Maier, Johann (ed.). *The Temple Scroll: An Introduction, Translation and Commentary*. JSOT Suppl. Series 34. Sheffield: JSOT Press, 1985.
Manns, F. "Exégèse rabbinique et exégèse johannique." *RB* 92 (1985) 525-38.
Mansoor, Menahem. *The Thanksgiving Hymns*. Studies on the Texts of the Desert of Judah, ed. J. Van Der Ploeg. Vol. 3. Leiden: E. J. Brill, 1961.
Marcus, R. and H. St-J. Thackeray (trans. and ed.). *Josephus*. Loeb Classical Library. Cambridge, MA: Harvard University Press & London: Heinemann, 1988.
Martínez, F. G. *See:* García Martínez, F.
Martyn, J. Louis. *History and Theology in the Fourth Gospel*. Nashville: Abingdon, 1968.
———. "Glimpses into the History of the Johannine Community. From Its Origin through the Period of Its Life in Which the Fourth Gospel Was Composed." In *L'Évangile de Jean: Sources, rédaction, théologie*, ed. M. de Jonge, 149-75. Leuven: Leuven University Press & Gembloux: Duculot, 1977.
———. *The Gospel of John in Christian History*. New York: Paulist, 1978.
Mastin, B. A. "A Neglected Feature of the Christology of the Fourth Gospel." *NTS* 22 (1976) 32-52.
Matera, Frank J. " 'On Behalf of Others,' 'Cleansing,' and 'Return:' Johannine Images for Jesus' Death." *LS* (1988) 161-178.
———. "Jesus before Annas: John 18, 13-14. 19-24." *ETL* 66 (1990) 38-55.
Mays, James Luther. "The David of the Psalms." *Int* 40 (1986) 143-55.
———. "The Place of the Torah-Psalms in the Psalter." *JBL* 106 (1987) 3-12.
———. "The Question of Context in Psalm Interpretation." In *The Shape and Shaping of the Psalter*, ed. J. Clinton McCann, 14-20. JSOT Supplement Series 159. Sheffield: Sheffield Academic Press, 1993.
McCann, J Clinton (ed.). *The Shape and Shaping of the Psalter*. JSOT Supplement Series 159. Sheffield: Sheffield Academic Press, 1993.
McCarter, P. Kyle Jr. "The Apology of David." *JBL* 99 (1980) 484-504.
———. "Plots, True or False: The Succession Narrative as Court Apologetic." *Int* 35 (1981) 355 - 67.
———. *1 Samuel* and *2 Samuel*. Anchor Bible Vol. 8-9. New York: Doubleday, 1984.
———. "The Historical David." *Int* 40 (1986) 117-29.
McNamara, Martin. *Targum Neofiti 1: Numbers* and Ernest G. Clarke, *Targum Pseudo-Jonathan: Numbers*. Edinburgh: T. and T. Clark, 1995.
McNeil, Brian. "The Quotation at John XII 34." *NovT* 19 (1977) 22-33.
McPolin, James. *John*. New Testament Message Series 6. Dublin: Veritas & Wilmington DE: Glazier, 1979.

Meeks, Wayne A. "Galilee and Judea in the Fourth Gospel." *JBL* 85 (1966) 159-69.

———. *The Prophet King: Moses Traditions and the Johannine Christology*. Leiden: E. J. Brill, 1967.

———. "Moses as God and King." In *Religions in Antiquity: Essays in Memory of E. R. Goodenough*, ed. Jacob Neusner, 354-71. Leiden: E. J. Brill, 1968.

———. "The Man from Heaven in Johannine Sectarianism." In *The Interpretation of John*, ed. John Ashton, 141-73. London: SPCK & Philadelphia: Fortress, 1986, Originally published in *JBL* 91 (1972) 44-72.

———. "Equal to God." In *The Conversation Continues: Studies in Paul and John in Honour of J. Louis Martyn*, ed. R. T. Fortna and B. T. Gaventa, 309-21. Nashville: Abingdon, 1990.

Meier, John P. *A Marginal Jew: Rethinking the Historical Jesus.* Vol. I, "The Roots of the Problem and the Person." Anchor Bible Reference Library. New York: Doubleday 1991.

Mendels, D. "Pseudo-Philo's Biblical Antiquities, the 'Fourth Philosophy,' and the Political Messianism of the First Century C. E." In *The Messiah*, ed. J. H. Charlesworth, 261-275. Minneapolis: Augsburg Fortress, 1992.

Menken, Maarten J. J. "Some Remarks on the Course of the Dialogue: John 6,25-34." *Bijdr* 48 (1987) 139-49.

———. "The Provenance and Meaning of The Old Testament Quotation in John 6:31. *NovT* 30 (1988) 39-56.

———. "The Old Testament Quotation in John 6,45: Source and Redaction." *ETL* 64 (1988) 164-72.

———. "Die Redaktion des Zitates aus Sach 9,9 in Joh 12,15." *ZNW* 80 (1989) 193-209.

———. "The Translation of Psalm 41:10 in John 13:18." *JSNT* 40 (1990) 61-79.

———. "The Old Testament Quotation in John 19:36: Sources, Redaction, Background." In F. van Segbroeck, C. M. Tuckett, G. Von Belle, S. Verheyden (ed.), *The Four Gospels, 1992. Festschrift F. Neirynck*, 2101-18. Leuven: Peeters, 1992.

———. "The Textual Form and Meaning of the Quotation from Zechariah in John 19:37." *CBQ* 55 (1993) 494-511.

———. "John 6, 51c-58: Eucharist or Christology?" *Bib* 74 (1993) 1-26.

———. "The Origin of the Old Testament Quotation in John 7:38." *NovT* 38 (1996) 160-75.

———. *Old Testament Quotations in the Fourth Gospel: Studies in Textual Form.* Contributions to Biblical Exegesis and Theology 15. Kampen: Kok Pharos, 1996.

Mérode, Marie de. "L'acceuil triomphal de Jésus selon *Jean*, 11-12." *RTL* 13 (1982) 49-62.

Merrill, Eugene H. *Qumran and Predestination: A Theological Study of the Thanksgiving Hymns.* Leiden: E. J. Brill, 1975.

Metzger, Bruce M. "The Formulas Introducing Quotations of Scripture in the New Testament and the Mishnah." *JBL* 70 (1951) 297-307.

———. *The Text of the New Testament: Its Transmission, Corruption and Restoration*, 3rd Edition. New York and Oxford: Oxford University Press, 1992.

Metzger, Bruce M. (trans.). "The Gospel of Thomas." In *Synopsis Quattuor Evangeliorum*, ed. Kurt Aland, 517-30. Stuttgart: Deutsche Bibelgesellschaft, 1985.

Meyers, Carol L. *The Tabernacle Menorah: A Synthetic Study of a Symbol from the Biblical Cult*. American Schools of Oriental Research Dissertation Series 2. Missoula MT: Scholars, 1976.

———. "Temple, Jerusalem." In *The Anchor Bible Dictionary*, ed. D. N. Freedman, Vol. VI, 350-68. New York and London: Doubleday, 1992.

Miller, Patrick D. "The Beginning of the Psalter." In *The Shape and Shaping of the Psalter*, ed. J. Clinton McCann, 83-92. Sheffield: JSOT Press, 1993.

Moloney, Francis J. "The Fourth Gospel's Presentation of Jesus as 'The Christ' and J. A. T. Robinson's *Redating*." *DRev* 95 (1977) 239-53.

———. "Reading John 2:13-22; The Purification of the Temple." *RB* 97 (1990) 432-51.

———. "A Sacramental Reading of John 13:1-38" *CBQ* 53 (1991) 237- 56.

———. *The Johannine Son of Man*. Biblioteca di Scienze Religiose 14. Rome: Las-Libreria Ateneo Salesiano, 1978.

Moo, Douglas J. *The Old Testament in the Gospel Passion Narratives*. Sheffield: Almond Press, 1983.

Moody Smith. *See:* Smith, D. Moody.

Moor, J. C. De and E. Van Staalduine-Sulman. "The Aramaic Song of the Lamb." *JSJ* 24 (1993) 226-279.

Moule, C. F. D. *The Birth of the New Testament*. London: Adam and Charles Black, 1962.

Mowinckel, Sigmund. *The Psalms in Israel's Worship*. Trans. D. R. Ap-Thomas. 2 Vols. Oxford: Blackwell, 1967.

———. *He That Cometh*. Trans. G. W. Anderson. Oxford: Basil Blackwell, 1959.

Mulder, Jan and Harry Sysling (ed.). *Mikra: Text, Translation, Reading and Interpretation of the Hebrew Bible in Ancient Judaism and Early Christianity*. CRINT 2.1. Assen: Van Gorcum & Philadelphia: Fortress, 1988.

Murphy, Roland. E. "Reflections on Contextual Interpretation of the Psalms." In *The Shape and Shaping of the Psalter*, ed. J. Clinton McCann, 21-28. JSOT Supplement Series 159. Sheffield: Sheffield Academic Press, 1993.

Murray, R. *Symbols of Church and Kingdom: A Study in Early Syriac Tradition*. Cambridge: Cambridge University Press, 1975.

Neusner, Jacob. *Messiah in Context: Israel's History and Destiny in Formative Judaism*. Philadelphia: Fortress, 1984.

Neyrey, Jerome. "Jacob Traditions and the Interpretation of John 4:10-26." *CBQ* 41 (1979) 419-37.

———. "'My Lord and my God': The Divinity of Jesus in John's Gospel." In *SBL 1986: Seminar Papers*, ed. K. Richards, 152-71. Atlanta: Scholars, 1986.

———. "Jesus the Judge: Forensic Process in John 8:21-29." *Bib* 68 (1987) 509-42.

———. *An Ideology of Revolt: John's Christology in Social-Science Perspective*. Philadelphia: Fortress, 1988.

———. "I Said: You Are Gods: Psalm 82:6 and John 10." *JBL* 108 (1989) 647-63.

Nolan, Brian M. *The Royal Son of God: The Christology of Matthew 1-2 in the Setting of the Gospel*. Orbis Biblicus et Orientalis 23. Göttingen: Vandenhoeck und Ruprecht, 1979.

Noth, Martin. *The Deuteronomistic History*. (2nd ed, 1957). Trans. Jane Doull, rev. John Barton, Michael D. Rutter, D. R. Ap-Thomas and David J. A. Clines. Sheffield: JSOT Press, 1981.

O'Day, G. R. "I have Overcome the World: Narrative Time in John 13-17." *Semeia* 53 (1991) 153-166.

Odeberg, Hugo. *The Fourth Gospel Interpreted in its Relation to Contemporary Religious Currents and the Hellenistic-Oriental World*. Amsterdam: B. R. Grüner, 1968.

Oesterley, W. O. E. *The Psalms: Translated with Text-Critical and Exegetical Notes*. London: SPCK, 1962.

O'Neil, J. C. "The Question of Messianic Expectation in Pseudo-Philo's Biblical Antiquities." *JHC* 1 (1994) 85-93.

Orr, William F. and J. A. Walther. *1 Corinthians: A New Translation, Introduction with a Study of the Life of Paul, Notes and Commentary*. Anchor Bible 32. New York: Doubleday, 1976.

Otto, J. C. D. (ed.). *S. Justini Philosophi et Martyris Opera*. Jena: F. Mauke, 1843.

Painter, John. "Quest and Rejection Stories in John." *JSNT* 36 (1989) 17-46.

———. "Tradition and Interpretation in John 6." *NTS* 35 (1989) 421- 50.

———. "Tradition, History and Interpretation in John 10." In *The Shepherd Discourse of John 10 and its Context*, ed. J. Beutler and R. T. Fortna, 53-74. Cambridge: Cambridge University Press, 1991.

———. "Theology, Eschatology and the Prologue of John." *SJT* 46 (1993) 27-42.

Pancaro, Severino. *The Law in the Fourth Gospel: The Torah and the Gospel, Moses and Jesus, Judaism and Christianity According to John*. Supplements to *NovT* 42. Leiden: E. J. Brill, 1975.

Patte, Daniel. *Early Jewish Hermeneutic in Palestine*. SBL Dissertation Series 22. Chico CA: Scholars Press, 1975.

Payne, David F. "Estimates of the Character of David." *IBS* 6 (1984) 54-70.

Perrin, Norman. "Mark XIV. 62: The End Product of a Christian Pesher Tradition?" *NTS* 13 (1966) 150-55.
———. *Rediscovering the Teaching of Jesus*. London: Harper and Row, 1976.
Perrot, Charles and Pierre M. Bogaert. *Pseudo-Philon, Les Antiquités Bibliques*. Tome II: Introduction Littéraire, Commentaire et Index. Sources Chrétiennes 230. Paris: Les Éditions du Cerf, 1976.
Pietersma, Albert. "David in the Greek Psalms." *VT* 30 (1980), 213-26.
Places, Edouard des (trans.). *Eusèbe de Césarée: La Préparation Évangélique, Livres VIII-IX-X*, Sources Chrétiennes 369. Paris: Les Éditions du Cerf, 1991.
Pomykala, Kenneth E. *The Davidic Dynasty Tradition in Early Judaism: Its History and Significance for Messianism*, SBL Early Judaism and its Literature Series 7. Atlanta: Scholars, 1995.
Pope, Marvin H. "Hosanna." In *The Anchor Bible Dictionary*, ed. D. N. Freedman, Vol. III, 290-91. London and New York: Doubleday, 1992.
Potterie, Ignace de la. "The Truth in Saint John." In *The Interpretation of John*, ed. John Ashton, 53-66. Issues in Religion and Theology 9. Philadelphia: Fortress & London: SPCK, 1986.
———. "La tunique sans couture, symbole du Christ grand- prêtre?" *Bib* 60 (1979) 255-269.
———. *The Hour of Jesus: The Passion and the Resurrection of Jesus According to John*. Trans. A. G. Murray. New York: Alba House, 1989.
Primentas, N. "'Ο'Άρραφο" Χιτώνα": Τεχνολογική και Ερμηνευτική Προσέγγιση" ("The Tunic without Seam: Technological and Hermeneutical Approach"). *DeltBibMel* 10 (1991) 38-50.
Puech, Émile. "11Q Ps Ap^a: Un Rituel d'Exorcismes. Essai de Reconstruction." *RevQ* 14 (1990) 377-408.
———. "La pierre de Sion et l'autel des holocaustes d'après un manuscrit hébreu de la grotte 4 (4Q522)." *RB* 99 (1992) 676-696.

Qimron, Elisha and John Strugnell. *Discoveries in the Judean Desert X: Qumran Cave 4*. Oxford: Clarendon Press, 1994.
Quasten, Johannes. *Music and Worship in Pagan and Christian Antiquity*. Trans. Boniface Ramsey. Washington D.C.: National Association of Pastoral Musicians, 1983.

Rahlfs, Alfred (ed.). *Septuaginta: Id est Vetus Testamentum graece iuxta LXX interpretes* (2 vols). Stuttgart: Deutsche Bibelgesellschaft, 1979.
———. *Psalmi cum Odis*. Septuaginta — Vetus Testamentum Graecum Auctoritate Academiae Scientiarum Gottingensis editum. Vol. 10. Göttingen: Vandenhoeck and Ruprecht, 1979.
Reim, Günter. *Studien zum altestamentlichen Hintergrund des Johannesevangeliums*. Cambridge: Cambridge University Press, 1974.
———. "Jesus as God in the Fourth Gospel: The Old Testament Background." *NTS* 30 (1984) 158-60.
———. *Jochanan: Erweiterte Studien zum Alttestamentlichen Hintergrund des*

Johannesevangeliums. Hessdorf-Hannberg: Verl. der Ev.-Luth. Mission, 1995.
Reinhartz, Adele. "Jesus as Prophet: Predictive Prolepses in the Fourth Gospel." *JSNT* 36 (1989) 3-16.
Richards, Kent H. "Psalm 34." *Int* 40 (1986) 175-80.
Richards, Kent H. (ed.). *SBL 1986: Seminar Papers.* Atlanta: Scholars, 1986.
Richardson, Alan. *An Introduction to the Theology of the New Testament.* London: SCM, 1958.
Riley, W. *King and Cultus in Chronicles: Worship and the Reinterpretation of History.* JSOT Supplement Series 160. Sheffield: JSOT Press, 1993.
Roberge, Michel. "Le discours sur le pain de vie: Jean 6, 22-59," *LTP* 38 (1982) 265-99.
———. "La composition de Jean 6, 22-59 dans l'exégèse récente." *LTP* 40 (1984) 91-123.
———. "La Composition de Jean 6, 25b-34." *LTP* 50 (1994) 171-86.
Roberts, J. J. M. "The Old Testament's Contribution to Messianic Expectations." In *The Messiah*, ed. J. H. Charlesworth, 39-51. Minneapolis: Augsburg Fortress, 1992.
Rogers, Cleon L., Jr. "The Davidic Covenant in the Gospels." *BSac* 150 (1993) 458-78.
Rordorf, Willy and André Tuilier (ed.) *La Doctrine Des Douze Apôtres (Didachè).* Sources Chrétiennes 248. Paris: Les Éditions du Cerf, 1978.
Rosenberg, Joel. "1 and 2 Samuel." In *The Literary Guide to the Bible*, ed. Robert Alter and Frank Kermode, 122-45. Glasgow: Collins, 1987.
Rost, Leonhard. *The Succession to the Throne of David* (1926). Trans. Michael D. Rutter and David M. Gunn. Sheffield: Almond, 1982.
Roure, D. *Jesús y la figura de David en Mc 2, 23-26: Trasfondo bíblico, intertestamentario y rabínico.* Analecta Biblica 124. Rome: Pontificio Istituto Biblico, 1990.
Rowland, C. "John 1,51, Jewish Apocalyptic and Targumic Tradition." *NTS* 30 (1984) 498-507.
Runia, David T. with David M. Hay and David Winston (ed.). *Heirs of the Septuagint: Philo, Hellenistic Judaism and Early Christianity. Festschrift for Earle Hilgert.* Studies in Hellenistic Judaism. Brown Judaic Studies – subseries Studia Philonica. Atlanta: Scholars, 1991.

Sabourin, Leopold. *The Psalms: Their Origin and Meaning.* New York: Alba House, 1974.
Safrai, Shmuel (ed.). *The Jewish People in the First Century: Historical Geography, Political History, Social, Cultural and Religious Life and Institutions.* CRINT 1, 2. Assen and Amsterdam: Van Gorcum, 1976.
———. (ed.). *The Literature of the Sages. First Part: Oral Torah, Halakah, Mishna, Tosefta, Talmud, External Tractates.* CRINT 2, 3. Assen: Van Gorcum & Philadelphia: Fortress, 1897.
Safrai, Shmuel. "The Synagogue. " In *The Jewish People in the First Century: Historical Geography, Political History, Social, Cultural and Religious Life and*

Institutions, ed. S. Safrai, 908-44. CRINT 1, 2. Assen and Amsterdam: Van Gorcum, 1976.

——. "The Temple." In *The Jewish People in the First Century: Historical Geography, Political History, Social, Cultural and Religious Life and Institutions*, ed. S. Safrai, 865-907. CRINT 1, 2. Assen and Amsterdam: Van Gorcum, 1976.

——. "Oral Torah," in *The Literature of the Sages. First Part: Oral Torah, Halakah, Mishna, Tosefta, Talmud, External Tractates*, ed. S. Safrai, CRINT 2, 3, 35-120. Assen: Van Gorcum & Philadelphia: Fortress, 1987.

Salters, R. B. "Psalm 82,1 and the Septuagint." *ZAW* 103 (1991) 225-39.

Sanders, E. P. *Jesus and Judaism*. London: SCM, 1985.

Sanders, J. A. *The Psalms Scroll of Qumran Cave 11 (11QPs^a)*. Discoveries in the Judean Desert IV. Oxford: Clarendon Press, 1965.

——. *The Dead Sea Psalms Scroll*. Ithaca, New York: Cornell University Press, 1967.

——. "The Qumran Psalms Scroll (11Q Ps^a) Reviewed." In *On Language, Culture and Religion: In Honor of Eugene A. Nida*, ed. M. Black and W. Smalley, 79-99. The Hague: Mouton, 1974.

——. *Canon and Community: A Guide to Canonical Criticism*. Philadelphia: Fortress, 1984.

——. "A New Testament Hermeneutic Fabric: Psalm 118 in the Entrance Narrative." In *Early Jewish and Christian Exegesis: Studies in Honour of William Hugh Brownlee*, ed. C. A. Evans and W. F. Stinespring, 177-90. Atlanta: Scholars, 1987.

Sandy, D. Brent. "John the Baptist's 'Lamb of God' Affirmation in its Canonical and Apocalyptic Milieu." *JETS* 34 (1991) 447-60.

Sarna, N. M. "The Psalm Superscriptions and the Guilds." In *Studies in Jewish Religious and Intellectual History Presented to Alexander Altmann on his Seventieth Birthday*, ed. Siegfried Stein and Raphael Loewe, 281-300. Alabama: University of Alabama Press, 1979.

Schiffman, Lawrence H. "The New Halakhic Letter (4QMMT) and the Origins of the Dead Sea Sect." *Biblical Archaeologist* 53 (1990) 64-73.

Schnackenburg, Rudolph. *The Gospel According to St John*. (1965, 1971, 1975). Vol. I, trans. Kevin Smyth. Vol. II, trans. C. Hastings, F. McDonagh, D. Smith and R. Foley. Vol. III, trans. D. Smith and G. A. Kon. London: Burns and Oates, 1980, 1980 and 1982.

Schneiders, Sandra M. *The Revelatory Text: Interpreting the New Testament as Sacred Scripture*. San Francisco: Harper, 1991.

Schniedewind, William M. "Notes and Observations, Textual Criticism and Theological Interpretation: The Pro-Temple *Tendenz* in the Greek Text of Samuel-Kings." *HTR* 87 (1994) 107-16.

Scholem, Gershom Gerhard. *The Messianic Idea in Judaism*. London: Allen and Unwin, 1971.

Schuchard, Bruce G. *Scripture Within Scripture: The Interrelationship of Form and Function in the Explicit Old Testament Citations in the Gospel of John*. SBL Dissertation Series 133. Atlanta GA: Scholars Press, 1992.

Schürer, Emil. *The History of the Jewish People in the Age of Jesus Christ*. Rev. and ed. Geza Vermes, Fergus Millar, Matthew Black and Pamela Vermes. 3 vols. Edinburgh: T and T. Clark, 1973-87.
Selms, A. van. "The Origin of the Title 'The King's Friend.' " *JNES* 16 (1957) 118-23.
Seynaeve, Jaak. "Les citations scriptuaires en Jn., 19, 36-37: une preuve en faveur de la typologie de l'agneau pascal?" *RevAT* 1 (1977) 67-76.
Sheppard, Gerald T. *Wisdom as a Hermeneutical Construct: A Study of the Sapientializing of the Old Testament*. BZAW 151. Berlin: de Gruyter, 1980.
———. "Theology and the Book of Psalms." *Int* 46 (1992) 143- 155.
———. "The Relation of Solomon's Wisdom to Biblical Prayer." *TJT* 8 (1992) 7-27.
Shimoff, Sandra R. "David and Bathsheba: The Political Function of Rabbinic Aggadah." *JEJ* 24 (1993) 246-56.
Shutt, R. J. H. "Letter of Aristeas: A New Translation and Introduction." In *The Old Testament Pseudepigrapha*, ed. J. H. Charlesworth, Vol. II, 7-34. New York: Doubleday, 1985.
Skehan, P. W. "Qumran and Old Testament Criticism." In *Qumrân: sa pieté, sa théologie et son milieu*, ed. M. Delcor, 163-82. Paris: Duculot & Gembloux: Leuven University Press, 1968.
———. "The Acrostic Poem in Si 51:13-30." *HTR* 64 (1971) 387-400.
———. "A Liturgical Complex in 11QPsa." *CBQ* 35 (1973) 195-205.
———. "Jubilees and the Qumran Psalter." *CBQ* 37 (1975) 343-47.
———. and A. A. di Lella. *The Wisdom of Ben Sira*. Anchor Bible 39. Garden City, New York: Doubleday, 1987.
Slomovic, Elieser. "Toward an Understanding of the Formation of Historical Titles in the Book of Psalms." *ZAW* 91 (1979) 350-380.
Smith, D. Moody. "The Use of the Old Testament in the New." In *The Use of the Old Testament in the New: Essays in honour of William Franklin Stinespring*, ed. James M. Efird, 3-65. Durham, NC: Duke University Press, 1972.
———. *Johannine Christianity: Essays on its Setting, Sources, and Theology*. Edinburgh: T. and T. Clark, 1984.
Smith, Dennis E. "Messianic Banquet." In *The Anchor Bible Dictionary*, ed. D. N. Freedman, Vol. IV, 788-91. New York and London: Doubleday, 1992.
Sonne, I. "Synagogue." In *The Interpreters' Dictionary of the Bible: An Illustrated Encyclopedia*, ed. George A. Buttrick, Vol. 4, 476-91. New York and Nashville: Abingdon, 1962.
Spicq, Ceslaus. "Τρώγειν: Est-il synonyme de φαγεῖν et d'ἐσθίειν dans le Nouveau Testament?" *NTS* 26 (1979-80) 414-19.
Stendahl, Krister. *The School of St. Matthew and its Use of the Old Testament*. Acta Seminarii Neotestamentici Upsaliensis. Lund: C. W. K. Gleerup, (2nd edition) 1968.
Stibbe, Mark W. G. *John*. Readings: A New Biblical Commentary. Sheffield: JSOT Press, 1993.

———. *John's Gospel*. London and New York: Routledge, 1994.
Stone, Michael (ed.). *Jewish Writings of the Second Temple Period: Apocrypha, Pseudepigrapha, Qumran Sectarian Writings, Philo, Josephus*. CRINT 2, 2. Assen: Van Gorcum & Philadelphia: Fortress, 1984.
Strugnell, John. "More Psalms of David." *CBQ* 27 (1965) 207-16.
———. "Notes on the Text and Transmission of the Apocryphal Psalms 151, 154 (=Syr II) and 155 (=Syr III)." *HTR* 59 (1966) 257-81.
Stuhlmueller, Carroll. *Psalms I : Psalms 1-72* and *Psalms 2: Psalms 73-150*. Old Testament Message, Vols 21 and 22. Wilmington, DE: Glazier, 1983.
Suggit, J. N. "John XVII.17: ὁ λόγος ὁ σος ἀλήθειά ἐστιν." *JTS* 35 (1984) 104- 17.
———. "John 2:1-11: The Sign of Greater Things to Come." *Neot* 21 (1987) 141-58.
Swanston, Hamish. *The Community Witness: An Exploration of the Influences at Work in the New Testament Community and its Writings*. London: Burns and Oates, 1967.

Talmon, Shemaryahu. "Pisqah be 'emsha 'pasuq and 11QPs^a." *Textus* 5 (1966) 11-21.
———. "The Textual Study of the Bible — A New Outlook." In *Qumran and the History of the Biblical Text*, ed. F. M. Cross and S. Talmon, 321-400. Cambridge MA and London: Harvard University Press, 1975.
———. *King, Cult and Calendar in Ancient Israel: Collected Studies*. Jerusalem: The Magnes Press, 1986.
———. *The World of Qumran from Within*. Jerusalem: The Magnes Press & Leiden: E. J. Brill, 1989.
Tournay, R. "Recherches sur la chronologie des Psaumes." *RB* 65 (1958) 321-57.
———. "Le Psaume CX." *RB* 67 (1960) 5-41.
Tov, Emmanuel, with the collaboration of Stephen J. Pfann. *The Dead Sea Scrolls on Microfiches*. Leiden: E. J. Brill, 1993.
Trocmé, Etienne. *The Passion as liturgy: A Study of the Origin of the Passion Narrative in the Four Gospels*. London: SCM, 1983.
Trudinger, L. P. "Davidic Links with the Betrayal of Jesus: Some Further Observations." *ExpTim* 86 (1974-75) 278-79.
———. "Hosanna to the Son of David!: St John's Perspective." *DRev* 109 (1991) 297-301.
Tsuchido, Kiyoshi. "Tradition and Redaction in John 12.1-43." *NTS* 30 (1984) 609-19.

Unnik, W. C. van. "The Quotation from the Old Testament in John 12:34." *NovT* 3 (1959) 174-79.

VanderKam, J. C. "Dedication, Feast of." In *The Anchor Bible Dictionary*, ed. D. N. Freedman, Vol. 2, 123-25. New York and London: Doubleday, 1992.

Vermes, Geza. *The Dead Sea Scrolls in English*. 3rd ed. London: Penguin, 1986.
Von Rad, Gerhard. *Old Testament Theology*. New York: Harper and Row, 1965.
Vosté, J. M. "Sur les titres des psaumes dans la Pešittā surtout d'après la recension orientale. *Bib* 25 (1944) 210-35.
Wacholder, Ben Zion. "David's Eschatological Psalter: 11Q Psalms^a." *HUCA* 59 (1988) 23-72.
Walker, W. D. "The Origin of the Son of Man Concept as Applied to Jesus." *JBL* 91 (1972) 482-90.
Walton, Brian [Brianus Vvaltonus]. *Biblia Sacra Polyglotta*. London: Thomas Roycroft, 1657.
Walton, John H. "Psalms: A Cantata about the Davidic Covenant." *JETS* 34 (1991) 21-31.
Wansbrough, H. (ed.). *The New Jerusalem Bible*. London: Darton, Longman and Todd & New York: Doubleday, 1985.
Weingreen, J. "The Rebellion of Absalom." *VT* 19 (1969) 263-66.
Weiser, Artur. *The Psalms: A Commentary* (1959). Trans. Herbert Hartwell. London: SCM, 1962.
Weren, W. J. C. "Psalm 2 in Luke/Acts: An Intertextual Study." In *Intertextuality in Biblical Writings: Essays in honour of Bas von I ersel*, ed. Spike Draisma, 189-203. Kampen: J. H. Kok, 1989.
Wernberg-Møller, P. *The Manual of Discipline*. Studies on the Texts of the Desert of Judah, ed. J. Van der Ploeg, Vol. I. Leiden: E. J. Brill, 1957.
Wilcox, Max. "The Denial Sequence in Mk XIV. 26-31, 66-72." *NTS* 17 (1970- 71) 426-36.
Willis, J. "Psalm 1 — An Entity." *ZAW* 9 (1979) 381-401.
Wilson, Gerald Henry. *The Editing of the Hebrew Psalter*. SBL Dissertation Series 76. Chico, CA: Scholars Press, 1985.
——. "The Qumran Psalms Scroll Reconsidered: Analysis of the Debate." *CBQ* 47 (1985) 234-42.
——. "The Shape of the Book of Psalms." *Int* 46 (1992) 129- 42.
——. "Understanding the Purposeful Arrangement of Psalms in the Psalter: Pitfalls and Promise." In *The Shape and Shaping of the Psalter*, ed. J. Clinton McCann, 42-51. JSOT Supplement Series 159. Sheffield: Sheffield Academic Press, 1993.
Wintermute, O. S. "Jubilees: A New Translation and Introduction." In *The Old Testament Pseudepigrapha*, ed. J. H. Charlesworth, Vol. II, 35-142. New York: Doubleday, 1985.
Witkamp, L. Th. "Jezus' laatste woorden volgens Johannes 19:28-30." *NedTT* 43 (1989) 11-20.
Wright, R. B. "Psalms of Solomon." In *The Old Testament Pseudepigrapha*, ed. J. H. Charlesworth, Vol. I, 639-70. London: Darton Longman and Todd, 1983.
Wyatt, Nicolas. "Supposing Him to be the Gardener (John 20, 15)." *ZNW* 81 (1990) 21-38.

Yarden, L. *The Tree of Light: A Study of the Menorah.* London: Horovitz, 1971.
Yee, Gale A. *Jewish Feasts and the Gospel of John,* Wilmington: Glazier, 1989.
York, Anthony D. "The Dating of Targumic Literature." *JSJ* 5 (1974) 49-62.
Young, Robert (ed.). *Untying the Text: A Post-Structuralist Reader.* Boston, London and Henley: Routledge and Kegan Paul, 1981.

Zenger, Erich. "New Approaches to the Study of the Psalms." *PIBA* 17 (1994) 37-54.
Zerwick, Maximilian. *Graecitas Biblica: Novi Testamenti Exemplis Illustratur.* Rome: Pontifical Biblical Institute, 1966.
——. *Analysis Philologica Novi Testamenti Graeci* Editio Quarta. Rome: Pontifical Biblical Institute, 1984.
Zvi, E. Ben. "The Authority of 1-2 Chronicles in the Late Second Temple Period." *JSP* 3 (1988) 59-80.

INDICES

INDEX OF BIBLICAL PASSAGES

Genesis
1:28	48
2 - 11	274
2:7	48
2:10	146
3:3	141
3:22	141, 286
3:24	141
12:6-7	99
15:7	126
15:7-21	126
18:14	25
21:17	269
22:2	47, 76, 232
22:6	232
22:7	232
22:8	128, 232
22:12	232
22:16	232
22:17	47
26:24-25	99
26:26	304-05
26:30	41
28:12	11, 30, 122, 157, 166, 275
28:18	99
31:54	41
37:3	216
38:2	123
45:4	216
49:8-12	179
49:10	266, 310
49:10-11	186

Exodus
4:16	171
4:20	138
7:1	137, 171
12:2	227
12:10	230-31, 231
12:46	29, 30, 40, 230-31, 234
13:2. 12	33
15:1	100
15:2	46, 71
15:17	78, 156
15:18	78
15:20-21	100
16:2-3	116
16:4	133, 135, 138, 139
16:15	133, 143
17:1-7	148, 149, 155, 226
17:2	227
17:3	227
17:6	159
18:15-16	171
20:21	171
23:20	269
24:8	227
25:9	75
32:32	43
33:7-11	122
33:11	298
34:6-7	44
34:35	100
40:34	122

Leviticus
9:24	126
10:2	126
14:4-5	227
23:40	180

Numbers
7:10-11	164
9:6	227
9:12	230-31
11:1	126
11:9	138
11:16-30	154
11:17	100
11:29	91
16:31-35	100
16:35	126
20:2-13	149
20:10-11	155
20:11	149
21:16-18	155
21:18	160
24:3-4	91-92

Deuteronomy
5:31	137
6:4-5	268

352 INDICES

6:7	280	18:18	82, 274
8:3	224	18:28	302
8:3-4	143	19:5	204, 308
8:15	160	19:2	302
11:26-28	279	19:6	63
17:18-20	96	20:6	245
18:18	154, 161, 170	21:1-7	292
18:18-19	204	21:5	292
28:39	125	21:10-16	237
30:15-20	279	21:13	237
31:24	5	22:16	299
32:1-43	80	22:23	297, 299
32:4	159	23:14	226
32:22	126	23:15	302
		24:1-22	211

Joshua
3:17	294

24:2	226
24:20	211
25:24	298
28:17	304

Judges
9:8-15	140
15:18-19	226

30:6	303
30:21-25	292
30:31	302

1 Samuel
1:11	25
2:1-10	25
2:26	25
9:9	92
10:6-7	91
13:14	253, 260, 313
15:10	260
15:27-28	211-12
16:1	89, 260
16:1-13	83, 265, 303, 307
16:2	260
16:3	303-04
16:6-10	304
16:7	62, 63
16:12	259
16:13	91, 100, 154, 304
16:14-23	61, 63
16:18	61, 97, 295
17:1-58	84
17:34-36	2-3, 94, 262
17:34-37	309
17:37	3
17:38-39	308
17:40	4
17:45	2, 185, 308
17:49	273
18 - 31	290
18:6-8	302
18:7	100
18:14	61, 295
18:16	302

2 Samuel
1:17-27	61
2:26	125
4:4	291
5:1-3	303
5:5	309
5:6 - 8:18	72
5:10	61, 295
6:12-19	72
6:14	73, 211
6:15	72
6:19	142, 303
7:1-29	5, 31, 72, 85, 90, 106, 247, 310
7:2-16	102
7:5-7	77
7:5-16	49
7:8	82, 274
7:8-16	53
7:11	77, 78, 128
7:12-13	246
7:12	30
7:13	77, 129
7:14	49, 78, 129, 172, 285
7:14-16	102
7:15	213
7:15-16	85
8:6	298
9 - 20	80
11:9	298
14:4	179

INDEX OF BIBLICAL PASSAGES

14:7	97	*1 Kings*	
15 - 18	289, 292, 302	1 - 2	76, 80
15:3-6	306	1:11	48, 277
15:7-9	298	1:33	226
15:14	298	1:33-40	301
15:15	291, 299	1:35	185, 211
15:21	298	1:38	185
15:21-22	207, 291, 294	1:43	48, 277
15:23	226, 293	1:44	185
15:23-24	294	1:47	48, 277
15:24-29	226	2:1-9	261
15:25	226	2:3	260
15:25-27	296	2:5-9	261
15:26	80	2:6	5
15:30	291, 299, 315	2:7	279
15:31	80, 112, 194, 291, 315	3:6-9	96
		3:9	5, 175
15:37	305	3:12	96
16:9	298	3:14	260
16:12	80	4:5	305
16:17	305	5:3	164, 274
16:23	194, 291	5:12	70
17:1	83, 291, 298	6:11	173
17:1-2	296	8:1-65	72
17:1-4	295	8:2	161, 180
17:2	291	8:15	92
17:23	290	8:17-18	102
17:29	226, 294, 303	8:25	247
18:28	195-96	8:65	161, 180
19:20	298	8:65-66	142
20:20-22	295-96	8:66	128, 180
20:21	195	9:4	260
21:17	306, 309	9:5	247
22 - 23	80	9:6	260
22:1	261	10:6-7	5
22:2	159	10:9	271
22:2-51	70, 86	11:10-11	260
22:5-6	164	11:29-31	210, 211, 264
22:15	91	11:32	211
22:21-24	261	11:36	211, 306
22:22	260	11:38	260
22:39	274	11:41	5
22:43	273	15:4	306
22:47	159	18:38	126
23:1	71, 91, 92, 318	19:10	126
23:1-7	70, 80, 286, 292	19:14	126
23:2	91, 95, 100	19:16	92
23:3-4	306	22:5-8	91
23:4	95, 305-06		
23:6	11	*2 Kings*	
23:13-17	226	3:16-17	226
24:17	309	4:42-44	142
24:18	157	6:26	179
24:18-25	76, 128, 160	8:19	306

11:18	98	35:15	91
12:2	260	35:25	5
13:20-21	235		
14:3.24	260	*Ezra*	
15:3	260	3:2	5, 98
18:3	109, 260	3:10	73, 98
19:15-18	295	6:16	164
19:15-19	72	7:6	5
19:31.39	295		
21:18. 26	300	*Nehemiah*	
22:2	109	1:7-9	5
25:4	300	3:15-16	301
25:7	309	3:16	300
		8:1.14	5
1 Chronicles		9:14	5
3:16-19	74, 311	9:15	133
10 - 29	73	9:20	133, 143
11:15-19	226	10:29	277
12:38	303	10:30	5
12:38-40	142, 303	12:36	73
16:3	142, 303	13:2	5
16:4	73	13:15-22	123
16:7	73, 81	13:19	134
17:1-14	102		
17:13	302	*Tobit*	
17:16-18	301	3:10	290
18:14	172		
22:1	75, 76	*Judith*	
22:8	173, 297	13:18	25
22:19	75	16:1-7	25
23:5	74		
25:1	91	*Psalms*	
25:1-8	74	1	94, 95
25:5	91	1 - 2	66, 90, 278-86, 322-23
27:33	195	1:1	99
28:3	297	1:1-3	323
28:8-21	261	1:3	148, 285
28:11-19	99	1:6	279, 285
28:19	75	2	49-51, 55, 56, 102
29:10-19	261	2:1-2	50
29:10-22	76	2:2	303
29:22	142	2:7	23, 36, 49, 172, 284, 285
2 Chronicles		2:9	234
3:1	75, 76, 157	2:10	100
6:7-8	102	2:11	284
6:41-42	90	2:12	35, 278-79, 284
6:42	85	6	257
7:1	126, 127	6:3	234
7:6	73	7:1	3
9:8	271	8	48-49, 270, 273
16:14	300	(8:2)8:1	277
23:18	98	(8:3)8:2	22, 33, 36, 48
29:29-30	73, 91	(8:5)8:4	273-74
33:12-13	88		

INDEX OF BIBLICAL PASSAGES

(8:6)8:5	82, 274, 277
(8:7)8:6	48, 54, 273-74, 277
(9)9 - 10	82, 279
(10)11:1	279
(10)11:6	223
(13)14:4	125
(15)16	102
(16)17	82
(16)17:9	164
(16)17:15	306
(17)18	70, 80, 81, 90, 261
(17:2)18:1	159
(17:3)18:2	159
(17:5-6)18:4-5	162
(17:22)18:21	260
(17:22-24)18:21-23	261
(17:28)18:27	26
(17:39)18:38	274
(17:44-45)18:43-44	86
(17:47)18:46	159
(17:51)18:50	92, 246
(18)19	279
(18:11)19:10	224
(20)21:9	126
(21)22	39-40, 56, 87, 111, 135, 214, 237, 241, 321
(21:2)22:1	10, 16, 23, 24, 32, 36
(21:7)22:6	214
(21:8)22:7	24, 36
(21:9)22:8	24, 36, 279
(21:10)21:9	214
(21:13)22:12	164
(21:14)22:13	214
(21:15)22:14	214
(21:16)22:15	214, 222
(21:17)22:16	164, 214-15
(21:19)22:18	24, 28, 31, 36, 190, 208-19, 254
(21;21)22:20	232
(21:22)22:21	215
(21:23)22:22	40, 216, 217
(21:27)22:6	215
(21:29)22:28	215
(22)23	92, 135, 308
(22)23:1	258-59, 262
(22)23:1-3	172
(22)23:2	262-63
(22)23:5	263-64
(24:1)25:2	279
(24:5-11)25:4-10	323
(24:15)25:16	232
(26)27	83
(26)27:1	265
(26)27:2	265
(26)27:4	89, 100
(26)27:6	61
(26)27:10	89, 265
(28)29:10	157, 158
(30)31	47-48, 65, 84, 257
(30:1)31:2	159
(30:6)31:5	25, 33, 36, 47, 207
(30:11)31:10	234
(30:14)31:13	47
(31)32	102
(31)32:7	164
(32)33	279
(32)33:2	61
(33)34	40-41, 56, 91, 233, 235, 321
(33:5)34:4	237
(33:6)34:5	100
(33:7)34:6	239
(33:9) 34:8	40-41
(33:12)34:11	238
(33:13-17)34:12-16	35
(33:13-24)34:12-23	40
(33:16)34:15	235, 236
(33:20-23(34:19-22)	235
(33:21)34:20	29, 30, 36, 40, 190, 229-40
(33:22)34:21	236
(34)35:4	252, 265
(34)35:10	234
(34)35:17	232
(34)35:19	35, 43, 202, 265
(34)35:23	51, 207, 265, 267
(35)36:8-9	301
(36)37:4	73
(36:37)10	280
(39)40	252-53
(39:4)40:3	87
(39:7-9)40:6-8	78, 183, 253
(39:9)40:8	151
(39:10-11)40:9-10	253
(39:15)40:14	252, 265
(40:)41	41-42, 56, 87, 241, 321
(40:10)41:9	4, 18-19, 23, 24, 28, 36, 41-42, 189, 191-201
(41)42	225
(41 - 42)42 - 43	253-253

(41:2)42:1	99	(68:23-24)69:22-23	43
(41:3)42:2	222-23, 228, 258	(68:25)69:24	43, 206
		(68:26)69:25	43, 290
(41:4)42:3	257	(68:29)69:28	43
(41:5)42:4	257	(69)70	84
(41:6)42:5	254-56	(70)71	84
(41:7)42:6	255	(71)72	82, 135, 186
(41:12)42:11	254-56	(71)72:5	247
(42)43:5	254-56	(71)72:6	138, 142
(44:5)45:4	266	(71)72:8	186
(44:7)45:6	51, 172, 266	(71)72:9-11.15	23
(44:7-8)45:6-7	265-66	(71)72:16	139
(44:9)45:8	211, 213	(71)72:20	128, 194, 203, 265
(48)49:1-3	100		
(50:3-7)51:1-5	83	(72)73:1	99
(50:9)51:7	227	(73)74:1	259
(50:10)51:8	234	(74:9)75:8	223
(50:12-15)51:10-13	100	(75)76:1	185
(51)52	88	(77)78	43-44, 56, 81, 161-63, 263, 321
(52:6)53:5	234		
(54)55	194, 195, 257		
(54:13-14)55:12-13	194-95, 212	(77)78:2	22, 29, 32, 37, 44, 162
(54:16)55:15	100		
(55)56	84	(77)78:3. 5. 8	162
(55:10)56:9	252, 265	(77)78:9. 12	162
(55:14)56:13	265	(77)78:14	155
(56:2)57:1	279	(77)78:15-16	137, 148, 150
(56:8)57:7	61	(77)78:16. 20	28, 30, 37, 117, 144-61, 188, 225, 245
(60)61:3	89		
(60)61:7-8	247		
(61:62:2	159	(77)78:20	263
(61)62:12	35	(77)78:21	162
(62)63	225-26	(77)78:22	162, 264
(62)63:1	222-23, 226, 228, 258	(77)78:24	27, 30, 37, 111, 117, 131-44, 188, 197
(62)63:2	100, 226		
(62)63:3	228	(77)78:25	137
(65)66:16-19	235, 236	(77)78:32	162
(67:20)68:19	17	(77)78:45	125
(67:36)68:35	268	(77)78:57	162
(68)69	42-43, 56, 102, 111, 219, 225, 237, 241, 257, 290, 321	(77)78:60	162, 163
		(77)78:67-68	162
		(77)78:69	78, 162
		(77)78:70	162
(68)69:4	28, 30, 35, 37, 42-43, 167, 189, 201-08,	(77)78:70-72	2, 163
		(78)79:7	125
		(78)79:13	259
(68:9)69:8	129	(79)80	286
(68:10)69:9	4, 27, 29-30, 37, 42, 76, 116, 118-31, 138, 188, 240	(81)82	44-45, 56, 164, 321
		(81)82:1	168, 174
		(81)82:5	174
(68:22)69:21	25, 29, 37, 42, 190, 219-29, 257	(81)82:6	28, 30, 37, 117, 164-76, 188, 278

INDEX OF BIBLICAL PASSAGES

(81)82:7	169-70, 174	(109)110:1	21, 23, 32, 37, 46, 48, 16-67, 226, 270-78
(83)84:10	73		
(85)86	82, 257		
(87)88:17	164	(109)110:4	54, 247, 277
(88)89	81, 245-51	(109)110:7	226, 276, 301
(88:2-3)89:3-4	30, 246	(110)111:9	26
(88:6)89:5	246, 247	(112)113:7	26, 48
(88:11)89:10	26	(112)113:8	185
(88:19)89:20	102	(113)114:8	151-52, 160
(88:21)89:20	102, 250, 307, 313	(113:16)115:8	279
		(115:7)116:16	323
(88:25-26)89:26-27	285	(117)118	45-46, 56, 321
(88:27)89:26	35, 232, 248	(117)118:8-9	279
(88:27-28)89:26-27	49	(117)118:12	164
(88:28)89:27	249, 277	(117)118:15-16	89
(88:36)89:37	246, 247	(117)118:16	46
(88:36-37)89:37-38	217	(117)118:18	46
(88:38)89:38	86	(117)118:22	36, 45-46, 181
(88:48)89:49	85	(117)118:22-23	22, 32
(88:49-50)89:50-51	206	(117)118:22-29	181
(88:52)89:51	247, 248	(117)118:24	46
(89)90:1	99	(117)118:25-26	176
(90)91	52, 87	(117)118:26	10, 22, 28, 29, 33, 37, 45, 118, 176-187, 188
(90)91:11	89		
(90)91:11-12	22, 32		
(92)93	157	(117)118:27	180
(94)95	102, 258, 263-64, 308	(118)119	94, 121
		(118)119:103	204
(94)95:1	159	(118)119:152	72
(94)95:7	172, 259, 263-64, 284	(118)119:161	203
		(120)121:5	89
(94)95:9	263-64	(121)122	128
(95)96	73-74, 81, 84	(121)122:1-5	162
(96)97	84	(121)122:2. 5	72
(97)98:3	26	(122)123	70
(99)100:3	259	(124)125:1	279
(100)101:8	306	(131)132	81, 90, 226
(101)102:26-28	51	(131)132:1	2, 76, 129, 309, 318
(102)103:17	26		
(103)104	70, 79	(131)132:5	102
(103)104:20	323	(131)132:17	306
(104)105	71, 73-74, 81	(133)134	70
(104)105:15	91	(134)135:5	277
(104)105:35	125	(134)135:18	279
(104)105:41	149, 150, 152	(140)141:2	78
(105)106	73-74, 135, 162-63	(140)141:7	72, 234
		(141)142:1	83
(106)107	81, 163	(142)143	83, 86, 257
(106)107:2	99	(142)143:8	306
(106)107:9	26	(143)144	81, 86, 87
(108)109	102, 290	(144)145	86, 87
(108)109:3	164, 202	(145)146:3	279
(108)109:8	290		
(109)110	52-56, 102, 104, 253, 270-78		

Proverbs
1:20	253
3:18	140
4:23	148
5:15	148
8:15	96
9:5	135, 199
12:28	279
14:2	279
16:1	78
18:4	148

Song of Songs
4:15	148

Wisdom
2:18	24
2:23	170
6:26	143
7:7-14	95
7:17 22	52
7:27	298
9:1-18	5, 96
9:3. 5. 7	276
9:8	75
9:10	138
9:12	276
16:24-26	224

Sirach
24:7-22	138
24:8-10	122
24:12-22	140
24:19-21	135, 224
24:21	140
24:23-29	151, 160
45:7.15	109
45:24-25	109
47:5	90
47:8-10	75, 109
47:11	109
48:2	126
48:3	126
48:11	278
49:4	109
49:10	235
49:11-12	74-75
51:13-30	95

Isaiah
4:2	140
4:3	43
5:1-5	158
6:1-5	104
6:9-10	31, 32
6:10	34, 43
7:13-14	246
7:14	32
8:14	45
9:1-2	32
9:6	172, 247
11 - 12	71, 138
11:1	71, 140, 246, 310
11:2	154, 307
11:3	96
11:6-8	110
11:10	246
11:10-11	71
11:13	309
12:1-4.	71
12:3	149, 153
14:13	185
16:5	292
22:21-22	211
23:8	123
25:4	226
25:6	135
28:16	145
29:13	32
31:8	125
33:10	276
38:9-20	83
40:3	32, 33, 104, 133, 304
40:11	172, 260
41:17-18	226
42:1	49, 303
42:1-4	32
43:10	217
43:20	149, 226
44:2	178
44:3	152
44:28	313
48:21-22	148, 149, 152
49:10	226
51:3	301
51:4	305
51:17. 22	223
53:1	30, 34
53:2	286
53:4	32
53:7	231, 232
54:13	30, 33, 131, 135
55:1	123, 148, 149, 161
55:1-3	145
55:1-5	219
55:1-13	85-87, 217, 310
55:2	135, 215
55:3-5	85-87

INDEX OF BIBLICAL PASSAGES

55:4	85, 217	37:24	6, 172, 173, 211, 307, 309-10
55:5	217, 218	37:25	247, 309-10
56:7	32, 122	37:26-28	313
58:11	148	37:27	314
61:1-2	33, 92	47:1-2	151
		47:1-14	149, 156, 160, 225

Jeremiah

2:13	148
2:30	125
4:10	170
5:14	126
7:11	122
17:13	148
17:27	126
21:8	279
23:5	140, 246, 309
24:7	131
30:9	6, 309-10,
31:15	32
31:33-34	131
32:1-17	223
32:6-9	32
33:15	140
33:23-26	309
34:5	300
39:4	300
25:7	300

Lamentations

3:22	310
4:20	5, 312
4:21	223

Baruch

3:36 - 4:4	138

Ezekiel

8:1-18	123
8:2	269
9:6	123
17:22-24	310
23:25	126
28:13-14	301
34:11	172
34:15	258, 314
34:16	173, 314
34:22	172
34:23	6, 139, 172, 173, 258, 260, 309-10, 314
34:30-31	258
37:1-14	235
37:17	313
37:21-24	260
37:22	309-10

Daniel

7:9	272
7:13	53, 182, 271-72, 273
7:13-14	275, 276, 292
7:14	247, 272
10:5	269
12:1	43

Hosea

3:5	6, 310
6:6	78
10:8	31
11:1	32, 33
12:7	123
14:3	78

Joel

2:27	131
2:28	153
3:1	91
4:18	139, 156

Amos

9:11	77-78

Micah

5:1	88
5:2	32, 245, 246
5:2-4	310
7:6	31

Habakkuk

2:3	182
2:14	131

Zephaniah

3:15	178

Haggai

2:20-23	74

Zechariah

3:8	140
4:12	140
6:12	140

9:7	32	5:31	33
9:9	34, 123, 139, 177-79, 185-87, 209	5:33	33
		5:38	33
9:9-10	179, 186	5:43	33
11:12	24, 32	8:17	32
11:17	123	9:13	33
12:7	240, 311	9:27	103
12:8	172, 240	10:35-36	31
12:8-9	240	10:41	184
12:10	30, 34, 123, 230, 240, 272	11:3	182
		12:1-8	291
12:12	240	12:7	33
13:1	123, 149, 180, 240	12:8	292
13:7	32, 123, 291, 295, 296, 297	12:18	32
		12:23	103
13:8	123	13:4	125
14:4	293	13:14-15	31
14:8	148, 149, 150-51, 152, 160, 225, 240	13:35	22, 29, 32, 44, 321
		14:19	197
14:8-10	156, 180	15:22	103
14:9	240	15:37	215
14:16	180	17:5	23, 49
14:21	123, 161, 180	18:20	45
		20:22-23	223
Malachi		20:30-31	103
3:1	32, 182	21:5	32
3:1-5	123	21:5-7	209, 219
4:5	25	21:9	22, 103, 177
		21:13	122
		21:15	103
1 Maccabees		21:16	22, 33, 48
2:57	90, 311	21:42	22
13:51	179	22:41-46	53, 102, 104
		22:44	21, 54, 55
2 Maccabees		23:13	125
1:18-36	126	23:39	10, 22, 29, 33, 183
10:7	179	26:1	116
11:17	291	26:3	196, 282
		26:3-4	47, 50
Matthew		26:3-5	282
1:2-17	103	26:15	24
1:23	32	26:20-25	291
2:1	103	26:23	24, 197
2:6	32	26:30	45
2:11	23	26:30-35	291
2:15	32	26:31	291
2:18	32	26:36-39	291
3:11	182	26:38	254
3:17	23, 49	26:39	223
4:1-11	32, 52	26:52	308
4:6	22, 32	26:64	23, 53, 55, 275
4:15	32	27:3-5	290
5:21	33	27:3-10	24
5:27	33	27:9	32

INDEX OF BIBLICAL PASSAGES

27:31	212	15:20	212
27:34	25, 219	15:23	25
27:35	208	15:24	24, 208
27:38	25	15:29	24
27:43	278-79	15:34	11, 23, 32
27:46	10, 16, 23	15:36	25, 219
27:48	219	15:37	225
27:50	225	16:19	23, 53

Mark

		Luke	
1:2-3	32	1:17	25
1:7-8	182	1:27	103
1:11	23, 49	1:32	103
1:13	2	1:37	25
2:23-28	291	1:46-55	25-26
2:28	292	1:49-54	26
3:11	153	1:63	16
4:4	125	1:67-79	25
4:12	31, 32	1:69	103
6:41	197	2:4	103
6:42	215	2:23	33
7:6-7	32	2:30	52
9:7	23, 49	3:4-6	33
10:38-39	223	3:16	182
10:47	153	3:22	23, 49-50
10:47-48	103	3:23	291
11:4	185	3:31	103
11:9	22, 103, 177	4:1-13	33, 52
11:17	32, 122	4:10-11	22
12:10	22, 32	4:18	47
12:10-12	181	4:18-19	33
12:35-37	53, 102	4:21	47
12:36	21, 32, 54, 55	6:1-5	291
13:3	293	6:5	292
13:26	272	8:5	125
13:37	116	8:10	31
12:40	125	9:16	197
14:1	47, 282	9:17	215
14:17-21	291	9:35	23, 49
14:18	23, 196	10:19	52
14:20	197	12:24	167
14:21	196	13:35	10, 22, 29, 49
14:26	45	15:30	125
14:27	32, 291, 297	16:31	279
14:29-31	291	18:8	273
14:30	291	18:38-39	103
14:32-33	291	19:14. 27	283
14:34	254-55	19:35	177
14:36	223	19:38	10, 22, 29, 177
14:49	204	19:46	122
14:61	129	20:17	22, 45, 181
14:62	23, 53, 55, 165, 272-73, 275, 276	20:41-44	53, 102, 104
		20:42	21
14:64	165	20:42-43	55

20:47	125	1:41	107, 150, 250
21:36	273	1:43	250, 307
21:37-38	116	1:45	104, 250
22:21	24, 29, 196	1:49	51, 166, 218, 275
22:21-23	291	1:51	12, 48, 122-23, 269, 272-73, 275
22:22	196		
22:33	291	2:3-5	129
22:39-43	291	2:11	51
22:42	223	2:12	129
22:53. 66	291	2:13-22	240
22:67	166	2:16	123
22:69	23, 53, 55, 275	2:17	4, 27, 29-30, 42, 116, 118-31, 138, 152, 159, 180, 191, 206, 219, 224, 238, 264
22:70	166		
23:6-12	50, 282		
23:30	31		
23:34	208	2:18	131
23:36	219	2:19	159
23:46	25, 33, 47, 225, 257	2:19-21	262
23:47	223	2:19-22	166
24:40	214	2:22	120-21, 186, 205, 208, 295, 318
24:44	6, 66, 102		
		2:51	30
John		3:1	203
1:1	51, 266-67	3:1-15	132
1:1-5	134	3:2	236, 295
1:1-18	251	3:9	295
1:2	278	3:10	205
1:4	265	3:11	217
1:4-5	306	3:12	251
1:5	115	3:13	137, 277, 278
1:7	51	3:14	302
1:8-9	304, 305	3:14-15	142
1:9-11	115, 174	3:16	232
1:11-12	115-16	3:19	174, 199, 298, 306
1:12	145, 174, 176, 216	3:21	217
1:12-13	190	3:29	304
1:12-18	115	3:31	106, 183
1:14	122, 232, 314	3:34	120-21, 122, 264
1:15	153, 182	3:35	264
1:17	102, 142	4:1-42	319
1:18	137, 232, 267, 277	4:6	224, 231
1:20	304	4:7-15	224
1:20-21	306	4:10	147
1:23	33, 104, 133, 304	4:12	136, 143
1:25	304	4:14	147
1:26	307	4:15	227
1:27	182	4:19	8
1:29	128, 231-33, 307	4:21-24	159
1:29-34	303, 307	4:22	163
1:30	182	4:25	107, 183
1:33	154, 304	4:26	106
1:34	303, 304	4:31-34	224
1:35-42	250	4:34	221, 223, 224, 252, 296
1:36	76, 128, 231		

INDEX OF BIBLICAL PASSAGES 363

4:42	185	6:62	278
4:48	131	6:64	197
5:2	134, 293	6:66	199
5:6	221	6:70	200
5:10	206	6:70-71	197
5:18	271	7:5	129, 206
5:18-19	55, 165	7:10	303
5:19	121, 184	7:17	252
5:19-23	55	7:22-23	167
5:21-24	174	7:24	174
5:22-23	276	7:25	303
5:25	264, 284	7:25-31	183
5:27	275	7:26	203
5:30	7, 55, 252, 266, 296	7:27	183, 307, 307
5:35	304-05	7:28	153, 218, 252
5:39	31, 119, 174, 205, 244, 318, 321	7:29	183
		7:37	85, 123, 228
5:43	183, 185	7:37-38	225
5:45	137	7:38	28, 44, 104, 117, 144-61, 228, 231, 240, 301
5:46	27, 102, 104, 182		
6:4	139, 262		
6:9	142	7:39	119, 153, 154
6:10	142, 262-63	7:40	8, 154
6:11	197, 303	7:40-41	153
6:12	215	7:40-43	103, 154
6:14	8, 141, 142, 154, 183	7:41	163
6:15	141, 142, 220, 303	7:41-42	108, 310
6:24	215	7:42	103, 228, 245-51, 286
6:27	85, 127, 215		
6:30-31	132	7:43	213
6:31	27, 44, 104, 111, 117, 131-144, 150, 152, 155, 161-62, 198, 216, 262, 263, 321	7:45-49	302
		7:48	203
		7:52	163
		8:12	140, 153-54, 265
6:31-33	142	8:14	106, 217
6:32-33	198	8:16	266
6:33	134, 138	8:17	217
6:35	140, 144, 147, 160, 259	8:21	174, 236, 285
		8:23	106, 134, 183
6:35-58	132, 134-35	8:24	259
6:36	215	8:28	259, 276, 302
6:37	141	8:29	209
6:38	183, 252, 296	8:32	298
6:39	145, 297	8:35	123
6:45	33, 104, 131	8:35-36	232
6:46	137	8:42	134
6:50	141	8:43	205
6:51	127, 141, 216	8:46	121
6:51c-58	198, 200	8:48	163
6:52-57	228	8:51	250
6:54. 56	192, 198	8:52	8
6:57	198	8:53	136
6:58	135, 192, 198	8:55	205
6:59	134, 143	8:56	232, 269

8:58	259, 265	11:47-53	127, 166, 283
8:59	303	11:49-52	224
9:16	213	11:50	127, 295
9:17	8	11:51-52	213, 314
9:22	106	11:52	213, 218
9:25	204	11:54	303
9:28	98	12:1	180
9:28-29	137	12:1-8	127
9:29	103	12:3. 7	299
9:31-32	236	12:10	177, 206
9:34	206	12:13	10, 28, 118, 164, 176-187, 179, 191, 218, 253
9:39	183, 183		
9:39-41	43, 174	12:14	209
10:1-21	172	12:15	34, 104
10:3-4	263	12:16	120, 124, 186, 187, 205, 220
10:6	174, 205		
10:9-10	262	12:17	177, 187
10:11	1, 4, 127, 164, 258-60, 262-63, 265, 308	12:19	302
		12:24-26	127
10:14	258-60, 262-63, 265	12:26	207, 294-95, 297, 298
10:15	1, 4, 308		
10:16	173, 213	12:27	255-56, 258
10:17	302, 308	12:27-28	200
10:17-18	261	12:27-33	256
10:18	262, 298, 308	12:28	51, 127
10:19	213	12:31	127, 179, 293
10:22-39	166, 172, 174, 270-71, 276	12:32	213, 218, 293, 302
		12:34	108, 167, 245-51, 277, 286, 302
10:24	202		
10:24-31	165	12:34-36	285
10:25	166, 184	12:36-43	285
10:26-27	172	12:38	34, 104, 221, 302
10:28	170, 263, 297	12:40	34, 43, 104
10:28-30	313	12:41	27, 102, 104, 269
10:29	263, 297	12:42	203
10:30	258	12:44	153
10:32-39	165, 166	12:45	184
10:33	55, 165	12:46	183
10:34	10, 28, 33, 93, 117, 164-76, 171, 204, 246	13:1 - 17:26	261
		13:1	220, 221, 224, 258
10:34-36	170, 175	13:1-3	202
10:35	169, 171	13:1-11	191
10:36	127, 164, 172	13:1-15	127
10:37	175	13:3	116
10:37-38	263, 313	13:4	210, 212, 213, 308
11:25	259	13:11	199
11:27	106, 154, 166, 183-84	13:12	210, 212
		13:12-20	191, 198
11:28	184	13:16	184, 298
11:33	256, 257, 258	13:18	4, 19, 28, 189, 191-201, 204, 221, 297
11:35	257		
11:41	236	13:19	259
11:44	323	13:21	191, 255-56, 258

INDEX OF BIBLICAL PASSAGES

13:26	197	16:13	183, 323
13:26-27	197	16:32	209, 295
13:27	293, 298	16:33	166, 283, 285
13:30	199, 293	17:1	236, 302
13:31	264	17:2	48, 127, 277
13:31-32	302	17:3	55, 107, 268
13:34	204, 261	17:4	221, 262, 302
13:36-37	315	17:5	51, 202, 228
13:38	308	17:6	40, 184, 202, 216, 218, 309
14:1	256, 258	17:8	121
14:1-2	257	17:11-12	184
14:1-9	243	17:12	196, 221, 297, 298, 309
14:2	297	17:14	106, 202
14:3,	183	17:17-24	151
14:6	259	17:19	127, 159, 309
14:15	261	17:21-22	213
14:18	183	17:23	302
14:21	261	17:24	228, 258
14:23	183	17:26	302
14:26	205, 323	18:1	293, 300
14:27	243, 256	18:4	221
14:28	183	18:5	265
14:30-31	293	18:6	252, 265, 296
14:31	262, 298, 302	18:8-9	296, 297
15:1	140	18:9	121, 297, 309
15:1-9	286	18:11	215, 223, 224, 227, 236, 308
15:2	145, 285	18:19	252
15:3	199	18:19-21	165
15:4	297	18:28	231
15:6	11, 286	18:36	249, 251
15:9	302	18:32	121
15:10. 12	261	18:33	218
15:12-13	262	18:33-35	302
15:15	298	18:36	308
15:18	208	18:37	86, 183, 217, 218, 253, 266
15:18-25	202, 204, 208	19:9	103
15:18 - 16:4a	202, 204, 205	19:12	299
15:19	202	19:13	293
15:20	203, 205, 207, 298, 299	19:14	224, 231
15:20 - 16:4	295	19:15	283, 296
15:21	205	19:17	159, 232
15:23	206	19:19	218, 238
15:25	28, 42, 93, 167, 201-8, 221, 246, 257, 265, 308	19:20	293
		19:20-21	230
15:26	183	19:23	210
16:1	206	19:23-24	213, 216, 219
16:2	200, 205	19:24	10, 28, 31, 104, 190, 208-19, 221, 254, 318
16:3	205		
16:7	183		
16:8-11	205		
16:9	236	19:28	28-29, 190, 219-29,
16:11	166		

	206, 240, 258, 265, 318	7:55-56	275
		7:55-58	272
19:28-30	276	7:56	166, 53, 275
19:29	224	7:59	47, 257, 267
19:30	221, 224-25, 227	8:21	44
19:31	231	8:30	16
19:34	147, 151, 152, 153, 159, 224	11:26	41
		13:22	102, 250, 253, 313
19:35	229, 240, 241	13:33	49-50, 51, 279, 282
19:36	28, 29, 40, 190, 229-40, 221, 241, 318	13:38-41	282
		15:26	308
19:37	34, 104, 180, 190, 230, 240, 241, 272	26:28	41
19:38	231	*Romans*	
19:39-40	213	1:3-4	106, 166
19:41	300	1:4	51
20:3	71	3:19	167
20:9	27, 119, 120, 121, 190, 205, 248	4:6-8	102
		8:34	54, 55
20:15	300	9:32-33	46
20:17	40, 216, 218, 248	10:16	30
20:22	147, 323	11:9	43
20:28	51, 207, 228, 266-67, 277	15:3	42, 124, 206
20:29	119, 278-79, 284	*1 Corinthians*	
20:30-31	184	1:24	160
20:31	106, 119, 142, 165-66, 241, 259, 322	3:11	46
		5:7	231
21:11	213	8:5	168
21:25	71	10:3	144
		10:4	153, 155
Acts		10:8	44
1:6-8	291	14:21	167
1:12	293	15:3-4	253
1:16-20	102	15:3-5	282
1:20	43, 88	15:4	27
2:23	282	15:20-28	48
2:24	282	15:25	54
2:25-36	102	15:25-27	274
2:29	300	15:27	54
2:30	94	16:22	277
2:30-31	121-22		
2:33-34	46, 53	*2 Corinthians*	
2:34-35	55	3:6-11	167
2:38	282	6:9	46
3:19-20	251		
3:20-21	54	*Galatians*	
4:11	45, 181	Gal 5:15	125
4:24-31	282		
4:25	102	*Ephesians*	
4:25-26	50	1:20	48, 54, 55
4:27	282	1:22	48, 54
5:31	45	4:8	16
7:46	102	6:5	284

INDEX OF BIBLICAL PASSAGES

Philippians
- 2:12 — 284
- 3:2 — 215
- 3:21 — 48
- 4:3 — 43

Colossians
- 2:8. 18 — 48
- 3:1 — 54, 55

2 Thessalonians
- 1:10 — 268

2 Timothy
- 3:11 — 40, 239
- 4:7 — 215

Hebrews
- 1:3 — 54, 55
- 1:5 — 5, 31, 51
- 1:8-9 — 266
- 1:8-12 — 51
- 1:13 — 54, 55
- 2:8 — 54
- 2:9 — 48
- 2:11-12 — 40, 216
- 4:7 — 102
- 5:5 — 51
- 5:6. 10 — 54
- 5:7 — 257
- 6:20 — 54
- 7:3. 17. 21 — 54
- 7:26 — 249
- 8:1 — 54, 55
- 10:5-7 — 252, 253
- 10:5-9 — 183
- 10:12-13 — 54, 55
- 10:27 — 125
- 10:37 — 182
- 11:17 — 232
- 11:32 — 94
- 12:2 — 54, 55
- 12:14 — 40
- 13:6 — 46

1 Peter
- 1:17 — 35
- 2:1-10 — 41
- 2:3 — 41
- 2:7 — 45
- 3:10-12 — 35, 40
- 4:14 — 206
- 4:16 — 41

2 Peter
- 1:17 — 49

1 John
- 1:1-4 — 44
- 3:5 — 231
- 3:6 — 262

Revelation
- 1:5 — 86, 232, 249
- 1:7 — 272
- 2:17 — 144
- 2:26-27 — 50
- 3:5 — 43
- 3:14 — 86
- 5:5 — 233
- 7:15 — 122
- 11:15 — 50, 215
- 12:4 — 125
- 12:5 — 50
- 12:12 — 122
- 13:6 — 122
- 14:10 — 223
- 15:3 — 100
- 17:7 — 223
- 16:1 — 43
- 16:4 — 44
- 16:19 — 223
- 19:5-6 — 215
- 19:7 — 46
- 19:11 — 86
- 19:15 — 50
- 19:19 — 50
- 21:3 — 122
- 22:1-5 — 158

INDEX OF ANCIENT TEXTS CITED

Apocalypse of Abraham
  31:1-2   303

Apocalypse of Moses
  22:3   158

Barnabas
  Ep. Barn. VIII   227
  Ep. Barn. XII, 10-11   103
  Ep. Barn, XVIII, 1-2   279
  Ep. Barn. XVIII, 1-21   285

2 Baruch
  3:7   63
  29:8   138
  30:1   97, 251

Bernard of Clairvaux
  De Div 100   4
  Sermo IVpP   4
  Sent. II, 68   4
  SC 32, 4. 8. 9   5
  SC 34, 25   5
  IV HM 11   5

Beth-ha-Midrash
  V, 167-68   100
  VI, 25-26   100

Dead Sea Scrolls
  CD III, 18 - IV, 10   78
  CD VI, 3-11   160
  CD VII, 10-11   104
  CD XIX, 7   104
  1QH I, 28   78
  1QH IV, 33-34   214
  1QH V,11   214
  1QH VI, 34   214
  1QH VIII   286
  1QH XI, 33-34   78
  1QH XII, 11   223
  1QH XV, 15   214
  1QH XVI, 6   78
  1QH XVII, 17   78
  1QpHab XII, 3-4   78
  1QpHab V, 9-12   291
  1QM XI, 7   91
  1QpPs 57   83
  1QS III, 13 - IV, 26   279, 285
  1QS VI   96, 280
  1QS VI, 7-8   95
  1QS VIII, 4-7   78
  1QS VIII, 8-9   78
  1QS IX, 4-5   78
  1QS X, 1. 8   78
  1QS X-XI   79
  1QS X, 6   280
  1QS X, 14. 22   78
  1QSa II, 12-21   96
  1Q30   65
  4 QFlor   77-78, 129, 285
  4QFlor 6-7   78
  4QFlor 8   280
  4QFlor 10-13   313
  4QMMT 110-11   65-66
  4QpIsa VIII-XI   96
  4QPs^a 280
  4QPs^c 83
  4Q161   96
  4Q174   303
  4Q246   268
  4Q400-07   169
  4Q500   158
  4Q522   75-77, 124, 157
  11Q5-6   169
  11QPsAp^a 52, 79, 83
  11QMelch   70-71, 169
  11QPs^a 27   63
  11QPs^a 27, 2-11 11QPs^{a}DavComp   68-72, 95-98, 140, 305
  11QPs^{a}Sirach   95-96
  11QT LVI, 20-21   96

Didache
  I - VI   279, 285
  IX   10
  X, 1   215
  X, 6   179

Dio Chrysostom
  1, 63-65. 66-67   64

INDEX OF ANCIENT TEXTS CITED

1 Enoch
- 47:3 — 43
- 48 — 148
- 48:2-3 — 250
- 48:10 — 250, 272
- 52:4 — 272
- 61:18 — 272
- 62:3 — 272
- 89 - 90 — 232-33
- 89:45 — 233
- 90:9-17 — 233

2 Enoch
- 8:4 — 140
- 8:4-6 — 158
- 29:1 — 63

Euripides
- *Bacchae* 556 — 73

Eusebius of Caesarea
- *In Psalmos* — 99
- *Praep. Evang.* IX, 30, 5 — 77

Extra-Canonical Psalms
- Ps 151 — 62, 68, 82, 84, 88, 89
- Pss 151-155 — 89-90
- Ps 152 — 3, 88
- Ps 154 — 95

Ezekiel the Tragedian
- *Exag.* 188-92 — 236

4 Ezra (2 Esdras)
- 7:29 — 272
- 12:32-34 — 97
- 13:3 — 272

Gospel of Bartholomew
- *Gosp. Bart.* 1, 32 — 277

Gospel of Peter
- *Gos. Pet.* 21 — 214
- *Gos. Pet.* 4:14 — 229

Gospel of Thomas
- *Gos. Thom.* 13 — 147

Hippolytus
- *Com. in Dan.* I, 17 — 146, 158

Ignatius of Antioch
- *IgRom* VII, 1 — 228
- *IgRom* VII, 2 — 228
- *IgRom* VII, 3 — 133, 228

Josephus
- *Ant.* I, 224 — 76
- *Ant.* I, 166 — 62
- *Ant.* III, 88.96 — 137
- *Ant.* IV, 302-06 — 101, 258
- *Ant.* V, 249-50 — 62
- *Ant.* V, 336 — 109
- *Ant.* VI, 214 — 62
- *Ant.* VI, 166 — 92
- *Ant.* VII, 75-79 — 77
- *Ant.* VII, 94 — 109
- *Ant.* VII, 305 — 63
- *Ant.* VII, 334 — 75, 77, 92
- *Ant.* VIII, 45-49 — 52
- *Ant.* VIII, 17 — 293
- *Ant.* VIII, 63-100 — 77
- *Ant.* VIII, 109 — 92
- *Ant.* VIII, 333-34 — 76
- *Wars* I, 33.9; 673 — 300
- *Wars* II, 433-34, 441-48 — 312
- *Wars* IV, 9. 7 — 109
- *Wars* IV, 510. 575 — 312
- *Wars* V, 70, 252 — 293
- *Wars* VI, 311-313 — 109
- *Wars* VII, 229-31 — 312

Jubilees
- 2:2 — 63
- 8:19 — 157, 158
- 18:13 — 76
- 31:18 — 311
- 49:13 — 236-37

Justin
- *Apol.* I, 32, 54 — 186
- *Dial.* 8, 4 — 306
- *Dial.* 38, 1 — 266
- *Dial.* 43, 3 — 266
- *Dial.* 52-54 — 186
- *Dial.* 53, 3 — 186
- *Dial.* 56, 14 — 266
- *Dial.* 69 — 146
- *Dial.* 86, 3 — 266
- *Dial.* 97, 3 — 214
- *Dial.* 114 — 146
- *Dial.* 135 — 146

Letter of Aristeas
- *EpAr* 88 — 158
- *EpAr* 89-91 — 75, 158

4 Maccabees
　18:13-14　　　　　　　　239
　18:15　　　　　　　　　　90, 200

Midrash on Psalms
　Midr. Teh. 1, 2　　　　　101
　Midr. Teh. 1, 18　　　　148
　Midr. Teh. 1, 5　　　　　99, 110
　Midr. Teh. 1, 6　　　　　84
　Midr. Teh. 2, 9　　　　　272
　Midr. Teh. 3, 4　　　　　195
　Midr. Teh. 5, 4　　　　　99, 249
　Midr. Teh. 5, 9　　　　　196, 298
　Midr. Teh. 8, 7　　　　　273
　Midr. Teh. 11, 1　　　　182
　Midr. Teh. 17, 5　　　　180
　Midr. Teh. 18, 29　　　272
　Midr. Teh. 18, 32　　　273
　Midr. Teh. 26, 5　　　　180
　Midr. Teh. 34, 1　　　　237
　Midr. Teh. 40, 2　　　　87
　Midr. Teh. 41, 7　　　　199
　Midr. Teh. 51, 3　　　　87
　Midr. Teh. 55:1　　　　 195
　Midr. Teh. 57, 3　　　　211
　Midr. Teh. 63, 1　　　　110-11, 182,
　　　　　　　　　　　　　 226
　Midr. Teh. 72, 1　　　　99
　Midr. Teh. 78, 5　　　　182
　Midr. Teh. 82, 1　　　　171
　Midr. Teh. 92, 6　　　　157
　Midr. Teh. 118, 21　　　182

Midrashim
　Abot of R. Nathan 37　　167
　Gen R. 99, 63b　　　　　266
　Exod. R. 2, 2-3　　　　 101
　Exod. R. 3, 1　　　　　 260
　Exod. R. 32, 7　　　　　169
　Exod. R. 15, 22　　　　 101
　Deut R. 2, 26-27　　　　101
　Midr. Tanh. Ps 3　　　　297
　Qoh. R. 1, 9, 1　　　　 139, 156
　On Song of Songs 1:18　139
　Sifrei Deut 306　　　　 170

Mishnah
　m. Aboth 3, 6　　　　　 45, 171
　m. Aboth 6, 3　　　　　 195, 212
　m. Sanh. 1, 6　　　　　 171
　m. Sanh. 10, 2　　　　　196, 298
　m. Sota 9, 12　　　　　 93
　m. Sota 9, 9-15　　　　 105, 311
　m. Sukk. 4, 5　　　　　 45, 180

　m. Tamid 7, 4　　　　　 164
　m. Yoma 5, 6　　　　　　159

Odes of Solomon
　30:1-3　　　　　　　　　148
　36:7　　　　　　　　　　148

Philo
　Agr. 6. 10　　　　　　　260
　Agr. 50-54　　　　　　　92
　Conf. 149　　　　　　　 64
　Deter. 115-18　　　　　 160
　Deter. 118　　　　　　　143
　Flac. VI, 40　　　　　　299
　Gig. 49　　　　　　　　 137
　Her. 79　　　　　　　　 143
　Her. 259-60　　　　　　 93
　Her. 290　　　　　　　　92
　Leg. All. II, 21. 86　　160
　Leg. All. III, 169-70　 143
　Mos. I, 27　　　　　　　101, 171
　Mos. I, 61　　　　　　　2, 101
　Mos. I, XXVIII, 158　　 101, 137
　Mos. I, XI, 60　　　　　101, 258
　Mos. I, XXVIII, 155　　 171
　Mut. 259-60　　　　　　 143
　Plant. II, IX, 39　　　 64, 65, 73
　Praem. 85-87　　　　　　110
　Praem. 94-95　　　　　　110
　Probus 19　　　　　　　 96
　Post. 28　　　　　　　　137
　Quaest. Gen. I, 10　　　140
　Sacr. 8-9　　　　　　　 137
　Somn. II, 189　　　　　 137
　Spec. Leg. I, 272　　　 79
　Virt. IX, 220-22　　　　110

Plato
　Pol. IV, 6　　　　　　　96

Prayer of Manasseh
　PrMan　　　　　　　　　 88

Psalms of Solomon
　PsSol 17 - 18　　　　　 97-98, 281,
　　　　　　　　　　　　　 313
　PsSol 17:22　　　　　　 281
　PsSol 17:23　　　　　　 280, 283
　PsSol 17:1　　　　　　　202
　PsSol 17:21　　　　　　 313
　PsSol 17:23-27　　　　　49
　PsSol 17:30　　　　　　 313
　PsSol 17:31　　　　　　 313

PsSol 18:5	251	*y. Ber.* 2,3	310
PsSol 18:6	97	*y. Shab*, 16, 1	312
		y. Sota 9:12	94
Pseudo-Philo		*y. Ta'an* 4, 68d	312
LAB 10: 7	133, 155, 162		
		Targumim	
LAB 11:15	155	TgPs-J Gen 2:7	157
LAB 12: 1	137	TgPs-J Gen 2:15	157, 158
LAB 16: 2	157	TgPs-J Gen 3:23	157
LAB 19:3.9	258	PgPs-J Gen 49:10	186
LAB 51, 3-4	304-05	TgNeof. Gen 49:10	186
LAB 51, 6	305	TgPs-J Gen 49:11	97
LAB 60: 2-3	62-63	TgNeof. Num 20:10-11	155
LAB 61: 5	4	TgPs-J Num 20:11	147, 155
LAB 56: 2	109	Tg1 Sam 15:27	211
LAB 56: 3	109-10	Tg 2 Sam 7:13-14	77
LAB 59: 4	89, 265	Tg 1 Chr 17:12-13	77
LAB 62: 5	89	TgPs 41:9	193, 195
LAB 63: 4	88	TgPs 45:2	266
		TgPs 55:14. 17	194
Sibylline Oracles		TgPs 78:24-25	137-38
Sib. Or. 7	139	TgPs 78:15	157
		TgPs 82:6	168
Suetonius		Tg Ps 89:19	89
Domitianus XIII, 2	267	Tg Ps 91	52
		TgPs 110:1	274
Talmud		TgPs 118:22-29	181
b. Abod. Zar. 5a	169	TgIsa 9:5	247
b. Ber. 5a	47	TgIsa 52:13	247
b. Ber. 6a	170	Tg Zech 6:12	77
b. Ber. 9b	279	TgZech 14:21	123
b. Bab. Bat. 14b-15a	81-82, 99, 110		
		Testament of Job	
b. Hag. 14a	272	*TJob* 33.3	271
b. Pesah. 50a	123		
b. Pesah. 117a	84, 99, 110	Testament of Solomon	
b. Sanh. 6b-7a	170	*TSol* 1:1-7	105
b. Sanh. 7	167	*TSol* 20:1	105
b. Sanh. 38b	271		
b. Sanh. 98b	186	Testaments of the Twelve Patriarchs	
b. Sota 47b	170	*TDan* 5:12	158
b. Sota 48b	94	*TJud* 22:3	186
b. Sukk. 53b	158	*TLevi* 3. 6	78
b. Sukk. 5 :55a	153	*TLevi* 8:3	271
b. Yoma 54a	157	*TSim* 4:9	125
b. Yoma 86b	101		

INDEX OF AUTHORS CITED

Achtemeier, P. 15-16
Ackerman, J. S. 168, 170
Aland, B. 30
Anderson, F. I. 140
Ashton, J. 7, 17, 101, 103, 107-08, 119, 121, 127, 142, 146, 147, 153, 154, 165, 169, 174, 184, 206, 213, 231, 233, 256, 303, 306, 314, 320
Aune, D. 7, 121, 259, 261, 264, 268, 269, 271, 272, 285, 286, 303
Auwers, J.-M. 299

Bampfylde, G. 220, 225, 247
Bar-Ilan, M. 87-88
Barker, M. 76, 140, 158
Barrett, C. K. 30, 133-34, 169-70, 180, 193, 209, 219, 231, 234, 259, 321
Barthélemy, D. 65
Barthes, R. 1-2, 13, 59, 111, 214
Barton, G. A. 239
Bassler J. M. 101, 291
Bauer, W. 46, 125, 197, 218, 232, 279, 308
Baumgarten, J. M. 158
Beaucamp, E. 2, 39
Becker, J. 85
Beckwith, R. 90, 163
Beetham, F. G. 227, 234
Berger, K. 105
Bergmeier, R. 220-21
Betz, O. 66
Beuken, W. A. M. 86
Beutler, J. 172, 222, 255-57, 260, 264
Bienaimé, J. 145, 146, 148, 149, 156, 161
Black, M. 273
Bloch, R. 18, 212
Boismard, M.-E. 7, 132, 147, 148, 149, 151, 154, 170, 173, 238, 248, 293, 306
Boman, T. 222
Borgen, P. 64, 121, 133, 134, 135, 137, 184, 192, 259, 269
Botha, P. J. J. 15
Braude, W. 17, 84
Braun, F.-M. 232

Brawley, R. L. 222, 227
Brodie, T. L. 272
Brooke, G. J. 77, 78, 178, 280, 281
Brown, F. 96
Brown, R. E. 17, 25-26, 30, 47, 50, 86, 105, 107, 115-16, 121, 122, 123, 129, 132, 134, 141, 142, 146, 147, 149, 151, 157, 164, 167, 171, 177, 178, 184, 187, 189, 190, 191, 192, 197, 198, 200, 203, 204, 209-10, 212, 213, 216, 218, 220, 221, 222, 224, 229, 230, 231, 232, 233, 234, 246, 256, 257, 259, 260, 265, 291, 293, 296, 298, 299-300, 302, 303, 247
Bruce, F. F. 154
Brueggemann, W. 48, 60, 66, 82, 102, 274, 310
Buchanan, G. W. 142
Bultmann, R. 64, 115, 132, 153-54, 164, 165, 166, 184, 186, 201, 202, 203, 204, 210, 217, 221, 246, 247, 285, 295-96, 298, 304, 307, 321

Carmignac, J. 79
Castelot, J. J. 161
Cathcart, K. J. 123
Cazelles, H. 81
Cazeau, J. 179, 186
Charlesworth, J. H. 3, 62, 63, 68, 95, 250
Childs, B. 82, 90, 94, 237
Chilton, B. C. 14, 15, 19, 102, 104, 247
Clark, D. C. 286
Conrad, E. W. 86
Cotterell, P. 11
Culler, J. 1, 59, 119
Culpepper, R. A. 103, 116, 119, 124-25, 144, 198, 199, 201, 293, 299

Dahl, N. A. 164, 166, 169, 238, 304, 322
Dahood, M. 38, 65, 125, 254
Daniélou, J. 209, 214, 216, 269
Daube, D. 17, 235, 236
Davila, J. 76

Derrett, J. D. M. 86, 130, 186, 217, 249, 298
Dillon, J. 65, 92
Dimant, D. 280
Dodd, C. H. 49-50, 115-18, 122, 127, 132, 134, 146, 148, 153, 173, 177, 184, 189-91, 193, 201, 203, 209, 215, 217, 222, 230, 233, 276, 321
Duling, D. C. 105, 106
Dunn, J. D. G. 129, 132, 142, 313
Dupont-Sommer, A. 96-97

Eaton, J. H. 176, 185
Ellis, E. E. 152, 167, 292
Eissfeldt, O. 85
Eliot, T. S. 8, 317
Emerton, J. A. 168-69
Evans, C. A. 104

Farrell, S. E. 69
Feldman, L. H. 64, 109
Ferguson, E. 79
Feuillet, A. 40
Finkel, A. 135
Fishbane, M. 317
Fischer, B. 4, 258, 269
Fitzmyer, J. 16, 94, 103-04, 268
Flanagan, J. W. 72, 79
Flusser, D. 63, 68, 89-90
Forr, W. 159
Fortna, R. T. 13, 121, 130, 166, 197
Freed, E. D. 106, 124, 133, 137, 148, 177, 178, 179, 185, 186, 192, 193, 203, 204, 219, 227, 230, 243-44, 257
Friedman, R. E. 5

García Martínez, F. 65-66, 75, 95, 193
Geiger, G. 162
Gerhardssohn, B. 18, 120
Geyser, A. S. 178, 213
Gibbs, J. M. 105
Ginzberg, L. 4, 251
Glasson, T. F. 7, 196, 290, 291, 314
Goldingay, J. 74
Goodwin, C. 30, 148
Goshen-Gottstein, M. H. 69
Goulder, M. 293, 299
Greenspoon, L. 14
Grelot, P. 93, 149, 155, 157, 234
Grigsby, B. H. 127, 151, 231, 232, 234
Guilding, A. 7, 123, 141, 152

Haenchen, E. 221, 228
Hamman, A. 267
Hanson, A. T. 20, 30-31, 148, 151, 169-70, 219, 234
Haran, M. 68, 70-71
Harrington, D. J. 62, 63, 71, 110, 155, 305
Harris, R.J. 39
Hart, H. St J. 179
Harvey, A. E. 24
Hay, D. M. 54, 64, 105, 271, 275, 276, 277
Hayes, J. H. 284
Hays, R. B. 12
Hecht, R. D. 110
Heinemann, J. 179
Hengel, M. 24-25, 238, 267, 268
Holladay, W. L. 39, 41, 167, 203
Hollander, J. 10, 11, 12, 13, 55, 112-13, 243, 245, 259, 302
Horsley, R. A. 109
Hoskyns, E. C. 147, 149, 222, 225, 300
Howard, D. M. Jr 65
Huerta, E. 299-300

Infante, R. 305
Isaac, E. 232
Iser, W. 119

Jacquet, L. 39, 41, 47, 52-53, 229, 234, 274
Jansen, G. 100
Jauss, H. R. 13, 59, 111
Jeremias, J. 139, 197
Johnson, A. R. 91-92
Jonge, M. de 8, 14, 97, 98, 103, 105, 132, 169, 183-84, 246, 281
Juel, D. 17, 31, 54, 77, 78, 79, 105, 124, 181, 232, 238-39, 253, 271, 308, 315
Jungmann, J. 268

Kasher, R. 152, 167
Keel, O. 72
Kiley, M. 286
Kilmartin, J. 135
Kingsbury, J. D. 105
Kister, M. 293
Klijn, A. F. J. 138
Kloppenborg, J. S. 22
Kaiser, W. C. Jr 86
Kaufman, Y. 312
Kraus, H. -J. 11, 23, 39, 44, 46-47, 49, 51, 53, 185, 209, 214, 226, 249

Lapin, H. 180
Leclercq, H. 3
Leclercq, J. 4
Léon-Dufour, X. 134
Levenson, J. D. 311
Liddell, H. G. 64
Lightfoot, R. H. 147, 149, 300
Lindars, B. 18, 42, 119, 121, 122, 123, 124, 125, 132, 134, 171, 178, 191, 193, 197, 198, 200, 201, 212, 219, 225, 229, 234, 241, 246, 247-48, 297
Lindsay, D. R. 217
Lipinsky, E. 279-80
Lohse, E. 48
Louw, J. P. 125, 196, 197

Mack, B. 110
MacRae, G. 59, 107, 115, 142
Magne, J. 3, 4
Magonet, J. 212
Maher, M. 120, 157
Maier, J. 96
Manns, F. 167, 178, 179
Mansoor, M. 68
Martyn, J. L. 7, 98, 107, 126, 141, 142, 143, 199, 205, 250, 303-04, 320
Mastin, B. 267
Matera, F. J. 127, 166
Mays, J. L. 75, 80-81, 94, 207, 281, 318
McCarter, P. K. Jr 61, 72, 80, 296
McNeil, B. 247
McPolin, J. 208
Meeks, W. 7, 64, 101, 103, 115, 129, 132, 135, 136, 137, 178, 202, 217, 266, 269, 278, 299
Meier, J. P. 17, 106
Mendels, D. 109-10
Menken, M. J. J. 14, 104, 118, 127, 128, 131, 132-33, 136, 145, 147, 149, 150, 151-52, 178, 185, 186, 192, 193-94, 200,
Mérode, M. de 185, 187, 234, 236-37, 238, 247, 291,304
Merrill, E. H. 79
Meyers, C. L. 140
Metzger, B. 41, 104
Miller, P. D. 279, 281, 284
Moloney, F. J. 103, 107, 131, 182, 184, 191, 197, 272
Moo, D. J. 186, 192, 201, 203, 219, 230

Moody Smith, D. 5, 177
Moor, J. C. de 100, 233
Moule, C. F. D. 102, 167
Moulon Beernaert, P. 217
Mowinckel, S. 38, 44, 226
Murphy, R. E. 90
Murray, R. 140-41

Neusner, J. 96, 199, 311
Neyrey, J. 122, 157, 164, 170, 202, 207, 213, 267, 269
Nolan, B. M. 289
Noth, M. 60

O' Day, G. R. 201
Odeberg, H. 132, 147, 149
Oesterley, W. O. E. 38, 40, 180, 235
O'Neill, J. C. 110
Orr, W. F. 160

Painter, J. 132, 173, 176, 299
Pancaro, S. 134, 136, 141, 170, 174, 203
Patte, D. 93
Perrin, N. 272-73
Perrot, C. 89, 155, 305
Pietersma, A. 82, 86
Pomykala, K. E. 74, 240, 310, 311
Pope, M. H. 179
Potterie, I. de la 210, 217, 221
Primentas, N. 212
Puech, E. 52, 75-76

Qimron, E. 65-66
Quasten, J. 92

Rahlfs, A. 15, 227
Reim, G. 8, 133, 145, 171, 178, 192, 219, 230, 235, 245, 259, 264, 265-66, 269, 284
Reinhartz, A. 121
Richards, K. H. 237
Richardson, A. K. 291
Riley, W. 73, 99-100
Roberge, M. 132, 134-35, 136
Roberts, J. M. 85
Rogers, C. L. Jr 106
Rordorf, W. 285
Rost, L. 60
Roure, D. 292
Rowland, C. 122-23

Sabourin, L. 39, 80, 237, 254
Salters, R. B. 168

Sanders, E. P. 130
Sanders, J. A. 3, 52, 62, 63, 66, 69, 70-71, 72, 79, 95-96, 97, 179
Sandy, D. B. 233
Sarna, N. M. 74, 81
Schiffmann, L. H. 66
Schnackenburg, R. 121, 127, 134, 142, 146, 147, 149, 152, 170, 180, 186, 192, 193, 203, 204, 205, 210, 213, 219, 221, 222, 224, 230, 245, 246, 247, 256, 262-63, 267, 275
Schneiders, S. M. 15, 244, 278, 319
Schniedewind, W. M. 77
Schuchard, B. 15, 106, 123, 124, 127, 136, 169, 171, 178, 185, 199, 203, 210, 222, 234, 238
Schürer, E. 64
Selms, A. Van 305
Seynaeve, J. 230, 238
Sheppard, G. T. 67, 81, 95, 102, 279, 281, 286, 317
Shutt, R. J. H. 158
Skehan, P. W. 69, 71
Slomovic, E 74, 82
Smith, D. E. 140, 142, 303
Sonne, I. 93
Spicq, C. 192
Stendhal, K. 24, 44
Stibbe, M. W. G. 13, 130, 178, 231-32, 238, 299, 300
Strugnell, J. 3, 63, 65-66, 68, 88
Stuhlmueller, C. 39, 40, 44, 226, 237, 248, 254
Suggit, J. N. 29, 121
Sylva, D. D. 299
Swanston, H. 162-63, 180, 267

Talmon, S. 69, 81, 88, 90, 105, 311
Tournay, R. 53

Tsuchido, K. 177
Tov, E. 83
Trocmé, E. 50, 254-55
Trudinger, L. P. 111-12, 175, 232, 291, 314-15

Unnik, W. C. Van 247

VanderKam, J. C. 126
Vermes, G. 78, 97, 291
Von Rad, G. 85-86
Vosté, J.-M. 87, 282

Wacholder, B. Z. 71, 91, 92
Walker, W. D. 273
Walton, B. 52
Wansbrough, H. 46
Weren, W. J. C. 50, 282
Weiser, A. 38, 80
Weingreen, J. 297
Wernberg-Møller, P. 79
Wilcox, M. 120
Willis, J. 280
Wilkins, M. J. 41
Wilson, G. H. 66-67, 68, 69, 94, 248, 279, 280
Witkamp, L. Th. 222-23
Wright, R. B. 97
Wyatt, N. 301

Yadin, Y. 68
Yarden, L. 140
Yee, G. A. 144
York, A. D. 16, 17
Young, R. 258

Zerwick, M. 46, 204, 218
Zvi, E. Ben 109